The International Handbook on Aging

The International Handbook on Aging

..■..

Current Research and Developments

Third Edition

Edited by Erdman B. Palmore, Frank Whittington,
and Suzanne Kunkel

Associate Editors, Elizabeth Lokon
and Samuel M. Mwangi

Foreword by George L. Maddox

PRAEGER
An Imprint of ABC-CLIO, LLC

A B C ■ C L I O

Santa Barbara, California • Denver, Colorado • Oxford, England

Library of Congress Cataloging-in-Publication Data

The international handbook on aging : current research and developments / edited by
Erdman B. Palmore, Frank Whittington, and Suzanne Kunkel ; associate editors,
Elizabeth Lokon and Samuel M. Mwangi ; foreword by George L. Maddox. — 3rd ed.
    p. cm.
  Rev. ed. of: Developments and research on aging. [Rev. ed.]. 1993.
  Includes index.
  ISBN 978-0-313-35230-0 (hardcopy : alk. paper) — ISBN 978-0-313-35231-7
(ebook) 1. Gerontology. 2. Aging. 3. Gerontology—Cross-cultural studies.
4. Aging—Cross-cultural studies. I. Palmore, Erdman Ballagh, 1930–
II. Whittington, Frank J. III. Kunkel, Suzanne. IV. Developments
and research on aging.
  HQ1061.I535 2009
  305.26—dc22   2009020864

13 12 11 10 9   1 2 3 4 5

This book is also available on the World Wide Web as an eBook.
Visit www.abc-clio.com for details.

ABC-CLIO, LLC
130 Cremona Drive, P.O. Box 1911
Santa Barbara, California 93116-1911

This book is printed on acid-free paper ∞

Manufactured in the United States of America

Dedicated to the gerontologists
around the world
who are helping to make
old age a good age

Contents

Foreword

This third edition of Erdman Palmore's pioneering handbook of aging around the world is a handy, updated introduction to aging in 46 countries worldwide. Excellent editing has assured very readable accounts of the demography and socioeconomic characteristics of aging populations globally, educational and training programs in gerontology and geriatrics, and the social policy issues designed to deal with identified challenges of older adults.

The initial editions appeared as *Developments and Research in Aging: An International Handbook* in 1993 and as the *International Handbook on Aging: Contemporary Developments and Research* in 1980. In this new edition, Suzanne Kunkel, Director of the Scripps Gerontology Center at Miami University (Ohio), and Frank Whittington, Associate Dean for Academic Affairs at George Mason University, join Palmore as co-editors. Also, Samuel Mwangi, a native of Kenya, and Elizabeth Lokon, who are graduate students at Miami University, serve as associate editors.

National and international media document the globalization of commerce, travel, and events, and increasingly call attention to the aging of populations around the world. The International Association of Gerontology and Geriatrics has provided periodic forums for scholars and scientists studying aging individuals and populations since 1950. In recent decades, the United Nations and the World Health Organization have outlined plans of action to identify and respond to the health and welfare needs of aging populations around the world, to suggest appropriate public policies for aging populations, and to promote training in gerontology and geriatrics.

The chapters on individual countries facilitate comparisons of population aging and societal responses by using a standard format that identifies population characteristics, training programs in gerontology and geriatrics, principal research issues and findings, and public policy issues. In addition, the regional chapters illustrate the usefulness of comparison by summarizing aging in four regions of the world.

The opening chapter focuses on sub-Saharan Africa, an area that includes 49 of Africa's 56 countries, and permits comparisons of demographics, research topics, training, and policy issues. The involvement of the United Nations World Assembly on Aging in 1982 and in the UN Madrid International Plan of Action in 2002 in assisting countries in the development of research training and public policies for aging in developing countries is illustrated. And scholars are cautioned against using models of aging in Western industrial societies to predict how populations in the developing world will age, against assuming that families in developing societies inevitably abandon their elderly, and against assuming that older adults do not make a contribution to society.

The second chapter also is a regional summary of 11 countries in Asia and covers the expected topics of demographics, research, training, and policy. Particular attention, however, is given to three priorities in the development of social policies for aging populations in Asia: the development of social protection of frail elderly; the strengthening of informal care services; and gender equality. The third and fourth chapters, on the European and Latin American regions, provide sharp contrasts to the first two regions.

The editors encourage and facilitate interaction of readers with authors by providing email addresses. In addition, the sources of many of the entries in the bibliographies of chapters are accompanied by Web addresses that direct the reader to original sources of documents that would otherwise be difficult to access.

This readable handbook connects a growing community of scholars and investigators around the world.

George L. Maddox, PhD
Professor Emeritus
Duke University Center for the Study
of Aging and Human Development

Preface

In 1980, the first edition of this book was published under the title *International Handbook on Aging: Contemporary Developments and Research*. It was considered a useful handbook by reviewers and won an award from *Choice* magazine as Outstanding Academic Book of the Year. The second edition was published in 1993 under the title *Developments and Research on Aging: An International Handbook*.

However, much of the material in those earlier editions is now out of date; several countries that now have gerontology and geriatrics programs and research were not represented in earlier editions, and most countries have undergone significant changes in their aging-related education, policy, and research endeavors. The first edition had chapters on 28 countries and the second edition included 25 countries. This edition updates the earlier information and adds new chapters on 47 individual countries, as well as four regional chapters and a chapter on international nongovernmental organizations (NGOs) concerned with aging. It also greatly expands the International Directory of Gerontological and Geriatric Associations.

Until recently, most work in gerontology and geriatrics has been limited to the United States and Western Europe. Consequently, most of what we know about aging processes and problems derives from data on whites in Western, capitalist countries. In fact, one analysis found that only about 10% of bibliographic references in American gerontological journals refer to foreign data and sources; furthermore, most of those studies were published in the United Kingdom or the United States.

For gerontology to become a truly international science and profession, scholarly inquiry must expand to include studies among all races and ethnic groups and in all countries around the world. This volume documents that we have made significant progress in that direction. It is an attempt to collect and summarize information on the educational programs, research in gerontology, and the policy initiatives in aging in most of the countries where substantial work is underway.

In order to obtain outstanding gerontologists as contributors to this volume, a letter was sent to the head of the main gerontological organization in each country listed in the International Directory of Gerontological and Geriatric Organizations, inviting each to prepare or revise a chapter on development in that country, or to suggest scholars who might be interested in the project. Most organizations agreed to assist, but if a contribution could not be secured from that source, we approached other eminent gerontologists or geriatricians referred by the International Federation on Aging or through personal contacts.

The resulting 46 countries represented in this volume include most of those with substantial organization, programs, and research on aging. Nevertheless, several countries that had been included in previous editions have been left out of this edition for various reasons: either no suitable author could be found, or the authors who agreed to write chapters were unable to do so by the deadline, for a variety of reasons. The major countries that had to be omitted are France and Russia. The reader is referred to the previous editions or the regional chapters for information on these countries. On the other hand, this edition contains 24 chapters on countries not included in the previous editions—all of which were added because of their recent growth in gerontology and their heightened national concern for societal aging and the growth of their older populations.

The countries surveyed in this edition include most of the world's largest nations (China, India, and United States) and some of the smallest (Singapore, Malta). These include highly urbanized countries and some less urbanized (developing) countries, and they represent all economic systems—capitalist, socialist, communist, and those with mixed systems. Included are countries with some of the highest proportions of older people (Japan, Germany, Greece) and countries with a very low proportion of older people (Botswana, Pakistan); countries with high birthrates (Kenya, Mexico), and many with low birthrates (Germany); some with relatively high death rates (Zimbabwe, Hungary), and some with low death rates (Israel, Canada).

The nations in this survey, however, are not a representative sample of all countries in the world. Gerontology research and programs have developed primarily in countries having two characteristics. The first is a high proportion of aged persons. The United Nations has defined populations as *aged* if a nation has more than 7% aged 65 or over; as *mature* if 4% to 7% are 65 or over; and as *young* if fewer than 4% are 65 or over. Most of the countries in this volume are classified as aged or mature countries. Those who are not yet at the "mature" stage are experiencing rapid population aging. The second characteristic that leads to a focus on gerontology is that high proportions of the country are urbanized and industrialized (usually 50% or more urban). However, this edition includes several new chapters on countries that have recently experienced significant growth in gerontology research, education, and/or policy (such as Austria, Botswana, and the Philippines).

It is understandable that the countries with the higher proportion of elders would have the most advanced gerontology programs and research. Yet the increase in proportion of aged has slowed in the highly developed countries, and it is the less developed nations that are facing the most rapid growth—in both size and proportion—of their older populations, with all the accompanying challenges. Perhaps the less developed nations have the greatest need to develop gerontological capacity and to create programs for the aged rapidly so that they can anticipate and reduce the problems of aging the industrialized countries have experienced.

This volume should be of use to researchers, students, program planners, administrators, and others interested in aging around the world. The differences among nations' responses to population aging provide rich information about the role of cultural, social, economic, historical, and political factors in shaping aging-related research, policy, programs, and education. Each author was asked to include a brief history of aging and gerontology in their country, the organization and state of aging research, the organization and state of gerontological education, and the current policy issues and programs for elders in their country. Many authors have chosen to emphasize some topics and de-emphasize others. Understandably, most also give more attention to work in their own disciplines. There is some variability in the length of chapters, largely dependent on the extent of gerontology and programs in their countries. Some have emphasized positive aspects, while others have been more critical.

We hope this volume will contribute to the growth of a truly international science and professional practice in gerontology and thereby improve the quantity and quality of life for the hundreds of millions of people already old, and those soon to be. Perhaps by improving international understanding in a field of pressing global need, this work also will make a small contribution toward a more tolerant and just world.

Finally, we would like to acknowledge the inspiration and support we each have received over the years from our colleagues and families. The International Task Force of the Association for Gerontology in Higher Education (AGHE) has been important for both Suzanne Kunkel and Frank Whittington as a source of gerontological contacts around the world and as a venue for nurturing our interest in global aging. Sharon King at Georgia State University provided Frank Whittington with the initial idea and opportunity to work in Africa, and she, along with Jenny Zahn of Georgia State, Steve Cutler at the University of Vermont, and, of course, his dear wife, Joy, continue to work collegially with him on global collaborations. Suzanne Kunkel is indebted to José Luis Vega Vega from University of Salamanca, who left this world too early, but not before he had planted the seeds for a European Union-United States collaboration that blossomed into Intergero, an international interdisciplinary exchange program for the study of aging and social policy. She also thanks her colleagues and students at Miami University, who have embraced and embodied the value of global perspectives in the field of gerontology.

And we all must thank Erdman Palmore for the pioneering work he did on the first two editions of this handbook, which inspired so many gerontologists to think globally—and for his generous invitation to us to share in the excitement (and painstaking editorial labor) of this third edition.

Erdman B. Palmore
Frank Whittington
Suzanne Kunkel

1

..■..

African Region

Isabella Aboderin and Monica Ferreira

Sub-Saharan Africa (SSA), sometimes referred to as "Black Africa," comprises 49 of Africa's 56 countries. The seven remaining countries make up North Africa, which is part of the Arabic-speaking world and differs from SSA in important demographic, economic, social, and cultural respects.

SSA is the world's poorest and least developed subregion. All 22 of the world's countries with low human development (United Nations Development Programme [UNDP] classification) and two-thirds of its low-income economies (World Bank classification) (UNDP, 2008; World Bank, 2008) are in SSA. It is also the world's youngest subregion: almost two-thirds (64%) of its population are younger than 25 years, and only 4.8% are aged 60 years or older. The median age is only 18 years. Due to persisting high fertility (currently 5.13 children per woman) and mortality rates, this population age structure is projected to remain largely unchanged until 2025 and to shift only gradually thereafter (United Nations Population Division [UNPD], 2008). SSA's population profile thus contrasts sharply with current rapid population aging in other developing regions and the already-matured populations of the developed world (see Figure 1.1).

Despite the continued youthfulness of SSA's population, international awareness of, and debate on, the implications and challenges of aging in the subregion are intensifying. This chapter aims to provide a broad review of the recent history and current scope of this debate. It charts the emergence of an international concern with aging in SSA, examines the body of accumulated gerontological research and evidence, and appraises

Figure 1.1

Trends in population share (%) of older persons aged 60+: SSA and other world regions, 1950–2050

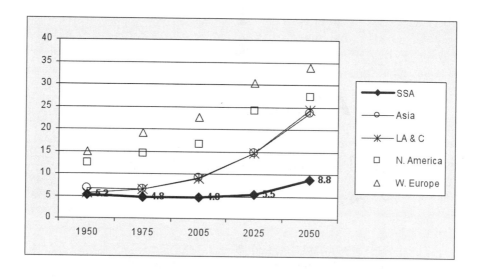

Source: United Nations Population Division (UNPD). (2008). *World population prospects. The 2006 revision.* Retrieved January 8, 2008, from http://esa.un.org/unpp/

the status of policy, and education and training on aging in the subregion. In so doing, the chapter sets out key directions and approaches needed for a strengthened gerontological endeavor in SSA.

A note of caution is due at the outset, however. Owing to language limitations, the review draws principally on published material from SSA's Anglophone countries. It fails therefore to do justice to the body of relevant work from the subregion's Francophone and Lusophone nations. Indeed, readers should note that the language barrier not only curbs the scope of the chapter, but also poses a real obstacle to a vibrant and unified African discourse on aging.

AWARENESS AND DEBATE ON AGING IN SSA: RECENT HISTORY

International awareness of issues of aging in SSA emerged in the early 1980s, as part of a United Nations (UN)-led drive to address perceived policy challenges of population aging in less developed countries (LDC).

The debate was effectively launched with the UN's First World Assembly on Ageing (WAAI), held in Vienna in 1982, and the ensuing Vienna International Plan of Action on Ageing (Vienna Plan) (UN, 1982).

Prior to WAAI, international interest in issues of old age in SSA was largely limited to a small body of U.S. and British anthropological studies and holocultural analyses that compared existing ethnographic data on age relations in different "preindustrial" societies. In addition, a handful of African and international scholars had conducted smaller social surveys on older persons, for example in Ghana (Apt, 1971; Caldwell, 1966).

Two main concerns shaped the UN's deliberations on aging in SSA (and other LDC) in Vienna. Both built on a notion, inspired by modernization theory, of development as a linear, uniform process from traditional to modern (Goode, 1963; Rostow, 1960). This perspective meant that contemporary LDC were expected to undergo the same transformations as historical preindustrial societies in the West, to eventually become like today's advanced industrialized Western nations (Neysmith & Edwardh, 1983).

The UN's first concern thus related to an anticipated rise in the number and proportion of older people in SSA populations, mirroring the process of population aging already underway in Western societies (see also Aboderin, 2008). The second concern centered on a contended erosion of traditional old-age family support systems as developing nations became progressively modernized and Westernized. The fear was that weakening family support would leave older people destitute and vulnerable, given the virtual absence of formal support structures in most SSA countries. It was presumed, moreover, that individual countries—given resource, institutional, and infrastructural constraints—would be unable to adequately meet an emergent need among a surging older population.

Significantly, the UN's expectation of waning customary family support for older persons was not based on any supporting empirical evidence (Marshall, 1990). Rather, it was a conjecture based on the tenets of modernization and aging theory. The theory, advanced by U.S. scholars in the 1960s and early 1970s, held that family support was high in traditional, preindustrial developing societies, but would, as in Western societies, erode with advancing industrialization, urbanization, and secularization, leaving older people abandoned and dependent on the state (Burgess, 1960; Cowgill, 1972, 1974; see also Aboderin, 2004b). The abandonment thesis was later solidly refuted by historical, contemporary, and ethnographic empirical evidence emerging in the 1960s, 1970s and 1980s, which showed the notion to fit neither with history nor with contemporary arrangements (O'Rand, 1990). Parallel theoretical critiques, moreover, exposed the fallacy of viewing development as a uniform process of change from traditional to modern (see Aboderin, 2004b). Yet, and perplexingly, the UN and WAAI embraced modernization and aging theory as a guiding perspective. Based on the theory, the Vienna Plan asserted a pressing humanitarian need for policy responses to preempt or redress a rising unmet need of older persons in areas of health, housing, family support, social welfare, and income security. Importantly, the Plan stressed the importance of research to inform such policy development (UN, 1982).

EARLY PHASE RESEARCH: 1982 TO MID-1990s

Stimulated by the Vienna Plan and subsequent consultations on the implications of aging in Africa—at a meeting of experts held in Versailles, France, in 1983 and a conference on aging in Africa held in Dakar, Senegal, in 1984 (Flesch, 1984), as well as by the African Gerontological Society (AGES), established in 1989 (Apt, 2005)—an early phase of research on older persons in SSA unfolded in the decade after the WAAI. Most investigations took the form of fairly small-scale, single-country quantitative surveys, and primarily collected basic descriptive data on older persons' health, economic, housing, family, and support status (e.g., Apt, 1987; 1996b; Brown, 1985; Dorjahn, 1989; Ekpenyong, Oyeneye, & Peil, 1987; Ferreira, Møller, Prinsloo, & Gillis, 1992; Nyanguru, Hampson, Adamchak, & Wilson, 1994; Nyanguru & Peil, 1993; Peil, Bamisaiye, & Ekpenyong, 1989). Additional studies examined the degree to which customary family obligation norms continued to be endorsed in African societies (e.g., Ohuche & Littrell, 1989; Togonu-Bickersteth, 1989; Togonu-Bickersteth & Akinnawo, 1990). Parallel ethnographic and qualitative studies described conditions of old-age and intergenerational support in various cultural contexts (e.g., Apt, Koomson, Williams, & Grieco, 1995; Campbell, 1994; Cattell, 1997; Everatt & Orkin, 1994; Foner, 1993; Keith et al., 1994; Møller, 1994; Sangree, 1992).

The budding research was accompanied by the founding of two new journals—*African Gerontology* (first issue in 1984) and the *Southern African Journal of Gerontology* (first issue in 1992)—which provided an important outlet for the sharing of generated evidence. The journals also offered a platform for raising awareness and a nascent discourse on what responses to aging were needed in SSA. Key perspectives that crystallized in the early debate (and remain salient in today's policy discourse) included a rejection of a simple reliance on Western models and an emphasis on solutions commensurate with African cultural values, as well as a focus on integration and participation of older persons (e.g., Menya, 1985; Shuman, 1984).

The emergent critical stance toward Western policy models did not, however, translate into a similar caution *vis-à-vis* Western scientific theories. Most of the early empirical research uncritically embraced modernization and aging theory as a dominant framework for exploration and analysis (Shapiro & Kaufert, 1983). Studies largely sought to establish to what extent processes of Westernization and urbanization had already impacted older persons' well-being. Little effort was made to scrutinize the modernization thesis, and/or to examine the *actual* nature, causes, and implications of changes in older persons' situation (Aboderin, 2004b; Ferreira, 1999).

The generated evidence documented, on the one hand, pervasive intergenerational co-residence, old-age family support, and customary norm endorsement. On the other hand, surveys found sizeable proportions of elders reporting inadequacies, especially in material family support, while anecdotal or ethnographic evidence highlighted instances of neglect of older persons. Some studies, moreover, suggested subtle shifts in customary normative expectations of old-age support. In keeping with modernization and aging theory, the findings were broadly interpreted as indicating a general continuity of traditional modes, but also an emergent decline in old-age family support, wrought by forces of modernization. Some authors additionally noted the effects of widespread economic strain (which took hold in SSA in the 1980s (Commission for Africa [CfA], 2005)) as a further negative impact on family support (e.g., Apt, 1992; 1996b; Mupedziswa, 1997). However, virtually no attempt was made to link such empirical insight to critiques of the modernization thesis or to other explanatory frameworks, such as political economy perspectives (Aboderin, 2004b). This omission highlights a clear disconnect that existed at the time between SSA research and salient theoretical debates in Western gerontology (e.g., Fennel, Phillipson, & Evers, 1988; Phillipson, 1982; Walker, 1981).

RECENT RESEARCH: LATE 1990S TO DATE

In the late 1990s and early years of the new millennium, research on aging in SSA began to expand in volume and scope, and in some countries was accompanied by important institutional developments—such as the founding of the multidisciplinary Institute of Ageing in Africa at the University of Cape Town, South Africa, in 2001. The growing research endeavor was bolstered by a raised awareness of very real need among

SSA's expanding older population and of the minimal progress that countries had made in forging policy responses (e.g., Ferreira, Apt, & Kirambi, 1999). Such awareness was reinforced by a series of key UN initiatives at the time, specifically the International Year of Older Persons and a fourth review of progress in implementation of the Vienna Plan, in 1999 (UN, 1999), and subsequent preparations for the UN's Second World Assembly on Ageing (WAAII) in Madrid, in 2002 (UN, 2002). The WAAII focused to a far greater extent on the challenges of aging in the developing world than did the Vienna Assembly.

The expanded body of recent SSA research on aging may be seen to comprise two distinct, yet overlapping strands: a more conventional academic track, and a body of explicitly advocacy-oriented work.

Academic Track

Much of the academic research has taken the form of small or moderately sized quantitative surveys, or secondary analyses of existing population survey data in a range of individual countries. Such investigations, like earlier studies, mainly generated descriptive data on the basic nature and patterns of older persons' demographic, health, economic, residential, or family support status. The findings point to several broad features of older people's circumstances in SSA. For example, a majority of older persons reside in rural areas (e.g., Mba, 2007; Nigeria Population Commission, 2004), and most live with at least one child. Only a minority lives alone or with a spouse only (e.g., Mba, 2007; UNPD, 2005; Zimmer & Dayton, 2005). A majority of older persons, especially in rural areas, remain economically active, with only very small proportions receiving pensions or income from formal assets or savings (e.g., Apt, 1996b; Baiyewu Bella, Adeyemi, Bamgboye, & Jegede, 1997; Ferreira, 2005a; Kuepie, 2007; Nigerian Population Commission [NPC], 2004). Sizeable proportions (though not always the majority) suffer from one or more mostly preventable or manageable disease conditions (e.g., Clausen, Romoren, Ferreira, & Kristensen, 2005; Ezeh, Chepngeno, Kasiira, & Woubalem, 2006; Kahn et al., 2006; Steyn, 2006; Steyn, Gaziano, Bradshaw, Laubscher, & Fourie, 2001). Several studies, for example in southern Africa, found large numbers of older persons reporting poor health and functional limitation (e.g., Clausen et al., 2005; Ferreira et al., 1992). Other surveys, for example in West African countries, typically found only a minority reporting these health conditions or limitations, thus indicating, possibly, the impact of sociocultural factors on measures of self-reported health and functioning in old age (e.g., Kuate-Defo, 2006; see Aboderin, 2009b).

Indications are that older people are marginalized in health service delivery and may receive less health care than younger adults, despite similar or higher incidence of disease (McIntyre, 2004; Ferreira, 2008). A considerable minority of those with functional limitations also are found to lack access to informal family care (Gureje, Kola, & Afolabi, 2007). Older persons' health status and living arrangements vary (though not uniformly) by gender and/or rural/urban residence, while employment and access to a pension or other income is consistently higher among older men than older women. Evidence of disparities in well-being by socioeconomic position (SEP) is more limited and conflicting. What exists (mainly regarding health) suggests that the risk of some conditions (e.g., depression) may rise with SEP (Gureje et al., 2007)—a pattern that differs from the social gradient in health found in the Global North (Ferraro & Shippee, 2007; World Health Organization [WHO], 2008b), while self-reported poor health and disability appear, as expected, to fall with SEP (Kuate-Defo, 2006; see Aboderin, 2009b). An ongoing multi-country study on global aging and adult health (SAGE) coordinated by the World Health Organization (WHO) is expected to generate more, including comparative, insights on patterns and determinants of health in old age in SSA countries (WHO, 2008b).

In addition to inquiries on older persons' basic sociodemographic, economic and health situation, a handful of recent studies have examined prevailing attitudes on old age and family support. The findings suggest that a considerable proportion of younger people hold ostensibly nontraditional attitudes regarding the value of old age and the provision of family support to older parents (e.g., Akinyemi, Adepoju, & Ogunbameru, 2007; Okoye, 2004).

Complementing the quantitative data, a number of qualitative investigations have offered more detailed descriptions of older persons' intergenerational relationships, support systems and health practices. Their findings have broadly highlighted older persons' experiences of unmet need for various dimensions of intergenerational family support and health care, but also their provision of support to younger generations (e.g., Cliggett, 2001; Ferreira, 2006a; Møller & Sotshongaye, 1996; Sagner & Mtati, 1999; Uwakwe & Modebe, 2007; Van der Geest, 1997, 2004, 2007).

A feature of much of the recent, especially quantitative, research has been its continued, uncritical embrace of modernization and aging theory as an explanatory framework. In response, a few scholars have forged explicit critiques of the theory's salience in African gerontology and, more generally, of an injudicious reliance on Western constructs and a limited use of interpretive microlevel analysis (Aboderin, 2004a, 2006; Ferreira, 1999; Makoni & Stroeken, 2002; Sagner, 1999). Building on such critiques, a single in-depth analysis has sought to examine and theorize the actual nature and causes of changes in material old-age family support, and, in doing so, has illuminated the complex interactions between individual motives and structural material and normative changes that have driven such shifts (Aboderin, 2004a, 2006). Sociolinguistic ethnographic analyses, meanwhile, have provided deep explorations of meanings of old age in various local contexts (Makoni & Stroeken, 2002; Sagner, 1999). Their findings have drawn attention, among others, to older persons' experiences of aging as a crisis or a generation gap between young trend-seekers and old tradition-keepers—and to their multiple concepts of self-conflict with common, unidimensional categorizations of the elderly (Devisch, Makoni, & Stroeken, 2002).

In addition to investigations into the situation and well-being of older people broadly, a burgeoning body of recent SSA research has sought to illuminate three specific areas. First, a growing number of studies have investigated the circumstances of older persons affected by the HIV/AIDS crisis. The investigations have primarily described older persons' roles as carers to ailing children and/or orphaned grandchildren, their loss of support from such younger kin, and, to a limited degree, their own infection with the virus, or risk thereof (e.g., Ainsworth & Dayton, 2003; Hosegood & Timaeus, 2006; Ingstad, Bruun, & Tlou, 1997; Merli & Palloni, 2006; Ntozi Ahimbisbwe, Odwee, Ayiga, & Okurut, 1999; see Ferreira, 2006b for an overview). Additional analyses have explored impacts of HIV/AIDS-related mortality on residential arrangements, pointing to reductions in older person's co-residence with adult children and increases in skipped-generation households in which grandparents live with orphaned grandchildren, with no middle-generation adult present (Zimmer, 2007).

Second, nascent research has focused on profiling the situation of older residents in urban slums as part of a broader concern for the conditions of slum-dwellers in SSA (United Nations Habitat [UN HABITAT], 2008). Emerging findings indicate extensive unmet health-care and economic needs among this population, and a lack of ability to realize desired return migrations to rural homesteads (e.g., Chepngeno & Ezeh, 2007; Ezeh et al., 2006). However, scant understanding exists as yet of older slum dwellers' own perspectives and the relative extent of their vulnerability, compared to younger slum and older non-slum populations (Nxusani, 2004).

Third, research attention is being paid increasingly to the implications of migration for older persons. A focus is on the impacts of massive rural to urban migration of younger kin and international out-migration of younger persons on intergenerational old-age support (e.g., Aboderin, 2005a; Ferreira, 2008), and late-life migration strategies of older persons themselves (e.g., Nxusani, 2004; Sagner, 1997).

Advocacy-oriented Research

A smaller body of explicitly advocacy-oriented investigations has emerged over the past decade. Frequently conducted or commissioned by key UN and international nongovernmental organizations such as UNFPA, WHO, and HelpAge International (HAI), the research has been geared toward forging a persuasive case on why it is imperative for national governments to introduce policies for the rising number of older citizens. Often in the form of small-scale studies (HAI, 2002), the participatory research has largely marshaled two main kinds of evidence.

First is documentation of older individuals' vulnerability to poverty and ill-health, which is attributed variously to combined effects of (a) physical, mental, and social changes, or attributes associated with chronological aging; (b) effects of rapid sociocultural change, economic stress, and acute crises such as HIV/AIDS or armed conflict, which strain family support and place added care burdens on older persons (see Ferreira, 2006b); and/or (c) the dearth of appropriate health and social provision for older people in most SSA countries, including in emergency and conflict situations (e.g., Bramucci & Erb, 2007; HAI, 2008; WHO, 2006).

Second, several articles present evidence of the significant contributions that older persons, in particular older women, make to the welfare and capacity development of younger generations in their family, and to their communities more generally (Ahenkora, 1999; Mohatle & de Graft Agyarko, 1999). Particularly emphasized are older people's care roles in the context of HIV/AIDS, and their use of pension income to support the education and health care of children and grandchildren (HAI, 2004, 2006; IDPM/HAI, 2003; see Ferreira, 2006b, 2008).

POLICY ON AGING IN AFRICA: ISSUES AND CHALLENGES

Building on the above evidence, an intensifying advocacy discourse on aging in SSA has forged three central arguments on the urgent need for national policy action for older persons.

First, governments have an obligation, under major international covenants, to realize the fundamental social and economic rights of older people, who are among the poorest and most vulnerable population groups—if not *the* most vulnerable—in contemporary SSA societies (Barrientos, 2002; Gorman & Heslop, 2002; HAI, 2006). Second, governments must acknowledge, encourage, and build on the valuable contributions that older persons make to their families and communities, and thus to the achievement of major development goals in general (HAI, 2004; WHO, 2002). Third, policies on aging need to be integrated or "mainstreamed" in core national development plans across sectors (Ferreira, 2008).

All three arguments, crucially, have been incorporated into and undergird the recommendations of two key international instruments presently available to guide SSA governments in forging comprehensive strategies on older persons: (a) the 2002 UN Madrid International Plan of Action on Ageing (MIPAA), which emanated from WAAII (UN, 2002), and b) the African Union (AU) Policy Framework and Plan of Action on Ageing (AU Plan), adopted in 2003 (AU/HAI, 2003). The instruments commit signatory countries to design and implement broad cross-sectoral policies to ensure, among others, that older persons are full beneficiaries of, and active contributors to, development (see Aboderin & Ferreira, 2009).

However, despite the plans' powerful message, little comprehensive policy on older persons has ensued in most SSA countries. The dearth of policy action is conspicuous and has been underscored in the UN's recent review and appraisal processes (United Nations, Department of Economic and Social Affairs [UN/DESA], 2008; United Nations Economic Commission for Africa [UNECA], 2007). Only one country (South Africa) has comprehensive legislation on older persons, and only nine nations (Botswana, Ghana, Lesotho, Mauritius, Namibia, Senegal, Seychelles, South Africa, and Zambia) have implemented concrete, national-level strategies targeted at older people (see Aboderin & Ferreira, 2009).

What is clear, moreover, is that the few policy steps taken have been narrow. Even though the MIPAA and the AU Plan call for multifaceted strategies to enhance older persons' quality of life holistically, existing policy action has focused mainly on the introduction or expansion of social protection in the form of noncontributory pensions and/or provision of free or discounted health care for older persons (for a discussion, see Aboderin & Ferreira, 2009).

CRITICAL REFLECTION ON THE CURRENT STATE OF POLICY AND RESEARCH DEBATES ON AGING IN SSA

The continued impasse in policy action on aging in SSA has ushered in what may be seen as a nascent reflective moment in African gerontology.

In recent years, a handful of SSA scholars and international bodies have begun to reflect critically on the present state of research and policy debates on aging in SSA. Such appraisal of the policy discourse (Aboderin & Ferreira, 2009) has highlighted important limitations in the coherence of dominant advocacy arguments—despite their apparent force. Specifically, the arguments fail to clarify sufficiently how rationales for policy on aging in SSA relate to, and concur with, countries' core development agendas. In particular, they omit four areas of ambiguity, namely over (1) focal cohorts and time horizons; (2) competing rights and needs of age groups; (3) policy priorities; and (4) policy approaches. The latter area specifically involves uncertainty about whether policy goals should be realized through family-based strategies aimed at strengthening traditional old-age support mechanisms or through measures to provide formal support to older individuals.

As a result, recommendations of the MIPAA and the AU Plan are passed over easily, as governments remain essentially insufficiently persuaded that the realization of policies for older people will concur with the pursuit of core national development goals, and/or insufficiently clear which policies to pursue and/or through what methods (Aboderin & Ferreira, 2009).

The recent reflections on the status of African research on aging have all begun from, and have reinforced, a premise that high-quality research evidence is a vital prerequisite for advancing apposite policy action on aging in SSA. Thus, evidence is required as a basis for both encouraging and informing policy development (e.g., Aboderin, 2005b; Aboderin & Ferreira, 2009; Cohen & Menken, 2006; Ferreira, 2005b, 2008; Ferreira & Kowal, 2006). At the same time, some assessments have asserted the importance—and real potential—of empirical evidence from SSA to advance core theoretical debates in gerontology and other relevant disciplines (Aboderin, 2005c, 2009a; Ferreira, 1999, 2005b).

Yet, the scientific and policy relevance of much SSA research remains deeply circumscribed. Inquiry on aging in the region has undoubtedly made great strides and covered important ground over the last two decades. However, the body of research remains fragmented and concentrated in a few countries and often lacks coherence, scale, rigor, and/or application. This impasse is due to three specific limitations. First are large deficiencies in the availability of even basic, reliable demographic and health data on the older population in most SSA nations. These gaps were clearly highlighted, among others, by a recent WHO-coordinated project to create a Minimum Data Set on aging and older persons in SSA (see Ferreira & Kowal, 2006).

Second are major gaps in the extent to which SSA research has thus far addressed particular issues and questions that are of chief relevance to both policy and scientific debates. In response, a number of African and international bodies—the UN Programme on Ageing in partnership with the International Association of Gerontology and Geriatrics (IAGG), the U.S. National Academies of Science (NAS), the African Research on Ageing Network (AFRAN), and individual scholars—have in recent years formulated research agendas that set out strategic priority directions and areas for future inquiry on aging in SSA (see Aboderin, 2005c; Aboderin & Ferreira, 2009; Cohen & Menken, 2006; UN/IAGG, 2008).

Third are the scant analytical endeavor and conceptual depth of much, if not most, SSA research on aging. Most studies have remained decidedly descriptive, with few attempts made to generate understanding, explanations, and theoretical ideas grounded in the perspectives, meanings, and motives of African actors—rather than derived from a reliance on *a priori* Western theories or concepts (Aboderin 2004b; Ferreira, 1999, 2005b). The scant attention paid to analysis and theory has gone alongside a neglect of certain conceptual and methodological bedrock elements (Baars, Dannefer, Phillipson, & Walker, 2006) that are vital to the study of aging, irrespective of geographical or cultural location. These elements include (a) the differentiation and comparative study of successive cohorts over time, in order to discern age and cohort effects (Riley, Foner, & Waring, 1988); (b) consideration of life-course exposures and trajectories in order to understand circumstances in old age (Elder, 1992); and (c) illumination of the interrelationships between micro (individual)-, meso (family)-, and macro (structural)-level factors in shaping experiences and conditions of old age (see Baars et al., 2006; Ryff & Marshall, 1999).

As part of the recent reflective endeavor, a few bodies, above all AFRAN, have drawn attention to, and are seeking to address, the major problems of capacity that underlie the present limitations in SSA research and policy action. Indeed, AFRAN's core mission, alongside the conduct of scientific and policy relevant research, is to promote the building of capacity on aging in SSA (Aboderin, 2005c). Shortcomings in capacity currently exist on two key levels.

First are grave limitations in the ability of scholars to produce high-quality, relevant research due to chronically under-resourced infrastructure and facilities—such as libraries, computing, and connectivity amenities, and data collection materials—at most SSA universities. The resource constraints are symptoms of a general crisis in tertiary education in the subregion (CfA, 2005), which greatly curtails opportunities for SSA scholars to access and partake in current research debates in their disciplines (Aboderin, 2005c; Assie-Lumumba, 2006; Ferreira, 2005b; World Bank, 2002). For example, the constraints limit access to relevant international literature, scientific conferences, and other fora for exchange with peers. The poor access to international publications is compounded by today's dearth of African scientific journals on aging—which again reflects a lack of requisite sustained external funding. The folding (due to a discontinuation of funds) of both the *Southern African Journal of Gerontology* (in 2000) and *African Gerontology* are an illustration of this situation. Second, capacity limitations arise due to a dearth, or the underdevelopment of, education and training on aging in SSA.

STATUS OF EDUCATION AND TRAINING ON AGING IN SSA

Formal instruction in the field of aging is a crucial stage in an effective research-policy-practice continuum. Scholars in both social sciences and medical sciences need to be grounded in gerontology and/or geriatrics in order to contribute to high-quality policy and scientific knowledge in this area. Similarly, new cadres of professionals, practitioners, and planners must be trained to implement policies and deliver services to meet the support needs of an exponentially growing older population.

Yet—and in contrast to North African nations, such as Tunisia and Egypt, where instruction in the field of aging has advanced—education and training on aging in SSA are hardly out of the starting blocks. Two surveys undertaken to assess the nature and extent of teaching on aging in African countries underscore the situation: a recent regional assessment conducted electronically through AFRAN in 2008 (Ferreira, Hoffman, & Aboderin, unpublished) and an earlier countrywide postal survey conducted in South Africa in 1994 (Ferreira, 1995). The findings of the 2008 assessment, which garnered information from 10 countries (Botswana, Ethiopia, Ivory Coast, Libya, Kenya, Nigeria, South Africa, Tanzania, Tunisia, and Zambia), offer a sketch of the current state of various types of instruction on aging in SSA.

Gerontology Education

Formal education in gerontology in the subregion's higher-education institutions is broadly lacking. African researchers on aging have been oriented and acquired research skills in gerontology largely by default—although a small number have received training abroad. Scholars have, in the past, attempted to introduce gerontology modules or programs, or at least concepts of aging, into departmental curricula and to encourage students to conduct studies on aging (Ferreira, 1995; Ntusi & Ferreira, 2004). However, they have typically met with institutional barriers at every step. As a consequence, only single gerontology instructional initiatives are available in some countries, while in others there are none. Where education is available—for example, in Tanzania, Kenya, Nigeria, and South Africa—it is offered primarily through social work departments, mainly as a module at fourth-year, master's (MSW) or certificate level, or in the form of unit courses covering aspects of gerontology in disciplines of demography, statistics, sociology, anthropology, psychology, nursing, and adult education. In two South African institutions, plans are underway (but have not been realized) to establish a full master's program in gerontological nursing. Significantly, despite the dearth of formal gerontology offerings, a growing number of master's and doctoral students at SSA universities are conducting dissertations based on aging-related topics. This situation points to a rising, and increasingly pressing, need for formal gerontology education.

Geriatrics Education

As with gerontology education, formal instruction in geriatric medicine appears to be nonexistent in the majority of SSA nations; in the remainder, it remains circumscribed. In Senegal and South Africa, some medical schools offer two-year specialist training programs at the master's level. Other institutions in these and some other countries incorporate aspects of geriatrics into medical school curricula—typically at fourth-year level and within a primary health care (PHC) focus. At two South African institutions, for example, geriatrics is taught in a Lifestyles module. Fourth-year medical students additionally spend two days in the geriatrics department during clinical rotation, while registrars in internal medicine complete a two- to three-month rotation in geriatrics. In Nigeria, Senegal, and South Africa, departments of psychiatry additionally give lectures on old-age psychiatry to medical students.

Training in Care of the Aged

Diversity (in terms of scope and content) of programs, target groups, and settings presently exists in which training is offered in care of the aged. The range includes initiatives led by government ministries, nongovernmental organizations (NGOs), and a few higher-education institutions.

The scope of the training is limited, however. Instruction offered by the government often takes the form of official meetings for discussion and staff development. NGO training can involve instruction for relevant practitioners in applied care for older persons (as offered, for example, by AGES's Nigerian chapter) and education to empower older persons themselves, or training workshops for interested community-based organizations (CBO) or other NGOs. HelpAge International's African Regional Development Centre (ARDC) in Nairobi, Kenya, for example, offers such workshops and works with partner organizations in several SSA countries to offer training to older people in human rights; literacy, numeracy, and health literacy; and skills development to foster livelihood security (Ferreira, 2008).

Training offered by higher education institutions includes (1) courses in geriatric care and management, delivered by medical school doctors, nurses, social workers, community nurses, and health officers to interest groups on an *ad hoc* basis, and (2) continuing medical education (CME) programs on aging for practitioners (as, for example, in South Africa and Senegal). In South Africa, additionally, several nursing agencies offer courses for nurses and carers. It is important to note that none of the above training is accredited—either because the countries lack a qualifications accreditation framework, or aging-related work is not recognized as a vocational occupation. However, certificates of participation or attendance may be awarded.

Impediments to Progress in Advancing Education and Training

Coupled with the findings of the 1994 South African survey (Ferreira, 1995), AFRAN's 2008 regional assessment also indicates the lack of progress made in SSA over the last 15 years in expanding instruction on aging in its countries. The reasons for this shortcoming are manifold and may be seen to include, variously, (1) a lack of government attention paid to older persons' issues, given the youthfulness of SSA populations and other priorities for administrations; (2) a lack of awareness of the implications of population aging and older people's needs in general; (3) a lack of familiarity with, or interest in, gerontology and geriatrics as specialist, multidisciplinary instructional areas; (4) traditional assumptions, now a myth, that extended family will care for its elders (see, e.g., Duodo, 1998); (5) a lack of interest of personnel and inadequate teaching resources; (6) an ill-defined job market for professionals and practitioners with skills in gerontology, geriatrics and/or care of the aged (only gerontological nursing is viewed as an occupational sector); (7) resistance of medical schools, by and large, to admit geriatric medicine as a subspecialty; (8) clinicians' perception of geriatrics as an insufficiently lucrative subspecialty (Ferreira, 2006a; Ntusi & Ferreira, 2004); (9) a lag in the development or review of relevant curricula; and (10) a lack of incentives, including financial support, for professionals and scholars to pursue education in geriatrics or gerontology.

Over the last decade, a number of pioneering international initiatives have attempted to overcome such barriers and to promote formal instruction on aging in the subregion. Two earlier initiatives were established by the African Foundation for Research and Interdisciplinary Training in Ageing (AFRITA) and HelpAge International's ARDC. AFRITA, founded in 1998, aimed specifically to build gerontology capacity in Africa through training to develop expertise in biomedical, rehabilitative, and social gerontology (Wilson, 1998; Wilson & Adamchak, 1997). To date, however, it is not clear what progress was made, and the foundation appears to be dormant.

Between 2001 and 2005, HAI's ARDC offered a number of five-day training courses on a wide range of aspects of Aging in Africa, targeted at practitioners, academics, researchers, and government officials. The training, which covered definitions, demographic trends, social, cultural and economic contexts, and implications of individual and population aging in SSA, was delivered by academics and development workers from across SSA. However, the courses were discontinued when a cycle of funding from abroad ended and the international agency reprioritized its core business activities. The faltering of these early projects, despite their initial promise, reflects an all-too-common constraint on academic and civil society initiatives in the SSA context—namely, a failure to mobilize sufficient internal and/or external resource support.

In the face of this constraint, however, two recent international initiatives remain active.

The first, the International Institute of Ageing (United Nations—Malta) (INIA) offers training programs to professionals, practitioners, academics, researchers, and government workers in developing countries. Each year, the organization provides several scholarships to individuals in African countries to participate in two-week training courses in Malta, on topics ranging from demographic, social, and economic aspects of population aging, to medical gerontology. A new program trains senior officials and other stakeholders to engage in review, appraisal, and follow-up of implementation of recommendations in MIPAA (Ferreira, 2008; UN, 2006). INIA has held *in situ* training courses in Egypt, Ghana, South

Africa, and Tunisia. (See www.inia.org.mt.) However, the programs rely largely on Western concepts and practice models as a reference point and contend implicitly that developing countries should emulate developed countries' responses to aging situations, which overlooks real problems of aging and dismisses viable solutions in African settings.

Second, AFRAN, in response, is pursuing the development of a stepwise program of education and training that is apposite to, and grounded in, African realities, perspectives, and contexts (see Aboderin, 2008, 2005c). As a component of this program, AFRAN has initiated and is presently coordinating plans for the design and delivery of (1) protocols to foster basic old-age care responsiveness at PHC level in SSA countries, and (2) basic geriatric and gerontological training for frontline health staff. The planned projects build on strategic partnerships between key African education/training institutions and practice and policy stakeholders. Nonetheless, AFRAN, too, faces considerable challenges in mobilizing sufficient funding support to sustain this and other training initiatives.

Ways Forward

What then may be a strategic way forward to sustainably foster a comprehensive expansion and improvement of education and training on aging in SSA? A first, and obvious, need is to develop a spectrum of germane academic and nonacademic instructional programs with a specialized but multidisciplinary focus. This effort requires, as a prerequisite, interdisciplinary collaboration among interested faculty members and with trainers in government and the NGO sector. An aim must be to galvanize interest in academic gerontology and geriatrics among relevant social science and medical science faculty, and to equip them with requisite knowledge and skills to enable them to deliver high-quality teaching. A second need is to determine the demand for, and supply of, practitioners, professionals, and private individuals trained in either subdiscipline and/or old-age care and to design tailored instruction for such groups. Where possible, such design should draw on expertise and examples of good practice where they exist in SSA. A third need is to establish an evolving accreditation system, with gerontology and care of the aged recognized as vocational occupations.

Ideally, individual countries should address these needs by forging, and then implementing, national plans for instruction and capacity building on aging. Concrete goals of such plans should be the establishment of (1) multidisciplinary instruction programs in gerontology and geriatrics, offered at an increasing number of higher education institutions; (2) multidisciplinary courses in care of the aged for professionals and private individuals offered at colleges and CBOs, and through university distance education programs; and (3) apposite training and relevant materials for empowerment and well-being in old age, targeted at aging individuals and provided through community and older-adult learning centers. A prerequisite for ensuring sufficient stakeholder and political support for the realization of such national plans is an effort to demonstrate compellingly the link between education and training, research, practice, and effective policy action—and its implications for overall development.

The forging of relevant education and training itself must be continually informed by systematic data collection to appraise progress in meeting instructional needs. Specifically, the survey database established by AFRAN in 2008 should be expanded and updated through regular research, to monitor trends in teaching needs and supply, and to evaluate education and training programs once established. Emerging leading centers of gerontological research in individual countries, in coalition with geriatrics departments, may be best equipped to lead a process toward an expanded research and training endeavor on aging in SSA.

CONCLUDING REMARKS

In this chapter, we sought to offer a broad overview of, and critical reflection on, the trajectory of international debate on aging in SSA, from its emergence in the early 1980s, the body of gerontology research that has been generated since then, and the present status of policy, education, and training on aging in the subregion. While we emphasize that the African gerontology endeavor has progressed over the past three decades, our concern has been to illuminate critical shortcomings in the forging of apposite policy for SSA's aging populations, and in the relevance of much research for science and policy in the subregion. We have argued that the shortcomings reflect profound limitations in resource capacity and formal training and education on aging—on the part of policy-makers, planners, practitioners, and scholars in SSA. Given these shortcomings and limitations, we have asserted a pressing need (and highlighted directions) for a comprehensive expansion of the paltry instruction on aging available in SSA countries at present. We have emphasized, moreover, that such extended education and training must be grounded in, and relevant to, African realities and perspectives on aging, rather than a simple and uncritical reliance on Western models and concepts. This prerequisite is notwithstanding the present SSA gerontology endeavor already having the potential to contribute to, and advance, gerontology in the developed world.

To this end, and in conclusion, we encourage scholars, students, and planners in developed nations and other developing countries to engage with the research and policy discourse on aging in SSA. However, a proviso in doing so should be that they do not attempt to impose Western (or other) solutions or perspectives on SSA's endeavors, but embrace the widened spectrum of perspectives and opportunities offered by the subregion for analysis, policy, and practice. In terms of the latter, insight into SSA policy and practice approaches may indeed point to novel solutions and responses to key universal aging-related challenges, such as the provision of health care and social care, and the management of HIV/AIDS. Analytically, an awareness of African realities, if coupled with a comparative, global approach to gerontology (see Aboderin, 2009a), can lead scholars to develop more refined understandings of aging in their own societies.

REFERENCES

Aboderin, I. (2004a). Decline in material support for older people in urban Ghana, Africa: Understanding processes and causes of change. *Journal of Gerontology: Psychological Sciences, Social Sciences, 5,* S128–S137.

Aboderin, I. (2004b). Modernisation and ageing theory revisited: Current explanations of recent developing world and historical Western shifts in material family support for older people. *Ageing and Society, 24,* 29–50.

Aboderin, I. (2005a). *Migration rationales and impacts among Nigerian nurses working in the U.K. eldercare sector: Implications for old age and intergenerational support in their families. A preliminary analysis.* Paper presented at the 34th annual conference of the British Society of Gerontology, Keele, United Kingdom.

Aboderin, I. (2005b). Research on ageing in Africa: The need to forge directions. *Generations Review, 15,* 3–4.

Aboderin, I. (2005c). Understanding and responding to ageing in sub-Saharan Africa. A strategic framework and plan for research. Report. Oxford, United Kingdom: University of Oxford, Oxford Institute of Ageing.

Aboderin, I. (2006). *Intergenerational support and old age in Africa.* Piscataway, NJ: Transaction Publishers.

Aboderin, I. (2008). Advancing health service provision for older persons and age-related non- communicable disease in sub-Saharan Africa: Identifying key information and training needs. African Research on Ageing Network (AFRAN) Policy-Research Dialogue Series, Report 01-2008. Oxford, United Kingdom: University of Oxford, Oxford Institute of Ageing.

Aboderin, I. (2009a). Global ageing: Perspectives from sub-Saharan Africa. In C. Phillipson & D. Dannefer (Eds.), *International handbook of social gerontology.* Newbury Park, CA: Sage. (Forthcoming.)

Aboderin, I. (2009b). West Africa. In P. Uhlenberg (Ed.), *International handbook of the demography of ageing*. New York: Springer.

Aboderin, I., & Ferreira, M. (2009). Linking ageing to development agendas in sub-Saharan Africa: Challenges and approaches. *Journal of Population Ageing*. (Forthcoming)

African Union/HelpAge International (AU/HAI). (2003). *The African Union Policy Framework and Plan of Action on Ageing*. Nairobi, Kenya: HelpAge International Africa Regional Development Centre.

Ahenkora, K. (1999). *The contributions of older people to development: The Ghana study*. London: HelpAge International.

Ainsworth, M., & Dayton, J. (2003). The impact of the AIDS epidemic on the health of older persons in northwestern Tanzania. *World Development, 3*, 131–148.

Akinyemi, I. A., Adepoju, O. A., & Ogunbameru, A. O. (2007). Changing philosophy for care and support for the elderly in south-western Nigeria. *BOLD, 18*, 18–23.

Apt, N. A. (1971). *Socio-economic conditions of the aged in Ghana*. Monograph. Accra, Ghana: Department of Social Welfare and Community Development.

Apt, N. A. (1987). *Aging, health, and family relations: A study of aging in the Central Region of Ghana*. Legon, Ghana: University of Ghana.

Apt, N. A. (1992). Family support to elderly people in Ghana. In H. L. Kendig, L. C. Coppard, & A. Mashimoto (Eds.), *Family support to the elderly: The international experience*. Oxford, United Kingdom: Oxford University Press.

Apt, N. A. (1996a). *Ageing in Ghana. Review studies*. Legon, Ghana: Centre for Social Policy Studies, University of Ghana.

Apt, N. A. (1996b). *Coping with old age in a changing Africa*. Aldershot, United Kingdom: Avebury.

Apt, N. A. (2005). 30 years of African research on ageing: History, achievements and challenges for the future. *Generations Review, 15*, 4–5.

Apt, N., Koomson, J., Williams, N., & Grieco, M. (1995). Family finance and doorstep trading: Social and economic well-being of elderly Ghanaian female traders. *Southern African Journal of Gerontology, 4*, 17–24.

Assie-Lumumba, N. (2006). Higher education in Africa: Crisis, reforms and transformation. CODESRIA Working Paper Series. Dakar, Senegal: CODESRIA.

Baars, J., Dannefer, D., Phillipson, C., & Walker, A. (2006). Introduction: Critical perspectives in social gerontology. In J. Baars, D., Dannefer, C., Phillipson, & A. Walker (Eds.), *Aging, globalization and inequality. The new critical gerontology*. Amityville, NY: Baywood.

Baiyewu, O., Bella, A. F., Adeyemi, J. D., Bamgboye, E. A., & Jegede, R. O. (1997). Health problems and socio-demographic findings in elderly Nigerians. *African Journal of Medical Science, 26*, 13–17.

Barrientos, A. (2002). Old age, poverty and social investment. *Journal of International Development, 14*, 1133–1141.

Bramucci, G., & Erb, S. (2007). An invisible population: Displaced older people in West Darfur. *Global Ageing, 4*, 23–34.

Brown, C. K. (1985). Research findings in Ghana: A survey on the elderly in the Accra Region. *African Gerontology, 4*, 11–37.

Burgess, E. W. (Ed.) (1960). *Ageing in western societies*. Chicago: University of Chicago Press.

Caldwell, J. C. (1966). The erosion of the family: A study of the fate of the family in Ghana. *Population Studies, 20*, 5–26.

Campbell, C. (1994). Intergenerational conflicts in township families: Transforming notions of respect and changing power relations. *Southern African Journal of Gerontology, 3*, 37–42.

Cattell, M. (1997). The discourse of neglect: Family support for elderly in Samia. In T. S. Weisner, C. Bradley, & P.L. Kilbride (Eds.), *African families and the crisis of social change*. Westport, C T & London: Bergin & Garvey.

Chepngeno, G., & Ezeh, A. (2007). "Between a rock and a hard place": Perception of older people living in Nairobi City on return-migration to rural areas. *Global Ageing, 4*, 67–78.

Clausen, T., Romoren, T. I., Ferreira, M., & Kristensen, P. (2005). Chronic diseases and health inequalities in older persons in Botswana. *Journal of Nutrition, Health and Ageing, 9*, 455–461.

Cliggett, L. (2001). Survival strategies of the elderly in Gwembe Valley, Zambia: Gender, residence and kin networks. *Journal of Cross-Cultural Gerontology, 16*, 309–332.

Cohen, B., & Menken, J. (2006). Report. In B. Cohen & J. Menken (Eds.), *Aging in sub-Saharan Africa: Recommendations for furthering research* Washington, DC: The National Academies Press.

Commission for Africa (CfA). (2005). *Our common interest. Report of the Commission for Africa*. London: Commission for Africa Secretariat.

Cowgill, D. O. (1972). A theory of aging in cross-cultural perspective. In D. O. Cowgill & L. D. Holmes (Eds.), *Aging and modernization* New York: Appleton-Century-Crofts.

Cowgill, D. O. (1974). Aging and modernization: A revision of the theory. In J. F. Gubrium (Ed.), *Late life*. Springfield, IL: Charles C. Thomas.

Devisch, R., Makoni, S., & Stroeken, K. (2002). Epilogue: African gerontology: Critical models, future directions. In S. Makoni & K. Stroeken (Eds.), *Ageing in Africa. Sociolinguistic and anthropological approaches*. Aldershot, United Kingdom: Ashgate.

Dorjahn, V. R. (1989). Where do the old folks live? The residence of the elderly among the Temne of Sierra Leone. *Journal of Cross-Cultural Gerontology, 4*, 257–278.

Duodo, Y. (1998). The need for geriatric services in Ghana. *Southern African Journal of Gerontology, 7*, 33–34.

Ekpenyong, S., Oyeneye, O., & Peil, M. (1987). Health problems of elderly Nigerians. *Social Science and Medicine, 24*, 885–888.

Elder, G. H., Jr. (1992). Models of the lifecourse. *Contemporary Sociology: A Journal of Reviews, 21*, 632–635.

Everatt, D., & Orkin, M. (1994). Families should stay together: Intergenerational attitudes among South African youth. *Southern African Journal of Gerontology, 3*, 43–48.

Ezeh, A., Chepngeno, G., Kasiira, A. Z., & Woubalem, Z. (2006). The situation of older people in poor urban settings: The case of Nairobi. In B. Cohen & J. Menken (Eds.), *Aging in sub-Saharan Africa: Recommendations for furthering research*. Washington, DC: The National Academies Press.

Fennell, G., Phillipson, C., & Evers, H. (1988). *The sociology of old age*. Milton Keynes: Open University Press.

Ferraro, K., & Shippee, T. P. (2007). *Aging and cumulative inequality: How does inequality get under the skin?* Paper submitted to the GSA Social Gerontology Award, sponsored by UMBC. Theoretical Developments in Social Gerontology.

Ferreira, M. (1995). *Gerontology and geriatrics education and training in South Africa. A survey report*. Cape Town: University of Cape Town, HSRC/UCT Centre for Gerontology.

Ferreira, M. (1999). Building and advancing African gerontology. Editorial. *Southern African Journal of Gerontology, 8*, 1–3.

Ferreira, M. (2005a). Advancing income security in old age in developing countries. Focus on Africa. *Global Ageing, 2*, 22–29.

Ferreira, M. (2005b). Research on ageing in Africa: What do we have, not have and should we have? *Generations Review, 15*, 32–35.

Ferreira, M. (2006a). Geriatric medicine in South Africa: A Cinderella subspecialty? Editorial. *South African Family Practice, 48*, 18.

Ferreira, M. (2006b). HIV/AIDS and older people in sub-Saharan Africa: Towards a policy framework. *Global Ageing, 4*, 56–71.

Ferreira, M. (2006c). The differential impacts of social pension income on poverty alleviation in three South African ethnic groups. *Ageing and Society, 26*, 337–354.

Ferreira, M. (2008). Ageing policies in Africa. In *Regional dimensions of the ageing situation* (ST/ESA/318). New York: United Nations Department of Economic and Social Affairs.

Ferreira, M., Apt, N. A., & Kirambi, A. (Compilers). (1999). *Ageing in changing societies. Africa preparing for the next millennium*. AGES workshop report. London: AGES International (Brook Green Print).

Ferreira, M., & Kowal, P. (2006). A Minimum Data Set on ageing and older persons in sub-Saharan Africa: Processes and outcome. *African Population Studies, 2*, 19–36.

Ferreira, M., Møller, V., Prinsloo, F. R., & Gillis, L. S. (1992). *Multidimensional survey of elderly South Africans, 1990–1991: Key findings*. Cape Town: University of Cape Town, HSRC/UCT Centre for Gerontology.

Flesch, J. (1984). Editorial. *African Gerontology, March*, 1–2.

Foner, N. (1993). When the contract fails: Care for the elderly in nonindustrial cultures. In V. L. Bengtson & W. A. Achenbaum (Eds.), *The changing contract across generations*. New York: Aldine de Gruyter.

Goode, W. J. (1963). *World revolution in family patterns*. New York: Free Press.

Gorman, M., & Heslop, M. (2002). Poverty, policy, reciprocity and older people in the South. *Journal of International Development, 14*, 1143–1151.

Gureje, O., Kola, L., & Afolabi, E. (2007). Epidemiology of major depressive disorder in elderly Nigerians in the Ibadan Study of Ageing: A community-based survey. *Lancet, 370*, 957–964.

Gureje, O., Ogunniyi, A., Kola, L., & Afolabi, E. (2006). Functional disability in elderly Nigerians: Results from the Ibadan Study of Ageing. *Journal of the American Geriatrics Society, 54*, 1784–1789.

HelpAge International (HAI). (2002). *Participatory research with older people: A sourcebook*. London: HelpAge International.

HelpAge International (HAI). (2004). *Age and security. How social pensions can deliver effective aid to poor older people and their families*. London: HelpAge International.

HelpAge International (HAI). (2006). *Why social pensions are needed now*. London: HelpAge International.

HelpAge International (HAI). (2008). *Annual Report*. London: HelpAge International. Retrieved January 4, 2009, from http://www.helpage.org/Worldwide/Africa/Resources#OhlD

Hosegood, V., & Timaeus, I. M. (2006). HIV/AIDS and older people in South Africa. In B. Cohen & J. Menken (Eds.), *Aging in sub-Saharan Africa: Recommendations for furthering research* Washington, DC: The National Academies Press. Retrieved October 19, 2008, from http://www.nap.edu/catalog/11708.html

Ingstad, B., Bruun, F. J., & Tlou, S. (1997). AIDS and the elderly Tswana: The concept of pollution and consequences for AIDS prevention. *Journal of Cross-Cultural Gerontology, 12*, 357–372.

Institute for Development Policy and Management/HelpAge International (IDPM/HAI). (2003). *Non-contributory pensions and poverty prevention. A comparative study of South Africa and Brazil*. London: HelpAge International.

Kahn, S., Tollman, S., Thorogood, M., Connor, M., Garenne, M., Collinson, M., & Hundt, G. (2006). Older adults and the health transition in Agincourt, rural South Africa: New understanding, growing complexity. In B. Cohen & J. Menken (Eds.), *Aging in sub-Saharan Africa: Recommendations for furthering research*. Washington, DC: The National Academies Press.

Keith, J., Fry, C. L., Glascock, A. P., Ikels, C., Dickerson-Putman, J., Harpending, H. C., & Draper, P. (1994). *The aging experience. Diversity and commonality across cultures*. Thousand Oaks: Sage.

Kuate-Defo, B. (2006). Interactions between socioeconomic status and living arrangements in predicting gender-specific health status among the elderly in Cameroon. In B. Cohen & J. Menken (Eds.), *Aging in sub-Saharan Africa: Recommendations for furthering research*. Washington, DC: The National Academies Press.

Kuepie, M. (2007, March 1). *The socioeconomic implications of ageing in Africa: Labour market participation and alternative sources of income*. Paper presented at the International Conference on Population Ageing, Towards an Improvement of the Quality of Life. Brussels, Belgium.

Makoni, S., & Stroeken, K. (Eds.). (2002). *Ageing in Africa. Sociolinguistic and anthropological approaches*. Aldershot, United Kingdom: Ashgate.

Marshall, V. W. (1990). *WHO health policy and United Nations aging policy: An analysis*. Paper presented at the International Sociological Association Meetings, XII World Congress of Sociology, Madrid, Spain.

Mba, C. J. (2007). Population ageing in Ghana and correlates of support availability. *Gerontechnology, 6, 102–111*.

McIntyre, D. (2004). Health policy and older people in Africa. In P. Lloyd-Sherlock (Ed.), *Living longer. Ageing, development and social protection*. London & New York: Zed Books.

Menya, M. J. (1985). Medical and social welfare of the elderly in Kenya. *African Gerontology, 4, 35–46*.

Merli, M. G., & Palloni, A. (2006). The HIV/AIDS epidemic, kin relations, living arrangements and the African elderly in South Africa. In B. Cohen & J. Menken (Eds.), *Aging in sub-Saharan Africa: Recommendations for furthering research*. Washington, DC: The National Academies Press. Retrieved October 19, 2008, from http://www.bap.edu/catalog/11708.html

Mohatle, T., & de Graft Agyarko, R. (1999). *The contributions of older people to development: The South African study*. London: HelpAge International.

Møller, V. (1994). Intergenerational relations in a society in transition: A South African case study. *Ageing and Society, 14, 155–189*.

Møller, V., & Sotshongaye, A. (1996). "My family eat this money too": Pension sharing and self-respect among Zulu grandmothers. *Southern African Journal of Gerontology, 5, 9–19*.

Mupedziswa, R. (1997). AIDS and older Zimbabweans: Who will care for the carers? *Southern African Journal of Gerontology, 6, 9–12*.

Neysmith, S., & Edwardh, J. (1983). Ideological underpinnings of the World Assembly on Aging. *The Canadian Journal on Aging, 2, 125–136*.

Nigeria Population Commission (NPC). (2004). *The elderly: Nigeria population census analysis*. Abuja, Nigeria: NPC.

Ntozi, J.P.M., Ahimbisbwe, F. E., Odwee, J. O., Ayiga, N., & Okurut, F. (1999). Orphan care: The role of the extended family in northern Uganda. In I. O. Orubuloye, J. C. Caldwell, & J.P.M. Ntozi, (Eds.), *The continuing HIV/AIDS epidemic in Africa: Responses and coping strategies*. Canberra: Australian National University Press.

Ntusi, N., & Ferreira, M. (2004). Medical practitioners' attitudes towards older patients. *South African Medical Journal, 94, 600–601*.

Nxusani, N. C. (2004). Late-life migration and adjustment of older persons. Between the Eastern and the Western Cape. In M. Ferreira & E. van Dongen (Compilers), *Untold stories. Giving voice to the lives of older persons in new South African society. An anthology*. Cape Town, South Africa: University of Cape Town, The Albertina and Walter Sisulu Institute of Ageing in Africa.

Nyanguru, A. C., & Peil, M. (1993). Housing and the elderly in Zimbabwe. *Southern African Journal of Gerontology, 2*, 3–9.

Nyanguru, A. C., Hampson, J., Adamchak, D. J., & Wilson, A. O. (1994). Family support to the elderly in Zimbabwe. *Southern African Journal of Gerontology, 3*, 22–26.

Ohuche, N. M., & Littrell, J. M. (1989). Igbo students' attitudes towards supporting aged parents. *International Journal on Aging and Human Development, 29*, 259–267.

Okoye, U. O. (2004). *The erosion of traditional forms of care for the elderly and its implication for the elderly in Nigeria*. Paper presented at the Union for African Population Studies (UAPS) African Conference on Ageing, Johannesburg, South Africa, August 2004 (pp. 18–20). Retrieved February 2, 2005, from http://www.uaps.org

O'Rand, A. M. (1990). Stratification and the life course. In R. H. Binstock & L. K. George (Eds.), *Handbook of aging and the social sciences* (3rd ed.). San Diego: Academic Press.

Peil, M., Bamisaiye, A., & Ekpenyong, S. (1989). Health and physical support for the elderly in Nigeria. *Journal of Cross-Cultural Gerontology, 4*, 89–106.

Phillipson, C. (1982). *Capitalism and the construction of old age*. London: Macmillan.

Riley, M. W., Foner, A., & Waring, J. (1988). Sociology of age. In N. Smelser (Ed.), *Handbook of sociology*. Beverly Hills, CA: Sage.

Rostow, W. W. (1960). *The stages of economic growth*. Cambridge, United Kingdom: Cambridge University Press.

Ryff, C., & Marshall, V. W. (Eds.). (1999). *The self and society in aging processes*. New York: Springer.

Sagner, A. (1997). Urbanization, ageing and migration: Some evidence from African settlements in Cape Town. *Southern African Journal of Gerontology, 6*, 13–19.

Sagner, A. (1999). Reflections on the construction and study of elderliness. *Southern African Journal of Gerontology, 8*, 1–6.

Sagner, A., & Mtati, R. Z. (1999). Politics of pension sharing in South Africa. *Ageing and Society, 19*, 393–416.

Sangree, W. H. (1992). Grandparenthood and modernisation: The changing status of male and female elders in Tiriki, Kenya and Irigwe, Nigeria. *Journal of Cross-Cultural Gerontology, 7*, 331–361.

Shapiro, E., & Kaufert, J. (1983). The role of international conferences—A theoretical framework. *Canadian Journal on Aging, 2*, 43–9.

Shuman, T. (1984). Aging in Africa. *African Gerontology, 1,* 3–9.

Steyn, K., Gaziano, T. A., Bradshaw, D., Laubscher, R., & Fourie, J. (2001). Hypertension in South African adults: Results from the Demographic and Health Survey 1998. *Journal of Hypertension, 19,* 1717–1725.

Steyn, K. (2006). Hypertension in South African adults: Results from the Demographic and Health Survey 1998. *Journal of Hypertension, 19,* 1717–1725.

Togonu-Bickersteth, F. (1989). Conflicts over caregiving: Discussion of filial obligation among adult Nigerian children. *Journal of Cross-Cultural Gerontology, 4,* 35–48.

Togonu-Bickersteth, F., & Akinnawo, E. O. (1990). Filial responsibility expectations of Nigerian and Indian university students. *Journal of Cross-Cultural Gerontology, 5,* 315–332.

United Nations. (1982). *Report of the World Assembly on Ageing, Vienna, 26 July to 6 August.* New York: United Nations.

United Nations. (1999). *Fourth review and appraisal of the implementation of the International Plan of Action on Ageing. Summary of findings.* Retrieved December 17, 1999, from http://www.un.org/esa/socdev/age4ra01.htm/

United Nations. (2002). *Report of the Second World Assembly on Ageing.* New York: United Nations.

United Nations. (2006). *Follow-up to the Second World Assembly on Ageing: Report of the Secretary-General.* (A/61/167.) New York: United Nations.

United Nations, Department of Economic and Social Affairs (UN/DESA). (2008). *Regional dimensions of the ageing situation.* New York: United Nations. Retrieved October 10, 2008, from http://www.un.org/esa/socdev/ageing/documents/publications/cp-regional-dimension.pdf

United Nations Development Programme (UNDP). (2008). *Human development report 2007/8. Fighting climate change: Human solidarity in a divided world.* New York: Palgrave Macmillan for UNDP.

United Nations Economic Commission for Africa (UNECA). (2007). *The state of older persons in Africa—2007. Regional review and appraisal of the Madrid International Plan of Action on Ageing.* Draft report. Addis Ababa, Ethiopia: UNECA.

United Nations Habitat (UN HABITAT). (2008). *State of the world's cities 2008/2009. Harmonious cities.* Nairobi, Kenya: UN HABITAT.

United Nations/International Association of Gerontology and Geriatrics (UN/IAGG). (2008). *Research agenda on ageing for the 21st Century.* New York: United Nations.

United Nations Population Division (UNPD). (2005). *Living arrangements of older persons around the world.* New York: UNPD.

United Nations Population Division (UNPD). (2008). *World population prospects: The 2006 revision.* New York: UNPD. Retrieved October 3, 2008, from http://esa.un.org/unpp/

Uwakwe, R., & Modebe, I. (2007). Community and family care responsibilities for persons with dementia in Eastern Nigeria. *Global Ageing, 4,* 35–44.

Van der Geest, S. (1997). Between respect and reciprocity: Managing old age in rural Ghana. *Southern African Journal of Gerontology, 6*, 20–25.

Van der Geest, S. (2004). "They don't come to listen": The experience of loneliness among older people in Kwahu, Ghana. *Journal of Cross-Cultural Gerontology, 19*, 77–96.

Van der Geest, S. (2007). Complaining and not complaining: Social strategies of older people in Kwahu, Ghana. *Global Ageing, 4*, 55–66.

Walker, A. (1981). Towards a political economy of old age. *Ageing and Society, 1*, 73–94.

Wilson, A. O. (1998). African Foundation for Research and Interdisciplinary Training in Ageing. *Southern African Journal of Gerontology, 7*, 36.

Wilson, A. O., & Adamchak, D. J. (1997). Linking priorities for training, research and policy on ageing in sub-Saharan Africa. *Southern African Journal of Gerontology, 6*, 41–42.

World Bank. (2002). *Constructing knowledge societies: New challenges for tertiary education*. Washington, DC: World Bank.

World Bank. (2008). *Country classification*. Washington, DC: World Bank. Retrieved July 4, 2008, from http://go.worldbank.org/K2CKM78CC0

World Health Organization (WHO). (2002). *Active ageing. A policy framework*. Geneva: WHO.

World Health Organization (WHO). (2006). *The health of the people. The African regional health report*. Brazzaville, Republic of Congo: WHO Regional Office for Africa.

World Health Organization (WHO). (2008a). *Closing the gap in a generation: Health equity through action on the social determinants of health*. Geneva: WHO.

World Health Organization (WHO). (2008b). *The WHO multicountry study on global ageing and adult health*. Retrieved December 20, 2008, from http://www.who.int/healthinfo/systems/sage/en/index.html

Zimmer, Z. (2007). HIV/AIDS and the living arrangements of older persons across the sub-Saharan African region. Institute of Public and International Affairs (IPIA) Working Paper 2007-11-21, IPIA, University of Utah. Retrieved from www.ipia.utah.edu/workingpapers.html

Zimmer, Z., & Dayton, J. (2005). Older adults in sub-Saharan Africa living with children and grandchildren. *Population Studies, 59*, 295–312.

2

..■..

Asia-Pacific Region

Sheung-Tak Cheng, David R. Phillips,
and Alfred C. M. Chan

TRENDS IN AGING IN THE ASIA-PACIFIC

The dynamics of population aging vary internationally, as the drivers, such as fertility and longevity, are not uniform (Kinsella & Phillips, 2005). Asia will be at the forefront of global aging in the next couple of decades, with China as the major country in terms of growth in numbers of older persons (Cheng & Heller, in press). However, demographic aging across the Asia-Pacific region is not uniform, although the patterns have been establishing for over a decade (Phillips, 1992, 2000) (Table 2.1). Subregionally, the countries of East Asia (China, Taiwan, South Korea, Hong Kong, and Singapore, demographically part of this group) will see the most rapid interim increases, with those in Japan, an already aged country, leveling off. Countries in Southeast Asia (such as Cambodia, Indonesia, the Philippines, and Laos) will in general see lower rates in increase in the initial part of this period, but many will see growth toward the middle of the century. Others, such as Thailand and Vietnam, are in an intermediate position, having a fairly well-established aging profile already (Kinsella & Phillips, 2005; Mujahid, 2006; Phillips, 2000; Yoon & Hendricks, 2006).

As elsewhere, the main reasons for the demographic aging of most countries in the Asia-Pacific region are falling and sometimes very low fertility rates, as well as gradually rising longevity (Cheng, Chan, & Phillips, 2008). UNESCAP[1] (2008) indicates that total fertility rates (TFRs)

Table 2.1
Key aging data for selected Asia-Pacific countries

Country or area and region	Mid-2008 population (thousands)	Crude birth rate (per 1,000)	Crude death rate (per 1,000)	Total fertility rate	Life expectancy at birth (years) males	Life expectancy at birth (years) females	% aged 0–14	% aged 60+	Ageing index (2008)	Per capita GDP (PPP US$)	Projected population 2025 (thousands)
EAST AND NORTH-EAST ASIA	1,546,983	12.6	7.2	1.7	72	76	19	14	70	–	1,653,959
China	1,336,311	13.1	7.1	1.7	71	75	20	12	58	6,757	1,445,782
Democratic People's Republic of Korea	23,867	13.3	9.9	1.9	65	69	22	14	62	–	25,228
Hong Kong, China	6,977	10.1	5.6	1.3	79	85	13	17	125	34,833	8,305
Japan	128,026	8.7	8.6	1.3	79	86	14	29	212	31,267	121,614
Macao, China	541	8.6	2.9	0.9	79	83	14	12	87	–	535
Mongolia	2,654	18.3	6.5	1.9	64	70	27	6	22	2,107	3,112
Republic of Korea	48,607	9.2	5.0	1.2	76	82	17	15	89	22,029	49,019

SOUTH-EAST ASIA	577,877	19	6.4	2.3	68	73	28	8	30	–	682,537
Brunei Darussalam	398	21.3	2.8	2.3	75	80	28	5	19	28,161	526
Cambodia	14,656	26.4	8.9	3.4	58	62	35	5	16	2,727	19,489
Indonesia	234,342	18.5	6.3	2.2	69	73	27	9	32	3,843	271,227
Lao PDR	5,963	26.6	7.0	3.2	63	66	37	5	14	2,039	7,713
Malaysia	27,663	17.6	4.4	2.6	72	77	30	7	25	10,882	33,769
Myanmar	49,221	18	9.6	2.1	59	65	26	8	32	1,027	55,374
Philippines	90,457	25.6	4.8	3.2	70	74	35	6	18	5,137	115,878
Singapore	4,490	8.1	5.3	1.3	78	82	17	15	85	29,663	5,104
Thailand	63,121	12.5	8.0	1.5	70	77	22	11	52	8,677	65,089
Timor-Leste	1,193	41.9	8.8	6.5	60	62	45	5	10	–	2,011
Vietnam	86,373	17.5	5.8	2.1	70	73	29	9	30	3,071	106,357

Source: UNESCAP. (2008). *Population data sheet 2008.* Bangkok, Thailand: UNESCAP.

in many Asian countries are lower than the world average of 2.6 and the natural replacement rate (2.1), with the Republic of Korea, Japan, Singapore, and Thailand at 1.2, 1.3, 1.3, and 1.5 respectively. Rates for Macao and Hong Kong—both approximately 0.9 to 1.0—are the lowest in the world. In such countries, rapid declines in fertility rates were accompanied by relatively rapid increases in longevity compared to the slower evolution in the West. The life expectancies at birth for Hong Kong and Japan (average life expectancy (ELB) 82 years), Macao and Singapore (80), Korea (79), and Taiwan (77) are now higher than the world and Asian averages (68). Moreover, women outlive men by four years or more (in the cases of Japan, Hong Kong, and Thailand) in many Asia-Pacific countries (Cheng et al., 2008; Population Reference Bureau, 2007; UNESCAP, 2008).

Asia cannot be ignored in demographic aging, as it has over half of the world's population of persons aged 65+, at a total of 495,126,000 in 2007, of whom 53.3% resided in Asia (UNPD, 2007).[2] Yet, the Asia-Pacific subregion is diverse in both population composition and socio-economic development. Japan, for example, is the oldest society in the world, with 21% of its population aged 65+. China is the world's most populous country and its rapid aging is underpinned by 30 years of a one-child policy. Its older population will double from 7% to 14% in just 26 years, from 2000 to 2026 (U.S. Census Bureau, n.d.); and South Korea, aging at a comparable pace to China, will achieve the same in just 22 years, starting from 2000 (Oh & Warnes, 2001). Hong Kong SAR China, Macao SAR China, Singapore, and South Korea, with roughly 10% of their population aged 65+ now will, similar to Japan, have around one-third of their populations aged 65+ by 2050. Therefore, relative to European and North American countries, many in Asia are aging within a compressed time scale. Developing countries like China and Thailand will reach a quarter of combined populations aged 65+; roughly 8% now. Henceforth, they will face challenges of population aging before being fully economically and technologically advanced (Phillips, 2000). They will also experience very important social and economic divides in ability to cope with demographic aging, and variations between urban and rural populations.

Some of the developing countries in the region—like Cambodia, Lao PDR, Myanmar, and Philippines—are still relatively young, with only 5–8% of the population aged 60+ and 3–4% aged 65+ in 2005. About one-tenth of their populations are expected to be aged 65+ by 2050 (UNPD, n.d.). Consequently, they have up to a two-decade window of opportunity in which to plan for the challenges of population aging. During the same two decades, they will have to meet the needs of economic development and a youthful population, which presents a dual challenge.

Because of increasing life expectancy, one of the fastest-growing population segments is the oldest-old population, sometimes defined as age 80+, although some feel this needs extending to 85+. This segment is expected to increase approximately fivefold between now and 2050 in most countries in the region. In Hong Kong, Japan, and other cities in the region where population aging is more pronounced, those aged 80+ will make up over 40% of the total older population by 2050 (UNPD, n.d.). Many among these older people may inevitably need long-term care (LTC). Support for community caregivers and the age structure calls for a wholesale reorientation of health, welfare, and support services toward smaller families and older populations, especially when there is not a concomitant increase in the economic and health status of the oldest-old populations (see later in this chapter). Care and support for the oldest old is likely to become of increasing significance in the coming decades, especially in the more rapidly aging countries of the region. It will impact societies and families. As recent UN reports point out (UNDESA, 2007a, 2007b),[3] people in their 50s or 60s will increasingly find themselves responsible for the care of one or more close family members aged 80 or over. The phenomenon of middle-aged adults in many Asia-Pacific countries becoming responsible for their very aging parents, as well as for their own children, is likely to be a pressing social and economic issue.

CHALLENGES OF POPULATION AGING IN THE ASIA-PACIFIC

The Madrid International Plan of Action on Aging (MIPAA; UN, 2002) outlined three priorities on which international efforts should focus in respect to population aging. These three priorities provide a perspective for the analysis of aging issues and policy development in the region: (1) older persons and development; (2) advancing health and well-being into old age; and (3) ensuring enabling and supportive environments. The ESCAP region's Shanghai Implementation Strategy (UNESCAP, 2003) shows how many countries have adopted such plans, with reference to special considerations—economic and political diversities; geographical barriers to service accessibility; social, cultural, and linguistic diversities. A UNESCAP-coordinated meeting in Macao in October 2007 provided a progress overview of the regions implementing MIPAA (UNESCAP, 2007). We now outline several significant issues of interest to many countries in the region identified in the MIPAA reviews, based on discussions

in Cheng et al. (2008). The UN has also issued a strategic implementation framework and advice for member states worldwide in their efforts
to implement the MIPAA up to 2012, based on results of the global first
review of the Madrid Plan in 2007–8. While it is hoped the framework
should be universal, it is recognized that many countries are at different
stages of economic and social development, as well as being in different
phases of population aging (UN, 2008).

Older Persons and Development

Social Protection

The nature and extent of social protection in countries of the Asia-
Pacific region are more diverse than in countries of the Americas and
European Union. Because there are relatively few advanced countries in
the Asia-Pacific region, poverty among most age groups, especially older
persons, is evident in many of its developing countries, where many people live on less than US$2 a day. This is especially common in rural areas
where older persons live in poverty or extreme poverty (Cheng et al.,
2008). Many older people tend to continue working or rely principally on
their families for social security, since they have, formerly, earned little.
In the region, only between 9% and 30% of the older population receive
any pension or social security benefits (UNESCAP, 2004). Many Asia-
Pacific countries lack universal benefits for the elderly as a group and, due
to financial constraints, their social security programs are rarely comprehensive and almost always tend to target only the very poor and disabled
persons. In addition to the limited coverage, levels of payment are very
small, so poverty has been identified as a prime issue of concern in many
countries in this region (Cheng et al., 2008). Countries such as Malaysia
are now addressing this and attempting to make benefits both wider and
more meaningful (Ong, Phillips, & Tengku-Aizan, 2009, in press).

A 2002 Survey of Elderly in Thailand conducted by the National Statistics Office found that only 50% of those aged 60+ were aware of social
security for older persons, and as few as 5% received aid (Knodel, Chayovan, Mithranon, Amornsirisomboon, & Arunraksombat, 2005). Many
among the current cohorts of older population in the developing countries
are unaware of existing benefits and social security systems, partly because
of their low education and illiteracy (Friedman, Knodel, Cuong, & Anh,
2003; Sobieszczyk, Knodel, & Chayovan, 2003; Zeng, Liu, & George,
2003). Women, residents of rural areas, and the oldest persons are often
left out of the safety net. In many countries, formal benefit systems are

limited principally to civil servants, the military or employees of state-owned enterprises (Malaysia, Thailand, the Philippines, Hong Kong) or employees in moderate- to large-sized, often international, enterprises (e.g., Indonesia, Laos, Vietnam, and Papua New Guinea; Office of Policy Data, 2005). This excludes most workers in small businesses or in informal types of jobs, who are very numerous in the region. Some countries have recently been trying to establish mandatory or provident fund systems, as in Hong Kong, Malaysia and a few others, but these schemes will take years to mature and benefit older people. Singapore's long-established Central Provident Fund is an exception to the rule.

In China, the transition to a market economy has effectively bank-rupted the pay-as-you-go pension fund of many state-owned enterprises, which meant that predominantly only civil servants and urban workers are truly covered. A new three-pillar system—social pooling, individual accounts, and voluntary supplementary corporate schemes—has been set up since, but its effect remains to be seen due to implementation delay, lack of incentive, and inability to pay for contributions (Béland & Yu, 2004; Williamson & Deitelbaum, 2005). Owing to a rapidly growing market economy, jobs and wealth are concentrated mainly in urbanized areas and in some richer villages, where vast pools of casual labor have been concentrated. Many workers who are not properly registered miss out on benefits, and there are considerable geographical variations. Workers in wealthier provinces or cities, such as Guandong or Shanghai, would, in theory, enjoy a fair pension, while people unable to pay or living in poorer provinces or rural villages would go without one. Perhaps more serious, there is effectively almost no formal pension coverage in rural areas in which roughly two-thirds of China's population reside. Many other regional countries that are less developed face similar challenges (Cheng et al., 2008).

In most countries, there is an ever mounting burden of providing social protection for rapidly expanding older populations, with fewer taxable workers supporting the increasing retirement beneficiaries. For example, there were 29 retirees supported by 100 working age persons in China in 2001; this is expected to increase to 55 in 30 years' time (Keran & Cheng, 2002). Countries such as China, the Hong Kong SAR, Singapore, the Philippines, and many others need to include individual accounts in their social security programs. Even the most affluent country in the region, Japan, finds it difficult to formulate a sustainable pension scheme for its citizens (Sakamoto, 2005). Other countries with pension systems or provident funds, such as Singapore, are also gradually increasing retirement or pensionable ages, and/or providing incentives to encourage employees to work beyond current retirement ages. Singapore's retirement age has been increasing from 55 to 62 (Teo, Mehta, Thang, & Chang, 2006). Other countries have taken different measures to deal with population aging, such as switching from defined benefits to defined contributions schemes. Many plan to adopt variants on the three-pillar system involving public and private sectors: (1) a minimal public pension, means tested or universal; (2) mandatory occupational contributions; and (3) voluntary support or contribution by individuals or family savings. However, pension reforms are intrinsically complex, long-term, and politically sensitive.

Strengthening the Informal Care System

Traditionally, in most Asian countries, the family has been the main source of both financial support and personal care. Sometimes this is referred to as "traditional Asian values" and concepts such as filial piety (family inter-responsibility). To date, many people have lived with or close by to their extended family households, drawing on each other's resources for psychological, social, and physical needs. This practice has certainly been undergoing considerable modification in recent years, especially amongst the growing urban classes; yet, almost everywhere in the region, there is a very strong emotional attachment to family informal care. This especially applies in the care of, and relationships with, older family members and the structure and relationships with ancestors. Partly due to the problems of providing official financial, welfare, and security support, almost every country in the region has been considering ways to bolster these traditional family-based informal systems (UNESCAP, 2003, 2004).

Stemming in large part from the influence of Confucian philosophies, people believe that the sense of well-being of older person depends largely on the filial devotion of their children, regardless of genuine needs (Cheng & Chan, 2006a). Therefore, young people have traditionally looked after older persons in the family with minimal state intervention, as part of the reciprocity for the care they received from their parents when they were young. This understanding is widespread in the region. For example, in Thailand, two representative surveys eight years apart found that the majority of elderly people (84.5% in 1994, 77.2% in 2002) received financial support from children, whereas the government contributes a very minor percentage (Knodel et al., 2005). Korea displays similar data; for example, in 2001, it was found that 59.4% of older persons had children as the main source of income, compared to just 2.7% in USA (UNPD, 2005). One could interpret these findings as a result of a lack of political and philosophical support for older people's welfare in Asia, thus requiring many family contributions in the region (e.g., Oh & Warnes, 2001). This is almost certainly true in part, but there is no denying the genuine importance of and attachment to familism and, especially previously, the strength of the extended family almost everywhere in the Asia-Pacific region.

However, in spite of this strong, almost overwhelming, tradition, family support for older persons has generally been declining in recent years, due to a combination of many factors. Underlying issues such as urbanization, migration of young people to cities, the emergence of the nuclear family as the norm for young adults, and increasing female education and involvement in the labor force have all combined to reduce the family's ability to provide continuing and sufficient care. Some also note the loss of status and economic resources of older persons, especially in the face of modernization and technology (Cheng & Chan, 2006a; Oh & Warnes, 2001). These factors have different significance for different places and people, but they certainly interact to redefine children's obligation to parents, and vice versa. Some see a substitution of indirect financial support in place of direct personal care or the growing importance of other older friends and neighbors as carers rather than children. Surveys in Chinese societies have consistently illustrated the trend of younger and even older generations to have less traditional attitudes toward co-residence and financial support for older persons. With fewer co-residences, what used to be the traditional duty of co-residing daughters-in-law (care being expected from a wife for her husband's family) is now assumed by daughters (Cheng & Chan, 2006a). In the longer term, this could be a serious issue as fewer girls are being born in China and several other countries of the region as well, so there will be fewer female carers available, and many of those will wish to work outside the home. It appears that who provides care and informal support can be both a source of added or reduced stress and well-being amongst older persons (Phillips et al., in press).

Although it is still relatively less likely in most parts of the Asia-Pacific region than elsewhere for older persons to live alone (overall, approximately 5% for men and 9% for women aged 60+, against the world mean of 8% and 19% respectively), there has been a noticeable increase across most Asian societies in the percentages of older people living with a spouse only (UNPD, 2005). Over a 20-year period, the percentage indicating children as the primary source of income for older persons also declined from 78.2% in 1981 to 59.4% in 2001 for Korea, and from 29.8% to 12.0% for Japan, compared with a steady 2.5% for the USA (UNPD, 2005). In the fast-developing Asia-Pacific economies, especially China,

Taiwan, Korea, Vietnam, and Thailand, there has been marked migration of younger adults from rural to urban areas, so it is increasingly common for older persons to be living alone or only with a spouse in rural areas, and these are places where formal support is often insufficient (UNPD, 2005). The informal care that absent children could have provided is often replaced by cash remittances to parents, but the close physical and emotional care is obviously lost. Ironically, as Knodel and Saengtienchai (2007) found in a Thai study, mobile phone communications can help parents keep in touch with their migrant children, but this still does not mean that daily care can be provided.

While many governments and organizations feel it is important to reinstate or bolster traditional family values in the years to come, others have claimed that the popular conception of a strong family care network has played a significant role in preventing the development of comprehensive public formal care networks, a debate that has arisen in Korea, China, and other countries. It is nevertheless something of a consensus that informal social networks such as family, friends, and neighbors can provide indispensable assistance to meet the growing needs of older persons. More developed places like Hong Kong SAR, Singapore, and Korea are using tax exemption to encourage adult children to live with or provide financial assistance to their parents. Malaysia, the Philippines, Singapore, China, and recently India have made it mandatory by law for children to support their parents, even if such laws are weak or seldom enforced (UNESCAP, 2004). However, with increasingly aged populations, it may be unrealistic to expect unskilled carers to take up the full challenge of caring for older people with complex conditions such as Alzheimer's disease. So, equipping caregivers with the necessary knowledge and skills to take care of family members and making available mutual support among caregivers are especially useful (Mittelman, 2005). Another view is that reliance on laws such as Singapore's Parental Maintenance Act (1996) has potential problems. The Act prioritizes the family as the first line of support and it could be interpreted as a form of empowerment for older people. It could, however, have adverse effects, and "the enforcement of filial piety may further fragment the already weakened intergenerational ties among family members when parents seek such drastic action" (Teo et al., 2006, p. 124).

Gender Equality

Women are often caregivers in the nuclear and extended families, but they often receive little support for their roles. For example, homemaking and informal caregiving will rarely give financial returns, as they are not recognized occupations, but many are bound to these roles for life. Cross-cultural studies have consistently shown female caregivers spending prolonged hours to provide personal care and do housework. They are more subjectively burdened than male caregivers primarily because of their tendency to internalize kinkeeping and caregiving roles (Bookwala & Schulz, 2000; Chiou, Chen, & Wang, 2005). Among married older persons in Thailand, more men than women chose their spouse to be the main personal care provider—71.2% and 49.7% respectively (Knodel et al., 2005).

In many ways, not solely through tradition, women are disadvantaged in many developing countries of the Asia-Pacific region. Due to their lack of education and consequent illiteracy, they are frequently dependent on men for land and income (Friedman et al., 2003; Sobieszczyk et al., 2003). The current generation of older persons, male and female, in most of the region, are poorly educated and many are illiterate, and older females almost consistently score worse in educational terms. Women in rural areas, in particular, are often treated as the property of their husbands or families. They may not be entitled to or be denied basic education, and they may be abused, so the future may not improve as rapidly as in economically advanced countries of the Asia-Pacific. Gender inequality can deprive women of their rights, and, at an extreme, segregate them from the rest of the community. Isolation (Sorkin, Rook, & Lu, 2002) and lack of formal support puts widows at greater risk of health and cognitive deterioration (UNESCAP, 2002). Education is the chief determinant of service utilization in these countries, particularly rural areas. It is important to recognize that older women can only participate fully in the society with equal status and financial security. Unfortunately, social insurance rarely covers homemakers in most countries in the region.

Though most discussion on gender issues focuses largely on the status of women in society, men also can suffer shortfalls from their position held in society. Consistently, men have shorter life expectancies than females, often by several years. Males may be less likely to maintain a broad social network as they age and they may tend to rely heavily on immediate family members, such as their wife, for emotional and active support. This may be workable when they still have a spouse, and when marriage has been more or less universal, but for future cohorts of men in the region, greater self-reliance may become necessary. Men may also find that their devotion to occupational and financial achievements will lead them to depend on their wives for social networks, emotional comfort, and household duties. Social norms may keep them distant from their own children and men often suffer more psychologically than women, when their spouses are incapacitated or depart (Cheng & Chan, 2006b). In conclusion, a gender-equitable society should benefit all.

Eliminating Age Discrimination and Promoting the Image of Older Persons

Unlike gender discrimination, age discrimination affects all in society as it encourages a form of segregation (Cheng et al., 2008). There are direct and indirect forms of discrimination: active discrimination happens when a person is denied an opportunity simply because of his/her age; indirect discrimination is when application of a requirement, condition, or practice places everyone else above the consideration of older persons. Historically, older persons have enjoyed a high status and esteem in the region; however, industrialization and urbanization may have encouraged age discrimination. Many urban dwellers may be denied jobs because they are considered "too old," even though they are experienced and competent. This view is shared by many in parts of the region. The UN view of a society for all ages calls for the elimination of age discrimination, as it damages intergenerational solidarity and hinders older people's full participation, but this is very hard to achieve. As in the West, negative stereotyping of older people can be a major obstacle to eliminating age discrimination (UN, 2008). In Asia, factors such as illiteracy and low education only reinforce the myth of the nonproductive, dependent, and frail older person.

One area that is of growing concern in the Asia-Pacific is the often unspoken topic of elder abuse and its prevention. The legislation for maintenance of parents in a number of countries has been noted, but aspects of cruelty and neglect, perhaps unintentional, perhaps deliberate, deserve attention. Another area is crimes against older persons. In general, older persons are at relatively low risk of being direct victims of violent crime and many Asian urban and rural environments are quite safe. Nevertheless, older persons are often targeted in petty theft, phone scams, and confidence-trick types of crime, as reports in Singapore suggest (Global Action on Aging, 2008). A study in Hong Kong has found the type of living environment, its security and social facilities can considerably affect older persons' levels of fear of crime and hence their well-being (Chan, 2008).

The concept of *productive aging* emphasizes that older people can contribute directly in terms of income generation, and indirectly by providing family care, freeing younger people to work, or by doing a wide range of voluntary activities. Direct and indirect economic participation by older persons is thus important. Not only can it improve the financial health of the economy and the later lives of individual workers, but it can also provide meaningful roles and a sense of identity for older people (Cheng et al., 2008; World Health Organization [WHO], 2002). Wider participation in the labor force can go a long way to eliminating ageism, as waged labor determines to a large extent one's value in modern economies. In fact, some developed regional economies (e.g., Australia and Singapore) note that older workers can benefit all parties in a business because their wisdom can be retained in the system, and they can also mentor younger workers. Internationally, it has been found that older workers can be more reliable than younger workers in many areas, especially in less glamorous service work. The main concern in many countries of the region is training and retraining older workers in today's rapidly changing economy in order to help alleviate the projected labor-force shortages (Teo et al., 2006). To expedite or enable these developments, legal changes may be needed to support older people's economic participation.

A related trend in *active aging* is for older persons to participate socially and economically in unpaid volunteer work. Volunteering creates social capital—it is productive work that carries economic value, despite its exclusion from the conventional gross domestic product. It also provides a compensation for individuals experiencing role loss (Greenfield & Marks, 2004) and a platform to build social ties in later life. Volunteer work is clearly a potential contributor to successful aging, and social participation is a key element in the WHO's (2002) Active Aging Policy Framework. Volunteering can take place in a variety of sectors, such as health and welfare (for example, at a local level in the Hong Kong Hospital Authority); even internationally, where retired professionals use their skills; or at an informal level, with a growing trend of old-to-old peer volunteering in Singapore (Teo et al., 2006). Older people's aspirations to volunteer and continue contributing in other ways will increase as the future cohorts in Asia are more educated (Cheng et al., 2004; Chou, Chow, & Chi, 2003). In the future, older people in the region will be more politically active and influential as they comprise a larger, better educated and wealthier segment.

Productive aging itself can take numerous forms. In addition to being productive economically and/or via volunteering, older persons in the region contribute to many other areas such as family welfare, child care and as carers for other older persons. A largely unquantified, if well-recognized, aspect of productive aging is the contribution of older persons to farming, animal care, and food production in rural areas. However, an important and growing phenomenon is what has been called in Japan the silver market of older persons. This has two aspects: older persons as consumers and as a major target or market for services such as finance, housing, vacations, leisure activities, and education (Phillips et al., 2009). The older group in many countries is often, as in the West, the main growing sector of the population and is often targeted both as consumers generally and for targeted goods and services for the age group. In some countries such as Japan, this is well established, and in others, such as Korea, Taiwan, and China, the silver market will become substantial. Elderly poverty has been stressed in many of the poorer and middle-income countries of the region and, while this is a key issue, middle-class older consumers are growing in numbers and in the future will form a major market segment, especially where birthrates and new younger consumers are falling. Recently in Asia, an organization called Silver has started to attempt to connect business and the 50+ segment in an innovative marketing strategy (Silvergroup, 2009).

Both demographic trends (declining fertility rates) and economic trends (increasing wealth) are making the silver market of increasing interest to many businesses. Sometimes older people are a market for gerontechnology applications and knowledge transfer between older and younger workers (HSBC, 2007). Older people increasingly have consumer power in their own right, as in many Western economies. They demand quality in goods and services, like any other consumers. Research in Malaysia has shown older adults to be rather discerning consumers, termed "canny consumers" by Ong and Phillips (2007). Contrary to many stereotypical images, older consumers were also able to discriminate and to select, especially on the basis of price and durability of products.

Advancing Health and Well-being into Old Age

Preventive and Primary Health Care (PHC)

Preventive and primary level health care are often deemed the best strategies for dealing with the challenges of population aging, especially in developing countries (WHO, 2004). Many developing and intermediate regional countries (such as Thailand, Vietnam, and the Philippines) do not have the infrastructure to deliver high-quality secondary and tertiary care, and many are moving increasingly toward a community-based model of health care. For the foreseeable future, it is practical for poorer countries to concentrate their resources on health promotion and disease prevention and on establishing comprehensive PHC. This will include environmental hygiene, a problem in most rural villages and many inner cities, where health promotion and education are needed, particularly about healthy behavior and sanitary practices. PHC has particular potential for providing care for older persons that is accessible, community based, and often culturally acceptable. It is often more appropriate than distant tertiary care, especially for the growing numbers with chronic diseases, as a five-country study in Asia by HelpAge International (2007) emphasizes. Many common health problems, like circulatory disorders and mobility problems, are often most appropriately supported by community-based LTC instead of higher-level hospital technology.

Some forms of universal health care have been experimented with for all ages, including older adults. Thailand's 30 baht (US$0.70) per visit gold card health-care scheme, introduced in 2001, is perhaps the best example in a transitional Asian economy (Coronini-Cronberg, Laohasiriwong, & Gericke, 2007). This gives access to public health care and hospitals nationwide and is politically popular, especially in the rural provinces, where costs previously kept many from hospital care. The program covers basic illnesses plus many expensive surgeries and treatments for AIDS and cancer. Almost 80% of 62 million Thais benefit from it. However, the scheme has practical drawbacks, and the user fee exemption works only partially with the poorest and senior citizens (Coronini-Cronberg et al., 2007). Some public hospitals and doctors feel the scheme was poorly thought out and too hastily implemented, overworking doctors, creating debt burdens for hospitals, and causing numerous doctors to leave the public system. The ambitious scheme nevertheless marked a major step toward universal health coverage in a transitional country in Asia, trying to provide a safety net for those who had been largely ignored in public health policy. Yet future governments must find the balance between serving the public and building a long-term health strategy. Other richer jurisdictions, such as Hong Kong and Singapore, have effective hospital-level care for the population, but the challenge here is to deliver universal, affordable PHC and community-based care to older groups.

Other Asian countries face similar challenges in covering their aging population with basic and long-term health-care needs. As Kaneda (2006) notes, China's health-care system, previously exemplary for a then low-income agrarian society, has deteriorated considerably in universal access, and costs have greatly increased in the last two decades. What was a system relying on public subsidies and providing classless access to basic health, especially PHC, has now shifted to a largely market-oriented system that relies heavily on private funding, characterized by expensive usage fees and costs. Older Chinese citizens are very concerned about rising medical and other costs and disparities in health-care access. They are especially concerned because they potentially have greater health-care needs and, at the same time, have fewer resources to meet these needs. Although it is now acknowledged that old age does not automatically bring worse health, with the growing number of older population, the numbers of older and frail people will grow. Many will have higher expectations (mainly due to rising income and education levels). Family care and community support services will require higher level skills to meet the needs, and round-the-clock attention may sometimes be required. This is especially true in the case of chronic diseases, which account for almost 70% of all deaths and much morbidity in the Asia-Pacific region (WHO, 2006a, 2006b). With demographic aging, chronic diseases generally increase; increasing numbers of older people have ischemic heart disease, chronic obstructive pulmonary disease, cerebrovascular disease, lower respiratory infections and, with their greater longevity, women often experience osteoporosis. Many such chronic and noncommunicable conditions are preventable or could be delayed by altering diet and behavior and with sustained treatments. Prevention of chronic diseases can lessen the perceived burden of aging on technology-intensive curative and hospital sectors (WHO, 2006b). Fortunately, regionally, chronic diseases have yet to reach the epidemic proportions attained in some Western societies. Epidemiological transition is very well established, especially in East Asia, where heart diseases, cancers, stroke, and other forms of noncommunicable diseases are increasingly becoming the major causes of morbidity and mortality.

Infectious diseases do remain important. For example, the HIV/AIDS epidemic in Thailand, and some other countries, such as Cambodia, which, while HIV tends to directly infect the young and middle aged, can have enormous effects on older family members. Often, older parents become the final safety net for their children with AIDS and suffer poverty (Knodel, 2008; Knodel & Saengtienchai, 2004; 2005; Wachter, Knodel, & VanLandingham, 2002). In Thailand, older persons cared for two-thirds of young adults who died from AIDS and almost half of the orphans (Knodel, VanLandingham, Saengtienchai, & Im-em, 2001). The lack of a formal safety net leaves most assistance before and after death to members of the family.

Living in the Community: Older People and Long-term Care (LTC)

The UN (2008) MIPAA implementation framework mentions that, in many countries worldwide, unsatisfactory arrangements for independent living undermine the opportunity of older persons to remain in their communities as they age, and this is clearly an important area of concern. In various developed countries in the region, LTC has tended to evolve along two main streams: residential care, and home- or community-based care. Some do define LTC as institutional living and end-of-life care facility, but in general, many Asia-Pacific countries can inspire the West with their example of traditional informal care by families and friends and truly home- and community-based LTC. Perhaps, thereby, Asia-Pacific countries can really achieve the mantra of *aging in place*.

This said, there is the widespread concern in the region that Westernization is reducing the ability of families to care for frail older members (Cheng et al., 2008; Oh & Warnes, 2001; Phillips, 2000). Aging in place encourages older persons to stay in their homes for as long as possible and to remain part of their communities, with formal community support services provided as needed. In much of the region, informal care in the community exists, provided by families, friends, and neighbors, but the formal support systems to supplement this informal care or to step in when it is inadequate (especially for dementias and other severe conditions) are often missing or feeble. Many programs that do exist are not cost effective, and recent reviews reveal that the current modes and delivery of community support services often do not match the needs of family and elderly members well, or are too expensive to be tailored to individual needs. Moreover, these services are often provided, unintentionally, in place of informal care. However, in the future, epidemiological transition will mean that the LTC needs and profiles will almost certainly change as populations age and more people enter the older-old cohorts. This means that countries in the region must start planning in anticipation for this population aging trend.

Dementia in particular will prove to be a serious challenge to LTC systems in the region, especially in places where there is a large number of older persons who are predominantly women suffering from diseases linked to dementia (Graham et al., 1997). It was estimated in 2000 that 46% of the world's 25.5 million demented persons aged 65+ lived in Asia, and 40% lived in China (Wimo, Winblad, Aguero-Torres, & von Strauss, 2003). Future increase in the world's demented population will tend to be concentrated in Asia, and a report for the Asia-Pacific members of Alzheimer's Disease International predicts that the number of people with dementia in the region will rise from about 14 million in 2005 to 65 million by 2050, and the number of new cases annually will rise from 4 million to 20 million (Access Economics, 2006). The report notes disparities within the region. For example, the Australian and South Korean governments have made dementia a health priority, but many of the developing countries have limited awareness of dementia and assume it is a natural part of aging. In these countries, there are inadequate human and financial resources to meet care needs. Various priorities and strategies for all Asia-Pacific governments are suggested. First, better education is needed to improve community attitudes to and awareness of dementia and to de-stigmatize the condition. Second, partnerships must be built between policy-makers, clinicians, researchers, caregivers, and people with dementia. Third, care services responsive to the needs of people with dementia and their family carers must be developed. Hopefully, this will reduce the excessive institutionalization of people with the condition. (Over 60% of residents in long-term care institutions have been found to have some forms of dementia [Matthews & Dening, 2002; Woo, Ho, Yu, & Lau, 2000].) Institutionalization of people with dementia is neither the only nor the best option. Early institutionalization is often associated with mortality and shortened survival time for persons with dementia (McClendon, Smyth, & Neundorfer, 2006). Nonetheless, we must guard against excessive reliance on the family, as care is exceedingly demanding, especially in the later stages of dementias for which treatment is limited and current prognosis is poor.

What are the directions for LTC? Clearly, for many in the Asia-Pacific, institutionalization of elderly relatives is anathema and only very reluctantly chosen. Yet sometimes older people themselves will opt for it, in spite of its implied stigma and the lack of quality controls in most countries. In most countries in the Asia-Pacific region, there is little coherent policy for LTC. Policies need to be developed to address the growing demands for institutional care, while at the same time supporting home- or community-based LTC. Without the latter, the rising demand for institutional care may overwhelm even the most prosperous countries. To date, Korea and Japan are among the few countries in the region to dedicate policies or legislation on LTC (Lee, 2004; Ministry of Health, Labor and Welfare, n.d.; Phillips et al., 2009). Japan established a program that uses a social insurance model supported by contributions from the government, for employees who are aged 40+. Hong Kong, Singapore, and Australia incorporate LTC into related policies like disability allowance under social security. Much needs to be done regionally to finance and organize sustainable LTC programs.

In China, although public funding for LTC of older persons is still limited, the government has decided to allocate more funding and opened new opportunities for entrepreneurship in the health service industry, stemming partly from China's ongoing and complex social welfare reform, which started in earnest in the 1990s. An increasing number of private homes and government-sponsored homes for the aged are providing alternative care to elder persons living by themselves with no other means of support, especially in urban areas (Kaneda, 2006; Wu, Carter, Goins, & Cheng, 2005; Zhan, Liu, Guan, & Bai, 2006). However, at this stage, the facilities are insufficient and often too expensive for the majority of older people and their families; standards vary considerably and there are great urban-rural variations.

Improving Accessibility

Various factors, such as geographic access, economic, cultural and language disparities, often block older persons, especially women and minority groups, from seeking health services even when these are provided. Accessibility can be affected by the characteristics of users (people's knowledge of health, services, and affordability) as well as the actual availability of services at the provider's end (locations, hours of services, user friendliness, etc.) (UNESCAP, 2002). This is a complicated issue in the Asia-Pacific region because of its geographical diversity and very uneven population distributions—for example, many older persons are concentrated in rural areas: 70% or more in China and 60% in Korea, and by differences in social, cultural, and political diversities. The differential access to health-care services may be a reason why mortality is generally much higher in rural than in urban areas (National Research Council, 2003).

CONCLUSIONS AND FUTURE PROSPECTS

There is clearly great interest and development of services and policies for older persons in most countries of the Asia-Pacific region, although the urgency varies greatly among and even within countries. A UN report found that 6 of the 15 countries of the East and Southeast Asian region reviewed (China, Japan, Republic of Korea, Singapore, Thailand, and Vietnam) view population aging as a major concern. The other nine countries note population aging as a minor concern, but almost all of them have also initiated steps at the national level to address issues associated with aging (Mujahid, 2006). This is promising and it is to be hoped that a combination of judicious policy, public investment, and support for families will help to avoid the panic and fear associated with the consequences of population aging (Cheng et al., 2008).

A pervasive demographic feature in the region, the gender gap in longevity, has considerable policy and practical relevance. As women live longer than men, older women outnumber older men in many countries, especially among the oldest-old cohorts. In 2000, women aged 80+ in East Asia outnumbered men in the age group by almost two to one and, while this gap is projected to narrow a little, by 2025 it is still expected that almost two-thirds of the age group will be female. Moreover, in East and Southeast Asia, the numbers aged 80+ will almost have tripled from the 2000 numbers. This has great social consequences, since older men are more likely than older women to be married, and are more likely than older women to receive assistance from their spouses if their health fails. Males, too, are most likely to have financial resources and pensions (if any), as few older females will ever have worked in paid employment. A significantly higher proportion of older women live alone when compared to older men. These solo dwellers may well need help from other family members or from service agencies in the public sector. Therefore, the gender gap highlights a major potential policy concern, especially with regard to providing care and preventing social isolation and economic deprivation of older women living alone (UNDESA, 2007a, 2007b).

Future Regional Strategies for Aging

There is considerable diversity in the region, but common themes have started to emerge. It is interesting to note that the UNESCAP region was the first UN region to have its own plan of action on aging, the 1997 Macao Plan of Action (UNESCAP, 1999), which followed several years of preliminary meetings among representatives of regional governments and civil society. This has meant a steady dissemination of knowledge and practices, collaboration and reporting, culminating after MIPAA (2002) in several regional surveys and the Shanghai Implementation Strategy. As Cheng et al. (2008) note, this recognized that families are still strong in providing support in the region, but governments should provide basic protection for the needy. Moreover, policies should be developed from the bottom up, thereby recognizing the needs of the people.

As a key regional organization, UNESCAP has coordinated a number of expert and country meetings to develop instrumental and outcome indicators, which have provided a common basis for understanding policies relevant for older persons regionally (UNESCAP, 2004, 2007). Regional cooperation can and will grow, perhaps via exchanges with developed countries both within and outside the Asia-Pacific region and helped by NGO networks and collaborative organizations such as HelpAge International. They can facilitate valuable exchanges, dissemination, and promulgation of good practices and learning on population aging amongst network members. Social protection, health care, and training are particular areas in which collaborative exchanges can be valuable. Health care may be an area where experience transfer would not be one-sided. Escalating health-care costs in many developed countries may eventually drive them to look for cheaper models from the developing countries through initiatives such as community-based PHC and family involvement in LTC.

Knowledge transfer may likewise operate in the training of informal caregivers and volunteers. For example, Singapore, Australia, and Hong Kong have begun to develop skill-based qualifications rather than traditional knowledge-based academic programs. The more advanced countries in the region are likely to be able to help develop international accreditation, help standardize curricula, and possibly disseminate teaching materials to other countries. It is clear that even within a diverse region such as the Asia-Pacific, international aid in the form of expertise and materials will remain crucial to parts of the region. Some countries will continue to need assistance and support from regional and international agencies, while others will increasingly be able to provide such assistance and share their experiences in the development of policies and provision for older persons, and especially in incorporating older people and their families into policy initiatives.

NOTES

1. UN = United Nations; ESCAP = Economic and Social Commission for Asia and the Pacific. The UN has five regional commissions around the world, which provide intergovernmental platforms for the formulation and implementation of regional and global policy agendas. ESCAP is one of these regional commissions.

2. UNPD = United Nations Population Division (of the UN Department of Economic and Social Affairs).

3. UNDESA = United Nations Department of Economic and Social Affairs.

REFERENCES

Access Economics. (2006). Dementia in the Asia Pacific—The epidemic is here. Report and executive summary for Asia Pacific Members of Alzheimer's Disease International. Retrieved August 21, 2008, from http://www.alz. co.uk/research/files/apreport.pdf

Béland, D., & Yu, K. M. (2004). A long financial march: Pension reform in China. Journal of Social Policy, 33, 267–288.

Bookwala, J., & Schulz, R. (2000). A comparison of primary stressors, secondary stressors, and depressive symptoms between elderly caregiving husbands and wives: The Caregiver Health Effects Study. *Psychology and Aging, 15*, 607–616.

Chan, A. C. M., & Phillips, D. R. (2005). *Report on the regional survey on ageing (2005)*. Bangkok, Thailand: UNESCAP.

Chan, O. F. (2008). *Fear of crime among older persons: An exploratory qualitative study in different environments in Hong Kong*. Unpublished M.Phil. thesis, Lingnan University, Hong Kong.

Cheng, S.-T., & Chan, A. C. M. (2006a). Filial piety and psychological well-being in well older Chinese. *Journal of Gerontology: Psychological Sciences, 61B*, P262–P269.

Cheng, S.-T., & Chan, A. C. M. (2006b). Relationship with others and life satisfaction in later life: Do gender and widowhood make a difference? *Journal of Gerontology: Psychological Sciences, 61B*, P46–P53.

Cheng, S.-T., Chan, A. C. M., & Phillips, D. R. (2004). Quality of life in old age: An investigation of well older persons in Hong Kong. *Journal of Community Psychology, 32*, 309–326.

Cheng, S.-T., Chan, A. C. M., & Phillips, D. R. (2008). Ageing trends in Asia and the Pacific. In *Regional dimensions of the ageing situation* (pp. 35–69). United Nations Department of Economic and Social Affairs. New York: United Nations.

Cheng, S.-T., & Heller, K. (In press). Global aging: Challenges for community psychology. *American Journal of Community Psychology*.

Chiou, C.-J., Chen, I.-P., & Wang, H.-H. (2005). The health status of family caregivers in Taiwan: An analysis of gender differences. *International Journal of Geriatric Psychiatry, 20*, 821–826.

Chou, K.-L., Chow, N. W. S., & Chi, I. (2003). Volunteering aspirations of Hong Kong Chinese soon-to-be-old adults. *Activities, Adaptation & Aging, 27*(3/4), 79–96.

Coronini-Cronberg, S., Laohasiriwong, W., & Gericke, C. A. (2007). Health care utilisation under the 30-Baht Scheme among the urban poor in Mitrapap slum, Khon Kaen, Thailand: A cross-sectional study. *International Journal for Equity in Health 2007, 6*(11). Retrieved from http://www.equityhealthj.com/content/6/1/11

Friedman, J., Knodel, J., Cuong, B. T., & Anh, T. S. (2003). Gender dimensions of support for elderly in Vietnam. *Research on Aging, 25*, 587–630.

Global Action on Aging. (2008). Singapore: Crimes against the elderly on the rise. *GAA Newsletter*, 18–22 August. Retrieved August 25, 2008, from http://www.globalaging.org/quickgo.htm

Graham, J., Rockwood, K., Beattie, B. L., Eastwood, R., Gauthier, S., Tuokko, H., et al. (1997). Prevalence and severity of cognitive impairment with and without dementia in an elderly population. *Lancet, 349*, 1793–1796.

Greenfield, E. A., & Marks, N. F. (2004). Formal volunteering as a protective factor for older adults' psychological well-being. *Journal of Gerontology: Social Sciences, 59B*, S258–S264.

HelpAge International. (2007). *Primary health care for older persons: A participatory study in five Asian countries.* Chiang Mai, Thailand: HAI, Asia-Pacific HAI Network.

HSBC. (2007). *HSBC Global Forum on Ageing and Retirement. 2007 Report: The future of retirement—The new old age. Global report.* Retrieved August 21, 2008, from http://www.hsbc.com/1/2/retirement/future-of-retirement

Kaneda, T. (2006). *China's concern over population aging and health.* Population Reference Bureau, June. Retrieved September 3, 2008, from http://www.popline.org/docs/1738/315087.html

Keran, M., & Cheng, H.-S. (2002). *International experience and pension reform in China* (Issue Paper no. 16). Burlingame, CA: The 1990 Institute.

Kinsella, K., & Phillips, D. R. (2005). Global aging: The challenge of success. *Population Bulletin, 60*(1), 1–40.

Knodel, J. (2008). Poverty and the impact of AIDS on older persons: Evidence from Cambodia and Thailand. *Economic Development and Cultural Change, 56*(2), 441–475.

Knodel, J., Chayovan, N., Mithranon, P., Amornsirisomboon, P., & Arunraksombat, S. (2005). *Thailand's older population: Social and economic support as assessed in 2002.* Population Studies Centre Research Report No. 05–471, Institute for Social Research, University of Michigan.

Knodel, J., & Saengtienchai, C. (2004). AIDS and older persons: The view from Thailand. In P. Lloyd-Sherlock (Ed.), *Living longer: Ageing, development and social protection* (pp. 249–274). London: ZED Books.

Knodel, J., & Saengtienchai, C. (2005). Older aged parents: The final safety net for adult sons and daughters with AIDS in Thailand. *Journal of Family Issues, 26,* 665–698.

Knodel, J., & Saengtienchai, C. (2007). Rural parents with urban children: Social and economic implications of migration for the rural elderly in Thailand. *Population, Space and Place, 13*(3), 193–210.

Knodel, J., VanLandingham, M., Saengtienchai, C., & Im-em, W. (2001). Older people and AIDS: Quantitative evidence of the impact in Thailand. *Social Science & Medicine, 52,* 1313–1327.

Lee, G. (2004). *Review of ageing policy in Korea.* Paper presented at the Regional Seminar on Follow-up to the Shanghai Implementation Strategy for the Madrid and Macao Plans of Action on Ageing, October 18–21, 2004. Macao, China.

Matthews, F. E., & Dening, T. (2002). Prevalence of dementia in institutional care. *Lancet, 360,* 225–226.

McClendon, M. J., Smyth, K. A., & Neundorfer, M. M. (2006). Long-term-care placement and survival of persons with Alzheimer's disease. *Journal of Gerontology: Psychological Sciences, 61B,* 220–P227.

Ministry of Health, Labour and Welfare, Japan. (n.d.). *Long-term care insurance in Japan.* Retrieved January 11, 2007, from http://www.mhlw.go.jp/english/topics/elderly/care/index.html

Mittelman, M. (2005). Taking care of the caregivers. *Current Opinion in Psychiatry*, *18*, 633–639.

Mujahid, G. (2006). *Population ageing in East and South-East Asia: Current situation and emerging challenges.* UNFPA Country Technical Services Team for East and South-East Asia, Bangkok.

National Research Council. (2003). *Cities transformed: Demographic change and its implications in the developing world.* Washington, DC: National Academic Press.

Office of Policy Data, Switzerland. (2005). *Social security programs throughout the world: Asia and the Pacific, 2004.* Retrieved August, 25, 2008 from http://www.segurosocial.gov/policy/docs/progdesc/ssptw/2004–2005/asia/index.html

Oh, K. M., & Warnes, A. M. (2001). Care services for frail older people in South Korea. *Ageing & Society, 21,* 701–720.

Ong, F. S., & Phillips, D. R. (2007). Older consumers in Malaysia. *International Journal of Ageing and Later Life, 2*(1), 83–115.

Ong, F. S., Phillips, D. R., & Tengku-Aizan, H. (2007). Ageing in Malaysia: Progress and prospects. In T. H. Fu & R. Hughes (Eds.), *Ageing in East Asia: Challenges for the twenty-first century.* London: Routledge.

Phillips, D. R. (1990). *Health and health care in the Third World.* London: Longman.

Phillips, D. R. (Ed.). (1992). *Ageing in East and Southeast Asia.* London: Edward Arnold.

Phillips, D. R. (Ed.). (2000). *Ageing in the Asia-Pacific region.* London: Routledge.

Phillips, D. R., & Chan, A. C. M. (Eds.). (2002a). *Ageing and long-term care: National policies in the Asia-Pacific.* Singapore: Institute of Southeast Asian Studies, and Ottawa, Canada: International Development Research Centre.

Phillips, D. R., Cheng, S.-T., & Chan, A. C. M. (in press). Ageing in a global context: The Asia-Pacific region. In C. Phillipson & D. Dannefer (Eds.), *Handbook of social gerontology.* London: Sage.

Population Reference Bureau (PRB). (2007). *2006 world population data sheet.* Washington, DC: PRB. Retrieved from http://www.prb.org

Sakamoto, J. (2005). *Japan's pension reform.* Social Protection Discussion Paper no. 0541. Washington, DC: World Bank.

Silvergroup. (2009). *Connecting to the 50+ market.* Retrieved from http://www.silvergroup.asia/

Sobieszczyk, T., Knodel, J., & Chayovan, N. (2003). Gender and wellbeing among older people: Evidence from Thailand. *Ageing & Society, 23,* 701–735.

Sorkin, D., Rook, K. S., & Lu, J. L. (2002). Loneliness, lack of emotional support, lack of companionship, and the likelihood of having a heart condition in an elderly sample. *Annals of Behavioral Medicine, 24,* 290–298.

Teo, P., Mehta, K., Thang, L. L., & Chan, A. (2006). *Ageing in Singapore: Service needs and the state.* London: Routledge.

United Nations (2002). *Report of the Second World Assembly on Ageing.* New York: United Nations.

United Nations. (2008). *Further implementation of the Madrid International Plan of Action on Ageing: Strategic implementation framework*. Report of the Secretary-General UN: Economic and Social Council, United Nations. E/CN.5/2009/5.

United Nations Department of Economic and Social Affairs (UNDESA). (2007a). *World economic and social survey 2007: Development in an ageing world*. New York: United Nations.

United Nations Department of Economic and Social Affairs (UNDESA). (2007b). *World population ageing 2007* (2nd ed.). New York: United Nations.

United Nations Economic and Social Commission for Asia and the Pacific (UNESCAP). (1999). *Macao Plan of Action on Ageing for Asia and the Pacific*. New York: United Nations.

United Nations Economic and Social Commission for Asia and the Pacific (UNESCAP). (2002). *Access to social services by the poor and disadvantaged in Asia and the Pacific: Major trends and issues*. Social Policy Paper no. 11. New York: United Nations.

United Nations Economic and Social Commission for Asia and the Pacific (UNESCAP). (2003). *Shanghai Implementation Strategy: Regional implementation strategy for the Madrid International Plan of Action on Ageing 2002 and the Macao Plan of Action on Ageing for Asia and the Pacific 1999*. 59th Session paper E/ESCAP/1280. Bangkok, Thailand: United Nations.

United Nations Economic and Social Commission for Asia and the Pacific (UNESCAP). (2004). *Report of the regional seminar on follow-up to the Shanghai Implementation Strategy for the Madrid and Macao Plans of Action on Ageing*. Bangkok, Thailand: United Nations.

United Nations Economic and Social Commission for Asia and the Pacific (UNESCAP). (2007). *The Macao outcome document of the high-level meeting on the regional review of the Madrid International Plan of Action on Ageing*. Bangkok, Thailand: UNESCAP.

United Nations Economic and Social Commission for Asia and the Pacific (UNESCAP). (2008). *Population data sheet 2008*. Bangkok, Thailand: UNESCAP.

United Nations Population Division (UNPD). (2005). *Living arrangements of older persons around the world*. New York: United Nations.

United Nations Population Division (UNPD). (n.d.). *World population prospects: The 2007 revision population database*. Retrieved June 1, 2008, from http://esa.un.org/unpp/

United States Census Bureau. (n.d.). *International database*. http://www.census.gov/ipc/www/idb/

Wachter, K. W., Knodel, J., VanLandingham, M. J. (2002). AIDS and the elderly of Thailand: Projecting familial impacts. *Demography, 39*(1), 25–41.

Williamson, J. B., & Deitelbaum, C. (2005). Social security reform: Does partial privatization make sense for China? *Journal of Aging Studies, 19*, 257–271.

Wimo, A., Winblad, B., Aguero-Torres, H., & von Strauss, E. (2003). The magnitude of dementia occurrence in the world. *Alzheimer Disease & Associated Disorders, 17*(2), 63–67.

Woo, J., Ho, S. C., Yu, A. L. M., & Lau, J. (2000). An estimate of long-term care needs and identification of risk factors for institutionalization among Hong Kong Chinese aged 70 years and over. *Journal of Gerontology: Medical Sciences, 55A*, M64–M69.

World Health Organization (WHO). (2002). *Active ageing: A policy framework.* Geneva: WHO.

World Health Organization (WHO). (2004). *International Plan of Action on Ageing: Report on implementation.* Executive Board paper EB115/29. Geneva: WHO.

World Health Organization (WHO). (2006a). *WHO, UNESCAP launch chronic diseases report.* Retrieved August 2, 2006, from http://un.by/en/who/news/world/2006/13–02–06–03.html/

World Health Organization (WHO). (2006b). *Preventing chronic diseases: A vital investment.* Geneva: WHO.

Wu, B., Carter, M. W., Goins, R. T., & Cheng, C. (2005). Emerging services for community-based long-term care in urban China: A systematic analysis of Shanghai's community-based agencies. *Journal of Aging and Social Policy, 17*(4), 37–60.

Yoon, H., & Hendricks, J. (2006). *Handbook of Asian aging.* Amityville, NY: Baywood.

Zeng, Y., Liu, Y., & George, L. K. (2003). Gender differentials of the oldest old in China. *Research on Aging, 25*, 65–80.

Zhan, H. J., Liu, G., Guan, X., & Bai, H. (2006). Recent developments in institutional elder care in China: Changing concepts and attitudes. *Journal of Aging and Social Policy, 18*(2), 85–108.

3

European Region

Marja Aartsen

> European citizens are getting older and greyer. By 2050, it is esti-
> mated that the average age in the European Union will be 49, up
> from 39 now. Coupled with a low birth rate, future generations will
> see more of their earnings going to support a geriatric Europe funding
> pension, health care and Cliff Richard albums.
>
> Gabriele Stauner, Member of the European Parliament, 2008

To understand European's socioeconomic and cultural heterogeneity in the macro-social context of aging, it is important to recognize the distinct political difference between the eastern and western parts of Europe. The definition of Western Europe and Eastern Europe, however, is not straightforward, as several descriptions have been given with different meanings at different times (Drake, 2005). Therefore, the focus of this chapter will not be exclusively on either Western or Eastern Europe, but mainly on the European Union (EU). The EU is a comprehensive, economic, and political partnership among 27 European countries, which started as an answer to the bloody and frequent wars in Europe until 1945. Before moving on to information about the aging European society, a short overview of Europe's recent past will be given (the official Web site of the EU: http://europa.eu).

RECENT HISTORY OF EUROPE

Twenty years ago, on November 9, 1989, the Berlin Wall fell. The Berlin Wall was a physical barrier between East and West Berlin, and part of the larger Iron Curtain dividing Europe into two politically and ideologically distinct parts. For many, the Berlin Wall and the Iron Curtain were symbols of the separation between the eastern European communism and the western European liberal democracy; a division between the two superpowers in the Cold War (Huntington, 1993). The fall of the wall was, therefore, an emotionally overwhelming moment for many German and other European citizens. However, the long-term consequences of this fairly sudden social change appeared to be not equally beneficial for all European citizens. For example, Westerhof (2001) found that six years after reunification, East Germans rated their material situation worse, and reported less life satisfaction, than West Germans.

The fall of the wall took place within the context of the unification of European countries into the EU. Based on the Schuman declaration of May 9, 1950, six countries (Belgium, France, Germany, Italy, Luxembourg, and The Netherlands) signed a treaty to run their heavy industries—coal and steel—under a common management. This cooperation prevented these nations from turning against each other, as in the past. The EU has grown from the treaty in heavy industry to a comprehensive, economic, and political partnership among 27 European countries in 2009. In 1973, Denmark, United Kingdom, and Ireland became members of the EU, followed by Greece in 1981, Portugal and Spain in 1986, Finland, Austria, and Sweden in 1995, Cyprus, Estonia, Hungary, Latvia, Lithuania, Malta, Poland, Slovakia, Slovenia, and Czech Republic in 2004, and finally Bulgaria and Romania in 2007. The EU currently is run by several main bodies, among which are the European Parliament, the Council of the European Union, and the European Commission. Decisions are made in three separate policy areas: the community domain, the common foreign and security policy, and the police and judicial cooperation in criminal matters domain (http://europa.eu).

DEMOGRAPHICS OF THE EUROPEAN UNION

In a recent study of the European Commission (2007), it was found that EU's demographic makeup will change dramatically over the coming decades. Populations are becoming older than ever before because of the baby-boom generation (which is approaching retirement age), low birthrates, and increased life expectancy (Table 3.1).

To deal with the growing number of older people, the European Commission identified five key areas for policy action: (1) helping

Table 3.1
Demographic trends in the European Union

	1960	1980	2004/5	2030	2050
Population in millions	378	426	457	469	450
Total fertility rate (number of children per woman)	2.6	1.9	1.5	1.6	1.6
Life expectancy at birth for women in years	73	76	80	84	86
Life expectancy at birth for men in years	67	69	74	78	81
Population share of persons under 25 in %	40	38	29	24	23
Population share of persons age 25–64 in %	54	49	54	51	47
Population share of persons age 60–79 in %	13	15	18	25	25
Population share of persons 80+ in %	1	2	4	7	11
Old-age dependency ratio (15–64) in %	15	21	25	40	53

Source: European Commission. (2007).

people balance work, family, and private life so that potential parents can have the number of children they desire; (2) improving work opportunities for older people; (3) increasing potential productivity and competitiveness by valuing the contributions of both older and younger employees; (4) harnessing the positive impact of migration for the job market; and (5) ensuring sustainable public finances to help guarantee social protection in the long term (European Commission, 2007).

RECENT RESEARCH ON AGING

The overview of research on aging in the European Union presented below is based on a literature search using various electronic databases, including PubMed, Medline, CINAHL, and SocIndex. The following search terms were used: "older" or "elderly," and "cross-national" and "Europe." In addition, the European Research Area in Ageing (ERA-AGE) database (http://era-age.group.shef.ac.uk/) was checked. As the European Commission is an important financial resource for cross-national research in Europe, the Web sites of the European Commission were also searched (http://ec.europa.eu/research/index.cfm) for additional studies. Only publications with a cross-national design (at least three different European countries) written in English and published between 2000 and 2009 are summarized below, in alphabetical (based on acronym) order. For each research project, one publication is highlighted as an example.

Cross-national Research Projects and Networks

The Aged in Home Care project (AdHOC) is designed to compare outcomes of different models of community care across 11 European countries (Carpenter et al., 2004). Participants in the study were 4,500 people aged 65 years and older who were already receiving home-care services within selected urban areas in each country. One of the AdHOC studies showed that in Nordic countries, older adults were five times more likely to live alone than in southern Europe. Recipients of community care in France and Italy are characterized by very high physical and cognitive impairment compared with those in northern Europe, who have comparatively little impairment in activities of daily living (ADL) and cognitive function. The provisions of formal care to people with similar dependency varies extremely widely, with very little formal care in Italy and more than double the average across all levels of dependency in the United Kingdom (Carpenter et al., 2004).

Activating Senior Potential in Ageing Europe (ASPA) is a collaborative project with partners from Poland, Italy, Denmark, Sweden, the United Kingdom, Germany, France, and the Netherlands. The project is coordinated by the Utrecht University in The Netherlands. The project aims to examine the forces and mechanisms behind employers' and governments' behaviors and the resulting societal arrangements. Data are from large-scale surveys, research, and interviews to map government behaviors. Statistical and focus group analyses are used to get insight into the participation and activity rates of people aged between 50 and 70. The ASPA study was just recently started, and therefore results are not yet available.

The Comparison of Longitudinal European Studies on Aging (CLESA) project is a research project on cross-national determinants of quality of life and health services for the elderly (Minicuci et al., 2003). CLESA aims to increase the knowledge of the predictors (sociodemographic, behavioral, psychological factors, and chronic conditions) of major health outcomes, such as decline in functional status, institutionalization, and mortality. It will allow the comparison of these health services in six different countries in relation to the above-mentioned health predictors and outcomes. The results should become instruments that contribute to a better quality of life for older people, also allowing the countries to better allocate their resources for health care. The CLESA project aims to investigate the determinants of quality of life among older people through six existing longitudinal studies: TamELSA (Tampere, Finland), CALAS (Israel), ILSA (Italy), LASA (The Netherlands), Aging in Leganes (Spain), and SATSA (Sweden). Results from one of the CLESA studies on depressive symptoms showed that depressive symptoms are higher in women than in men in every country, except Sweden (Zunzunegui et al., 2007).

The ENABLE-AGE project (http://www.enableage.arb.lu.se/) aims to explore the home environment as a determinant for autonomy, participation, and well-being in very old age. More specifically, the project aims to explore country-specific, housing-related societal support as represented in personal situations and to provide an update of housing policies and legislations. Five countries participated in the ENABLE-AGE study: Sweden, Germany, the United Kingdom, Hungary, and Latvia. The project was coordinated by Lund University, Sweden. Data were collected at home visits with 1,918 very old people aged 75–89 years, living alone in urban areas (Oswald et al., 2007). The consortium of the ENABLE-AGE project produced many articles and contributions to conferences. In one of the studies of this research project, the relationships between aspects of objective and perceived housing were explored in very old adults (Nygren et al., 2007). It was concluded that very old people living in more accessible housing perceived their homes as more useful and meaningful in relation to their routines and everyday activities, and that they were less dependent on external control in relation to their housing. The patterns of these relationships were similar in the five countries involved.

The EURODEP Concerted Action was conducted by a consortium of 14 research groups from 11 European countries (The Netherlands, Germany, Ireland, Iceland, United Kingdom, Italy, Spain, France, Belgium, Sweden, and Finland), all engaged in population-based research into the epidemiology of late-life depression. The overall sample size of the pooled EURODEP data set comprises 22,570 individuals (Copeland et al., 1999). One of the studies of the EURODEP research group, on cross-national differences in the association between physical health and depressive symptoms, showed that the association of depressive symptoms with functional disability was stronger than with physical conditions. Associations were slightly more pronounced in the United Kingdom and Ireland (Braam et al., 2005).

The EUROFAMCARE research project collected detailed information on the situation of caregiver support in six countries: Germany, Greece, Italy, Poland, Sweden, and the United Kingdom (http://www.uke.de/extern/eurofamcare/). Due to existing cross-national differences in terms of family care roles, female employment, public/private mix of care expenditures, and residential/home/monetary share of care provision, these countries represent heterogeneous European care regimes

(Lamura et al., 2008). This study indicated, ". . . European Union-wide efforts to improve caregiver support need to focus on improving the care system's ability to provide timely, high-quality care delivered by staff who treat the older person with dignity and respect, and to enhance cooperation between health professionals (in all countries), informal networks (especially in southeastern Europe), social services (particularly in Sweden and the UK), and voluntary organizations (in Germany and the UK)" (Lamura et al., 2008, p. 752).

The Family Support for Older People (FAMSUP; www.lshtm.ac.uk/cps/famsup/) is an international network of researchers from different universities, aimed at examining the effect of demographic variables such as marital status, socioeconomic status, employment, and living arrangements on the provision of care and long-term care facilities (Glaser, Wolf, & Tomassini, 2006). In one of the studies of the FAMSUP network, it was found that older people in low socioeconomic status groups in the United Kingdom and The Netherlands were more likely to use informal help from outside the household than their counterparts in Italy, and similarly, that older people in The Netherlands were more likely to use formal help than their Italian peers (Broese van Groenou, Glaser, Tomassini, & Jacobs, 2006).

Healthy Ageing: a Longitudinal Study in Europe (HALE) aimed to study changes in and determinants of usual and healthy aging in 13 European countries (Knoops et al., 2004). For the HALE project, longitudinal data of three older international studies were used: the Seven Countries Study database (five of the seven countries were from Europe) and the combined database of the FINE and SENECA Study (3,805 elderly men and women followed for 10 years in 12 European countries). As the Seven Countries Study database and FINE and SENECA were launched more than 10 years ago, their design is not described further here. One of the intriguing findings of the HALE study is that among individuals aged 70 to 90 years, adherence to a Mediterranean diet and healthful lifestyle is associated with a more than 50% lower rate of all-causes and cause-specific mortality (Knoops et al., 2004).

Old Age and Autonomy: The Role of Service Systems and Intergenerational Family Solidarity study (OASIS; Lowenstein, 2007) is based on a sample of 2,064 older adults (aged 75 and older) living in Norway, England, Germany, Spain, and Israel. The study indicates that family solidarity was high in all five countries, whereas conflict and ambivalence were low. In addition, it was found that reciprocal intergenerational support and ambivalence predicts quality of life (Lowenstein, 2007).

The PRevention in Older people—Assessment in GEneralists' Practices Project (PRO-AGE study; Stuck et al., 2007) is an international randomized controlled study on health risk appraisal among older persons registered as patients of general practitioners conducted in London (United Kingdom), Hamburg (Germany), and Solothurn (Switzerland). The study aimed to test the effectiveness of Health Risk Appraisal (HRA) intervention strategies to prevent or delay disability in older people. HRA interventions were originally developed in the United States and tested in working-age adults with the aim of identifying risks and decreasing the rate of premature illness and mortality. Based on the PRO-AGE database, Lubben and others validated the abbreviated version of the Lubben Social Network Scale (LSNS) used to screen for social isolation among community-dwelling older adults. Their main conclusion was that screening older persons based on the LSNS-6 provides quantitative information on their family and friendship ties, and identifies persons at increased risk for social isolation (Lubben et al., 2006).

The Survey of Health, Ageing and Retirement in Europe (SHARE; www.share-project.org) is a multidisciplinary and cross-national panel database of micro data on health, socioeconomic status, and social and family networks of more than 30,000 individuals aged 50 and over. Eleven countries—Denmark, Sweden, Austria, France, Germany, Switzerland, Belgium, the Netherlands, Spain, Italy, and Greece—contributed data to the 2004 SHARE baseline study. Further data were collected in 2005–06 in Israel. Two new EU member states—the Czech Republic and Poland—as well as Ireland joined SHARE in 2006 and participated in the second wave of data collection in 2006–07. The survey's third wave of data collection, SHARELIFE, currently collects detailed retrospective life histories in 16 countries, with Slovenia joining in as a new member. SHARE is coordinated centrally at the Mannheim Research Institute for the Economics of Aging. It is harmonized with the U.S. Health and Retirement Study (HRS) and the English Longitudinal Study of Ageing (ELSA). SHARE has resulted in a wide variety of research papers, books, and book chapters. For example, Hank and Schaan (2008) studied the correlation between frequency of prayer and health. Based on the 2004 SHARE baseline study, they found that frequency of prayer was negatively correlated with self-perceived general health, general physical health, functional limitations, and mental health, and that these correlations were roughly the same for all participating countries, and thus for the different "religious regimes" (Hank & Schaan, 2008).

Inequalities in healthy life years comprised the topic of a study by Jagger et al. (2008). Based on data of 25 countries in Europe, the researchers calculated life expectancies and healthy life years (HLY) at 50 years by age and sex. They found that an average 50-year-old man in 2005 could expect to live until 67.3 years, free of activity limitation, and a woman to 68.1 years. HLY at 50 years for both men and women varied more across the participating countries. HLY for men ranged from 9.1 years in Estonia to 23.6 years in Denmark; for women: from 10.4 years in Estonia to 24.1 years in Denmark.

Voracek and Marusic (2008) investigated the pattern of geographic variation in European suicide rates in individuals aged 65 years and over. Based on analysis of the national suicide rates of older people from 34 European countries, the researchers concluded that there is a J-shaped belt of high-suicide-rate countries spanning from Central Europe (Austria, Hungary, and Slovenia) to northeastern Europe (Finland and the Baltic countries). There are early historical and genetic communalities among the populations inhabiting this area, but in terms of culture, recent history, political systems, and socioeconomic factors, there is great diversity among these countries.

CURRENT STATE OF EDUCATION IN GERONTOLOGY

In this section, only cross-border gerontology programs in higher education are described. For national educational programs, the readers are referred to the national chapters. An overview of national academic programs in gerontology can be found in a study by Meyer (2003). As far as we know, there are two international educational initiatives in Europe: the European Master's program in Gerontology (EuMaG) and the Nordic Master's Degree Program in Gerontology (NordMaG). Next to this is an international exchange program (INTERGERO) running from 2005 till 2009, which facilitates students from three European and three United States universities to visit each other's programs.

The idea of a joint European master's degree, as provided by the EuMaG, is rooted in the demographic shifts and socio-structural changes in Europe, which have made common efforts and strategies related to the gerontological training useful (Meyer, 2003). Based on the description of the state of gerontological education throughout Europe, it was concluded that there was a clear imbalance in the Europe-wide distribution of study programs; that there were gaps in the gerontological education map; and that training programs in Eastern Europe were deficient due to the social and political changes in the past years (Meyer, 2003).

The European Master's program in Gerontology (EuMaG; www. eumag.org) was started in 2003, and is a modular, two-year, part-time international training program about the aging process and its societal implications. The multidisciplinary curriculum emphasizes international comparison, focusing on current European debates concerning—among other things—policy and care for the elderly population. The program is delivered by members of several gerontology programs across Europe: VU-University Amsterdam (The Netherlands), Institute of Gerontology of the University of Heidelberg (Germany), Keele University (United Kingdom), and the Université du Versailles Saint-Quentin-en-Yvelines in Paris (France). All institutes are involved in current aging research, which serves as a resource to inform students about the latest research. Part of the standard curriculum is the Summer School, which is a collaborative endeavor of the VU-University Amsterdam and one of the partner universities of the larger European network. The Summer School is open to professionals and students from all parts of the world (Heijke, 2004).

The NordMaG was launched in the autumn of 2008 and is a multidisciplinary and jointly implemented degree program in higher education in the Nordic countries in the field of gerontology (more information available at: http://www.jyu.fi/nordmag). It combines the expertise of three Nordic universities: University of Jyväskylä (JyU) in Finland (coordinator), University of Iceland (UI), and Lund University (LU) in Sweden. NordMaG is integrated into a local master's degree program at the three universities. NordMaG covers topics related to aging of individuals and populations, the consequences of aging, as well as the factors that underlie the aging processes. The program explores the most common issues of well-being in old age and ways to promote successful and healthy aging. The studies at JyU and UI are organized into four academic terms. At LU, the program can be completed in two years through an individual study plan, but presently the program consists of part-time studies over a four-year period. The joint NordMaG curriculum is taught in English and consists of an introduction to gerontology, intensive courses at the respective universities, studies abroad, and a master's thesis, with a topic in gerontology (www.jyu.fi/nordmag).

The European Commission, together with United States Department of Education, provided a grant for the purposes of implementing an international, interdisciplinary program for teaching gerontology in Europe and the United States. This program, called INTERGERO (Interdisciplinary

Program for Teaching Gerontology: A Consortia Implementation Project), consisted of three European and three American universities. The selected European universities are Universidad de Salamanca (Spain), Universität Heidelberg: Institut fur Gerontologie (Germany), and Vrije Universiteit Amsterdam (The Netherlands). The American universities are Miami University (Ohio), Oregon State University (Oregon), and San Francisco State University (California). INTERGERO provides financial support for students from the participating universities to stay overseas for a maximum of four months to learn the language of the host country, to delve into the different approaches to gerontology and to acquire firsthand professional experience by means of apprenticeships and work placements at qualified centers in the field of gerontology (www.intergero.org).

CONCLUSIONS

Despite the ongoing unification of European countries, Europe can still be described as a continent with large, international differences in the socioeconomic and political-cultural context of aging societies, resulting in a wide variety of threads and potentials shaping the individual life course. Especially countries that were under the political range of influence of the communistic ideology—Estonia, Slovenia, Bulgaria, or Romania, for example—are under-represented in cross-national research projects or in international programs for higher education in gerontology. To gain a more thorough understanding of factors influencing the aging process, we need to actively enhance participation of former Eastern European countries in cross-national studies. This may also help to stimulate the exchange of best practices in care programs and encourage participation in educational programs of higher education in gerontology.

REFERENCES

Braam, A. W., Prince, M. J., Beekman, A.T.F., Delespaul, P., Dewey, M. E., Geerlings, S. W., et al. (2005). Physical health and depressive symptoms in older Europeans. Results from EURODEP. *British Journal of Psychiatry, 187,* 35–42.

Broese van Groenou, M., Glaser, K., Tomassini, C., & Jacobs, T. (2006). Socioeconomic status differences in older people's use of informal and formal help: A comparison of four European countries. *Ageing & Society, 26,* 745–766.

Carpenter, I., Gambassi, G., Topinkova, E., Schroll, M., Finne-Soveri, H., Henrard, J. C., et al. (2004). Community care in Europe: The Aged in Home Care project (AdHOC). *Aging Clinical and Experimental Research, 16*(4), 259–269.

Copeland, J., Beekman, A., Dewey, M., Hooijer, A., Lawlor, B., Lobo, A., et al. (1999). Depression in Europe: Geographical distribution among older people. *The British Journal of Psychiatry, 174,* 312–321.

Drake, M. A. (2005). *Encyclopedia of library and information Science.* Boca Raton, FL: CRC Press.

European Commission. (2007). *European research in social trends: Demography, migration, cohesion and integration. 7th Framework Program.* Brussels: Directorate-General for Research Communication Unit.

Glaser, K., Wolf, D. A. & Tomassini, C. (2006). Guest editorial: The FAMSUP network and its comparative studies of family support for frail older people. *Ageing & Society, 26,* 689–692.

Hank, K., & Schaan, B. (2008). Cross-national variations in the correlation between frequency of prayer and health among older Europeans. *Research on Aging, 30,* 36–54.

Heijke, L. (2004). The European Master's programme in Gerontology. *European Journal of Ageing, 1,* 106–108.

Huntington, S. P. (1993). The clash of civilizations. *Foreign Affairs, 72*(3), 22–49.

Jagger, C., Gillies, C., Moscone, F., Cambois, E., Van Oyen, H., Nusselder, W., et al. (2008). Inequalities in healthy life years in the 25 countries of the European Union in 2005: A cross-national meta-regression analysis. *Lancet, 372,* 2124–2131.

Knoops, K.T.D., De Groot, L.C.P.G.M., Kromhout, D., Perrin, A. M., Moreiras-Varela, O., Menotti, A., et al. (2004). Mediterranean diet, lifestyle factors, and 10-year mortality in elderly European men and women: The HALE Project. *Journal of the American Medical Association, 292,* 1433–1439.

Lamura, G., Mnich, E., Nolan, M., Wojszel, B., Krevers, B., Mestheneos, L., et al. (2008). Family carers' experiences using support services in Europe: Empirical evidence from the EUROFAMCARE Study. *The Gerontologist, 48,* 752–771.

Lowenstein, A. (2007). Solidarity-conflict and ambivalence: Testing two conceptual frameworks and their impact on quality of life for older family members. *Journal of Gerontology, 62B,* S100–S107.

Lubben, J., Blozik, E., Gillmann, G., Iliffe, S., Von Renteln Kruse, W., Beck, J. C., et al. (2006). Performance of an abbreviated version of the Lubben Social Network Scale among three European community-dwelling older adult populations. *The Gerontologist, 46,* 503–513.

Meyer, M. (2003). The current state and developments in gerontology in European higher education. *Educational Gerontology, 29,* 55–69.

Minicuci, N., Noale, M., Bardage, C., Blumstein, T., Deeg, D.J.H., Gindin, J., et al. (2003). Cross-national determinants of quality of life from six longitudinal studies on ageing. The CLESA project. *Aging Clinical and Experimental Research, 15*, 187–202.

Nygren, C., Oswald, F., Iwarsson, S., Fänge, A., Sixsmith, J., Schilling, O., et al. (2007). Relationships between objective and perceived housing in very old age. *The Gerontologist, 47*, 85–95.

Oswald, F., Wahl, H. W., Schilling, O., & Iwarsson, S. (2007). Housing-related control beliefs and independence in activities of daily living in very old age. *Scandinavian Journal of Occupational Therapy, 14*(1), 33–43.

Stuck, A. E., Kharicha, K., Dapp, U., Anders, J., Von Renteln-Kruse, W., Meier-Baumgartner, H. P., et al. (2007). The PRO-AGE Study: An international randomised controlled study of health risk appraisal for older persons based in general practice. *BMC Medical Research Methodology*. Retrieved from http://www.biomedcentral.com/1471–2288/7/2

Voracek, M., & Marusic, A. (2008). Testing the Finno-Ugrian suicide hypothesis: Geographic variation of elderly suicide rates across Europe. *Nordic Journal of Psychiatry, 62*, 302–308.

Westerhof, G. J. (2001). Wohlbefinden in der zweiten Lebenshälfte [Well-being in the second half of life]. In F. Dittmann-Kohli, C. Bode, & G. J. Westerhof (Eds.), *Die zweite Lebenshälfte –Psychologische Perspektiven. Ergebnisse des Alters-Survey* (pp. 79–128). Stuttgart: Kohlhammer.

Zunzunegui, M. V., Minicuci, N., Blumstein, T., Noale, M., Deeg, D., Jylha, M., et al. (2007). Gender differences in depressive symptoms among older adults: A cross-national comparison. *Social Psychiatry and Psychiatric Epidemiology, 42*, 198–207.

4

▪▪■▪▪

Latin American Region

Nelida Redondo

DEMOGRAPHIC TRANSITION AND THE AGING OF POPULATIONS IN LATIN AMERICAN COUNTRIES

Latin America comprises a group of countries located in Central and South America. These countries share a common cultural and institutional origin, which dates from Spanish colonization. In all these countries, except Brazil, the Spanish language is spoken. Despite this common origin, each of the countries is differentiated by its particular geography, climate, racial composition, size, and structure of the population, and the degree of human, social, and economic development achieved.

At the start of the 21st century, Latin America presented a diverse social and demographic scenario. The countries in the region—and the different groups that make up each country—feature multiple individual aging and population aging structures.

The temperate portion of South America—Uruguay, Argentina, and Chile—and Cuba in Central America present aging populations that date from the last decades of the 20th century. Although all the countries in the region have begun this demographic transition, the speed and magnitude of the changes differ widely. While Bolivia and Haiti are still at an incipient stage, mortality rates have already started to drop in El Salvador, Guatemala, Honduras, Nicaragua, and Paraguay. The remaining countries of South and Central America also feature a drop in birth rates, and have therefore entered a full transition phase (ECLAC/CEPAL, CELADE, 2001).

Additionally, two Latin American nations—Brazil and Mexico—are among the 10 countries on the planet with the greatest number of people aged over 60 years, with 14.1 and 7.3 million, respectively (UN, 2001, cited in WHO, 2002).

LIVING CONDITIONS OF AGED PEOPLE
IN THE LATIN AMERICAN COUNTRIES:
POLICIES AND INSTITUTIONS

Latin America is a region of the world with great inequalities. In each country, the differences between population groups belonging to the same cohort are significant. Sharp differences are also observed in the wealth of the different cohorts of elderly people, attributed mainly to the highly volatile macro-economy of these countries. Furthermore, in the region there are huge differences in living conditions of the elderly populations among countries.

In order to analyze living conditions of the Latin-American elderly populations, it is convenient to divide the region into two groups of countries: (a) the group of pioneering countries: Argentina, Chile and, Uruguay—with aged populations and higher social security institutional development. Brazil is currently approaching membership in this group; and (b) the remaining countries, which have initiated their demographic transition more recently and possess smaller institutional development in aging matters.

In the pioneering countries, there are broad policies of social protection directed at old age, which cover two bodies of basic politics: (a) the provision of monetary incomes, and (b) the coverage of health care. In the pioneering countries from South America, the institutional framework of social protection to the elderly has been consolidated and extensively developed since the second half of the 20th century, although it suffered successive reforms. Brazil is at present included in this group of countries.

In Bolivia, in the year 2002, the Supportive Bond (Bono Solidario—BONOSOL) was established, providing monetary income to people over 65 years old as part of a more complex institutional framework that includes integral attention and promotes active aging and the rights of older people (ECLAC/CEPAL, 2006a).

In Peru, the National Network of Old People (Red Nacional de Personas Adultas Mayores) was formed and established to fulfill the National Plan for Old People 2002–2006 (Plan Nacional para las Personas Adultas Mayores).

Despite the fact that in all the countries of the region, fundamental rights of older people are legally protected by national constitutions, some countries have enacted specific laws: the Special Law of Elders in Ecuador (Ley Especial del Anciano en Ecuador), the Law of Adult People in Paraguay (Ley de las Personas Adultas en Paraguay), a law that includes preferential attention to older people in Peru (Ley que incluye la atención preferencial de las personas mayores), a law called Statute of Older Persons in Brazil (Estatuto do Idoso do Brazil) and the Law of Integral Promotion of the Older Adults in Uruguay (Ley de Promoción Integral de los Adultos Mayores en Uruguay). This legislation promotes equality in dealing with the aged: protections to ensure employment in satisfactory conditions and gradual retirement with economic security; fair access to health services; medicine supply and long-term services; and regulation in the area of health, as well as sanctions against abuse or neglect of elderly persons (ECLAC/CEPAL, 2006a).

PENSIONS AND POVERTY IN LATIN AMERICA'S ELDERLY POPULATIONS

In most of the countries in the region, policies directed at providing economic security to older people and guaranteeing their rights have recently been implemented. These policies have a greater impact on the living conditions of the elderly populations.

In the urbanized and industrialized or semi-industrialized societies of the region, the elderly need sufficient monetary income to survive. Throughout the 20th century, the pension fund systems that were established in the countries of the region aimed to eliminate poverty. To date, the countries of the region with aged populations—those in the Southern Cone—have successfully met the challenge of insuring some level of economic support. Furthermore, Bolivia, a country whose population is still young, recently achieved success with the implementation of its universal pension program for the elderly. In recent years, the proportion of households with elderly adults whose income is below the Indigence Line dropped noticeably in those countries. This is attributed to the extension of benefits provided by noncontributory or social assistance old-age pension systems, the implementation of pension programs for poor elderly people in rural areas, or a greater involvement of the state pillar in the private pension fund systems, especially directed at elderly people with a low contributory density.

In Argentina, in 2003, noncontributory pensions or assistance was extended with no budgetary restrictions to all individuals aged over 70 who did not receive a pension or retirement pay and had insufficient monetary income, and whose families were unable to provide adequate support; in other words, the support program covers all eligible individuals (Argentina, 2003). In Brazil, the FUNRURAL program grants pensions to elderly people in rural areas who lack retirement rights and have insufficient material resources. Bolivia also put in place a pension program called BONOSOL for all people over 65 years old. In Chile, the social security reform extends the public pillar to cover the sector of the population without sufficient contributions to obtain a minimum pension. Furthermore, in Chile, the PASIS Vejez program grants pensions to elderly people who lack retirement rights and do not have enough material resources. PASIS grants were included in the more comprehensive system for social protection for elderly population, reformed in 2007. Finally, Uruguay has a traditional pension program—dating from 1919—that covers people over 70 years old who do not receive retirement pay and do not have enough material and familial resources (ILO/OIT, 2002).

Through these measures, the states of Argentina, Bolivia, Brazil, Chile, and Uruguay are complying with the constitutional mandate of guaranteeing monetary income or support for people who are unable to work and obtain a means of sustenance due to their advanced age.

The rest of the countries in Latin America do not have pensions or retirement systems that protect the elderly against poverty. Despite progress made in the field of economic benefits for elderly people who lack material resources, in many countries, poverty associated with old age continues to be a pressing problem. This is the case of the structurally young countries of the continent, where the elderly must continue to work until a very advanced age—and often in deplorable physical conditions—to avoid indigence, or they must be supported by their families.

The impact of poverty is different for different age groups of the countries in the region. In only five Latin American countries, the proportion of the elderly (60 years of age and older) in poverty is larger than that in the younger population (0 to 59 years old): in Colombia, Costa Rica, Dominican Republic, Honduras, and Mexico, aged persons are likely to be poorer than younger people. For the other countries, the average aged person is less likely to be poor than the rest of the population, indicating that policies with the aim of preventing poverty among the aged have been somewhat effective in their positive impact on living conditions (Gasparini, Alejo, Haimovich, Olivieri, & Tornarolli, 2007).

South American countries with aging populations feature a marked urban concentration of elderly people. Demographic aging also goes hand in hand with a change in housing arrangements for the elderly, with a tendency toward mono-generational arrangements and an increase in one-person households. In this context, the integration of elderly people depends essentially on their consumption capacity in the urban goods and services market. The inflation and wage adjustment of social security benefits in line with the economically active population are essential components to ensure economic independence and suitable social inclusion of the elderly, since this allows them to continue functioning as active consumers. The benefits provided by the social security systems in the countries of the region are generally low and do not adequately replace active wages. Because the consumption capacity of public or private contributory pensions is very limited, this constitutes one of the main problems for older people in the middle social strata in the main cities of South American countries.

POLICIES IN THE FIELD OF HEALTH COVERAGE

Health coverage for the elderly in the countries of the region presents problems of a different nature. The public health-care systems are mainly directed to maternal and child care. Access to highly complex medical care, such as that required for degenerative diseases—like cardiovascular disorders and cancer—is affected by unequal availability. This type of service is available in the large cities of the region, although with serious accessibility problems. However, in small urban centers and rural areas, complex diagnostic technology and treatment is not available for the elderly. Consequently, the life expectation differentials at the age of 65 vary considerably from one jurisdiction and social stratum to another. The main negative impact of the regional inequalities is the differing life expectancy and life expectancy free of disabilities. For this reason, South American countries need to improve their health care policies for the elderly in order to reach the goals of the Madrid International Plan of Action on Aging (MIPAA).

Only one South American country, Argentina, offers a specific health-care plan for its elderly population under the social security system. In Argentina, health coverage for the elderly through the social security system is very broad. However, it already presents accessibility problems related to services; these challenges are particularly significant for very old people with physical disabilities. On the other hand, benefits provided through price discounts on medication are far-reaching and freely available to people without resources or with prevalent chronic diseases.

Remediar, a program for the free supply of generic medication, has been in place since 2002. This is added to the traditional discount system on prescription drugs offered by health-care organizations and private health care.

Chile features an interesting pioneering project, which promotes monthly visits by elderly people to centers that offer primary medical attention. During this monthly visit, patients receive nutritious food packages provided under the Golden Years program, and receive a functional physical checkup as per a guideline specially validated for Chile under the framework of a technical cooperation project with the Pan American Health Organization (PAHO). The functional checkup is designed to prevent dependence stemming from physical or cognitive disability in elderly people.

Bolivia recently established free medical insurance for elderly people without social security coverage, and Peru incorporated issues related to older people into the national health system. Despite these recent improvements, a common feature in the medical-care and health-care systems in the countries of the region is the lack of programs designed specifically for the elderly. At this time, maternal and child-care programs are more important issues than geriatric care in almost all South American national health-care systems.

POLICIES IN THE FIELD OF SOCIAL
AND POLITICAL PARTICIPATION
OF OLDER PERSONS

Starting three decades ago, organizations run by elders in the countries of the region have developed recreational, cultural, and educational activities. These organizations typically originate in neighborhoods and provide a sphere for integration among elders, which facilitates close social interaction. Educational establishments, including universities, also offer a growing number of formal and informal courses for the elderly, among which it is worth noting the so-called universities of the third age programs.

In Argentina, the Federal Council of Older Persons was formed in 2002. The Council provides coordinating and advisory functions focused on policies for older persons. At present, it comprises 12 provincial representatives from older persons' organizations. In 2004, Brazil created the National Council for the Rights of the Elderly, formed by 14 governmental representatives and 14 NGO representatives. The Council is involved in the elaboration of guidelines and norms that establish priorities in the matter of national politics for older people. Uruguay created similar advisory councils of older persons, focused on specific policies for the elderly population (ECLAC/CEPAL, 2006b).

IMPROVEMENTS IN THE FIELDS
OF GERIATRICS AND GERONTOLOGY

In spite of different processes of demographic aging, the disciplines of geriatrics and gerontology have been developing in most of the countries of the region. In 1951, the Argentinean Society of Geriatrics and Gerontology (Sociedad Argentina de Geriatría y Gerontología) was created with the support of the Medicine Nobel Prize-winning doctor Bernardo Hussay; this was the first scientific association of those disciplines in Latin America. The academic interest in developing the specialty derived from professional concerns regarding new health problems related to the increasing number of aged persons who had been requiring attention in the private and public hospitals in the largest Argentinean cities.

Since the second half of the 20th century, in many other countries of the region there has been an expansion of the medical and professional associations focused on both disciplines. Currently, in Brazil, Chile, Colombia, Costa Rica, Equator, Mexico, Panama, Paraguay, Peru, Uruguay, and Venezuela, there are associations or scientific societies related to geriatrics and gerontology. The Latin American Committee of the International Association of Gerontology and Geriatrics (COMLAT-IAGG) brings together the existing Latin American associations, creating an invaluable environment for the formation of human resources and academic exchange on the specialty.

In many Latin American countries, international programs of technical cooperation and empirical research have been carried out, focused on policy design and innovative institution development in order to adapt both policies and institutions to the familiar and demographic changes that have occurred in the region. During 2004 and 2005, the Ministers of Health (Ministerios de Salud) of Argentina, Chile, Uruguay, and Canada were involved in an international cooperation program with a specific focus on Integral Services for Dependent Elderly Persons (Servicios Integrales para personas mayores dependientes). This technical cooperation program, coordinated by the Older Adult section of the PAHO (OPS), provided a forum for exchanging experiences in each country, and led to the development of a common regulatory framework aimed at unifying the goals of the actions taken by each Southern Cone nation.

From 2005 to 2007, the international research project Social Exclusion of Dependent Persons Living in Long-Term Institutions (Exclusión social de las personas dependientes que residen en instituciones de larga estadía) was carried out by national teams from Argentina (ISALUD Foundation— Fundación ISALUD), Chile (Catholic University—Universidad Católica of Chile) and Uruguay (Catholic University—Universidad Católica of Uruguay). The international project was supported by the Interamerican Development Bank (BID) and PAHO (OPS). During 2006 and 2007, empirical investigations were started in cities in Brazil and Argentina within the framework of the Age-friendly Cities project, promoted and coordinated by the World Health Organization (WHO). The general aim of the investigation was to find out what the key actors thought of the advantages and disadvantages offered by each city toward the daily welfare of older people. In 2005 and 2006, governmental, NGOs and mass media representatives, researchers and professionals of several South American countries participated in the U.S. National Alliance for Caregiving initiative for the Planning Meeting for the Pan American Family Caregiving Conference. The First Pan American Family Caregiving Conference, which took place in the United States in 2006, introduced family caregiving issues into the policy agenda in most South American countries. The next two Pan American Family Caregiving Conferences are planned to take place in Argentina and in Brazil.

The SABE (Salud y Bienestar de las Personas Mayores en América Latina—Aging, Health and Well-being in Latin America) survey is a pioneer cross-national research project, supported by PAHO, which was conducted in seven cities on the American continent during October 1999 and the first trimester of 2000. The study is a cross-sectional survey of random samples of older persons residing in urban areas selected by the study: Buenos Aires in Argentina; Bridgetown in Barbados; Havana in Cuba; Mexico City in Mexico; Montevideo in Uruguay; Santiago in Chile; and Sao Pablo in Brazil. SABE has been used extensively in the preparation of policy documents throughout the region and provided basic core data for the implementation of policies related to aged populations (SABE, 2007).

REFERENCES

Argentina. (2003). Decreto 582/03. Retrieved from http://www.infoleg.gov.ar

ECLAC/CEPAL, CELADE. (2001). *Características sociodemográficas y socio-económicas de las personas de edad en América Latina* [Socioeconomic and sociodemographic characteristics of the aged persons in Latin America]. Fabiana del Popolo. Serie población y desarrollo. Santiago, Chile: ECLAC/CEPAL.

ECLAC/CEPAL. (2006a). *Informe de la reunión de gobiernos y expertos sobre envejecimiento en países de América del Sur* [Report of the meeting of governments and experts on aging in countries of South America]. November 2005. Buenos Aires. LC/L. 2547. Santiago, Chile: ECLAC/CEPAL.

ECLAC/CEPAL. (2006b). *La protección social de cara al futuro: Acceso, financiamiento y solidaridad* [Social protection facing the future: Access, financing and solidarity]. Santiago, Chile: ECLAC/CEPAL.

Gasparini, A., Alejo, J., Haimovich, F., Olivieri, S., & Tornarolli, L. (2007). *Poverty among the elderly in Latin America and the Caribbean.* United Nations.

ILO/OIT. (2002). *Pensiones no contributivas y asistenciales. Argentina, Brasil, Chile, Costa Rica y Uruguay* [Assistance and noncontributory pensions. Argentina, Brazil, Chile, Costa Rica and Uruguay]. Edited by F. M. Bertranou, C. Solori, & W. van Ginneken. Santiago, Chile: OIT.

Salud y Bienestar de las Personas Mayores en América Latina (SABE) [Aging, health and well-being in Latin America]. (2007). Retrieved from http://www.paho.org

World Health Organization (WHO). (2002). *Active aging. A policy framework. Contribution to the Second United Nations World Assembly on Aging, April 2002.*

5

■ ■ ■ ■ ■

International Nongovernmental Organizations (NGOs) Related to Aging

Samuel M. Mwangi

All over the world, populations are aging rapidly, even in developing nations. This phenomenon is characterized by increasing longevity and declining fertility due to 20th century advances in the prevention of infectious diseases, prenatal, and infant mortality (Aboderin, 2005). A body of evidence from aging studies and statistical data shows that older populations will supersede those of children under the age of 14 in the next few decades. The population 60 years and older is projected to increase eightfold, from 205 million people in 1980 to 1.6 billion people in 2050. Over the same period of time, the proportions will increase from 6.2% to 21% of the global population (Aboderin, 2005).

Population aging has put a stamp on the systems of many countries of the world. Some nations have made significant progress in addressing the social, economic, and health needs of the aging populations. However, many other countries, especially those in the developing world, are currently facing political, cultural, economic, and social constraints in their efforts to deal with the welfare of their aged populations. Global aging has received a great deal of attention since the early 1980s, after the first United Nations World Assembly on Ageing in Vienna, Austria. From this convention, the first International Plan of Action on Ageing (IPAA) ensued (United Nations [UN], 1982). Since then, global aging has become a shared experience of both the developed and developing nations (Gokhale, 1997; Gorman, 2002).

In response to the growing needs of the older populations and reduction in social welfare expenditures by national governments worldwide, national, regional, and international nongovernmental organizations (NGOs) have mounted numerous initiatives. The guiding objective of NGOs is to empower older adults, which, in turn, helps them to become aware of issues affecting them (Gokhale, 1997). Empowerment propels self-efficacy among older adults, which in many ways helps them discover their capabilities and share their power, which benefits other generations as well (Gokhale, 1997; Gorman, 2002). On top of assistance provision, NGOs also supplement the efforts of national governments, communities, and families by providing services to older consumers (Gokhale, 1997; Smith, 2003).

Some NGOs provide their services indirectly through research and dissemination of information and knowledge that is meaningful to older people, as well as family members and the community as a whole. Provision of services by NGOs to the older people also ensures that they age gracefully and with dignity. These organizations play a key role in influencing global policies on aging (Gokhale, 1997). NGOs, through their advocacy and representational roles at various intergovernmental meetings, serve the necessity of empowerment and participation for older adults (Gokhale, 1997). The main issues that the NGOs in aging address through their operations include, but are not limited to, population growth and longevity; health problems and health-care provision for elders; long-term care provision; infectious diseases, including HIV/AIDS; income maintenance and economic security; elder rights; housing and environment; and information linkage and referral.

This chapter summarizes the activities and operations undertaken by principal international nongovernmental organizations (INGOs) in the field of aging. For each INGO, we will describe briefly its history, goals and objectives, main functions, operations, and services provided, member organizations and global partners, and publications, if any.

AARP INTERNATIONAL

AARP International grew out of the American Association of Retired Persons' (AARP) quest for an international focus. For decades, the organization has been at the forefront of advocating for aging policy changes by providing relevant information on issues affecting aging populations around the world. Its aims are to help people live longer, healthier, more financially secure and productive lives by identifying the best ideas and practices in key policy areas. In order to address these needs more effectively and in a timely manner, AARP International has a team of experts drawn from various disciplines that touch or work on issues affecting older people. The areas of operations include aging and society, economic and retirement security, health care and wellness, livable communities, and long-term care. The organization maintains a collection of global resources under these areas of expertise, in which people interested in various topical issues can find information. The same resources are categorized by regions of the world.

AARP International also convenes international opinion leaders and policy-makers to share their expertise and develop research on health and long-term care, livable communities, older workers, and retirement income. In the end, it acts as a partner and catalyst to governments and decision-makers in all sectors to help address and favorably shape the social and economic face of aging worldwide. The goal of these collaborations is to change the perceptions and experience of aging around the world. To ensure that global aging is adequately covered, AARP International has interactive country profiles for most countries of the world that are considered global aging partners of AARP International.

Information and news from around the world also are collected and published on AARP International's Web site and in *The Journal*, a biannual journal covering such topics as demography of aging, health policy, and financial security issues facing a global aging population. Listing of major aging events such as conferences, annual meetings, aging expos, and forums in which aging issues are likely to be key are a major part of AARP International's database of resources (American Association of Retired Persons [AARP], 2008).

GLOBAL ACTION ON AGING (GAA)

Global Action on Aging (GAA), a nonprofit organization with special consultative status to the United Nations Economic and Social Council, was founded in 1994. GAA conducts research on critical emerging topical issues and publishes the results on its Web site. GAA staff and interns conduct research on aging policy and programs, in both the United States and worldwide. The research areas are divided into income support, health access, and human rights. GAA posts its materials in all six of the United Nations official languages: Arabic, Chinese, English, French, Russian, and Spanish. GAA also monitors United Nations activities on aging through the Aging Watch at the UN Web site section, and documents the situation of older persons caught in armed conflict. The mission of this organization is to report on older people's needs and their potentials within the global economy. Its programs include:

Elder Rights. GAA advocates for the protection of older persons as a key facet of the human rights movement, which includes choice of sexuality and sexual activity, suitable housing, novel caregiving programs, and more control over end-of-life decisions.

Health. GAA examines older persons' access to health care and medicine, both in the United States and worldwide, and the effect of the market system by monitoring actions by for-profit firms in the health field that restrict or compromise older persons' chance of living healthy lives.

Pension Watch. GAA observes how income support in old age, either public or private, shapes older people's experience out of the work force. It monitors reforms that affect older people's income and tracks policy changes and debates about dependence, entitlements, generational equity, and other income-security related issues in many countries of the world.

Rural Aging. The majority of the older people in the world dwell in rural areas and are largely isolated from journalists, policy-makers, and researchers, making them especially vulnerable to rapidly changing policies, environmental disasters, disease, and wars. Therefore, GAA seeks to document the barriers that rural elderly face and point to ways to overcome their isolation.

Armed Conflict & Emergencies Project. This project produces and posts research on legal, humanitarian, and physical challenges facing older persons caught in armed conflict and advocates at the United Nations for the Security Council's adoption of comprehensive international policies that address the problems and potential contributions of older persons at all stages of an armed conflict.

Aging Watch at the UN. A section of GAA's Web site tracks the reports, decisions, and other actions in the major United Nations organs charged to follow up decisions made at the Second World Assembly on Ageing, which was held in Madrid, Spain, in 2002.

Foreign Language Programs. In an attempt to reach a wider global audience, GAA's Web site publishes its articles and reports in the six official languages of the UN. Each language section covers U.S. and world stories, as well as country-specific issues about aging (Global Action on Aging, 2008).

HELPAGE INTERNATIONAL (HAI)

HelpAge International is a global network of not-for-profit organizations with a mission to improve the lives of disadvantaged older people. HAI also embraces a vision to create a world in which all older people can fulfill their potential to lead dignified, healthy, and secure lives. The HAI network was established in 1983 by five agencies in Canada, Colombia, India, Kenya, and the United Kingdom. The network also carries its activities in partnership with community-based organizations (CBOs) and works closely with academic institutions, local and national governments, and international agencies. To date, HAI is the only global network of not-for-profit organizations with such a mission. The network does this by supporting practical programs, giving a voice to older people, and influencing policy at local, national, and international levels.

The main areas of emphasis are economic and physical security, health care and social services, and the caregiving role across generations. HelpAge International's approach to work is based on a commitment to: (1) developing grassroots work that directly supports older people; (2) supporting and strengthening organizations that are working in practical ways to improve the lives of older people; and (3) giving a voice to older people, especially the most disadvantaged.

Most of HAI's activities are carried out in partnership with older people's organizations, community development organizations, and other NGOs. They also work closely with academic institutions on research projects and with local and national governments and international agencies to ensure that aging issues are at the center of development policies. Working in partnership helps HAI to: (1) strengthen the capacity of organizations working with older people; (2) connect grassroots experience with government thinking; and (3) build a global alliance of organizations working to raise the voice of older people in development processes. HAI also manages programs directly, especially in difficult circumstances such as during conflicts.

Global Affiliates/Partners. As a network of affiliates, HAI is able to share best practice on aging and development issues and gather evidence from around the world to support advocacy work at local, national, and international levels. Organizations affiliated with HAI benefit from links with other affiliates, contact with an HAI regional office, and regular information and publications. Affiliates play an important role in governing HAI, with representatives holding at least 6 of the 12 seats on the board of trustees.

Publications. Research and policy briefs, detailed research reports, and two regular newsletters, *Ageways* and *Ageing and Development*, are the resources used by the HAI network to disseminate information and data that result from its work.

INTERNATIONAL ASSOCIATION OF GERONTOLOGY AND GERIATRICS (IAGG)

The International Association of Gerontological Societies was founded in Liege, Belgium, in July 1950, and later it became the International

Association of Gerontology (IAG). From 1951 to 1981, IAG held a World Congress of Gerontology every three years. Since 1985, there has been a four-year interval between congresses. In recognition of IAG's historical background, its logo is subtitled "Founded 1950," and its flag represents the international community and the presence of gerontologist members all over the world, supporting the promotion and development of gerontology as a science. In 2005, the IAG Council approved adding "Geriatrics" to the name, and the association is now known as the International Association of Gerontology and Geriatrics (IAGG). This action was taken to promote and develop geriatrics as a medical specialty that focuses on the diseases of older people.

IAGG draws its member organizations from five regions: Africa, Asia/Oceania, Europe, Latin America and the Caribbean, and North America, with 70 member societies in 63 countries. The mission of IAGG is to promote the highest levels of achievement of gerontological research and training worldwide and to interact with other international, intergovernmental, and nongovernmental organizations in the promotion of gerontological interests globally and on behalf of its member associations. The Association pursues these activities to promote the highest quality of life and well-being of all people as they experience aging at individual and societal levels.

IAGG's ultimate goal is to have collaborative centers, at least one in each country, and to be in permanent contact with them, helping with the development of actions on gerontological and geriatrics education and research. This will also enhance exchange of experiences, open doors for international relationships, and support actions for qualifying students from less-developed countries in the fields of gerontology and geriatrics. The centers will be instrumental in the organization of congresses (regional and worldwide) and will help people working in the fields of gerontology and geriatrics to become acquainted.

Fostering high-quality education and training of personnel to plan, administer, and deliver services to older adults is a major objective of IAGG. Resolution 37/51 of the United Nations 1982 World Assembly on Ageing endorsed the agenda of promoting training and research, as well as the exchange of information and knowledge in order to provide a basis for social policies and action. IAGG promotes training institutes to act as a practical bridge between and among developed and developing nations. Over the years, IAGG has assisted the UN Programme on Ageing in the development of a Research Agenda on Ageing for the 21st Century. The agenda was endorsed by the IAGG Council in 2002 and was presented at an official roundtable at the World Assembly on Ageing in Madrid later that year.

IAGG publishes an official journal, the *International Journal of Experimental, Clinical and Behavioural Gerontology*, and a newsletter reporting on strategic plans, ongoing initiatives promoting research and education/training in gerontology, and international issues relevant to the member organizations (IAGG, 2008).

INTERNATIONAL ASSOCIATION OF HOMES AND SERVICES FOR THE AGEING (IAHSA)

IAHSA was founded in 1994 by a group of visionary aging services leaders from across the globe who realized that the global aging crisis would have a profound impact on care for the elderly. IAHSA is an international, not-for-profit educational and charitable organization with multinational composition, both in governance and membership. IAHSA's global network comprises provider organizations, businesses, researchers, individuals, and government officials from over 30 countries. The provider members represent all ownership types, including for-profit, not-for-profit, and government. Members of IAHSA benefit from shared knowledge, professional development, educational resources, leadership opportunities, and access to a global network of personal and professional contacts. Provider members range from single-site facilities to large provider-focused associations. The main vision of IAHSA is to create a platform for policy-makers, researchers, businesses, and aging services providers to collectively share their knowledge and best practices to enhance quality of care for the elderly.

As a partner of IAHSA, companies benefit in a number of ways: (a) faster, easier, and more affordable ways to showcase the company's products and services; (b) access to key decision-makers in the provider organizations; and (c) increased name and brand recognition throughout the aged care community.

During its decade of global aging leadership, IAHSA has conducted six international conferences, developed an international research agenda, and become recognized across the globe as the only international organization representing aging service providers. IAHSA currently has two main programs: (1) the Excellence in Aging Services Award, which is an annual international award program created to recognize organizations and individuals for models of innovation and excellence that contribute significantly to the quality of life of the individuals served; and (2) the International Design for Aging Symposium and Showcase, a program initiated in 2007 that features a survey and exhibit of the state of the art and trends in senior living and aged care. IAHSA's newsletter, *Alliance*, provides up-to-the-minute news about trends and issues on the global aging agenda, references to resources and reports of interest to providers, valuable insights about best practices, and profiles of aging services in countries around the globe (International Association of Homes and Services for the Ageing, 2008).

INTERNATIONAL FEDERATION ON AGEING (IFA)

IFA is a membership-based network of organizations, bodies, and individuals with a mission to improve the quality of the lives of older people around the world through policy change, grassroots partnerships, and strengthening bridges between public and private sectors concerned with aging issues. The IFA has a long-established and wide-ranging network of organizations in membership from across the globe. The network extends to 62 countries around the world, covering every region and together representing over 45 million older people globally, with two categories of membership: full members, comprising local, regional, provincial/ territorial or national not-for-profit or nongovernmental organizations; and associate members, including all individuals and sectors of society interested in understanding the issues and improving the lives of older people.

IFA works to influence and promote positive change for older people globally. Its work is based on the United Nations Principles of Older Persons: Independence, Participation, Care, Self-fulfillment, and Dignity. The strategic plan for the years 2003–2008 focused on: (1) alleviating the burden of poverty on older people and supporting policies that encourage economic independence to the fullest extent; (2) promoting policies and practices that enable older people to live healthy and active lifestyles; (3) raising awareness that older people may face abuse and neglect as part of their daily lives; (4) raising awareness about the extent to which ageism and age discrimination undermine people's right to dignity and quality of life; and (5) improving understanding of the fact that older women face a triple jeopardy, due to their social status, economic conditions, and illnesses and disabilities associated with longer life.

The IFA produces several useful publications, including Global Ageing— Issues and Action, a journal published regularly with the aim of informing debate on policy and practice issues vital to the well-being of older persons. A former publication, Ageing in Focus (Intercom), focused on the main aspects of policy, practice, and their impact on older persons. To supplement Global Ageing, IFA publishes reports and a new publication titled Ageing in Africa (International Federation on Ageing, 2008).

CONCLUSION

This summary chapter has described six key international nongovernmental organizations (NGOs) that work in the field of aging, as recognized by the United Nations Programme on Ageing. Resources that are helpful to the stakeholders in aging, as well as to older people themselves, were highlighted. The increasing number of global initiatives and activities on aging undertaken by these NGOs is an indication of the powerful trend of population aging. This chapter also recognized the most critical undertakings of these organizations to alleviate destitution and isolation of older adults as their numbers increase all over the world. For further information on nongovernmental organizations working in the field of aging around the world, see the Directory of International Gerontological and Geriatrics Societies and Associations in the Appendix of this volume.

REFERENCES

Aboderin, I. (2005). Changing family relationships in developing nations. In M. L. Johnson (Ed.), *The Cambridge handbook of age and ageing* (pp. 469–475). Cambridge, United Kingdom: Cambridge University Press.

American Association of Retired Persons (AARP) International. (2008). Retrieved November 2008, from http://www.aarpinternational.org

Global Action on Aging. (2008). Retrieved November 11, 2008, from http://www.globaging.org

Gokhale, S. D. (1997). Community experiences in active ageing: An NGO perspective. *International Ageing, 24,* 154–162.

Gorman, M. (2002). Global aging: The nongovernmental organization role in the developing world. *International Journal of Epidemiology, 31,* 782–785.

HelpAge International. (2008). Retrieved November 9, 2008, from http://www.helpageinternational.org

International Association for Gerontology and Geriatrics. (2008). Retrieved November 11, 2008, from http://www.iagg.org.br

International Association of Homes and Services for the Ageing. (2008). Retrieved November 9, 2008, from http://www.iahsa.org

International Federation on Ageing. (2008). Retrieved November 11, 2008, from http://www.ifa-fiv.org

Smith, S. R. (2003). Government and nonprofits in the modern age. *Society, 40,* 36–45.

United Nations. (1982). *Report of the World Assembly on Ageing, Vienna, 26 July to 6 August.* New York: United Nations.

6

··■··

Argentina

José R. Jauregui and Isidoro Fainstein

DEMOGRAPHY

Argentina, a large country situated at the southern end of the Americas, covers 3.7 million km² and has a population of about 40,000,000 people. Just as a comparison, India has 20 times the population of Argentina with almost the same territory (ARGENTINA-INDEC National Census, 2001).

The vastness of the territory, the relatively low density of the population, and an impressive immigration movement at the turn of the 19th century have shaped a country with singular sociodemographic characteristics and an unusual degree of urbanization. Nearly 85% of the population is Caucasian, and the remainder is native Indian and mestizo offspring (ARGENTINA-INDEC National Census, 2001).

It is estimated that 70% of the persons over 60 inhabiting our planet in the near future will be living in the developing world. Latin America (LA) is not an exception. It expects a sharp increase in its elderly population from 7% in 1980 to 15% in 2025. Argentina is experiencing the same process, with an increase of its aged population from 9% in 1987 to an expected 16% by 2025 (ARGENTINA-INDEC-CELADE, 2001). Over the last three decades, Argentina has witnessed a growth in its older population (>65 years) from less than 7% to nearly 10%. These figures place Argentina among the countries with the oldest population in LA. This trend is even more evident in Buenos Aires city, where more than 17% of the population is aged 65 and higher, which is comparable to many European cities.

In Argentina, the population doubled every 20 years until 1914, when foreigners amounted to 30% of the population. The flow of European migration stopped in 1930, but resumed at the end of World War II, although with much lower intensity; a little more than half a million people arrived between 1945 and 1948.

These new Americans settled mainly in the region's largest cities, such as Buenos Aires, Sao Paulo, Montevideo, or Santiago, turning LA into a highly urbanized subcontinent, almost as urbanized as Europe. Seventy per cent of the population of LA lives in urban areas; that is about twice the proportion of Asians and three times that of Africans who are living in cities. We are like Chile and Uruguay in being one of the most urbanized countries in the world. In spite of having a strongly developed agrarian economy, more than the 80% of the Argentine population live in the cities (Strejilevich, 1990).

AGING OF THE ARGENTINE POPULATION

Over the last decade, the elderly population has also increased in absolute terms, and the population pyramid has witnessed a change as a result of demographic variations. The base of the pyramid has narrowed due to a lower fertility rate, and the peak of the pyramid has widened because of an increase in life expectancy.

In many developed countries, it took a century for the older population to rise from 8% to 12%; in Argentina, similar changes have taken place in only 40 years. Projections to 2025 predict that more than one million people will be aged 80 and older.

Argentina, like many other countries in LA, will become older without necessarily becoming richer, as has been the case in Western Europe and North America. Current population life expectancy at birth is 74 years (Kalache, 1998).

Most seniors live alone in their households or with their spouse. As a result of the unemployment rates in our country, many young people have depended on the pension of an elder living at home over the last decades.

Finally, most Argentine older people are under the care of the Instituto Nacional de Servicios Sociales para Jubilados y Pensionados (PAMI—National Health Insurance Program for the Elderly), or remain uninsured. This latter group of senior citizens accounts for nearly 20% of the population aged 65 and more, and constitutes one of the most unprotected sectors of the population (see Figure 6.1) (Redondo, 1990).

Figure 6.1
Population pyramid of Argentina, 2001

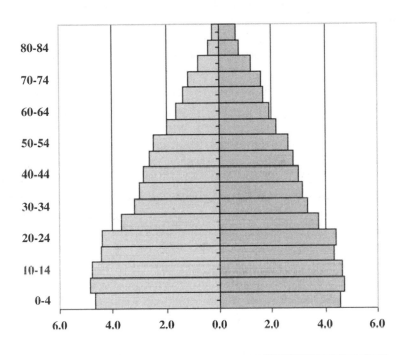

HEALTH CARE

The Argentine health-care system is characterized by excessive fragmentation. On the one hand, there is a public sector whose national, provincial, and municipal levels have a high degree of autonomy. On the other
hand, there are a series of heterogeneous agencies that deliver medical care
and that are supported by the social security system (Kaplan, 1987). And
lastly, there is an important private sector based on mutual benefit societies,
prepaid health care systems, and for-profit hospitals (Stocker, Waitzkin, &
Iriart, 1999; Barrientos, 2000). A recurrent lack of coordination within
each of these sectors makes the interrelation among them very complex.

The public system was strongly enhanced in the 1940s under a legal entitlement (Universal Coverage Dogma), which promised free access to health care
for the whole population, covering the costs of inpatient and outpatient care.
This coverage is provided by federal or state authorities and benefits approximately 45% of the population. Unfortunately, it has failed to provide effective
medical care because of its huge bureaucratic structure and limited resources.

The social security system provides assistance to 50% of the population, inpatients and outpatients in acute and chronic conditions. Union health systems (Obras Sociales) and PAMI offer this medical care only to their members (Kaplan, 1987).

The private health care system has been growing since the 1980s as a result of changes in the regulatory framework allowed by a more free-market economy, although this growth has stopped in recent years. This sector accounts for only 7% of health-care services, but new governmental regulations are being enacted to integrate the social security and private systems.

There are 265 medical doctors per 100,000 inhabitants. Although these numbers clearly exceed those necessary to satisfy health-care needs, nurses are scarce, with only 77 per 100,000 inhabitants. Volunteer workers, junior physicians in training, and relatives partially balance this shortage. Although both of these professions, including social workers, receive some training in geriatrics, there is no specific training for pharmacists (Lloyd-Sherlock & Novick, 2001).

Argentina still lacks a nationwide health-care system specifically designed for the elderly; and proper health-care coverage is not guaranteed to some in the country. Despite this situation, medical insurance provided by the social security health care system (PAMI or Union Health Services) or by the private system give assistance to almost 80% of senior citizens. The main institution is PAMI (Integral Medical Assistance Program), which provides state-run coverage for disabled or senior citizens, covering services analogous to American Medicare and Medicaid. It is offered to all ages as an entitlement for those with a defined level of disability. There are other eligibility requirements for PAMI, but their complexity is beyond the scope of this chapter. PAMI gives assistance to 65% of the approximately 4 million older people now living in Argentina.

The union health systems, which provide services to approximately 400,000 senior beneficiaries, represent the second type of health coverage (social security system). These services cover acute inpatient, outpatient, limited nursing home, and home care (including doctor's visits). Patients may be treated at different hospitals but with varying financial coverage.

The private health-care system is composed of health companies, HMOs, and health insurers. Only the higher socioeconomic classes can afford their high fees, and that is why only 8% of Argentine seniors have a private health insurance provider. The prepaid systems cover acute care, outpatient care, and doctor's visits.

Home care is an option, especially after hospital discharge, but nursing home (NH) care is not usually covered, resulting in a great financial burden for many families. Although many elderly remain without any health coverage (approximately 18% of them), it is interesting to note that many others have double or triple health coverage.

The number of long-term care facilities has grown significantly since 1970 through entrepreneurial initiatives, as well as the contracts PAMI signed with privately owned NHs. There are currently about 70,000 long-term care beds in Argentina, placed in 600 facilities, and they render a wide diversity of services. NHs must have a medical director, regardless of whether he is or is not a geriatrician (Chalita, 1992).

Although NH clinical guidelines do exist, they are seldom fully followed; an undertrained and overworked staff frequently takes care of institutionalized elderly. Unfortunately, accurate data on the quality of the services delivered by different health providers are not available.

Home care is still in a developing stage and most of the medical doctors practicing home care medicine do so as a second job. Only 2% of senior citizens live in adapted housing, residential homes, or NHs. One possible explanation for this low rate in comparison with that found in other countries could be the strong influence of Catholic and Jewish religions, which emphasize that the care of older people is primarily a family responsibility.

Under a new Argentine law enacted in 2002, physicians must primarily prescribe medications using their generic names, and they can be purchased in pharmacies. A considerable discount is given (usually ranging from 40% to 70%) on the total cost, depending on the type of medications and health coverage. Drugs for some chronic illnesses, such as insulin, are supplied at no cost. Before 2002, medications were prescribed and purchased under their brand names, and generics were not available.

EDUCATION IN GERIATRICS

The Secretary of Health, a branch of the Health Ministry, recognized geriatric medicine as a specialty in 1977. Since then, almost 600 doctors have completed their postgraduate training in the specialty.

It is not uncommon for the practice of geriatric medicine to be closely integrated with the practice of internal medicine. Therefore, geriatricians perform general medical care for adult senior patients, spending just a small percentage of their time on specific geriatric tasks.

There are two basic routes for obtaining the specialization in Argentina. On the one hand, there is an additional two-year geriatric fellowship after board certification in internal medicine or family medicine. Currently, only three Argentine faculties certify graduate doctors as geriatricians in this way. On the other, the Sociedad Argentina de Gerontología y Geriatría (Argentine Society of Gerontology and Geriatrics) gives a two-year course whose conditions include being a graduated physician with at least three years' previous training in internal medicine (Sociedad Argentina de Gerontología y Geriatría, 2008).

No comprehensive training program is available for nurses who want to specialize in geriatrics. Physical medicine and rehabilitation are not well-recognized medical specialties, as a result of the poor salaries offered. Moreover, the country lacks a reasonable number of physiotherapists to provide adequate care to Argentine seniors.

Since 2007, the Sociedad Argentina de Gerontología y Geriatría has given an elective course in geriatrics for medical students at Buenos Aires University.

SUMMARY

Argentina does not yet have a formal nationwide health program for the elderly. This situation has resulted in huge differences in the quality and entitlement of health care for senior citizens.

Academic affairs in developing countries such as Argentina have insufficient infrastructure, and this situation prevents geriatrics from becoming a rewarding specialty.

Teaching and research in this field is usually unpaid and *ad honorem*. Yet, a committed minority of teachers and health professionals are confident that their efforts are worthwhile and a new generation of geriatricians is starting to participate actively in international forums, to publish in recognized medical journals, to participate in Latin American academic forums, such as ALMA (Latin American Academy of Senior Adults Medicine), and to foster geriatrics as a specialty (Montero Odasso, 2004).

REFERENCES

ARGENTINA-INDEC (National Census). (2001). *B series, selected characteristics*. Federal District, N1, Prat 2.

ARGENTINA-INDEC (National Census). (2001) *General characteristics*. Retrieved from http://www.indec.gov.ar

ARGENTINA-INDEC-CELADE. (2001). *Projections of population according to gender and age; 1990–2010*. Series 2, Demographic Analysis. Buenos Aires: INDEC.

Barrientos, A., & Lloyd-Sherlock, P. (2000). Reforming health insurance in Argentina and Chile. *Health Policy Plan, 15*, 417–423.

Chalita, E. (1992). Modelos de asistencia geronto-geriátrica. Artículo original, *Rev. Arg. Ger y Ger, 12*, 129–154.

Kalache, A. (1998). Future prospects for geriatric medicine in developing countries. In R. C. Tallis (Ed.), *Brocklehurst's textbook of geriatric medicine and gerontology* (5th ed., pp. 1513–1520). London: Churchill Livingstone.

Kaplan, R. (1987). Care for the elderly: Could teaching nursing homes be of value in Argentina? *Dan Med Bull, suppl. 5*, 28–32.

Lloyd-Sherlock, P., & Novick, D. (2001). "Voluntary" user fees in Buenos Aires hospitals: Innovation or imposition? *Int J Health Serv, 31*, 709–728.

Montero Odasso, M., et al. (2004). Health care for older persons in Argentina: A country profile. *Journal of the American Geriatrics Society, 52*, 1761–1765.

Redondo, N. (1990). *Poverty and aging. Research in urban popular sectors in Buenos Aires*. Buenos Aires: CEPEV-Humanitas.

Sociedad Argentina de Gerontología y Geriatría. Retrieved October 17, 2008, from http://www.sagg.org.ar/

Stocker, K., Waitzkin, H., & Iriart, C. (1999). The exportation of managed care to Latin America. *New England Journal of Medicine, 340*, 1131–1136.

Strejilevich, M. (1990). Consequences of the sudden urbanization and of the immigration of the Argentine aged population. In M. Strejilevich (Ed.), *Subject for gerontopsychiatrics*. Buenos Aires: Ediciones.

7

Australia

Laurie Buys, Evonne Miller, and Karen Robinson

RECENT HISTORY OF AGING

Australia's population is aging, both numerically and proportionately. In the next 40 years, the proportion and number of Australians aged 65 or older will almost triple, from 2.5 million in 2002 (13% of the total population) to 6.2 million in 2042 (25% of the total population). The number of Australians aged over 100 years will also significantly increase: in 2005, 2,055 Australians were older than 100, but by 2055, there will be 78,000 centenarians (Department of Health & Ageing, 2006). Most notably, by 2018, the number of Australians aged 65 years and over is projected to exceed the number of children aged 0–14 years (Australian Bureau of Statistics [ABS], 2007). Given such predictions, the anticipated social, economic, and health impact of an aging population has become a major public policy issue within Australia.

Although population aging varies among Australia's states and territories, due to differences in fertility, mortality, and migration trends, the basic demographic profile of Australia has aged significantly over the past century. In 1870, only 2% of the population was aged 65 years or older, with this proportion increasing to 8% in 1971 and 13% today (ABS, 2003). The life expectancy for Australian men has increased from 55 years in 1900 to 77 years in 2000, while the life expectancy for Australian women has increased from 58 years in 1900 to 82 years in 2000 (ABS, 2002). Unfortunately, the majority of indigenous people in Australia do not reach old age; the life expectancy for Indigenous Australians is approximately 17 years less than non-Indigenous Australians, with only 3% of Indigenous Australians older than 65 years. In 2006, 35% of older Australians (953,702 people) were born overseas, with approximately two-thirds from non-English-speaking countries, predominantly Italy and Greece (Australian Institute of Health and Welfare [AIHW], 2007). Residing primarily in Sydney and Melbourne, this culturally and linguistically diverse group relies predominantly on their language of origin for communication with service providers (AIHW 2007).

The majority of older Australians are married and own their own home in a metropolitan area; approximately two-thirds of the 85 years and older age group are widowed, with one-third (783,000) living alone (AIHW, 2007). Approximately 6% of older Australians reside in alternative accommodation, predominantly retirement villages and residential care facilities. While the vast majority of older Australians view their health positively and lead active lives, the major determining factors precipitating entry to residential care are disability, falls, and dementia (which currently affects over 227,300 Australians; Alzheimer's Australia, 2008). Over half of all older Australians (1.4 million) have at least one disability that restricts everyday activities, while 23% of older people (58% of the 85 years and older cohort) reported severe disability, requiring assistance with self-care, mobility, or communication (ABS, 2003).

Australia abolished the previous fixed age of retirement of 65 years in 2001, with 2% of the Australian work force now aged 65 years or older (Abhayaratna & Lattimore, 2006). However, despite policy efforts to increase mature-age work-force participation, Australia's current labor force participation rates for older people (aged 55 to 64 years) remains at 48.6%, slightly below the international OECD average of 50.8% (Department of Families, Housing, Community Services and Indigenous Affairs, 2006). While the transition to retirement is now a more gradual process and very fluid, approximately half of all Australian men currently retire between ages 55 and 64, with a third of women retiring before the age of 45 (AIHW, 2007). At 65, Australians with income and assets below a certain amount are eligible for an aged pension (Department of Communications, Information, Technology and the Arts [DCITA], 2004). Australia began a compulsory superannuation scheme in 1992. Total balances are still relatively low, with average retirement payouts (of the total balance) in 2006 of A$136,000 (about US$106,000) for men, and A$63,000 (about US$49,000) for women; indeed, only 3% of new retirees in 2006 had superannuation of A$500,000 or more (about US$392,000), which is the amount needed to support a comfortable retirement lifestyle in Australia (Association of Superannuation Funds of Australia, 2008).

RECENT RESEARCH ON AGING

Australia has a significant research base that addresses a wide range of topics and disciplines, from biomedical to social research issues. While Australian researchers publish in quality journals across the world, we would like to refer readers to the *Australasian Journal on Ageing*, which features research outcomes on gerontology and geriatric medicine in the Asia-Pacific region.

Currently, there is no one aging-specific national research or grant-funding body in Australia, with the government primarily funding aging research through two national generic research bodies: the Australian Research Council (ARC) and the National Health and Medical Research Council (NHMRC). In 2004–2005, the NHMRC allocated $109 million (about US$85 million) (32% of its total expenditure) to various competitive funding research in the priority area of Ageing Well, Ageing Productively (AWAP), with a further $4.5 million (about US$3.5 million) awarded to a new Health Services Research Program project to investigate innovative analyses of health insurance, aging, and economic burden of illness and injury.

Three large aging research initiatives have been funded recently. The Australian government has named dementia as a national priority area, setting up three national dementia collaborative research centers: Assessment and Better Care Outcomes in Dementia (University of New South Wales); Prevention, Risk Reduction, and Early Detection (Australian National University); and Consumers, Carers, and Social Research (Queensland University of Technology). A second recent initiative is the jointly funded ARC/NHMRC Research Network in Ageing Well (RNAW), to "increase the scale, focus, and capacity of Australian research to inform national efforts to respond constructively to an aging society" (RNAW, n.d.). The RNAW brings together over 360 researchers in aging from a broad range of disciplines and institutions across Australia. The Network has strong links with a wide range of aging constituencies that provide input on priority research needs, promotes research partnerships, communicates with key individuals and organizations, and participates in Network activities. The focus of the Network is on building research agendas and partnerships in four key research theme areas essential to quality of life and national impacts, specifically: healthy aging; productivity and economic participation; independent living and social participation; and population research strategies. Third, the ARC and NHMRC recently collaborated to advance the priority goal of Ageing Well, Ageing Productively, by awarding six AWAP grants investigating the topics of (a) the economic and workplace adjustments that population aging will generate; (b) predictors of aging well, utilizing two existing longitudinal studies; (c) gene-environment interaction in healthy brain aging; (d) developing statistical and microsimulation models to optimize healthy aging; (e) developing guidelines for managing poly-morbidity in older people; and (f) exploring the health of the older Indigenous population.

Key Aging Research Areas

In an attempt to quantify aging research areas in Australia, the RNAW recently commissioned a review of aging research conducted in Australia or by Australians from 1999 to 2005. This review identified a total of 2,176 studies addressing the RNAW priority areas; healthy aging (1,355 studies) and independent living (1,133 studies) were the predominant topics. Although falls, vision, and dementia were particularly well covered, there were gaps in general health promotion within healthy aging and the role of social and environmental factors in the priority area of independent living and social participation. The review also identified deficits in volume and scope in two themes, population research (310) and productivity (201), potentially attributable to the relative lack of maturity of current Australian longitudinal studies.

Australian Longitudinal Studies

In a recent review, the AIHW identified 21 key Australian longitudinal studies that focused on aging issues, concluding that longitudinal data coverage was least comprehensive in the area of age-friendly infrastructure and built environment, specifically assistive technology, carer stress and elder abuse (AIHW, 2004). Overall, this review concluded that the Australian knowledge base from these longitudinal studies was strongest for healthy aging, condition-specific research and mental health. While it is impossible to list all these longitudinal studies, among the best known is the Australian Longitudinal Study on Ageing. More than 200 publications have resulted from this bio-psycho-social and behavioral study, which began in 1992 and followed 2,087 older adults (aged 70 and over) residing in the community and in residential care in South Australia (Andrews, Cheok, & Carr, 1989). Other major Australian longitudinal studies focusing on specific aspects of aging include the Sydney

Older Persons Study (commenced in 1991, focusing on the health of community-dwelling World War II veterans, aged 75 years and older), the Healthy Retirement project (commenced in 1998, exploring preparation and impacts of retirement among 590 workers aged 50 and over) and the Dubbo Study of the Health of the Elderly (commenced in 1988, focusing on biomedical and social science aspects of healthy aging). Two major gender-specific longitudinal aging studies are the Australian Longitudinal Study on Women's Health (ALSWH) and the Perth Health in Men Study (HIMS). ALSWH is the largest of its kind ever conducted in Australia, surveying over 40,000 Australian women aged 18–23, 45–50, and 70–75 years when the study began in 1995, and it is scheduled to continue investigating a wide range of biological, social, psychological, and lifestyle factors (including use and satisfaction with health-care services) until at least 2016 (Lee et al., 2005). HIMS began as a West Australian Trial of Screening for Abdominal Aortic Aneurysms in approximately 12,000 men aged 65–83 years in 1996; now, the focus has widened to understanding the diverse factors that influence the health of older men (Norman et al., 2008). Thanks to joint funding from NHMRC and ARC (through AWAP), ALSWH and HIMS data currently are being integrated to explore successful aging in men and women and to investigate potentially modifiable factors that may contribute to aging well.

Research Centers

The expansion of the number of research centers with a specific focus on aging also provides evidence of the growing awareness of aging as a research issue in Australia; research centers have successfully fostered research students and early career researchers, as well as the recruitment of experienced researchers from other fields. In 2003, the Stocktake of Australian Ageing Research and Policy Initiatives identified nine centers engaged in aging-related research. Currently there are more than 20 such centers, with most Australian universities now having a group specifically focusing on aspects of aging research. This is extremely positive for the long-term future of aging research. Outside universities, another positive development has been the growing role that provider organizations are taking in research, both in direct funding and with in-kind collaborations. With providers of community and residential health services—such as Silver Chain, Blue Care, the Royal District Nursing Service, and Rural Doctors Network Australia in Victoria—having taken the lead some years ago, an increasing number of organizations are developing their own in-house research capacity.

Professional Organizations

Finally, there are two key professional aging associations in Australia. Founded in 1964, the Australian Association of Gerontology (AAG) is Australia's largest, multidisciplinary, peak, professional association for professionals working in the broader field of aging. With approximately 800 members, AAG aims to expand knowledge of aging, with the purpose of improving the experience of aging. The AAG has two specialist subsections, the Aboriginal and Torres Straight Islander Division and the Student Division. The Aboriginal and Torres Straight Islander Division commenced in 2006 and has a growing membership of interested participants interested in aging issues affecting this population. The Student Division is also expanding. Notably, there has been significant growth in the number of students taking an active interest in aging research, which is reflected in the expansion of the AAG student group, its high profile and general level of enthusiasm. It also suggests that attitudinal barriers to aging-related research are gradually being overcome, with the field now attracting a growing group of emerging researchers willing to make a career in this area. As one indicator of this, from 2004 to 2006, there has been a marked increase in the number of student delegates to the national AAG conferences, and an associated significant increase in student membership of the AAG. The second key association is the Australian and New Zealand Society for Geriatric Medicine (ANZSGM), which is for medical practitioners engaged in the practice of geriatric medicine and has over 600 members.

CURRENT STATE OF EDUCATION IN GERONTOLOGY

In Australia, education in gerontology is available through universities and the Technical and Further Education (TAFE) system (equivalent to community colleges in the United States and the polytechnic system in the United Kingdom). All Australian states and territories offer courses on aging or aged care, with a significant number of these courses offered in flexible delivery formats, including distance-education options, or packaged so that they are available in short, intense modules. Universities include gerontology education in most undergraduate training programs for medical, allied health, and social work professionals, as well as offering postgraduate gerontological courses. Beyond traditional specialized aged care courses focusing on palliative and pastoral care, most Australian universities also offer courses that specialize in specific key issues concerning aging, such as social planning (specifically, building communities for aging in place), housing, financial management, leisure therapy, and cultural aspects of aging. With dementia identified as a national health priority, many universities are also developing and offering courses that specifically focus on dementia care. Therefore, there are several opportunities for those interested in aging, wherever they reside, to enroll in tertiary aging education.

In Australia, TAFE offers a range of Aged Care qualifications in the Community Services Training Package, which provide the knowledge and skills required to work as an assistant in nursing or personal care assistant in an aged care facility, a community support worker, a home-care assistant or a community care worker. Statistics from the National Centre for Vocational Education Research (2004) indicate that 8,060 students were enrolled in an Aged Care course in 1999; by 2003, however, 23,180 were enrolled. Notably, the vast majority of students were female (20,220) and older than 25 years (18,380). Unfortunately, poor perceptions of career opportunities may lead students to other specialization choices. An example of this is the typical pay rates for community care workers: the National Community Care Coalition recently reported that a personal care worker (who must have a TAFE Certificate III in aged care) is paid less than a checkout operator in a supermarket (Allen Consulting Group, 2007, p. 7).

All Australian universities offer specialist aged care nursing courses, covering the basic daily activities, knowledge, and skills required for health care professionals working in the aged care environment. These courses typically cover a wide range of topics, including evidence-based practice, the life cycle and experience of aging, quality of life, palliative care and dementia, management, and leadership, and different approaches for acute, community, and residential care. Aged care is a compulsory component of the undergraduate nursing curriculum, and students can choose to complete further study in the area within diplomas, graduate certificates, and master's degrees. Unfortunately, aged care nursing generally has a poor image due to a variety of factors such as ageism, the perceived lack of status and/or excitement associated with non-acute nursing, and poor pay and working conditions (Nay & Pearson, 2001). It is estimated that 38,272 Registered Nurses are employed in geriatrics and gerontological nursing (8% fewer than in 1993; Nay & Pearson, 2001), and they generally are assisted by Enrolled Nurses (who have completed a one-year Vocational Education Training (VET) course and by Nursing Assistants (most hold a Certificate in Aged Care).

A wide range of occupations are included under the broad allied health category, including pharmacists, physiotherapists, occupational therapists, psychologists, social workers, and dieticians. Both the qualifications required (which range from a diploma to a bachelor's degree) and the exposure to aging curricula vary, although all may work with older people at some stage in their careers. For geriatricians, 40 sites in Australia provide advanced training in geriatric medicine, with an estimated 52 physicians currently in training (ANZSGM, 2008).

Finally, a range of gerontology postgraduate courses is available in Australia, covering a diverse range of topics including dementia care, bio-statistics for health professionals, community analysis and health-care planning, law in health service management, rural health, aging diversity, gender and culture, quality management, social planning, epidemiology, and contemporary issues in gerontology (e.g., elder abuse, social isolation, health, dementia, theories of aging, environmental influences, financial management, leisure, housing, social support, and spirituality). In recent years, new courses have been offered in end-of-life management, which includes palliative care and pastoral care designed to prepare students for the challenges they will face when working with death, dying, loss, and grief issues on a daily basis. The majority of students attracted to further education in gerontology are practicing health professionals, typically already working in some form of aged care. This means that the demand has predominantly been for part-time and flexible study opportunities, especially online education (Russell, Mahony, Hughes & Kendig, 2007).

CURRENT PUBLIC POLICY ISSUES IN AGING

Recent aging policy in Australia has been driven predominantly by the fiscal and economic implications of population aging; while not perceived as a crisis, it is accepted that population aging will require innovative policy approaches designed to increase labor force participation and economic productivity, while minimizing public expenditure on health, aged care, and welfare (Costello, 2004; Productivity Commission, 2005). Indeed, the current dependency ratio in Australia is five working people per person over 65, with projections that by 2041, the ratio will be 2.5 working people per person over 65 (Healy, 2004). Australia's long-term strategic approach to population aging is outlined in the National Strategy for an Ageing Australia (NSAA), which was released in 2001 (DoHA, 2001). The Strategy, designed to provide a coordinated national response and guiding policy framework for future action by governments, business, communities, and individuals, focuses on four key theme areas: (1) independence and self-provision (includes employment for mature age workers); (2) attitude, lifestyles and community support; (3) healthy aging; and (4) world-class care.

The first NSAA theme emphasizes self-provision, specifically encouraging individual contributions to retirement savings, changing the culture of early retirement in Australia, and removing the barriers that inhibit ongoing participation in the work force. While the age pension remains a safety net, NSAA and other policy papers (e.g., Costello, 2002) have highlighted that Australia is moving from "inter-generational transfers (the working population supporting the retired population) to intra-generational self-sufficiency (people funding their own retirement and old age)" (Healy, 2004, p. 2). The second NSAA theme, "Attitude, Lifestyles, and Community Support," outlines two associated goals, designed to highlight both the significant contributions of older Australians (especially as caregivers and volunteers) and the importance of supporting the needs of older people (through appropriate infrastructure, technology, and information). Specifically, Goal 1 specifies that "society has a positive image of older Australians, appreciates their diversity and recognises the many roles and contributions they continue to make to the economy and the community," while Goal 2 is "That public, private and community infrastructure is available to support older Australians and their participation in society" (DoHA, 2001, p. 34). There is also an increasing acknowledgment that the built environment has a critical impact on older Australians' mobility, independence, and quality of life, with state and local governments working to create age-friendly communities (Australian Local Government Association, 2005).

The third NSAA theme, "Healthy Aging," encapsulates the importance of maintaining and optimizing older Australians' physical, social, and mental well-being, advocating a life-course approach to wellness. This theme emphasizes the need for sound research to develop the evidence base required to support policy decision-making about aging issues, with research needed "to drive the healthy ageing evidence base to understand what works and why" (DoHA, 2001, p. 39). The Framework for an Australian Ageing Research Agenda (FAARA; DoHA, 2003) subsequently outlined a broad direction for aging research in Australia, providing six Strategic Priorities for Building Ageing Research Capacity (BARC):

1. Excellence in aging research;
2. Translation of research into practice;
3. Better use and dissemination of existing research;
4. Emphasis on multidisciplinary research;
5. Address gaps in existing research; and
6. International collaboration.

Six Strategic Ageing Research Themes also were proposed:

1. Sustained economic growth;
2. Adequate retirement income;
3. Positive images of aging and social participation;

4. Age-friendly infrastructure;

5. Healthy aging; and

6. High-quality health and aged care.

BARC has aimed to develop and encourage maximum collaboration between Australian researchers and policy-makers on aging issues; one example of this is the Ageing Research Online Web site, which acts as a clearinghouse of aging-related research conducted across Australia.

The final NSAA theme, "World Class Care," focuses on providing a high-quality, affordable, accessible, and appropriate care system. Issues such as expanding the evidence base, future patterns of health and disease, improving service planning and resource allocation, and health work force shortages are discussed in this theme. The provision of aged care involves all tiers of government and is complex; briefly, the *Aged Care Act 1997* provided the main vehicle for structural reforms in residential and community aged care packages, with a range of subsequent initiatives, including a Review of Pricing Arrangements in Residential Aged Care Report in 2004, and the development of an online source of information on culturally appropriate aged care (for example, the Centre for Cultural Diversity in Ageing). Via Medicare, older Australians have access to a free public hospital system (including doctors, specialists, and participating optometrists or dentists), with Aged Care Assessment Teams assessing the level of care they may need. In mid-2008, a new funding instrument was introduced for residential aged care (Age Care Funding Instrument), while community care programs are becoming increasingly important as the majority of older Australians prefer to age in place. For example, each year, approximately 750,000 older and disabled Australians access Home and Community Care, which seeks to maximize older people's independence by providing assistance with the activities of daily living and delivers low-level nursing care, cooking, and cleaning services. Overall, the focus is on developing strategies and initiatives that enhance health in later life. Notably, although Australia is well prepared to deal with the challenges of an aging population, "the prominence of ageing policy over the next two decades appears to be as 'absolutely inevitable' as the growth of the older population itself" (Jones, de Jonge & Phillips, 2008, p. 24).

REFERENCES

Abhayaratna, J., & Lattimore, R. (2006). *Workforce participation rates—How does Australia compare? Productivity Commission Staff Working Paper.* Retrieved February 20, 2008, from http://ssrn.com/abstract=1018871

Allen Consulting Group. (2007). *The future of community care: Report to the community care coalition*. Retrieved April 10, 2008, from http://www.agedcare.org.au/General_PDFs/ACG_CCC_future_community_care_280207F.pdf

Alzheimer's Australia. (2008). *Living with dementia: Dementia facts & statistics*. Retrieved February 18, 2008, from http://www.alzheimers.org.au/upload/StatisticsMar08.pdf

Andrews, G., Cheok, F., & Carr, S. (1989). The Australian Longitudinal Study of Ageing. *Australian Journal on Ageing, 8*, 31–35.

Association of Superannuation Funds of Australia Ltd. (2008). *Retirement balances on the increase—But more savings effort still required*. Retrieved February 1, 2008, from http://www.superannuation.asn.au/mr080211/default.aspx

Australian and New Zealand Society for Geriatric Medicine (ANZSGM). (n.d.). Retrieved April 22, 2008, from http://www.asgm.org.au/training.asp

Australian Bureau of Statistics (ABS). (2002). *Australian demographic statistics*. Catalogue No. 3101.0. Canberra: ABS.

Australian Bureau of Statistics (ABS). (2003). *Population projections Australia, 2002–2101*. Catalogue No. 3222.0. Canberra: ABS.

Australian Bureau of Statistics (ABS). (2004). *Australian social trends*. Catalogue No. 4102.0. Canberra: ABS.

Australian Bureau of Statistics (ABS). (2006). *Australian social trends*. Catalogue No. 41020.0. Canberra: ABS.

Australian Bureau of Statistics (ABS). (2007). *Population by age and sex: Australian states and territories*. Catalogue No. 3201.0. Canberra: ABS.

Australian Institute of Health and Welfare (AIHW). (2004). Logie H, Hogan R & Peut A. Longitudinal studies of ageing: Implications for future studies. AIHW Cat. No. AGE 42. Canberra: AIHW.

Australian Institute of Health and Welfare (AIHW). (2007). *Older Australia at a glance* (4th ed.). Canberra: AIHW.

Australian Local Government Association. (2005). *Age-friendly built environments: Opportunities for local government*. Canberra: Australian Local Government Association. Retrieved February 15, 2008, from http://www.alga.asn.au/policy/healthAgeing/ageing/resources/publications/Agefriendly_built_environment_paper.pdf

Costello, P. (2002). *Intergenerational report: 2002–03*. Canberra: Australian Government.

Costello, P. (2004). *Australia's demographic challenges*. Canberra: Australian Government. Retrieved February 1, 2008, from http://demographics.treasury.gov.au

Department of Communications, Information, Technology and the Arts (DCITA). (2004). *A more flexible and adaptable retirement income system*. Canberra: Author.

Department of Families, Housing, Community Services and Indigenous Affairs. (2006). *Occasional Paper No. 8: Inquiry into long-term strategies to address the ageing of the Australian population over the next 40 years*.

Retrieved February 12, 2008, from http://facs.gov.au/research/op08/contents.htm

Department of Health and Ageing (DoHA). (2001). *National strategy for an ageing Australia.* Canberra: Australian Government.

Department of Health and Ageing (DoHA). (2003). *Framework for an Australian ageing research agenda.* Canberra: Australian Institute of Health and Welfare.

Department of Health and Ageing (DoHA). (2006). *Aged care in Australia.* Canberra: Australian Government.

Healy, J. (2004). *The benefits of an ageing population. Discussion Paper No 63: The Australia Institute.* Retrieved February 15, 2008, from http://www.tai.org.au/documents/dp_fulltext/DP63.pdf

Jones, A., de Jonge, D., & Phillips, R. (2008). *The impact of home maintenance and modification services on health, community care and housing outcomes in later life: Positioning paper No. 103.* Canberra: Australian Housing and Urban Research Institute.

Lee, C., Dobson, A., Brown, W., Bryson, L., Byles, J, Warner-Smith, P., et al. (2005). Cohort profile: The Australian Longitudinal Study on Women's Health. *International Journal of Epidemiology, 34,* 987–991.

National Centre for Vocational Education Research. (2004). *Submission to Senate Community Affairs References Committee Inquiry into Aged Care.* Retrieved February 18, 2008, from http://www.aph.gov.au/senate/committee/clac_ctte/completed_inquiries/2004-07/aged_care04/submissions/sub44.pdf

Nay, A., & Pearson, R. (2001). *Australian aged care nursing: A critical review of education, training, recruitment and retention in residential and community setting.* Retrieved February 10, 2008, from http://www.dest.gov.au/archive/HIGHERED/nursing/pubs/aust_aged_care/3.htm

Norman, P. E., Flicker, L., Almeida, O. P., Hankey, G. J., Hyde, Z., & Jamrozik, K. (2008). Cohort profile: The Health in Men Study (HIMS). *International Journal of Epidemiology.* (In press.)

Productivity Commission. (2005). *Economic implications of an ageing Australia.* Canberra: Productivity Commission. Retrieved February 10, 2008, from www.pc.gov.au/study/ageing/docs/finalreport

Research Network in Ageing Well (RNAW). (n.d.). Retrieved April 22, 2008, from http://www.ageingwell.edu.au/

Russell, C., Mahony, M. J., Hughes, I., & Kendig, H. (2007). Postgraduate education in gerontology in the Asia-Oceania region. *Gerontology & Geriatrics Education, 27,* 99–111.

Weston, R., Qu, L., & Soriano, G. (2003). Australia's ageing yet diverse population. *Family Matters, 65,* 6–13.

8

▪▪■▪▪

Austria

Kathrin Komp

Austria sometimes prides itself on being the cradle of modern geriatrics. In 1909, I. L. Nascher, a physician of Austrian origin living in New York, wrote an article on a Viennese nursing home for older persons, in which he coined the term *geriatrics* and argued that geriatrics should constitute an autonomous specialty (Amann, Doberauer, Doberauer, Hoerl, & Majce, 1980). Whether Austria remains the front-runner of 21st century geriatrics is for each reader to determine. But independent of its position in an international comparison, Austria is noteworthy because of the latest developments it has seen in the field of aging. Those developments will be described in the following pages.

THE RECENT HISTORY OF AGING

Austria entered the 21st century with a comparatively old population, which is still aging. In 2000, every fifth Austrian was aged 60 or older. In 2020, every fourth Austrian will be in this age group, and in 2040, it will already be every third Austrian. Likewise, the share of persons aged 75 and older will double from about 7% in 2000 to about 15% in 2040 (Statistik Austria, 2005, 2007). This trend of population aging is expected to slow down from 2030 on, when the smaller birth cohorts of the 1970s reach the age of 60. A development that lasted for about 120 years will come to an end then, heralding a new era characterized by a comparatively balanced age structure and a declining population (Kytir & Münz, 2000).

Besides demographics, the social structures among older persons have also been changing recently. The most prominent of those changes relate to social structures created by gender, ethnicity, and geographical location. Perhaps most notably, there has been a defeminization of old age. In the last 150 years, there have been more older women than older men, and this will probably not change in the decades to come. The exact proportion of women among persons aged 60 and older, however, has been changing markedly. It reached an all-time high in 1985, when there were about twice as many women as men in this age group. Since then, it has been decreasing again. One explanation is that lately, persons from the cohorts dominated by war widows have been dying (Kytir & Münz, 2000).

Apart from defeminization, an ethnicization of old age has also recently occurred. During the 1950s and 1960s and beyond, Austria recruited additional labor, especially from southern Europe. The aim was to create a group of labor migrants who would spend their productive working years in Austria and then return to their home countries upon retirement (Brockmann & Fisher, 2001). Due to various reasons, among them economic factors and the existence of social networks, many labor migrants have decided to remain in Austria even after retiring (Fernandez de la Hoz & Pflegerl, 2000). Moreover, there has been an inflow of refugees to Austria, particularly from Central and Eastern Europe. Both developments have led to an increasing ethnic diversity among older Austrians. In 2008, only 3% of the inhabitants of Austria aged 65 and older did not have Austrian citizenship (Statistik Austria, 2008). This share is expected to increase considerably within the next decades. Because most labor migrants are men, the ethnicization of older age is also assumed to further enhance the defeminization of old age.

Finally, the geographical distribution of older persons in Austria has been changing slowly for some time now. This is mainly due to internal and international migration. In the 1960s, Vienna, the capital of Austria, was the oldest demographic region within Austria. Since then, the aging and eventual death of larger cohorts, as well as international migration, rejuvenated Vienna. In 2005, the population of western Austria had a comparatively low proportion of older persons (around 20%), southeast Austria a comparatively high proportion (around 23%), and Vienna an intermediate proportion (22%) (Kytir & Münz, 2000; Statistik Austria, 2005). Such an uneven age distribution within a country has an impact on older persons' social integration and on the organization of social services provided to them.

RECENT RESEARCH ON AGING

With the aging and changing composition of the older population, Austrian research on aging has increased in volume, scope, and multidisciplinarity. Generally speaking, this research on aging can be separated into two kinds: scientific and social scientific. I will present both kinds of research in succession.

The Austrian scientific research on aging is carried out by scholars from a range of disciplines, such as medical science, veterinary medicine, and microbiology. Their research is often not explicitly labeled as gerontological research, which makes it harder to identify. The Austrian Society for Geriatrics and Gerontology increased the visibility of scientific research on aging by presenting the Walter Doberauer Scholarship for Gerontological Research and the Viennese Award for Humanistic Research in Aging (Böhmer, 2005). The 2008 holder of the Walter Doberauer Scholarship, Associate Professor Dr. Johannes Attems of the Otto-Wagner-Spital in Vienna, studies secretagogin, a protein related to Alzheimer's disease (Lindengrün, 2008). Recent recipients of the Award for Humanistic Research were Professor Ilse Kryspin-Exner from the Institute of Psychology at the University of Vienna, who was honored in 2004 for her work on cognition in old age, and Professor Georg Wick from the Institute of Pathophysiology at the University of Innsbruck, who was honored in 2006 for his work on immunology in old age ("Univ-Prof Dr. Ilse Kryspin-Exner," 2005; "Vom programmierten," 2007). A few years before he received the Award for Humanistic Research in Aging, Professor Wick took stock and pointed out the following universities and institutes as leading institutions in experimental gerontology research in Austria: the Medical Schools of the Universities of Vienna, Graz, and Innsbruck; the School of Veterinary Medicine in Vienna; the Institute for Applied Microbiology of the Vienna University for Agricultural Sciences; the Faculty of Natural Sciences of the University of Salzburg; the Ludwig-Boltzmann-Institute for Aging Research in Vienna; and the Institute for Biomedical Aging Research of the Austrian Academy of Sciences in Innsbruck (Wick, 2000).

Austrian social scientific research on aging is as diverse as its scientific counterpart and similarly well documented. The merit for this lies largely with the Seniorenbericht 2000, a concise report on the social situation of older persons in Austria (Bundesministerium für soziale Sicherheit, Generationen und Konsumentenschutz, 2000). The report, published by the former Federal Ministry for Social Security, Generations and Consumer Protection, covers topics ranging from housing and financial issues to volunteering and leisure in old age. It even contains a chapter on the situation of social gerontology in Austria (Amann, 2000). One conclusion of this chapter is that social scientific research on aging often has direct practical relevance. Today, eight years after the report was published, this conclusion still holds true: common research topics in recent years have been the organization of care for older persons, the state of social insurance, the retirement transition, and education in later life.

The organization of formal and informal care of older persons is usually analyzed separately. The Institute of Sociology at the University of Vienna, for example, analyzes the situation of informal caregivers (e.g., Berger, 2005; Horak, 2003), whereas the Institute for Social Policy at the Vienna University of Economics and Business Administration focuses on the costs of care (e.g., Schneider, 2006; Trukeschitz & Buchinger, 2007). Some studies, however, also point to the interrelation of both forms of care (Brockmann & Fisher, 2001; Grilz-Wolf, Strümpel, Leichsenring, & Komp, 2004). In research on the situation of social insurances, the long-term care insurance and pension schemes receive special attention. This is, on the one hand, because they are pay-as-you-go financed, which means that the current workers' contributions cover the benefits currently distributed. It is also because early retirement is more common in Austria than in most other European countries, which decreases the amount of contributions to those insurances. Studies on this topic are often designed as European comparisons (e.g., Da Roit, Le Bihan, & Österle, 2007; Fischer & Schneider, 2007; Zaidi, 2006a).

Investigations into the retirement transition and into learning in later life, finally, are motivated by two facts. First, most concepts of welfare state reforms include increasing the effective retirement age, which necessitates maintaining the employability of older workers; for example, through continued education (Organisation for Economic Co-operation and Development [OECD], 2005). Second, the number of years that persons spend in good health after they retire constantly increases (Kytir & Münz, 2000). This gives old age a new facet: a time for leisure and the possibility for productivity (Amann & Ehgartner, 2007). Learning is one way to embrace this new facet of old age (Kolland, 2005; Simon, 2007). Besides the research topics already named, there has also been a variety of other social scientific research on old age in previous years. It covered topics such as cultures of aging (e.g., Kolland & Kahri, 2004), poverty (e.g., Zaidi, 2006b), and palliative care (e.g., Heimerl, Heller, & Kittelberger, 2005). Until recently, the Ludwig Boltzmann Institute for Social Gerontology and Life-span Research also contributed a significant number of studies to the Austrian body of literature, but unfortunately this institute was closed down in 2005 (Ludwig Boltzmann Gesellschaft, 2008). One of its last studies was on whether demographic change caused a generational conflict in Austria—a hypothesis that could not be confirmed in that study (Majce & Rosenmayr, 2005).

THE CURRENT STATE OF EDUCATION IN GERONTOLOGY

Currently, there is no complete study program in gerontology at Austrian universities. There are, however, several courses and postgraduate programs in gerontology, mainly at non-university institutes. Most of the programs are interdisciplinary and with emphasis on applicability (Kolland, 2007). The postgraduate programs in gerontology currently offered are in geriatrics, in interdisciplinary gerontology, and in *geragogy* (educational gerontology).

The Austrian Medical Association offers a diploma program in geriatrics. The program was set up in cooperation between the Austrian Medical Association, the Austrian Society for Geriatrics and Gerontology, and the Ludwig Boltzmann Institute for Research of the Elderly. Its aim is to provide both physicians in general medicine and specialists of all fields with geriatric and gerontological knowledge at a postgraduate level. The knowledge is imparted in eight two-day seminars within a time span of two years. These seminars cover diverse topics, such as the etiology and pathophysiology of illnesses of elderly people, nutrition, occupational therapy, and basics in social welfare (Österreichische Gesellschaft für Geriatrie und Gerontologie, 2008). Holding a diploma in geriatrics in addition to the Austrian Medical Association's diploma in palliative care is a precondition for participating in the master's program in geriatrics at the Danube-University Krems. The master's program is designed as an in-service training, lasting two years (Donau-Universität Krems, 2008).

The second program in gerontology is the course on interdisciplinary gerontology offered by the University of Graz. It was established in 1999 as continuing education for professionals who already work with older persons (Kolland, 2007). Within two years, the participants in this course learn about four topics: demographic development and social contexts; the human as an individual in the process of aging; stimulation, companionship, and caregiving in aging and old age; and social changes for generational solidarity and for human aging (Institut für Erziehungs-und Bildungswissenschaft der Universität Graz, 2008). An evaluation of the first cohort of students (1999–2001) showed that generally they were satisfied with the course, reported acquiring relevant information and skills, and expected to progress in their career thanks to the course. The heterogeneity of students, however, was not necessarily seen positively, because it made finding common ground in class more difficult. This point of criticism will most likely apply to the other study programs in gerontology as well (Kolland, 2007).

The third program in gerontology is the master's program in geragogy in Vienna. Geragogy is sometimes also called educational gerontology. It focuses on the education of older persons, education on aging, and education of professionals and volunteers in the field of aging. A master's program in geragogy is offered at the Church University College of Teacher Education in Vienna, in cooperation with two welfare associations (the Caritas Vienna and the Diakonie Austria), the Forum of Catholic Adult Education, and an institute for long-term care (Haus der Barmherigkeit). Its target group is postgraduates in an area related to pedagogies or geriatrics. After passing an entrance exam, students attend classes for three years. This program began only in the fall of 2007, which makes it the youngest of the three study programs presented (Gründungsstudienkommission der Kirchlichen Pädagogischen Hochschule in Wien, 2007; Kolland, 2007).

Beside the postgraduate programs described above, also available to interested Austrians are a Ph.D. program in medical gerontology and an international master's program in gerontology. The program in medical gerontology is organized by the Institute for Biomedical Aging Research in Innsbruck and Innsbruck Medical University. It focuses on the aging of biological communication systems, in particular on the mechanisms of cellular and systemic aging and the development of age-related diseases (Köllersperger, 2008). The international master's program mentioned is EuMaG, the European Master's Program in Gerontology. For two years, EuMaG participants attend a number of courses on psycho-, social- and health gerontology, which are held in different European countries (European Masters in Gerontology, 2008). In 2002, the Austrian Society for Geriatrics and Gerontology joined the EuMaG program, which made the degree available to Austrian participants and therewith broadened the Austrian landscape of education in gerontology (G. Pinter, personal email regarding the Austrian EuMaG membership, June 12, 2008).

CURRENT PUBLIC POLICY ISSUES IN AGING

The aging of society and the increasing life expectancy of individuals are topics present in most current political debates in Austria. The reason is that the demographic change creates internal as well as external pressure for change on the Austrian welfare state—internal pressure, because the demographic change challenges existing structures in social insurances and in health and social care services; external pressure, because international organizations such as the United Nations and the European Union attempt to support their member states in their efforts to deal with the demographic change. As a result, existing policies needed to take into account the demographic change, and policies explicitly targeting old age were developed. The current state of both kinds of policies will be described consecutively.

Of the existing policies that needed to incorporate the demographic change into their considerations, retirement regulations received the most attention. This is firstly because retirement regulations affect how long persons pay contributions to and receive benefits from social insurances. Secondly, even without the demographic changes, the retirement regulations in Austria were in need of reform. Until 2000, early retirement due to reduced work capacity had been possible from the age of 55 years on, and disability schemes remain easily accessible for persons over 57 years of age (OECD, 2005). This led Austria to have one of the lowest employment rates of persons aged 50–65 years in Western Europe in 2005 (Zaidi & Fuchs, 2006). Consequently, pension reforms were implemented in 2000, 2003, and 2004/05, aimed at raising the effective retirement age and increasing the link between individual contributions and benefit payments. However, the OECD (2005) remarked that those reforms might still not go far enough to completely counter the challenges brought about by the demographic change.

Policies explicitly targeting old age in Austria are usually developed by the Federal Ministry of Social Affairs and Consumer Protection. In its self-description, the ministry stresses the cross-sectional quality of policies for old age and the new character of old age as a time of health, financial independence, and active engagement with society. Moreover, it names four priorities in its policies for old age: the participation of older persons, older workers, lifelong learning, and active aging. The participation of older persons in society, politics, economy and culture is intended to be promoted through legislative measures, the federal senior citizens advisory committee, social planning for senior citizens, and the support of innovative projects. Increasing the share of older workers is a goal set in the Lisbon Strategy, an action plan developed by the European Union. To reach this goal, awareness raising and public-oriented measures are taken, such as giving awards to companies that support older workers. The promotion of lifelong learning is closely connected to this goal and mainly pursued through project grants (Bundesministerium für Soziales und Konsumentenschutz, 2008). In addition, a number of studies on learning in old age have been commissioned by the ministry (e.g., Kolland, Ahmadi, Benda-Kahri, Kranzl, & Neururer, 2007; Simon, 2007). Active aging, finally, is understood as a combination of good health, social integration, and a high level of well-being in old age. It is enhanced, *inter alia*, through measures on anti-discrimination and equal opportunities, quality certificates for nursing homes, and support of volunteers (Bundesministerium für Soziales und Konsumentenschutz, 2008).

Though current public policies on aging cover a wide range of topics, research reports still point out some blind spots. They mainly concern the situation of older women and of migrants. In their review of political papers on productivity and resources in old age, Amann and Ehgartner (2007) found that such papers approach unemployment in old age only from a male perspective. The situation of older working or unemployed women usually was not addressed. Strümpel (2007) confirmed this finding, reporting that the situation of older women in general was not usually explicitly dealt with in old-age policies. She saw this as the result of a general gender-blindness in Austrian policies for old age. It can be assumed that the ethnicization of old age changes the demands on social and health care services for older persons. Brockmann and Fisher (2001), however, argued that the change in demands might not be countered by an actual change in the services, as working migrants are still largely expected to return to their home country upon retirement, which gives them no voice in political discussions on old age. In addition, a new kind of work migrant is coming to Austria: women from Central and Eastern Europe, who provide care to older persons on the black and grey market (Lenhart, 2007; Lenhart & Österle, 2007). While those women's work migration might help to buffer the increasing need for affordable care to older Austrians, the migrants run the risk of finding themselves in a precarious social situation in their later years.

CONCLUSION

Aging and old age are important topics in Austria at the beginning of the 21st century. Society, culture, economy, and the welfare state are affected by the demographic change and striving to find ways of dealing with it. Unfortunately, not all these efforts have been given the label *gerontology*, which is partly due to the fact that gerontology is not yet fully developed as a scientific discipline in Austria. The blossoming of study programs in gerontology within the last years, however, gives cause for optimism.

REFERENCES

Amann, A. (2000). Altersforschung in Österreich [Research into aging in Austria]. In Bundesministerium für soziale Sicherheit, Generationen und Konsumentenschutz (Ed.), *Seniorenbericht 2000: Zur Lebenssituation älterer Menschen in Österreich* [Report on senior citizens 2000: On the life situation of older persons in Austria] (pp. 504–531). Vienna: Bundesministerium für soziale Sicherheit, Generationen und Konsumentenschutz.

Amann, A., Doberauer, B., Doberauer, W., Hoerl, J., & Majce, G. (1980). Austria. In E. Palmore (Ed.), *International handbook on aging: Contemporary developments and research* (pp. 3–38). Westport, CT: Greenwood Press.

Amann, A., & Ehgartner, G. (2007). *Projekt Produktivität und Ressourcen des Alter(n)s in Österreich. Eine Pilotstudie. Endbericht* [Project productivity and resources for old age in Austria. A pilot study. Final report]. St. Pölten: Zentrum für Alternswissenschaften, Gesundheits- & Sozialpolitikforschung.

Berger, M. (2005). *"Der Sturm vor der letzten Ruhe"—Entwicklung im Leben der BegleiterInnen unterstützungsbedürftiger alter Menschen* ["The storm before the last calm"—Development in the life of persons accompanying older persons in need of care]. Unpublished master's thesis, Institute of Sociology, University of Vienna.

Böhmer, F. (2005). 50 Jahre ÖGGG: Eine Gesellschaft im Wandel [50 years ÖGGG: An association in the process of change]. *Geriatrie Praxis, 02.* Retrieved July 6, 2008, from http://www.medical-tribune.at/dynasite.cfm?dssid=4171&dsmid=63430&dspaid=481527

Brockmann, M., & Fisher, M. (2001). Older migrants and social care in Austria. *Journal of European Social Policy, 11,* 353–362.

Bundesministerium für soziale Sicherheit, Generationen und Konsumentenschutz (Ed.). (2000). *Seniorenbericht 2000: Bericht zur Lebenssituation älterer Menschen in Österreich* [Report on senior citizens 2000: On the life situation of older persons in Austria]. Vienna: Bundesministerium für soziale Sicherheit, Generationen und Konsumentenschutz.

Bundesministerium für Soziales und Konsumentenschutz. (2008). *Themenbereich Senior/innen* [Subject area senior citizens]. Retrieved July 11, 2008, from http://www.bmsk.gv.at

Da Roit, B., Le Bihan, B., & Österle, A. (2007). Long-term care policies in Italy, Austria and France: Variations in cash-for-care schemes. *Social Policy and Administration, 41,* 653–671.

Donau-Universität Krems. (2008). *Geriatrie: Master of Science.* Retrieved July 11, 2008, from http://www.donau-uni.ac.at/de/studium/geriatrie/index.php

European Master's in Gerontology (EuMaG). (2008). *EuMaG programme.* Retrieved July 12, 2008, from http://www.eumag.org/component/option,com_frontpage/Itemid,74

Fernandez de la Hoz, P., & Pflegerl, J. (2000). Ältere MigrantInnen in Österreich [Older migrants in Austria]. In Bundesministerium für soziale Sicherheit, Generationen und Konsumentenschutz (Ed.), *Seniorenbericht 2000: Zur*

Lebenssituation älterer Menschen in Österreich [Report on senior citizens 2000: On the life situation of older persons in Austria] (pp. 454–471). Vienna: Bundesministerium für soziale Sicherheit, Generationen und Konsumentenschutz.

Fischer, T., & Schneider, U. (2007). Die Finanzierung der solidarischen Pflege-versicherung in Deutschland und in Österreich. Ein Vergleich unter Fair-nessaspekten [The financing of solidaristic long-term care insurance in Germany and in Austria. A comparison with regard to aspects of fairness]. *Soziale Sicherheit, 60,* 526–535.

Grilz-Wolf, M., Strümpel, C., Leichsenring, K., & Komp, K. (2004). Providing integrated health and social care for older persons in Austria. In K. Leich-senring and A. M. Alaszewski, (Eds.), *Providing integrated health and social care for older persons—A European overview of issues at stake* (pp. 97–137). Aldershot: Ashgate Publishing.

Gründungsstudienkommission der Kirchlichen Pädagogischen Hochschule in Wien. (2007). *Curriculum des Studienganges Geragogik. STUKO GZ 3/2007* [Curriculum of the degree programme in geragogics. STUKO GZ 3/2007]. Vienna: Kirchliche Pädagogische Hochschule.

Heimerl, K., Heller, A., & Kittelberger, F. (2005). *Daheim sterben. Palliative Kultur im Pflegeheim* [Dying at home. Palliative culture in nursing homes]. Freiburg im Breisgau, Germany: Lambertus Verlag.

Horak, K. (2003). *Hilfe und Pflege durch Angehörige in der Altenbetreuung unter besonderer Berücksichtigung der Rolle der Frau* [Help and care provided by relatives in the context of care for older persons with special consideration of the role of women]. Unpublished master's thesis, Institute of Sociology, University of Vienna.

Institut für Erziehungs- und Bildungswissenschaft der Universität Graz. (2008). *ULIG—Interdisziplinäre Gerontologie* [ULIG—Interdisciplinary gerontology]. Retrieved May 30, 2008, from http://www-gewi.uni-graz.ac.at/ulig

Kolland, F. (2005). *Bildungschancen für ältere Menschen. Ansprüche an ein gelungenes Leben* [Chances for education in later life. Demands on a successful life]. Münster, Germany, & Vienna, Austria: Lit Verlag.

Kolland, F. (2007). Gerontologie- und Geriatrieausbildung in Österreich [Education in gerontology and geriatrics in Austria]. *Zeitschrift für Gerontologie und Geriatrie, 40,* 433–437.

Kolland, F., Ahmadi, P., Benda-Kahri, S., Kranzl, V., & Neururer, M. (2007). *Lern-bedürfnisse und Lernarrangements von älteren Menschen. Endbericht* [The need and arrangements for learning in later life. Final report]. Vienna: Büro für Sozialtechnologie und Evaluationsforschung.

Kolland, F., & Kahri, S. (2004). Kultur und Kreativität im späteren Leben: Zur Pluralisierung der Alterskulturen [Culture and creativity in later life: On the pluralization of cultures of ageing]. In G. Backes, W. Clemens, & H. Künemund (Eds.), *Lebensformen und Lebensführung im Alter* [Life forms and lifestyles in later life] (pp. 151–172). Wiesbaden, Germany: Verlag für Sozialwissenschaften.

Köllersperger, M. (2008). *The aging of biological communication systems*. Retrieved July 12, 2008, from http://www.i-med.ac.at/phd/aging

Kytir, J., & Münz, R. (2000). Demographische Rahmenbedingungen: die alternde Gesellschaft und das älter werdende Individuum [The demographic framework: The aging society and the aging individual]. In Bundesministerium für soziale Sicherheit, Generationen und Konsumentenschutz (Ed.), *Seniorenbericht 2000: Zur Lebenssituation älterer Menschen in Österreich* [Report on senior citizens 2000: On the life situation of older persons in Austria] (pp. 22–51). Vienna: Bundesministerium für soziale Sicherheit, Generationen und Konsumentenschutz.

Lenhart, M. B. (2007). Die Migration von (weiblichen) Pflegekräften [The migration of (female) care workers]. *Kurswechsel, 2*, 28–35.

Lenhart, M. B., & Österle, A. (2007). Migration von Pflegekräften: Österreichische und Europäische Trends und Perspektiven [The migration of care workers: Austrian and European trends and perspectives]. *Österreichische Pflegezeitschrift, 12*, 8–11.

Lindengrün, C. (2008). Walter-Doberauer-Preis für Alternsforschung: "Verhungern ist nicht würdevoll" [Walter-Doberauer-Award for research into aging. "Starving is not dignified"]. *Geriatrie-Praxis, 02*. Retrieved July 6, 2008, from http://www.geriatrie-online.at/dynasite.cfm?dssid=4285&dsmid=92210&dspaid=700827

Ludwig Boltzmann Gesellschaft. (2008). *Institut für Sozialgerontologie und Lebenslaufforschung* [Institute for social gerontology and life-course research]. Retrieved July 3, 2008, from http://www1.lbg.ac.at/gesellschaft/institute_info.php?a_id=88

Majce, G., & Rosenmayr, L. (2005). *Generationensolidarität in Österreich 2005. Empirisch-soziologische Untersuchung der Alternsforschung in Österreich* [Generational solidarity in Austria 2005: An empirical-sociological study on the research in aging in Austria]. Vienna: Ludwig Boltzmann Institut für Sozialgerontologie und Lebenslaufforschung.

Organisation for Economic Co-operation and Development (OECD). (2005). *Ageing and employment policies: Austria*. Paris: Organisation for Economic Co-operation and Development.

Österreichische Gesellschaft für Geriatrie und Gerontologie. (2008). *ÖAK Diploma— Geriatrics*. Retrieved May 30, 2008, from http://www.geriatrie-online.at/dynasite.cfm?dssid=4285&dsmid=62661&dspaid=476193

Schneider, U. (2006). Informelle Pflege aus ökonomischer Sicht [Informal care from an economic perspective]. *Zeitschrift für Sozialreform, 52*, 493–520.

Simon, G. (2007). *Lernen und Bildung im Interesse älterer Menschen. Untersuchung der wichtigsten Konzepte zum lebenslangen Lernen im 3. und 4. Lebensalter. Projekt im Auftrag des Bundesministeriums für Soziales und Konsumentenschutz. Endbericht* [Learning and education in the interest of older persons. Study on the most important concepts of lifelong learning in the third and fourth life-phase. Project commissioned by the Federal Ministry for Social Issues and Consumer

Protection. Final report]. Vienna: Bundesministerium für Soziales und Konsumentenschutz.

Statistik Austria. (2005). *Demographisches Jahrbuch 2004* [Demographic yearbook 2004]. Vienna: Statistik Austria.

Statistik Austria. (2007). *Bevölkerungsvorausschätzung 2007–2050 für Österreich (Mittlere Variante)* [Population projection 2007–2050 for Austria (intermediate model)]. Vienna: Statistik Austria.

Statistik Austria. (2008). *Bevölkerung am 1.1.2008 nach zusammengefasster Staatsangehörigkeit, Geschlecht und Altersgruppen* [Population on January 1, 2008, by cumulated nationality, gender and age groups]. Retrieved July 6, 2008, from http://www.statistik.at/web_de/static/bevoelkerung_am_1.1.2008_nach_zusammengefasster_staatsangehoerigkeit_gesch_031407.pdf

Strümpel, C. (2007). *Gender Mainstreaming in der Österreichischen Politik für Seniorinnen und Senioren. Expertise erstellt im Auftrag des Bundesministeriums für Soziales und Konsumentenschutz* [Gender mainstreaming in Austrian politics for senior citizens. Expertise commissioned by the Federal Ministry for Senior Citizens and Consumer Protection]. Vienna: Bundesministeriums für Soziales und Konsumentenschutz.

Trukeschitz, B., & Buchinger, C. (2007). Finanzierung mobiler Dienstleistungen der Altenpflege und –betreuung [The financing of mobile support services for older persons]. *Kontraste, 8*, 13–18.

Univ-Prof. Dr. Ilse Kryspin-Exner: Ehrung für Gerontolopsychologin [Univ-Prof. Dr. Ilse Kryspin-Exner: Distinction for gerontopsychologist]. (2005). *Clinicum, 03*. Retrieved July 6, 2008, from http://www.medical-tribune.at/dynasite.cfm?dssid=4171&dsmid=62972&dspaid=476601

Vom programmierten Zelltod zur Pensionsreform [From programmed cell death to pension reform]. (2007, February 13). News release from the Medical University Innsbruck. Retrieved July 6, 2008, from http://www.i-med.ac.at/mypoint/news/2007021301.xml

Wick, G. (2000). Summary: Experimental gerontology in Austria. *Experimental Gerontology, 35*, 513–519.

Zaidi, A. (2006a). *Pension policy in EU25 and its possible impact on elderly poverty. Policy brief*. Vienna: European Centre for Social Welfare Policy and Research.

Zaidi, A. (2006b). *Poverty of elderly people in EU25. Policy brief*. Vienna: European Centre for Social Welfare Policy and Research.

Zaidi, A., & Fuchs, M. (2006). *Transition from work to retirement in EU25. Policy brief*. Vienna: European Centre for Social Welfare Policy and Research.

9

..■..

Botswana

Akpovire Oduaran and Keneilwe Molosi

Aging has come under very close scrutiny and investigations by scholars and practitioners, whose business it is to ensure populations are healthy in the later years of life. As a nation, Botswana has been making efforts to ensure that policies are in place to ensure that our people enjoy their later years fully, as they make valuable contributions to national growth in every area. In this chapter, we address some of the socioeconomic, cultural, and political factors that influence aging in Botswana. The chapter begins by addressing the context of the discussion, moves through an exploration of recent history, aging population, and health systems, and pays attention to current public policy issues and research on aging in Botswana. It concludes by making some proposals that might help in giving stronger direction to aging and development in our nation.

THE CONTEXT

Geopolitical Data

Botswana is geographically located in the southern subregion of Africa, a continent acclaimed to be the world's second largest and second most populous continent, but which has acquired a reputation, unfortunately, as the poorest economically. Botswana occupies a land area of approximately 566,730 square kilometers, nestled among South Africa, Namibia, Zimbabwe, and Zambia. Botswana's total population in 2003 stood at

1.7 million people. The country is democratically ruled, and it is well known for its exemplary democratic governance since its independence in 1966. Botswana features a growing economy and a stable political environment. It has some of Africa's last great wildernesses, including the famous Okavango Swamps and the Kalahari Desert. Botswana is the largest exporter of gemstone diamonds in the world, as well as a large beef exporter to the European Union (Botswana Review, 2008; Republic of Botswana, 2004). When compared with many other sub-Saharan African nations, Botswana could be described as an epitome of stability and rapid socioeconomic transformation, guided by meticulously implemented, monitored, and regularly evaluated national development plans and policies.

At the time of its political independence from Britain in 1966, Botswana was classified as one of the poorest nations in the world. Indeed, it was observed that there was a lack of infrastructure, which manifested itself in low income, poor standards of living, and high incidence of poverty (Bank of Botswana, 2006). In 2008, it could be said that the tide of inadequate infrastructure was gradually being reversed for good, and the nation could be ranked among the few African countries that can be counted among the middle-income countries of the world.

Today, with a stable political environment, Botswana is frequently cited by international agencies as good in policy-making and service delivery, including health policies. For example, the 2003 Report of the United Nations Commission for Africa ranked Botswana number one in Africa for its expanded policy support index, macro policies, poverty-reduction policies, and institution building. Botswana is not counted among the indebted nations of Africa. The 2003 Report also ranked Botswana as high in terms of ongoing government commitment to sustainable macroeconomic, financial, and social policies (Botswana Review, 2008; Republic of Botswana, 2004). The same cannot be said of many other African nations.

Botswana's population comprises many ethnic groups, with a majority being those who speak Setswana (the national language), but there are a number of minority groups, like the Bakalanga in the Northeast, Basarwa (San) in the western and northern parts, Babirwa and Batswapong in the northern part, and the Ovaherero, originally from Namibia, who live in different parts of Botswana, especially the western part. Botswana also has other African ethnic groups and people of Asian and European origins. All these communities have enjoyed equal rights and privileges under the constitution of Botswana (Ministry of Finance and Development Planning, 2003).

It is estimated that 53% of the population live in urban areas. The urban areas consist of towns and big or urban villages, and these are occupied by more than 5,000 people, who do not depend solely on agriculture for livelihood. In contrast, about 47% of the population lives in the rural areas. The rural dwellers depend mainly on agriculture for their living. Botswana's demographics are interesting in many ways. It is estimated that Botswanans aged 0–14 comprise 38%, and those aged 15–59 make up 57%. Those who are 60+ constitute 5% of the entire population, and this is the main group that this chapter is highlighting for discussion. The demographics seem to suggest that the majority of the population is still very young. That is probably the reason that education is considered to be a very important public service. It is made available to all school-going children who are within a reasonable distance to schools, and it is free but not compulsory. As of 2005, Botswana's literacy rate was 81%, with 76% for males and 82% for females.

The Botswana Review (2008) hints that the nation is committed to pursuing vigorously the UN's guiding principles for Millennium Development Goals (MDGs), which include making efforts to eradicate poverty and hunger, achieve universal access to primary education, promote gender equality, reduce child mortality, improve maternal health, and combat HIV and AIDS. In addition to education, the nation pays serious attention to the health of its people, and this has implications for longevity.

As noted above, Botswana enjoys a stable democracy. Politically, it has steadfastly pursued a multiparty approach, resulting in nine consecutive elections since Independence.

The Government of the Republic of Botswana has been engaged in a number of economic reforms that have been very beneficial to its citizens and others who reside in the nation. Economists are quick to draw attention to the fact that some of the critical indicators of economic success should include, among others, the lowering of poverty, unemployment, reducing income disparities in the nation, and an extended life span.

Economic Situation

We have noted above that Botswana is perhaps the largest exporter of gemstone diamonds in the world. It is also a large exporter of beef to the European Union. It has risen from the unenviable posture of being counted among the 10 poorest countries in the world at the time of independence in September 1966, to among the middle income human development index. Whereas in 1966, Botswana's per capita annual income (at current prices) stood at about P3,000 (US$361) (Pula, the national currency = US$0.12), the situation has seen a positive reversal over the years. In 2005/06, the annual per capita income was about P33,000 (US$3,976). The official records also show that between 1965/66 and 2005/06, Botswana's real gross domestic product (GDP) growth averaged 9%. Whereas the government's total expenditure was about P10 million (US$1.2 million) in 1965/66, this had grown to P22.4 billion (US$2.7 billion) by 2006/07. At the same time, financing of the government budget from foreign grants has since declined from 51% to less than 2% over the same period (Republic of Botswana, 2007b), and these developments surely have implications for this discourse, as we shall soon demonstrate.

It should be noted at the same time that while the economy has made remarkable improvements in the last four decades, Botswana is faced with the challenge of how to sustain its high economic growth in the light of so many other equally important issues that are competing for attention. For example, Botswana has been examining how it might best diversify its economy beyond the diamond mining sector. To direct its search for sustained growth, the nation has been pursuing the objectives enunciated in its policy document titled "Vision 2016 and the United Nations MDGs." The nation remains committed to achieving the UN MDGs of eradicating extreme poverty and hunger; achieving universal primary education; and promoting gender equality and empowerment. It also committed to reducing child mortality; improving maternal health; combating HIV/AIDS, malaria and other diseases; ensuring environmental sustainability; and developing a global partnership by the year 2015.

These developments certainly have implications for aging. For example, rapid increases in GDP could mean paying more attention to public policies of, and programs for, the aged in our societies. That is almost a universal truth.

DEMOGRAPHICS

The first challenge facing any scholar who wishes to explore the largely unexplored area of scholarship in aging in Botswana is that of defining or classifying who is old. Some cultural expectations could help or even constrain such an effort. Globally, the standard policy development approach of defining older persons is to assign all those aged 60 or above to the status of "older person" (UN, 2008b, p. 3). In Africa, this approach is problematic because many Africans believe you are as old as you think you are. In that sense, for example, you can be politically, socially, and economically very active, engaged, and relevant in most African communities, even at 60 or beyond, and no one could confine you to playing essentially socially constructed and defined functions. No one is free to tag you as too elderly to be socially, economically, and politically engaged. In fact, we have observed in Nigeria that in some instances, there are politicians who are 60 years old and above who classify themselves as still young and contest for the position of youth leaders in the political parties to which they belong. In Botswana, however, public policy regards age 60 as the benchmark for describing anyone as an elderly citizen. Therefore, the demographics depicted in the next few paragraphs take the official and legal age of 60 as basic and recognizable.

Botswana can be counted among the few African countries to have undergone substantial demographic transition. Botswana's Population Reference Bureau (2001) has reported that between 1950 and 1990, the country's infant mortality rate was reduced from 130 per thousand to 53 per thousand live births, and that life expectancy reached 63 years for females and 59 years for males in 1990, and fertility declined from a total rate of 6.6 children per woman in 1971 to 4.9 children per woman in 1988. By 2001, Botswana had an estimated total fertility rate of 3.9 children per woman (Population Reference Bureau, 2001).

Data from the Economic Commission for Africa (2001) suggest that Botswana will experience a marked increase in the number of people who are 60 years old or above, which implies that policies and programs related to the aged would become a bit more visible and urgent. Unfortunately, the nation has been battling the scourge of HIV and AIDS, and this has been a major cause for concern for everyone in Botswana. It has been reported in several places that the recent upsurge of the prevalence of HIV/AIDS in the country is taking its toll on life expectancy. It was estimated that life expectancy in 2001 reached a low of 42 years for females and 45 years for males. The implication of this reversal in life expectancy for the population structure of the country is not clearly known. But since fertility (among all factors of population dynamics) has the most noticeable influence on a country's age structure, it can be surmised that if sustained fertility decline continues to prevail in Botswana, the country will experience a rapidly increasing proportion of its population who are elderly. This has serious socioeconomic implications for the welfare of the population, especially for the elderly, if the government does not institute appropriate measures to cater to their needs.

RECENT HISTORY OF AGING IN BOTSWANA

It is estimated that the total number of Botswanans 50 years and above is 177,000, comprising 10.5% of the country's total population. Among those, 54.2% are females and 45.8% are males (Central Statistics Office [CSO], 2001). It is now estimated that the aged will constitute over 250,000 of the country's total population by the year 2011 (World Health Organization [WHO], 2003). It is believed that despite the scourge of pandemic diseases like HIV and AIDS, tuberculosis, malaria, and others, the population 50 years and above will increase from the current 10.5% to 12.5% by 2011 (CSO, 2001). However, despite this projected increase in the elderly population, life expectancy continues to drop tremendously in Botswana. From a life expectancy of 63 years for men and 59 years for women, between 1950 and 1990, life expectancy has now dropped to 45 years and 42 years for men and women respectively (Population Reference Bureau, 2001).

The Botswana population is shifting from younger to older ages. This situation is known as an aging population (Economic Commission for Africa, 2001). It should be noted that social and economic challenges are likely to flow from an aging population (Sembajwe & Kalasa, 1999). For instance, there would be fewer productive people in the population, and this may well mean that sectors such as agriculture may suffer. Also, because of older people's dependency, government spending for social and health services to the elderly would increase, overstretching the government to some extent.

For Botswana, the aging population might also be a result of a decline in fertility, previously cited. This decrease in fertility may be attributed to the HIV/AIDS pandemic that is claiming the lives of most of the younger and fertile Botswana.

CURRENT PUBLIC POLICY ISSUES ABOUT AGING

The increasing number of elders in Botswana will have clear policy implications. The nation, for example, will have to pursue policies that would guarantee the continuous nourishing of the elderly, who in most African countries would constitute the bulk of the food-insecure segments of the population. For the Government of Botswana, this concern will be particularly stressful, because it would have to care for its elderly even as it tries to implement a range of policies geared toward meeting national targets in the provision of physical infrastructures, improved human development processes, committed financial management, transparency, diversification of the economy, and the implementation of incentives aimed at attracting investors, especially in the private sector. Even as the Government of the Republic of Botswana aims to ensure that it engages seriously in developing the infrastructures of the country, it has never lost sight of the need to strengthen social policies that recognize the needs of its elderly citizens. Here, it might suffice to attempt a brief historical illustration of the point made.

Since 1968, Botswana has had a pension scheme for the elderly. The scheme was improved in 1996 to include additional benefits such as a World War II pension benefit. This benefit is meant only for Botswanans who fought on the side of the British Empire troops during World War II. That means the elderly who did not fight in that war cannot have this benefit that could have enriched the pension that existed at that time.

By far the most important policy initiative on aging was enacted in 1996, when the government passed an Act of Parliament on Social Security. The Act was aimed at protecting elderly citizens by providing a universal pension program for all citizens 65 years old and above. The special pension scheme for public officers was a flat pension rate of P100 (US$12) per month. With the inflation being experienced everywhere, it hardly needs to be mentioned that the pension scheme is already invalid.

The Government of Botswana has several policies and services that can be viewed as its effort to help the elderly. The introduction and existence of improved health systems and other social amenities are efforts toward helping elders lead a healthy and improved life in their old age. For instance, the increase in the number of hospitals and social safety nets could go a long way in enhancing the prospects for productive aging in the nation. Another policy to note is the destitute policy. Elders who live in poverty can be included in the destitute program and be provided with a monthly food basket. Also, considering the retirement age of 65 years, one would hope that some elderly people will retire and continue to live a comfortable life, since they would have their retirement package.

Already, the government has begun systematic support for the elderly in Botswana, especially for public officers. In 2001, for example, the government published a document titled "Planning for the Future: Botswana Public Officers' Pension Fund." In that document, public officers are educated about their contributions to the fund, their employers' contributions, benefits on retirement, benefits on leaving service, benefits on death, benefits on ill health, planning ahead for retirement, and the rules of fund management. These issues are so well laid out that all public officials know exactly what to expect at the point of retirement.

The major concerns about aging at this point in time should be over how much attention the public sector of society should pay to the elderly in the light of other competing national issues. For one thing, the government cannot afford to neglect its elderly people, who have made valuable contribution to the development of the nation. That is why, perhaps, it is common nowadays to find a number of private-sector initiatives that appear to significantly complement public policies and programs for the elderly. For example, a number of insurance companies have begun marketing life insurance schemes and pension funds for workers who may want to save toward securing comfort for themselves when they are old. This is a positive step forward and one that would enhance the utility of the African extended family system, which encourages support for the elderly in our families, even if the younger ones are not immediate members of the family.

RESEARCH ON AGING IN BOTSWANA

Why research on aging? Properly articulated and relevant research on aging in Botswana could generate reliable data that should be valuable to policy formulation and programs. For example, research information on aging could reveal how the phenomenon affects production, consumption, savings, investments, labor economics, and socioeconomic transfers. It also could reveal how much of intergenerational programs the government would need to put in place to guarantee productive relationships between grandparents and their grandchildren, and this is a scenario that is often ignored.

Yet, aging in Africa (Ferreira, 2008, p. 71) and in Botswana is not a well-researched area. In fact, research on aging in Botswana is underdeveloped and probably has been hindered by inadequate capacity, capability, and infrastructure, since much of the research funding seems to be directed at more "serious" and urgent national concerns like the HIV and AIDS pandemic, unemployment, and citizen empowerment.

Even when some work is done, far too little has been documented. However, one study looked at the impact of modernization on the elderly's socioeconomic life and revealed that, due to modernization, there is a collapse of traditional sources of the elderly's economic and social support structures. As such, the government has to design more safety nets and other social programs from which the elderly may benefit.

THE FUTURE OF AGING AND POLICY ON AGING IN BOTSWANA

Even if this chapter has not been able to capture astutely all the major developments on aging and relevant policies in Botswana, due mainly to the underdeveloped nature of research on the matter, it is anticipated that major international actions should soon drive the nation toward meeting the set priorities for research and policies on aging. In this direction, we hope that the collective research agenda propelled by the international community should help us get to our destination. It might be useful for us to identify some of these actions.

- The research agenda on aging for the 21st century, revised in 2005. As it affects sub-Saharan Africa, to which Botswana belongs, it is important. Therefore, the United Nations and the International Association of Gerontology and Geriatrics should make Botswana a sample case when they begin to study chronic poverty, changing family structures and functions, access to health care, HIV and AIDS, income security, and urbanization.
- The Council for the Development of Social Science Research in Africa and the Oxford Institute on Aging in the United Kingdom should factor Botswana into their research agenda when the time comes for them to explore poverty among the aged, health, and family, among others.

Even as we look out for external involvement in the discourse on aging in Botswana, we are aware that we have to work toward meeting the requirements of several international resolutions, some of which we have subscribed to as a nation. Toward that goal, we note the importance of United Nations General Assembly Resolution 55/2 of September 2, 2000, which included a special commitment to support Africa's development needs. As well, the Madrid International Plan of Action on Aging, which has broad macroeconomic goals that seek to resolve issues of poverty reduction and the promotion of social development and human rights, is important to us. Botswana has subscribed already to the African Union Policy Framework and Plan of Action on Aging (African Union & HelpAge International [HAI], 2003). That means we would take the necessary steps to examine the social, cultural, and environmental realities shaping aging among our people, and we should be well on the way to having enviable policies and programs for the elderly in our nation.

CONCLUSION

This chapter has highlighted some of the major developments in aging in Botswana. In particular, we have attempted to examine briefly the contexts within which aging could be discussed in Botswana. We explored the demographic parameters and the trends on aging in Botswana from the point of view of projections and estimation. We made the point that Botswana will, in the years ahead, begin to witness increasing numbers of elderly people, despite the scourge of HIV and AIDS. We observed that the government may have put in place the right programs that may help the elderly. We explored the research and policy dynamics of aging in our contexts and came to the conclusion that we still have a lot more work to do in terms of implementing all the protocols and resolutions to which the nation might have been signatory. This is not a mean expectation, but with increasing government involvement, coupled with the support of the civil society and private sector, Botswana could well be in the league of African nations that have good plans for the elderly on the continent.

REFERENCES

African Union & HelpAge International. (2003). *African Union Policy Framework and Plan of Action on Ageing*. Nairobi, Kenya: HAI.

Bank of Botswana. (2006). *Bank of Botswana annual report*. Gaborone, Botswana: Bank of Botswana.

Botswana Review. (2007). *Botswana review of commerce and industry* (27th ed.). Gaborone, Botswana: B & T Directories.

Botswana Review. (2008). *Botswana review of commerce and industry* (28th ed.). Gaborone, Botswana: B & T Directories.

Central Statistics Office (CSO). (2001). *National population census*. Gaborone, Botswana: CSO.

Economic Commission for Africa. (2001). *Booklet on population, environment, development and agriculture (PEDA) model. PEDA Advocacy Booklet: Projections on aging for Botswana*. CA/FSS/01/5 November, 2001.

Ferreira, M. (2008). Ageing policies in Africa. In United Nations, Economic and Social Affairs (Ed.), *Regional dimensions of the ageing situation*. New York: United Nations.

Government of Botswana and United Nations Development Program. (2000). *Botswana human development report 2000*. Gaborone, Botswana: United Nations Development Program.

Ministry of Finance and Development Planning. (2003). *National Development Plan IX 2003/04–2008/09*. Gaborone, Botswana: Government Printer.

Population Reference Bureau. (2001). *World population data sheet*. Washington, DC: Author.

Republic of Botswana. (1997). *Vision 2016: Towards prosperity for all*. Gaborone, Botswana: Ministry of Finance and Development Planning.

Republic of Botswana. (1998). *Consumer protection Act no. 21 of 1998*. Gaborone, Botswana: Government Printer.

Republic of Botswana. (2003). *Botswana national strategic framework on HIV/ AIDS, 2003–2009*. Gaborone, Botswana: National AIDS Coordinating Agency.

Republic of Botswana. (2004). *Botswana: Millennium Development Goals status report*. Gaborone, Botswana: Tiger Design and Graphics.

Republic of Botswana. (2007a). *Botswana review of commerce and industry.* Gaborone, Botswana: Ministry of Trade and Industry and B & T Directories (PTY) Ltd.

Republic of Botswana. (2007b). *Budget speech 2007 and the National Development Plan 9, presented by the Honorable B. Gaolathe, Minister of Finance and Development Planning.*

Sembajwe, I., & Kalasa, B. (1999). *Aging in Africa: The foreseen situation and its security, health, social and economic implications.* APC 8A (111). Abuja, Nigeria: OAU.

United Nations. (2002). *Report of the Second Assembly on Aging, Madrid, 8–12 April, Sales No. E. 02. Iv. 4.* New York: Author.

United Nations, Department of Economic and Social Affairs. (2008a). *Guide to the national implementation of the Madrid International Plan of Action on Ageing.* New York: United Nations.

United Nations, *Department of Economic and Social Affairs.* (2008b). Regional dimensions of the ageing situation. New York: United Nations.

U.S. Social Security Administration, Office of Policy (OP). (1999). *Social security programs in selected African countries.* Washington, DC: Author.

World Health Organization (WHO). (2003). *Country cooperation strategy, 2003–2007: Botswana.* Geneva: WHO.

10

Brazil

Renato Maia Guimarães

The social scenario in Brazil still includes thousands of children begging in the streets. Despite recent advances, a significant proportion of children face the social risk of not achieving the educational and health standards modern society demands. However, it would be wrong to interpret this as evidence of a typical developing country social demographic pattern, where poverty, high fertility rates, high infant mortality, and low life expectancy prevail. Brazil is among the 10 major world economies in which the total fertility rate is low (2.2 per woman), infant mortality is declining fast, and life expectancy at birth is around 72 years. A silent demographic revolution is taking place. A youthful country in the 1970s, Brazil is now a mature one. Those who survived the challenges of a poor and insufficiently structured society in the past are now assured of a life expectancy of 21 years at the age of 60, not too different from a more developed society like the United States, where life expectancy at this age is 22.2 years (United Nations, 2007). Thus, despite not solving the structural inequality that victimizes children, Brazil is facing a new challenge imposed by the survivors. They do not constitute an exception, since there are more than 16 million people aged 60 and over. In the district of Copacabana (Rio de Janeiro), famous for its beaches, older persons constitute a third of the total population, a proportion that resembles London or Paris. This imposes a polarization in the social-economic agenda of Brazil, where improving living standards of the poorest and having children at school (not in the streets) is as important as setting up adequate policies for the aged.

Because of the demographic changes at the end of the past century, Brazilian authorities were faced with the growing expenses of social security. It can be said that the early predominant approach to aging was based on economic impact. Apart from demographic data, there was insufficient information about aging; even demographers were relatively silent about the demographic transition. However, in 1988, the Brazilian Association of Population Studies (Associação Brasileira de Estudos Populacionais [ABEP], 1988) reserved important space at its national meeting for population aging. It was clear that the trajectory of the Brazilian population had changed. The debate about population control by state programs that had dominated the last decades of the last century gave way to a new reality, in which better education, access to birth control information, urbanization, and the inclusion of women in the labor market had a greater impact on fertility rate than was expected by the demographic projections. The Brazilian population in 2000 was 30 million lower than had been estimated 30 years earlier.

Some evidence of the awareness of population aging was the retirement policy that allowed people to retire at as young as 40 years old. The growing national budget deficit due to retirement and pensions urged authorities to change this benevolent situation. Despite low benefits (as low as US$200/ month), the deficit attributed to social security was around US$20 billion a year. Up to a third of the expenses of the Brazilian health system are related to old people, but a special health policy for the aged has not been implemented so far.

THE GRAY HAIR OF A YOUNG COUNTRY

This was the title of the first national publication for dissemination of information on aging, at a time when few institutions and researchers were working on gerontology. However, in the last 20 years, many institutions and researchers have been attracted to the field of aging. Sound evidence of this growing interest is the increasing number of scientific papers submitted to the National Congress of Gerontology and Geriatrics, which in 2008, was over a thousand. It is believed that 40% of the total presentations were relevant and consistent with good practice in gerontology. There are, however, important barriers for developing gerontological research. Gerontology itself is not recognized as an independent field of research by the National Council for Scientific Development and Technology (CNPq), so all proposals for research are evaluated by a board whose expertise relates to the main subject of the study, such as epidemiology or health. This process makes research funding more difficult and does not contribute to the development of gerontology.

Despite lacking incentives, many research efforts are filling the gap in gerontology in Brazil. The Institute of Applied Economic Research (Instituto de Pesquisa Econômica Aplicada [IPEA]), a national institute of applied economics research, has produced an important data set on demography and characteristics of the Brazilian older population (Camarano, 2006). IPEA researchers have just finished an extensive analysis of older people living in institutions, a study used as reference for setting up governmental regulations for nursing homes. The study found nursing homes all over the country without any public subsidy, where residents were living in inadequate conditions, many in poor health. As there is no health policy for older people who need continuing care, the nursing homes are used as substitute institutions for dependent patients, many of them demented, who need highly specialized care.

Other researchers are also making great contributions to a better understanding of aging in Brazil. There is a five-year difference in life expectancy between the richest states, located in the southeast and south regions, and the poorest ones in the northeast regions. Messias (2003) studied the impact of income inequality and illiteracy rates on longevity; this author concluded that the elimination of illiteracy and improvement in education standards should be the main strategies for increasing life expectancy and reducing inequality.

Two population-based studies on aging are underway in Brazil. The EPIDOSO is a cohort study of 1,667 people aged 65 plus years living in Sao Paulo (Ramos et al., 1998; Ramos, Simoes, & Albert, 2003). It focuses on functional, clinical, and psychological aspects of aging, and recently included the evaluation of different strategies to improve the capacity of the older adults. The Bambuí Health and Aging Study (BHAS) is a long-term prospective cohort study of 1,606 older Brazilian adults living in the community (Lima-Costa et al., 2001). The study has been carried out in Bambuí city (15,000 inhabitants) in southeast Brazil. The study started in 1997 and completed its 10th wave in 2007. The objective of the study is to assess predictors of adverse health outcomes in old age (mortality, hospitalization, physical functioning and cognitive decline, complications due to Chagas' disease, hypertension, and depressive symptoms). The study emphasizes the influence of both infectious and noninfectious diseases on the abovementioned outcomes. The baseline study carried out in 1997 included a comprehensive interview regarding risk factors, blood tests, and medical examination. Blood samples and DNA aliquots were stored for further investigations. The study participants were identified through a complete census carried out in the town. All residents aged 60 or more years (n = 1742) were selected for the study (92% participated). Annual follow-up consists of interviews and death certificate verification. At predetermined intervals, medical examinations, and blood tests are repeated. During the first 10-year follow-up, total losses were about 8%. This study is conducted by researchers from the Fundação Oswaldo Cruz and the Universidade Federal de Minas Gerais Medical School. Up to now, around 60 papers have been published with results of both the survey and initial follow-up, and around 25 Ph.D. and master's students have used the project data set to develop their theses.

EDUCATION IN GERONTOLOGY

There is a growing interest in gerontology, but most universities are not aware of the importance of education in this area. Only five universities offer master's degrees or Ph.D. programs in gerontology. On the other hand, there are widespread informal courses that attract a large audience. Most have a limited content that includes basic demography and principles of gerontology and geriatrics. An important contribution has been made by the University of the Third Age (U3A) in Rio de Janeiro. It started 20 years ago, promoting cultural activities for older people, and also progressively created training programs for young professionals who want to qualify in gerontology or geriatrics. The U3A is very active in getting support from the community and also in disseminating gerontology by publishing books and a scientific journal (*Revista Brasileira de Gerontologia e Geriatria*).

A large number of groups work with older persons all over the country, and most of them are involved in some sort of education. Aging is a theme quite often presented on TV, and some programs are dedicated to senior audiences.

The Brazilian Society of Geriatrics and Gerontology offers a diploma in gerontology that evaluates candidates by their curricula and also by a test. Each year, at least 20 people submit their applications. This has made it possible to attract highly qualified people from top universities, and the number of researchers and lecturers in gerontology is increasing. Half of the 4,000 attendants at the International Association of Gerontology and Geriatrics congress held in Rio de Janeiro in 2005 were Brazilian. This was a fair indicator of the interest in all aspects of aging. In contrast, there were no federal government representatives at that meeting.

The Statute of the Aged is a legal instrument intended to implement a policy for the aged and that urges the inclusion of gerontological topics in high schools and in universities' curricula. However, up to now, little progress has been made. Gerontology remains relatively absent from our schools. Only a third of Brazilian medical schools teach geriatrics. For a large country projecting 35 million older people in 20 years' time, it is necessary to make a complete review of our policy for education in gerontology.

PUBLIC POLICIES

Brazil, with its cultural tradition of producing elegant and politically feasible legislation, has good policies for its aging citizens, but implementation efforts are scarce. In 1994, a National Policy for the Aged was established, and in 2003, the Statute of the Aged. Both are comprehensive legislations that include points such as human rights, social protection, health, education, and leisure. Public transport is free, including, in some cases, interstate travel. Older people are given priority in assistance at any public service, but a lot remains to be implemented, such as free medication, education in gerontology and geriatrics, and adequate health assistance. Programs that demand investment have been postponed. However, a program for promoting tourism for the aged was implemented with 50% reduction in cost of travel and hotels.

Social security is relatively well organized in Brazil. More than 18 million families receive payments from social security, with an estimated cost of 12% of the gross national product. Those who did not contribute to social security are assured a pension when they reach 65 years, but are considered poor. This is part of an overall policy that is producing positive results, including reduction of poverty. Since this policy was implemented, there has been a 10% increase in the self-rated health status and a similar decrease in hospital admission of older people (Neri & Soares, 2007).

In Brazil, there is a free and universal health care system. In large cities, the system is overstressed and the quality of assistance is criticized. Aging patients use 35% of the national health budget, but despite the high costs, medical care for the aged is poor. Historically, the Brazilian health system has been hospital oriented, but in the last 10 years, priority has been transferred to the Health of the Family Program (PSF). This is why the health system for over 60 million inhabitants is one of the largest primary care programs in the world (Stein & Harzheim, 2006). Thus, an important window for improving the health of old people demands training those involved in this community program.

A major barrier for implementing policies is illiteracy among the aged, reflecting a difficult and deprived past. Many NGO programs are teaching senior citizens to read and write, but it is difficult to repair errors of political ignorance of that past.

REFERENCES

Associação Brasileira de Estudos Populacionais (ABEP). (1988). *Transição demográfica*. Anais-VI Encontro Nacional de Estudos Populacionais. Olinda, Brazil: Associação Brasileira de Estudos Populacionais.

Camarano, A. A. (2006). *Sixty plus: The elderly Brazilians and their new social roles*. Rio de Janeiro, Brazil: Instituto de Pesquisa Econômica Aplicada.

Lima-Costa, M. F., Barreto, S. M., Uchoa E., Firmo, J. O., Vidigal, P. G., & Guerra, H. L. (2001). The Bambuí Health and Aging Study (BHAS): Prevalence of risk factors and use of preventive health care services. *Revista Panamenha Salud Publica, 9*(4), 219–222.

Messias, E. (2003). Income inequality, illiteracy rate and life expectancy in Brazil. *American Journal of Public Health, 93*, 1294–1296.

Neri, M. C., & Soares, W. L. (2007). Estimando o impacto da renda na saúde através de programas de transferência de renda aos idosos de baixa renda no Brasil. *Ensaios Econômicos da EPGE* [Economics Working Papers], *number 645*.

Ramos, L. R., Simoes, E. J., & Albert, M. (2001). Dependence on daily living and cognitive impairment strongly predicted mortality among elderly residents in Brazil: A two-year follow-up. *Journal of the American Geriatrics Society, 49*, 1168–1175.

Ramos, L. R., Toniolo Neto, J., Cendoroglo, M. S., Garcia, J. T., Najas, M., Perracini, M., et al. (1998). Two-year follow-up study of elderly residents in São Paulo, Brazil: Methodology and preliminary results. *Revista de Saúde Pública, 32*, 397–407.

Stein, A. T., & Harzheim, E. (2006). Effectiveness of primary health care evaluated by a longitudinal ecological approach. *Journal of Epidemiologic Community, 60*(1), 3–4.

United Nations. (2007). *World population ageing*. New York: Department of Economic and Social Affairs Population Division.

11

.. ■ ..

Canada

Neena L. Chappell

RECENT HISTORY

Aging in Canada reflects the fact that the country is a developed nation. Just over 12% of her population is aged 65 and older; this figure will be 15% in 2011 as the baby-boom generation enters old age, and will be over 24% around 2035. The fastest-growing segment of the population is those who are oldest old; that is, those who are aged 80 and over. At birth, men can expect to live to their mid-70s and women to their early 80s; at age 65, men can expect to live to their early 80s and women to their mid-80s. Circulatory diseases such as heart disease and stroke, cancers, and respiratory diseases such as chronic degenerative diseases, including emphysema and chronic bronchitis, are the major causes of death. Women outnumber men and do so by greater differentials the older they become in the age spectrum.

Politically, 10 provinces and 3 northern territories comprise political federalism. Older adults, like the population as a whole, are concentrated in the south of the country. Provinces that are more economically prosperous, such as Alberta, show lower percentages of older adults within their provincial population, due to the in-migration of the young for jobs. Provinces such as Manitoba and Saskatchewan, which are less economically prosperous, reveal higher percentages of older adults as young individuals move elsewhere. There is, of course, variation within the provinces as well and from city to city in terms of the percentage of older adults living there.

Canada's older adults reflect a multicultural mix, more so than younger generations because there are more foreign-born among those who are seniors today. That is, past immigration policies have structured the ethnic composition of today's elderly population. The majority of foreign-born among the senior population are therefore from other Western countries and speak one of Canada's two official languages—English or French. A currently small proportion consists of visible minorities from Asia, Africa and the Caribbean, but this will increase in future cohorts because of recent immigration from these countries. A small proportion are also currently First Nations people, small because of the higher fertility and higher mortality rates amongst First Nations people at the present time and in the past than is evident in the general population. However, the aging of their population is expected to double their percentage of persons aged 65+ by 2016.

Older adults in Canada reveal declines in their physical health, suffering more from chronic conditions than acute illnesses, with over three-quarters of those living at home diagnosed with at least one chronic health condition. Most commonly, they report having arthritis and rheumatism, then high blood pressure, then food or other allergies. Functional health problems also increase with age, although fewer older adults suffer from them than from chronic conditions. Functional disabilities, referring to basic and instrumental activities of daily living, are reported by about one-third of the older population. Cognitive impairment, specifically dementia, also increases with age, from less than 10% for those 65+, to over 20% for those 80+. However, recent data suggest that older Canadians are becoming healthier for longer; overall levels of disease and disability are being postponed to later in life.

It is important to note that subjective evaluation of their overall quality of life, or their mental well-being, such as happiness, life satisfaction, and morale—including subjective assessment of physical health—do not decline with age. Over three-quarters of older adults rate their health as good to very good, or excellent.

To sum up, older adults in Canada live relatively long lives with physical health declines that are occurring later and later. Their psychological well-being or overall quality of life is excellent and often better than that revealed for younger adults.

RECENT RESEARCH ON AGING

Research on aging in Canada is healthy and multidisciplinary. There are a number of university-based research centers at several universities across the country, some with more of a biomedical focus, some with more of a social science focus. All of the initial centers established in the 1980s by the Social Sciences and Humanities Research Council of Canada (SSHRC), are thriving (except for one at Guelph University, which closed). That strategic initiative by the SSHRC had a major effect on facilitating social science research on aging in Canada (Lesemann, 2001). Funding in Canada, as elsewhere, often has the ability to steer research. For this reason, it was important that the Canadian Institutes of Health Research (an expanded version of the earlier Medical Research Council) established an Institute on Aging as one of its 13 institutes. This too provides a focal point for the field. Not only does government conduct its own research (notably, in aging, important information is released through Statistics Canada) but in addition, different groups within the federal government, such as Health Canada and the Social and Human Development Directorate, fund special competitions, time limited on specific areas (such as home care and pharmaceuticals). One was the Seniors' Independence Program and another, the Health Transition Fund. Such announcements have done much to ensure Canadian research in targeted areas.

A major tendency of funders at the present time in Canada, as elsewhere, is to promote and facilitate applied collaborative research with nonacademic partners, including budgets targeted to translation and dissemination. This trend is evident in virtually all health research; it is not restricted to that related to aging, per se. Networking is considered part of the collaborative effort. It is too early to say what the benefits of this major thrust for funding research will be, but it is not obvious that either more research, better research, or more research uptake is resulting from such efforts. Only time will tell.

Other large initiatives, usually spearheaded by a few individuals, although definitely collaborative and supported by many agencies, include the Canadian Study on Health and Aging, Canada's first and only national study to establish the prevalence of dementia. That longitudinal study is due to the persistence of individuals in cobbling together many different sources of funding. There is, at the present time, no mechanism to fund expensive longitudinal studies despite their critical importance for answering fundamental questions in aging. For the last several years, many researchers across the country have been working toward the Canadian Longitudinal Study on Aging, a planned 20-year multidisciplinary study that will include the collection of biological, psychological, and social data on the determinants of health, beginning with individuals in middle age. While the baseline was due to go into the field in 2008, the dollars necessary to ensure its longevity for the 20 years is far from certain.

Although often the large and expensive research undertakings are most visible, this is in no way to undervalue research conducted by individuals alone or in small groups within their local universities. Indeed, research conducted by lone researchers and small groups of researchers is arguably the backbone of the research enterprise in Canada. Canadian research has a focus on the traditional problems and challenges faced in old age, as well as a more recent concern with healthy aging. The past several years have seen a major focus on frailty, recognizing that multiple causations and a chronic course are typical of clinical problems in old age. Canadian researchers, especially in the Maritimes and in Quebec, examine frailty as a complex state of increased risk, rising from both medical and social determinants (Rockwood, MacKnight, & Powell, 2001). The researchers are multidisciplinary, including both geriatricians and social scientists. Pharmaceutical epidemiological research and brain, memory and cognition research are also being conducted. Research involving the importance of the social determinants of health for quality of life in old age is strong, characterizing much of Canadian research. The older gerontological focus on life satisfaction and morale is evidenced in current research on quality of life and well-being, including notions such as independence and autonomy. There has been a major focus on the family and caregiving within Canadian research, demonstrating the resilience of individuals coming together when needed and the essential role played by seniors (Chappell & Penning, 2001). Concern with inequality and disadvantage for older individuals is evident in much Canadian research, whether in the area of health-care services, housing, welfare, poverty, or employment and the older worker.

There is an overwhelming focus in Canada, as elsewhere, on old age rather than on the aging process *per se*. This is partly related to the difficulty of funding longitudinal studies. Research on dementia includes a focus on formal care, pharmaceuticals, and family caregivers. Canadian research in gerontology and geriatrics is also largely applied, dealing with real-world problems and focusing on potential solutions often through examination of government programs. A common underlying thread of much research is how can we improve quality of life as we age? Much gerontological research is either directly or indirectly related to the health-care system, health policy, and public policy, more generally.

CURRENT STATE OF EDUCATION

Gerontology is now well established in many fields. Virtually all Canadian universities have a variety of courses, in many different departments, that focus on aging, and many more that focus partially on aging. It is more common in Canada to enroll in an established discipline or area and specialize in aging than it is to receive a degree in Aging or Gerontology. There are exceptions. For example, one university offers an undergraduate option in aging and has just established a similar program at the graduate level. There are a couple of universities that offer a master's in gerontology, and a Ph.D. in gerontology is being established. There is also a separate master's degree in health, aging, and society at another university. It is safe to speculate that in the future, more of these interdisciplinary degrees will be provided. At the present time, however, it is still most popular for students to enroll within established disciplines, such as sociology or psychology, and to specialize in gerontology. There have been for some time, and continue to be, certificates and diplomas in gerontology offered at a variety of community colleges and also out of continuing education divisions of universities.

In Canada, as elsewhere, one is no longer a gerontology expert, but rather the field has grown so substantially in the last three decades that one specializes within particular aspects of gerontology, such as caregiving or retirement or medicine. Within the medical school system, a specialty of geriatrics can be taken as part of internal medicine. Despite major shortages of geriatric specialists, few students are choosing this field. Within the health professions, there is much variation as to the emphasis placed on gerontology training within the educational curriculum and from school to school. While there are some in Canada who argue that gerontology is a discipline with an integrated body of knowledge of its own, most would disagree that gerontology is quickly heading to that status. Instead, most refer to it as a substantive area to which many disciplines—indeed, almost all disciplines—have something important to contribute.

CURRENT PUBLIC POLICY

In Canada, physician and hospital services are universally accessible through publicly insured services—Medicare. However, Canada's formal health care system is not socialized medicine; physicians are guaranteed remuneration for their work, but operate mainly as private entrepreneurs with guaranteed incomes from government. Medicare rests on five principles: universality, affordability, accessibility, comprehensiveness, and non-profit administration by a public agency. It is often referred to as defining the Canadian identity, distinct from the powerful U.S. neighbor to the south, where no universal health-care system exists. The Medicare program is especially important in a country such as Canada, where the delivery of health care is a provincial, not federal responsibility. However, the federal government exercises considerable influence through its funding power. Funding arrangements have changed throughout the years; at the present time, the federal government transfers dollars to the provinces to assist them in meeting the terms of the Canada Health Act and Medicare. Nevertheless, and similar to most other industrialized countries, Medicare serves as a universal system in which most citizens have access, without expenses out of their own pocket, to physician and acute hospital care. Issues of availability and access arise largely in rural and remote areas.

Nevertheless, Medicare has been criticized because of its medical focus and its exclusion of nonmedical services, especially for an aging society. Notably, nursing homes and home care are not included within Medicare. Yet gerontologists, including geriatricians, in Canada as elsewhere, argue that an aging society requires both forms of long-term care, due to the primarily chronic nature of their conditions (Chappell, 2008). Given that the delivery of health services falls within provincial and not federal jurisdiction, this results in varying levels and types of services in continuing care that fall outside of the acute care sector.

There have been many jurisdictional, provincial, and federal reports, commissions, and task forces on the health care system since 1990. All call for a definition of health that is broader than biomedicine, recognition of informal caregivers, more health promotion and disease prevention from the health-care system, and a shift from institutional-based to more community-based care (Chappell, 2008). However, despite this consensus (see Romanow, 2002, as an example of one of the more recent reports), health reform since the early 1990s has seen a retrenchment of vested medical interests, rather than a broadening from medical to health care (Williams, Deber, Baranek, & Gildiner, 2001). Indeed, the current global neoliberal agenda has seen the rhetoric of health reform used to close hospital beds, including entire hospitals; drastically increase outpatient surgeries; and turn home care from a community support system for those with chronic illness (primarily seniors) to a post-acute care hospital support system with little, if any, attention to health promotion and the broader determinants of health.

There is major concern at present that Canada's signature on numerous international trade agreements will seriously affect the health care it can deliver to its citizens, since those agreements contain provisions that will see Canada having to reimburse private companies for lost future earnings should it decide to convert any private services to public ones. The Romanow Report (2002) argues that Canada must, at every opportunity, explicitly state that her health care is not subject to these provisions. That is, long-term care, which is so important for the chronic health problems experienced in old age, is currently in jeopardy as health reform retrenches back to a medical focus.

During the public debates on health reform in the 1990s, there was a newfound political recognition of caregivers and the large contributions that they make to providing care to older adults. And much Canadian research before, during, and after that time has revealed the role of family and friends in providing the vast majority of care to seniors. The particular role of women, notably of wives and daughters, has been emphasized. However, this political recognition has turned into little by way of supportive resources to assist families. Services are not by and large available for caregivers *per se* (as opposed to the individual they care for); caregivers have not been integrated into a partnership with the formal health care system; and there are few signs that the work that informal caregivers undertake is any more valued than it was in the past.

Both the health care system *per se* and the role of family care in old age have been and continue to be emphases of Canadian gerontologists.

REFERENCES

Béland, F. (1997). Éditorial: Bâtir la gerontology d'ici: Un tremplin pour la reconnaissance international? ["Editorial: Building Canadian gerontology: A springboard for international recognition?"] *Canadian Journal on Aging,* 16(1), 19–33.

Chappell, N. L. (2008). The future of aging in health care. In D. Cloutier-Fisher, H. Foster, & D. Hultsch (Eds.), *Vulnerability and resilience in health and aging.* Canadian Western Geographical Series, Victoria, BC: Western Geographic Press. (Forthcoming.)

Chappell, N. L., & Penning, M. J. (2001). Sociology of aging in Canada: Issues for the millennium. *Canadian Journal on Aging,* 20, 82–111.

Lavoie, J. P. (2001). Are there two solitudes in Canadian gerontology? *Canadian Journal on Aging,* 20, 76–82.

Lesemann, F. (2001). Twenty years of Canadian social research on aging: An attempted understanding. *Canadian Journal on Aging,* 20, 58–67.

Rockwood, K., MacKnight, C., & Powell, C. (2001). Clinical research on older adults in Canada: Summary of recent progress. *Canadian Journal on Aging,* 20, 1–16.

Romanow, R. J., Commissioner. (2002). *Building on values. The future of health care in Canada. Commission on the future of health care in Canada. Final report*. National Library of Canada, Ottawa: Government of Canada Publications.

Williams, A. P., Deber, R., Baranek, P., & Gildiner, A. (2001). From medicare to home care: Globalization, state retrenchment, and the profitization of Canada's health-care system. In P. Armstrong, & D. Coburn (Eds.), *Unhealthy times. Political economy perspectives on health and care in Canada* (pp. 7–30). Toronto, Canada: Oxford University Press.

12

China

Du Peng and Yang Hui

POPULATION AGING

After the founding of the People's Republic of China in 1949, the population mortality rate decreased by a large margin in a short time, along with an improvement in the living standards and medical service conditions. At the same time, the fertility level went through a sweeping transformation in a limited period of time as a result of the decreasing birthrate, especially after 1973, when the Family Planning policy was implemented in China. Since that time, the number of new births in China has dropped dramatically, and the percentage of elderly in the population has started to rise. The Third National Population Census in 1982 attracted a lot of attention to the trend of population aging in China. With its increasing life expectancy, the increasing size of the senior population, and the rising percentage of seniors in the population, China stepped onto the stage of aging society in the year 2000.

From 1982 to 1990, the elderly population aged 65 and over in China grew from 49.5 million to 63.15 million, and the percentage of the population 65 and over increased from 4.91% to 5.57%. In the new century, the speed of aging has further accelerated. Between 2000 and 2007, the number of seniors aged 65 and above rose from 88.1 million to 106.36 million, and the percentage rose from 6.96% to 8.1%. In general, the population of the aging increased by 115%, with a 3.19% increase from 1982 to 2007.

The elderly population is defined as those aged 60 and over by the related laws in China. The speed of aging for people over 60 is faster than that for those aged 65 and above. From 1982 to 2008, the population of those aged 60 and over rose from 76.6 to 159.9 million, and the proportion of the elderly population to the total population increased from 7.6% to 12%. The elderly population aged 60 and above in China is so large that it equals the total population of elderly in all of Europe, which was 153.5 million in 2007.

One of the prominent characteristics of the aging population in China is that it occurred when China's economy was still underdeveloped (Du & Yang, 2009). Due to the large elderly population and higher aging proportion, support for the elderly and the socioeconomic development of China faces numerous challenges. As the young and middle-aged work forces migrate from the rural areas to the cities, it is seniors who are left at home in the countryside. (The rural elderly comprise 58% of the total senior population in China, and compared with the aging proportion in the cities, the proportion of aged population in the rural areas is 1.6 percent higher than in urban areas.) However, family support is still the major way to provide for the elderly in rural areas. Under the current condition of an insufficient social security and pension system, the huge transient labor force renders a severe blow to the traditional Chinese type of family support for the elderly, revealing a major social problem of stay-at-home elderly (i.e., those left behind when children have moved away). Another social problem regarding how only-child families should support their parents also deserves close attention. The aging of the population in China not only has an enormous impact on the health, income, and social security for seniors in China, but also exerts a certain influence on the world population and socioeconomic development. Therefore, gerontological institutions, experts, and scholars, both in China and abroad, devote a vast amount of interest and effort to understanding the issues created by the aging of the Chinese population.

RESEARCH ON AGING IN CHINA

The family planning policy in China has resulted in a dramatic shrinkage of the birthrate and an increasing emergence of single-child families. The number of households with only one child aged 17 or under amounted to 95.4 million in 2000, and is expected to reach 114 million by 2020. By that time, the total population of single children under 30 will soar to 150 million (Yang & Wang, 2007). Family planning reduces the size of families and resources available to families, fosters nuclear families, and weakens the functions of families to support the elderly, all of which threaten the traditional method of family support for seniors in China and raise huge risk for the future. This is especially true because the social security system is a long way from completion, and community-oriented support for the elderly is still limited. How to care for their parents now is a big concern for many only-sons and only-daughters. This problem absorbs attention in academia, and a number of studies have been done to find solutions to this problem. Government also attaches great importance to this problem, and some public policies have begun to play a positive role.

In the process of population aging and urbanization in China, more and more young and middle-aged workers have flown to the cities. The number of elders left in villages sharply increased, from 17.9 million in 2000 to about 50 million in 2007 (Sun, 2008; Zhou, 2006). Chinese society's ability to support elders in the rural areas is much weaker than in the urban areas in terms of the resources available, community services, and spiritual lives. The significant impacts those migrating children have on their stay-at-home parents have enticed scholars to shift their attention from research on the floating population to the stay-at-home elderly. The special term *floating population* is used in China to refer to migrants who are working and living away from their hometown, but who have not been registered in the local household registration system, so they are not totally identical to migrants.

According to the studies, the floating population has two types of influence on the stay-at-home elderly. On the negative side, the migrant population leads to a higher percentage of lonely home-stay and empty-nest elders, a rise from 23.8% to 44.2%, and to fewer resources available to take care of them. As many as 12% of elders are left with serious illness and no one nearby to take care of them. Apart from the heavy burdens laid on the shoulders of elders, the floating population also heightens seniors' feeling of loneliness. On the other side, adults earning their living in the cities will enhance their financial capability to provide for their parents staying at home (Du, Yi, Zhang, Qu, & Ding, 2004; Ye & He, 2008). The larger migrant population is an unavoidable socioeconomic trend in contemporary China, but apparently, the total number of stay-home elderly will continue to increase as a result. Research findings urge the government to take effective measures through scientific research on the problems related to the home-stay elderly, thus relieving some of their burden. The plan to support the elderly through community services should be further propounded, so as to solve the difficulties in their daily lives. It is a shared duty and responsibility of the government, society, and the transient population to improve the living standards of the stay-home elderly.

Like older people everywhere, Chinese seniors have a higher chance of chronic diseases, and they consume a significant amount of medical resources. It is of great importance for individuals, families, and societies that people enter old age in good health. It has been demonstrated that there is a high correlation between the health of the elderly and their sex and age. To be more specific, the self-rated health of males is better than that of females; the health of the elderly in rural areas is better than that in the cities; the health of the younger old is better than the older old. Even the extent of education and living environment of the elderly tremendously affects their health conditions (Wang & Ye, 2006; Yu, 1999). The healthy elderly in Beijing have some common characteristics, including being younger, male, and having received more education (Du, 2007; Du & Andrews, 2003).

According to research on the life expectancy of the elderly, females tend to live longer than their male counterparts. However, they will be less self-supporting and self-reliant than males. Due to the increase in average life expectancy, the proportion of the years that the elderly can be self-sufficient and self-reliant to their total years of life becomes lower and lower (Du & Li, 2006). Prevention of functional disability is vital to slowing organ decline and to helping elders maintain independence (Tang & Xiang, 2001). Du Peng and Yang Hui (Du & Yang, 2008) conducted systematic research on both the disabled condition of the Chinese elderly and their needs. Ding Zhihong (Ding, 2008) carried out a study on the current condition and characteristics of the disabled elderly in China. Zheng Sun, and Liu (2008) suggested methods for preventing disabilities. Health condition is closely interrelated with life quality (Zheng et al., 2008). At present, China is implementing policies to support healthy aging and assist elders to enter the aging stage in good health, which is significant for diminishing the elderly's risk of being disabled and keeping them self-reliant.

It is a tradition for Chinese seniors to spend as much as they earn, so their income will determine their standard of living. The major sources of income for elders in China are money provided by the children, pensions, and salary. The importance of the three economic sources changed from 1994 to 2004. Support from sons, daughters, and other relatives ranks as the primary resource (accounting for 59.6%) for elders in rural areas, and 70% of female seniors depend on their family members to support them (Du & Wu, 2006). There is a disparity between the amount of money the elderly can receive from their sons and from their daughters. However, the outflow of labor reduces the gap (Song & Li, 2008).

Retirement pensions serve as the primary source of income for seniors in the cities, among whom 60% depend on the pension. The number of female elders relying on their children and family to support their lives is bigger than that of their male counterparts (Du & Wu, 2006). An income gap derived from salary exists between the elderly in the rural areas and urban areas, among which rural elders who depend on labor and salary are four times more than those in the cities, but their income is only two-thirds of those in the cities (Du & Wu, 2006; Zhang, 2008). To relieve economic pressure and improve quality of life, it is very important that we have more information on the resources elders draw up and on the variables that influence their income. Scholars are studying a variety of topics in addition to the above, such as daily care, spiritual life, and health care.

The Development of China's Undertakings for the Aged (China National Commission on Ageing, 2006) summarizes the efforts and achievements in the development of undertakings for the aged in China in terms of seven aspects, including (1) the state mechanism of initiatives for the aged; (2) the old-age security system; (3) health and medical care for the aged; (4) social services for an aging society; and (5) elderly people's legitimate rights and interests. *The Elderly Population of China: A Century-long Projection* (Du, Zhai, & Chin, 2005) enunciates the severe challenges that the aged will have to face.

Scholars and experts at Renmin University, integrating the current situation of population aging and problems related to aging into their research, have conducted several studies and issued the following reports: *Population Ageing and Socioeconomic Development* (2006), *Research on the Community Services for the Elderly in Chongwen District in Beijing* (2007), *Research on the Income of Rural Elderly in Beijing* (2007), *Disability and Development in Rural China* (2008), *The Floating Population and Their Impacts* (2008), *Comparative Study on Welfare System for the Elderly* (2008), *Research on the Pension System in Rural Areas in Baoji, Shaanxi Province* (2008), *Policy Research on Population Ageing in Shunyi District in Beijing* (2008), and *The Need for Social Security for the Disabled in China* (2008).

The State Statistics Bureau began to collect specific information on aging in 1994 as part of the annual population sample survey, and some key questions were integrated into the 2000 Population Census and the 2005 1% Population Survey. The first national survey on the senior population was conducted in 1987 by the China Social Science Academy, and the first longitudinal survey of elderly persons was carried out by Beijing Geriatric Centre in 1994. Peking University has conducted a longitudinal survey on healthy longevity since 1998 and continued it over three data points. The China Research Centre on Ageing took two national sample surveys on the senior population in China, in 2000 and 2006, respectively. Part of these samples can be used as longitudinal data. In addition, the Second China National Sample Survey on Disability conducted in 2006 also provided very informative data on health and disability of the senior population. The above surveys have provided quantitative and statistical evidence for researchers in this field and have offered a favorable database for training students majoring in gerontology, which will help optimize the policies on aging and improve their life quality.

The studies described above have focused on the positive aspects of the aging population, as well as problems related to aging, retirement, and so on. In addition, other studies and reviews, both at home and abroad, are ongoing on sociological theories on aging in regard to its development, process, and significance (Li & Du, 2005). They are of immense help in facilitating the growth of aging theories.

GERONTOLOGICAL EDUCATION IN CHINA

The problems related to aging are so comprehensive and strategic that they play a major role in maintaining the stability and development of society in various ways, including cultural, political, social, and economic. In 1987, Renmin University in Beijing was the first Chinese university to have courses on gerontology. In 2003, a new specialty in gerontology was established at Renmin, and both a master's and doctoral degree in gerontology were created. These degrees provide a platform for research on population aging and related problems in China and complement the scientific study of aging (Du, P., 2003).

Renmin University initiated its postgraduate programs in gerontology in 2004, followed by Peking University in 2005. Currently, a number of universities offer gerontological courses, including Beijing Normal University, Capital Normal University, Capital University of Medical Sciences, Beijing City University, China Civil Affairs College, Women's Academy in Shandong, and Qinghai Normal University. Renmin University held four consecutive seminars on the topic of establishing the discipline of gerontology and three training programs on gerontology and policies on aging from 2005 to 2008. Meanwhile, Peking University held four forums on gerontology from 2005 to 2008.

The above seminars, trainings, and forums perform an incomparable function in establishing the discipline, publicizing gerontological knowledge, and promoting the development of gerontology. The Research and Teaching Committee on Gerontology in Higher Education and the Students' Committee of Gerontological Society of China, based at Renmin University, also facilitate research on this subject and prepare professionals and experts in this field.

As at Renmin University, the courses offered in the field of gerontology in Chinese universities include Introduction to Gerontology, Research Methodology in Gerontology, Demography of Aging, Economics of Aging, Psychology of Aging, Sociology of Aging, Aging and Social Work, Social Security, Aging and Health, Classics Reading in Gerontology, and Aging and Policies.

The Institute of Gerontology at Renmin University of China has been leading the way in developing textbooks on gerontology in China. Efforts have been made from two perspectives, the first being to translate the leading international textbooks on gerontology. In the past three years, *The Series of Translated Books on Gerontology in the 21st Century*, edited by Du Peng (2007), as the first set of translated textbooks on gerontology in Chinese in the new century, was published with the full support of the United Nations Population Fund (UNFPA). This series consists of *Gerontology: An Interdisciplinary Perspective* (by John C. Cavanaugh and Susan Krauss Whitbourne), *Social Gerontology: A Multidisciplinary Perspective* (by Nancy R. Hooyman and H. Asuman Kiyak), and *Handbook of Theories of Aging* (by Vern L. Bengtson and K. Warner Schaie), which illuminated various arguments and theories on aging and introduced the latest research results to China.

At the same time, years of efforts and sweat have been repaid by the harvest of publications on aging by Chinese scholars and experts. Over the past decade, a large number of books have appeared, including *Social Gerontology; Epidemiology and Ageing; Social Work on Ageing; Analysis of the Factors of Healthy Longevity; Geriatrics; Social Security on Ageing: History and Transformations; Theory and Practice of Informal Support; Study on the Value and Status of Elderly in Society; Syllabus of Gerontology Curriculum; Lecture Notes on Population Ageing and Ageing Issues for Senior Officials; Population Ageing in China: Changes and Challenges; Introduction to Gerontology; Research on the Service System for the Elderly in Cities; Psychology of Ageing; Research on Life Quality of the Elderly in China; Social work on Ageing;* and *Research on the Current Situation and Policy on Nursing Homes in Shanghai*. The above works fill in the blanks of the gerontological monographs and make a huge contribution to the development of gerontology in China by providing sufficient materials and disseminating gerontological knowledge to the general public.

POLICY RESEARCH ON AGING IN CHINA

Population aging in China is having an enduring impact on the development of policies and public services. Due to the declining birthrate and increase in the aging population, the growth of the newborn population will slow down, resulting in limited welfare for the general public and enlarging the income gap between generations (Feng, 2004). To meet the challenges raised by population aging in China, scholars are promoting the development of a social security system, Medicare, and long-term care insurance. Meanwhile, other policies closely related to the welfare of the elderly and harmonious development of the economy and society are being considered, such as the age of retirement, the public pension insurance mechanism, long-term care for the elderly, and others.

Delaying the Retirement Age

The interaction of population aging and the pension system attracts attention from all levels of society, and academia has been involved in a heated debate on whether to postpone the retirement age so as to relieve pressure on the pension system. Those who support this policy believe that population aging will cause a shortage of labor, whereas longer life expectancy will add to the huge pressure on the pension year by year. In order to keep the pension system in balance, according to these advocates, the retirement age should be delayed (Dong, 1998; Du W. L., 2003; Shi, 2001; Xiong, 2003). Some other scholars view this problem from the perspective of gender equality and regard earlier retirement for females as a kind of discrimination that hinders their development (Chen & Li, 2004).

Other scholars opposed to the idea of later retirement claim that the priority should be on how to increase the employment rate for the young rather than encouraging later retirement. They base their argument on numerous factors, such as Chinese life-span characteristics, labor resources and their utilization, sustainable development of the economy, the work force, sources of income, and so on. Based on these factors, they argue, later retirement is not suitable in China at present (Jiang & Chen, 2004). The experience of other developed countries has shown that delayed retirement age has not resolved the crisis of population aging and imbalance of pensions; rather, it has only resulted in a low rate of work participation. To better deal with the pressure on pensions, mobilizing elders to participate in work is of great importance (Yuan & Wan, 2006).

In our opinion, although China is aging rapidly, labor resources are still sufficient, in contrast with many developed countries. China has been regarded as getting old before getting rich. A better solution to relieve the pressure of aging is to boost the employment rate for the young, raise productivity, and encourage economic development. What's more, under the current system, postponing the age of retirement will extend the time for the elderly to pay for their Medicare and add to their burden. It would lower the level of welfare for the majority of elders and goes against the purpose of an equal society. In sum, the current situation in China makes it improper to delay the retirement age for the elderly. However, it should be put on the agenda for public debate in two or three decades.

The Public Pension System

The reform and completion of the public pension system will guarantee sufficient income for the elderly. As a result of the policy in past decades calling for high employment rate, low salary, and low reserves in the pension system in China, the system was based on a pay-as-you-go model. However, population aging fosters an increase of pension expenditures and leads to a deficit for the public pension account in the transition period. In order to avoid an empty account, raising the pension charge (or tax) is inevitable, which will lay the economic burden on the shoulders of investors and employees. To deal with this dilemma, a method that combines social pooling and individual accounts came into being.

The method of partially accumulated public pension insurance that combines social pooling with individual accounts will prevent the problem of uneven charges paid by individual employees in cash, and also diminish the inflation risk and investment risk caused by full accumulation. However, the oversized funds of personal accounts require further adjustment of structure between social pooling and individual accounts. In addition, scholars also estimate how the risks of political, economical, social, and legal environments shape the basic risk of public pension insurance through institutions (Luo, 2005).

The Medicare System

It is very important to develop the public health system, to speed up the establishment of a rural Medicare mechanism, and promote the reform of the urban medical system, all of which will ensure the health of citizens in both rural and urban areas. The new Cooperative Medical Service of Counties is a solution to the problem that seeing a doctor in the countryside is both difficult and expensive. However, this type of medical service still needs further improvement, due to its high initial cost and low percentage of reimbursement. Thus, the development of commercial medical insurance would complement the insurance system for the elderly, in both cities and rural areas.

In terms of the Medicare system in urban areas, a series of reforms has been carried out since 1999, based on the *Decision of the State Council on Setting Up a Basic Medical Insurance System for Staff Members and Workers in Cities and Towns* guide (State Council, 1998). Though the coverage of Medicare has been extended, it is still not available to two-fifths of employees in cities and towns. The expansion of Medicare coverage to all members will break down and prevent the cycle from poverty to illness and from illness to poverty. A fully functional Medicare system, plus health education and a nutrition plan, is irreplaceable for the realization of healthy aging.

Long-Term Care for the Elderly

Age is one of the most important factors for the deterioration of health. Population aging leads to more care for the elderly. The process of lower birthrate, rapid population aging, and modernization diminishes the family resources available to take care of the elderly and weakens the function of the family to support their elderly members. Public support for the elderly becomes inevitable. However, the shortage of facilities, nursing professionals, and related experts pushes the burden of long-term care back to the family members. In order to tackle the problems of long-term care, it will be necessary to strengthen the formal long-term care system for the elderly by legalization, institutionalization, and regulation; by encouraging society to build care centers for the elderly; and by establishing a network of caring under the guidance of the government, stretching to all communities (Xu & Tang, 2007).

Aging policies in China provide the momentum for the development of *silver industries* and legal rights protection. Even though public policy in the field of aging lags behind policies in the economic sector and other social sectors, the prominence of the problems related to aging absorbs the attention of relevant government branches. By means of policies and media influence, the government can create a friendlier social environment for the development of the aging sector and guide the public toward greater concern regarding aging affairs. These attitudes would support the development of the silver industry, thus improving the country's overall ability to face the challenges of an aging population.

Above all, the rapid decline of both the birthrate and the mortality rate leads to an aging population. Under the condition that population aging occurs when the national economy is still underdeveloped and the social security system is still incomplete, a *floating population* and a strong *family planning policy* bring about huge challenges to the traditional method of supporting elderly members—through individual families. Therefore, income and health condition determine their life quality. The development of gerontology in China is of great use and significance to establish a knowledge base through research, to spread that knowledge to the public and to policy-makers, train professionals in this field, and provide intellectual support for making favorable policies on insurance for aging, Medicare, and long-term care.

REFERENCES

Chen, W. M., & Li, Y. (2004). The impacts of retirement age on sexual difference in old-age pension among China's urban employees. *Collection of Women's Studies, 1,* 28–31.

China National Commission on Ageing. (2006). *The Development of China's Undertakings for the Aged (White Paper).* Retrieved December 8, 2008, from http://www.china.org.cn/english/aged/192020.htm

Ding, Z. H. (2008). The current status and characteristics of the disabled elderly in China. *Population Research, 4,* 66–72.

Dong, Z. Y. (1998). *Resource development of the elderly and modern civilization society.* Beijing: Management of Economy Press.

Du, P. (2003). The first gerontology major in China established at Renmin University of China, postgraduate programs in gerontology. *Population Research, 3,* 11.

Du, P. (Editor-in-chief). (2007). *The series of translated books on gerontology in the 21st century.* Beijing: China Population Press.

Du, P., & Andrews, G. R. (2003). Successful ageing: A case study on Beijing old persons. *Population Research, 3,* 4–11.

Du, P., Ding, Z. H., Li, Q. M., & Gui, J. F. (2004). The effect on the left-behind elderly of out-migration adult children in rural China. *Population Research, 6,* 44–52.

Du, P., & Li, Q. (2006). Disability-free life expectancy of Chinese elderly and its change between 1994 and 2004. *Population Research, 5,* 9–16.

Du, P., & Wu, C. (2006). The change in main source of income of the elderly in China between 1994 and 2004. *Population Research, 2,* 20–24.

Du, P., & Yang, H. (2008). The disability status and rehabilitation demands of the disabled elderly in China. *Journal of Capital Medical University, 3,* 262–265.

Du, P., & Yang, H. (2009). Comparative studies on population ageing between China and Asian countries. *Population and Development, 2,* 75–80.

Du, P., Yi, M., Zhang, P., Qu, J. Y., & Ding, Z. H. (2007). A study of the healthy elderly population in Beijing. *Population & Economics, 2,* 55–59.

Du, P., Zhai, Z. W., Chen W. (2005). *The elderly population of China: A century-long projection. Population Research, 6,* 90–93.

Du, W. L. (2003). An analysis of population aging and retirement age reduction. *Population Research, 2,* 66–67.

Feng, J. (2004). The welfare effects of population structure change—A model and explanation of social security. *Economic Science, 1,* 35–44.

Jiang, X. Q., & Chen, Y. (2004). A debate on postponing the current retirement age. *Population Research, 5,* 69–74.

Li, B. G. (2007). *Paying attention to the elderly.* Beijing: Huaxia Press.

Li, B., & Du, P. (2005). Theories in sociology of aging: Current situation and policy implications. *Population Research, 5,* 66–72.

Luo, J. X. (2005). The risks of system circumstance of the endowment insurance fund of employees in urban China. *Journal of South-Central University for Nationalities (Humanities and Social Sciences), S2,* 11–13.

Shi, B. N. (2001). Retiring age and the payment of pension. *Population & Economics, 2,* 71–76.

Song, L., & Li, S. Z. (2008). Out-migration of young adults and gender division of intergenerational support in rural China. *Population Journal, 3,* 38–43.

State Council. (1998). *Decision of the State Council on setting up a basic medical insurance system for staff members and workers in cities and towns.* From http://www.china.com.cn/chinese/zhuanti/yg/933896.htm.

Sun, J. J. (2008). Issues and enlightenments of the stay-at-home elderly. *Proceedings of the Conference on the Stay-at-home Elderly, December 2008.* Beijing.

Tang, Z., & Xiang, M. J. (2001). An analysis of ADL evaluation and its related factors of the elderly in Beijing. *China Population Science, S1,* 92–96.

United Nations Economic and Social Affairs. (2008). *World population 2007.* Retrieved December 28, 2008, from http://www.un.org/esa/population/publications/WPA2007/wpp2007.htm

Wang, D. W., & Ye, W. Z. (2006). Gender differences in health among the Chinese elderly and contributing factors. *Collection of Women's Studies, 4,* 21–26.

Wu, C. P, & Du, P. (1999). *Social gerontology.* Beijing: Publishing House of Renmin University of China.

Xiong, B. J. (2003). The comprehensive construction of an affluent society and the challenge of population aging. *Chinese Academy of Social Sciences Newspaper, 1.*

Xu, Q., & Tang, Z. (2007). Long-term care in China: Current status and future trend. *Population & Economics, 2,* 6–12.

Yang, S. Z., & Wang, G. Z. (2007). An indirect method of estimation of the number of only children. *China Population Science, 2007*(4), 58–64.

Ye, J. Z., & He, C. Z. (2008). *Lonely sunsets: The elderly left behind in rural China.* Beijing: Social Sciences Literature Press.

Yu, X. J. (1999). A study on the elderly health in China. *China population science, 4,* 1–11.

Yuan, X., & Wan, N. (2006). Postponing retirement age and its effectiveness on alleviating aging pressure, *Population Research, 4*, 47–54.

Zhang, W. J. (2008). The impact factors and regional disparities of labor income of the elderly in China. *Population Research, 6*, 69–75.

Zheng, X. Y., Sun, X. B., & Liu, M. (2008). *A study on the preventive countermeasure for the disabled person*. Beijing: Huaxia Press.

Zhou, F. L. (2006). *Study on the elderly left at villages in China*. Beijing: Publishing House of China Agriculture University.

Zhou, W. B. (2002). The actuarial analysis of the public endowment insurance of China. *Statistical Research, 1*, 42–45.

13

▪ ▪ ■ ▪ ▪

Costa Rica

Jim Mitchell, Don E. Bradley, and Alejandro Gutierrez Delgado

Costa Rica is a Central American nation situated between Nicaragua and Panama, with an estimated population of 4,476,614 as of July 1, 2007 (Costa Rican National Institute of Statistics and Census, n.d. a). The Pacific Ocean is to the west and south, and the Caribbean Sea is to the east. The capital city and focus of political and economic activity is San José. San José and surrounding communities are in the Central Valley, defined to the north and south by volcanic mountains. The cantón of San José boasts more than 1.5 million residents (Costa Rican National Institute of Statistics and Census, n.d. b).

BRIEF HISTORY, PUBLIC HEALTH, AND HEALTH CARE

During the colonial era, the region's remoteness, mountainous terrain, and disease-related decimation of indigenous peoples compromised its economic value to the Spanish. Colonists generally worked their own land, fostering egalitarianism that persists today (Shafer, 1994).

The official language of Costa Rica is Spanish. One of the more consolidated democracies in Central America, Costa Rica has maintained political stability in spite of economic and social difficulty the past two decades. Costa Rica gained international recognition when its army was abolished in December 1948 by President José Figueres. Funds allocated previously to the army were transferred to support education and other social programs. As a result, Costa Rica is one of the higher-ranked Latin American nations among those classified as high human development by the United Nations Development Programme (2007), behind Argentina, Chile, and Uruguay. Costa Rica also ranks fifth among nations according to the Yale Center for Environmental Law and Policy's (2008) Environmental Performance Index.

The reallocation of funding under President Figueres targeting education and social programs was indicative of an emphasis upon social welfare. Enhanced technology, including foreign investment in a railroad system tied to banana production in the Caribbean coastal region beginning in the late 1930s (Cerdas, 2004), increased agricultural productivity capitalizing upon rich alluvial and volcanic soils. According to Trejos (1995), the government encouraged education and occupational training. While the Central Valley emerged as the economic and political center, the rest of the country was primarily agricultural. More recently, ecotourism and associated development, primarily along the Pacific coast, have played an increasingly important role in the nation's economy.

Mohs (1982) describes sporadic efforts at public health and welfare reform up to the 1970s. These efforts include publication in 1943 of a National Health Code. A General Medical-Social Assistance Law was passed in 1950, including coordination of medical assistance and provision of social protection institutions. The 1950 Law also included an Illness and Maternity Program. A key feature of the 1950 Law was the establishment of the National Health System. The System included in its plan increased life expectancy, a 50% reduction in infant mortality, and a supply of potable water throughout most of the country.

The 1970s set the stage for several government-supported social reform initiatives in the face of rising unemployment and economic uncertainty (Simpson, 1983; Trejos, 1995). They included the National Plan of Economic and Social Development, expanded educational opportunity and basic health care, and preventive medicine and maternal and child health for Costa Rican citizens. Significant government reorganization and aggressive public health measures resulted in large part from the efforts of re-elected President Jose Figueres, formerly Chief of State (1948–1949) and President (1954–1958). Figueres's efforts were continued following the election of President Oduber in 1978. By 1980, all-cause mortality had dropped to 4.1/1,000 and infant mortality to 10/1,000 live births.

Despite an economic crisis in the early 1980s, including devaluation of the Costa Rican currency by 600%, 100% increase in inflation, and 10% unemployment (Mohs, 1991), the positive effects of public health reforms continued. By the latter part of the decade, Costa Rica, with other nations, was exploring mixed public and private sector involvement in health care. With continued work through the National Health System and general economic improvement, infant mortality decreased by another 25% in the late 1980s, mortality rates dropped to 3.7/1,000, and life expectancy increased to 76 years. By the mid- to later-1980s, programs for elderly people began to appear in discussions of goals for the national health care system (e.g., Mohs, 1991).

Costa Rica offers an intriguing example of a nation experiencing population aging in the face of sporadic and somewhat limited economic development and expansion. Rosero-Bixby (1986) describes social expansion, likely stemming from the reform initiatives described above, started during the 1970s. He points to increased life expectancy, illiteracy less than 10%, almost universal school attendance among children, 78% of the population covered by social security (a term used differently than in the United States), and indoor plumbing for 84% of the nation's population. Between 1972 and 1980, infant mortality declined by an average 8.7% per year (Rosero-Bixby, 1986). The sharp decline can be attributed primarily to reduction in diarrheal diseases and respiratory infections accompanied by improved pre- and neonatal care and improvement in the diagnosis and early treatment of diseases such as septicemia.

Among Costa Ricans, access to medical care is viewed as a basic human right that the government is compelled to provide. As evidence of this commitment, despite recent macroeconomic fluctuation reflected by rising and falling gross domestic product (World Health Organization [WHO], 2007), Costa Rica ranked 45th among 191 member nations of the World Health Organization in overall health system achievement, situated between United Arab Emirates and Kuwait, based upon 1999 data (Murray, Lauer, Tandon, & Frenk, 2000). Neighboring Panama and Nicaragua ranked 70th and 101st, respectively. Based upon 2006 World Health Organization national profile data (WHO, 2008), life expectancy at birth for Costa Rican males is 76 years compared to 80 for females, surpassing comparable figures for the United States.

The Costa Rican government instituted its national health-care system in the early 1970s under the guidance of the National Plan of Economic and Social Development. Health-care services are purchased from the Costa Rican Cooperative (COOPESALUD), by way of the Costa Rican Social Security Fund (CCSS). The Plan was implemented in order to provide health education and basic health care to rural and urban populations (Simpson, 1983), including reliable birth control (Gallagher, 1980).

The Costa Rican health-care system has two primary components. Preventive care falls under the purview of the Ministry of Public Health.

Medical and hospital-based care is the responsibility of the Costa Rican CCSS. A health and health-care system profile of Costa Rica provided by the Pan American Health Organization (1998) suggests a hierarchical system of medical care. Primary care is provided by general practitioners stationed at 103 clinics throughout the country. The second level of care includes a network of 7 hospitals and 13 peripheral hospitals, with general practitioners as well as specialists in basic medical fields. The third level of specialty and tertiary care is provided in three national and six specialized hospitals located in the primary cities. Communication among providers in the system takes place through a referral system.

Some have looked at the effectiveness of Costa Rica's health-care system reforms. Hill's (1994) analysis points to improvements in health-care access in rural areas from a macro or system perspective, with problems remaining at the micro or individual level. In his spatial analysis of access to health care among Costa Ricans, Rosero-Bixby (2003) describes variability by area in improvement in physical access to health care and in physician consultation time. In her analysis of mechanisms to evaluate the effectiveness of the Costa Rican health-care system, Abramson (2001) points to the need for quantifiable results through measureable indicators of system effectiveness. She describes reliance upon population coverage in lieu of measureable indicators of treatment effectiveness and quality as well as the efficient use of resources.

GOVERNMENT POLICY AND SERVICES TARGETING OLDER ADULTS

Unlike the United States and other nations impacted demographically by the increase in children born after World War II, population aging in Costa Rica is attributed to the sharp decline in infant mortality beginning in 1972 (Rosero-Bixby, 1986) described previously, and declining fertility due in part to availability of reliable birth control (Gallagher, 1980). Comparative U.S. Census data suggest a steady increase in longevity and the population of retirement-eligible adults, with dramatic growth beginning around 2050.

In 1999, the National Assembly defined older adults as persons aged 65 years and older. Costa Rican law (Public Law 7935) stipulates that elderly people are guaranteed equal opportunity, a dignified life, and participation in the formulation and application of policies affecting them. The Law also promotes the principle that older adults will stay with their families and in their communities and it recognizes the right of older adults to organize and participate in activities that allow their community and nation to capitalize upon their experience and knowledge. Finally, the Law promotes public and private institutional care and oversight of services and programs, and it promotes social security and the protection of elderly people. The same public law also establishes the National Council of the Elderly (CONAPAM) with its Board of Directors. The Board is charged with the administration of retirement funds, elder rights, and policy and national plan formation; it promotes program creation, continuity, and accessibility; it recommends the distribution of public funds for services; keeps records of accredited service providers; provides for older adult victims of abuse or those at risk; supports research; ensures compliance with government regulations; and funds rehabilitation and treatment programs. Subsequent public laws designate a portion of lottery proceeds for social welfare, including programs and services for the elderly. Further, 31% of alcohol and cigarette tax revenue are allocated to fund CONAPAM services, such as day-care centers, shelters, and other social projects.

A Golden Citizen Programme was implemented by the Caja Costarricense del Seguro Social in 1997. The Programme offers older people discounts at retail establishments, public events, workshops, parks, hotels and travel, and museums. In general, policy initiatives and programs encourage older adults to participate in physical activity and in the social life of the country.

Raul Blanco Cervantes National Hospital for the Elderly of the University of Costa Rica serves as a focal point for the clinical care of older adults, as well as graduate training in geriatric medicine. Beyond this, elderly people in Costa Rica are cared for through the hierarchical system of medical care described above. Raul Blanco Cervantes National Hospital is included among the three national specialty hospitals.

Nongovernmental organizations (NGOs) serving older adults or their care providers include those with an advocacy function, such as the National Crusade for the Protection of the Elderly. The Costa Rican Geriatrics and Gerontology Association of health professionals is charged with the provision of continuing medical education. The Costa Rican Gerontology Association (AGECO) provides public education about aging, combats discrimination targeting older adults, and fosters integration and active participation of older adults in social life. Intervention with and on behalf of older adults is also widespread among Catholic churches and other faith-based organizations.

Beginning in 1976, the Raul Blanco Cervantes National Hospital began efforts to promote the creation of day-care centers in communities across Costa Rica. This effort gained impetus in 1980 with funding from the Board of Social Protection, supplemented by other governmental and private agencies. Much like United States senior centers, there are approximately 50 such facilities across the country. They are intended to delay and provide an alternative to institutionalization by complementing family support through opportunities for socialization, education, and participation in leisure activities.

There are approximately 79 public and private institutional long-term care facilities across Costa Rica registered by the Ministry of Public Health. There are also homes not registered by the Ministry, placing their residents at risk. Gilliland and Picado (2000) describe the problem of domestic elder abuse in Costa Rica. They describe a country in which the family is a focal institution for the care of older people, and the sense of filial obligation is strong. They describe unintentional elder abuse stemming from overprotection by family members, threatening the autonomy and independence of older adults. They also mention the problem of abandonment of older adults, citing the lack of facilities or resources to accommodate older people.

Although documentation of numbers, volume, and dynamics is vague at best, Nicaraguan immigrants to Costa Rica are a significant source of care for older adults in the homes of Costa Ricans. Quesada (1997) estimated that in 1999, about 8% of the population of Costa Rica consisted of Nicaraguan immigrants, and this proportion has since increased dramatically. Castro and Morales (1998) and Morales (1999) describe unemployment and other conditions in Nicaragua pushing immigrants into Costa Rica and the labor sector involvement of Nicaraguan immigrants, including domestic work.

The Central Valley of Costa Rica is densely populated and home to approximately half of the nation's people. Areas outside the Central Valley are largely rural, with scattered communities and relatively large regional population centers. This difference in population density and diffusion presents service design and delivery challenges shared by other nations with significant rural populations. Strategies for delivering services in urban locations may not be suitable or effective in rural environs. Those who formulate policy and design services to meet the needs of Costa Rica's aging population will be challenged by this population dynamic, particularly in the face of migration from urban locations to pacific coast communities. The migration of working-aged people may be significant for the maintenance and effectiveness of traditional family-centered care of older people.

EDUCATIONAL PROGRAMS AND INITIATIVES

The first author has visited the country four times, beginning in 2003, to confer with faculty members and administrators at the National

University of Costa Rica (Universidad Nacional de Costa Rica or UNA), the University of Costa Rica (UCR), long-term care facility staff, and government officials. UCR in San José was established in 1940 during the reformist administration of President Guardia. It is the largest publicly supported university in the country. The Costa Rica Institute of Technology and UNA in Heredia are relatively young public institutions of higher education, established in 1972 and 1973, respectively. UCR offers an interdisciplinary master's degree in gerontology, the sole degree-granting educational program in gerontology in Costa Rica. Established in 1994, the program has conferred 44 degrees. According to the program's Web site, degree recipients have pursued careers or advanced education in psychology, pharmacy, social work, sociology, engineering, theology, education, medicine, and administration. Of the five master's-prepared faculty members affiliated with the program, two received their degrees in the United States, two from UCR, and one from Universidad Latina de Costa Rica, specializing in science and medicine. As stated, training in geriatric medicine is available through the Raul Blanco Cervantes National Hospital for the Elderly of the University of Costa Rica. Several Web-based graduate programs in gerontology offered by U.S. universities advertise their courses and programs to Costa Rican students.

The emphasis of services targeting older adults in Costa Rica is medical care available through the Raul Blanco Cervantes National Hospital, the various regional and community hospitals throughout the country, and the national network of primary care providers. Persons employed or volunteering in preventive recreational and activity programs are prepared educationally in related disciplines, or they gravitate toward aging services out of personal interest or desire. Those working in a residential care setting and formally educated apply their educations in disciplines such as social work, nursing, or nutrition.

During the first author's second visit to the country in 2004, he was asked by UNA faculty and administrators to assemble a team of gerontological educator-researchers from the United States to participate in a conference in Costa Rica to be held the following year. The purpose of the conference was to stimulate interest in gerontological research and practice in Costa Rica through presentations featuring various research examples and best practice interventions. The UNA-sponsored conference, "UNA—Gerontologia y Desarrollo Humano Integral," was held in May 2005, at a regional UNA campus in Nicoya in northwestern Costa Rica. This first international gerontology conference featured 13 presentations over two and a half days. In addition to the first author, presenters from the United States included Dena Shenk (UNC—Charlotte), Karen Roberto (Virginia Polytechnic and State University), and John Krout (Ithaca College). Six Costa Rican colleagues also contributed presentations. Conference proceedings are in a 2005 volume, *I Encuentro Internacional Universitario UNA—Gerontologia Y Desarrollo Humano Integral*, published in Spanish by the UNA academic press.

Costa Rica is represented in the International Association of Gerontology by Sr. Francisco Carrillo Castro, President of the Costa Rican Gerontological Association (Asociación Gerontológica Costarricense). The Association participates in international conferences on aging and offers topical educational opportunities to professionals as well as the public. The organization receives funding from Cost Rican exit tax revenue.

CONCLUSION

Although several government-sponsored programs provide services, care of elderly Costa Ricans remains largely a family responsibility. The government provides minimal income maintenance for older people who are poor, and employers, workers, and the state contribute to a pension system. Still, about 30% of Costa Ricans over age 60 were not covered by a pension plan a decade ago (World Bank, 1997). Through its nationalized system of primary-care clinics and national and regional hospitals, including the specialty hospitals described above, health care is widely available to those aged 60 years and over.

Nursing-home residents and people in shelters for the elderly are indigent, without family members to care for them (Laake & Morales, 1998). Nursing home versus shelter designation is contingent upon the degree of independence. Nursing homes provide total care, whereas shelter care for those more independent consists of meals and social activities. Day-care centers are available primarily in urban locations.

Amid economic fluctuation, Costa Rican policy and programs reflect commitment to a basic level of services and reform legislation targets the more pressing needs of older persons. Formal training for persons caring for older adults is primarily topical and episodic rather than sustained when provided by government-funded organizations and institutions, as well as NGOs.

Amid efforts to keep pace with immediate needs in the face of economic challenges in this developing nation, the dynamics of population aging offers time to develop a proactive approach to aging policy and service provision. Population aging in this Latin American nation is a result of improvement in primary care in the 1970s, enhancing infant survival. The initial beneficiaries of life extension will enter the ranks of people aged 60 and over in 2050. This period preceding a literal wave of older people offers an opportunity to design and implement university-based graduate programs in applied gerontological research. The efforts described previously to evaluate the effectiveness of health-care reforms in Costa Rica illustrate the need for educational preparation in program outcomes assessment grounded in quantitative descriptive and explanatory analyses. Such educational programs can provide workers equipped to guide culturally appropriate and proactive government policy and programs targeting Costa Rica's older adult population. Exemplified by the health-care reform and restructuring spearheaded by President Figueres and others, Costa Rica is a Latin American nation with a history of reform policy and programs when needed. There is time for educational program design and implementation before the full effects of population aging in this progressive Latin American nation are felt.

REFERENCES

Abramson, W. (2001). Monitoring and evaluation of contracts for health service delivery in Costa Rica. *Health Policy and Planning, 16*, 404–411.

Castro, C., & Morales, A. (1998). *La inserción laboral de la fuerza de trabajo nicaragüense en el sector de construcción, la producción bananera y el servicio domestico en Costa Rica* [The insertion of the Nicaraguan labor force into the construction sector, banana production, and domestic service in Costa Rica]. San José, Costa Rica: FLACSO.

Cerdas, A. L. (2004). From rainforest to banana plantation: A worker's eye view. In S. P. Palmer, I. Molina, & I. M. Jiménez (Eds.), *The Costa Rica reader: History, culture, politics* (pp. 293–309). Durham, NC: Duke University Press.

Costa Rican National Institute of Statistics and Census. (n.d. a). *Cuadro 1. Población total proyectada por sexo, según años calendario Hipótesis recomendada 2000–2050* [Figure 1. Population totals projected by sex, according to recommended assumptions for calendar years 2000–2050]. Retrieved October 2, 2008, from http://www.inec.go.cr

Costa Rican National Institute of Statistics and Census. (n.d. b). *Cuadro 1. Población total cerrada por sexo, según provincia, canton, y distrito: Al 31 de diciembre del 2007* [Figure 1. Total population by sex, according to province, canton, and district: December 31, 2007]. Retrieved October 2, 2008, from http://www.inec.go.cr

Gallagher, C. F. (1980). Demography and development: The lessons of Costa Rica. *American Universities Field Staff Reports: North America, 16*, 1–14.

Gilliland, N., & Picado, E. L. (2000). Elder abuse in Costa Rica. *Journal of Elder Abuse and Neglect, 12*, 73–87.

Hill, C. E. (1994). National and cultural influences on economic development, political decision-making, and health care changes in the rural frontier of Costa Rica. *Human Organization, 53,* 361–371.

Laake, K., & Morales, F. (1998). *Elementos practicos para la attencion de las personas mayors* [Practical elements of the care of older persons]. CENDEISS-CCSS.

Mohs, E. (1982). Infectious diseases and health in Costa Rica: The development of a new paradigm. *Pediatric Infections Disease, 1,* 212–224.

Mohs, E. (1991). *Politicas y estrategias de salud durante dos decades. 1970–1990 (documento medito)* [Health policies and strategies during two decades, 1970–1990 (medical document)]. San José, Costa Rica.

Morales, A. (1999). *Amnestía migratoria en Costa Rica: Análisis de los alcances sociales y del impacto del regimen de excepción migratoria para los inmigrantes de origen centroamericano en Costa Rica* [Migration amnesty in Costa Rica: Analysis of the social reach and impact of the migration exception rule for immigrants to Costa Rica from Central America]. San José, Costa Rica: FLACSO.

Murray, C.J.L., Lauer, J., Tandon, A., & Frenk, J. (2000). *Overall health system achievement for 191 countries.* Discussion Paper Series No. 28, EIP/GPE, World Health Organization.

Pan American Health Organization. (1998). General situation and trends: Socioeconomic, political, and demographic overview. Retrieved from http://www.paho.org/english/sha/prflcor.htm

Quesada, C. Q. (1997). Flujo migratorio de Nicaragua a Costa Rica: Un problema al margen de la integración regional [Migration influx from Nicaragua to Costa Rica: A problem at the margin of regional integration]. *I Brecha, 16,* 8–9.

Rosero-Bixby, L. (1986). Infant mortality in Costa Rica: Explaining the recent decline. *Studies in Family Planning, 17,* 57–65.

Rosero-Bixby, L. (2003). Spatial access to health care in Costa Rica and its equity: A GIS-based study. *Social Science and Medicine, 58,* 1271–1284.

Shafer, D. M. (1994). *Winners and losers: How sectors shape the developmental prospects of states.* Ithaca, NY: Cornell University Press.

Simpson, S. H. (1983). National health system and popular medicine: The case of Costa Rica. In J. H. Morgan (Ed.), *Third World medicine and social change: A reader in social science and medicine* (pp. 210–241). Lanham, MD: University Press of America, Inc.

Trejos, M. E. (1995). Socioeconomic factors for the understanding of health policy during the 1970s. In C. Muñoz & N. S. Scrimshaw (Eds.), *The Nutrition and health transition of democratic Costa Rica* (Chapter 5). Boston: International Nutrition Foundation for Developing Countries. Retrieved from http://www.unu.edu/unupress/food2/uin05e/uin05e00.htm

United Nations Development Programme. (2007). *Human development report 2007/2008.* New York: Author.

World Bank. (1997). Costa Rica: Identifying the social needs of the poor. Latin America and the Caribbean Region. Retrieved from http://www-wds. worldbank.org/external/default/main?pagePK=64193027&piPK=641879 37&theSitePK=523679&menuPK=64187510&searchMenuPK=641872 83&theSitePK=523679&entityID=000009265_3971110141107&search MenuPK=64187283&theSitePK=523679

World Health Organization (WHO). (2007). *Costa Rica: Country cooperation strategy at a glance.* Retrieved September 10, 2008, from http://www.who. int/countryfocus/cooperation_strategy/ccsbrief_cri_en.pdf

World Health Organization (WHO). (2008). *Costa Rica.* Retrieved September 10, 2008, from http://www.who.int/countries/cri/en/

Yale Center for Environmental Law and Policy & Center for International Earth Science Information Network at Columbia University. (2008). *Environ-mental performance index 2008, Costa Rica: All metrics.* Retrieved October 2, 2008, from http://epi.yale.edu/CostaRica

14

Cuba

James T. Sykes and Enrique Vega

A LOOK BACKWARD

The dynamics of growing old in Cuba changed with the expulsion of Dictator Batista in 1959 by revolutionary forces under Fidel Castro. A nation that had experienced a huge gap between privileged landowners, government, and military officials and an overwhelming majority of the Cuban population discovered that reform could bring universal educa tion, land reform, and a comprehensive primary health-care system that guaranteed equal access to all Cubans. Cuba began slowly to emerge into a new era, marked by hope and promise, despite hardships and limited resources to spur development.

With the establishment of the revolutionary government and a commitment to the social well-being of the people, Cuba began a long and difficult journey toward a society in which all Cubans, including older persons, received equal protection and opportunity under the law. While opportunities were constrained by the underdevelopment of the economy and its over-reliance on sugar cane, nonetheless the benefits of centralized planning enabled Cuban citizens to receive education, health care, and jobs without sacrificing the vibrant cultural milieu deeply appreciated by Cubans, young and old.

In the 1960s and 1970s, Cubans experienced a dramatic increase in literacy and received widespread benefits from both a primary health-care system that served Cubans effectively in urban and rural areas and a social security system that ensured that all persons, including those no longer in the work force, had housing and a small pension, as well as the services of physicians. However, despite these policy reforms, Cubans continued to struggle for adequate nutrition, necessary services for impaired persons, and a transportation system that facilitated movement within communities and between towns.

While Cuban society was undergoing substantial changes, Cuban elders received not only the support of their families, but also immediate access to a family physician for acute interventions and a wide range of services often described as social medicine. Additionally, every family, including those headed by older persons, could call on a neighborhood community leader to intercede with problems relating to such matters as living arrangements and dysfunctional families. This social care system, developed after the revolution, created conditions for positive changes throughout the nation, including assuring older persons the personal and economic security they needed.

In 1985, Cuba launched a family health-care program that ensured coverage to every neighborhood across the nation. This was also the year in which Cuba began a serious effort to train geriatricians and enhance the training of family physicians to care for older persons. Neighbors were encouraged to care for neighbors. Grandparents' Circles, a voluntary association of older persons who engaged in physical exercise activities, socialization, and mutually supportive relationships, emerged across the island. Daily exercise programs were organized, often led by a vigorous elder from the neighborhood. With nearly year-round good weather, the groups met in parks and other community spaces.

With the withdrawal of Soviet aid at the same time that Cuban products could not be delivered to Eastern European markets, the people of Cuba faced extreme hardships; the economy floundered. Severe shortages of basic food, uncertain transportation, and limited medicines affected the quality of life for all Cubans. However, the basic social structure remained in place. The 1990s, referred to as the "special period" due to widespread shortages, was also a decade in which Cuba launched numerous innovations in the services elders provided and received. Neighborhood homes were opened and staffed as senior centers and adult day-care centers, where adult children brought their parents and picked them up at the close of the workday. Volunteers from the neighborhood provided assistance and entertainment to vulnerable persons, including especially frail elders.

During the 1990s, Cuba consolidated its numerous programs for older persons. Influenced by the United Nations' call for each member nation to develop a report on the status of older persons, Cuban officials at the national and local levels developed information about the extent to which older Cubans were receiving the care they required. Their findings were reported at the UN Second World Assembly on Ageing in Madrid in 2002. Various ministries investigated ways and means of improving the quality of life of older persons and reported to a special committee of the Parliament assigned responsibility for coordinating aging policy initiatives in the government. Cuban leaders urged the government to improve and expand services to those needing skilled care both within nursing homes and in the community.

Las Universidades de la Tercera Edad (Third Age Universities) were organized in diverse venues, including universities, to offer learning opportunities for retirees. Serious older adult students attended classes, wrote a thesis, and received a certificate for their work. Nearly every municipality in Cuba has a Universidad de la Tercera Edad. Within a recent four-year period, these third age universities had graduated more than 30,000 persons. Cuba's commitment to the principles of lifelong learning is clearly established in all parts of the island nation.

In his report to the World Assembly on Ageing, Alfredo Morales, Minister of Work and Social Security, described Cuba's integrated, multisectorial approach to ensuring that all older persons were guaranteed health care, social services, modest pensions, continuing education including physical and social activities, housing, and a network of informal programs to enhance their well-being.

The following section provides information about economic realities that constrain Cuba's ambitious social agenda for older Cubans.

ECONOMIC CONTEXT

Since the revolution of 1959, Cuba has had a centralized planning system. However, due in part to policies of the United States that have severely constrained trade and tourism, Cuba has struggled economically to generate the resources needed to implement its ambitious social agenda. Cuba was successful in establishing trade relations with countries closely aligned with the Soviet Union, which produced revenues to underwrite such programs as universal education, health-care services for all, and a transportation system fueled by subsidized petroleum products and paid for through the sale of sugar. Nonetheless, Cuba did not achieve economic self-sufficiency.

In fact, with the collapse of the Soviet Union, Cuba's principal source of foreign exchange revenue was cut off. Between 1989 and 1993, Cuba faced an economic crisis: its gross domestic product fell 35% and exports declined by 75%. The loss of trade with nations aligned with the Soviet Union was exacerbated by the U.S. economic blockade, a policy first imposed on Cuba in 1962 that forced the nation to curtail many programs important to the elders of Cuba, families, and those whose employment depended on trade.

Despite Cuba's lack of resources needed to flourish economically, the citizens valiantly accepted drastic measures to enable the nation to survive during the "special period." In the early 1990s, Cuba adopted various policies to increase its economic self-sufficiency, including broadening its tourism industry to earn the hard currency Cuba needed to purchase products from abroad. Before the 1959 revolution, tourism was a principal economic engine for Cuba. Since 1995, foreign companies have invested substantial resources to develop international resort areas on the coasts east and west of Havana. In addition, Cuba has begun to host international conferences, not only to enable Cuban professionals to enhance their skills and expand their knowledge, but also to stimulate the Cuban economy.

DEMOGRAPHIC AND LABOR FORCE TRENDS

While Cuba has demographic markers similar to a developed country, many of its economic indicators are like those of a developing country. The inconsistency between developed and developing country characteristics in Cuba is a recurring theme. For example, the large proportion of women in the work force is characteristic of a developed country; in 1999, approximately 38% of all workers, 60% of professional workers, and 70% of workers in the Ministry of Health were female (Cuban Ministry of Health, 1999).

A brief summary of significant trends shows that persons 60 and older in 1950 comprised 7.3% of Cuba's population; by 1975, they represented 9.9%, rising to 13.7% in 2000. By 2025, one of every four Cubans will be 60 or older. Life expectancy has a similar trend, from 59.3 years (at birth) in 1950–1955 to 76.4 in 2000–2005. Labor force participation of older people fell dramatically between 1950 and 2000. Fifty-seven percent of males over 65 were employed in 1950 compared with only 9% still working in 2000. While older women in Cuba have not traditionally been found in the formal work force, in 1950, 8.5% of older women had jobs outside the home; by 2000, that number had fallen to 1.4% (UN, 2002).

EMERGING AWARENESS

With the considerable increase in longevity, in 2003 Cuba launched the 120 Club—a public health initiative led by Fidel Castro's physician,

Dr. Eugenio Selman—calling for national efforts to improve nutrition, expand exercise programs, stop smoking, and for older persons to become involved in their communities. The promoters of the 120 Club insisted that to reach 120 was an attainable goal, but only if people began to live healthy lives in healthy environments early on. The idea of living to 120 captured the attention of many older Cubans.

Cuba's preparation for its aging society underwent important shifts during the 1990s. The National Institute for Sports, Physical Education and Recreation (INDER) promoted strategies for active aging. Concerns of the 60-plus population were partially addressed with better-trained primary care physicians serving neighborhoods. Medical schools began providing training in geriatrics. Universities and ministries developed research agendas to investigate broadly the growing needs for medical and social interventions and chronic care associated with long life. Clearly the effect of INDER initiatives promoting health and supporting older person initiatives is substantial and continuing to achieve positive results.

Family physicians live in the neighborhood they serve. Their homes are also their clinics. State planning guidelines suggest that one primary care physician serves about 120 families, a ratio that ensures that persons in need get not only medical care, but also health education (on disease prevention and health promotion), counseling, and personal support. Additionally, the primary health care system offers assessments and treatments in the community and referral to tertiary-care centers when one needs a specialist or hospitalization. The physician follows the patient and retains responsibility to see that care is appropriate, timely, and monitored.

With the aging of individuals and younger persons moving from rural communities, more Cuban elders are finding their family support system inadequate. Communities are responding with various community-based services, including personal care; most large communities have nursing homes, many of which are at capacity, leaving some older frail Cubans to be cared for in long-term-stay hospitals, occupying beds that are also needed for patients with acute-care needs. Emerging in some communities are assisted living arrangements, small homes where staff and volunteers provide limited care; modest rooms are available for those who lack alternative accommodations. Despite the emergence of neighborhood-based services, Cuba's policy is based on the premise that the bulk of care will be provided by the individual's family in the home or neighborhood with assistance from a family physician. In fact, an overwhelming number of Cubans believe it is improper and inhumane to place an older person in a nursing home, an attitude that explains, in part, that throughout Cuba, there are only 143 nursing homes serving 8,805 patients (Gericuba, 2008).

LAYING THE FOUNDATION

During the period between 1997 and 2005, Cuba's Ministry of Health, with principal responsibility for the care of elders and persons with disabilities, responded to problems exacerbated by "special period" losses and launched several initiatives, as described below.

Primary Health-Care Team

While responsibility for the care of older persons rests primarily with a family physician, the team leader has access to the insights, skills, and knowledge of a social worker, a nurse, and a psychologist to assist in diagnosis, the development of care plans, and ensuring compliance with a plan of care through monitoring. Additionally, the team's mission includes leading health promotion programs, alerting the community to environmental hazards and specific disease-prevention efforts, training family members in caregiving, and informing patients about self-care strategies. The team members are awarded a certificate in community gerontology, indicating their competence to provide comprehensive services to older residents. Today there are 246 geriatric medicine specialists and 36 geriatric departments in hospitals with a total of 739 beds (Gericuba, 2008).

Long-Term Care Initiatives

Despite the fact that there is a clearly defined growing number of frail elders, some of whom are not adequately cared for by families, Cuba has only just begun to address seriously the need for a long-term care system—a set of services and interventions for addressing chronic care needs—parallel to Cuba's highly effective primary-care system. Clearly, the lack of resources has constrained the development of long-term care programs, services, and facilities. However, Cuba needs additional long-term care beds and expanded efforts for early diagnoses and treatment for persons with such conditions as diabetes, cardiovascular diseases, stroke, and cancers. To lead this effort, Cuba has prepared specialized teams trained to identify emerging chronic conditions and to initiate treatment plans. In addition, family members who provide continuing care to a frail member may be paid by the State for such services. There are 436 multidisciplinary gerontological teams assisting the nation's primary-care physicians (Gericuba, 2008).

Hospital-Based Care

The policy regarding health care is clear: to the fullest extent possible, care should be provided in one's home in the community. Nonetheless, hospitals and nursing homes are essential community assets; unfortunately, many hospitals lack sophisticated diagnostic equipment and costly medicines, impairing the quality of medical care a patient may require. And, indeed, there is a wide range of quality among care facilities, especially when one considers the physical environments of many institutions.

While the policy is clear—all citizens of Cuba are to receive quality care—circumstances are mixed due to insufficient resources to upgrade care facilities. Making improvements in hospital-based care requires upgrading diagnostic equipment, rehabilitating patient rooms, improving sanitary services, and scheduling in-service education to prepare hospital personnel to give appropriate attention to long-term-stay patients.

Work Force Development

Cuba's health-care system is designed to encourage the development of professionals in areas of health care required by an aging population. Physicians, therapists, nurses, and social workers are assigned to neighborhoods by health officials in each of the provinces. Recent increases in the number of physicians trained in geriatrics will improve the quality of chronic care for frail persons. The Ministry of Health is acutely aware of the current and widening gap between an adequate professional work force and the number of Cuban elders who will need specialized services. The Ibero-American Center on Aging (CITED) provides informed and substantial leadership both in raising awareness about the broad consequences of Cuba's rapidly aging population and in championing specific training programs to increase the skills of trained professionals and their capacity to deliver quality care. It is noteworthy that 125,136 older Cubans live alone in their neighborhoods (Gericuba, 2008). Of course, they are served by family physicians and receive the attention of multidisciplinary gerontological teams.

Beginning in 1985, leaders in the field of aging, principally medically trained individuals, created a network of practitioners and researchers to strengthen the scientific foundation for the care of Cuba's elders. Pioneers in this field, including Osvaldo Prieto Ramos, were successful in their efforts to establish a training center and chronic care teaching hospital within the confines of Havana University to provide care, undertake research, and conduct ongoing training and annual conferences. CITED was assisted by numerous overseas experts who collaborated with CITED's leadership to strengthen the content of training courses. Invited colleagues from overseas reviewed research methodology and results, guided Cuban gerontologists as they improved assessment tools and updated care protocols, and ensured that current science supported the training modules.

LOOKING FORWARD

Cuba faces challenges on many fronts, including the following: disabilities, caregiving, work force development (medical and nonmedical), appropriate living arrangements, self-care, and adequate pensions.

Health Care

Older persons should have access to the care they need as part of a universal health-care system. Cuba is committed to ensuring that older persons will be cared for in their homes and neighborhoods, counseled, and supported by a care team and thoughtful neighbors. There is little evidence to suggest that Cuba's tradition of family caring for elders will change, even though an increasing number of very old Cubans may outlive their support system. The introduction of assistive devices, along with a willingness of the nation to cover the costs of in-home care—including paying family members—should enable the old old of tomorrow to expect that they, too, will be cared for. It seems clear that until the general economic conditions improve, Cuban elders may be unable to receive the medications and treatments they need to cope with chronic conditions.

Social Security

Cuba has instituted a national pension system that provides modest income to nearly all citizens. However, the amount the typical pensioner receives provides barely enough income to meet their subsistence needs. Fortunately, most elders have families that contribute to their resources; housing and health care are provided without cost; public transportation is cheap. The government provides food vouchers to pensioners, ensuring that all Cuban elders receive the minimum daily food sustenance they need.

Employment

Five percent of Cuba's older persons continue to be employed (UN, 2002), most in the informal economy. An increasing number serve as volunteers in various community settings. A remarkable feature of Cuban life is the large number of musical groups that entertain in social clubs and bars throughout the island; many of these bands include a parent and child and persons ranging in age from very old to rather young. Elders living in rural families, especially those working the land, find many ways to help, from working in the fields to caring for children in the home.

Care and Residential Facilities

About 50% of Cuban households include an older relative; 11% of persons over 60 live alone, while another 11% live with other older persons without children present. While a large number of older people own their homes, there remains severe pressure on housing. Many young families share housing with their families, living in crowded conditions while waiting for an apartment or home to become available.

Most neighborhoods in Cuba have centers where elders may go for the day, for a nutritional lunch and limited care services. Third age universities often utilize these centers for educational and cultural programs; however, this exciting development is in its early stages. Many neighborhood day-care centers provide not only such services as hair grooming, bathing facilities, and meals, but also overnight accommodations for those who need a place to stay when ill or when their care providers are away. A recent survey indicates that there are 146 senior centers and day-care centers in Cuba (Gericuba, 2008).

Unfortunately, for those who need to be admitted to a hospital, Cuba's hospitals show the effects of poor maintenance, marginal sanitation, and crowded conditions. Cuba's tight economy has limited the nation's investment in quality hospitals, whether to upgrade those in place or to develop new hospitals to replace some very much in need of replacement. It is fair to note that the quality of hands-on care in teaching hospitals and in Ameijeieas, Havana's principal hospital, is high. And some observers will note that Cuba's priority attention to neighborhood-based clinics and to self-care make the lack of adequate acute-care beds less onerous.

Life Satisfaction

Recent research findings suggest that most of Cuba's elders describe their lives as good or very good. They live with their families and receive the attention and opportunities to be useful for extended periods of time following an active work life and raising a family. Their basic needs for shelter, food, health care, and a little cash income are met by government-guaranteed entitlements. While it is evident that a short-age of medicines, poor transportation services, and crowded living arrangements negatively affect the quality of their lives, in a nation where expectations for material goods are low, the self-described quality of life is relatively good.

REFERENCES

Cuban Ministry of Health. (1999). *Anuario estadistico.* Havana, Cuba: Cuban Government Publications.

Gericuba. (2008). *Red Cubana de gerontología y geratría.* Retrieved October 21, 2008, from http://www.sld.cu/sitios/gericuba/

United Nations Department of Economic and Social Affairs/Population Division. (2002). *World population ageing: 1950–2050.* New York: UN. Retrieved from http://www.un.org/esa/population/publications/worldageing19502050/index.htm

15

·· ■ ··

Czech Republic

Eva Topinková and Lucie Vidovicová

The Czech Republic, formed in 1991 by the partition of the former country of Czechoslovakia, has slightly more than 10 million residents, of whom 14.6% are aged 65 or above. Life expectancy at birth in the Czech Republic is 73.7 years for males and 79.9 years for females; at age 60, this 6.2-year advantage for females shrinks to 3.9 years (18.4 years for males vs 22.3 years for females) (Institute for Health Information and Statistics, 2008).

HISTORY OF AGING IN THE CZECH REPUBLIC (CR)

The history of Czech gerontology goes back to the mid-1920s, when Rudolf Richard Eiselt, Professor of the Medical Faculty at Charles University in Prague, founded the first specialized Internal Department for Diseases of Old Age in 1924; several years later, he became chair of the medical faculty. Prof. Eiselt is considered a founder of clinical gerontology in CR. Unfortunately, during World War II (WWII), when Czech universities had to be closed, the department stopped its activity. After the end of WWII, it was never reopened (Pacovský & Virsík, 1986).

In 1958, the Gerontological Section of the Czech Society of Internal Medicine, Czech Medical Association was established by Bohumil Prusík, Professor of Internal Medicine at Charles University and a founding member of the International Association of Gerontology. Later on, in

1962, the Section was renamed the Czech Society of Gerontology. This professional organization led the effort in developing and promoting the field of gerontology, particularly in the medical and social areas. The membership grew slowly, and from the beginning it was multidisciplinary (Přehnal & Topinková, 2001). But it was only during the 1970s that societal interest in aging issues emerged. In 1972, the Czech-Slovak government recognized the needs of the country's rapidly aging population and requested restructuring of care services for elderly and chronically ill citizens. Two years later, a Sub-Department of Gerontology and Geriatrics was established at the Postgraduate School of Medicine in Prague. Its role was primarily to develop the national postgraduate training program in geriatrics for physicians, but also to conceptualize the specialty of geriatrics and define its content and relations to other disciplines. Further activities of the newly established department included methodological leadership in the system of care and services for the elderly and coordination of gerontological research. The work was led by Vladimír Pacovsky, professor of Internal Medicine at Charles University in Prague, who had a long-standing interest in geriatric medicine and who served as chair of the department and president of the Czech Society of Gerontology for almost 20 years. Due to the successful development of gerontology, in 1979 the Czech government accepted the national health program Care for Old and Chronically Ill Citizens. The 1970s were years of major changes in health and social care and service provision for older people: first, nursing homes (e.g., care homes for long-term patients) were established as health care–based facilities for chronically sick people; second, a network of district visiting nurses for old and disabled persons started working under supervision of general practitioners (one nurse per 2–3,000 inhabitants); and third, new forms of board and care homes (old people's homes and sheltered housing) under the social care sector were developed. In addition to Prague, university-based research in social gerontology was promoted by Prof. Rudolf Bures and, later, by his coworkers (V. Zaremba, H. Zavázalová a.o.) in the Department of Social Medicine in the city of Plzen.

But it was only in the early 1980s when demographic aging of the population and a growing number of older persons, together with their increasing needs for medical, rehabilitative, nursing, and community care, sped further development of the field. In 1982, geriatric medicine was approved by the Czech Ministry of Health as an independent medical specialty and a new system of elderly health care and care services was accepted by the government. In 1987, Charles University in Prague started a program of university studies for seniors, University of the

Third Age, which has run very successfully and been copied by other universities.

After the Velvet Revolution in the 1990s, the transformation of the political and economic system was taking place, followed by transformation of other sectors, including education and health care. In 1992, a National Gerontological Program was launched by the Ministry of Health, but due to a shortage of money and low political priority, it was stopped three years later. However, even during its short existence, at least a dozen geriatric centers were financially supported by this program. Transformation of chronic care began, but almost 20 years later is still ongoing, with endless discussions about the optimal division of acute and chronic care provision, responsibility of health and/or social sectors, care quality and methods of financing. Currently, many problems persist, including, for example, an insufficient number of acute geriatric beds (545 beds per 10 million population); shortage of chronic care beds and facilities (9.6 nursing care beds per 1,000 persons 65+); uneven geographic distribution and availability; long waiting lists for placement; low staffing and financing; and low quality of care (Přehnal 1999; Topinková, 2007; Topinková, Szczerbinska, Čeremnych, & Gindin, 2006). Compared to institutional long-term care, new and positive developments occurred in community care. Home care agencies started operating in the early 1990s and currently are providing a full spectrum of home services from home help, Meals on Wheels, personal assistance, home nursing, and, in some regions, even rehabilitative or palliative care and end-of-life care.

Growing interest in health gerontology was reflected in the renaming of the professional society in 1992, to the Czech Society of Gerontology and Geriatrics (CGGS). New goals were established for the near future to respond to the challenges caused by demographic changes, the political transition, and new societal expectations and changing values. The mission of the CGGS (www.cggs.cz) was to improve care practice and care delivery to older people. This mission is being accomplished through complex tasks stemming from medical care, service provision, and education in research and policy:

- Promote and disseminate best clinical practice and care for elderly
- Improve knowledge and skills in the field of geriatrics and gerontology by supporting and organizing professional education in medical care and care delivery
- Promote research, interdisciplinary cooperation and networking, both nationally and internationally, and disseminate and implement research results

- Influence health and social policy for senior citizens by serving as the consulting body for the Ministry of Health, Ministry of Welfare, Czech Chamber of Physicians, and regional authorities
- Combat ageism and age discrimination, improve image and prestige of the specialty and of those working in the field both, among professionals and the public

Since the 1990s, the activities of CSGG have not only encouraged professional activity but also established contacts and cooperation with older people themselves, their carers, voluntary associations, and nongovernmental organizations in the CR and internationally (e.g., Czech Association of Retired People, Life 90, EURAG). More emphasis has been given to mutual dialog with policy-makers, health and social care managers and administrators, media, politicians, and the trade union organization of health workers (Přehnal & Topinková, 2001).

RECENT RESEARCH ON AGING IN THE CZECH REPUBLIC

Gerontological research in the CR can be traced back to the mid-1970s. It was in the area of health gerontology where the first research was conducted and covered the newly developing concept of disability and comprehensive assessment of health, psychological, and social needs of elderly patients. The First Faculty of Medicine of the Charles University in Prague took the lead in gerontological research in the 1980s and 90s, with a broadening spectrum of research areas: medicine (geriatric research), ethical issues, palliative care, gerontological nursing, and public health issues. Though originally based predominantly at medical faculties (Charles University in Prague and Plzen; Masaryk University in Brno), at the turn of the century, sociological and policy research in aging began to grow at the Faculty of Social Sciences of Charles University in Prague, the Faculty of Social Studies of Masaryk University, and several other institutes (Institute of Postgraduate Medical Education in Prague, Research Institute for Labor and Social Affairs in Prague, and Sociological Institute of the Academy of Sciences CR). No research center specializes specifically in biological research on aging in the CR.

Research in Health Gerontology and Geriatric Medicine

Currently, three medical faculties—in Prague, Brno, and Hradec Králové—have established chairs of geriatrics. They are the leading

centers in geriatric research. Other geriatric centers and academic nursing centers conduct research in some areas. Health gerontology research
covers such geriatric syndromes as falls, incontinence, impaired cognition, and disability (First Faculty of Medicine in Prague, Brno), selected
medical conditions, nutrition, and metabolism (Hradec Králové), diabetes mellitus (Brno), dementia (Prague, Brno, Hradec Králové), chronic
wound care (Pardubice), geriatric rehabilitation (Liberec), geriatric
nursing (Prague, Brno, České Budějovice, Ostrava), and public health
issues and health system research (Prague, Plzeň). The safety of pharmacological treatment in older patients has become an important topic,
and a comparative European epidemiological study on drug inappropri-
ateness has been published by researchers from the CR (Fialová et al.,
2005).

Despite the existence of several successful centers and European
projects, research in gerontology in the CR suffers from low financing.
According to Topinková and Přehnal (2002), only 3% of the overall
medical research budget of the Internal Grant Agency of the Czech
Ministry of Health was spent on gerontological research. This situation
was criticized by CGGS and research priorities set for the development
of research facilities. To improve the situation, the CGGS in 2003 began
publishing a quarterly scientific journal, *Česká Geriatrická Revue* (www.
geriatrickarevue.cz), with the intention of bringing the latest reviews
from clinical research and publishing original research articles in the
field of geriatrics and gerontology. However, despite some attempts at
improvement, the situation has not changed substantially in recent
years, and the financing of research on aging is still disproportionately
low, mainly because of (1) overall low resources spent on Czech research
(below 1% of the gross domestic product); (2) comparatively low activity of geriatric research centers; and (3) poorer quality of research
applications and insufficient participation of Czech scientists in international research projects and networking. The situation described is
not exclusively a Czech national trait, but reflects the current situation
in most European countries (Andrews et al., 2006). Therefore, the recognized future goals for national gerontological research are to increase
participation of Czech scientists in European gerontological network
structures, and to promote and support contacts and cooperation with
other research centers in Europe (Topinková & Přehnal, 2002). One of
the recent positive achievements is the involvement of the Department
of Geriatrics, First Faculty of Medicine of Charles University in Prague
in the European research centers network, GERONTONET (Abellan
van Kan, Andrieu, & Vellas, 2007).

Research in Social Gerontology and Sociology of Old Age

Research in social gerontology and/or sociology of old age has a shorter history than research in geriatric medicine. However, the political changes in the 1990s and population aging with steadily increasing life expectancy brought a renewed interest in aging issues. Currently in the CR, four main research areas in social gerontology are identified as general attitudes toward aging and old age; family and intergenerational issues; labor market issues and financial implications of aging; and life conditions of older people.

According to a recent survey of the general public, aging is perceived as a highly unpopular demographic development: only 5% of respondents evaluated aging of society as a "good" or "excellent" process. However, knowledge of the exact percentage of older people in the CR was surprisingly low. The respondents estimated the percentage of people 65 and over as about 30%, more than double the actual situation (14.6%) (Vidovicová & Rabušic, 2003). Another survey showed high prevalence of negative as well as positive stereotypes about older people and old age. Older people are mostly seen as wise, dear, but poor, asexual persons who have too much political influence (Vidovicová, Chromková-Manea, & Rabušic, 2008).

Another problem in the Czech population seems to be ageist attitudes, with up to 66% of women and 57% of men aged 70–80 reporting they have experienced age-differentiating behavior. According to this survey, age discrimination was the most often reported (18% of respondents) and increased between 2003 and 2007. The most common ageist incidents occurred in (1) interpersonal relationships and communication (ageist language, under-representation of old age in media, etc.); (2) the labor market (age being an important criterion for hiring, remuneration, training, and dismissal); and (3) the health-care system (longer waiting periods for older patients, age restrictions on preventive checkups). Two pilot studies were recently published on elder abuse and neglect in institutional settings (Vidovicová & Lorman, 2008; Zpráva, 2007) and on domestic violence against elderly people (Burijánek & Kovařík, 2006). The former study, performed in homes of elderly people in the CR, was looking for reports of different kinds of abuse and neglect from the staff as well as family. Although the situation had improved during the last few years, some issues endangering dignity and integrity of the residents were reported: insufficient privacy (i.e., several residents living in one room, lack of lockers, the impossibility of meeting relatives or friends in a private place, lack of privacy during hygiene) and lack of control over one's life (daily routines, meal selections, etc.) (Vidovicová & Lorman, 2008).

Despite the negative findings in institutions, Czech older people seem to be well positioned within their primary networks and communities. According to Vidovicová and Rabušic (2003), nearly 70% of people aged 45–59 years frequently help their older parents. Such close relationships are enabled by the relatively low mobility of the Czech population. The survey showed that about 26% of children live in the same flat with parents, 53% in proximity within 30 minutes' reach, and only 21% families are separated by longer distances. Even though families tend to be close and supportive, separate living is unambiguously the most preferred option in old age, even if health is deteriorating.

In 2002, Kuchařová, Rabušic, and Ehrenbergerová published the first large survey on general life conditions of elderly Czech citizens, Life in Old Age. This population cohort was confronted with deep and rapid social and economic changes brought by the Velvet Revolution in 1989, which started the transformation from a socialist to a capitalist regime. Elderly people perceive the following as the most problematic: difficulty keeping up with technological innovations; some activities becoming unaffordable; difficulty understanding the political and social context of events; and difficulty dealing with administrative tasks. The most preferred activities are passive forms of entertainment: watching TV, reading newspapers or magazines, followed by "meeting relatives and friends," and working in the garden or farming.

According to the Labour Force Survey performed regularly by the Czech Statistical Office (www.czso.cz), less than 10% of the 60+ population is involved in the active labor market. However, attitudes about pensioning are mixed: some preferred early retirement, but 35% of respondents supported continuing employment after reaching the official retirement age. These mixed attitudes have been referred to as the Czech retirement paradox (Rabušic, 2004; Vidovicová et. al., 2008). As the body of research grows, new projects are being financed from governmental resources. Some of the new topics involve financial literacy and preparedness for retirement (Research Institute for Labour and Social Affairs in Prague, www.rilsa. cz) and pension surveys carried out by the Ministry of Labour and Social Affairs (www.mpsv.cz); care of older parents by their daughters and sons (Přidalová, 2007a, 2007b; Veselá, 2003); older people and computer literacy (Herzmann, 2008); lifelong learning (Rabušic, 2006); and quality of life in old age (Dragomirecká, 2007). Complex and broader studies concerned with different areas of life conditions of the older generation are rare and, as far as we know, no longitudinal studies on social aspects of aging in the CR have been done.

EDUCATION IN GERONTOLOGY IN THE CZECH REPUBLIC

Specialty of Geriatrics and Old-Age Psychiatry (Psychogeriatrics)

Since the 1970s, training of physicians in geriatrics has been recognized as an important issue in health education. Since 1974, the newly established Sub-Chair of Geriatrics and Gerontology at the Institute of Postgraduate Medical Education in Prague has provided postgraduate education and training to all Czech physicians specializing in geriatric medicine. The Board certification started in 1986 and since then, the number of board-certified geriatricians has grown steadily. Over the years, more than 240 geriatricians have completed geriatric fellowship training and board certification. Currently 90 fellows are in training (Topinková & Neuwirth, 2004). The estimated number of geriatricians needed in the country is 400. During the last decade, postgraduate training of physicians has been undergoing restructuring. Geriatrics remains an independent specialty, and since 2000, a Czech representative has sat on the Board of the European Union of Medical Specialties—Geriatric Medicine Section (UEMS—GMS). Its main goal is to standardize and harmonize medical education in Europe so that the free migration of physicians would be possible. This mission is being accomplished by publishing a unified European curriculum, requirements for accreditation of training centers, and continuing medical education. Further work is underway in preparation for a European board certification in geriatrics. In the CR, a new fellowship program has been developed compatible with UEMS—GMS recommendations. Psychogeriatrics (old-age psychiatry) is another distinct medical specialty in the CR, but the number of specialists is very low. Continuing medical education in geriatric medicine for geriatricians and other medical specialists is ensured by several bodies: the Institute of Postgraduate Medical Education, Chamber of Czech Physicians, universities, and CGGS, through courses, clinical training programs, and congresses. Recently, the importance of training general practitioners (GPs) in basic geriatric knowledge has been recognized, and the CR participated in an international project to develop and pilot nationwide training of GPs (Krajčík, Gabanyi, & Topinková, 2006). A new geriatric textbook and guidelines for GPs were published recently (Topinková, 2005b; Topinková et al., 2007).

Undergraduate Training in Gerontology and Geriatrics

Undergraduate training of health professionals has a much shorter history than professional training. Officially recognized courses in geriatric medicine and social gerontology for medical students were introduced in Prague in 1991. The situation is changing very slowly; despite the international and national recommendation to establish independent chairs and clinical departments of geriatrics at each medical faculty, only three out of seven medical faculties follow these recommendations (Topinková, 2005a). The barriers to nationwide dissemination of geriatric teaching programs are the low number of potential faculty, the low priority of the field, and insufficient scientific production. A well-established program in social gerontology for medical students exists at the Medical Faculty of Charles University in Plzen (Zavázalová, 2001). In recent years, undergraduate training of other paramedical staff (e.g., nurses, occupational and physiotherapists) was introduced at several universities. Its acceptance and results are promising (Mádlová, Neuwirth, & Topinková, 2006). An important achievement in 2002 was the accreditation of the first research Postgraduate Doctoral Studies in Gerontology at Charles University in Prague for students from different backgrounds—medicine, biological sciences, and social sciences. The program will enable the promotion of research in gerontology and geriatrics. This is an important way to attract young students to the field and improve the academic position of geriatric medicine as a scientific discipline. The First Faculty of Medicine of Charles University in Prague is participating in the international European Master's Studies in Gerontology program (EuMaG; www.eumag.org), offering training for Czech and foreign students.

CURRENT PUBLIC POLICY ISSUES IN AGING

More than 70% of the Czech adult population believes the government is significantly or even fully responsible for caring for older people, while only 7% in 2001 said the government has little or no responsibility in this area (Vidovicová & Rabušic, 2003). Government intervention is most expected in health care and community care and services. These trends persist as stereotypes inherited from the previous regime, when the state was providing care "from the cradle to the grave" and held full responsibility for the social security of its citizens (Rabušic, 2004). Another important issue researched in several public opinion polls is the participation of the elderly in work after retirement. In recent years, policy has changed in favor of a prolonged working life. After retirement age, there is now more flexibility, enabling one to receive a pension and work concomitantly, or to postpone retirement to a later age with an increased pension. However, some would say that barriers in the number of suitable jobs and age discrimination on the labor market still exist. An important milestone was the adoption of the National Program for Preparation for Population Ageing 2003–2007 (NPPA) in May 2002 by the government, which set goals for responding to population aging and to the newly emerging needs of older citizens. The declared goal was to "support the development of society for people of all ages, enabling people to age in dignity and safety and to continue their contribution to the life of the entire society as respectable citizens." Unfortunately, upon the final evaluation in 2007, NPPA was considered ineffective because its goals were mainly declarative and there was insufficient political support on the national as well as regional level to accomplish necessary changes. In January 2008, a new plan for the period 2008–2012 was launched by the government with the main goal of improving quality of life of seniors. This newly adopted National Program is based on the following principles: lifelong and gender-sensitive approach; cooperation of the government, local authorities, and NGOs; intergenerational relations and cohesion; special focus on disadvantaged and frail groups; reaching for social and geographical equity, individual responsibility; and evidence-based decision-making. Building on these principles, the Program aims to achieve five strategic goals: (1) active aging; (2) age-friendly environment and community; (3) improvements in health and health care in old age; (4) support for family and family carers; and (5) social empowerment and human rights protection. It is hoped that this program will advance more successfully than the NPPA.

Apart from the described governmental national programs, several important changes have taken place in the course of the last 10 years, significantly influencing the lives of Czech seniors. The transformation of social services led to significant changes in their financing. One of the very positive aspects of this reform was concern with the quality of services. A new concept of quality standards was introduced, and accreditation of service providers took place. This in turn substantially improved the quality of social services. Second, reform of social benefit systems took place by changing eligibility for some benefits, particularly with the new methods for assessing disability and changing disability allowances. Probably the most important reform for future pensioners is the ongoing reform of public finances in which pension reform plays a major role. The sustainability of the current pay-as-you-go pension system and concerns for its future have been ongoing since the 1990s. Given the political difficulties involved, it has seemed almost impossible to find a consensus across the political spectrum and among the many stakeholders on how to transform the pension system. Recent development has turned the discussions from total abolition of the pay-as-you-go system to moderate modifications, such as (1) introducing individual savings through private pension funds; (2) a gradual increase in the statutory retirement age; (3) prolongation of the social security payment period; and other specific actions (e.g., support of older unemployed persons). The statutory retirement age is increasing gradually for both men and women (in 2006, it was 62 for men and 57–61 for women, according to the number of children), and it is expected to reach 65 for both sexes in the next 10 years. However, the actual age of leaving the labor market remains rather lower than these targets, due often to unemployment. Surprisingly, gender differences in statutory retirement age are considered highly just and nondiscriminatory in the public opinion (Rabušic, 2004; Vidovicová & Rabušic, 2003). Financial security of older people also has been debated in relation to old age poverty. About 27% of Czech pensioners claimed to be poor, according to Kuchařová et al. (Kuchařová, Rabušic, & Ehrenbergerová, 2002), but poverty in late life is actually not that common. The average pension in the CR is rather low, only a little above 40% of the average salary, and for 70% of pensioners, it is the only source of income. Therefore, after retirement, older people report a significant decrease in lifestyle. Despite the fact that the average pension is about US$520 per month, much above the official subsistence level (US$280 per month) (Bulletin No 22, 2007), older people can be regarded as the population segment at the highest risk of social exclusion.

Since older people are the major consumers of health services, liberal reform of the health care system influences their life significantly. At the health-system level, a wide spectrum of specialized services for older people exists in the CR (acute care geriatrics, post-acute and long-term care and nursing, outpatient geriatric clinics, home care, and palliative care). However, inequalities exist in the distribution throughout the country, and accessibility of some services is rather poor. Despite the national health insurance for a majority of elderly persons (97%), there is a rather high and increasing out-of-pocket co-payment of about 12% of total medical spending.

REFERENCES

Abellan van Kan, G., Andrieu, S., & Vellas, B. (2007). GerontoNet: A network of excellence for clinical trials with geriatric patients. *Journal of Nutrition, Health and Aging, 11*(3), 251–253.

Andrews, G. R., Sidorenko, A. V., Gutman, G., Gray, J. E., Anisimov, V. N., Bez-rukov, V. V., et al. (2006). Research on ageing: Priorities for the European region. *Advances of Gerontology, 18*(1), 7–14.

Burijánek, J., Kovařík, J.(Eds.). (2006). *Domácí násilí na mužích a seniorech.* [Domestic violence on men and seniors]. Prague, Kroměříž, Czech Republic: Triton.

Dragomirecká, E. (2007). *Prediktory kvality života ve vyšším věku* [Predictors of quality of life in higher age]. Dissertation, Faculty of Philosophy, Charles University, Prague, Czech Republic.

Fialová, D., Topinková, E., Gambassi, G., Finne-Soveri, H., Jónsson, P., Carpenter, I., et al. (2005). Potentially inappropriate medication use among elderly home care patients in Europe. *Journal of American Medical Association, 293*(11), 1348–1358.

Herzmann, J. (2008). *Spojitost mezi počítačovou gramotností a kvalitou zaměstnání* [Connection between computer literacy and job quality]. Conference presentation, SENIOŘI—NAŠE ŠANCE!? Diskriminace starších lidí v ČR aneb Antidiskriminační zákon nebo mainstreaming? May 19, 2008. Prague, Czech Republic.

Institute for Health Information and Statistics (UZIS). (2008). *Demographic situation in the Czech Republic in 2007, Aktuální Informace No. 11.* Prague, Czech Republic: UZIS.

Krajčík, Š., Gabanyi, J., & Topinková, E.(2006). Teaching geriatric medicine in primary care—Experience of Slovakia, Hungary and Czech Republic. *Journal of Nutrition, Health and Aging, 10*(4), 341.

Kuchařová, V., Rabušic, L., & Ehrenbergerová, L. (2002). *Život ve stáří. Zpráva o výsledcích empirického šetření* [Life in old age. Report on results of an empirical survey]. Prague, Czech Republic: Research Institute for Labour and Social Affairs, Socioklub.

Mádlová, P., Neuwirth, J., & Topinková, E. (2006). Efektivita výuky teoretické i klinické gerontologie u studentů 1. Lékařské fakulty UK v Praze [Effectiveness of teaching gerontology and geriatrics to students of the 1st Faculty of Medicine, Charles University in Prague]. *Časopis lékařů českých, 145*(9), 733–737.

Ministry of Labor and Social Affairs. (2008). *Quality of life in old age: National programme of preparation for ageing for 2008–2012.* Prague, Czech Republic: Author.

Pacovský, V., & Virsík, K. (1986). Vývoj české a slovenské gerontologie [History of Czech and Slovak gerontology]. *Praktický Lékař, 66*(7), 233–235.

Přehnal, J. (1999). Péče o geriatrické a chronicky nemocné pacienty [Care for geriatric and chronically ill patients]. *Zdravotnické noviny, 48*(8), 1–2.

Přehnal, J. & Topinková, E. (2001). Czech Society of Gerontology and Geriatrics, Czech Medical Association—Its history and future. Abstract, 17th World Congress of Gerontology. *Gerontology, 47*(Suppl. 1), 6.

Přidalová, M. (2007a). *Mezi solidaritou a konfliktem: Zkušenost pečujících dcer a synů* [Between solidarity and conflict: Experience of caring daughters and sons]. Sociální studia, Brno, Czech Republic: FSS Masarykovy university.

Přidalová, M. (2007b). *Pečující dcery a pečující synové—rozhodnutí, se kterým můžu žít* [Caring daughters and caring sons—decision I can live with]. IVRIS Working Papers 4, 1-116. Brno, Czech Republic: Institut pro výzkum integrace a reprodukce společnosti.

Rabušic, L. (2004). Why are they all so eager to retire (on transition to retirement in the Czech Republic)? *Czech Sociological Review, 40*(3), 319–342.

Rabušic, L. (2006). Vzdělávání dospělých v předseniorském a seniorském věku. *Sborník prací filozofické fakulty brněnské univerzity* [Adult education in předseniorském and senior age. Proceedings of the work of the Brno University Faculty of Arts]. Vol. U 11 (11), 79–99U. Brno, Czech Republic: Masarykova univerzita.

Topinková, E. (2005a). Doporučení pro pregraduální vzdělávání lékařů v geriatrii v Evropě. Závěry pracovní skupiny Evropské akademie nadace Yuste 2004 [Recommendations for undergraduate education of physicians in geriatrics in Europe]. *Česká geriatrická revue, 3*(1), 34–38.

Topinková, E. (2005b). *Geriatrie pro praxi* [Geriatrics for practice]. Prague, Czech Republic: Galén.

Topinková, E. (2007). Co je a co není geriatrie [What is and what is not geriatrics]. *Zdravotnické noviny, Lékařské listy, 56*(12), 3–5.

Topinková, E., Červený, R., Doleželová, I., Jurašková, B., Holmerová, I., & Kalvach, Z. (Eds.) (2007). *Geriatrie–Doporučený diagnostický a léčebný postup pro všeobecné praktické lékaře.* [Geriatrics—Guideline for general practitioners]. Prague, Czech Republic: Společnost všeobecného lékařství ČLS JEP.

Topinková, E., & Neuwirth, J. (2004). Třicet let postgraduálního vzdělávání v gerontologii a geriatrii v České republice [Thirty years of postgraduate training in gerontology and geriatrics in the Czech Republic]. *Česká geriatrická revue, 2*(1), 6–12.

Topinková, E., & Přehnal, J. (2002). Prioritizing research on ageing in a global context: The agenda in Europe. In *Valencia forum, book of abstracts* (pp. 128–129). Valencia, Spain: International Association of Gerontology.

Topinková, E., Szczerbinska, K., Čeremnych, J., & Gindin, J. (2006). Development of geriatric services in the Czech Republic, Poland and Lithuania during 1990–2000. *Journal of Nutrition, Health and Aging, 10*(4), 322–323.

Veselá, J. (2003). *Sociální služby poskytované seniorům v domácnostech* [Social services provided to seniors at home]. Prague, Czech Republic: Research Institute for Labour and Social Affairs.

Vidovicová, L., Chromková-Manea, B. E., & Rabušic, L. (2008). Only fools rush in? On transition to retirement. In *People, population change and policies: Lessons from the population policy acceptance study—Volume 2: Demographic Knowledge-Gender-Ageing* (pp. 267–288). The Hague, The Netherlands: Springer.

Vidovicová, L., & Lorman, J. (2008). *Život v domovech pro seniory* [Life in seniors' homes]. Prague, Czech Republic: Úřad vlády ČR (Governmental Office CR).

Vidovicová, L., & Rabušic, L. (2003). *Senioři a sociální opatření v oblasti stárnutí v pohledu české veřejnosti* [Seniors and social measures in the area of aging reflected by Czech public]. Prague, Czech Republic: Research Institute for Labour and Social Affairs.

Zavázalová, H. (Ed.) (2001). *Vybranné kapitoly ze sociální gerontologie* [Selected chapters from social gerontology]. Prague, Czech Republic: Univerzita Karlova.

Zpráva z návštěv zařízení sociálních služeb pro seniory [Report from social care facilities for seniors] (2007). Veřejný ochránce práv—ombudsman. Retrieved June 28, 2008, from http://www.ochrance.cz/dokumenty/doku ment.php?back=/cinnost/ochrana.php&doc=780

ACKNOWLEDGMENT

The work of Lucie Vidovicová was supported by the Institute for Research on Social Reproduction and Integration (MSM 002 1622408).

16

▪ ▪ ■ ▪ ▪

Denmark

Karen Munk

Denmark is a small country, one-tenth the size of Sweden and one-eighth that of Germany. It is one of the five Scandinavian welfare states (besides Norway, Sweden, Finland, and Iceland), and part of the European Union. Being a welfare state means a high level of equality and rights to common goods such as equal access to the health system, community care, retirement and disablement pension, day-care institutions for children, unemployment support, and education. The other side of the coin is relatively high taxes, but one is spared expenses on health insurances, education fees, and fear of doctors' bills if one gets ill. For the last 10 years, the Danish economic system has become world famous because of the unusual combination of high taxes and a very flexible and well-educated labor force; the so-called flexicurity economy. It is easy for companies to get rid of superfluous manpower, because the state guarantees a minimum salary to the unemployed, and the labor force dares to take chances with new employment areas because of this security. It has been difficult for international economists to understand how Denmark has managed to become one of the richest countries in the world with that system, in contrast to what is dictated by the economic textbooks (Albæk, Eliason, & Nørgaard, 2008).

Denmark has few natural resources. Apart from farm production, which means increasingly less to the economy, only oil from the North Sea gives a substantial—but not ever-lasting—contribution to the economy. This means that in the long run, the economy is dependent on a highly qualified labor force. In 2008, Denmark reached the highest level of employed persons in modern times, and the number of unemployed is about 45,600 persons (below 1%); both the number and the proportion of unemployed persons are historically low. However, being a trade nation, the global crisis also has consequences for Denmark. The number of unemployed is still historically low, but was increasing at the beginning of 2009. Due to a healthy economy, it is estimated that Denmark has a good chance of going through the crisis without overly serious consequences for the population. For the moment, however, nobody knows how deep and protracted the crisis is going to be.

Culturally, the Danish population was originally very homogenous, but through the last decades, a substantial amount of immigration has taken place, from Asian and not least from Muslim countries; the Danish population now also consists of about 478,000 (8.8%) ethnic minorities (immigrants and descendants) out of a population totaling 5,489,022, which includes ethnic elderly who will spend the last part of their lives in Denmark. The growth of the Danish population during the last half of the 1980s and the 1990s was primarily caused by immigration.

DEMOGRAPHY

As in the rest of Europe, Denmark's percentage of old-age population is high. But in contrast to southern Europe, Denmark has a relatively high birthrate, in spite of the fact that it also has the highest percentage in Europe of women in the labor market; this relatively high fertility and high labor-force participation of women are partly due to an extensive organization of day-care institutions for children. However, the relatively higher percentage of births and of immigrants cannot compensate for the growing imbalance in the age structure created by the high growth of the elderly population. A substantial number of persons born in the 1940s (the highest number of 60–64-year-olds ever in the country's history) are leaving the labor market these days; due to relatively low birthrates (20–24-year-olds: 303,797; 15 % fewer than 10 years ago), Denmark is having an increasing problem with vacant jobs, especially in hospitals and nursing homes (Statistics of Denmark, 2008).

The 60+ population in 2007 constituted about 22.5 % of the total population, and in 2030 will be about 26 %. The 80+ population reached 4.3% in 2007, will reach 5% in 2030, and 10 % in 2050. Table 16.1 provides the percentage of the total population for three age groups for the year 2007 and projected percentages for the year 2030. Demographic predictions say that half the girls born in Denmark in the 2000s will reach 100 years

Table 16.1
Percentage distribution of age groups, 2007–2030

Years	2007	2030
0–59	77.5	74
60–79	18.2	21
80+	4.3	5

Source: Statistics of Denmark, 2008

of age, assuming that the conditions of life continue in the same track as seen in recent years. The number of 90-year-olds is 355,000, and the number of centenarians was about 731 in 2008. Most of the 90+ live alone. It is a general pattern that the oldest old live alone, mostly as widows or widowers, for the last years of their lives.

The numbers illustrate the aging of Denmark. It is estimated, however, that the aging process of Danish society is not going to culminate until 2040, with a further reduction of approximately 1% of persons below 60 years, and increase of the 60+ group of 1.4%.

ROLES, STATUS, AND PROBLEMS
OF THE AGED

At the beginning of the 1980s, the Danish Parliament introduced an early retirement pension to the Danish population as a means of solving the problem of the many unemployed young people; the government policy offered the aging members of the work force an opportunity to enjoy early retirement and freedom. However, the popularity of this arrangement has now become a burden to Danish society, because of a decrease of persons in the work force. For the moment, politicians are offering economic and other kinds of incentives to encourage the elderly to stay in the labor market longer. These policies indicate a clear shift in attitudes to working elderly. Earlier prejudices about elderly persons being poor laborers are very quickly disappearing. This means that the status of the elderly has improved very much in recent years. The effect is that the pension age is going up, so far to 62.3 years. As of 2008, the official retirement age is 65 years. A pension reform in 2007 introduced a dynamic formal retirement limit, which will follow the demographic development of aging; every five years, Parliament will estimate whether the formal retirement age should be gradually changed—due to demographic development— and every change will be only one year at a time. The gradual change implemented means that the retirement age of 65 years is maintained for people born before January 1, 1959, and gradually increases to a limit of 67 for people born before July 1, 1960. A projection of a gradual increase means that the formal retirement age in 2100 is going to be 75.5 years. Likewise, the early retirement pension will gradually disappear.

Due to tax reductions, pensions, and savings over approximately the last 30 years, a substantial proportion of the new elderly in Denmark are very well off; they typically experience no difference in income after retirement. Because of many other kinds of new pensions related to the labor market, only 20% of retirees receive the full income-related pension from the state; these 20% are the poorest elderly in Denmark. Among those, we find 60% of the unmarried or widowed elderly. About 44% of elderly on public pension only live alone. The poorest elderly are more likely to be living alone, and they are the most vulnerable to actual increases in the prices of food and energy. During the last 20 years, we have experienced a yet-larger gap in wealth among Danish elderly.

With the growth of wealth among the elderly, there is also a growing number of elderly who own their home. From 1981 to 2006, there was an increase from 47% to 52% of elderly owning their house. This growth is found among the young elderly of 65–79 years. Owning is one thing, but living by yourself is another; 77% of the 80+ live by themselves, and the other 23% live in nursing homes or special protected homes for the elderly, where they can live on their own but receive help from nurses and home help when needed. The elderly in Denmark have a global record in receiving free public home help; not because they are less healthy or less wealthy than in other countries, but because home help is free and is an obligatory public service to every frail citizen in Denmark.

There seems to be a close connection between low income and bad health. Not surprisingly, it is this group that receives most help from society. However, 80% of the 65+ do not receive home help at all, and every second person above the 80+ mark does not receive any help.

In the last 10 years, the family has become more important in relation to identity and in receiving practical help. In general, elderly Danes have supportive relatives, but the oldest old are more often alone and lonely, because they survive their relatives.

Not only are still more elderly living good, healthy lives, but there is also a growing number of elderly with chronic illnesses due to an increase in medical treatment. Two-thirds of the capacity of the medical wards is used by elderly patients. However, while the need for geriatric medicine is growing due to more elderly and to still more treatment possibilities, geriatric professionals (nurses and doctors) are shrinking in number. The age limit for a geriatric patient is no longer 65 years, but 75–80 years.

PROGRAMS FOR THE AGED

As a welfare state, Denmark considers it a common good that elderly who are in need of different kinds of help can receive it freely. The overall policy in Denmark is to help the elderly to maintain an active and independent life in their own home as long as possible. If this is not possible in a person's own home, the public administration is obliged to provide a residency in a nursing home or a protected elderly home. This was fixed by a number of social laws, primarily throughout the 20th century. The services are administrated and provided by the local governments of the municipalities. In the 1990s, there were further initiatives related to prevention. Parliament decided that the municipalities should be obliged to offer every person over 75 a prevention visit twice a year. In general, it is also public policy to offer frail and ill elderly rehabilitation.

Home Care

Free home-help services are provided by the municipality for more than 20% of people aged 65 and older. According to individual assessments, normally made by home nurses, the services are provided, including individual practical assistance with personal hygiene, dressing, and cleaning the most necessary parts of the home. There is a one-year educational scheme for home helpers, based on an education reform called social- and health-helpers. People who participate in the educational program are obliged to assist the elderly to an independent life if possible and to not provide unneeded assistance, which can damage the rehabilitation process of the home-help recipient. Because more elderly are in need of much help and due to work force shortages, the procedure for individual assessment and eligibility has become stricter in the last 10 years. A part of this restriction is that the home help no longer cooks for clients. Individual cooking has been replaced by Meals on Wheels. Apart from home help for cleaning and personal hygiene, it is also possible to receive home nursing, if needed.

Aides

Being able to live in one's own home with frailties and illnesses can sometimes only be possible with help from aides, which is provided for free, regardless of the economic situation of the elderly person, from the municipality. In cases where the person has to bear part of the cost, but has no means, financial support can be granted from the social welfare. In all municipalities are established centers for aides.

Housing

In the effort of supporting the elderly to have an independent life, Parliament has made it possible to give practical and financial assistance to frail elderly in remodeling their houses or creating minor alterations to make the home more suitable for persons with different frailties or handicaps. If the arrangement involves a considerable expense in modifying the elderly's own house and if an improvement increases the value of the home, the support will be granted in the form of an interest-free loan. The local government can also take over the payment of taxes on real property, converting them to a mortgage debt, if there is equity in the house.

Nursing Homes and Other Kind of Homes

The local government is also responsible for providing special housing for elderly people with handicaps. The policy objective is in the long run to remove traditional impersonal elderly institutions in the country. In 1987, Parliament decided that there should no more institutions built for the elders in Denmark, and that every older person's home should as a minimum have 67 square meter of space with two rooms, kitchen, and bathroom. Every frail older person should have his or her own home and should not be institutionalized in the last part of life.

There are four kinds of public homes for the elderly: nursing home apartments, "protected houses," nursing houses, and elderly houses. The nursing home apartments constitute the traditional old-age institutions, with one room per resident, which are going to disappear. They have a nursing staff and connected services, such as welfare services, and various types of health services, such as physiotherapy, occupational therapy, and chiropody. The protected houses are situated near old-age institutions and almost all of them are connected to the same nursing staff and other services. The nursing houses have the same facilities as the nursing home apartments. The difference is that these houses are meant to be successors to the traditional old-fashioned elderly institutions. The last category is elderly houses for elderly and for younger handicapped persons. They are organized in a way that makes them more comfortable to live in. These houses are meant for persons who can manage without help from a nursing

staff person. Typically, these new kinds of elderly homes are built in connection with day-care centers where it is possible to buy a daily meal and
participate in diverse activities. About 23% of the elderly aged 80+ are
living in some of these kinds of elderly homes.

Since 1987, the concept of an institution has gradually changed into
a home in the neighborhood of a 24-hour home-nursing centre. This
means that nursing homes in most municipalities have been changed
into centers with combined individual elderly apartments and home-
nursing centers with 24-hour services.

Health Services

The National Health Service is run by regions. The general practitioner (GP) is paid by the region both according to fee-per-capita and
fee-for-services. Only a small percentage of the population has chosen
not to join an arrangement with free appointments with a particular GP.
Normally, the GP is the gatekeeper to other health services.

Geriatric hospital departments have been developed at several hospitals, replacing the former long-term care units, with more emphasis on
short-term stay and on acute and sub-acute services to the elderly patient with multiple medical problems. Further, there was also an extension of geropsychiatric services in the 1990s, and a new kind of clinic is
now being offered to the elderly to detect early dementia, the so-called
memory clinics.

In general, there is also a growing optimism in the health service related
to initiating all kinds of treatment for the elderly. There is a new understanding that the prognosis of elderly patients depends on their clinical
condition and not on their formal age. This more aggressive treatment
attitude has resulted in a yearly decrease in the death rate of 1–2% among
the elderly over 80 and 90. However, although geriatric medicine is a
growing and modernized field, it is difficult to recruit enough doctors to
the discipline (Winding, 2008a, 2008b).

GERONTOLOGY

The first scientific society of old-age research was founded in 1946 by
medical doctors only, and for many years Danish gerontology was a single
science. But after the 1960s, the Danish Gerontological Society developed into a cross-scientific society with the following disciplines represented: psychology, sociology, anthropology, history, economy, nursing
science, occupational therapy, architectural science, and so on. All kinds

of sciences that have anything to contribute to practical and theoretical knowledge about aging and old age are now welcome under the umbrella of the Danish Gerontological Society. The Society publishes a quarterly on scientific and practical gerontological issues and arranges Nordic conferences every 10 years, taking turns with the other gerontological societies in Scandinavia.

RESEARCH AND EDUCATION

Since the 1940s, different kinds of gerontological research on biological, clinical, epidemiological, psychological, and social issues have been carried out at universities and research institutes, beginning with geriatric medicine, cross-cultural social studies, and longitudinal population studies. Especially worth mentioning is the Glostrup Population Studies, founded in 1964, examining cohorts from 1897 and on.

In the 1990s and at the beginning of 2000, four research centers on aging and old age were founded. The metropolitan hospitals and the municipality of Copenhagen run a Centre for Research and Development in society's efforts for the elderly, with the agenda of studying the effect of new institutional initiatives related to care and rehabilitation. At the University of Southern Denmark, the Centre for Research in Old Age is conducting research on the process of aging with the National Register of twins as a database, and is studying Danish centenarians. Now the Centre has made an extended common data platform, the Biobank at the Department of Social Medicine, University of Copenhagen, studying the influence of social conditions and inflammations in middle adulthood to aging; and with the Centre for Research in gerocytology, University of Aarhus, is studying the aging of human cells. Further, a Centre for Healthy Aging opened in late November 2008 at the University of Copenhagen, with a huge grant from private funding. This Centre is an extension of the Biobank, with several new subprograms run by medical doctors, psychologists, and ethnologists. The medical doctors and psychologists focus on causes of early aging, while the ethnologists are concerned with lifespan and concepts of health and the good life. With the founding of the new center, one of the researchers, Kirsten Avlund, Ph.D., was promoted to become the first professor of gerontology at the University of Copenhagen. In 2000, the Centre for Research in Gero-odontology was founded at the University of Copenhagen with the purpose of doing research in oral health and aging.

In 1992, the first chair and Centre for Geropsychology was established at the Institute of Psychology, the University of Aarhus, and the

University Hospital of Psychiatry in Risskov, Aarhus. The agenda of the Centre was to study healthy mental development and mental illness in old age. Unfortunately, the Centre was closed on February 1, 2009, because the two institutions behind it did not want to support it with the necessary economic resources. However, the chair in geropsychology at the Institute of Psychology is maintained. In 2007, the Centre published the first textbook in Danish on geropsychology, meant for doctors, psychologists, and students.

The Institute of Psychology, University of Aarhus, is the only university in Denmark where students in psychology are introduced to the psychology of aging. In general, it has been difficult to establish education programs in gerontology. In 2004, a master's degree in gerontology was established at the University of Southern Denmark, but only one group of about 20 persons completed the degree in 2006. However, in the following years, there were not students enough to continue, so the program was stopped after two years.

REFERENCES

Albæk, E., Eliason, C. L., & Nørgaard, A. S. (Eds.) (2008). *Crisis, miracles and beyond: Negotiated adaptation of the Danish welfare state.* Aarhus Universitets Forlag: Statistics of Denmark.

Winding, K. (2008a). Vokseværk i geriatrien [Growth of geriatrics]. *UFL, 13*(42), 3304–3305.

Winding, K. (2008b). Mangel på geriatere [Lack of geriatricians]. *UFL, 13* (42), 3305.

17

Egypt

Abdel Moneim Ashour

DEMOGRAPHY

Egypt is suffering from three demographic problems that determine all other aspects related to aging and the status of the aged in Egypt. First, its population growth rate is far beyond the capacity of the country to contain it. Second, there is a concentration of the population in urban areas that impedes proper development and creates a false feeling of overcrowding. Third, the high dependency ratio and illiteracy rate impede productivity and efficiency.

This dangerous demographic situation has its roots in a diminishing mortality rate, coupled with a rising or stable birthrate in the last four or five decades. The crowding is exemplified by the fact that 99% of the population live on 4% of the land. Some urban areas now have monumental density figures. That 29% of all persons over 10 years of age are illiterate tells how helpless this population is in facing problems of development in a modern world. The current policy trend is to improve the quality of the existing labor force as an immediate rescue measure. As for long-term policy, there are indicators that the population growth will slow down as a consequence of several factors.

The Egyptian population census of 1897 recorded about 9 million people. This number doubled to 18 million by 1947; that is, in 50 years. It took only 29 years to double again, to 36 million by 1976. This number has doubled again, to over 70 million by 2006. However, the annual growth rate has dropped from 2.8% in 1976, to 2.05% in 2006. This is because both the death rate has dropped (from 9 per 1,000 in 1976 to 6.3 per 1,000) and the birthrate has dropped from 29 per 1,000 to 26 per 1,000.

In 1927, the urban to rural ratio was 27 to 73. In 1986, it became 44 to 56. In 2006, it was 42 to 58. This urbanization from the country to the cities was the result of socioeconomic necessity and is a controversial issue. At any rate, it is not healthy and is an impediment to development (Al-Housseini, 1985). One result of this concentration in a few urban centers is overcrowding. Density is about 24 persons per square kilometer in Cairo City, which accommodates 10% of the population. The total population per square kilometer is 78.7.

The 2006 census shows a very youthful profile: younger than 5, 15%; 5–15, 44%; 60 and over, 6.3%. The dependency ratio (below 15+ above 64) divided by 15–64 years of age = .77.

The illiteracy rate among those over 10 years of age has diminished from 84% in 1937 to 49% in 1986 to 29% in 2006. However, the female illiteracy rate is about 1.5 times that of males. The rural illiteracy rate is almost twice that of the urban rate.

DEMOGRAPHICS OF THE AGED

The percentage of aged (60+) among the total population has increased from 5.1 in 1950 to 6.1 in 1990 and 6.3 in 2006. The figures projected by the United Nations show an increase from 2.9 million in 1985 to 10.6 million in 2025, an increase of 266%. The proportion that will be 60+ will increase to 11.3 by 2025.

This aging trend is also shown in the following indicators. The ratio of 60+ to the total population in 2025 (11.1%) will be higher than the average for all of Africa and equal to the average for all developed countries in 1950. The median age was about 20 up until 1990, but the expected age in 2025 will be 31 years, which is close to the world average.

The rise in the proportion of aged will be caused by a drop in the fertility ratio from 15 per 1,000 in 1990 to 12 per 1,000 in 2025. Some resources will have to be shifted from care of children to care of the aged.

Life expectancies at birth have also been rising: for males, it has increased from 60.0 in 2000 to 68.3 in 2006, and for females has increased from 64.4 to 73.6.

The Aged Labor Force

The labor force over 60 constitutes about 21% of the aged population, but only 5% of the nation's labor force. About 60% of the aged in the labor force are 60 to 64 years old.

The majority of the aged labor force (56%) is self-employed and works in agriculture or hunting (60%). This is quite different from the national profile, which shows about 58% working for wages.

Income

The main sources of income are work (37% for men; 13% for women), pensions (31% for men; 29% for women), savings (18% for men and for women), and children (11% for men; 18% for women).

The pensionable age in Egypt is 60. Besides pensions, some elders receive a compensation lump sum. A 10-month salary as indemnity is also available to some retiring persons. The elders receiving retirement pensions are entitled to other benefits, such as reduced rates on the railways and loans. The official policy is to increase the overall and minimum rates of pensions and to assure better increases with inflation.

The elders not covered by insurance schemes may apply to one of two social aid schemes (Act No. 30/1977 or Act 112/1080). However, the amount received is only nominal.

Health Insurance

Medical insurance was introduced to Egypt by Act. No. 75/1964, as an offshoot of the social security system. Pensioners contribute to the health insurance scheme by just 1% of their pension. Eighty-three percent of government employees and 31% of the public and private sector employees are covered by this system.

On the whole, elders do not use this system much because the service is sparse. The trends are to increase the resources of the system and use modern geriatric concepts to improve the quality of care.

Homes and Clubs for the Aged

Before 1900, Egypt had only three homes for elders. The number increased to 81 by 1980. There has been no increase since then. These homes accommodate less than 1% of elders 60+.

There are also over 50 day centers for the elderly and over 60 nongovernmental local organizations working especially with elders in different fields of service.

Informal Support System

The laws of Islam rule that one is legally obligated to support one's parents and grandparents. This obligation works the other way around, too. These principles are behind the prominent role played by sons in providing support for the aged. About half of Egyptian elders receive income from their children.

Elders can also count on sons and daughters and spouses for help with daily tasks, such as housekeeping and preparing meals. Sons and daughters are also the main source of emotional support.

Religious Institutions

Religion is a source of strength and comfort to most old people. For the retired, religious practice is a compensatory activity that structures their time and gives purpose to life. Religious institutions also provide the aged with a network of friends and fellow worshipers.

Roles and Status of the Aged

The reciprocal nature of human relations never changes, and underneath all the cultural values and traditions, reciprocity persists as the basis of human relations. Of special importance in Egypt are the nuances related to authority within the family, conflict of interests, and reciprocity in family relations.

Most Egyptian elders experience a narrowing of their lives. Men experience the trauma of forced retirement, barrenness in daily living, and lack of outlets for substitute activities. Women feel threatened by the diminishing support of their children after the children marry. For a large number of men and women, pensions are insufficient, and for the poorest, pension support is negligible. Meanwhile, due to cultural expectations, the family, especially the oldest son, provides most of the support.

On the other hand, elders seeking emotional fulfillment and status reciprocate services.

Marriage and Literacy

About 57% of people 60+ are married and 36% are widowers. This compares to 65% of all adults and only 8% widowed for all adults.

About 80% of the aged are illiterate compared to about 50% for all adults.

CURRENT POLICY ISSUES AND PROGRAMS

The Social Security Pensions system has been boosted to cover more of those without other pensions. Elders have been targeted to ensure that they can afford to meet their basic needs. They now have a right to subsidized food and energy, as well as loans for income to support basic activities.

The Ministry of Health and Population plans to extend the coverage of medical insurance to more of the population, including the retired and elders. The Ministry is focusing on health promotion and prevention as a means of medical cost containment. The World Health Organization plans and efforts are in line with this policy.

Informal care of elders is guaranteed by religious and cultural commitments. It is stated as a holy duty in the 1971 Constitution. The problems here are:

1. Lack of resources caused by the general national poverty;
2. The diminishing numbers of family caregivers, because more women are working outside the home; and
3. The government's reluctance to contribute to specific health and housing for frail elders.

The United Nations Program that monitors Development and Human Rights is busy with more basic issues, such as reducing poverty and hunger, empowering women, and freedom of expression. This is related to problems of elders in Egypt.

Education and training for all Egyptians is growing, and training in care of elders, especially those with dementia or Alzheimer's disease, has become mainstream.

The main government office concerned with elders is the Ministry of Social Affairs, Department of Family Care, Elders Office (Cairo, Egypt).

RESEARCH ON AGING

Two large-scale surveys with adequate methodology form the spearhead for exploring the needs and services of elders in Egypt.

The first was a study of the social support systems for the aged in Egypt (Azer & Affifi, 1990), which was sponsored by the National Center for

Social and Criminological Research and the United Nations University. The study entailed an ethnographic and household survey of an urban area in Greater Cairo. It surveyed 5,463 households, with a total of 996 aged persons. Case studies were performed on a sample of the elderly surveyed.

The study concluded that the situation calls for policy reassessment and considerations of possible social interventions, such as home delivery of services and alleviation of the heavy financial burden that is shouldered by the families of the poorest elderly persons. The study concludes with recommendations to insure that the elderly enjoy equality and the development of their abilities.

The second survey was called *Aging in the Eastern Mediterranean Region* (Andrews & Kotry, 1991), and its results have been summarized in the preceding sections. It underlines the failure of the present system to meet the needs of Egyptian elders.

There have been several other research projects in gerontology. The following was one of the most noteworthy projects. An *Epidemiological Study of the Conditions, Biological Changes, Nutritional and Drug Requirements Among Elders in Alexandria* (El Sherbini & Hassan, 1989) was sponsored by the Academy of Scientific Research and Technology, Council of Health and Drug Research. The study documents the excess of physical and mental complaints among elders.

Eleven studies on psychiatric and geriatric problems of elders in Egypt were published in *Geriatrics and Gerontology* (Ashour, 1989). In addition, there have been over 400 titles (theses, dissertations, and books) in Arabic about geriatrics and gerontology published in the last 20 years.

The Fulbright Commission has published several studies on *Health Care of the Elderly in Egypt* (Palmore & Ashour, 1992).

GERIATRICS

The University of Alexandria Medical School has material relevant to geriatrics in its undergraduate teaching. The University of Ain Shams Medical School runs a master's degree program to qualify leaders in geriatrics, with emphasis on primary care. The Ismailia and Menofia Community-based medical schools integrate care of elders into their clinics. The Minia Medical School has a growing program sponsored by the community medicine department. In 1990, the Helwan University Cairo School of Social Services launched a diploma program in social care for the aged.

National congresses on geriatrics and gerontology are being held more and more frequently. A geriatric section in the *Journal of the Egyptian Medical Association* has been established.

The main geriatric societies are:

- The Egyptian Association for Geriatrics and Gerontology, established in 1987, with membership at around 100;
- The Egyptian Society for Health Care of the Elderly, established in 1982, with multidisciplinary membership; and
- The Egyptian Society for General Care of the Elderly, established in 1981, which runs homes and clubs nationwide.

REFERENCES

Al-Housseini, S. (1985). *The city: A study in urban sociology*. Cairo: Al-Maaref.

Andrews, G., & Kotry, A. (1991). *Aging in the Eastern Mediterranean region*. Cairo: WHO & Ministry of Public Health—Egypt.

Ashour, A. (Ed.) (1989). *Geriatrics and gerontology. Proceedings of a congress, March 5–8, 1988*. Cairo: Ain Shams University.

Azer, A., & Affifi, E. (1990). *Social support systems for the aged in Egypt*. Cairo: National Center for Social and Criminological Research and the United Nations University.

El Sherbini, F., & Hassan, M.N.R. (1989). *An epidemiology study of geriatric conditions in Alexandria*. Cairo: Academy of Scientific Research and Technology Council of Health and Drug Research.

Pulmore, E., & Ashour, A. (Eds.) (1992). *Health care of the elderly in Egypt*. Cairo: Fulbright Commission.

18

▪

Estonia

Kai Saks

DEMOGRAPHIC CHANGES IN ESTONIA

Estonia is experiencing one of the fastest population aging processes in Europe. The demographic transition started in the middle of the 19th century and followed the so-called French type with simultaneous mortality and fertility decline. As a result, there was a relatively small increase in the number of the population—Estonia numbered nearly a million in 1897 and only slightly more in 1934 (Katus, Puur, Põldma, & Sakkeus, 1999). In the course of the Second World War, Estonia fell to the Soviet occupation, which lasted for almost 50 years, but Estonia regained its independence in 1991. Between 1940 and 1953, the population losses of Estonia, due to war activities and sovietization (tens of thousands of people were deported from Estonia to Siberia), have been estimated to be at least 17.5% of the total population. On the other hand, these losses were exceeded in number by mass immigration from different parts of the Soviet Union, mainly from Russia. During 1945–1950 alone, more than 240,000 people immigrated. During the next 30 years, Estonia grew mainly due to migration (Population: Composition by sex and age, 2008). According to the census data, over 1.5 million people lived in Estonia in 1989, and the foreign-born population, together with their second generation, comprised 36% of the total population (Population of Estonia by population census, 1997).

After the country regained independence in 1991, the size of the population started to decrease quickly. In 2000, Estonia had about 1.37 million people; that is, 13% less than at the time of the previous Population Census. Negative net migration and negative natural increase were the reasons for the decrease of population. Decrease of the population also continued after the year 2000 (Population: Composition by sex and age, 2008). At the beginning of 2008, 1.34 million people resided in Estonia (Statistical database: Population, 2008).

After World War II, the aging of the population decelerated due to intensive immigration, as immigrants were mostly younger working-age persons. At the beginning of the 1990s, when immigration was replaced by emigration, and fertility also decreased considerably, the aging of the population accelerated. Numerous persons of the generation that had immigrated to Estonia at a young age had been reaching pension age (Katus et al., 1999).

Due to the demographic changes described above, the natural population aging process in Estonia was delayed for 40 years, but accelerated rapidly at the end of the 20th century. According to the data from the Population Census of 1922, the number of persons 60 years of age and older comprised 12% of the population, while in 2000, that proportion was 21%. According to recent population prognosis, the proportion of persons 60 years of age and older will reach 33% by 2050. The number of persons 65 years of age and older was about 230,000 at the beginning of 2008 (17.2% of the total population), and the number 85 and older was nearly 18,000 (1.3% of the total population). The mean life expectancy at birth in 2006 was 73 years (males = 67.4 and females = 78.5 years); at the age of 65, it was 16.2 years (males = 13.2 and females = 18.2 years); at the age of 85, it was 5.5 years (males = 5.0 and females = 5.6 years) (Statistical Database: Population, 2008).

In conclusion, due to historical peculiarities, population aging in Estonia is one of the fastest in Europe, and the proportion of older people is high despite a relatively short life expectancy at birth.

RESEARCH ON AGING

There is neither a specialized gerontological nor geriatric research institution in Estonia. Aging-related research is an interest of scientists in different universities: University of Tallinn (demography, social politics, and social work), University of Tartu (biomedicine, medicine, nursing, kinesiology, and social work), and Tallinn University of Technology (aging and work). In addition, the Estonian Association of Gerontology and Geriatrics (EGGA) has conducted several national and international surveys (health and social services; coping and well-being of the older population).

Studies of the aging of the population were launched in the 1980s by Prof. Kalev Katus (1955–2008). He and his colleagues implemented new methods in demographics and made public the meaning of population aging for Estonian society (Katus et al., 1999; Katus, Puur, & Põldma, 2002). Age-related changes in muscles, bones, and joints is another topic of interest connecting scientists from biomedical, sport, and medical sciences (Jürimäe & Jürimäe, 2007; Pääsuke, Ereline, & Gapeyeva, 2003; Pääsuke et al., 2004). Social gerontology research was initiated at the end of 20th century, including studies of pension system reforms (Leppik, 2006; 2007), coping and well-being of older population (Saks et al., 2008; Saks, Oja, & Kivisaar, 2004a; Tiit, Saks, & Vaarama, 2008; Tulva, 2005; 2007). Medical topics of aging are, as a rule, from different medical specialties (neurology, orthopedics, etc.) but also from comprehensive population studies. Examples of medical research topics include osteoporosis, osteoarthrosis and joint replacement (Haviko, Kirjanen, Martson, & Parv, 2004; Haviko, Maasalu, & Seeder, 1996); stroke (Kõrv & Roose, 2004); Parkinson's disease, dementia (Linnamägi & Asser, 2004; Taba & Asser, 2003; Taba et al., 2005); epidemiology of diseases among older population (Saks et al., 2001; Saks, Kolk, Soots, Takker, & Vask, 2003; Saks, Tiit, Käärik, & Jaanson, 2002)

In conclusion, research on aging is a relatively new field in Estonia, fragmented and not well coordinated. Nevertheless, formal and informal networks of Estonian scientists and research teams have been created both nationally and internationally.

EDUCATION IN GERONTOLOGY

Education in gerontology and geriatrics was rather sporadic in Estonia until the beginning of the 21st century. Traditionally, some age-related topics were included in several courses for students of health sciences and social work, but coordination was weak. In 2008, almost all curricula in health and social sciences include at least some mandatory courses in gerontology: social workers and physical and occupational therapists have a course in gerontology (2–4 credit points) during their undergraduate studies. Nurses learn gerontology in the module Healthy Older Person and geriatrics in the module Sick Older Person during their basic studies. Occupational therapists and physical therapists also have geriatrics included in their curricula. Students in social work have a special course called Social Work for the Older Population at the undergraduate level.

Unfortunately, there are no mandatory courses in gerontology/geriatrics for medical students, although some topics have been included in other subjects (e.g., health promotion of the older population, geriatric pharmacology).

A master's degree in gerontology is not available in Estonia. Nevertheless, social workers and physical therapists have the possibility of learning about gerontological problems in more depth at the master's level. Tallinn University has a master's curriculum in social work with a specialization in gerontological social work. A master's curriculum for physical therapists at the University of Tartu includes geriatrics and geriatric physical therapy.

For nurses and medical doctors, there are no postgraduate curricula for specializing in gerontology or geriatrics. Nevertheless, the Tartu School of Health Care will implement specialist training in gerontological nursing in the near future. During 2007–08, the first group of medical doctors graduated from a 1.5-year specialist training in geriatrics at the University of Tartu. Since geriatrics is not an approved medical specialty in Estonia, regular training for specialization in geriatrics is missing but needed. Courses for continuing education in gerontology and geriatrics are offered not only by educational institutions but also by hospitals, local authorities and professional organizations.

In conclusion, education in gerontology in Estonia in 2008 is just beginning to receive formal acknowledgement. Development of a master's curriculum in gerontology, implementing geriatric training for medical students, and specialist training for gerontological nursing and geriatricians are the next important issues to solve in Estonia.

PUBLIC POLICY ISSUES IN AGING

The conception of policy for older people in Estonia was approved by the Estonian government in 1999 (Policy for the Elderly in Estonia, 1999). The Estonian policy for the elderly is based on the consideration that society comprises people of different age groups who must all have the opportunity to participate in social life, irrespective of their age. Estonian policy for the elderly is mainly focused on supporting the elderly to cope independently. The conception holds that the needs of the elderly can and must not be standardized, but depend on the person's economic situation, sex, marital status, education, biological and psychological age, physical and mental health, and lifestyle. Of importance is devising a flexible service system, which would help increase the number of elderly persons capable of coping by themselves. The policy for the elderly focuses on the following issues: family and environment, health care and social welfare, employment and coping, education, cultural activities and sports, nongovernmental organizations and self-help, and regional and international cooperation. The conception serves as the frame for developing regulations and services for older population.

Pension reform was begun in 1998, when Estonia opted for a three-pillar pension system. The first pillar is the renewed state pension scheme. The second pillar, a mandatory funded pension scheme, was implemented in 2002. The third pillar, enacted in 1998, is a voluntary supplementary pension scheme that is supported by the government through tax deductions (Pension, 2008). The mean old-age pension in January 2008 was 240 EUR (around 40% of the mean net salary) (Statistics Estonia, 2008).

The Health Insurance Act, effective January 1, 1992, started the financing of health care based on the principle of solidarity, which covers almost 95% of Estonian residents, including all old-age pensioners. Compulsory health insurance covers 80–90% of the health care costs of insured people. Voluntary health insurance has been available since 2002, but is still not widespread. Private medical services, where the patient pays for the whole service or the payment is a combined payment by the health insurance fund and the patient, are used far more frequently. People who have state health insurance receive medical care fully financed by the health insurance fund. The health insurance fund pays the insured for primary care and hospitalization, with minor extra charges for the persons themselves. The greatest public expense is for dental care and the purchase of drugs. Patients have to pay most of the dental care costs and for approximately half the price of prescription drugs. The cost of dentures is compensated for seniors once per three years, and they can get certain drugs at a bigger discount than working-aged people can. The health services costs for people 65 years old and older formed 29% of the total for the country, and the subsidized drug expenditure 42% of the total respective spending in 2003. The share of long-term nursing care formed 2.8% of all hospital expenses and just 0.8% of the total health care costs in 2001. In 2002, a home nursing service was started in Estonia. At this point, the supply of this service is still limited as the retraining of providers in home nursing started only in 2002. The availability of medical rehabilitation services is quite limited as well, and often clients have to pay for it themselves, since the health insurance fund does not finance home medical rehabilitation. Geriatric care is not available in Estonia (Saks et al., 2004b).

Provision and development of social care services is the responsibility of local authorities. Social services include social counseling, providing prosthetic, orthopedic and other appliances, domestic services and home care, housing services, and care in rehabilitation and welfare institutions (temporary and permanent placement, day care). Welfare institutions for adults include senior centers, support homes, care homes, and social rehabilitation centers (Saks et al., 2004a. Financing of social care services consists mainly of two sources: local authorities and clients and their families. In a few cases, mainly for services to persons with mental health problems, central state financing is available. The services provided in the day centers are free of charge for clients or at a discount. Financing of home and institutional services depends on the family of the client. According to the Family Law, children and grandchildren have to take care of their parents/grandparents (§ 64 Täisealiseks saanud lapse kohustus vanemat ülal pidada and § 66 Lapselapse kohustus ülal pidada vanavanemat; Perekonnaseadus, 2008). An older person who does not have children or grandchildren gets home services free of charge and pays 85% of the personal income for institutional care. Local authorities pay the remainder of the cost. In cases where a person has children/grandchildren, they must pay for the service. In certain cases, it means that an older person who has family could be in a very unpleasant situation, becoming dependent on children but getting no help from society.

Current developments in health and social care for the older population in Estonia are oriented toward guaranteeing the required amount and choice of services, implementing comprehensive Web-based assessment for care-dependent persons, and introducing principles of integrated care with care managers and individualized service packages.

REFERENCES

Haviko, T., Kirjanen, K., Martson, A., & Parv, M. (2004). Total hip arthroplasty: Clinical results. *Journal of Bone and Joint Surgery—British Volume* (Suppl. III), 250.

Haviko, T., Maasalu, K., & Seeder, J. (1996). The incidence of osteoporotic fractures at the University Hospital of Tartu, Estonia. *Scandinavian Journal of Rheumatology, 25,* 13–15.

Jürimäe, J. & Jürimäe, T. (2007). Plasma adiponectin concentration in healthy pre- and postmenopausal women: Relationship with body composition, bone mineral, and metabolic variables. *American Journal of Physiology: Endocrinology and Metabolism, 293,* E42–47.

Katus, K., Puur, A., & Põldma, A. (2002). *Eesti põlvkondlik rahvastikuareng* [Cohort population development in Estonia] (p. 364). Tallinn: Grafica Malen, Eesti Kõrgkoolidevaheline Demouuringute Keskus [Estonian Inter-university Population Research Centre].

Katus, K., Puur, A., Põldma, A., & Sakkeus, L. (1999). *Rahvastikuvananemine Eestis* [Population ageing in Estonia] (pp. 31–33). Tallin: Eesti Korgkoolidevaheline Demouuringute Keskus [Estonian Inter-university Population Research Centre].

Kõrv, J. & Roose, M. (2004). Stroke epidemiology in Estonia. *Atherosclerosis Supplements*, 5, 32–33.

Leppik, L. (2006). Coordination of pensions in the European Union: The case of mandatory defined-contribution schemes in the Central and Eastern European countries. *European Journal of Social Security*, 8, 35–55.

Leppik, L. (2007). Experiences with international social security conventions: A point of view from Central and Eastern European states. In F. Pennings (Ed.), *International social security standards: Current views and interpretation matters* (pp. 80–92). Tilburg, The Netherlands: Intersentia.

Linnamägi, Ü., & Asser, T. (2004). Dementne inimene, koormus ühiskonnale [Persons with dementia–burden for the society]. *Eesti Arst* [Estonian Physician], 83, 256–261.

Pääsuke, M., Ereline, J., & Gapeyeva, H. (2003). Age-related differences in knee extension rate of isometric force development and vertical jumping performance in women. *Journal of Sports Medicine and Physical Fitness*, 43, 453–458.

Pääsuke, M., Ereline, J., Gapeyeva, H., Joost, K., Mõttus, K., & Taba, P. (2004). Leg extension strength and chair rise performance in elderly women with Parkinson's disease. *Journal of Aging and Physical Activity*, 12, 511–524.

Pension. (2008). Retrieved June 30, 2008, from http://www.sm.ee/est/pages/index.html

Perekonnaseadus [Family law]. § 64 Täisealiseks saanud lapse kohustus vanemat ülal pidada *(Resposibility of an adult child to take care of his/her parents)*; § 66 Lapselapse kohustus ülal pidada vanavanemat *(Responsibility of an adult grandchild to take care of his/her grandparents)* (2008). Retrieved June 30, 2008, from https://www.riigiteataja.ee/ert/act.jsp?id=1011053

Policy for the elderly in Estonia. (1999). Retrieved June 30, 2008, from http://www.sm.ee/eng/pages/index.html

Population: Composition by sex and age. (2008). In T. Rosenberg (Ed.), *The statistical collection (Aegamööda asi kaunis)* (pp. 11–16). Tallinn: Greif Ltd.

Population of Estonia by population census. (1997). Tallinn: Statistical Office of Estonia.

Saks, K., Kolk, H., Soots, A., Kõiv, K., Paju, I., Jaanson, K., et al. (2001). Health status of the older population in Estonia. *Croatian Medical Journal*, 42, 663–668.

Saks, K., Kolk, H., Soots, A., Takker, U., & Vask, M. (2003). Prevalence of cardiovascular disorders among the elderly in primary care in Estonia. *Scandinavian Journal of Primary Health Care*, 21, 106–109.

Saks, K., Oja, K., & Kivisaar, S. (2004a). *Marginaliseerumise riski vähendamine eakatel: pensionisüsteem, tervishoiuteenused, sotsiaalteenused. Olukorra kirjeldus Eestis 2003.a* [Reduction of the risk of marginalization in older people: Pension system, health and social care services. State of the Art in Estonia 2003] (pp. 52). Tartu.

Saks, K., Oja, K., & Kivisaar, S. (2004b). Services for elderly at risk of marginalization in Estonia. In *Care services for elderly: State of the art and perspectives* (pp. 147–158). *Proceedings of the Seminar Fano, November 4.* COOSS Marche, Italy.

Saks, K., Tiit, E., Käärik, E., & Jaanson, K. (2002). Depressive symptoms in older Estonians: Prevalence and models. *Journal of American Geriatrics Society, 50*, 1164.

Saks, K., Tiit, E-M., Muurinen, S., Mukkila, S., Frommelt, M., & Hammond, M. (2008). Quality of life in institutional care. In M. Vaarama, R. Pieper, R., & A. Sixsmith (Eds.), *Care-related quality of life in old age: Concepts, models, and empirical findings* (pp. 196–216). New York: Springer.

Statistical Database: Population. (2008). Retrieved June 30, 2008, from http:// pub.stat.ee/px-web.2001/Dialog/varval.asp?ma=RV021&ti=RAHVA STIK+SOO+JA+VANUSER%DCHMA+J%C4RGI%2C+1%2E+J AANUAR&path=../Database/Rahvastik/01Rahvastikunaitajad_ja_ koosseis/04Rahvaarv_ja_rahvastiku_koosseis/&lang=2

Statistics Estonia. (2008). Retrieved June 30, 2008, from http://www.stat.ee/ main-indicators

Taba, P., & Asser, T. (2003). Incidence of Parkinson's disease in Estonia. *Neuroepidemiology, 22*, 41–45.

Taba, P., Kanarik, E., Krikmann, Ü., Macht, M., Simons, G., Spliethoff-Kamminga, et al. (2005). Cognitive behavioural education programme for Parkinsonian patients and carers. *Journal of the Neurological Sciences, 238*, S372.

Tiit, E-M., Saks, K., & Vaarama, M. (2008). Care keys data and statistical methods. In M. Vaarama, R. Pieper, & A. Sixsmith (Eds.), *Care-related quality of life in old age: Concepts, models, and empirical findings* (pp. 45–61). New York: Springer.

Tulva, T. (2005). Eakate aktiivsest eluhoiakust [Active attitude in old age]. *Sotsiaaltöö* [Social Work], *6*, 58–59.

Tulva, T. (2007). Ageing in Estonia and challenges for professional growth. In Saari, S., & Varis, T. (Eds.), *Ammatillinen kasvu* [Professional growth] (pp. 448–456). Keuruu: Otavan Kirjapaino OY.

19

··■··

Germany

Andreas Kruse and Eric Schmitt

RECENT HISTORY OF AGING IN GERMANY

Over the course of the 20th century, life expectancy (at birth) in Germany has increased by more than 30 years. At the beginning of the 20th century, German women had a life expectancy of 48.3 years. For German men, life expectancy was even shorter: 44.8 years. Continuous increases can also be observed over the last decade. Today, average life expectancy in Germany has reached 83.1 years for women and 78.7 years for men. According to life tables for 2005/2007, 60-year-old German women can expect to live another 24 years, and 60-year-old men another 20 years. An 80-year-old woman has a life expectancy of 8.9 more years, and an 80-year-old man 7.6 more years (Statistisches Bundesamt, 2008).

In projection of population development, it is regularly assumed that life expectancy will continue to increase. However, it is also expected that future increases will not be as pronounced as those observed in the last decades (a hypothesis that recently became the subject of substantial discussion in German demography; see Vaupel, 2008). In Western Germany, fertility rates have been relatively low for decades, with barely 1.4 children per woman since the 1970s. Due to family policy in the former GDR, fertility rates in Eastern Germany temporarily increased—up to 1.9 children per woman—but decreased after German reunification to an historical low of 0.8. Since the mid-1990s, fertility rates in Eastern Germany have approximated those in the western part of the country. The German

Bureau of Statistics proceeds in this actual model of future population development from the assumption that until the year 2050, average life expectancy at birth will gain five more years and fertility rates will be stable at 1.4 children per woman.

Following the prognosis of the German Bureau of Statistics, the age structure of the German population will reverse between 1950 and 2050. By the end of 2005, 19.3% of the German population was 65 years and older. Proceeding from a surplus of 100,000, in 2050, 33.3% of the German population will be age 65 years and older; 51.7% will be between 20 and 65 years old; and only 15.1% will be younger than 20 years. Based on a net immigration rate of 200,000 people, which is more than twice the actual net immigration rate, 31.8% will be age 65 years and older; 52.8% will be between 20 and 65 years old; and 15.4% will be younger than 20 years. Only with a surplus of 3,400,000 people would the actual ratio of older to younger people hold constant. Whereas in 1950, when the number of people less than 20 years old was twice that of people 65 years and older, there will be twice as many people age 65 years and older as people younger than age 20 in the year 2050. From a sociopolitical perspective, development of dependency ratios is particularly important because an increase in these ratios is assumed to imply an increased burden on the productive part of the population to maintain the pensions and other costs related to those outside of traditional working years. There are direct impacts on financial programs such as social security.

The (total) dependency ratio is an age-population ratio of those typically not in the labor force (the dependent part) and those typically in the labor force (the productive part). In Germany's statistical reports, the dependent part usually includes those under the age of 20 and those aged 65 years and older. The productive component is composed of the population in between; that is, ages 21–64. The (total) dependency ratio (number of people aged 0–20 years + number of people aged 65 years and older divided by the number of people aged 21–64 years x 100) can be partitioned into the child dependency ratio (number of people aged 0–20 years divided by the number of people aged 21–64 years x 100) and the aged dependency ratio (number of people aged 65 years and older divided by number of people aged 21–64 years x 100). Following the German Bureau of Statistics' prognosis of population development (scenario 1), the old age dependency ratio will increase from 32.6 (per 100 workers) in 2010, to 47.3 in 2030, and 54.5 in 2050. The (total) dependency ratio will increase from 61.0 in 2000 to 77.8 in 2030 and 84.2 in 2050.

Since frailty and the need for care show a marked increase in the 9th and 10th decades of life, it is also important to consider population growth of people aged 80 years and older. According to the second scenario (net immigration of 200,000) of the German Bureau of Statistics, there were 2,280,000 German women and men in need of care at the end of 2006, with 78.4% of these aged 80 years and older. The absolute number of people aged 80 years and older is expected to increase from 4,300,000 (5.2% of the total population) in the year 2010 to 5,900,000 (7.3%) in 2020; 6,300,000 (7.9%) in 2030; 8,000,000 (10.3%) in 2040; and 10,000,000 (13.5%) in 2050.

The aforementioned changes in German life expectancy reflect German statistics on causes of death. Infectious diseases were eliminated as dominant causes of death. Because of advances in curative medicine, people can live much longer with chronic disease. In contrast to the situation at the beginning of the 20th century, to survive no longer implies being in good health. Consequently, the relationship between mortality and morbidity—and not only in Germany—has gained more and more interest in gerontological research (and politics).

The competing hypotheses of "compression of morbidity" (Fries, 1980) and "failure of success" (Gruenberg, 1977) have stimulated considerable research in the last two decades. Cohort-sequential analysis of data from the German Socioeconomic Panel suggests that increases in life expectancy particularly imply gains in active life expectancy; that is, the number of years people lead an independent and self-responsible life. German women and men born in 1917, at ages 67 to 70 years old, had spent barely three-quarters of their years in activity (women: 72.5%, men: 73%). By contrast, German men who were born in 1927, at ages 67 to 70 years old, had spent 81.5% of their years in activity, and German women born in 1927 had spent 77% of their years in activity. Additionally, research indicates that, for both sexes, increases in education contribute to reduced rates of poor health in younger cohorts (Klein & Unger, 2002).

Notwithstanding general physical and cognitive decline, older people also possess potential and strength enabling them to successfully compensate for age-related deficits, in working contexts as well as in everyday life. Moreover, most older Germans have at least a satisfactory amount of financial resources at their disposal. The Third National Report on Poverty and Prosperity shows that the risk for poverty in older people is lower than that for every other age group. In Germany, poverty rates reach a maximum in childhood and adolescence. To be a single parent implies a threefold poverty risk compared with the risk of poverty for older people. However, financial resources of future cohorts of older people are expected to reflect increases of discontinuous employment, unemployment, and early retirement (Bundesministerium für Arbeit und Soziales, 2008).

Considering the experience and potential of older people to continue to contribute to their communities in their later years, an aging society cannot dispense with the civil engagement of its older people. Older persons as well as younger persons are able to contribute innovations to society and sharpen its competitive edge (Kruse & Schmitt, 2006a). Indeed, it is more and more apparent, not only in scientific but also in public (and political) discourse, that changes in age do not necessarily imply losses in economic competitiveness. Intergenerational equity and solidarity appear to be on the rise.

However, these more optimistic scenarios of population aging presuppose that older people already are, or can be, motivated to use their strengths and potential for society; that older people are adequately engaged in, accepted by and rewarded through their interactions with society at large. In Germany, older people already contribute to intergenerational solidarity and social cohesion by means of social and political engagement with and/or for younger generations (Kessler & Staudinger, 2007; Tesch-Römer, Engstler, & Wurm, 2006). It is apparent from the available survey data that even in the ninth decade of life, family relationships reflect reciprocity in exchange of instrumental and emotional support. Numerous associations, clubs, and initiatives could not exist without the voluntary activities of older people. Older people contribute considerably to the socialization of younger generations (not only in their own families) and to the functioning and sustainability (and affordability) of the German social security system (Pohlmann, 2002).

RECENT RESEARCH ON AGING IN GERMANY

In German gerontology, the notion is commonly accepted that continuity and change of human development cannot be explained by a single general theory of human aging. The idea of a differential gerontology able to take into account both interindividual variability and context-specific variations in developmental processes was put forth primarily by Hans Thomae and Ursula Lehr's theoretical, methodological, and empirical contributions to the development of a biographical perspective on human aging (Thomae & Lehr, 1986). In the 1990s, Paul Baltes' propositions of life span developmental psychology (Baltes, 2003) were influential for the further establishment of a differential gerontology. Today, multidimensionality, multidirectionality, plasticity, and contextual embeddedness belong to the basic premises of theoretical perspectives in German gerontology. Examples may be found regarding cognitive aging (Lindenberger, 2008; Singer, Verhaeghen, Ghisletta, Lindenberger, & Baltes, 2003);

control-related behavior (Heckhausen & Schulz, 1995); developmental tasks (Freund & Baltes, 2005); age stereotypes (Kruse & Schmitt, 2006b); personality development (Staudinger & Kunzmann, 2005); social relationships (Carstensen & Lang, 2007); resilience (Greve & Staudinger, 2006); and dependency (Baltes, 1996).

The biology, sociology, and psychology of aging are equally interested in differentiating patterns of aging (Wahl & Weisman, 2003). Biology of aging is particularly interested in interindividual variation at the cellular, organ, and organism levels. Contributions to behavioral genetics focus on interactions between genes and environmental conditions, as well as constructs such as functionality, and explicitly deny a close, uniform, and linear relationship between chronological age and adaptive capacity. In sociology of aging, individuals are conceived of as reasonable actors who make rational decisions among available alternatives. Accordingly, developmental paths do not simply reflect normative societal expectations or differences in social status, social roles, and social resources, but also individual judgments and preferences. Life span contextualism explicitly differentiates between age-graded, historical, and non-normative factors that interact in influencing human development in specific environments (Wahl, 2006). In the context of aging patterns, it should also be mentioned that after a long period of neglecting gender distinctions in aging research, differences between women and men in health status, psychological functioning, social resources, and social participation have become main topics in current German gerontology (Kruse & Schmitt, 2004).

Another important trend in German gerontology is the conception of individuals as agents of their own development. Processes of developmental regulation have attracted much interest from German theorists in the last two decades. For instance, Baltes and Baltes (1990) introduced their model of selective optimization and compensation. This model is not only essential for a comprehensive understanding of successful aging, but also serves as a meta-theory able to integrate a huge number of different theoretical contributions to gerontology in the last decades. Also, Heckhausen and Schulz proposed a life-span theory of control, which is based on the distinction between primary and secondary control originally introduced by Rothbaum et al. (Rothbaum, Weisz, & Snyder, 1982). Additionally, Brandtstädter and colleagues enriched our understanding of stability and change of the self with their dual-process model of assimilative and accommodative coping. Socioemotional selectivity theory was further developed in empirical studies of Lang and Carstensen (2002).

The distinction between the third and the fourth age became a prominent frame of reference for theoretical conceptions and empirical studies during the second half of the 1990s. This was particularly due to the results of the Berlin Aging Study and its follow-ups (Baltes & Mayer, 2001). Whereas the so-called third age is characterized by preserved skills and capabilities, enhanced vulnerability becomes more and more evident in the fourth age. This is particularly the case in findings on cognitive functioning and plasticity in old and very old age (Baltes & Lindenberger, 1997; Li et al., 2008; Singer, Lindenberger, & Baltes, 2003). But it also holds true for comprehensive studies of psychological functioning and general adaptive capacity, which suggest that positive cohort effects (e.g., today's 70-year-olds are highly similar to those 65-year-olds three decades ago) might not expand to very old age.

Instead, there is growing evidence that the fourth age is characterized by cognitive de-differentiation (Ghisletta & Lindenberger, 2003), a strong relationship between declines in cognitive and sensory functioning (Ghisletta & Lindenberger, 2005) and an enhanced probability of at least mild (subdiagnostic) depression, and losses in subjective well-being (Smith & Baltes, 1999). In his theoretical conception of the incompleteness of the architecture of human ontogenesis, Baltes (2003) postulates three general principles that might establish a qualitative difference between third and fourth age: the first principle states that biological capacity decreases with age; the second that with advancing age, more culture is needed to extend stages of life; and the third that efficacy of culture decreases with age. However, some recent contributions from German gerontology show that accentuating the distinction between the third and fourth age is problematic for at least three reasons: first, this generalization overlooks the marked interindividual variability in health status and psychological functioning in very old age. Whereas associating the fourth age with enhanced vulnerability might suggest decreases in interindividual variability, some empirical studies suggest further increases of interindividual variability in very old age. Second, this generalization neglects the multidimensionality and multidirectionality of human development, which is also evident in very old age. Third, research on coping with borderline situations suggests that there is the potential for psychological growth even in the highest age groups (Lehr, 2007).

Quality of life and aging has been one of the major issues in gerontological research in Europe supported by the European Union Fifth Framework Programme (FP-5), in which quality of life was one of its Key Actions. Examples of European research on quality of life are the EQUAL and OASIS Projects, both supported by FP-5 (Fernández-Ballesteros, Kruse, Zamarrón, & Caprara, 2007). From a population aging perspective, the EQUAL Project covered five European countries (Germany, Italy, the

Netherlands, Sweden, and United Kingdom). In every country, a set of quality of life conditions was revised from the existing aggregate data. These conditions were environmental (housing, neighborhood, transport, and new technology); physical and mental health; employment and networks; family and support networks; participation and social integration; health and social services; life satisfaction and subjective well-being; and inequality and variation in quality of life (see also Walker, 2005).

Recently, quality of life also became a key concept in comprehensive diagnostics of inpatients suffering from dementia. Under the assumption that the planning and implementation of intervention measures must not be based exclusively on an assessment of cognitive impairments, but should also consider individual aspirations and preferences in a given situation, the Heidelberg Instrument for Assessment of Quality of Life in Demented Nursing Home Residence (HILDE) was developed as an option for a more individuated care for patients in nursing homes. In a sample of 362 residents from 22 nursing homes, four patterns of competence were identified and independently cross-validated (Becker, Kaspar, & Kruse, 2006). Each of these four different dementia syndrome groups is characterized by specific needs and values. They can be used as points of reference within, as well as between, these competence groups in order to plan individual interventions with competence-oriented expectations.

The results of the HILDE study support the theoretical conception of Veenhoven (2000), which focuses particularly on the empirical relationships between the four dimensions suggested in the original Lawton model (i.e., well-being, behavioral competence, perceived quality of life, and environmental or objective quality of life) in terms of income or antecedent and outcome variables. In line with this theoretical position, quality of life is defined as a constellation of personal and environmental material and immaterial resources, along with subjective well-being. Recently, the Heidelberg research group began a further step of the project aimed at enabling members of staff in nursing homes to use the HILDE instrument—independent from the supervision of the researchers—for assessment of quality of life, planning, and evaluation of individual intervention measures.

GERMANY'S CURRENT STATE OF EDUCATION IN GERONTOLOGY

Three types of gerontological courses can be differentiated at German universities: (a) BA courses (Vechta); (b) M.A. courses (Dortmund, Erlangen-Nürnberg, Heidelberg, and Vechta); and (c) extra-occupational courses (Dortmund). Moreover, gerontology content can be found in the context of nursing science at a number of German universities of applied sciences. E-learning courses in gerontology are currently under preparation (e.g., at the University of Stuttgart). All gerontology courses at German universities have an interdisciplinary orientation, with some differences in interdisciplinary profiles. Besides courses that accentuate relationships between and among sociology, political science, and economic science, there are other courses that accentuate an integration of psychological, sociological, medical, and ethical perspectives.

In Germany, education in geriatric medicine is embedded in advanced vocational training for physicians, with training modules offered by different institutions. Following a successful examination process, physicians are awarded the additional denomination Physician of Geriatric Medicine. Significantly, geriatrics has become an obligatory subject in the education of medical students. These developments reflect a general trend in which medical practitioners are more and more concerned with older patients, implying that the treatment of chronic disease is gaining in importance.

Gerontological knowledge is also available in the context of an extra-occupational course, occupational training/adult education (Heidelberg), as well as through M.A. courses in theology, and in Catholic (Caritas) and Protestant (Diaconia) social welfare work (Heidelberg). Also, a number of postgraduate programs focusing on areas of gerontological research have been established recently. Four model programs should be mentioned here: Multimorbidity in Old Age in Berlin (founded by the Robert-Bosch Foundation); Cognitive Impairment in Old Age and the Spatial Everyday Environment (founded by the University of Heidelberg); Dementia (founded by the Robert-Bosch Foundation); and the International Max Planck Research School for Demography (founded by the Max Planck Foundation and the University of Rostock).

Education in gerontology is substantially enriched by international programs. An outstanding example in this regard is the Max Planck International Research Network on Aging (MaxNetAging), a virtual institute for the advancement of research on the causes, patterns, processes, and consequences of aging. MaxNetAging was founded by Paul Baltes in 2004. It is intended to provide a platform for international collaboration between 12 Max Planck Institutes and outstanding scholars from other institutions, such as the University of Virginia or the Karolinska Institute, Stockholm. MaxNetAging has an interdisciplinary focus, including political science, law, sociology, anthropology, economics, history, art history, history of science, demography, mathematics, biology, medicine, cognitive and brain sciences, psychology, and human development. The network contributes to the accumulation and dissemination of gerontological knowledge and education in gerontology through its fellowships, a doctoral program, and research workshops.

Heidelberg University is involved in two programs that will also have an impact on the development of future curricula. The European Master's in Gerontology (EuMaG) program offers outstanding international training that enables participants to gain a deeper knowledge and understanding of the aging process and its societal implications. EuMaG was developed and delivered by a network of more than 20 European universities. The curriculum is multidisciplinary, with a strong emphasis on international comparison in regard to current debates in Europe concerning policy and care for the elderly. The modular program includes an introductory course in gerontology (Vrije Universiteit Amsterdam), a psychogerontology module (University of Heidelberg), a social-gerontology module (Keele University), a health-gerontology module (Université Versailles Saint Quentin en Yvelines), and a summer school. The consortia implementation project, INTERGERO (Implementation of an International interdisciplinary program for teaching Gerontology), is a cooperative effort between three universities from the United States (Miami University, Oregon State University, and San Francisco State University) and three universities from Europe (Heidelberg University, Universidad De Salamanca, and Vrije Universiteit Amsterdam). The program is supported through collaboration between the U.S. Dept. of Education and the European Union. In addition to curricula development, exchange of students and lecturers between the United States and the European Union is also a key part of this program.

In German gerontology, it is increasingly realized that a closer international interconnectedness presents the opportunity to improve the richness, value, and attractiveness of courses in gerontology. Existing international cooperation is seen as a first step in the development of joint degrees. Moreover, strengthening cooperation with universities in Eastern Europe is seen as another priority of German gerontological institutes in furthering education in gerontology. Particularly in the behavioral and social sciences, courses reflect a more general life span perspective. Old age is systematically integrated into the teaching of psychologists and sociologists who offer courses on life-span developmental psychology, or life-span sociology. Further, in Germany there is a markedly growing interest in aging research in the humanities (e.g., in ethnology or practical philosophy).

CURRENT PUBLIC POLICY ISSUES IN AGING

Aging policy has long been a topic of major importance in Germany, especially given the voter participation of older people and their growing

numbers. Political parties designated civil servants responsible for senior citizen policy and established working groups for senior citizens.
The recently increasing significance of aging policy is reflected in the
work of the Federal Government and the German Bundestag. The German Bundestag negotiated three main inquiries on aging policy in 1978,
1986, and 1999. And in 1992, the German Bundestag constituted an
Enquete Commission on Demographic Change: Challenges Posed by
Our Aging Society to Citizens and Policy-makers. The Federal Government commissioned several national reports—one on family affairs and
six on aging—which are exclusively concerned with specific aspects of
the situation of older people in Germany. Plus, the German government
took the initiative for the preparation of the Second International Plan
of Action on Aging (approved in Madrid in 2002) and hosted the ECE
Ministerial Conference on Aging in Berlin, which adapted the ECE Regional Implementation Strategy. Aging policy in Germany is not only an
important issue at the national level, but also at the state, district, and
community levels.

Initially, aging policy primarily focused on the frailties and limitations
of older people and welfare policy to address those issues. Aging policy
was understood as something to be done *for* rather than *with* older people.
The traditional view was gradually replaced by a new perspective that
focused more on the attributes, independence, and self-determination of
older people. New concepts that also considered more vigorous older people were developed and implemented. Additionally, demographic change,
once discussed only in terms of a burden on social security systems, is now
seen as an opportunity for the development of a more productive and ac-
commodating society.

In order to understand the political discourse on aging in Germany,
it is important to differentiate between aging as an individual phenomenon and as a collective phenomenon. Individual aging refers to
the processes of individual development that are influenced by cohort
membership. Today, aging for the majority of people implies preserved
physical, psychological, and intellectual competences, adequate social and financial resources and—due to a higher educational status—
knowledge that can be used creatively and productively for self and
others. Collective aging refers to the growing (absolute and relative)
number of older people due to constantly low fertility rates and gains in
average life expectancy.

As a basis of political discourse on aging and demographic change,
it is commonly stated that, as a consequence of collective aging, people have to take more responsibility for their own aging processes.

Otherwise, it would be impossible to sustain the current level of social security funds for old age in Germany. The sociopolitical model
of subsidiarity (Nell-Breuning, 1977) is even more important today.
Likewise, the national reports on aging and demographic change pro-
ceed from the individual's increasing responsibility for his or her own
aging process. However, such a statement must be qualified in different
ways.

First, it is argued that most older people possess the resources necessary for leading an independent and self-responsible life. This includes
maintaining social participation and civil engagement and taking shared
responsibility for others and the development of society as a whole. It is
argued that society and politics must not focus exclusively on resources
for preserved independence in old age, but also need to consider resources
for shared responsibility in the sense of a continuous engagement or
re-engagement after retirement. Likewise, the recommendations of the
Second International Plan of Action on Aging focus on improving participation of older people in sociocultural, economic, and technological
progress. This line of argument can be found in several reports, including
the Third and Fifth National Report on Aging (Bundesministerium für
Familie, Senioren, Frauen und Jugend, 2000, 2006); the two Enquete-
Commissions, Demographic Change: Challenges Posed by Our Aging
Society to Citizens and Policy-makers (Deutscher Bundestag, 2002a);
the Future of Civil Engagement (Deutscher Bundestag, 2002b); and the
Progress Report of the Federal Government (Bundesregierung, 2004).
The two Reports on Aging and the reports of the two Enquete-Commis-
sions expand on the contributions of older people to intergenerational
solidarity. Noticeable communication and transfer of knowledge and
skills between old and young equally comprises material and nonmaterial resources. In all the aforementioned reports, addressing older people
as responsible citizens possessing indispensable potential for society is
considered a precondition for successfully meeting the challenges of demographic change.

Second, there is agreement in the National Reports that due to the pronounced heterogeneity of old age—which is reflected in marked interindividual differences in life situation and competence—it is indispensable
to develop differentiated societal and political concepts and implementation strategies that must consider social inequalities in both resources
and risks. Potential risks must be met adequately—not only in technical
terms, but also in ethical terms. As mentioned, poverty is no longer a
prevalent risk of old age in Germany. Still, poverty on any level remains
an important problem, particularly among single older women.

Need for care, which implies psychological and social burden for both older individuals and their relatives, is considered an important risk of old age. Hence, prevention and care-improvement have become central topics of German aging policy. Strengthening rehabilitation, promoting cooperation between professionals, relatives, and volunteers, and striving for better consideration of the special needs and requirements of people suffering from dementia have been described as central aims of further development of German long-term care insurance.

Referring to development, maintenance and societal application of old-age potential and strengths, the Fifth National Report of Aging (Bundesministerium für Familie, Frauen, Jugend und Senioren, 2006) proceeds from five guiding principles that summarize the important directions evident in aging policies in Germany today:

1. Shared Responsibility and Solidarity: This principle refers to the concept of subsidiarity, which is founded in the Christian social ethics of Nell-Breuning (1977) and states that matters of social welfare, ideally, should be handled in their immediate place of origin; that is, by the smallest, lowest, or least centralized competent authority. Central authority should have a subsidiary function, performing only those tasks that cannot be performed effectively at a more immediate or local level. The concept of subsidiarity refers to both the utilization of existing potentials (of the individual, the family, municipalities) to manage tasks and challenges, and the obligation of more global social structures to offer the necessary structures and support. Accordingly, the principle of shared responsibility and solidarity accentuates both obligations of older people and obligations of society: Older people should take responsibility for development and maintenance of old-age potential and use them in support of self and others; and society must guarantee the underlying conditions necessary for development, maintenance, and realization of old-age potential.

2. Old Age as a Driving Force for Innovation: This principle is based on the assumption that society's prosperity cannot be maintained by utilization of younger people alone. As a consequence of an aging labor force, companies' competitiveness depends more and more on their ability to recognize, support, and effectively use older employees' experience and potential for innovation and creativity. Design of protective working environments, adjustment of working conditions, and offering opportunities for extended vocational training belong to the criteria of the companies' demographic fitness. Moreover, the principle of old age as a driving force for innovation accentuates that an aging society's economic growth depends increasingly on fulfillment of the consumer needs of older people.

3. Sustainability and Generation Equity: This principle reflects that chances and opportunities available for different groups can be negatively interdependent. As a consequence, the pronounced promotion of development, maintenance, and utilization of old-age potential might imply decreasing opportunities for development and realization of potential in later-born cohorts, particularly when available resources are scarce. Therefore, promotion of old-age potentials must also be considered in the context of developing a child-friendly society. In the long range, an anti-children society is not capable of surviving, and a sustainable realization of old-age potential is only possible in a child-friendly society. In this context, it should be considered that societal innovation is perceived and evaluated subjectively and is not necessarily congruent with objective standards. Consequently, enhanced labor force participation of older workers might be perceived as an age-based discrimination by younger people, even if they themselves benefit from a respective development. Accordingly, a sustainable promotion of old-age potential requires an intergenerational perspective and continuous effort to establish transparency of aims and measures of aging policy.

4. Lifelong Learning: This principle emphasizes that accelerated technological innovation and increases in life expectancy imply a risk that experiences and knowledge systems developed in earlier phases of the life span might become obsolete in later years. In the last few decades, the traditional understanding of education (which was exclusively oriented toward formal learning in childhood and young adulthood) has been broadened to include and embrace the concept of lifelong learning. Different versions of this concept contain a common thread that learning in different phases of the life span—and learning in formal, non-formal, and informal contexts, as well as learning in the context of a variety of personal experiences—are conceived as indispensable components of lifelong learning. The necessity to intensify investment in lifelong learning follows from four principal aims: (a) The elevation of economic growth and improvement of competitiveness: Due to demographic change and globalization of markets, the economic growth and competitiveness of Western societies increasingly depends on the innovative potential and qualification of employees. As a consequence, there is a need for enhanced investment in education, including investment in extended vocational training for older workers; (b) The support of individual employability: Rates of employment and unemployment differ according to the level of qualification of the workers. Typically, those who reached a higher level of qualification and who continuously used opportunities for further education are employed until retirement; (c) The promotion of independence in old age: Good health and mental flexibility are essential preconditions

for leading an independent and satisfying life in old age. Numerous studies confirm that everyday competence, as well as physical and mental capability, can be improved by adequate training programs, regardless of age or mental and physical capacity of the participants; and (d) The strengthening of societal cohesion: General political and cultural learning mediates basic orientations and competences, which are a precondition for social participation in a continuously changing complex society. The contents of learning are essential for civil engagement in all phases of the life span. Without this engagement, social cohesion and social security in modern societies would be impossible.

5. Prevention: This principle stresses that the foundations for realization of old-age potential are laid in the earlier phases of the life span, that health and productive capacity can still be increased in old age, and that capacity for new learning expands over the entire life span. As with health status and education, self-responsibility and shared responsibility in old age also depend on previous developmental processes and social inequalities. Those who perceived their individual development in childhood, middle, and older adulthood as other-directed and uncontrollable (and therefore had only limited opportunities to develop skills, competences, and habits promoting self-responsibility and shared responsibility) will probably not develop an optimal lifestyle in old age. Similarly, it could be shown that early learning experiences are a good predictor of learning motivation and activities in older adulthood and old age. Nevertheless, people are always agents of their own development, regardless of social status, biography, and chronological age (e.g., avoiding risk factors, health-promoting nutrition, and physical activity have a marked impact on health status also in very old age).

REFERENCES

Baltes, M. M. (1996). *The many faces of dependency in old age*. New York: Cambridge University Press.

Baltes, P. B. (2003). On the incomplete architecture of human ontogeny: Selection, optimization, and compensation as foundation of developmental theory. In U. M. Staudinger & U. Lindenberger (Eds.), *Understanding human development: Dialogues with lifespan psychology* (pp. 17–43). Boston: Kluwer.

Baltes, P. B., & Baltes, M. M. (Eds.). (1990). *Successful aging: Perspectives from the behavioral sciences*. Cambridge, UK: Cambridge University Press.

Baltes, P. B., & Lindenberger, U. (1997). Emergence of a powerful connection between sensory and cognitive functions across the adult life span: A new window to the study of cognitive aging? *Psychology and Aging, 12,* 12–21.

Baltes, P. B., & Mayer, K. U. (Eds.). (2001). *The Berlin Aging Study: Aging from 70 to 100*. Cambridge, UK: Cambridge University Press.

Becker, S., Kaspar, R., & Kruse, A. (2006). Die Bedeutung unterschiedlicher Referenzgruppen für die Beurteilung der Lebensqualität demenzkranker Menschen. *Zeitschrift für Gerontologie und Geriatrie, 39,* 350–357.

Bundesministerium für Arbeit und Soziales. (2008). *Lebenslagen in Deutschland— Der 3. Armuts- und Reichtumsbericht der Bundesregierung.* Berlin: BMAS.

Bundesministerium für Familie, Senioren, Frauen und Jugend. (2000). *Dritter Altenbericht: Alter und Gesellschaft.* Berlin: Bundesministerium für Familie, Senioren, Frauen und Jugend.

Bundesministerium für Familie, Senioren, Frauen und Jugend. (2006). *Fünfter Altenbericht: Potenziale des Alters in Wirtschaft und Gesellschaft.* Berlin: Bundesministerium für Familie, Senioren, Frauen und Jugend.

Bundesregierung. (2004). *Fortschrittsbericht 2004: Perspektiven für Deutschland.* Berlin: Presse- und Informationsamt der Bundesregierung.

Carstensen, L. L., & Lang, F. R. (2007). Sozioemotionale Selektivität über die Lebensspanne: Grundlagen und empirische Befunde. In J. Brandtstädter & U. Lindenberger (Eds.), *Entwicklungspsychologie der Lebensspanne* (pp. 389–412). Stuttgart, Germany: Kohlhammer.

Deutscher Bundestag. (2002a). *Bericht der Enquete-Kommission "Demografischer Wandel".* Berlin: Deutscher Bundestag.

Deutscher Bundestag. (2002b). *Zukunft des bürgerschaftlichen Engagements.* Berlin: Deutscher Bundestag.

Fernández-Ballesteros, R., Kruse, A., Zamarrón, M. D., & Caprara, M. (2007). Quality of life, life satisfaction, and positive aging. In R. Fernández-Ballesteros (Ed.), *Geropsychology—European perspectives for an aging world* (pp. 197–223). Cambridge, UK: Hogrefe & Huber.

Freund, A., & Baltes, P. B. (2005). Entwicklungsaufgaben als Orientierungsstrukturen von Entwicklung und Entwicklungsoptimierung. In S.-H. Filipp & U. M. Staudinger (Eds.), *Entwicklungspsychologie des mittleren und höheren Erwachsenenalters* (pp. 37–79). Göttingen, Germany: Hogrefe.

Fries, J. F. (1980). Ageing, natural death, and the compression of morbidity. *New England Journal of Medicine, 3,* 130–135.

Ghisletta, P., & Lindenberger, U. (2003). Age-based structural dynamics between perceptual speed and knowledge in the Berlin Aging Study: Direct evidence for ability dedifferentiation in old age. *Psychology and Aging, 18,* 696–713.

Ghisletta, P., & Lindenberger, U. (2005). Exploring structural dynamics within and between sensory and intellectual functioning in old and very old age: Longitudinal evidence from the Berlin Aging Study. *Intelligence, 33,* 555–587.

Greve, W., & Staudinger, U. M. (2006). Resilience in later adulthood and old age: Resources and potentials for successful aging. In D. Cicchetti & A. Cohen (Eds.), *Developmental psychopathology* (pp. 796–840). New York: Wiley.

Gruenberg, E. M. (1977). The failure of success. *Mil-bank Memorial Foundation Quarterly/Health and Society, 55,* 3–24.

Heckhausen, J., & Schulz, R. (1995). A life span theory of control. *Psychology and Aging, 17,* 125–139.

Kessler, E.-M., & Staudinger, U. M. (2007). Intergenerational potential: Effects of social interaction between older adults and adolescents. *Psychology and Aging, 22,* 690–704.

Klein, T., & Unger, R. (2002). Aktive Lebenserwartung in Deutschland und in den USA. Kohortenbezogene Analysen auf Basis des Sozio-ökonomischen Panels und der Panel Study of Income Dynamics. *Zeitschrift für Gerontologie und Geriatrie, 35,* 528–539.

Kruse, A., & Schmitt, E. (2004). Differentielle Psychologie des Alterns. In K. Pawlik (ed.), *Enzyklopädie der Psychologie—Angewandte Differentielle Psychologie* (pp. 533–571). Göttingen, Germany: Hogrefe.

Kruse, A., & Schmitt, E. (2006a). Adult education. In J. E. Birren (Ed.), *Encyclopedia of gerontology* (pp. 312–332). Oxford, UK: Elsevier.

Kruse, A., & Schmitt, E. (2006b). A multidimensional scale for the measurement of agreement with age stereotypes and the salience of age in social interaction. *Ageing & Society, 26,* 393–411.

Lang, F. R., & Carstensen, L. L. (2002). Time counts: Future time perspective, goals and social relationships. *Psychology and Aging, 17,* 125–139.

Lehr, U. (2007). *Psychologie des Alterns.* Wiebelsheim, Germany: Quelle & Meyer.

Li, S.-C., Schmiedek, F., Huxhold, O., Röcke, C., Smith, J., & Lindenberger, U. (2008). Working memory plasticity in old age: Practice gain, transfer, and maintenance. *Psychology and Aging, 23,* 731–742.

Lindenberger, U. (2008). Was ist kognitives Altern? Begriffsbestimmung und Forschungstrends. In U. M. Staudinger & H. Häfner (Eds.), *Was ist Alter(n)? Neue Antworten auf eine scheinbar einfache Frage* (pp. 69–82). Heidelberg, Germany: Springer.

Nell-Breuning, O. V. (1977). *Soziallehre der Kirche.* Freiburg, Germany: Herder.

Pohlmann, S. (Ed.). (2002). *Facing an aging world—recommendations and perspectives.* Regensburg, Germany: Roderer.

Rothbaum, F., Weisz, J. R., & Snyder, S. S. (1982). Changing the world and changing the self: A two-process model of perceived control. *Journal of Personality and Social Psychology, 42,* 5–37.

Singer, T., Lindenberger, U., & Baltes, P. B. (2003). Plasticity of memory for new learning in very old age: A story of major loss? *Psychology and Aging, 18,* 306–317.

Singer, T., Verhaeghen, P., Ghisletta, P., Lindenberger, U., & Baltes, P. B. (2003). The fate of cognition in very old age: Six-year longitudinal findings in the Berlin Aging Study (BASE). *Psychology and Aging, 18,* 318–331.

Smith, J., & Baltes, P. B. (1999). Trends and profiles of psychological functioning in very old age. In P. B. Baltes & K. U. Mayer (Eds.), *The Berlin Aging Study: Aging from 70 to 100* (pp. 197–226). Cambridge, UK: Cambridge University Press.

Statistisches Bundesamt. (2008). *Statistisches Jahrbuch für die Bundesrepublik Deutschland 2008*. Retrieved from http://www.destatis.de

Staudinger, U. M., & Kunzmann, U. (2005). Positive adult personality development: Adjustment and/or growth? *European Psychologist, 10*, 320–329.

Tesch-Römer, C., Engstler, H., & Wurm, S. (Eds.) (2006). *Altwerden in Deutschland. Sozialer Wandel und individuelle Entwicklung in der zweiten Lebenshälfte*. Wiesbaden, Germany: VS Verlag für Sozialwissenschaften.

Thomae, H., & Lehr, U. (1986). Stages, crises, conflicts and life-span development. In A. B. Soerensen, F. E. Weinert, & L. R. Sherrod (Eds.), *Human development and the life-course* (pp. 429–444). Hillsdale, NJ: Erlbaum.

Vaupel, J. W. (2008). Lifesaving, lifetimes and lifetables. In E. Barbi, J. Bongaarts, & J. W. Vaupel (Eds.), *How long do we live? Demographic models and reflections on tempo effects* (pp. 93–107). Berlin: Springer.

Venhooven, R. (2000). The four qualities of life. Ordering concepts and measures of the good life. *Journal of Happiness Studies, 1*, 1–39.

Wahl, H.-W. (2006). The person-environment perspective in ageing research. In H.-W. Wahl, H. Brenner, H. Mollenkopf, D. Rothenbacher, & C. Rott (Eds.), *The many faces of health, competence and well-being in old age* (pp. 3–6). Dordrecht, The Netherlands: Springer.

Wahl, H.-W., & Weisman, J. (2003). Environmental gerontology at the beginning of the new millennium: Reflections on its historical, empirical, and theoretical development. *The Gerontologist, 43*, 616–627.

Walker, A. (Ed.) (2005). *Growing older in Europe*. London: Open University Press.

20

··■··

Great Britain

Kate Davidson

This chapter will first outline the recent demographic history of aging in Great Britain (GB); second, discuss current research projects and the development of education in gerontology; and finally, give an overview of early 21st century public policy issues in aging. The geopolitical profile of the United Kingdom is somewhat complex and here I offer a very brief explanation. Mainland Great Britain (the focus of this chapter) comprises England and Wales (customarily coupled for statistical purposes), and Scotland. The province of Northern Ireland (six counties of Ulster) completes the political entity that is the United Kingdom (UK). Northern Ireland will be covered within another chapter in this volume. However, the Census data are usually for the four countries of the UK, and this will be indicated in the text. The GB political landscape changed dramatically with the advent of devolution of governance for Scotland (1997) and Wales (1999) and the implications for older people will be further discussed in the section on public policy.

While still lagging behind the United States, it is pleasing to report that since my colleague Prof. Tony Warnes' contribution to the previous edition of this volume in 1991, Great Britain has witnessed a marked advance in the quantity and quality of research on aging. This fundamental paradigm shift has taken place within academia, government departments, and non-governmental organizations (NGOs), and the media. There is widespread acknowledgment of the importance of research and education in aging, stimulated by demographic realities.

AGING IN GREAT BRITAIN

The UK 2001 Census (carried out every 10 years) reveals that for the first time, the population of people over the age 60 is greater than that of children under the age of 16, at 21% and 20% respectively (Office of National Statistics, 2006a). By the 2011 Census, most of the immediate post-War baby boomers will have reached 65, thus swelling the numbers and proportion even more. The UK experienced a more sustained population growth in the late 1960s and early 1970s, and this larger second wave of boomers will impact on the aging population profile into the third decade of the 21st century.

For the first time, the 2001 Census asked for ethnic origin. The question was not compulsory, but there was a 92% response. Just under 12% of the population reported ethnic origin other than British. This included white Irish and white other (European, Australasian, North American, etc.) as well as non-white ethnicity. White ethnic groups have an older age structure than other ethnic groups, reflecting past immigration and fertility patterns. Among the white British population in the UK, 17% were aged 65 and over in 2001. Among the non-white groups, African Caribbeans had the largest proportion of people aged 65 and over (11%), partly reflecting their earlier migration to Britain in the 1950s. Large-scale migration from South Asia began in the 1960s, so these groups have the next oldest population structures—between 4% and 7% were aged 65 and over. Only 2% of black Africans were 65 and over, large-scale migration to Britain having only begun since the 1980s (Office of National Statistics, 2006b). So although the numbers and proportions are currently quite small, as the migrants and their families age, we are likely to encounter many more in the next Census, of 2011.

As in all developed countries, the fastest-growing population is that of people over the age of 85. The percentage of the UK population over 85 will increase from 1.9% (1.1 million people) in 2001 to 3.5% (2.2 million people) in 2021. It is projected that by 2056, 5.2% of the UK population will be over 85 (3.3 million people) (Office of National Statistics, 2006b). We face the paradox of celebrating a longer living, healthier, wealthier old age, but bewail the increased burden on the public purse in supporting frail elderly people.

GERONTOLOGICAL RESEARCH AND EDUCATION IN GREAT BRITAIN

To date, the major topics of research interest, especially those funded by government departments and NGOs, have focused on the plight of elders: poor health, acute and chronic disabilities, income inequalities, dependency, loneliness and isolation, elder abuse, and so on. Highlighting these issues led to greater and much needed investment in health and social programs for older people and, importantly, their carers. An unintended consequence of such investigation has been to taint all research into aging as relentlessly depressing. Only recently has attention been paid to issues of quality of life and aging well, recognizing the growth of a healthier, wealthier, better educated, more knowledgeable cohort who are demanding a say in their future as they age.

Academic and institutional gerontology have grown substantially in Britain over the last two decades, with the development of centers of excellence in universities, the blossoming of master's courses and the encouraging increase of Ph.D. topics in aging. While it used to be that institutions with departments or centers dedicated to study and education on aging could be counted on one hand, happily, there are now too many to list in a short chapter. More institutions of further and higher education are establishing specialist undergraduate and postgraduate courses within mainstream subjects such as medicine, nursing, social work, psychology, sociology, social policy, and criminology. This has been largely due to state investment resulting from the pioneering work of academics and researchers in the 1980s and 1990s (Warnes, 1993).

Government statistical services such as the General Household Survey, the British Household Panel Survey, the Family Expenditure Survey, the National House Condition Survey, the Retirement Survey, and the Labour Force Survey now ask questions specific to old age and have more banded age categories instead of "all over 55," as was customary. The relatively new and much welcomed English Longitudinal Study of Ageing (ELSA), started in 2002, will give important data over time.

Although funding continues to be a bone of contention for all disciplines, and no one thinks that funding is sufficient for their scholarly interest, research into aging has recently been boosted by three major programs funded by national research councils (RCs). These councils are supported by the government and set the current research agenda. Until recently, the RCs principally relating to gerontology were the Economic and Social Research Council (ESRC) and the Medical Research Council (MRC). Relatively little nonclinical gerontological (as opposed to geriatric) research is supported by the MRC. The ESRC has historically funded modest, formula-led grants, which tended to be awarded to interested individual academics in disparate institutions.

However, from 1999 to 2004, the ESRC funded the Growing Older Programme: Understanding Quality of Life in Old Age directed by

Prof. Alan Walker of Sheffield University (ESRC GO Programme, 1999–2004). Never before had such an ambitious, multidimensional call gone out for applications for funding social research in gerontology. The program comprised 24 qualitative and quantitative projects that examined quality of life around topics including cognition, early and late old age, the environment, ethnicity, frailty, gender, grandparenthood, health, income, lifelong learning, lone living, residential care, social networks, spirituality, and transportation. The individual projects introduced a whole new generation of full-time researchers to aging research and established more experienced ones in British gerontological circles. The findings have been presented to and taken up by government departments such as health, social security, work and pensions, housing, and education.

More recently, and building on the success of the Growing Older Programme, there has been a unique collaboration between five UK research councils: the ESRC and MRC have joined with the Arts and Humanities RC (AHRC), the Biotechnology and Biological Sciences RC (BBSRC), and the Engineering and Physical Sciences RC (EPSRC) to offer the largest and most ambitious research program on aging ever mounted in the UK. The New Dynamics of Ageing Program: Collaborative Research Projects (NDA CRP) is a seven-year multidisciplinary research initiative with the ultimate aim of improving quality of life of older people, and is again under the Directorship of Professor Alan Walker (New Dynamics of Ageing, 2008). The program aims to develop practical policy and implementation guidance, as well as novel scientific, technological, and design responses to help older people enjoy better quality lives as they age. This requires integrating understandings of the changing meanings, representations, and experiences of aging, and the key factors shaping them (including behavioral, biological, clinical, cultural, historical, social, economic, and technological), through direct engagement with older people and user organizations. The program has opened vistas for many more researchers, academics, emerging scholars, and students to become involved with gerontology in the UK.

Another important source of funding is the European Union, which offers opportunities to study national and international comparisons within 27 widely diverse countries (European Commission, 2008). As with the NDA CRP program, collaborative work is complex and requires sensitivity to cultural and disciplinary allegiances and traditions and can be a political minefield. However, such teamwork highlights the heterogeneity of the experience of aging and serves to remind us of the imperative to recognize its importance.

On a more modest scale, research grants are also available from several medical and social welfare foundations such as the Joseph Rowntree Foundation, the Beth Johnson Foundation, the Leverhulme Trust, the Nuffield Foundation, as well as specific calls from such bodies as the British Academy and the Wellcome Trust. The research councils discussed above also support small-scale individual research project on aging.

An important consequence of the burgeoning interest in aging and the willingness to fund research projects has been the significant increase in the quality and quantity of publications on gerontology. In the past, mainstream academic social scientific journals would rarely consider publishing articles about older people; they now encourage guest editorials and special issues. There are also academic journals devoted to social gerontology and social policy, and professional journals that cover specific aspects of social care and physical and mental health. These journals enjoy a readership among professionals, lecturers, researchers, and students. The most encouraging aspect of the increasing readership is that the dissemination of knowledge is reaching people with wide interests in aging issues.

Although they have maintained their individual academic identity, the three learned societies representing the medical (British Geriatric Society: BGS), social (British Society of Gerontology: BSG) and biomedical (British Society for Research on Ageing: BSRA) interest in aging recently formed a British Council of Ageing (BCA). This body offers the government a collective and concerted voice on aging matters in the UK responding to policy initiatives and sitting on parliamentary committees.

CURRENT PUBLIC POLICY

Most health and welfare benefit services are delivered by the state in the UK and, to some extent, driven by the political ideology of the incumbent government. As mentioned in the introduction, devolution of power to the Scottish and Welsh Assemblies has meant that there are some regional differences in service delivery and benefit eligibility for older people. For example, in Scotland, the personal (as well as medical/nursing) component of residential care is free, and in England, personal care is means tested and charged for by the Local Authority. The Welsh Assembly pioneered free bus and highly subsidized community transport for older people. However, throughout the UK, National Health Service (NHS) medical prescriptions are free for all over the age of 60.

Recent policy initiatives and commissions include the NHS Framework for Older People (2001), which identified eight standards to be achieved: Rooting out Discrimination; Person Centred Care; Intermediate Care;

General Hospital Care; Stroke Services; Falls; Mental Health; and Health Promotion.

Legislation on standards in residential home care set targets for improving the environment (room size and access to bathrooms, for example), training of staff, medication protocols, nutrition and inspection (Office of Public Sector Information, 2001). This has led to the closure of many of the smaller, private residential care homes, which was encouraged by the "new right" agenda of the 1980s, because of lack of funds to make the alterations and inflexibility of some of the older accommodation. Most provision is now through major conglomerates, both commercial, such as Bupa, and the not-for-profit homes, such as Anchor Homes. There has been no return to the large-scale state provision that was reined back under Margaret Thatcher's Conservative government.

To a large extent, the policy that as far as possible and as long as possible, care should be in people's own homes, supported by Community Care provided by the Local Authority, has worked for most older people with physical limitations. A consequence of this, however, is that the profile of nursing-home residents has changed, inasmuch as they are older when they enter, they tend to be highly dependent, and there is a greater turnover owing to deaths. The residential homes therefore have much higher mortality rates than in the 1960s and 1970s. The younger residents tend to suffer from some form of dementia and cannot be looked after by families or live independently in the community. The workload for residential care staff is therefore much heavier and demanding and there tends to be a high staff turnover as well as resident turnover. One solution has been to encourage migrant workers from the European Union, the Philippines, and Africa. There can be difficulties with communication in terms of language barriers, sensory impairment, and cultural differences within the residential homes. There is also the ethical issue of poaching skilled workers from countries that need their own labor force. This is a source of tension within the care-home sector.

The complex pension systems in the UK are constantly under review and recommendations have been made to alleviate the poverty experienced by those with low-paid, interrupted or patchy employment histories, such as women and ethnic minority groups (Turner, 2005). In order to make these changes affordable, the government has legislated that between 2010 and 2020, the age for eligibility to claim the state pension will equalize at 65 years for men and women. Currently women can claim at 60; this reform will affect those born after 1950. Every two years from 2010 to 2020, the age of eligibility will be raised one year; so, for example, a woman born in 1956 will not be able to claim until she is 63.

From 2020, all women will need to have reached their 65th birthday for eligibility. However, occupational and private pensions will be negotiated between the employee and the pension scheme provider, as now.

In October 2006, the Age Discrimination Act deemed it illegal to discriminate against a person on the grounds of (older) age. The Act deals principally with discrimination in employment in terms of hiring and firing (DirectGov, 2006), but media hype initially highlighted some absurdities such as regulating wording on humorous birthday cards. Two years down the road, the legislation has settled into what information is given on the application form and what may be asked at interview that does not indicate a person's age.

Policy is also influenced by academic research, NGO (usually charities) and voluntary organization advocacy, and media pressure. The Centre for Policy on Ageing (CPA) has the one specialist gerontology library in the UK. It not only holds a comprehensive collection of current journals, but also maintains a database of all research projects and reports related to aging and as such is the most valuable resource for study, research, and literature searches. It also hosts the Better Government for Older People (BGOP) organization, which is supported by central and local government and has been at the forefront of developing successful new approaches to enable services to meet the challenges for today's and tomorrow's older population.

There are numerous local and national pressure groups and charities that address specific conditions of older people: Alzheimer's disease, arthritis, stroke, heart disease, Carers' Association, and so on. However, in the UK, there are two large national generic charities: Age Concern and Help the Aged. Age Concern has autonomous governance in England, Wales, Scotland, and Northern Ireland. Within their countries, they coordinate a federation of more than a thousand local voluntary service-providing groups. Help the Aged funds local action projects and is very active in international projects. These two major charities are about to amalgamate and bring to the table a combination of their expertise in advice and information, research, training, advocacy, and a strong political voice and commitment to Britain's aging population.

CONCLUSION

So, as we approach the end of the first decade of the 21st century, it is true to say that there has been a significant improvement in the lives of older people, who are now healthier, wealthier, and better educated than any previous cohort (Marmot, Banks, Blundell, Lessof, & Nazroo, 2003).

A major shift has been the involvement of older people themselves in academic, governmental, and NGO research on aging. Instead of a top-down, we-know-what-is-good-for-you approach, increasingly older people are being consulted and listened to for decision-making at local and national levels.

Nevertheless, there is room for even greater progress in understanding and responding to the experience of aging in Great Britain. Yes, older people are more involved, more visible, and audible in expressing their opinions and needs, but these are most frequently those of articulate, white, better-educated men and women. We still have a long way to go to address the needs of the poorest, most physically and mentally frail, ethnic minority elders, and other minority groups, such as the gay, lesbian, bisexual, and transgender elders. But we are steadily getting there.

USEFUL SOURCES IN GREAT BRITAIN USED IN THIS CHAPTER

Age Concern UK. *Working with and for older people.* http://www.ageconcern.org.uk
Arts and Humanities Research Council. http://www.mrc.ac.uk/index.htm
Beth Johnson Foundation. http://www.bjf.org.uk/
Biotechnology and Biological Sciences Research Council. http://www.bbsrc.ac.uk/
British Council on Ageing. http://www.bcageing.org.uk/
Better Government for Older People. http://www.bgop.org.uk/home.aspx
British Geriatrics Society. http://www.bgs.org.uk/
British Society for Research on Ageing. http://www.bgs.org.uk/
British Society of Gerontology. http://www.britishgerontology.org/
Centre for Policy on Ageing. http://www.cpa.org.uk/
Economic and Social Research Council. http://www.esrc.ac.uk/
Engineering and Physical Sciences Research Council. http://www.epsrc.ac.uk/
English Longitudinal Study on Ageing. http://www.ifs.org.uk/elsa/
Help the Aged. *Help the Aged: We Will.* http://www.helptheaged.org.uk/
Joseph Rowntree Foundation. http://www.jrf.org.uk/
Medical Research Council. http://www.mrc.ac.uk/
Nuffield Foundation. http://www.nuffieldfoundation.org/
The British Academy. http://www.britac.ac.uk/
The Leverhulme Trust. http://www.leverhulme.ac.uk/
Wellcome Foundation. http://www.wellcome.ac.uk/

REFERENCES

DirectGov. (2006). *Age Discrimination Act.* Retrieved August 6, 2008, from http://www.direct.gov.uk/en/Employment/DiscriminationAtWork/DG_10026429

ESRC GO Programme. (1999–2004). *Growing Older Programme: Understanding quality of life in old age.* Retrieved August 6, 2008, from http://www.growin golder.group.shef.ac.uk/Contents.htm

European Commission. (2008). *7th Framework Programme (FP 2007–2013).* Retrieved August 1, 2008, from http://ec.europa.eu/grants/index_en.htm

Marmot, M., Banks, J., Blundell, R., Lessof, C., & Nazroo, J. (Eds.). (2003). *Health, wealth and lifestyles of the older population in England: The 2002 English Longitudinal Study of Ageing.* London: Institute for Fiscal Studies.

New Dynamics of Ageing. (2008). *The New Dynamics of Ageing: A cross-council research programme.* Retrieved August 1, 2008, from http://www.newdy namics.group.shef.ac.uk/about/

Office of National Statistics. (2006a). *Population statistics.* Retrieved August 1, 2008, from http://www.statistics.gov.uk/CCI/nscl.asp?ID=7433

Office of National Statistics. (2006b). *Social trends 36.* London: HMSO.

Office of Public Sector Information. (2001). *The Care Homes Regulations.* Retrieved August 1, 2008, from http://www.opsi.gov.uk/si/si2001/20013965.htm

Turner, A. (2005). *Pensions, challenges and choices.* Retrieved August 6, 2008, from http://www.atl.org.uk/atl_en/images/Turner%20report%20exec%20 summary_tcm2–18545.pdf

Warnes, A. M. (1993). United Kingdom. In E. Palmore (Ed.), *Developments and research on aging. An international handbook* (p. 335–353). Westport, CT: Greenwood Publishing Group.

Co-director: Centre for Research on Ageing and Gender (CRAG) Past President: British Society of Gerontology (BSG)

21

‥■‥

Greece

Efstathios S. Gonos, Ioannis P. Trougakos, and Niki Chondrogianni

Aging is a natural biological process characterized by a progressive failure of homeostasis and multiple biochemical, molecular, and cellular changes that lead to increased disability, morbidity and, inevitably, death. Although much aging research focuses primarily on its biological etiology, it is evident that biological data must be combined with analysis of various socioeconomic factors, which also determine the rate of aging, in order to maximize a healthy and disease-free lifespan. Biological aging research in Greece is well established. Several groups, located mainly in research institutes and universities, are studying the various factors that determine human aging. These activities were first recorded in a review article in 2002 (Gonos et al., 2002). This chapter summarizes not only the various aging research activities, but also comments on the current state of education in gerontology as well as the public policy issues in relation to aging in Greece.

AGING RESEARCH IN GREECE

Laboratories at the National Center for Scientific Research (Demokritos) initiated aging research activities in Greece in the early 1990s. Dr. Stathakos's laboratory focused on the regulation of tissue homeostasis during development and aging and the role of growth factors during these processes. The qualitative alterations during the fetal-to-adult transition in the cells' response to exogenous growth factors, especially to TGF-β, as well as to autocrine growth factors, were the major research areas of this group (Kletsas & Stathakos, 1992; Kletsas, Stathakos, Sorrentino, & Philipson, 1995; Psarras, Kletsas, & Stathakos, 1994). Dr. Kletsas, who is now the director of the laboratory, is interested in tissue homeostasis and wound repair and its alteration during aging (Kletsas et al., 1998). Emphasis is also given to the study of tissue degeneration that promotes age-associated dysfunction (Pratsinis & Kletsas, 2007). Recent work in this laboratory has focused on the role of oncogene-induced senescence as tumorigenesis barrier and inhibitor of the malignant progression as imposed by DNA damage checkpoints (Bartkova et al., 2006). Furthermore, the regulation of crucial receptors in the cell-cell interactions, like intercellular adhesion molecule-1 (ICAM-1), that have a central role during all forms of injury are studied (Gorgoulis et al., 2003). At the same center, Dr. Sekeri-Pataryas's laboratory, now directed by Dr. Sourlingas, concentrates on the role of histones, their gene expression and acetylation during aging in human diploid fibroblasts and T-lymphocyte cell cultures (Happel, Doenecke, Sekeri-Pataryas, & Sourlingas, 2008; Sourlingas, Kypreou, & Sekeri-Pataryas, 2002; Sourlingas, Tsapali, Kaldis, & Sekeri-Pataryas, 2001).

In the mid-1990s, the laboratory of molecular and cellular aging was established by Dr. Gonos at the National Hellenic Research Foundation. This laboratory focuses on the genetic and environmental factors that influence human aging and longevity. The laboratory has cloned several age-associated genes by taking advantage of conditionally immortalized fibroblast cell lines that undergo senescence (Gonos et al., 1996, 1998; Powell et al., 1999). One of the cloned genes encodes for Clusterin/ Apolipoprotein J (CLU), which is found overexpressed *in vitro* under a variety of stress conditions and *in vivo* in samples from patients suffering from various age-related diseases, as well as in primary tumors that have acquired chemotherapeutic drug resistance (Dumont et al., 2000; Lourda, Trougakos, & Gonos, 2007; Trougakos et al., 2002). In addition, it has been demonstrated that inhibition of endogenous CLU expression by RNA interference induces growth retardation and higher rates of endogenous cellular death and sensitizes human cells to stress (Trougakos, Lourda, Agiostratidou, Kletsas, & Gonos, 2005; Trougakos, So, Jansen, Gleave, & Gonos, 2004). Thus, CLU is a novel survival factor being implicated in both aging and cancer.

Given that homeostasis is a key feature that determines organismal lifespan, Dr. Gonos's laboratory also studies the proteasome function in replicative senescence and cell survival (Chondrogianni et al., 2003; Chondrogianni et al., 2005; Chondrogianni, Trougakos, Kletsas, Chen, & Gonos, 2008). In search of natural compounds that may activate proteasome, it was identified that the main constituent of olives, oleuropein, exerts stimulatory effects on proteasome. Moreover, continuous treatment of human fibroblasts cultures with oleuropein delays senescence by approximately 15% (Katsiki, Chondrogianni, Chinou, Rivett, & Gonos, 2007).

Finally, the laboratory has also developed banks of cells (skin fibroblasts and peripheral blood monocytes), RNA, and DNA of healthy centenarians and long-lived sib pairs that has allowed study of the genetic and environmental factors that relate to longevity (Chondrogianni, Petropoulos, Franceschi, Friguet, & Gonos, 2000; Chondrogianni, Simoes, Franceschi, & Gonos, 2004; Mondello et al., 1999).

Research activities at the Foundation of Research and Technology in Crete, led by Dr. Tavernarakis, focus on the elucidation of the basic molecular mechanisms underlying the progressive decline in cellular function that accompanies aging based on the *Caenorhabditis elegans* model system. Special effort is made to identify the specific biochemical steps underlying alterations of protein turnover during aging and under caloric restriction (Tavernarakis & Driscoll, 2001). As protein synthesis and degradation are the two essential cellular processes responsible for maintaining functional protein content, this group has shown that decrease in protein synthesis can extend lifespan in *C. elegans* (Syntichaki, Troulinaki, & Tavernarakis, 2007; Tavernarakis, 2008). In parallel, Dr. Tavernarakis's group is investigating the mechanisms responsible for the degeneration and necrosis of neuronal cells in an attempt to simulate the human neurodegenerative diseases and their regulation (Syntichaki, Xu, Driscoll, & Tavernarakis, 2002).

Age-related activities at the University of Patras, Department of Chemistry, initially directed by Prof. Tsigganos, now led by Prof. Karamanos, are focused on the alteration of proteoglycans/glycosaminoglycans in cartilage, brain, and blood vessels. The group also studies the factors that contribute to the development of abdominal aortic aneurism (Theocharis, Tsolakis, Tsegenidis, & Karamanos, 1999).

Given that oxidative stress is a major challenge to all living cells, research efforts in the University of Ioannina, School of Medicine, directed by Prof. Galaris, concentrate on understanding the molecular mechanisms of action of cytotoxic agents that are generated *in vivo* (Doulias, Barbouti, Galaris, & Ischiropoulos, 2001). Moreover, the role of redox-active iron and copper ions is investigated (Barbouti, Doulias, Nousis, Tenopoulou, & Galaris, 2002; Galaris, Mantzaris, & Amorgianiotis, 2008), along with the role of a variety of substances that are able to protect cells from H_2O_2-induced DNA damage (Tselepis et al., 2001). Another research activity at the University of Ionnina, directed by Dr. Koletas, relates to the study of oncogenes and their activation in the process of aging. Comparison of human diploid fibroblasts with their immortalized and transformed counterparts revealed multiple molecular changes, mainly in the expression of growth factor and receptor genes, as well as extracellular matrix (Kolettas, Khazaie, & Rosenberger, 1997).

Apart from the above-mentioned biological research activities on "normal aging," other groups work on several age-related diseases. Studies on the regulation of Alzheimer's disease—particularly on the biochemistry, molecular, and cell biology of the amyloid precursor protein (APP) and presenilin 1 (PS1)—are performed in the Department of Biology at the University of Athens (Efthimiopoulos et al., 1998), as well as at the Biomedical Research Foundation at the Academy of Athens, where the molecular basis of neuronal degeneration and plaque formation in Alzheimer's disease are investigated using transgenic animal models (Georgopoulos, McKee, Kan, & Zannis, 2002). At the same institute, the pathogenesis of Parkinson's disease and the role of α-synuclein are also investigated (Clough & Stefanis, 2007). Finally, the detailed understanding of the molecular and cellular mechanisms underlying immunological disease initiation, progression, and chronicity is the goal of research in the Biomedical Sciences Research Center called Alexander Fleming, where animal models for chronic immunopathologies and autoimmunity have been developed (Armaka et al., 2008; Douni, Armaka, Kontoyiannis, & Kollias, 2007).

CURRENT STATE OF EDUCATION IN GERONTOLOGY

Regardless of the rapid expansion of aging research, medical specialization in gerontology and geriatrics remains to be established in Greece. The only relevant educational activity is a European postgraduate program; namely, the European Master's in Gerontology degree (EuMaG; www.eumag.org). The flexible schedule of EuMaG caters especially to professionals working in the field of (public) health and social welfare, offering the possibility of a full master's program as well as participation in individual modules that meet specific professional interests or needs. This program focuses on training young scientists and professionals through various education centers of gerontology in several European countries, including Greece.

Gerontology and geriatrics in Greece is represented by the Hellenic Society of Gerontology and Geriatrics, which was founded in 1977. The aims of this society are the study of aging (basic and applied research), prevention of premature aging, education in gerontology, and close collaboration with governmental organizations to ameliorate the quality of life of aged people. To this end, the Society organizes conferences, seminars and symposia to promote scientific knowledge for gerontology. The Society also represents Greece in international organizations, informs the public about age-related issues, and has established the Alzheimer's Centre. In this center, patients with Alzheimer's disease can be diagnosed, receive medical treatment and therapy, and acquire psychological help to improve their quality of life. Finally, Greece also participates in the European Society of Preventive, Regenerative and Anti-Aging Medicine (ESAAM) in its local branch, which will organize the 2nd European Congress of Preventive, Regenerative and Anti-Aging Medicine in Athens in 2009.

CURRENT PUBLIC POLICY ISSUES IN AGING

To address public issues in aging, the Hellenic Ministry of Health and Care established the Centers for the Open Care for the Elderly in 1984. Today there are more than 300 such centers throughout the country. The main goal of this institution is the protection of social rights of the elderly over the age of 60, regardless of their financial and social status. The aims of these centers are: (a) prevention of biological, psychological, and sociological problems of the elderly, allowing them to remain equal and active members of the society; (b) medical care of the elderly (vaccinations, checkups, etc.); and (c) constant updating of the society regarding the problems and needs of the elderly. In these centers, psychological and emotional help is offered as well as physiotherapy, ergotherapy, indoor and outdoor diversion, medical care, social lectures, excursions, organized visits to museums, and various social events aimed at maintaining and even revitalizing the personal interests of the participating individuals.

CONCLUDING REMARKS

Biological aging research in Greece is well established. As described earlier, many groups, mainly at research institutes and universities, are studying the various and complementary aspects of biological aging. Their research activities are recognized by the international scientific community and are reflected in numerous publications in eminent scientific journals, as well as in various labs' participation in international (mainly European) research grants and other relevant activities (e.g., journal editorial boards and various committees). Despite this international recognition, at the domestic level, substantial and continuous financial support is essential to maintain the country's achievements in this competitive research field. To this end, the establishment and funding of a Hellenic network on aging research is required to strongly facilitate these efforts. In addition, the introduction of a medical specialization in geriatrics is a prerequisite if Greece wishes to offer high-quality medical treatment to its elderly citizens.

REFERENCES

Armaka, M., Apostolaki, M., Jacques, P., Kontoyiannis, D. L., Elewaut, D., & Kollias, G. (2008). Mesenchymal cell targeting by TNF as a common pathogenic principle in chronic inflammatory joint and intestinal diseases. The *Journal of Experimental Medicine, 205,* 331–337.

Barbouti, A., Doulias, P. T., Nousis, L., Tenopoulou, M., & Galaris, D. (2002). DNA damage and apoptosis in hydrogen peroxide-exposed Jurkat cells: Bolus addition versus continuous generation of H(2)O(2). *Free Radical Biology and Medicine, 33,* 691–702.

Bartkova, J., Rezaei, N., Liontos, M., Karakaidos, P., Kletsas, D., Issaeva, N., et al. (2006). Oncogene-induced senescence is part of the tumorigenesis barrier imposed by DNA damage checkpoints. *Nature, 444,* 633–637.

Chondrogianni, N., Petropoulos, I., Franceschi, C., Friguet, B., & Gonos, E. S. (2000). Fibroblast cultures from healthy centenarians have an active proteasome. *Experimental Gerontology, 35,* 721–728.

Chondrogianni, N., Simoes, D.C.M., Franceschi, C., & Gonos, E. S. (2004). Cloning of differentially expressed genes in skin fibroblasts from centenarians. *Biogerontology, 5,* 401–409.

Chondrogianni, N., Stratford, F.L.L., Trougakos, I. P., Friguet, B., Rivett, A. J., & Gonos, E. S. (2003). Central role of the proteasome in senescence and survival of human fibroblasts: Induction of a senescence-like phenotype upon its inhibition and resistance to stress upon its activation. The *Journal of Biological Chemistry, 278,* 28026–28037.

Chondrogianni, N., Trougakos, I. P., Kletsas, D. Chen, Q. M., & Gonos, E. S. (2008). Partial proteasome inhibition in human fibroblasts triggers accelerated M1 senescence or M2 crisis depending on p53 and Rb status. *Aging Cell, 7,* 717–732.

Chondrogianni, N., Tzavelas, C., Pemberton, A. J., Nezis, I. P., Rivett, A. J., & Gonos, E. S. (2005). Overexpression of proteasome beta 5 subunit increases the amount of assembled proteasome and confers ameliorated response to oxidative stress and higher survival rates. The *Journal of Biological Chemistry, 280,* 11840–11850.

Clough, R. L., & Stefanis, L. (2007). A novel pathway for transcriptional regulation of alpha-synuclein. *FASEB Journal., 21,* 596–607.

Doulias, P. T., Barbouti, A., Galaris, D., & Ischiropoulos, H. (2001). SIN-1-induced DNA damage in isolated human peripheral blood lympho-cytes as assessed by single cell gel electrophoresis (comet assay). *Free Radical Biology and Medicine* , 30, 679–685.

Douni, E., Armaka, M., Kontoyiannis, D. L., & Kollias, G. (2007). Functional genetic and genomic analysis of modeled arthritis. *Advances in Experimental Medicine and Biology*, 602, 33–42.

Dumont, P., Burton, M., Chen, Q. M., Gonos, E. S., Frippiat, C., Mazarati, J. B., et al. (2000). Induction of replicative senescence biomarkers by sublethal oxidative stresses in normal human fibroblast. *Free Radical Biology and Medicine*, 28, 361–373.

Efthimiopoulos, S., Floor, E., Georgakopoulos, A., Shioi, J., Cui, W., Yasothorn-srikul, S., et al. (1998). Enrichment of presenilin 1 peptides in neuronal large dense core and somatodendritic clathrin-coated vesicles. *Journal of Neurochemistry, 71*, 2365–2372.

Galaris, D., Mantzaris, M., & Amorgianiotis, C. (2008). Oxidative stress and aging: The potential role of iron. *Hormones, 7*, 114–122.

Georgopoulos, S., McKee, A., Kan, H. Y., & Zannis, V. I. (2002). Generation and characterization of two transgenic mouse lines expressing human ApoE2 in neurons and glial cells. *Biochemistry, 41*, 9293–9301.

Gonos, E. S., Agrafiotis, D., Dontas, A. S., Efthimiopoulos, S., Galaris, D., Karamanos, N. K., et al. (2002). Ageing research in Greece. *Experimental Gerontology. 37*, 735–747.

Gonos, E. S., Burns, J. S., Mazars, G. R., Kobrna, A., Riley, T.E.W., Barnett, S. C., et al. (1996). Rat embryo fibroblasts immortalized with simian virus 40 large T antigen undergo senescence upon its inactivation. *Molecular and Cellular Biology, 16*, 5127–5138.

Gonos, E. S., Derventzi, A., Kveiborg, M., Agiostratidou, G., Kassem, M., Clark, B.F.C., et al. (1998). Cloning and identification of genes that associate with mammalian senescence. *Experimental Cell Research, 240*, 66–74.

Gorgoulis, V. G., Zacharatos, P., Kotsinas, A., Kletsas, D., Mariatos, G., Zoum-pourlis, V., et al. (2003). p53 activates ICAM-1 (CD54) expression in an NF-kappaB-independent manner. *The EMBO Journal, 22*, 1567–1578.

Happel, N., Doenecke, D., Sekeri-Pataryas, K. E., & Sourlingas, T. G. (2008). H1 histone subtype constitution and phosphorylation state of the ageing cell system of human peripheral blood lymphocytes. *Experimental Gerontology., 43*, 184–199.

Katsiki, M., Chondrogianni, N., Chinou, I., Rivett, A. J., & Gonos, E. S. (2007). The olive constituent oleuropein exhibits proteasome stimulatory proper-ties *in vitro* and confers lifespan extension of human embryonic fibroblasts. *Rejuvenation Research, 10*, 157–172.

Kletsas, D., Caselgrandi, E., Barbieri, D., Stathakos, D., Franceschi, C., & Otta-viani, E. (1998). Neutral endopeptidase-24.11 (NEP) activity in human fibroblasts during development and ageing. *Mechanisms of Ageing and Development, 102,* 15–23.

Kletsas, D., & Stathakos, D. (1992). Quiescence and proliferative response of normal human embryonic fibroblasts in homologous environment: Effect of aging. *Cell Biology International Reports, 16,* 103–113.

Kletsas, D., Stathakos, D., Sorrentino, V., & Philipson, L. (1995). The growth inhibitory block of TGF-β is located close to the G1/S border in the cell cycle. *Experimental Cell Research, 217,* 477–483.

Kolettas, E., Khazaie, K., & Rosenberger, R. F. (1997). Overexpression of *c-erbB* (EGF receptor) proto-oncogene fails to alter the lifespan or promote tumourigenic growth of normal and SV40-transformed human fibroblasts. *International Journal of Oncology, 11,* 1071–1080.

Lourda, M., Trougakos, I. P., & Gonos, E. S. (2007). Development of resistance to chemotherapeutic drugs in human osteosarcoma cell lines largely depends on up-regulation of clusterin/apolipoprotein. *International Journal of Cancer, 120,* 611–622.

Mondello, C., Petropoulou, C., Monti, D., Gonos, E. S., Franceschi, C., & Nuzzo, F. (1999). Telomere length in fibroblasts and blood cells from healthy centenarians. *Experimental Cell Research, 248,* 234–242.

Powell, A. J., Darmon, A. J., Gonos, E. S., Lam, E.W.F., Peden, K.W.C., & Jat, P. S. (1999). Different functions are required for initiation and maintenance of immortalisation of rat embryo fibroblasts by SV40 large T antigen. *Oncogene, 18,* 7343–7350.

Pratsinis, H., & Kletsas, D. (2007). PDGF, bFGF and IGF-1 stimulate the proliferation of intervertebral disc cells *in vitro* via the activation of the ERK and Akt signaling pathways. *European Spine Journal, 16,* 1858–1866.

Psarras, S., Kletsas, D., & Stathakos, D. (1994). Restoration of down-regulated PDGF receptors by TGF-β in human embryonic fibroblasts: Enhanced response during *in vitro* aging. *FEBS Letters, 339,* 84–88.

Sourlingas, T. G., Kypreou, K. P., & Sekeri-Pataryas, K. E. (2002). The effect of the histone deacetylase inhibitor, trichostatin A, on total histone synthesis, H1(0) synthesis and histone H4 acetylation in peripheral blood lymphocytes increases as a function of increasing age: A model study. *Experimental Gerontology, 37,* 341–348.

Sourlingas, T. G., Tsapali, D. S., Kaldis, A. D., & Sekeri-Pataryas, K. E. (2001). Histone deacetylase inhibitors induce apoptosis in peripheral blood lymphocytes along with histone H4 acetylation and the expression of the linker histone variant, H1°. *European Journal of Cell Biology, 80,* 726–732.

Syntichaki, P., Troulinaki, K., & Tavernarakis, N. (2007). eIF4E function in somatic cells modulates ageing in *Caenorhabditis elegans*. *Nature, 445,* 922–926.

Syntichaki, P., Xu, K., Driscoll, M., & Tavernarakis, N. (2002). Specific aspartyl and calpain proteases are required for neurodegeneration in C. elegans. *Nature, 419,* 939–944.

Tavernarakis, N. (2008). Ageing and the regulation of protein synthesis: a balancing act? *Trends in Cell Biology*, *18*, 228–235.

Tavernarakis, N., & Driscoll, M. (2001). Cell/neuron degeneration. In S. Brenner & J. Miller (Eds.), *The encyclopedia of genetics* (Vol. 1). New York: Academic Press.

Theocharis, A. D., Tsolakis, I., Tsegenidis, T., & Karamanos, N. K. (1999). Human abdominal aortic aneurism is closely associated with compositional and specific structural modifications at the glucosaminoglycan level. *Atherosclerosis*, *145*, 359–368.

Trougakos, I. P., Lourda, M., Agiostratidou, G., Kletsas, D., & Gonos, E. S. (2005). Differential effects of clusterin/apolipoprotein J on cellular growth and survival. *Free Radical Biology and Medicine*, *38*, 436–449.

Trougakos, I. P., Poulakou, M., Stathatos, M., Chalikia, A., Melidonis, A., & Gonos, E. S. (2002). Serum levels of the senescence biomarker clusterin/apolipoprotein J increase significantly in diabetes type II and during development of coronary heart disease or at myocardial infarction. *Experimental Gerontology*, *37*, 1175–1187.

Trougakos, I. P., So, A., Jansen, B., Gleave, M. E., & Gonos, E. S. (2004). Silencing expression of the clusterin/apolipoprotein J gene in human cancer cells using small interfering RNA induces spontaneous apoptosis, reduced growth ability, and cell sensitization to genotoxic and oxidative stress. *Cancer Research*, *64*, 1834–1842.

Tselepis, A., Doulias, P. T., Lourida, E., Glantzounis, G., Tsimogiannis, E., & Galaris, D. (2001). Trimetazidine protects low-density lipoproteins from oxidation and cultured cells exposed to H_2O_2 from DNA damage. *Free Radical Biology and Medicine*, *30*, 1357–1364.

22

Hungary

Bálint Boga

In the previous editions of this book, Prof. Edit Beregi described in detail the situation of elderly people, and the formation and development of gerontology in Hungary until 1993. I will now give an overview of these topics since 1993, mainly using data from recent years.

DEMOGRAPHY

Hungary is a country in Eastern-Central Europe. Its geographic site and position between West and East have played an essential role in its history, as well as at the present time. The country recently became a member of NATO and the European Union. However, even before 1989, when our regime changed, some influence from the West could be felt. Despite these recent changes, catching up with the West is difficult and requires more time.

Demographically, the process of aging in our society is similar to that of most developed countries. In the past few years, the proportion of the population aged 60 or over has increased by 20% (1980: 17.1%; 2007: 21.6%). This fact can be explained not only by the increase in average life expectancy, but also by the decrease in the birthrate. This means that the decline in the number of younger people has contributed to this demographic phenomenon: in 1980, 21.9% of the population was 0–14 years old; in 2006, this proportion was 15.2%. The aging index (65+ divided by 0–14 years old) is very high: 102.9 in 2006, while in 1960, it was 35.2.

In general, we observe a slow increase in average life expectancy, although the trends are not straightforward. In 1980, it was 69.0 years at birth, and in 2006, it was 73.2 years. This has been the consequence of the amelioration in general living conditions, the development of medicine and health care, as well as better access to its facilities for the elderly population—as in most countries. Nevertheless, this increase, which was greatest mainly in most recent years, is still four to seven years behind the most developed countries (e.g., France: 76.9 years for males, 84.0 for females); but it is better than in the majority of the Eastern European countries (e.g., Ukraine: 61.5 years for males, 73.4 for females). Clearly, there is a relationship between the gross domestic product (GDP) per person and life expectancy in each country, and our data also fit with this relationship.

In addition, an important tendency in our country is the decrease in total population, in spite of the fact that the mortality rate has declined in almost all age groups. The number of deaths exceeds the number of births. Immigration alters this trend slightly.

A remarkable difference occurs between the average life expectancy of men and that of women: 68.6 and 76.9 years at birth, respectively (2006). This phenomenon can be observed in all developed countries (in the United Kingdom: four years, 2006); but it is more striking in our country and the difference has been increasing during the last 25 years (in 1980: 7.2; in 2006: 8.5 years). Besides biological causes, working conditions and societal frustration are also responsible for this, and have been present in everyday life and cause family problems, such as the high rate of divorce. Anomie, as a psychological phenomenon, affects men more than women. Family tasks and everyday duties of women generally compensate better for the societal contradictions that were stressful during the so-called socialist era. These social stressors are still present today, in new forms. This problem of anomie among men has been reflected in the high mortality rate among middle-aged men. Their mean life expectancy decreased between 1970 and 1990 from 66.3 to 65.1 years. Since 1990, there has been a slow increase.

Other relevant data are as follows: in 1960, out of 1,000 men aged 45–49, 5.2 died; in 1990, this number was 11.5; and in 2005, 10.7. For men aged 50–54, the corresponding death rates are 8.9, 16.7, and 15.5; for those 55–59 years old: 15.6, 24.6, and 20.8, respectively.

In the older age groups, there has been a continuous decrease in death rates from 1980: in age group 70–74, from 71.2 to 53.3; in those above 85 years, from 275.2 to 187.2. Life expectancy (19 years for those aged 60, and 12.3 years for those aged 70, in 2006) is acceptable in comparison to more developed countries. So this is an explanation for the relatively large and increasing proportion of the older age group within the population.

Similar to other nations, women outnumber men in the elderly group, and this trend has accelerated in recent decades. In 1980, the ratio of women to men aged 60–64 was 1.23; in 2001, it was 1.33, and for those over 85 years, these numbers were 2.33 and 2.52, respectively (KSH [Central Statistical Office], 2007).

HEALTH STATUS AND HEALTH CARE

Some surveys have been performed in recent years that registered the subjective (perceived) health status of the elderly population. The OLEF 2000 (Országos Lakossági Egészségfelmérés: National Survey of Population Health) demonstrated perceived bad health in a remarkable share of persons aged 65 or over: 36.9% of females and 32.0% of males evaluated their health condition as bad or very bad (Bácskay, 2004b). In the VÉKA (Változó Életkörülmények Adatfelvétel: Survey of Changing Living Conditions) of 2006, 40% of people aged 70 or over felt their health status was bad, and 14% very bad. This survey is important because recent international surveys verified that subjective health evaluation is frequently a better predictor of health status, occurrence of major pathological events, and death than objective parameters. Of course, health status significantly influences the capacity to conduct daily living activities. Approximately 44% of both genders in this age group are restricted in daily living activities. The Microcensus (KSH, 2006) demonstrated more detailed and more unfavorable data. 50–60% of those 60 or older were limited in their daily living activities; moreover, three-quarters of females aged 70 or over were so limited. These unfavorable data, different from those in Western Europe, are consequences of the social, economic, occupational, and other circumstances of political changes that occurred in the last century in our geographical region. Many of the old cohorts have lived through and endured them. They bear the psychic, psychosomatic, and somatic impacts of these periods.

Health care of ill older persons is carried out in the ordinary way in the framework of the general adult health-care system. At each level of the health-care system, a large proportion of the patients belong to the old age group. This fact is obvious because of the higher frequency of morbidity and the phenomenon of multimorbidity in the elderly population. Two-thirds of those treated in the basic health-care system are 60 years old or older. The proportion of 65 years old or over is 20% for outpatient specialist care, and 33% in hospital care. Also in 2001, 50% of those 75 or older were treated in hospitals (Paksy, 2004).

Among the causes of mortality—as in other modern countries—cardiovascular and neoplastic diseases occupy the first two places: 60% and 23% of deaths, respectively (Paksy, 2004). With advancing age, the relative rate of these diseases increases progressively. It is remarkable that the number of incidents is relatively high (e.g., it is twice as high as in the United Kingdom).

However, we can observe one favorable phenomenon, as mentioned before: the relative decrease in the death rates of older persons. The average age at death is 75.2 years in females and 67.1 in males.

The special geriatric care started to function only after considerable delay and even now—in the period of transformation of the health care system—there are many difficulties. The Board of Geriatrics, as an advisory council of the Minister of Health, has been functioning since 1996. Since 2000, geriatric medicine has been accepted as a medical specialization with separate examination. In 2003, a decree of the Ministry of Health, Social Affairs and Family defined the concept of a geriatric patient, and three levels of special geriatric care: consulting (for out-patients), mobile team (in-hospital for all departments), and geriatric hospital department. The latter can have three sub-departments: acute, readaptive/rehabilitative, and day-hospital sub-departments (Ministry of Health, Social Affairs and Family, 2003). Long-term departments are available for all ages. In fact, up to now special geriatric care has been functioning only in a few places, and even in these places, it functions only partially. Even now, the chronic and geriatric hospital care overlap, mainly for patients in an incurable or terminal state, regardless of their age.

SOCIAL CARE

The regulation of this sphere has undergone manifold changes in the last decades. Social care is the responsibility of local governments and in most cases, they fulfill the needs well. The so-called basic provision includes home care (personal assistance) and Meals on Wheels service (delivery of food). The placement of individuals into institutions must be decided by a council in the local government. Recently, the precondition for this has been a need for immediate personal help lasting for more than four hours.

The number of persons provided by home care is about 15,000; by Meals on Wheels about 75,000; by both, about 28,000. Altogether, the basic care system gives help to 120,000 persons, mainly for elderly (Bácskay, 2004a). This number was 143,000 in 2006, including home care for 45,000, and Meals on Wheels for 106,000 persons. Of those provided for by the home-care system, 75% to 80% are aged 70 or over. There is probably a large hidden need for this, if we take into account the results of surveys mentioned in the section on health. This survey verified that 7% of the aged 70 or over need assistance in everyday living. A helper cares for 5.5 persons, on a national average.

About 45,000 persons receive so-called intermediary provision, which means they obtain care in the day-care system (we call them clubs for the elderly). There are about 1,200 such clubs in the country. This is a relatively small number, for only 2% of persons over 60 participate in this kind of provision. A significant problem is the access to these clubs from small villages.

There are about 45,000 people living in homes for elders. This number is 2% of those aged 60 or over. Thirty percent need permanent nursing care. Twenty-nine thousand of these beds are administered by the local governments, the others by churches, associations, foundations, and so on.

RELATIONSHIPS IN THE FAMILY AND HOUSING

The so-called modified extended family is common in our country. This is a situation in which relatives provide emotional and financial support while living apart. Earlier, to have a common flat was one of the determinant factors of intergenerational links. As a consequence of our societal changes, the rate of living together is decreasing. In 1970, the percentage of elders living on their own in apartments/flats was 16.1%; in 2002, this figure was 23.8%. In 14.5% of households, elders live together with members of the younger generation (Lakatos et al., 2005). More than 56% of one-person households are run by old people. There are differences in the usual facilities between the flats of the elderly and those of younger people, for example in terms of water supply and toilet facilities.

Earlier, due to lower wages and salaries, younger people were not able to afford a home of their own. At present, however, the majority of old couples and widows or widowers live separately from the younger members of the family. Because of this, there are difficulties in assisting with the everyday needs of frail elderly parents.

The difference in the mortality rates of men and women causes a higher rate of widowhood among females than males (52.2% of women aged 60 or over are widowed, compared to 14.8% of men). A special problem for the widower living alone is how to keep house; because it was usually run by their wives, they are inexperienced in this activity.

PARTICIPATION IN WORK AND RETIREMENT

Very few elderly persons participate in official work: only 1.3% of those aged 60 or over is an active breadwinner and only 3.7% of them work in addition to receiving a pension (Lakatos et al., 2007). Only 4.8% of men aged 62–64, and 1.7% of the women in this age interval have a salaried job. In comparison, 33.6% of the aged 55–64 are at work. Due to the social changes of recent decades in our country, the number of persons who retire early is very high, because of the large number of old age and disability pensions available. One consequence, among others, is a low rate of active earners even in the 50–60 age group. Of course, unemployment also contributes to this unfavorable phenomenon. More precisely, in the 50–54 age group, 61.9% of males and 58.8% of females are at work, and at age 59, these rates are 46.9% and 10.3%, respectively (Lakatos et al., 2005). This latter difference can be explained by the fact that a few years ago, 55 years was the official retirement age for women, but now it is 62 years for both genders. The low employment rate further increases the age-based dependency ratio. Over 56% of pensioners are below the official retirement age. Even nowadays, there is a problem in pension provision because of the low number of people contributing as paying earners.

Our pension system stands on three pillars: (1) pay-as-you-go, the state social security pension system, the main form; (2) privately managed and funded pension systems with mandatory contribution; and (3) privately managed and funded pension systems, with voluntary contribution (Gál, Iwasaki, & Széman, 2008).

The average old-age pension is about 67% of average salary (it was 60% in 2000). There is a part inflation and part average salary follow-up mechanism (the inflation rate was 8% in 2007).

The proportion of the aged 60 or over among parliament representatives is lower than in the population. In civil organizations, this proportion is higher (for example, in the retired section of trade unions).

EDUCATION OF OLDER PERSONS

We have had good traditions in this field since 1982. In our capital, the Free University of the Retired and the Old Age Academy at Batthány-Strattman are functioning.

In the framework of people's college, some elderly persons take part in informal education. In a few towns, there are special colleges for older people. The community cultural centers organize cultural clubs for the elderly population. There were 200,000 participants in 2004. Moreover, social institutions and organizations for older adults run educational programs.

More than 4% of the population over 60 participate in formal adult education, which is a very low number compared to that of other Western countries; for example, in the United Kingdom, 29.1% are involved.

In artistic amateur groups, there are about 14,000 elderly persons. There are a few Internet courses for the elderly; for example, the "Click, granny!" program in Budapest. The rate of Internet users is low in the old age group, due to the delay of the introduction of the Internet in our country: 6.3% of persons aged 65–74 are able to use it and 8% of all retired.

EDUCATION IN GERONTOLOGY

Since 1998, geriatrics has been a component of the curriculum in university medical schools. There are different forms of teaching at each university. At the Semmelweis University in Budapest, medical students are required to take 32 hours of geriatrics in their last semester. At the University of Debrecen, students can choose 32 hours of geriatrics as their electives. At the University of Szeged, students attend 14 hours of lectures on geriatrics and 14 hours of practicum. At the University of Pécs, students complete a single-semester course in gerontology (two hours per week in the sixth or eighth semester). Gerontology, social gerontology, and social work for elders are taught at the faculties of social sciences and at Eötvös Lóránd University, Budapest, as well.

RESEARCH

Hungary has a deep-rooted tradition in the field of gerontology. Nowadays, experiments and follow-up surveys are in progress at some research centers. These are as follows:

- Semmelweis University Budapest, Medical School, Geriatric Department and Institute of Clinical Experimental Research and Human Physiology, where the role of sexual hormones and free radicals in postmenopausal changes is being investigated
- University of Pécs, Institute of Anatomy: pathogenesis of Parkinson's syndrome; Department of Pathophysiology and Gerontology: regulation of age-related changes in the metabolism, body weight and composition, obesity, anorexia, role of peripherial factors and neuropeptids
- University of Szeged, Institute of Anatomy: microvascular lesion in the brain; Laboratory of Neurobiology: investigation into c-FOS in the aging process; Clinic of Psychiatry: gene polymorphism in Alzheimer's disease; Section of Behavioural Sciences: health promotion and sociological

aspects of aging, thanatology; Geriatric Teaching Hospital Department, Institute for Biochemistry and Clinic of Internal Medicine: relationships between membrane fluidity, thermoshock proteins and aging

- University of Debrecen, Division of Geriatric Medicine, Department of Internal Medicine: immunology and endocrinology of aged people, cross-sectional survey of nonagenerians (clinical and social status); Centre for Medical and Health Sciences: aging processes, social gerontology

- Institute of Sociology, Hungarian Academy of Sciences: outdoor and indoor mobility of the elderly, intergenerational equity, aging in the labor market, employment and care, migrant labor eldercare sector, pension system and accessibility within the home

THE ASSOCIATION OF GERONTOLOGY

The Hungarian Association of Gerontology changed its name to the Hungarian Association of Gerontology and Geriatrics in 2005. The majority of the members of our association are geriatricians who work in different parts of our country, mainly in geriatric departments. Our Association has a close relationship with the professional Board of Geriatrics, for example, giving opinions on the regulations and state of health care. Every year, we organize a conference with postgraduate education programs and give reports on scientific research. We are a member of the IAGG and participate in its international congresses.

PLANNING FOR THE FUTURE

This year, a comprehensive strategy for elders in the future was begun by experts of different fields of science. This strategy will cover all aspects of living for the next decades.

REFERENCES

Bácskay, A. (2004a). *Az idősek szociális gondozása* [Social care for the elderly]. Budapest: KSH (Central Statistical Office).

Bácskay, A., et al. (2004b). *Old people in Hungary*. Budapest: KSH (Central Statistical Office).

Gál, R. I., Iwasaki, I., & Széman, Z. (2008). *Assessing intergenerational equity*. Budapest: Akadémiai Kiadó.

KSH (Central Statistical Office). (2006). *Microcensus 2005*. Budapest: Department of Census.

KSH (Central Statistical Office). (2007). *Demographic yearbook, 2006*. Budapest: Department of Census.

Lakatos, J., et al. (2005). *Társadalmi jellemzök* [Characteristics in the society]. Budapest: KSH (Central Statistical Office).

Lakatos, J., et al. (2007). *Ezüstkor, idöskorúak Magyarországon* [Silver age, old people in Hungary]. Budapest: KSH (Central Statistical Office), Ministry of Social and Labour Affairs.

Ministry of Health, Social Affairs and Family. (2003). *ESZCSM* [Ministry of Health, Social Affaires and Family] *60/2003 decree*. Budapest: Author.

Paksy, A. (2004). *Az idöskorúak egészségi állapotának jellemzöi* [Health status of the elderly population]. Budapest: KSH (Central Statistical Office).

23

··■··

India

P. V. Ramamurti and D. Jamuna

India is a secular democracy of diverse cultures. Though Hindus are in the majority, there are a considerable number of Muslims, Buddhists, Christians, Sikhs, and smaller numbers belonging to other faiths. Despite industrialization and modernization being fast afoot, agriculture continues to be the mainstay. Its population of 1.2 billion is second in size only to China, the most populous nation in the world. About 7.5% of the Indian population is above 60 years of age, with average life expectancy around 65 years. At 60 years of age, individuals are expected to live on an average for another 17 years, with women outliving men. About two-thirds of older people live in rural areas and approximately 60% of the elderly have not had any formal schooling. Older people constitute the fastest-growing segment of the population, and by 2025, they are expected to increase to about 180 million, equating to 14% of the population (National Sample Survey Organization [NSSO], 1998; Rajan, Mishra, & Sharma, 1999; Ramamurti & Jamuna, 2004).

DEVELOPMENTS SINCE 1990: GOVERNMENT PROGRAMS

Since we wrote for an earlier edition of this book (Ramamurti & Jamuna, 1993), a good number of developments have taken place. India was a signatory to the declaration at the first World Assembly on Aging in 1982, and again at the second world meeting on Aging, held in Madrid in 2002. In consonance with these developments, the government of India announced the National Policy for Older Persons (NPOP) in 1999 with the Ministry of Social Justice and Empowerment (MSJ & E) as the nodal agency coordinating the implementation of policy by different ministries as applicable to them.

The NPOP of 1999, prepared by the MSJ & E and adopted and promulgated by the Government of India, is a comprehensive document. The policy encompasses a wide range of programs and measures that pertain to the overall welfare of older persons and seek to improve their quality of life in all spheres of life, including medical (geriatric) services, social and financial security, supplemental income generation, old age pensions for the destitute and retirement benefits for the employed, support for the family as a primary care provider, education and training, and increased public awareness of aging.

As a follow-up on the national policy, a National Council for Older Persons (NCOP) was constituted as an advisory and monitoring body. An action plan for the implementation of the policy was prepared. The MSJ & E coordinates the activities of various ministries involved in the implementation of the action plan. The action plan stresses the following programs, which are under the jurisdiction of various ministries: (a) strengthening of primary health care and special training of medical and paramedical staff to meet the needs of older persons; (b) promoting healthy aging; (c) encouraging nongovernmental agencies to provide health and physical care of the elderly; (d) subsidizing basic necessities of life for the elderly; (e) assisting local bodies and self-help groups to extend eldercare through day care and residential care for senior citizens; (f) providing financial savings schemes specially intended to provide for returns in older years; (g) establishing legal provisions for care of elderly by adult children; and (h) providing for the utilization of the capabilities and skills of senior citizens and empowering them.

In 2007, the Indian Parliament passed a legislation, *viz.*, The Care and Maintenance of Parents and Senior Citizens Act 2007, which mandates the care of parents by their adult children. It also provides for free medical care for destitute old people in hospitals and free long-term care for them in old-age homes. The governments at the state level are expected to implement the provisions of the Act. Parents can seek maintenance through a simple procedure within a local district level tribunal constituted for this purpose by the state government. The government has also implemented a number of other measures based on the action plan for the national policy for older people. These measures include an old-age pension for those in poverty, transportation concessions, subsidized rations of food grains (to those below the poverty line), and priority for older people in queues at hospitals and other consumer counters. The government has also asked universities and other institutions to introduce courses in gerontology and to create greater public awareness about aging. (The details of various governmental welfare measures for the senior citizens can be accessed through the Web site www.http://socialjustice.nic.in/sdciop/ministries.htm and also india.gov.in/citizens/seniorcitizens/policiesschemes.php [National Portal of India: citizens: Senior citizens corner].)

The government encourages and assists nongovernmental organizations (NGOs) in establishing and running old-age homes, day-care centers, and mobile medical units and in providing other types of services (Gokhale, 2004). HelpAge (India), the biggest of the NGOs, has regional units spread throughout the country, through which it provides a number of services, such as free cataract surgery, an adopt-a-granny scheme, day-care centers, and training programs. HelpAge (India) also publishes a periodical in regional languages, designed for the elderly; a research journal; and a resource centre. Several other NGOs in the country—like the Dignity Foundation, the Silver Innings, the Harmony Foundations, the Elders Forum, a Yahoo discussion group (SSS-global@yahoogroups.com), and a host of similar organizations spread the length and breadth of the country—offer a variety of services, including security for seniors, Alzheimer's care, emergency help lines, and hospice services.

GERONTOLOGY IN HIGHER EDUCATION

Gerontology as a subject of study in higher education was first introduced at the Sri Venkateswara University (Department of Psychology); since then, gerontology has been offered at Tirupati as an optional paper in 1976; as a specialization at the master's level in 1990 and as a Post-Masterate Diploma in 1993–94. A Center for Research on Aging was started in the department in 1983–84. In spite of these developments, it took some time for gerontology to gain momentum as a specialty in higher education in India. As part of the implementation of the NPOP, the Government of India has asked universities and other educational institutions to start courses in aging. To date, several universities and colleges in the country have started teaching the subject of aging, both at the graduate level and at the research level, as part of psychology, home science, anthropology, and social work courses (e.g., M.S. University, Baroda; Sri Padmavathi Women's University, Tirupati; SNDT Women's University, Bombay; Tata Institute of Social Sciences, Bombay; Bharathi Dasan University, Madurai; and Mother Teresa University, Kodai Kanal).

Organizations like the Indian Council of Social Science Research, the University Grants Commission, Indian Council of Medical Research, the Department of Science and Technology, and the Ministry of Social Justice and Empowerment have come forward to fund research on aging as an area of emphasis. During the current year (2008–2009), the government of India is poised to start a National Institute on Aging, which will assume responsibility for carrying out coordination and assistance in aging research, and play an advisory role to the government and other agencies on all matters pertaining to aging. An adequate allotment in the national budget for this has been provided.

The Government of India, through its National Institute of Social Defence (NISD), organizes short-term training programs in geriatrics, geriatric nursing, and training in bedside care. The NISD also collaborates with and encourages other organizations in conducting similar training programs. The National Council of Educational Research and Training, the University Grants commission, and several other bodies have developed curricula for a variety of professional courses in gerontology and geriatrics for adoption in education and training programs.

An Association of Gerontology (India), affiliated to the International Association of Gerontology and Geriatrics (IAGG), has been in existence since 1982, as has the Geriatric Society of India. An International Longevity Centre (ILC) (India) with UN recognition has been set up at Pune (in Maharashtra). Academic journals, for example the *Indian Journal of Gerontology* from Jaipur, and the *Journal of Ageing and Society* from Calcutta, are devoted to publication of research in aging. A number of popular periodicals have appeared in recent years, providing plenty of reading material on aging, meant especially for senior citizens. Over the years, academic and professional institutions interested in aging have organized a large number of seminars and conferences and conducted outreach programs toward homeless, widowed, childless, and economically poor older persons. The print and electronic media also play a significant role in creating awareness of aging among the public.

RESEARCH

Research output in the multidisciplinary field of gerontology may be categorized under three broad headings: medicine, biology, and behavioral and social sciences. The research effort in India can be traced back to the late 1950s and 1960s, but growth of research in the field was slow. It picked up in the post-1982 period (following the World Assembly on Aging) and accelerated from early 1990s onward. The bulk of research publications fall into the area of behavioral and social sciences. Books and articles in this area significantly outnumber those in bio-gerontology and medicine. Several reviews of the work on aging in India are available (Karkal, 1999, 2000; Ramamurti & Jamuna, 1995, 2004; Ruprail, 2002).

THE MEDICAL SCIENCES

As in other parts of the world, India is in the grip of the health transition, a shift from communicable diseases to degenerative chronic age-related disorders. Work in geriatric medicine has mostly been an application of the principles of general medicine to age-related disorders and conditions. Departments of geriatric medicine are just beginning to come into being (two or three for the whole country), and so are postgraduate courses in geriatrics. However, in the next decade, this trend is expected to increase considerably (Gangadharan, 2003).

Basic research in geriatrics is sparse. However, annual meetings of the geriatric societies do discuss newer developments in the practice of medicine for older adults. The Indian Council of Medical Research has a division on noncommunicable diseases (NCD), which deals with aging issues, funds research projects in the area of aging, and conducts consultancy meetings on important topics. A special issue of the *Indian Journal of Medical Research on Ageing* (1997) by the Indian Council of Medical Research (ICMR) is indicative of the trends in the medical field. Good sources of literature on the practice of geriatrics in India are Sharma (1999); Dey (2003); and Rosenblatt & Natarajan (2002).

Much of geriatric research output pertains to studies on the prevalence of various aging related disorders (Rao, 1997, 2004). The commonly reported ailments in the elderly are arthritis (47%), hypertension (16%), and diabetes (17%) (NSSO, 1998). Of significance is the increasing interest in dementia, especially Alzheimer's disease (Chandra, 1997; Rajkumar, Samuel, & Sahabudi, 1996). The Alzheimer's and Related Disorders Society of India (ARDSI) provides a forum for dissemination and discussion of research and practical concerns about dementia. Another development is the revival of interest in Indian systems of medicine and therapy such as Siddha, Ayurveda, Yoga, and Unani in the treatment of age-related disorders. The National Institute of Nutrition (NIN) Hyderabad and several university departments of nutrition have done some work on the recommended daily allowances (RDA) for the aged, and have conducted studies on nutrient intake among the elderly. They also conduct outreach programs for the benefit of the elderly in the community (Dey, 2003; Natarajan, 1995; Puri & Khanna, 1999; Shah, 2004; Ramamurti, S., 2004).

BIO-GERONTOLOGY

Research in the biology of aging, which started in the 1960s at Benaras Hindu University by a group of molecular biologists, has progressed modestly. In addition, work is being carried out at the University of Hyderabad, University of Bhopal and at the Indian Institute of Science in Bangalore. The work being done at these places focuses on gene regulation, hormonal modulation, antioxidant manipulation, and telomere role and repair, all of these in relation to aging (Kanungo, 2004a, 2004b; Subbarao, 1997; Thakur, 2003, 2004). Most of this research output is presented at international meetings and at the meetings of the Association of Gerontology (India).

BEHAVIORAL AND SOCIAL GERONTOLOGY

There is a view that the phenomenon of aging is a social construction. Even though there are physical aspects of aging, the impact of aging is very significant on the behavioral and social dimensions, including interactions among individuals. The number of scholars working on aging in the behavioral and social sciences is considerably higher than those in the clinical or in the biological fields. Given the greater number of scholars involved in this aspect of aging, the academic output in this area is substantial (Ramamurti & Jamuna, 2004).

As in the United States, in India the early work in the field of aging was focused on the problems of adjustment in old age, on the status of the aged in the family and society, and on intergenerational interactions and perceptions (Ramamurti & Jamuna, 1995). Reviews and bibliographies on the developments of aging studies in India have been several (Karkal, 1999, 2000; Ramamurti & Jamuna, 1995, 2004; Ruprail 2002). A variety of topics have been touched upon, including problems, attitudes, adjustments, intergenerational interactions, personality, social supports and networks, physical and mental health, health behavior, disability, loneliness, eldercare issues, caring stress, elder abuse, neglect, centenarian studies, longevity models, institutional and day-care issues, the elder in the family, gender aging, death anxiety, religiosity and spirituality, leisure utilization, successful and productive aging.

The findings of the studies on psychological and social aspects carried out from 1991 to date are briefly and selectively summarized here below. However, a detailed account of these findings is available in a review that is part of the Indian Council of Social Science Research's fifth survey of psychology (Ramamurti & Jamuna, awaiting publication).

Ageist attitudes are widely prevalent despite India being steeped in a tradition that honors elders. Positive attitude toward the aged is found to increase with age, though negative perception of aging is present even among the elderly themselves (Jamuna & Ramamurti, 1995; Reddy, 1995). Health and economic problems continue to affect the elderly as a majority of the aged (70%) are poor, rural/slum dwelling, uneducated and in occupations with unsteady income in the unorganized sector (i.e., agricultural or other casual labor, petty vendors, artisans and the like) (Muthayya, 2004; NSSO, 1998; Ramamurti, 2003a).

The majority of the elderly live in families with a spouse and adult children. There is a growing trend of children migrating away from aged parents, in pursuit of education or jobs. Parents who have adequate and dependable income tend to live independently, but they help children in times of need (such as childbirth and infant care). Property conflicts, incompatibility between sons/daughters-in-law and parents and parents-in-law have caused strained relationships and, in some cases, resulted in overt or covert elder abuse and neglect (Bambawale, 1996; Jamuna, 2003). Older people who are subjected to such abuse or those who are destitute are relegated to old-age homes. Apart from these options, there are a number of older people with reasonable means, seeking to stay independently in retirement homes or communities (Ara, 1995; Kalavar & Jamuna, 2002; Prakash, 1998; Ramamurti & Jamuna, 1997, 2004)

Wherever they stay, loneliness is a commonly reported problem among the elderly, but degree of loneliness varies. Empirical studies show that the widowed and those in old-age homes reported feeling more lonely than other older people, and those in joint or extended families felt least lonely (Patel, Asgarli, & Broota, 2000; Prakash, 2004; Ramamurti, 1997a).

Eldercare is increasingly becoming a problem in India as joint and extended families are on the decline, while migration among children, dual careers among younger couples, and costs of caring for older persons are on the rise. India is at a stage when familial care of the elderly is decreasing and the state and community care has yet to step in adequately. There is a feminization of caring for the elderly despite difficulties experienced by women. Many caregiving women have reported stress. (Bagchi, 2000; Jamuna, 2000, 2001, 2004, 2007; Singh, 1999).

In the last two decades, a good number of studies have been carried out on life satisfaction, quality of life, successful aging, and active and productive aging. These are well-worked areas of gerontology in India. Several psychosocial factors, such as self-perception of health, level of functionality, self-acceptance of aging changes, social and family supports, economic security, self-confidence, living arrangements, flexibility of behavior, belief in Karma philosophy, and life review—were found to be correlated to life satisfaction and successful aging. Moreover, life satisfaction, quality of life, successful aging, and active aging were found to be intercorrelated variables (D'Souza, 1993; Easwaramoorthy & Chadha, 1999; Ramamurti & Jamuna, 1995, 1999; Singh, 2002; Sinha & Singh, 1997; Ushasree & Basha, 2003).

Examining the characteristics of long-lived individuals (nonagenarians and centenarians), several variables are significant, including both biological and psychosocial variables. Family history and lineage (parental longevity) is a significant factor. Long-lived individuals are generally slim or of moderate body build, belong mostly to the middle economic class, are active for their age, do not have any major disease, and suffer only from visual and/or auditory defects. They are largely self-reliant in carrying out their activities of daily living. Most of them are widowed. Like others, they too have passed through the usual stresses and strains of life, but maintain a calm, unagitated temperament and take challenges in stride and cope well. They generally have a confident outlook, are god-fearing and enjoy good social relationships with children, grandchildren, and relatives (Jamuna & Ramamurti, 2000; Ramamurti, 1997b; Ramamurti, Jamuna & Reddy, 1996, 2000; Sudha Rani, 2000).

Most of the research studies reported above on sociopsychological aspects of aging are on cross-sectional samples and not of a longitudinal type (which follows the same individuals over a period). Therefore, there is the possibility of time or period effects confounding the age effects to some extent (Ramamurti, P. V., 2003a, 2003b, 2004; Ramamurti & Jamuna, 1999).

The foregoing may be considered a selective summary of the developments in the field of aging in India since 1990. The volume of literature generated is substantial. Today, there is greater awareness of human aging both in the government and among the people, though the common man among the aged is yet to secure a square deal.

WHAT THE FUTURE MAY HOLD

Conjecturing about the future could result in both apprehension and optimism. The ominous signs of the projected swift growth of the older population in a populous country such as India may forebode a crisis situation that requires a careful assessment and long-range planning at the highest levels. A strategy for efficient use of elderly person-power would turn the elderly from an economic liability into an asset. Another reason to think about opportunities for older people to remain involved in productive activity is the decreasing trend in total fertility, which is a welcome sign for a population that is bursting at the seams. It carries the hope that the population will stabilize at around 1,500 million, putting the lid on the uncontrolled population growth of the second half of the last century. The national economy, which appears to be showing a positive trend at the moment, may put behind an era of shortages caused by phenomenal growth of the population.

The 60+ and 80+ age groups, which are today the fastest-growing segments of the population, will substantially grow in size and proportion, requiring more efficient services for the elderly and a more open employment market for the elderly. Otherwise, the 20-odd years that are available on average, post-retirement (at 60), would remain empty and become wasted person power. Engagement of some kind during these years, coupled with adequate activity, promotes both physical and mental health of the older person, reduces his disability (Ramamurti, 1996, 1997a, 1997b), and cuts the costs to the state exchequer.

Simultaneously, to meet the growing demand for services to the elderly, there is a need for concerted efforts to develop professional careers in gerontology and geriatrics and in-service/short-term supplementary training for existing staff, providing a wide variety of courses. Third age universities and special training programs for developing the human resource of older people also need to be instituted (Ramamurti, 2003a). A string of seniors' service centers may be organized, offering information and a variety of services within easy reach of the elderly; for example, to cater to the financial, health, therapeutic, and disability needs of elderly at home or in residential homes (Ramamurti & Jamuna, 2007). To reimburse health expenditures in the elderly, health insurance schemes may be extended to all senior citizens.

To keep old age active, healthy, and free from disability, we need a multipronged national strategy that would provide for a healthy and active lifestyle across the life span, beginning in the young years, along with an economy that would efficiently employ people at all ages, according to capability, and without age discrimination. India as a developing country would need to reset its sights with regard to mainstreaming the elderly into the development agenda, and work to realize them instead of allowing them to remain as mirages. In achieving this end lies the very future of the country.

REFERENCES

Ara, S. (1995). Old-age homes, the last resort. *Research and Development Journal, Help Age (India)*, 2(1), 3–10.

Bagchi, K. (2000). Healthy aging. *Research and Development Journal, Help Age (India)*, 6(3), 36–43.

Bambawale, U. (1996). Abuse of the aged. In V. Kumar (Ed.), *Aging: Indian perspective and global scenario* (pp. 298–382). New Delhi: Author.

Chandra, V. (1997). Alzheimer's disease and other dementias. In K. Bagchi (Ed.), *Elderly females in India: Their status and suffering* (pp. 89–100). New Delhi: Society for Gerontological Research and HelpAge India.

D'Souza, V. S. (1993). The concept of active aging. *Indian Journal of Social Work, 54*(3), 334–344.

Dey, A. B. (2003). *Aging in India.* New Delhi: Ministry of Health and Family Welfare and WHO.

Easwaramoorthy, M., & Chadha, N. K. (1999). Quality of life of Indian elderly: A factor analytic approach. *Social Change: Journal of the Council for Social Development, 29* (1 & 2), 32–46.

Gangadharan, K. R. (2003). Geriatric hospitals in India: Today and in the future. In P. S. Liebig and S. Irudayarajan (Eds.), *An aging India: Perspectives, prospects and policies* (pp. 143–158). New York: The Haworth Press.

Gokhale, S. D. (2004). Aging in India—Policy issues. In P. V. Ramamurti and D. Jamuna (Eds.), *Handbook on Indian gerontology* (pp. 437–462). New Delhi: Serials Publications.

Indian Journal of Medical Research. (1997). *Special issue on aging in India.* New Delhi: ICMR.

Jamuna, D. (2000). Aging in India: Some key issues. *Aging International, Spring,* 16–31.

Jamuna, D. (2001). Intergenerational issues in eldercare. *Indian Journal of Gerontology, 15*(3&4), 287–295.

Jamuna, D. (2003). Issues of elder care and elder abuse in the Indian context. In P. S. Liebig & S. I. Rajan (Eds.), *An aging India: Perspectives, prospects and policies* (pp. 125–142). New York: The Haworth Press, Inc.

Jamuna, D. (2004). The statics and dynamics of elder care in the Indian context. In P. V. Ramamurti and D. Jamuna (Eds.), *Handbook on Indian gerontology* (pp. 208–242). New Delhi: Serials Publications.

Jamuna, D. (2007). Elder women in India—Roles and status. In J. Troisi & A. Powliczko (Eds.), *The elderly woman in Asia—Her roles and position* (pp. 75–98). Malta: International Institute on Aging, United Nations.

Jamuna, D., & Ramamurti, P V. (2000). *Psychological correlates of long-lived individuals. Project report.* New Delhi: University Grants Commission.

Jamuna, D., & Ramamurti, P. V. (2007). Perceptions of ageism across the generations. *Indian Journal of Gerontology, 21*(2), 206–215.

Kalavar, J. M., & Jamuna, D. (2002). Old-age homes: The experience of elderly in Bangalore, India. *Journal of the Aging Family System, 1,* 21–36.

Kanungo, M. S. (2004a). Genes and aging. In P. V. Ramamurti and D. Jamuna (Eds.), *Handbook on Indian gerontology* (pp. 69–95). New Delhi: Serial Publications.

Kanungo, M. S. (2004b). Mechanism of aging. *Proceedings of the Indian National Science Academy,* New Delhi.

Karkal, M. (1999). *Elderly in India. An annotated bibliography* (Vol. I). Bombay: TISS.

Karkal, M. (2000). *Elderly in India. An annotated bibliography* (Vol. II). Bombay: TISS.

Lalitha, K., & Jamuna, D. (2004). Memory status in the elderly and its correlates: An intervention study. *Indian Journal of Gerontology, 18*(1), 151–158.

Liebig, P. S. (2003). Old age homes and services: Old and new approaches to aged care. In S. Liebig & I. Rajan (Eds), *An aging India: Perspectives, prospects and policies* (pp. 159–178). New York: Haworth Press.

Muthayya, B. C. (2004). The rural elderly in India. In P. V. Ramamurti and D. Jamuna (Eds.), *Handbook on Indian gerontology* (pp. 369–381). New Delhi: Serials Publications.

Natarajan, V. S. (1995). *Nutrition in the elderly.* Madras: Natarajan.

National Sample Survey Organization (NSSO). (1998, November). *The aged in India: A socio-economic profile—52nd round* (July 1995–June 1996). New Delhi: Author.

Patel, J. M., Asgarli, & Broota, A. A. (2000). Perception of loneliness and ways of resolving it. *Indian Journal of Gerontology, 14*(1 & 2), 55–60.

Prakash, I. J. (1998). Social network and functional competence and well-being of the elderly. *Indian Journal Clinical Psychology, 25*(1), 6–12.

Prakash, I. J. (2004). Mental health of older people in India. In P. V. Ramamurti and D. Jamuna (Eds.), *Handbook on Indian gerontology* (pp. 176–208). New Delhi: Serials Publications.

Prakash, I. J. (2008). Mushrooming of gerontology courses: Making them more relevant & effective. *Research and Development Journal, Help Age (India), 14*(2), 34–36.

Puri, S., & Khanna, K. (1999). *Health and nutrition profile of middle-class elderly women in New Delhi.* New Delhi: HelpAge India.

Rajan, S. I., Mishra, U. S., & Sharma, P. S. (1999). *India's elderly: Burden or challenge.* New Delhi: Sage.

Rajkumar, S., Samuel, R., & Sahabudin. (1996). Burden in caregivers of Alzheimer's disease patients. In V. Kumar (Ed.), *Aging: Indian perspective and global scenario* (pp. 249–252). New Delhi: AIIMS.

Ramamurti, P. V. (1996). *Health behavior among the middle aged and elderly. Project report.* New Delhi: Indian Council of Medical Research.

Ramamurti, P. V. (1997a). Coping with aging. *Indian Journal of Medical Research; Aging in India, 106,* 376–380.

Ramamurti, P. V. (1997b). *Contributions to longevity: The Tirupati Centenarian Study.* Paper submitted November 1997 to the First Asian Symposium at Kaulalampur, Malaysia.

Ramamurti, P. V. (2002). Geropsychology—East–west scenario. *Journal of Community Guidance and Research, 19*(2), 265–272.

Ramamurti, P. V. (2003a). Empowering the older persons in India. *Research and Development Journal, Help Age (India), 9*(1), 16–21.

Ramamurti, P. V. (2003b). Perspectives of research on aging in India. In P. S. Liebig & S. I. Rajan, *An aging India: Perspectives, prospects and policies*. New York: The Haworth Press.

Ramamurti, P. V. (2004). Psychosocial aspects of aging in India. In P. V. Ramamurti and D. Jamuna (Eds.), *Handbook on Indian gerontology* (pp. 268–327). New Delhi: Serials Publications.

Ramamurti, P. V. & Jamuna, D. (1993). Developments and research in aging. In E. Palmore (Ed.), *Developments and research on aging: An international handbook* (pp. 145–158). Westport, CT: Greenwood Press.

Ramamurti, P. V., & Jamuna, D. (1995). Perspectives of geropsychology in India: A review. *Indian Psychological Abstracts and Reviews, 2*(2), 207–267.

Ramamurti, P. V. & Jamuna, D. (1997). *Evaluation of old age homes, day care centers, mobile Medicare of Andhra Pradesh. Project report*. New Delhi: Ministry of Welfare, Government of India.

Ramamurti, P. V., & Jamuna, D. (1999). Frontiers of aging research in India. In S. D. Gokhale et al. (Eds.), *Aging in India* (pp. 205–215). Mumbai: Somaiya Pubs. Pvt. Ltd.

Ramamurti, P. V., & Jamuna, D. (2004). *Handbook on Indian gerontology*. New Delhi: Serials Publications.

Ramamurti, P. V., & Jamuna, D. (2007). Senior citizens' service and information centres. *Research and Development Journal, Help Age (India), 13*(3), 33–36.

Ramamurti, P. V., Jamuna, D., & Reddy, L. K. (1996). Psychosocial profiles of centenarians: The Tirupati Centenarian Study. In V. Kumar (Ed.), *Aging: The Indian perspective and global scenario* (pp. 63–65). New Delhi: Vinod Kumar.

Ramamurti, P. V., Jamuna, D., & Reddy, L. K. (2000). *The Tirupati Centenarian Study*. Tirupati: CEFRA, S. V. University.

Ramamurti, S. (2004). Nutrition in the elderly. In P. V. Ramamurti & D. Jamuna (Eds.), *Handbook of Indian gerontology*. New Delhi: Serials Publications.

Rao, A. Venkoba. (1997). Psychiatric morbidity in the aged. *Indian Journal of Medical Research, 106*, 3361–369.

Rao, A. Venkoba. (2004). Psychiatry of old age. In P. V. Ramamurti & D. Jamuna (Eds.), *Handbook on Indian gerontology* (pp. 117–152). New Delhi: Serials Publications.

Reddy, L. K. (1995). Public attitudes towards the elderly. In S. Vijayakumar (Ed.), *Challenges before the elderly: An Indian scenario* (pp. 143–150). New Delhi: MD Publications.

Reddy, L. K. (1996). Health and attitude towards health among elderly. In V. Kumar (Ed.), *Aging: The Indian perspective and global scenario* (pp. 231–234). New Delhi: Vinod Kumar.

Rosenblatt, D. E., & Natarajan, V. S. (2002). *Primer on geriatric care*. Cochin: Printers Castle.

Ruprail, N. (2002). *Silver generation in India*. New Delhi: ICSSR.

Shah, B. (2004). Health care delivery systems of the elderly. In P. V. Ramamurti and D. Jamuna (Eds.), *Handbook on Indian gerontology* (pp. 96–116). New Delhi: Serials Publications.

Sharma, O. P. (1999). *Geriatric care in India: Geriatrics and gerontology.* Delhi: A & B Publishers Ltd.

Singh, R. R. (1999). Self-help groups and pressure groups for older persons. *Research and Development Journal, Help Age (India)*, 5(3), 34–44.

Singh, S. (2002). Issues of emotional integration, peace and happiness—The Vedantic view. *Journal of Gerontology*, 17(1 & 2), 205–212.

Sinha, S. P., & Singh, R. (1997). Time structure and well-being among retired persons. *Indian Journal of Gerontology*, 11(3&4), 72–77.

Subbarao, K. (1997). DNA damage and DNA repair in aging brain. *Indian Journal of Medical Research*, 106, 423–437.

Sudha Rani, N. N. (2000). *Psychosocial correlates of long-lived individuals.* Unpublished doctoral dissertation, S. V. University, Tirupati.

Thakur, M. K. (2003). Hormonal interventions of aging and longevity. In S. S. Rattan (Ed.), *Biology of aging and its modulation: Modulating aging and longevity.* Dordrecht, The Netherlands: Kluwer Academic Publisher.

Thakur, M. K. (2004). Biological aspects of aging. In P. V. Ramamurti and D. Jamuna (Eds.), *Handbook on Indian gerontology* (pp. 39–68). New Delhi: Serials Publications.

Ushasree, S., & Basha, S. A. (2003). Religiosity as a contributor to meaning in life. *Indian Journal of Gerontology*, 17(1&2), 85–98.

24

Ireland

Desmond O'Neill, Cillian Twomey, and Eamon O'Shea

The role and position of older people in Ireland has ebbed and flowed over the centuries. In pre-Christian Irish civilization, there was a strong tradition of a culture that prioritized the position of older people under a system of laws known as the Brehon laws (Robins, 1986). With colonization by the Normans in the 12th century, these laws fell into disuse and the position of older people was probably of the same nature as was common in the rest of Europe.

A COUNTRY OF YOUNG PEOPLE?

By European standards, Ireland is a relatively youthful nation; 11% of the population were aged 65 and over in 2006 (Central Statistics Office, 2007). Ireland has the lowest proportion of its population aged 65 and over in the European Union (EU), well below the EU average of nearly 17%. Life expectancy of men at age 65 increased from 13.8 years in 1995–1997 to 15.4 years in 2001–2003; corresponding figures for women were 17.4 and 18.7 years.

AGING-SPECIFIC POLICY IN IRELAND

Although certain branches of government have developed policies specific to older people (in particular in health), overall level of awareness of aging as a core issue for government policy is low. Ireland is one of the few European countries that has not responded to the UN Madrid Action Plan on Aging, and the key UN concept of intergenerational solidarity (United Nations, 2002) finds little echo in official policy. It does not appear in *Towards 2016*, the Ten-Year Framework Social Partnership Agreement (Department of the Taoiseach, 2006), in a recent Pensions Green Paper (Department of Social and Family Affairs, 2007), or a recent report of the National Economic and Social Council on the developmental welfare state (National Economic and Social Council, 2005).

Although there has been a junior Minister for Older People for over a decade, and an Office of Older People was initiated in 2008 to develop a National Strategy on Positive Ageing (Department of Health, 2008), no new line of funding has been organized for this work, and in the first instance the Office will incorporate the work and staff of the National Council on Ageing and Older People (www.ncaop.ie). Founded in 1981 as an advisory body to the Department of Health, it has been a vital catalyst in the development of policies on aging, acting as a center for social and health gerontology when such activity was at an embryonic stage in Irish universities. It has published over 100 reports on various aspects of aging in Ireland, including health, mental disease, disability, the law, and older people, which are excellent source books on aging in Ireland.

INCOME AND FINANCES

Income and support for older people in Ireland arise from a combination of pensions and benefits in kind. The pension system is of the Beveridge type, with the aim of providing a safety net rather than income replacement. The result is that the risk of relative poverty is one of the highest in Europe: older Irish people rank second highest for risk of relative poverty in the EU after the social transfers and pensions are taken into account (Central Statistics Office, 2007). Older women are at a higher risk of poverty than men. However, overall poverty rates are significantly lower than for people of working age (Fahey, Maitre, Nolan, & Whelan, 2007).

Between 1996 and 2005, there was a considerable shift from State noncontributory pensions (a means-tested basic pension) to State contributory pensions (a taxable, but higher, flat-rate basic pension linked to social insurance payments). Overall, the take-up of occupational pensions is low in Ireland, with less than half of all workers covered by such schemes (Whelan, 2003).

The most important benefit in kind has been provision of free access to primary care, medications, and hospitals to those over 70, not means tested, which has been shown to have had a dramatic effect on uptake of preventive health care for older people in the first Irish longitudinal study on aging (Health and Social Services for Older People II; HeSSOP-2) (O'Hanlon et al., 2005). Unfortunately, this was curtailed in the 2008/9 budget. More controversial are the benefits in kind of free public transport, telephone rental, and an allowance for electricity; critics point to the inevitable erosion of access that occurs with piecemeal benefits, and challenges to less able-bodied older people in using existing public transport (O'Neill, Bruce, Kirby, & Lawlor, 2000). A helpful initiative in this regard has been Department of Transport support for social economy models of rural transportation (Roberts, Drazin, Basi, & O'Neill, 2007).

EMPLOYMENT, SOCIAL PARTICIPATION, AND POLITICAL PROFILE

Although industrial policy and lifelong learning opportunities in Ireland do not favor older workers (Basten, Irwin, & Heaney, 2002), as a result of persistence of a legacy economy of farming, fishing, and agriculture, Ireland had the sixth highest employment rate for people aged 65 and over among EU countries, particularly for men (Central Statistics Office, 2007). Since 2004, there is no longer mandatory retirement in most of the public sector in Ireland, but age discrimination is the most common form of complaint of discrimination in the workplace reported to the Irish Equality Authority (Equality Authority, 2008).

A high proportion of older Irish people vote—in the 2002 general election, 86% of persons aged 65 and over—but their public advocacy profile is not commensurate with this voting strength. Advocacy has involved a relatively large number of organizations, most notably Age Action Ireland (www.ageaction.ie), but also the Irish Senior Citizens' Parliament (a coalition of 380 organizations, most not specific to older people: http://iscp.wordpress.com/about/), and the Irish Association of Older People (www.olderpeople.ie). In conjunction with a number of other organizations, they have formed a coalition called Older and Bolder (www.olderandbolder.ie), although it is disappointing that they have no formal links with academic or professional gerontology groups. The Irish government has also funded an agency, Age and Opportunity (www.olderinireland.ie), to promote positive attitudes to aging: its most successful activities include *Go For Life*, a nationwide exercise network for older people, and *Bealtaine*, an annual festival of creativity and later life.

LIVING CIRCUMSTANCES

With 5.5% of older Irish people resident in nursing homes and other long-stay hospitals in 2006 and another 3.5% in acute hospital care at any one time, Ireland has the second highest proportion of older people living in nursing homes and hospitals in the EU. Social supports are strong— two-thirds of older people talk to their neighbors most days, with most of the rest doing so once or twice a week (Fahey et al., 2007). The majority of older people said they are never or not very often bothered by loneliness and 85% report a high level of emotional and social support.

HEALTH STATUS

The first Irish longitudinal study on ageing (HeSSOP-2) found that the health of older Irish people in the community was generally good (O'Hanlon et al., 2005). In the first wave, 80% rated their quality of life as very good or good (Garavan, Winder, & McGee, 2001). In the second cohort, over 75% reported being self-sufficient in their abilities to perform tasks of daily living and 60% reported no functional disability. Eighty per cent rated their quality of life as good or very good and over 75% scored high on morale. In terms of need, 12% usually needed help with one or more tasks of daily living. Almost half of older people receive informal help from one or more people on a regular basis (O'Hanlon et al., 2005), and older people are often the people providing informal care (O'Neill & McGee, 2007). The level of disability rises with advancing age. In the 2006 census, 30% of those aged 65 and over indicated they had a disability compared to 9% among the total population. Almost 90% of those in nursing homes have at least one disability (Falconer & O'Neill, 2007).

HEALTH SERVICES

The health system is a mixed public and private system (O'Neill & O'Keeffe, 2003), with older people largely using the public service, often supplementing it with their own money. The health services also provide and fund services—home helps, nursing home subsidy, Meals on Wheels, et cetera—which in many other countries would be provided by a separate social services budget, making it difficult to accurately compare health and social care spending on older people in Ireland with other countries (Organisation for Economic Co-operation and Development [OECD], 2006), but the level of health spending is also likely to be below the OECD and EU averages. Social-care spending is also low relative to countries of similar prosperity, and significant investment is also required, particularly with respect to community-based services and supports (National Economic and Social Council, 2005). In terms of private health care, a troubling development for older people has been sustained pressure by private health insurance companies on "community rating," whereby health insurance premiums cannot be increased on age grounds. Despite support by the government for community rating, a recent Supreme Court decision has opened the way for erosion of the scheme in practice.

The general practitioner (GP) and public health nurse (PHN) are the key elements of the primary care system. The GP is a pivotal health professional contact for older people, with 93% having consulted their GP in the previous year. The PHN has a less prominent profile, with 15% having been visited by the PHN in the past year. Use of other services was very limited, with many older people stating that they would like to use them, but are deterred by lack of information, and barriers to access including cost, availability, stigma, and transport. This is a major challenge, as more than a third of older people in the community found to be "severely impaired" in carrying out activities of daily living had not received any home services in the past year. One in 10 people experiencing extreme disruption to their lives through illness had not received any of the home or community-based services studied (O'Hanlon et al., 2005).

SPECIFIC HEALTH-CARE POLICIES FOR OLDER PEOPLE

The aging-preparedness of the health system represents a mixed scorecard. On the positive side, Ireland was one of the first countries in Europe to develop a strategic plan for the development of services for older people, *The Years Ahead* (Working Party on Services for the Elderly, 1988). Adopted as official government policy in 1993, it has been influential in shaping health policies for older Irish people, but a review of its effect after eight years found many recommendations unfulfilled and noted that almost no extra spending had been directed to older people (Ruddle, Donoghue, & Mulvihill, 1997).

At a strategic level, the health service has appointed an Expert Advisory Group (EAG) on Older People, to advise it on policy. The EAG has no statutory power or authority, its deliberations are largely confidential, and there has been limited collaboration or consultation with the relevant professional bodies, for example with geriatricians or old-age psychiatrists. Concern has been raised about whether the resultant decisions of the health services represent either the best of gerontological science, or the best use of the cumulative expertise of the very many highly trained health gerontologists in Ireland.

In terms of gerontological orientation of the health service, perhaps the most important development has been the support for geriatric medicine, old-age psychiatry and gerontological nursing. With almost 60 geriatrician posts, each acute hospital in Ireland has at least one specialist geriatrician on staff. Not only do these provide foci of expertise in the secondary care system, but have a wider impact: for example, increasing numbers of future hospital doctors and GPs are spending a period of their training in geriatric medicine. The structure of training is similar to that adopted by the European Union of Medical Specialists (Geriatric Medicine Section of the European Union of Medical Specialists, 1999). The representative body for Irish geriatricians, the Irish Society of Physicians in Geriatric Medicine, was founded in 1979. Old-age psychiatry has also developed greatly in the past 20 years, with a representative body, the Irish Association of Consultants in Psychiatry of Old Age. Another positive development has been a national strategy on elder abuse, with a network of senior caseworkers, and a national research and advisory center (O'Dwyer & O'Neill, 2008).

On the debit side, a wide range of services is under-provided in terms of both funding and gerontological expertise. Services for age-related diseases such as stroke and dementia are under-resourced or nonexistent (Horgan, Hickey, McGee, & O'Neill, 2008); it is therefore not surprising that death rates and disability for stroke in Ireland are among the worst in Europe (Gray et al., 2006). Services in community and long-term care facilities, despite the best efforts of under-resourced and under-supported staff, also represent a major area of concern (Murphy, O'Shea, Conney, & Casey, 2007; Murphy et al., 2006; O'Shea et al., 2008). The government-funded breast cancer screening program stops at 65, despite evidence that the risk of developing and dying from breast cancer increases sevenfold after this age.

Only 35% of people in Ireland give a positive assessment of the quality of nursing homes in the country (satisfaction ratings in France and Belgium were 78% and 75%, respectively) (European Commission, 2007). This mirrors long-standing concerns about standards of care in nursing homes (National Council on Ageing and Older People, 2001; O'Neill, Gibbon, & Mulpeter, 2001) which were substantiated in the review of the first Irish nursing home scandal. This revealed a system unaware of the lessons of other countries from previous decades, unresponsive to developments in gerontological research in long-term care, and lacking in expertise, funds, and procedures (O'Neill, 2006). It is hoped that the Irish government will fully implement the 12 recommendations arising in the inquiry, which address the deficits at many levels. Some of these recommendations are addressed in new standards for residential care to be enacted in 2009 (Health Information and Quality Authority, 2007).

ACCESS AND ELIGIBILITY

Access to and eligibility for health and social services is a cause for concern for older Irish people, their advocacy organizations and professional groups. There is no overt government statement linking needs to entitlement to care provision in the community, and the provision of such services is highly variable. Almost two-thirds of Irish people believe that dependent older people have to rely too much on their relatives (European Commission, 2007). An important recent development was the provision of a set number of home-care packages designed to support independent living at home. These are means–tested, and tend toward cash payments rather than direct service provision; the challenges inherent in this choice include quality assurance, adding an employer role to the caring role, training of care assistants, and prevention of elder abuse (Timonen, 2004). Only one-third of Irish citizens believe that professional care at home is available at reasonable cost (European Commission, 2007).

Access to nursing-home care is even more vexed. After a major scandal involving charging older residents of nursing homes, which entailed a potential reimbursement of €1.5 billion, the Irish Supreme Court ruled that those in need of nursing home care were entitled to it free, apart from a weekly sum equivalent to 80% of the noncontributory pension (Office of the Ombudsman, 2005). However, accessing this care is difficult, with system-wide resistance, informational opacity, and limited provision (particularly in the larger cities) driving many older people and/or their families to self-fund nursing home care. Almost the only way to exercise the right to a publicly funded bed is by a final common pathway of critical functional failure in the community, admission to hospital, and subsequent placement in a public nursing home or fully publicly funded bed in a private nursing home. A separate route is by applying for a means-tested nursing home subvention, which in most cases covers only a fraction of the total cost.

Currently, there is general agreement that major horizontal and vertical inequities exist in relation to access to long-stay care in Ireland, leading to calls for reform in the financing of long-term care (Donnison, O'Shea, & Larragy, 1991; O'Shea, 2002; O'Shea & Hughes, 1994). It is not possible at this time to say with certainty what financing model will eventually emerge in Ireland, but current government thinking promotes cost sharing among older people, their families, and the state (Doyle et al., 2006) in a way that would not be tolerated for health and social care for illnesses such as cancer. A government bill proposing a charge for nursing homes of 80% of disposable income and collection of up to 15% of the estate after death is currently before the Irish parliament.

EDUCATION AND RESEARCH

The scientific body associated with aging is the Irish Gerontological Society (IGS; www.gerontology.ie). Founded in 1951, it is one of the oldest gerontological societies in Europe. It is the Irish affiliate to the IAGG, and membership is open to both the Republic of Ireland and Northern Ireland. The IGS has an interdisciplinary membership and despite a strong health-care orientation, strives in its constitution, board, membership, and activities to represent all branches of gerontological inquiry. It produces a journal, *Irish Ageing Studies Review,* and a newsletter, as well as running an annual scientific meeting, an annual focused study day, and Ph.D. study days. This latter activity provides a forum for doctoral candidates in all branches of gerontology to present their research and network in a supportive environment.

There has been considerable development in teaching various disciplines at both undergraduate and postgraduate levels in care of older people. Trinity College Dublin had the first academic department of medical gerontology, the first Chair in Psychiatry of Old Age, and offers diploma and master's courses in gerontological nursing. Academic developments are underway also in Cork and Galway, and the University of Limerick has appointed a geriatrician as the Professor of Medical Science in its medical school. The Royal College of Physicians in Ireland confers a postgraduate Diploma in Medicine for the Elderly, directed toward family doctors who wish to take specialist interest in older people, particularly those who may be appointed as medical officers for nursing homes.

In social gerontology, postgraduate programs exist at the National University of Ireland Galway (www.icsg.ie) and Trinity College Dublin (www.sparc.tcd.ie), and no undergraduate degree in gerontology exists in Ireland as yet.

ATLANTIC PHILANTHROPIES

In the absence of dedicated rubrics for aging research in Irish research councils, funding for research and advocacy in Ireland was given a major boost by significant financial support from Atlantic Philanthropies, a

philanthropic foundation. They have co-funded many projects supporting aging in Ireland. The areas co-funded include:

a. Advocacy projects, including substantial funding for the advocacy
   groupings and their coalition (The Older and Bolder Consortium),
   capacity-building funding for Age and Opportunity, and a high level
   network, the Ageing Well Network;
b. Social economy projects, including the Senior Citizens' Helpline;
c. Academic developments in social and health gerontology—the Irish
   Centre for Social Gerontology (www.icsg.ie) and a Chair in Social Gerontology at National University of Ireland Galway, the Social Policy
   and Ageing Research Centre (www.sparc.tcd.ie), a Ph.D. program in
   dementia studies and a Chair in Neural Engineering and Aging in
   Trinity College Dublin, a proposed Centre in Clinical Gerontology &
   Rehabilitation at University College Cork, and a Chair in Geriatric
   Medicine and support staff in St James's Hospital, Dublin;
d. An all-island body to coordinate and promote research on aging in
   Ireland, the Centre for Ageing Research and Development in Ireland
   (www.cardi.ie);
e. Funding toward a major longitudinal study on ageing in Ireland, The
   Irish Longitudinal Database on Ageing (www.tilda.ie), involving three
   Irish universities, an independent medical school, and the Economic
   and Social Research Institute; and
f. A grant of nearly €17 million for the Centre for Successful Ageing
   involving St James's Hospital and some of the staff in the Department
   of Medical Gerontology, Trinity College Dublin (The Atlantic Philanthropies, 2007).

NEW MAJOR RESEARCH PROGRAMS

The application of existing and new technologies has the potential to
enhance the independence and well-being of older people and increase the
probability of remaining in their own homes. Intel Corporation, a leading global manufacturer of microprocessors and associated technologies,
has combined with the Irish government, through its Industrial Development Authority, to establish a health research and innovation program in
Ireland, Technology and Research for Independent Living (TRIL; www.
trilcentre.org). This new program involves cooperation among scientists,
ethnographers, engineers, designers, and clinicians in three Irish universities, NUI Galway, UCD, and Trinity College.

The outcomes are technologically based products, policies, and measures for optimizing health promotion, health enhancement, and living

conditions, so that freedom of choice for older people is maintained as fully as possible for as long as possible. The current focus is on exploring technologies across three strands: falls prevention, social connection, and cognitive function, but the range of areas covered by TRIL is likely to increase as the program expands. The ethnographic component, based at NUI Galway, centers on the content and meaning of older people's narratives concerning experiences of dependence and disability, felt need for new technologies, and experiences with that technology as part of a holistic home care model.

TILDA (www.tilda.ie) is a major longitudinal exploration of aging in Ireland. A multidisciplinary, collaborative, cross-institutional national study led by Trinity College, with initial funding coming from Atlantic Philanthropies and Irish Life, the overall aim is to examine aging as a dynamic process incorporating physical, psychological, and cognitive function over time; economic and social influences on these functions; and adaptive responses that contribute to successful aging. The study will cover approximately 10,000 people aged 50 years and over, with a minimum follow-up of 10 years. TILDA will play a major role in planning for an aging population in Ireland, through its contribution to evidence-based research, policy formulation and implementation, and international comparative analysis.

SUMMARY

Overall, research and practice in Ireland have developed steadily over the last five decades, with significant academic developments in health, and increasingly social gerontology. Government policy reflects this pattern of development, with strongest orientation toward the new demography seen in health policy, and less clear direction in other areas of policy. Funding for research has been largely driven by philanthropy and industry, with no focus on aging in the research programs of the Irish health, humanities or sciences research councils.

However, developments in the last few years have seen the emergence of more academics with formal training in gerontology, the beginnings of a more informed dialogue on aging in Ireland, and increasing levels of seminars and colloquia on the topic. If such developments continue to multiply, we may eventually realize the speculative opinion on longevity and Ireland from 1901 that: "Taking all the data together and estimating their significance, it would seem that we ought not to consider Ireland a bad country to live in, but must infer that possibly the green island averages fairly well among the other parts of the earth" ("Longevity in Ireland," 1901).

REFERENCES

Basten, A., Irwin, G., & Heaney, D. (2002). *Labour market inequalities for older people in Ireland: Listening to the views of older persons*. Dublin: Equality Authority.

Central Statistics Office. (2007). *Aging in Ireland*. Dublin: Central Statistics Office.

Department of Health. (2008). *Press release*. Dublin: Department of Health.

Department of Social and Family Affairs. (2007). *Green paper on pensions*. Dublin: The Stationery Office.

Department of the Taoiseach. (2006). *Towards 2016: Ten-year framework social partnership agreement 2006–2015*. Dublin: The Stationery Office.

Donnison, D., O'Shea, E., & Larragy, J. (1991). *Role and future development of nursing homes in Ireland*. Dublin: National Council on Aging and Older People.

Doyle, M., Shaw, J., Hennessy, L., Smyth, D., Devitt, D., Wolfe, D., et al. (2006). *Report of the Long-Term Working Group*. Dublin: Department of Social and Family Affairs.

Equality Authority. (2008). *The Equality Authority Annual Report 2007*. Dublin: Equality Authority.

European Commission. (2007). *Health and long-term care in the European Union: Special Eurobarometer*. Brussels: European Commission.

Fahey, T., Maitre, B., Nolan, B., & Whelan, C. (2007). *A social portrait of older people in Ireland*. Dublin: The Stationery Office.

Falconer, M., & O'Neill, D. (2007). Profiling disability within nursing homes: A census-based approach. *Age Aging, 36*(2), 209–213.

Garavan, R., Winder, R., & McGee, H. (2001). *Health and social services for older people*. Dublin: National Council on Aging and Older People.

Geriatric Medicine Section of the European Union of Medical Specialists. (1999). *Training in geriatric medicine in the European Union*. Brussels: European Union of Medical Specialists.

Gray, L. J., Sprigg, N., Bath, P. M., Sorensen, P., Lindenstrom, E., Boysen, G., et al. (2006). Significant variation in mortality and functional outcome after acute ischaemic stroke between Western countries: Data from the tinzaparin in acute ischaemic stroke trial (TAIST). *Journal of Neurology, Neurosurgery, and Psychiatry, 77*(3), 327–333.

Health Information and Quality Authority. (2007). *National quality standards for residential care settings for older people in Ireland*. Dublin: Health Information and Quality Authority.

Horgan, F., Hickey, A., McGee, H., & O'Neill, D. (2008). *National audit of stroke care*. Dublin: Irish Heart Foundation.

Longevity in Ireland. (1901). *Journal of the American Medical Association, 37*, 1682–1683.

Murphy, K., O'Shea, E., Conney, A., & Casey, D. (2007). *The quality of life of older people with a disability in Ireland*. Dublin: National Council on Aging and Older People.

Murphy, K. et al. (2006). *Improving quality of life for older people in long-stay care settings in Ireland*. Dublin: National Council on Aging and Older People.

National Council on Aging and Older People. (2001). *Framework for quality in long-term residential care for older people in Ireland*. Dublin: National Council on Ageing and Older People.

National Economic and Social Council. (2005). *The developmental welfare state (no. 113)*. Dublin: National Economic and Social Council.

O'Dwyer, C., & O'Neill, D. (2008). Developing strategies for the prevention, detection and management of elder abuse: The Irish experience. *Journal of Elder Abuse and Neglect, 20*(2), 169–180.

Office of the Ombudsman. (2005). Nursing home charges. Dublin: Office of the Ombudsman.

O'Hanlon, A., McGee, H., Barker, A., Garavan, R., Hickey, A., Conroy, R., et al. (2005). *Health and Social Services for Older People II (HeSSOP II): Changing profiles from 2000 to 2004*. Dublin: National Council on Aging and Older People.

O'Neill, D. (2006). *A review of the deaths at Leas-Cross nursing home 2002–2005*. Dublin: HSE. O'Neill, D., Bruce, I., Kirby, M., & Lawlor, B. (2000). Older drivers, driving practices and health issues. *Clinical Gerontology, 10*, 181–191.

O'Neill, D., Gibbon, J., & Mulpeter, K. (2001). Responding to care needs in long-term care. A position paper by the Irish Society of Physicians in Geriatric Medicine. *Irish Medical Journal, 94*(3), 72.

O'Neill, D., & McGee, H. (2007). Oldest old are not just passive recipients of care. *British Medical Journal, 334*(7595), 651.

O'Neill, D., & O'Keeffe, S. (2003). Health care for older people in Ireland. *Journal of American Geriatric Society, 51*(9), 1280–1286.

Organisation for Economic Co-operation and Development (OECD). (2006). *OECD health data, 2006*. Paris: OECD.

O'Shea, E. (2002). *Review of the nursing home subvention scheme*. Dublin: The Stationery Office.

O'Shea, E., & Hughes, J. (1994). *The economics and financing of long-term care in Ireland*. Dublin: National Council on Aging and Older People.

O'Shea, E., Murphy, K., Larkin, P., et al. (2008). *End-of-life care for older people in acute and long-stay care settings in Ireland*. Dublin: National Council on Aging and Older People.

Roberts, S., Drazin, A., Basi, T., & O'Neill, D. (2007). An ethnographic study of the Rural Transport Programme and older people. *Irish Journal of Medical Science, 176*(Suppl 6), S252.

Robins, J. (1986). *Fools and mad*. Dublin: Institute of Public Administration.

Ruddle, H., Donoghue, F., & Mulvihill, R. (1997). *The years ahead report: A review of the implementation of its recommendations*. Dublin: National Council for the Elderly.

The Atlantic Philanthropies. (2007). *Ireland's first centre of expertise in geriatric care*. Retrieved from http://atlanticphilanthropies.org/grantees/profiles/15253_ st_james_s_hospital

Timonen, V. (2004). *Evaluation of homecare grant schemes in the NAHB and ECAHB*. Dublin: Eastern Regional Health Authority.

United Nations. (2002). *Report of the Second World Assembly on Aging*. New York: United Nations.

Whelan, S. (2003). Promises, promises: Defined benefit schemes in a cynical age. *Irish Banking Review* (Spring), 48–62.

Working Party on Services for the Elderly. (1988). *The years ahead—A policy for the elderly*. Dublin: The Stationery Office.

25

▪

Israel

Howard Litwin and Jenny Brodsky

AGING IN ISRAEL

The Israeli population numbers some 7.2 million persons. The proportion of adults aged 65 and over is currently 10%, or about 702,000 persons. Jews comprise the majority group in Israel and 11.5% of them are elderly. Among the Arab minority, only 3.4% are over age 65, due to their higher fertility. Israel ranks 5th in the world for men's life expectancy at birth (78.5 years), but only 14th for women's life expectancy at birth (82.2 years). This gender gap in the relative rankings has yet to be adequately explained.

Israel is one of the youngest of the developed countries primarily because of its high fertility (2.9 children per woman). Nonetheless, the country also has had an exponential increase in the absolute numbers of its older people, due to a combination of natural increase and immigration. For example, while the general population increased four times during the past 50 years, the elderly population grew by eight times. The rate of increase of those over the age of 75 has been even more pronounced—11.5. In general, it is projected that the proportion of older adults will remain stable until 2010, but will rise to 12.7% by 2025, numbering some 1.2 million persons.

The elderly dependency ratio in Israel is 18 persons aged 65 and over per 100 persons of working age (20–64). This ratio is forecast to rise by the year 2025 to 23.7. While the elderly dependency ratio is still lower than in other developed countries, the child dependency ratio in Israel is the highest among the developed countries and stands at 68. The high combined dependency ratio (children and elderly) poses a major challenge to the Israeli social and health systems. Moreover, while the relative proportion of children is expected to decline, this decrease will not balance the increased need for resources generated by the growing proportion of older people.

Migration has also affected the age structure in Israel. The relatively high proportion of elderly immigrants since the establishment of the country in 1948 is unique. Some 8% of all immigrants since 1948 were at least 65 years of age on arrival in Israel, and about 18% were between 45 and 64 years of age. Of particular note is the recent re-emergence of large-scale immigration, mainly from the former Soviet Union (FSU). Since 1989, almost one million immigrants have arrived from the FSU, including 155,000 persons aged 65 and over (about 15% of the current immigration cohort). These newcomers now constitute more than one-fifth of the elderly cohort. The absorption of this group, which arrived without economic resources, presents new challenges to Israeli society and to its social and health-care systems (Litwin, 1995).

The proportion of Arab elders among the total elderly population in Israel remains low (7%), due to high fertility in this group, but their share will increase to 9% by 2025 (Azaiza & Brodsky, 2003). Yet, the number of Arab-Israeli elders is projected to show an increase of 150% in the period from 2006 to 2025 (the corresponding expected increase among Jewish Israeli elders is only 62%). In addition to the Arab-Jewish population differences already noted, several other demographic developments also have affected the structure and the character of the Israeli elderly population. Thus, while Jewish citizens constitute 93% of the elderly population, they are nevertheless quite heterogeneous. The vast majority (86%) were born abroad, two-thirds of them in Europe. Moreover, some 36% of Israel's aged population comprises Holocaust survivors, who experienced traumatic life histories and have special needs (Shmotkin, Blumstein, & Modan, 2003).

RECENT RESEARCH ON AGING

Research on aging in Israel is carried out at several academic centers of gerontology and by many investigators from a range of institutions. We summarize several major initiatives.

1. The Israel Gerontological Data Center (IGDC), at the Hebrew University in Jerusalem, was launched in 2005 as a Web-based facility that works to pool data and to link researchers across Israel's universities and

research institutes (http://igdc.huji.ac.il/). Its goal is to promote analysis of the dynamics of aging in the Israeli population and their social, economic, and health-related concomitants. The IGDC database reports some 1,500 articles and other publications in Israeli gerontology that have appeared since 2000 and cites some 900 different investigators who have published the results of gerontological research.

2. SHARE-Israel is the Israeli component of the Survey of Health, Ageing and Retirement in Europe. The SHARE survey is a major empirical enterprise that seeks to better understand the status of persons aged 50 and over (Litwin, 2008). It combines an international and interdisciplinary approach that allows comparison of the health, social life, and economic situations of older people in 15 different countries, including Israel. The structure and design of SHARE is based upon the American Health and Retirement Survey (HRS). The effective sample in each participating country numbers about 2,500. The first wave of SHARE-Israel, funded primarily by the U.S. National Institute on Aging and the Israeli National Insurance Institute, was executed in 2005–2006 by the IGDC. Data from the survey on demographics, physical health, behavioral risks, cognitive function, mental health, health care, employment and pensions, children, social support, financial transfers, housing, household income, consumption, assets, activities, and expectations are available to all researchers.

3. The Center for Research on Aging at the Myers-JDC-Brookdale Institute is a national center for applied research on aging (http://brookdale.jdc.org.il/). Its aim is to improve the effectiveness of social policies and services by generating knowledge about social needs and by evaluating programmatic efforts that are intended to meet them. The center provides up-to-date information to assist policy-makers and service planners in enhancing the quality of life of Israel's older population. In 2005, the center completed a multi-year project with the World Health Organization to support policy development around the world in the area of long-term care. In 2006, the Center joined a Canadian-headed international initiative aimed at improving the understanding of the causes and trajectory of frailty among older persons and identifying priorities for further development of research. In collaboration with the Association for the Planning and Development of Services for the Elderly (ESHEL), the Center also publishes an Annual Statistical Abstract on the Elderly that contains a wealth of current data on Israel's older population (Brodsky, Schnoor, & Be'er, n.d.). A computerized version of the publication equipped with a Web-based search function has been developed in conjunction with the IGDC.

4. The Herczeg Institute on Aging (http://spirit.tau.ac.il/herczeg/) has fostered interdisciplinary research between the Faculty of Social Sciences and the Faculty of Medicine at Tel-Aviv University since 1992.

Its current work focuses on dementia, cognition, health and mental health promotion, quality of life, trauma, and the long-term effects of the Holocaust. The Institute is also currently responsible for CALAS (the Cross-sectional and Longitudinal Aging Study), which began in 1989 at the Sheba Medical Center and other hospitals through a grant from the U.S. National Institute on Aging, and for the subsequent allied Israeli Multidisciplinary Aging Study (IMAS) (Ben-Ezra & Shmotkin, 2006). Among the findings reported on the basis of the CALAS are new insights into the gender paradox of health and new evidence as to the centrality of resilience among the old-old population (Walter-Ginzburg, Blumstein, & Guralnik, 2004).

5. The Geriatric Institute of Education and Research at Kaplan Medical Center in Rehovot has used the CALAS data to incorporate Israel as a member of the CLESA project (Comparison of Longitudinal European Studies on Aging). In this effort, a harmonized data set was established from longitudinal studies in Finland, Sweden, Spain, Italy, the Netherlands, and Israel. Its aim is to compare the determinants of health and quality of life in older people in Europe and Israel.

6. The Center for Research and Study of Aging (http://hw.haifa.ac.il/gero/CenterResearchAging/) at the University of Haifa has served as a databank for methods of treatment and care techniques, conducted qualitative and quantitative research, and developed educational programs since 1990. The Center was also the prime initiator of Old Age and Autonomy: The Role of Service Systems and Intergenerational Solidarity (OASIS), a project funded by the European Commission 5th framework, in 2002. OASIS examined the interplay between family culture, intergenerational relations, and service systems as they impact elders' autonomy and quality of life in large cities in Israel as well as in Norway, England, Germany, and Spain. Results of the study revealed that intergenerational solidarity was substantial in all countries but also that filial obligations were higher in Israel (and in Spain) than in the northern countries (Lowenstein & Daatland, 2006).

7. The Jerusalem Longitudinal Cohort Study was established in 1991 by the Department of Geriatrics and Rehabilitation at Hadassah-University Hospital and focuses upon West Jerusalem residents born 1920–1921. Based upon three phases of data collection at cohort age 70, 77, and 85 years old, the primary study goals included a basic description of the patterns of aging; the isolation of elements of lifestyle, health factors, biological, and disease states, which are harbingers of morbidity and mortality; and the identification of potential strategies and predictors of successful aging. Among the findings to emerge thus far are the contribution of maintained regular activity to successful aging and the strong association of socioeconomic status with improved health measures into advanced age (Stessman, Hammerman-Rozenberg, Maaravi, & Cohen, 2002).

8. The Center for Multidisciplinary Research in Aging was established in 2000 in the Faculty of Medical Sciences at Ben-Gurion University of the Negev (BGU) and Soroka University Medical Center (http://cmra.bgu.ac.il/). Its goal is to foster interdisciplinary research and education in geriatrics and gerontology. The research program of the Center addresses health and welfare services and policies, physical and cognitive capabilities, frailty and disease, nutrition, and physiology and biology. The Center was also recognized as one of the independent units of the International Longevity Center, a nonprofit international research, policy, and education organization, the aim of which is to educate on how to live longer and better.

9. The Belle and Irving Moller Center for the Biology of Aging, established in 1979, at the Weizmann Institute of Science in Rehovot, focuses upon the biological determinants of cellular aging. In addition, the Faculty of Biology at the Technion in Haifa instituted one of the first research projects on the molecular mechanisms of aging in Israel.

10. The Central Bureau of Statistics (CBS) is a governmental body that collects a wide range of data on the Israeli population at large (http://www1.cbs.gov.il/). Specific surveys of the cohort aged 60 and older that were carried out in 1985 and 1997 have served as the basis for numerous scientific articles. In addition, the Social Survey carried out periodically by the CBS allows age-related analysis of important social trends.

11. The Israel Gerontological Society (IGS) (http://www.gerontology.org.il/), a professional member organization for the advancement of gerontology in Israel, currently functions as the conduit for distribution of research grants provided by the Ministry of Pensioners' Affairs. The competitive grants are uniquely for the study of aging. Thirteen such grants were awarded in 2007. The IGS also issues Israel's premier journal in the field of aging, *Gerontologia*. Articles in this Hebrew publication are anonymously refereed by leading academic experts and represent the state of the art of Israeli gerontology. Special issues of the journal are periodically organized around selected themes. Thus, for example, recent special issues have focused on cognition and aging, geriatric physical therapy, nutrition in the elderly, and intergenerational justice and economics.

THE CURRENT STATE OF EDUCATION IN GERONTOLOGY

The study of gerontology has increased steadily in Israel in the past years. Since the year 2000, some 30 Ph.D. dissertations in the field of aging have been registered, and dozens of master's theses have been written. The academization of the study of aging has been furthered much to the credit of two M.A. programs in gerontology (Carmel & Lowenstein, 2007). The program at Haifa University—now 10 years old—is multidimensional in character and geared to students from a range of professions, among them the medical and legal professions, the behavioral sciences, social work, and education. The academic program is composed of courses in (1) basic interdisciplinary studies that include psychology, biology, and epidemiology of aging; (2) research methods; (3) management and organizational behavior; (4) micro- and mezzo-interventions such as elderly assessment and psychogeriatrics; (5) macro-interventions such as aging policy and the pension system; and (6) electives, such as art and aging and environment and aging. Since its founding, the program has produced more than 170 graduates who have entered or returned to the field.

The M.A. program at BGU, in Beersheba, was established to train researchers and experts in the care of older people. The curriculum of the program, located in the School of Health Sciences, is sociomedical and interdisciplinary in nature. Students may choose to specialize in one of three tracks of study: case management, administration, or research. In each track are three main clusters of courses: (1) the fundamentals of scientific inquiry and basic courses on various aspects of aging; (2) specialty courses according to each track of study; and (3) course electives. Major themes that are addressed in the program of study include quality of life and meaning of life in the face of loss, clinical topics of particular relevance to elderly patients and policy analysis. The program is affiliated with the Geriatrics ward of the Soroka Medical Center and with the Ben-Gurion University Center for Multidisciplinary Research in Aging. Since its founding, in 1999, the program has produced some 280 graduates.

In addition to these two full-fledged degree programs, courses on various aspects of aging and their social and health concomitants are offered at other institutions of higher learning in Israel as well. Several such settings maintain concentrations or specialty tracks in gerontology within regular degree programs for other disciplines, such as social work, nursing and occupational therapy. Gerontology also is offered as a field of study in the private sector of higher education in Israel. For example, the Israel College, a private academic institution founded in 1994 for academic education to mid-career professionals, maintains a subspecialty in gerontology within its master's degree program in Health Systems Management. The studies are co-sponsored by Clark University in the United States, but are delivered mostly at its branch campus in Tel Aviv.

Another wing of gerontology education in Israel is earmarked to enrich those who serve the elderly population in a variety of capacities. The Glickman Center for Education and Training at the Sheba Medical

Center in Tel Hashomer was established in 1989 by JDC-ESHEL to improve the quality of elder care. The Center offers more than 50 courses for professionals and paraprofessionals in the field of aging. Courses have been developed uniquely for directors of homes for the aged and day care centers, nurses, social workers, primary care physicians, home care workers, and volunteers. Over the past 10 years, more than 10,000 individuals have participated in such programs. Continuing professional education tracks operate at other sites as well, such as the program at Haifa University, which is also supported by ESHEL.

Yet another wing of gerontology education focuses upon the educational needs of older people. For example, the Bar-Ilan Brookdale Program in Applied Gerontology, at Bar-Ilan University in Ramat Gan, promotes the contribution of older adults to society through continuing education. It operates several programmatic initiatives, which include: (1) the Open Door College, a framework through which persons over the age of 55 audit regular university classes; (2) the Center for Third Age Learning, which offers courses and workshops in areas not available in the regular university curriculum, such as improving study skills, memory, and computer literacy; (3) the Senior Community Leadership Program, which provides skills and knowledge for a post-retirement career as leaders in the public voluntary and civic sector, and (4) a program of inter-generational home visitation in which university students maintain contact with isolated elderly people living in localities near the university. Similar learning opportunities for older adults exist at other Israeli universities as well.

CURRENT PUBLIC POLICY ISSUES IN AGING

As in many other countries, aging-related issues are frequently at the forefront of policy debates and legislative initiatives in Israel. Although there are several such matters on the public agenda, we focus on four public policy issues that have particular relevance for the well-being of Israel's aging population. They include (1) maintaining a sufficient standard of living and preventing poverty; (2) participation in the labor market; (3) ensuring health care; and (4) ensuring appropriate care for elders with disabilities.

Maintaining a Sufficient Standard of Living and Preventing Poverty

The incomes of older people in Israel stem from three principal sources or tiers: governmental allotments, occupational pension payments, and private savings and insurance arrangements. The first tier comprises governmental transfer payments at two levels: (a) a basic old-age allowance from the National Insurance Institute (Israel's Social Security System) in the form of a flat-rate benefit that is universal from a specific age; and (b) an income supplement allowance and other welfare benefits designed exclusively for persons lacking other sources of income. The second tier is composed of occupational pensions, the rights to which employees accrue during their years of employment, most frequently on the basis of collective wage agreements reached with labor unions. The third tier of income consists of savings, private insurance schemes and other forms of income. In addition, a small percentage of the elderly population continues to derive income from some form of paid employment.

Poverty among the elderly in Israel is still relatively extensive. In 2006/2007, the incomes of 23.5% of households headed by an elderly person were below the poverty line, even after taking into account the effect of old-age social security allowances and other governmental transfers. Without receipt of social security and transfer payments, up to 56% of the households headed by an elderly person would be considered poor (i.e., they have an available income below 50% of the median income per standard person). This high risk of poverty stems from a combination of issues related to the current value of the old-age allowances, to the prevalence of immigrants within the elderly cohort, and to the corresponding limited coverage they have from occupational pensions.

First, although Israel furnishes a universal old-age allowance, the allotment provides only minimal basic support (about 16% of the average wage). This requires pensioners to obtain additional income sources in order to maintain an acceptable standard of living in late life, the principal source of which is the occupational pension. However, since a good part of the current elderly cohort immigrated to Israel as adults, many of them did not accrue sufficient employment pension benefits over their working lives. The influx of immigrants from the FSU since 1990 has significantly exacerbated this problem. At present, only about 35% of retirees have an occupational pension (42% of the men and 31% of the women). Thus, a high proportion of elders must rely mainly on public old-age allowances and other governmental transfers for their livelihood.

We should point out that until recently, a compulsory employment pension scheme existed only in the public services and in entities governed by collective wage agreements. Expanding access to occupational pensions thus became a national priority, and at the end of 2007, the government introduced a compulsory employment pension that is based on an agreement signed with the General Labor Federation and the Manufacturers

Association. This agreement is a first step in extending the much-needed pension coverage, but it also has several drawbacks. As a result, the issue of ensuring an adequate occupational pension system in Israel remains a formidable challenge.

Participation in the Labor Market

We have already noted that high dependency rates prevail in Israel. An additional trend of contemporary concern has been a decline in the proportion of older workers in the labor force, particularly among men aged 55–64. In order to reverse the potentially negative effects of these trends upon the actuarial soundness of the social security system, the Israeli government has recently instituted changes with regard to eligibility for retirement benefits. Up until July 2004, women had been eligible for old-age allowance and employment pension from the age of 60 and men from the age of 65. From that point, the age of eligibility was scheduled to increase gradually, so by the end of the process, it will be 67 for men and 64 for women.

In principle, delayed retirement should constitute a means to guarantee that people reach retirement age with sufficient pension coverage. It also should offer several potential benefits for Israeli economic development. However, the opportunities for older workers to maintain an active role in the labor force are subject to two conflicting forces. On the one hand, structural changes in the economy have put pressure on redundant and declining economic sectors to retire their older workers, limiting the number of jobs available to them. On the other hand, the recently legislated increase in the retirement age, along with longer life expectancy and better health among elderly people, underscores the need for continued employment over the life course and into older age. Maintaining employment opportunities for older workers is thus a major challenge that will require new approaches to education and ongoing training throughout life.

Ensuring Health Care

The Israeli health system is characterized by a high degree of concern with assuring access for all segments of the population. A major step in this regard was the implementation of the National Health Insurance (NHI) Law in 1995, which mandates universal health coverage and defines a basket of services to which all citizens are entitled. Health services covered by the law include primary care, acute hospitalization, medications, laboratory tests, medical rehabilitation, and professional home care for the disabled. Clinical care is organized and provided through one of four publicly financed and -administered nonprofit health plans (similar to the Health Maintenance Organizations in the United States). All Israeli citizens have the right to register in the health service plan of their choice.

The health system is funded partly by general tax revenues and via a progressive payroll tax. The unemployed, the elderly, and those receiving disability and income support pay only a minimal tariff. These monies are transferred to the National Insurance Institute, which then distributes them to each of the four health plan organizations according to a capitation mechanism. Health plans' revenues are a function of the number of members in the plan and their age profile. This system currently favors higher reimbursement to the health plans for those over age 65 and for those who suffer from a selected list of diseases (e.g., severe renal failure). This financial arrangement provides an incentive for health plans to develop and deliver services for their elderly members. Nevertheless, one of the remaining challenges facing the Israeli health system is the need to balance the currently heavy emphasis on curative care and to invest in public health measures that promote health and prevent disability.

Ensuring Appropriate Care for Elders with Disabilities

The system of health and welfare services for elders with disabilities in Israel has developed considerably in the past two decades. In particular, there has been accelerated development of home care and other community-based services. The vast majority of elderly people live at home and are cared for at home or in the community. Only 4.5% of older Israelis reside in an institutional setting of any kind (with less than 3% living in a nursing facility).

"Aging in place" in one's community is the currently preferred option for older people. Even among older persons with physical or other impairment, 78% live in the community. This is due to the extensive care that is provided by families in Israeli society, along with the development of formal services, some quite innovative, that are intended to strengthen families' caregiving capacity. Such services include (1) personal care delivered at home (provided through an insurance mechanism enacted by the Community Long-Term Care Insurance Law); (2) personal care, meals, and recreational services provided at day-care centers; (3) locally based monitoring of older people and fostering their social involvement in associations termed "supportive communities"; (4) social work therapy and advocacy services to elderly individuals and their families; (5) home adaptations to maximize mobility and independence; (6) the loaning of medical equipment and other devices for personal use, primarily through a national voluntary organization called Yad Sarah; (7) information and advice provided through counseling centers; and (8) friendly home visits conducted by volunteers.

In recent decades, Israel has increased the allocation of resources earmarked for the community. This has resulted in a more balanced distribution of public resources between institutional and community care and a better balance of responsibility between the family and the state. Nevertheless, research continues to show that families remain the primary caregivers of frail and disabled elderly persons in Israel. Research also shows that family caregivers experience a great deal of burden and stress. Thus, Israel has an urgent need to further develop policies aimed to support informal caregivers and in turn to augment the quality of care delivered to frail and disabled older people at home.

REFERENCES

Azaiza, F., & Brodsky, J. (2003). The aging of Israel's Arab population: Needs, existing responses, and dilemmas in the development of services for a society in transition. *Israel Medical Association Journal, 5*(5), 383–386.

Ben-Ezra, M., & Shmotkin, D. (2006). Predictors of mortality in the old-old in Israel: The Cross-sectional and Longitudinal Aging Study. *Journal of the American Geriatrics Society, 54*(6), 906–911.

Brodsky, J., Schnoor, Y., & Be'er, S. (Eds.). (n.d.). *The elderly in Israel—The statistical abstract.* Mashav—Planning for the Elderly A National Database. Jerusalem: JDC-Brookdale & ESHEL. Retrieved from http://www.jointnet.org.il/mashav/eng/

Carmel, S., & Lowenstein, A. (2007). Addressing a nation's challenge: Graduate programs in gerontology in Israel. *Gerontology & Geriatrics Education, 27*(3), 49–63.

Litwin, H. (1995). *Uprooted in old age: Soviet Jews and their social networks in Israel.* Westport, CT: Greenwood Press.

Litwin, H. (2008). Understanding aging in a Middle Eastern context: The SHARE-Israel survey of persons aged 50 and older. *Journal of Cross-Cultural Gerontology, 24*(1): 49–62. doi: 10.1007/s10823-008-9073-7.

Lowenstein, A., & Daatland, S. O. (2006). Filial norms and family support in a comparative cross-national context: Evidence from the OASIS study. *Ageing & Society, 26,* 203–223.

Shmotkin, D., Blumstein, T., & Modan, B. (2003). Tracing long-term effects of early trauma: A broad-scope view of Holocaust survivors in late life. *Journal of Consulting and Clinical Psychology, 71*(2), 223–234.

Stessman, J., Hammerman-Rozenberg, R., Maaravi, Y., & Cohen, A. (2002). Effect of exercise on ease in performing activities of daily living and instrumental activities of daily living from age 70 to 77: The Jerusalem Longitudinal Study. *Journal of the American Geriatrics Society, 50*(12), 1934–1938.

Walter-Ginzburg, A., Blumstein, T., & Guralnik, J. M. (2004). The Israeli kibbutz as a venue for reduced disability in old age: Lessons from the Cross-sectional and Longitudinal Aging Study (CALAS). *Social Science & Medicine, 59*(2), 389–403.

26

■■■■■

Italy

Antonio Cherubini, Beatrice Gasperini,
Francesco Orso, and Mauro Di Bari

The rapid and intense aging of the Italian population during the last century has had profound implications within our society. New needs, as well as challenges and opportunities, have developed as a consequence of this demographic change and this implies a need for politicians, decision-makers, researchers, service providers, and citizens to be aware of the characteristics of aging. The paradox of aging of the population is that, while on one side it represents a success—being the consequence of a significant improvement in living conditions and in health care—on the other hand, it poses several questions that society is not yet able to fully answer. These encompass the large number of older subjects who suffer from chronic diseases and/or disability, the inability of the health-care system to satisfy their needs and expectations, the widespread persistence of ageism, and the limited economic viability of the social protection system, particularly due to the growing expenditure for pensions (Kunkel, 2008).

DEMOGRAPHICS AND EPIDEMIOLOGY

Italians presently enjoy one of the longest life expectancies worldwide, about 78 years for males and 84 years for females at birth. Predictions have been made that Italians will continue to experience a three-month increase in life expectancy per calendar year, for many years to come (ISTAT, 2006).

During the last half of the 20th century, aging of the Italian population progressed at one of the fastest paces among developed countries, as a consequence of both a reduction of mortality and a very low birthrate (Kohler, Billari, & Ortega, 2002).

About 11.5 million persons are aged 65 or more, which corresponds to almost 20% of the total population, a proportion that is expected to increase further because of the very low birthrate. These demographic changes have profound implications for the structure and composition of families, moving from the traditional A-shaped pattern—that is, one living grandfather or grandmother and several grandchildren—to the current V-shaped pattern, characterized by three or four living grandparents and, at most, only one grandchild. Also, the average number of members in Italian families has dramatically decreased in the last 50 years, from 3.6 to 2.5.

As in other Western countries where a full-blown demographic transition has occurred, Italian women live longer than men. However, this differential in total life years is unfortunately largely represented by years of dependency: in fact, whereas at the age of 65 men have about 16 years of total life expectancy, with probably two of these of disabled life, at the same age, total life expectancy is about 20 years in women, with at least five of these to be spent as disabled years (ISTAT, 2007).

According to national statistics, based on telephone interviews, loss of autonomy in activities of daily living involves nearly one out of five older Italians, with prevalence figures of 19.3% in persons aged 65 years or more and up to 47.8% in those aged 80 years or more. Epidemiologic surveys, where more strict definitions of disability have been used, reported lower prevalence data, showing that approximately 10% of persons aged 65 years or more, and one-third of those above the age of 80, need assistance in at least one of the classic basic activities of daily living (BADL), such as eating, dressing/undressing, transferring from bed to chair, using the toilet, bathing, and maintaining urine and stool continence. Regardless of the specific definition applied, the prevalence of disability is greater in women, a disadvantage that cannot simply be explained by the longer longevity of women, because it persists also when genders are compared within age-specific strata from 65 years onwards.

The age-associated increase in the prevalence of disability accompanies, and of course largely stems from, the high prevalence of chronic diseases in late life (ISTAT, 2007). National statistics report that about 47% of persons aged 75 years or more have at least one severe chronic disease and that 56% may be affected by three chronic conditions. Bone and joint diseases (particularly osteoarthritis) are the most frequent, with more than 50% of elders in this age range affected, followed by hypertension (42%), cardiac diseases (20.2%), and diabetes (15.2%). For these reasons, it is not surprising that more than 80% of these subjects are taking at least one medicine per day, with painkillers being the most frequently used. Data derived from the ASSET study, conducted in three Italian regions, show a mean annual cost for medications of €652.75 and €481.20 for men and women aged 75 years or more, respectively (Favato & Catapano, 2007).

At present, the Italian National Health Service covers most health-care expenses, but with the continuous increase in life expectancy and in the prevalence of chronic conditions, it is possible that in the near future, this will change. A consistent amount of economic burden on the National Health Care Service is still related to hospitalizations. According to the most recent data available, hospitalizations of patients aged 65 years or more were 3.6 million in the year 2005, accounting for more than 40.2% of all hospitalizations (Ministero della Salute, 2008). Length of hospital stay was longer in older persons, 9.2 and 10.6 days for those aged 65–74 and ≥75 years, respectively, compared to 7.4 days in younger patients.

SOCIAL PROTECTION FOR ELDERS

The Pension System in Italy

In Italy, there are three main types of pensions to safeguard older people:

- Old-age pension: obtained after reaching the pensionable age, provided that a minimum number of years of contributions have also been achieved
- Seniority pension: independent of age, the worker can enjoy pension after a minimum number of years of contribution (usually 35) have been collected
- Social pension: the minimum social protection, assigned based on age alone, to citizens who do not fulfill the criteria to obtain any other pension

The total pension expenditure is very high in Italy; that is, 12.7% of the gross domestic product (GDP), while the total expense for old-age and disability pensions, including that assigned to the survivor after bereavement in case the spouse had a pension, accounts for 16.7% of the GDP. In comparison, the mean expenditure in the EU 25 countries is 10.9% and 14.2%, respectively. Of the total pension expenditure, 76% is accounted for by the old-age pension, 8% by cash allowance for disability, and 15% by survivor pensions. This situation is due not only to the very long life expectancy of the Italian population, but also to the fact that for some decades, it was possible to receive a seniority pension even after a relatively short period of time; that is, 20 years of contribution, lowered to 15 years for women who were married or had at least one child (so-called baby-pensioners). The money necessary to cover the pension expenditure comes from the mandatory payment of a percentage of salaries. Workers who are employees have to pay one-third of the contribution, while two-thirds are paid by the employer; self-employed workers are required to provide the whole contribution.

Although there has been an increase in the minimum pension in recent years, poverty is still a widespread problem in the older population. Poverty level was approximately €986 per month in 2007. While 11% of all families and 12.8% of individuals were below this poverty threshold, this percentage was 11.8% in families that had one older person and increased to 16.9% among families with two or more older persons (ISTAT, 2008).

THE LONG-TERM CARE (LTC) SYSTEM

This estimate of the prevalence of disability reported above does not include nursing-home residents, who have the highest rate of disability. According to a recent national research performed in nursing homes, almost 80% of nursing-home residents have at least one disability in basic activities of daily living (Lattanzio et al., n.d.). Older disabled subjects are those who make the highest use of LTC.

Public LTC for older people includes three main types of services: home care, residential care, and cash allowances. A general picture will be provided here, although there are large differences between different areas of the country, with the north of Italy having the highest provision of public services and the south the lowest one. National and local taxation are the main financing sources of public LTC, since in Italy, there is not a specific tax to cover the cost of disability. A fund to cover the assistance of disabled older persons has been recently created at a national level as well as in some regions, but it is currently thought to be underfinanced.

Therefore, private expenses make up a large percentage of costs in some areas, for example home care. In Italy, health services and social care are still not integrated, despite some successful local experiences, since the former, which is usually more developed, is under the control of health-care agencies, and the latter of municipalities.

Health care-related activities are managed by the Italian National Health Service (Servizio Sanitario Nazionale—SSN), through its Regional Health Authorities. The Italian SSN was established in 1978 and is intended to be universalistic, by providing health care to the whole population according to their needs. From 1998, the major financing responsibility has been shifted from the central government to the regional authorities (there are 20 regions, with corresponding governments). The national government produces the legislation, defines the aims and provides general rules, while the regional authorities establish the provision of health-care services as well as the allocation of resources to each of them. Many services are provided by authorized private providers, which are directly reimbursed by the public system.

On the other hand, domestic and personal care tasks provided within home or nursing home are usually managed at a local level by municipalities, which are also in charge of supporting half of the expenses of residential care for poor subjects. While health services are free of charge, social care is often charged for, at least for those who have an income above a specified threshold.

HOME CARE

In the Italian traditional culture, care for older persons is a responsibility of the families: maintaining an older person at home continues to be seen as a priority, while moving him/her to a nursing home is considered the final choice to provide adequate assistance, when all other chances have had to be abandoned (Gori, Di Maio, & Pozzi, 2003).

However, this situation is rapidly changing, due to the low birthrate, which is reducing the size of families and therefore the availability of caregivers (Kohler et al., 2002) and the higher participation of women in the labor force.

The main form of public care for older subjects with disability is home care, called integrated health care (ADI, Assistenza Domiciliare Integrata), which should include both home help and home health care. Home care is a complex and expensive service, involving physicians, nurses, physiotherapists, psychologists, and social workers, with the primary aim of maintaining older disabled persons at their own home for as long as possible, therefore preventing or delaying their admission to nursing homes. Multi-professional, social and health-care services are delivered at the patients' home with a level of intensity proportional to the patients' needs. Although home care has grown in recent years in Italy, this service is clearly underdeveloped, with a coverage of less than 2.5% of the older population and often unable to satisfy the increasingly complex needs (Bernabei, Landi, & Zuccalà, 2002; Carpenter et al., 2004). Moreover, the quality of services, as well as the integration between social and health care provided within ADI, is extremely heterogeneous, even within the same region.

As a consequence of the low availability of home care, associated with a low number of beds in nursing homes, in the past 15 years there has been a constant growth of private home care for frail older people. According to the last available statistics, this is used by 2% of all Italian families and 4.2% of households with a member aged 65 and over.

It has been estimated that the number of privately paid care workers (called "badanti") is between 700,000 and 1.1 million. They come mainly from foreign, for example Eastern European, countries and often provide 24-hour care without adequate training to care for older disabled subjects (Spano, 2006). A significant percentage work in the grey market.

In the ASSI study (Di Bari et al., 2008), a survey of older community-dwellers living in an urban setting, participants with BADL disability received most of the help they needed (58.3%) from close relatives, followed by paid assistants (20.5%), other relatives (19.5%) and less than 1% (0.6%) from public health-care services.

RESIDENTIAL CARE

The availability of residential care is insufficient to meet the requests, with less than 2% of older adults living in nursing homes. Moreover, there is an uneven distribution within the country: while northern Italy has a large number of facilities, central and southern Italy suffer from underdevelopment of this type of LTC.

Residential care is provided in different types of institutions, which can host older people based on their degree of disability, from those who are completely self-sufficient to those severely disabled or in terminal conditions. Residenze Sanitarie Assistenziali (RSA) are the nursing homes assisting older subjects with a high burden of multimorbidity and severe disability.

Most of the nursing home residents (73%) are women, because they live longer and, in general, older persons do not leave their homes as long as their spouse is alive. In spite of the profound changes in the structure of the families described above, older Italians are admitted to nursing homes late in life and in poor functional status (Lattanzio et al., n.d.).

Although until few years ago, these nursing homes were mainly devoted to assisting older subjects for all their remaining life, now a significant percentage of beds are reserved for short-stay residents; that is, those who stay up to 2–3 months, usually after discharge from an acute care hospital.

Within residential services, there are also day-care centers for older patients, in particular those suffering from dementia, which are becoming increasingly available in some areas (Mossello et al., 2008).

According to the national health-care plan, access to nursing homes, as well as to public home care, is decided by a multidisciplinary team led by a geriatrician, called geriatric evaluation units (Unità Valutativa Geriatrica, UVG), which should also design and implement an individualized health-care plan, making periodic assessments of older patients. However, the composition and role of UVG are extremely varied, and almost always its role is limited to the initial assessment, with no further evaluation over time.

CASH ALLOWANCES FOR DISABILITY

A significant amount of public resources are used to maintain a public allowance for severely disabled subjects; that is, those unable to walk without the help of another person or dependent for the majority of basic activities of daily living. This allowance, called *indennità di accompagnamento*, is also granted to blind and deaf subjects, regardless of age. This allowance, which corresponds to around €470 per month and is neither linked to contributions nor means-tested, is not restricted to older adults, but they do represent 45% of recipients, which was 5.8% of the older population in 1999.

EDUCATION

The demographic scenario described above would clearly imply a growing need for widespread education on aging issues. Unfortunately, this is still underdeveloped in Italy, although some progress has been made in recent years. Education on aging is much more developed in the medical field, due to the introduction of gerontology and geriatrics in medical and allied health sciences professional curricula, which probably reflects the priority assigned to the care of a new category of patients, characterized by multimorbidity, disability, and a greater use of drugs and health-care services (Senin, Cherubini, & Mecocci, 2003). In other words, the increasing need for geriatric and gerontological education of physicians and other health-care professionals (e.g., nurses and nursing aides, physiotherapists, occupational and speech therapists, podologists, and psychologists), determined, in recent years, changes in the corresponding academic curricula, which now include gerontological and geriatric topics. However, duration and quality of education on these topics is extremely variable across the country, and it is still possible to find some universities or curricula where the geriatric track is not implemented or is underdeveloped, sometimes being left to professionals who lack specific expertise in the field.

Only in the last 10 years has a course in gerontology and geriatrics been mandatory in undergraduate medical education. This course is always held in the last year of medical school, but has variable duration, format and content in different universities and is sometimes taught by a teacher who lacks specific expertise in the field. Indeed, the majority of medical schools in Italy have at least one faculty member who specializes in geriatric medicine, although in some of them, the teaching of geriatrics is provided by non-geriatricians, because current legislation allows assignment of chairs of geriatrics to internal medicine professors. Usually, the attention devoted to purely gerontological topics is rather small. A further issue, particularly for physicians, is that the practical training is still performed mainly within the acute-care hospital, and only a few medical schools provide the opportunity to experience the multifaceted aspects of geriatrics practice in different health-care services and settings in the community, such as home care, rehabilitation services, and nursing homes (Cherubini, Huber, & Michel, 2006; Michel, Huber, & Cruz-Jentoft, 2008).

Almost all medical schools have ongoing residency programs in geriatrics, with a well-defined curriculum. Geriatrics is an independent specialty, meaning that trainees enter a four-year postgraduate training in geriatric medicine directly after medical school. At the present time, the geriatric training programs remain extremely varied even within the same region, mainly due to the fact that training programs have been historically organized on the basis of the services that were locally available, and were not considered based primarily on the educational needs of the geriatric specialists (Cherubini et al., 2006; Michel et al., 2008).

However, an important change will occur shortly in postgraduate training in geriatrics, to fulfill the requirements of the European Union: the duration of the training will increase by one year and rotations across internal medicine and different health-care settings where older people are cared for will be implemented, for postgraduate curricula to be accredited by the Ministry of Education.

GERIATRIC RESEARCH

The Italian Society on Gerontology and Geriatrics (Società Italiana di Gerontologia e Geriatria [SIGG], 2009) was founded in 1950 by Enrico Greppi, Professor of Medicine at the University of Florence, with the mission "to promote and coordinate studies on pathophysiology of aging and to face the severe and complex problem of old age also in its social aspects." Since its foundation, SIGG has contributed substantially to the growth of geriatrics as an established medical discipline, as witnessed by the institution, back in 1961, of the first Chair and Specialty School of Geriatrics in the world, held in Florence by Prof. Francesco M. Antonini.

In more recent years, SIGG has become a major promoter of the scientific and professional growth of geriatricians across the country, directly or via its emanation, the Italian Foundation for Ageing Research (FIRI), established in 1999 with the intent of supporting and promoting scientific research in the bio-gerontological and behavioral fields. Several study groups originated from SIGG and FIRI, which also directly designed and coordinated large nationwide research studies. The Italian Group of Pharmacoepidemiology in the Aged (Carosclla et al., 1999) aimed to assess the quality of in-hospital care for the elderly and evaluate drug-related problems and their risk factors. The ULISSE study (an informatics link for healthcare of older people) Lattanzio et al. (n.d.) was designed to define the characteristics of older patients admitted to health-care services and to verify quality of care for older subjects in hospitals, home-care services, and nursing homes in Italy. The Depression in the Aged Female National Evaluation (DAFNE) study (Lattanzio et al., 2009), a multicenter, cluster randomized clinical trial, evaluated whether a training intervention can improve the ability of geriatricians to recognize depression in older persons.

Other important contributions to geriatric research in Italy, developed outside the SIGG and FIRI direct involvement, although sometimes with their general endorsement, should be mentioned. The Italian Longitudinal Study on Aging (ILSA) Working Group (1997), promoted and funded by the National Research Council, was an epidemiological, population-based, longitudinal study of the health status of older Italians, designed to study prevalence and incidence rates of common chronic conditions in older Italians, and the identification of their risk and protective factors. The CRONOS project (Bellelli et al., 2005), supported by the National Health Service, was initially designed to improve early diagnosis of cognitive disorders and Alzheimer's disease and subsequently contributed to the widespread and appropriate use of specific prescription drugs for this condition, via the creation of a national network of Alzheimer Evaluation Units. Finally, we would like to acknowledge the Insufficienza Cardiaca negli Anziani Residenti a Dicomano (ICARe Dicomano) study (Di Bari et al., 2004)—mostly directed to the epidemiological assessment of cardiovascular diseases in late life—and the InCHIANTI study (Ferrucci et al., 2000), which combined epidemiological and biological aspects of aging research to provide a better understanding of the process leading to loss of walking ability in old age.

The wealth and depth of Italian research on aging is further documented by the impressive increase, in recent years, in the number of publications by Italian scientists that are indexed in PubMed. Using the keywords "Elderly OR Ageing OR Aging" and "Italy" in the search, and limiting it to human studies, the number of titles retrieved was negligible in the decade 1970–1979 (when the world scientific production already exceeded 15,000 studies) and increased substantially thereafter, to reach more than 2,000 publications in 1990–1999 and more than 3,500 publications from 2000 through 2008.

CONCLUSIONS

Public policy for aging in Italy is still underdeveloped, despite the fact that life expectancy and the percentage of older subjects within the population are among the highest in the world. Critical areas are the insufficient availability of gerontology and geriatrics within the education and health-care systems, and the lack of an adequate fund to cover the growing expenses for the assistance of older disabled people. This situation causes a lack of long-term care services in many areas of the country and a high out-of-pocket expenditure to pay for private care workers, who often do not have adequate training to carry out their work. On the other hand, research on aging is currently well developed in Italy.

REFERENCES

Bellelli, G., Lucchi, E., Minicuci, N., Rozzini, L., Bianchetti, A., Padovani, A., et al. (2005). Results of a multi-level therapeutic approach for Alzheimer's disease subjects in the "real world" (CRONOS project): A 36-week follow-up study. *Aging Clinical and Experimental Research, 17*, 54–61.

Bernabei, R., Landi, F., & Zuccalà, G. (2002). Health care for older persons in Italy. *Aging Clinical and Experimental Research 14*, 247–51.

Carosella L, Pahor M, Pedone C, Zuccalà G, Manto A, Carbonin P. (1999)-Pharmacosurveillance in hospitalized patients in Italy. Study design of the 'Gruppo Italiano di Farmacovigilanza nell'Anziano' (GIFA). Pharmacological Research, 40, 287-95.

Carpenter, I., Gambassi, G., Topinkova, E., Schroll, M., Finne-Soveri, H., Henrard, J. C., et al. (2004). Community care in Europe. The Aged in Home Care project (AdHOC). *Aging Clinical and Experimental Research, 16*, 259–69.

Cherubini, A., Huber, P., & Michel, J. (2006). Geriatric medicine education in Europe. In M.S. John Pathy, A. J. Sinclair, & J. E. Morley (Eds), *Principles and practice of geriatric medicine* (pp. 1783–8). UK: John Wiley & Sons, Ltd.

Di Bari, M., Pecchioli, A., Mazzaglia, G., Marini, M., Maciocco, G., Ferrucci, L., et al. (2008). Care available to severely disabled older persons living at home in Florence, Italy *Aging Clinical and Experimental Research, 20*, 31–9.

Di Bari, M., Pozzi, C., Cavallini, M. C., Innocenti, F., Baldereschi, G., De Alfieri, et al. (2004). The diagnosis of heart failure in the community. Comparative validation of four sets of criteria in unselected older adults: The ICARe Dicomano Study. *Journal of the American College of Cardiology, 44*, 1601–1608.

Favato, G., & Catapano, A. L. (2007). Gli anziani e l'uso di farmaci in Italia. Dati dallo studio ASSET [Old people and drug prescription in Italy. Results of ASSET study]. *Giornale di Gerontologia, 55*, 191–192.

Ferrucci, L., Bandinelli, S., Benvenuti, E., Di Iorio, A., Macchi, C., Harris, T. B., et al. (2000). Subsystems contributing to the decline in ability to walk: Bridging the gap between epidemiology and geriatric practice in the InCHIANTI study. *Journal of the American Geriatrics Society, 48*, 1618–25.

Gori, C., Di Maio, A., & Pozzi, A. (2003). Long-term care for older people in Italy. In A. Comas-Herrera & R. Wittenberg (Eds.), *European study of long-term care expenditure* (pp. 59–76). London: PSSRU, LSE Health and Social Care, London School of Economics.

ISTAT. (2006). *Previsioni Demografiche Nazionali 1° gennaio 2005–1° gennaio 2050* [Census population projections January 1, 2005–January 1, 2050]. Retrieved March 31, 2009, from http://www.istat.it

ISTAT. (2007). *Condizioni di salute, fattori di rischio e ricorso ai servizi sanitari—Anno 2005* [Health conditions, risk factors and use of health services—Year 2005]. Retrieved March 31, 2009, from http://www.istat.it

ISTAT. (2008). *La povertà relativa in Italia nel 2007* [Relative poverty in Italy in 2007]. Retrieved March 31, 2009, from http://www.istat.it

Italian Longitudinal Study on Aging (ILSA) Working Group. (1997). Prevalence of chronic diseases in older Italians: Comparing self-reported and clinical diagnoses. *International Journal of Epidemiology, 26*, 995–1002.

Kohler, H., Billari, F. C., & Ortega, J. A. (2002). The emergence of lowest-low fertility in Europe during the 1990s. *Population and Development Review, 28*, 641–680.

Kunkel, S. (2008). Global aging and gerontology education. *Annual Review of Gerontology & Geriatrics, 28*, 45–59.

Lattanzio, F., Di Bari, M., Sgadari, A., Baccini, M., Ercolani, S., Rengo, F., et al.; for the Depression in the Aged Female National Evaluation Study Group. (2009). Improving the diagnostic accuracy of depression in older persons: The depression in the aged female national evaluation cluster randomized trial. *Journal of the American Geriatrics Society*. (In press.)

Lattanzio, F., Mussi, C., Scafato, E., Ruggiero, C., Dell'Aquila, G., Pedone, C., et al.; for the ULISSE study group. (n.d.) Health care for older people in Italy: The ULISSE Project: A computerized network on health-care services for older people. *Journal Nutrition Health and Aging* (In press.)

Michel, J., Huber, P., & Cruz-Jentoft, A. (2008). Europe-wide survey of teaching in geriatric medicine. *Journal of the American Geriatrics Society, 56,* 1536–1542.

Ministero della Salute. (2008). *Relazione sullo stato sanitario del Paese—Anni 2005–2006* [Report on health status of the country—years 2005–2006]. Retrieved March 31, 2009, from http://www.ministerosalute.it/dettaglio/phPrimoPianoNew.jsp?id=150

Mossello, E., Caleri, V., Razzi, E., Di Bari, M., Cantini, C., Tonon, E., et al. (2008). Day care for older dementia patients: Favorable effects on behavioral and psychological symptoms and caregiver stress. *International Journal of Geriatric Psychiatry, 23,* 1066–72.

Senin, U., Cherubini, A., & Mecocci, P. (2003). Impact of population aging on the social and the health care system: Need for a new model of long-term care. *Annali Italiani Medicina Interna, 18,* 6–15.

Società Italiana di Gerontologia e Geriatria. (2009). *Storia* [History]. Retrieved March 31, 2009, from http://www.sigg.it/societa.asp?riferimento=storia

Spano, P. L. (2006). Convenienze nascoste. Il fenomeno badanti e le risposte del welfare [Hidden conveniences. The phenomenon carers and answers welfare]. Nuova Dimensione.

27

Japan

Daisaku Maeda

At the beginning of the 21st century, typical elderly Japanese people, aged approximately 70 years old, have lived through one of the stormiest periods in their country's long history. When they were born, Japan was one of the many underdeveloped countries of Asia. During and after the Second World War, many of these people had painful experiences, such as the loss of family members and relatives; physical injury from air raids; and even hunger from lack of food due to economic ruin caused by the war.

During their upper teens, Japan surrendered and gave up its ultra-nationalistic policies, totally abolishing its military forces forever. Thus it can be safely said that the typical Japanese elderly person of today has experienced a complete political and cultural revolution, from ultra-nationalism, totalitarianism, and militarism, to internationalism, democracy, and pacifism, during the most sensitive stage in life.

In short, the older Japanese persons of today have lived under two completely different sets of national goals and ideologies. They have also experienced very rapid change in the standard of living in accordance with the shift from an agricultural to an industrialized country. Their unique life experiences should always be kept in mind when problems of aging in Japanese society are considered.

RECENT HISTORY OF AGING IN JAPAN

Demographic Features

In 2005, the total population of Japan was 128 million, and the number of elderly persons aged 65 and over was 25.7 million, or 20.1% of the total population. At the beginning of the 21st century, Japan was one of three countries with the most aged populations (Italy, Japan, and Sweden) in the world (Health and Welfare Statistics Association, 2007, p. 36).

The age structure of Japan's population was quite stable from the beginning to the middle of the 20th century. The very high birthrate, promulgated by national policy, offset the gradual increase in the aged population resulting from advances in medicine and public health, as well as general improvements in the standard of living. However, from 1949, four years after the end of the Second World War, the birthrate decreased very sharply, from 33.0 per 1,000 in 1949 to 17.2 per 1,000 in 1960, and 9.5 per 1,000 in 1997 (Health and Welfare Statistics Association, 2007, p. 378). Japan now belongs to the group of countries with the lowest birthrate in the world (Japan Aging Research Center [JARC], 2007, p. 326). In addition, its low birthrate is combined with a great extension of life expectancy in older people. This tendency is expected to continue, and it is estimated that Japan will continue to lead the world in the population aging race until at least 2050, when the proportion of the elderly aged 65 and over of Japan will reach 37.7%.

Regarding population aging in Japan, the impact of the high increase in Japan's oldest population (80+) cannot be overemphasized. The number of older persons aged 80 and over will increase and exceed 17 million (a 2.7-times increase from 2005) and its proportion of the total population will reach 19.1% in 2055 (a nearly four-times increase from 2005), while the increase in the total number of older persons aged 65 and over is only about 1.4 times that of the years 2005 and 2055 (from 22.8 million to 36.5 million). It is to be noted, however, that as described above, its proportion in the total population will increase from 20.2% to 40.5% between 2005 and 2055 (a two-times increase) (JARC, 2007, p. 74; JARC, 2007, p. 85). As the increase in the number of very old persons necessarily brings about the increase of mentally and/or physically impaired older persons, health-care services for such older persons will become increasingly more important in the coming half-century.

The Impact of Population Aging on Japanese Society

In parallel with the aging of the population and the accompanying socioeconomic changes, it is predicted that the tradition of family care for aged parents cannot help but decline significantly. In most Western industrialized nations, almost all the older persons aged 65 and over live alone or only with spouses. It seems quite certain that Japan will follow the same direction in light of very high industrialization, urbanization, and Westernization. It should be strongly emphasized that Japan has to exert every possible effort in the construction of a solid and efficient system of health and social services for the elderly, before it is too late.

RESEARCH IN GERONTOLOGY

In Japan, research on aging is a relatively new field. Organized scientific research on aging was started in the 1920s in the field of medicine at Tokyo University School of Medicine and the Yokufukai Institution, a large, multifunctional voluntary institution for the aged in Tokyo.

In 1953, after the long and difficult period of World War II and the ensuing economic distress, the National Society for the Study of Geriatrics was organized. This is the forerunner of the current Japan Geriatrics Society (Nihon Ronen Igakukai). Modern psychological research on aging was also started at the Yokufukai Institution in 1930s, but the number of psychologists devoted to this area has not increased much and it is still considerably smaller than the other areas of research on aging.

Organized efforts for the development of social science research on aging also started very late—at the beginning of 1950s. In 1954, the Japan Society for the Study of Longevity (Nihon Jumyo-Gaku Kenkyukai) was established, enlisting the participation of most of the leading researchers in the social and behavioral sciences interested in gerontological study at that time.

In the meantime, the activities of the International Association of Gerontology, which was organized in 1950, gave rise to an awareness of the necessity of interdisciplinary efforts in the study on aging. In 1960, under the initiative of these two organizations, the Japan Gerontological Society (Nihon Ronen Gakkai) was established as a federation of the two independent societies—the Japan Geriatrics Society and the Japan Socio-Gerontological Society (Nihon Ronen Shakai-Kagakukai). The first National Congress of the Japan Gerontological Society was held in 1959, a year before the formal establishment of the federal society. Since then, the joint national congress has been held every two years, and in the year between the joint congresses, each of the two societies has a national congress of its own.

In 1972, 12 years after the Japan Gerontological Society was established, the Tokyo Metropolitan Institute of Gerontology (TMIG) was set up by the Tokyo Metropolitan Government. This is a multidisciplinary research institute dedicated solely to the study of aging and related problems. Since the turn of the century, because of the Tokyo Metropolitan Government's financial difficulties, TMIG has been gradually reduced in size. It is, however, still one of the largest and best-equipped research institutions in the field of gerontology and geriatrics in the world. In 1977, the Japan Society for Biomedical Gerontology (Nihon Kiso Roka Gakkai) was established and later joined the Japan Gerontological Society.

In 1991, the Japanese Society of Geriatric Dentistry (Nihon Ronen Shika Gakkai) was organized and joined the Japan Gerontological Society. Since then, a number of academic associations devoted to geriatric and gerontological study have been set up and some of them joined the Japan Gerontological Society, which is now a federation of the following six academic organizations: Japan Geriatrics Society (approximately 6,400 members); Japan Socio-Gerontological Society (approximately 1,500 members); the Japan Society for Biomedical Gerontology (approximately 300 members); the Japanese Society of Geriatric Dentistry (approximately 1,700 members); the Japanese Psychogeriatric Society (approximately 2,500 members); and the Japanese Society for the Study of Case Management (approximately 2,500 members).

The National Congress of Gerontology, which is sponsored by the Japan Gerontological Society, is held every two years. Naturally, this is a multidisciplinary congress, like the International Congress of Gerontology. In the year when a multidisciplinary congress is not held, each organization holds its own national congress.

In addition to the societies in the field of gerontology and geriatrics mentioned above, there are many small and specialized societies of researchers. Among them, the Japanese Society of Applied Gerontology seems to be worth mentioning. So far, the studies in the field of social gerontology have tended to be too academic to be useful in practice. This society aims at promoting practical studies that can produce useful outcomes in the field of health and social services for the elderly.

The growing interest in population aging has anticipated many serious problems, and has gradually influenced policy-makers at the national level. In 1995, the national government established a geriatric research institute in one of the national hospitals located in Aichi Prefecture. This research institute was given a rather unique name, the literal translation of which is the Center for the Study of Longevity Medicine. At the time of its establishment, it had 8 research departments and 21 laboratories. In

2004, this Center was given the status of an independent national research institute composed of 13 research departments and 42 laboratories. Unfortunately for social and behavioral gerontologists, however, this Center is devoted solely to the study of longevity medicine, namely the study of geriatric medicine. In the field of social policies, the National Institute of Social Security and Population Problems has been playing a significant role. It is a part of the Ministry of Health, Labor, and Welfare.

In the field of social sciences, the following two organizations seem to be worth mentioning. The first is the Japan Aging Research Center (JARC), and the other is the International Leadership Center—Japan (ILC-Japan). Though they have no full-time researchers, through the utilization of sociologists, demographers, economists, and other specialists belonging to universities and other academic organizations, they are making a significant contribution to the study of aging in the field of social sciences in Japan.

In accordance with the aging of Japanese society, the care of demented older persons has become one of the most pressing national issues. In response to this need, the national government decided to appropriate a special grant to three voluntary organizations for the establishment of a Dementia Care Research and Training Center in the year 2000. Each center has a number of full-time researchers and trainers for the care of people with dementia. The trainees are mainly nurses and care workers.

Recently, there was also a small but significant movement in the study of social gerontology. A multidisciplinary research center for the study of social gerontology was established in the faculty of human sciences of Tokyo University. As Tokyo University is one of the leading academic institutions in Japan, this will give a significant stimulus to the progress of research in social gerontology in the future.

EDUCATION IN GERONTOLOGY

Physicians

In the field of medicine, the importance of gerontology and geriatrics has been recognized widely in the last half-century. At present, there are 80 schools of medicine in Japan, of which 23 have some kind of special section or unit for education and research in geriatrics and gerontology. Even at schools that do not have such a section or unit, geriatrics is regarded as one of the most important subjects.

Recently, the Japanese Geriatrics Society started the Certified Geriatric Specialist System. At present (December 1, 2007), there are 1,497 Certified Geriatric Specialists throughout Japan.

Nurses

Government regulation regarding the education of nurses requires that all schools of nursing should have at least one teacher who is specialized in geriatric nursing. Unlike physicians, however, there is no certification system for geriatric nursing.

Social Workers

Japan has had a national examination for Registered Social Workers since 1991. Because subjects regarding gerontology, as well as knowledge of various public services for the elderly, are regarded as very important, all the schools of social work in Japan place emphasis upon the field of gerontology and knowledge about various services for the elderly. There is no certification system for social workers specializing in gerontology.

Care Workers

Japan has a national system for Registered Care Workers. In order to become a Registered Care Worker, one must either pass the national examination or graduate from a designated school for care workers. Most of the designated schools for care workers are two-year vocational schools. However, a number of colleges have a department or section for registered care workers.

School for Advanced Study in Gerontology

In Japan, there is only one graduate school solely devoted to education and training on social gerontology: the Department of Social Gerontology at J. F. Oberlin University, which is located in Tokyo. It has both master's and doctoral degree programs. Though it is a small department (20 students a year at the master's degree level), it places emphasis on research. Every year it publishes a number of research papers of high quality.

CURRENT PUBLIC POLICY ISSUES

Coping with Rapidly Expanding Social Security Cost

Mainly because of the enormous increase in the elderly population, Japan's social security cost is expanding rapidly. The speed of this increase is much faster than economic growth, which is one of the slowest among industrialized countries. The gap between the expanding social security cost and economic growth will probably continue to exist in the coming two decades. Needless to say, the measures that need to be taken are obvious: cutting expenditures and increasing income. The cutting of expenditures, however, has almost reached the limit. To further cut expenditures will greatly damage the quality of life of elderly Japanese, which seems to be significantly lower compared to that of other industrialized countries.

Thus, more and more economists, politicians, and even businesspeople have begun to express the opinion that consumption tax, which is 55% now, should be raised. Some progressive politicians even propose that consumption tax should be used only for social security and related services and that the name should be changed from *consumption tax* to *social security tax*. However, Japanese public opinion, expressed through the media, regarding an increase in consumption tax, seems to be rather negative. It will take at least several years for the rate of the consumption tax to be raised so as to cover the expanding social security costs.

Because of population aging, the number of older persons needing care services is increasing rapidly. On the other hand, the number of younger people who are expected to serve older persons as care workers is decreasing significantly. The reasons are the decline in wages of care workers, due to the general decrease in remuneration paid to service providers by the Public Long-Term Care Insurance. This is due to the excessively fast increase in the total demand on the Public Long-Term Care Insurance, which in turn is caused by the rapid increase in the older population, especially that of frail and/or impaired very old persons. This problem is especially acute in large metropolitan areas, where the number of jobs with higher income and social status is increasing due to the recovering national economy.

The measures to be taken are, needless to say, the improvement of remuneration to the service providers and/or the import of foreign care workers. The latter is, however, difficult to realize because of the general attitude of Japanese people toward foreign workers. On the other hand, improving remuneration to service providers is also hard to realize, because of the very tight balance between the current income and expenditures of the Public Long-Term Care Insurance. Many insurers, especially in rural areas, feel that the level of the contribution of the insuree to the Public Long-Term Care Insurance is already at its maximum. In order to solve this problem, the proportion of the contribution of the governments (national, prefectural, and local governments) which is presently one-half, should be raised considerably, however difficult it may be at the present state of the national economy.

Shortage of Institutions and Assisted Living for the Frail and/or Impaired Elderly

Because of the rapid increase in the population of the very old, the need for institutions for nursing care and assisted living is growing significantly. The increase in these services, however, cannot catch up to the growing needs because of the slow economic growth over the past several decades. The shortage is especially serious in large metropolitan areas, where family care of older parents is weakening rapidly because of the increase of older persons living alone or with only a spouse, which, in turn, is caused by the further progress of industrialization and urbanization. In many cases, grown-up children are working far away from where their older parents live. On the other hand, due to the high price of land, the shortage of manpower and, above all, the insufficient provision of government grants, the speed of the increase of institutions for nursing care, as well as assisted living, is very slow. Though long-term life-care–type retirement homes are increasing rapidly, especially in large metropolitan areas, they are too expensive for ordinary middle-class older persons.

CONCLUSION

Regrettably, it can rightfully be said that, in spite of the very long average life expectancy at age 65, the present level of quality of life for older Japanese persons is considerably lower in comparison with that of other industrialized countries. This is mainly due to the slow development in health and social services for the elderly, especially assisted living and institutional care services over the past several decades. As a result, there are quite a number of severely impaired older persons cared for in their own homes by their spouses, who are themselves frail and/or impaired. In addition, many severely impaired older persons are cared for by their children, whose health status is not good enough to care for their aged parents, or who are physically or mentally handicapped. The services provided by the Public Long-Term Care Insurance to such families are too low to secure a minimum level of quality of life. Thus, in Japan, almost not a single day passes without news being reported by mass media about double suicides by older couples, as well as elder abuse by family caregivers.

After the first oil shock of 1973, the speed of economic growth of Japan has been very slow. The policy of the national government of Japan toward economic stagnation was just to cut to the fullest extent the growing costs for social security, as well as health and social services on the whole. The effects of such negative social policies came to the surface around the turn of the century. The severest influences are felt in the services for the elderly and the disabled. It seems that it will take at least another couple of decades for Japan to catch up to the level of other industrialized countries of the West.

REFERENCES

Health and Welfare Statistics Association (Kousei Toukei Kyoukai). (2007). *Kokumin eiseino doukou* [Trends of nation's health]. Tokyo: Health and Welfare Statistics Association.

Japan Aging Research Center (JARC). (2007). *Kourei Shakai Kiso Shiryou— 07–08 nenban* [Data book on aging in Japan 2007–2008]. Tokyo: JARC.

28

·· ■ ··

Kenya

Samuel M. Mwangi

HISTORY OF AGING IN KENYA

The Kenyan older population has not risen significantly over the last few decades. In 1989, a little over 1 million individuals were aged 60 and above (U.S. Census Bureau, 2000). A decade later, in 1999, this number had risen to 1.3 million (Gondi, 2007). In 2007, older Kenyans had marginally increased to about 1.5 million (Gondi, 2007; U.S. Census Bureau, 2000). Projections show that by the year 2020, they will have increased to slightly over 2 million. A dramatic increase will be expected in the decades leading to 2050, with an older population of 8.2 million (HelpAge International, 2007; U.S. Census Bureau, 2000). The proportion of older Kenyans has remained fairly stable as well over the last few decades, averaging around 4% over the period from 1989 to present (Gondi, 2007). This population is expected to increase over five-fold from 2007 to 2050. Figure 28.1 below summarizes the demographic transition for Kenyans aged 60+ from 1989 to 2050.

As do most other countries, Kenya has more elderly women than men. Women constitute 55% of older people globally and 52% of older people in Kenya (Ministry of Gender, Sport, Culture and Social Service [MGSCSS], 2006). Another interesting observation about Kenyan older people is that 64% live in rural areas (MGSCSS, 2006). In spite of the fact that the HIV/AIDS pandemic has reduced life expectancy in Kenya, older people will continue to live longer. In fact, over the next 30 years,

Figure 28.1
Kenyan population 60+ in millions between 1989 and 2050

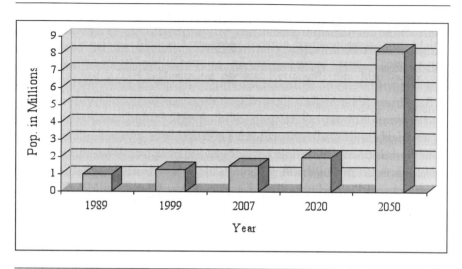

Source: U.S. Census Bureau International Database. (2000). *Country summary: Kenya.*
Washington, DC: U.S. Census Bureau. Retrieved June 22, 2008, from http://www.census.
gov/cgi-bin/ipc/idbsprd

the older population in Kenya will grow to more than double its current
size (MGSCSS, 2006).

Kenya has adopted and institutionalized the United Nations definition
of old age as age 60 and older (Gondi, 2007), despite the fact that the
mandatory retirement age is 55 years. The implication is that Kenyans
exit the labor force long before attaining old age. However, the definition of old age by chronological age in sub-Saharan Africa has been criticized severely (Kimuna & Adamchak, 1999). Instead, social definitions
that view old age as both a process and a stage have been recommended
because they are much closer to the perceptions and notions of old age by
indigenous people (Ezeh, Chepngeno, Kasiira, & Woubalem, 2006).

Most of the older people in Kenya are confronted by a host of challenges,
ranging from economic, health, social, and other personal problems that
are created by the larger social and economic forces in the country. The
keys areas of concern for older people were identified as follows: (1) high
levels of poverty among the elderly; (2) poor health and lack of proper nutrition; (3) effect of HIV/AIDS pandemic causing the burden of providing
care for orphaned children and risk of infection; (4) lack of decent housing
and shelter; (5) lack of income security in older age and nonexistence of

social services appropriate for the elderly; (6) abuse, neglect, and violence against older Kenyans; (7) illiteracy and lack of participation in adult education; (8) lack of recognition of elderly rights by the legal systems; and (9) employment discrimination in old age (Gondi, 2007). It should also be noted that a number of elderly Kenyans are infected with the HIV virus, and little is known about them (E. O. Nyambedha, personal communication, October 2, 2008).

AGING RESEARCH IN KENYA

A dramatic increase in the older population in Western countries has led to an explosion of research on health and aging. Conversely, very few aging-related studies have been conducted in developing countries. This is despite the fact that many developing countries will be aging faster than many other regions of the world. Aging in Kenya has been occurring in an environment of social and economic hardships, widespread poverty, HIV/ AIDS, and the rapid transformation of the traditional extended family structure (Gachuhi & Kiemo, 2005). The Madrid International Plan of Action of Ageing (MIPAA) in 2002 identified the major aging problems in Africa that can be investigated through scientific studies.

The major aging research issues identified are: (1) risk of marginalization of older adults as they lose traditional family support and social networks as people move to the cities; (2) the HIV/AIDS crisis, which forces many older people to become caregivers to their orphaned grandchildren; and (3) the weakening of social security and health systems that support older adults (Gachuhi & Kiemo, 2005). All these issues present opportunities for research that can be, or has been, undertaken in Kenya. As previously noted, a few research studies on aging have been conducted and published in Kenya (E. O. Nyambedha, personal communication, October 2, 2008). Research conducted in Kenya and published in foreign publications typically have been done in collaboration with faculty and scholars from developed countries. Kenyan universities seldom get involved in the process of aging data collection (Gachuhi & Kiemo, 2005).

LIMITATIONS ON AGING
RESEARCH IN KENYA

Before embarking on the status of current aging research in Kenya, it is worthwhile noting some of the limitations identified as impediments to aging research on the African continent. According to Gachuhi and

Kiemo (2005), the main reasons are: (1) aging research in Africa in general has been given low priority in most countries and in the universities, because population aging has not been an explicit issue of concern at the academic or government policy level; (2) enormous amounts of public resources in Kenya are invested in support of young people, channeled through health, education, and employment needs, as opposed to the needs of older people; (3) lack of trained gerontologists to provide leadership on aging research and lack of training in social science research methods hamper development of this kind of research; (4) academic sources and past published research on aging issues is limited in African universities, hindering the teaching of gerontology; and (5) teaching materials available in aging use examples from developed countries, which may also prove difficult for students to conceptualize.

Other limitations are: inadequate computer software and hardware; a lack of specialized tools and equipment in geriatrics at the universities and research centers; large-scale research is constrained by unavailability of older human subjects at particular times like planting and harvesting seasons, and impassable rural roads during rainy seasons (other reports suggest this problem may be overstated [E. O. Nyambedha, personal communication, October 2, 2008]); as in many African countries, poverty has crippled research endowment funds; and there is a shortage of academic forums where researchers on aging can meet, deliberate, and share/discuss ideas and research findings. Similarly, no publications in Africa are dedicated to empirical research on aging on the African continent. The implication is that findings based on African studies are disseminated through foreign publications, which rarely become available in places where the research was originally conducted. This underscores the need to think about alternative approaches to the dissemination of research evidence on aging in Kenya and Africa in general.

To surmount these problems, a number of suggestions have been brought forward for increasing aging research capacity in Kenya and the rest of Africa. The milestone of this move is the establishment of the African Research on Ageing Network (AFRAN), which is a network of dedicated key African and international scholars, policy-makers, civil society representatives, and African graduate students with a common interest in aging research in Africa. AFRAN was established as a standing committee of the International Association of Gerontology and Geriatrics (IAGG) in Rio de Janeiro in 2005. This initiative has formally been endorsed by United Nations Programme on Ageing as a platform for furthering aging research and implementation of MIPAA guidelines in Africa.

Particular Aging Studies in Kenya

Aging research in Kenya, as it has been pointed out, is mostly based on collaborations between international scholars and Kenyan professors and/ or postgraduate students. Kenya National Bureau of Statistics (KNBS), the central governmental data-collecting agency, has some limited data related to aging for secondary analyses. KNBS data, however, are limited and inadequate for gerontological research purposes because measures related to aging are insufficient in these data sets. Basic data collected include demographics, labor force participation, literacy and education, health-care consumption, and HIV/AIDS status. Particular aging studies in Kenya are summarized below.

Kenyan Grandparents Study on Health (KGS)

This ongoing research project examines the impact of caregiving for AIDS orphaned children on the health and well-being of Luo elders in a rural setting in western Kenya. Gillian Ice, an associate professor at Ohio University, United States, is the principal investigator. This research is usually conducted during summer, when her U.S. students assist with data collection. The focus is on the health of 287 grandparents (age 65 to 81) who are examined using multiple methods, including objective measures, clinical history, physical examination, and a modified version of the Short Form (36) Health Survey (SF-36) (Ice, Zidron, & Juma, 2008).

Grandparents Empowered to Nurture Orphans (GENO)

GENO is an ongoing collaborative project between Georgia State University in the United States, Global Health Action (an Atlanta-based NGO), and several African nonprofit organizations. This project started on a small scale, providing support to Kenyan elders who are taking care of their AIDS-orphaned grandchildren. Data collection for this project began in 2006, with support from Georgia State University and the Coca-Cola Africa Foundation, and work continues on data analysis and the search for additional funds to expand the intervention study to a larger number of families in Kenya, Uganda, and Tanzania. The ultimate goal of the project is to reduce the risk of transmission of the virus to the younger generation through support of their elders, education of service providers, and improving communication between generations.

Widowhood among Abaluyia and Samia in Kenya

This is an anthropological and sociohistorical study in western Kenya that has been ongoing since the early 1980s under the leadership of Maria Cattell, an American anthropologist affiliated with the Field Museum in Chicago. In her most recent publication, Cattell (2008) provided narrative accounts of ways in which modernization and social change, such as the disappearance of African families and declining family support to the elderly, have transformed the daily lives of older people in the Abaluyia and Samia communities. Numerous publications have resulted from this ethnographic research.

Nairobi Urban Health and Demographic Surveillance System (NUHDSS)

NUHDSS is a small-scale study under the auspices of the African Population and Health Research Centre (APHRC). Data for this research study are collected at surveillance sites at two urban slum settlements in the capital, Nairobi. The main areas of investigation in this study are sociodemographics, living arrangements, and the economic and health status of older adults in those settlements.

Kenya Demographic and Health Survey (KDHS)

KDHS is based on a nationally representative sample for demographic and health indicators conducted by KNBS in partnership with Ministry of Health (MoH). The study was jointly funded by the United States Agency for International Development (USAID), the U.K. Department for International Development (DFID/UK), the United Nations Development Programme (UNDP), and the United Nations Population Fund (UNFPA). The most recent data were collected in 2003, with prior data collection in 1989, 1993, and 1998 (KNBS, 2003). Several studies focusing on older adults have used KDHS secondary data.

Research on aging in Kenya is predominantly carried out on a small scale, with the exception of KDHS, which was a national survey. The examples cited above reveal that most aging research in Kenya is related to HIV/AIDS and elders' caregiving for AIDS-orphaned children. The high prevalence of HIV/AIDS in western Kenya has attracted more funding AIDS-related research, unlike in other parts of the country. Other aging-related issues, like income maintenance and poverty, housing, long-term care, health care access and provision, and nutrition, have not attracted much funding or research attention.

GERONTOLOGY EDUCATION IN KENYA

Gerontology as an academic discipline is very new to many African universities including those in Kenya. The major challenge of gerontology education in Africa is that universities do not even have course units on aging that are offered in any of the academic disciplines (Gachuhi & Kiemo, 2005). Therefore, gerontology education as an academic discipline is yet to take root in the East African region's institutions of higher learning. Early in 2004, Kenyatta University was the first university in the region to establish gerontology education in partnership with Georgia State University in Atlanta (King, Gachuhi, Ice, Cattell, & Whittington, 2005).

Dr. Mugo Gachuhi, an associate professor of sociology at Kenyatta University, has been at the forefront of introducing gerontology as an academic discipline and an area for public policy development in Kenya (King et al., 2005). The quest for gerontology education through this partnership was also to focus on the short-term courses to service providers from communities and organizations dealing with older persons and aging (King et al., 2005). Kenyatta University has started offering both undergraduate and diploma (equivalent to an associate degree in the United States) programs in gerontology.

Courses offered under these programs are structured to provide education for people working both directly and indirectly with older persons, especially those working in social services and community development (King et al., 2005). In addition, a number of graduate students in related fields of study are researching aging issues for their master's theses and doctoral dissertations. Other Kenyan universities are yet to establish curricula for courses in gerontology. The KU-GSU partnership called for more collaboration between Kenyan universities and those in developed countries where gerontology programs have been established. Formation of the Inter-University Gerontology Research Committee for universities in the East African region will encourage and support other educational institutions to establish gerontology courses (King et al., 2005).

PUBLIC POLICY ISSUES

Kenya is one of the signatories to the Madrid International Plan of Action on Ageing (MIPAA) adopted in Vienna, Austria, in 1982, during the first World Assembly on Ageing. Kenya also recognizes the aging concerns identified by the African Union (AU) Policy Framework and

Plan of Action on Ageing. As claimed previously, a large proportion of older Kenyans remain at significant risk of poverty. Many are unable to work due to either age or disability, or they work under very stressful conditions. Some suffer a great deal of sickness and usually have below-average educational attainment (Kakwani & Son, 2006). In order to protect older Kenyans from economic and social risks, the Kenyan government has committed itself to supporting the welfare and activities of older persons. This is evidenced by a number of proposed initiatives for ways of reducing vulnerability among older adults. In this section, we will discuss these initiatives by government, nongovernmental organizations, and local community levels. The key policy proposals and initiatives intended to improve the quality of lives of older adults in Kenya are listed below.

Sessional Paper No. 1 of 2000 on National Population Policy

This document recognizes the problems of elders in Kenya as a result of declining social and material support from families, and also due to lack of comprehensive government support programs for this age group. This policy attempts to address elders' basic needs and care by formulating long-term programs to ensure their socioeconomic support and security. Creation of private social security programs and encouraging positive traditional support networks are also enhanced in this policy.

Ninth National Development Plan (2002–2008)

With the change and even disintegration of traditional family structures in Kenya due to urbanization and modernization, the support system for older people has been strained, making them more vulnerable to poverty. The government has therefore collaborated with other stakeholders to undertake a number of activities to lift older people out of poverty: (a) operationalizing the National Policy for Older Persons to ensure that programs for older persons are well coordinated; (b) designing appropriate capacity-building programs for all organizations dealing with issues of older people; (c) creating advocacy programs to sensitize the public to the needs and rights of older people; and (d) mainstreaming aging issues in the national development and budgeting process.

Kenya National Policy on Ageing and Older Persons (2006)

This is the major policy document aimed at integrating and mainstreaming needs and concerns of the older people in the national development process. This policy also envisions creating an environment where older people are recognized, respected, and empowered to actively and fully participate in the society and its development. The priority issues covered in the National Policy include legal rights of older people; poverty reduction and sustainable development; health and active life; family culture; gender; food security and nutrition; housing and physical amenities; education, training, and media; employment and income security; social security and social welfare; preparation for retirement; and conflict and disaster preparedness.

Constitutional Amendment (in Process)

Legislation was enacted in Kenya in 2003 to allow amendment of the current constitution. Article 36 of the draft document has provisions for older people, including the rights and entitlements to: (1) full participation in the affairs of society; (2) pursuit of personal development; (3) protection against all forms of discrimination, exploitation, and abuse; (4) live with dignity and respect; and (5) entitlement to reasonable care and assistance from both family and state. It also provides that older people have a duty to plan their retirement, share their knowledge and skills with others, and remain active and independent in the society. An NGO, HelpAge Kenya, made several presentations to improve this section of the draft document and to advance a more comprehensive statement of old-age issues (Gondi, 2007).

Budgetary Allocations

During the annual budget speeches, the Minister for Finance presents to the National Assembly proposed appropriations for different government ministries and departments. Appropriations for the social services department include those for the most vulnerable people in society. In the 2008/09 fiscal year, the minister proposed several budgetary allocations in favor of older Kenyans. For the first time, caregivers for HIV/AIDS orphans will receive financial support from the government. A separate fund of 550 million Kenya Shillings (about US$7 million) was set up to provide social protection to vulnerable children and elderly Kenyans in the current fiscal year. Other initiatives that were made in the current budget were exempting monthly pension benefits from taxation as well as lump-sum benefits upon retirement, and allowing and encouraging pension schemes to provide benefit drawdown to ensure regular benefits are received by retirees. These are major financial incentives to allow growth of the retirement benefits sub-sector that were previously not available (Ministry of Finance, 2008).

CONCLUSION

This chapter has reviewed the demographic and socioeconomic profile of older Kenyans. Since Kenya is entering demographic transition, its population is expected to age over the coming decades. Although the current population size of older people may not sound alarm bells, it is evident that most older Kenyans are poor and in need of socioeconomic and health support. To address such needs, collaboration between institutions of higher learning, research institutions, civil society organizations, and government policy agencies should be strengthened to initiate research studies of aging issues. This process strengthens institutional mechanisms for aging research, gerontology education, and aging policy formulation. To this end, the government and other stakeholders have prepared strategies to be included in the National Policy on Ageing. The challenge remains to ensure that issues affecting older people will be addressed comprehensively as stipulated in the several ongoing policy initiatives.

REFERENCES

Cattell, M. (2008). Aging and social change among Abaluyia in western Kenya: Anthropological and historical perspectives. *Journal of Cross-Cultural Gerontology, 23*, 181–197.

Ezeh, A. C., Chepngeno, G., Kasiira, A. Z., & Woubalem, Z. (2006). The situation of older people in the case of urban settings: The case of Nairobi, Kenya. In B. Cohen and J. Menken (Eds.), *Aging in sub-Saharan Africa: Recommendations for further research* (pp. 117–135). Washington, DC: The National Academies Press.

Gachuhi, J. M., & Kiemo, K. (2005). Research capacity on ageing in Africa: Limitations and ways forward. *Generations Review, 15*, 36–38.

Gondi, H. O. (2007). *Report on status and implementation of national policy on ageing in Kenya.* New York: United Nations Department of Economic and Social Affairs.

HelpAge International. (2007). *Kenya country profile.* London: Author.

Ice, G., Zidron, A., & Juma, E. (2008). Health and health perceptions among Kenyan grandparents. *Journal of Cross-Cultural Gerontology, 23*, 111–129.

Kakwani, N., & Son, H. H. (2006). *Poverty, old age and social pensions in Kenya. Working Paper (24)*. Rio de Janeiro, Brazil: UNDP International Poverty Centre.

Kenya National Bureau of Statistics (KNBS). (2003). *Kenya demographic and health survey (KDHS) preliminary report*. Nairobi, Kenya: Author.

Kimuna, S. R. & Adamchak, D. J. (1999). Population ageing and elderly support: A Kenyan profile. *BOLD Journal of the International Institute on Ageing, 10*(1), 6–16.

King, S. V., Gachuhi, M., Ice, G., Cattell, M., & Whittington, F. (2005). Gerontology education and research in Kenya: Establishing a U.S.-Africa partnership in aging. In D. Shenk & L. Groger (Eds.), *Aging education in a global context* (pp. 117–149). New York: The Haworth Press.

Ministry of Finance. (2008). *Budget speech for the fiscal year 2008/2009*. Nairobi, Kenya: Author.

Ministry of Gender, Sport, Culture and Social Services (MGSCSS). (2006). *The national policy on older persons and ageing*. Nairobi, Kenya: Author.

U.S. Census Bureau International Database (IDB). (2000). *Country summary: Kenya*. Washington, DC: U.S. Census Bureau. Retrieved June 22, 2008, from http://www.census.gov/cgi-bin/ipc/idbsprd

Waithaka, J. K., Anyona, F., & Koori, A. (2003). *Ageing and poverty in Kenya. Country report*. Paper presented at the Regional Workshop on Ageing and Poverty in Sub-Saharan Africa, October 29–31, 2003, in Dar-es-Salaam, Tanzania. Nairobi, Kenya: The Government Printer.

29

．．■．．

Luxembourg

Dieter Ferring

DEMOGRAPHIC ASPECTS

Comparable to all other Western European countries, the demographic changes in Luxembourg are characterized by a progressively declining and low birthrate, greater longevity, and increasing female participation in the paid labor market. Though comparable to its neighbors, Germany, France and Belgium, in these aspects, Luxembourg has distinctive characteristics, including a relatively small population, which amounts to about 484,000 persons (50.5% women), who speak up to three languages (Luxembourgish, French, and German). Table 29.1 summarizes the total population in its absolute and relative numbers of women and men in three age groups, using data provided by the National Statistical Bureau of Luxembourg (STATEC, 2008).

Data in Table 29.1 illustrate that the ratio of children to those in the third age in Luxembourg is still in favor of the first group. Present estimations show that the crude death rate amounts to 8.0 deaths per 1,000, and the crude birthrate averages 11.7 births per 1,000. The fertility rate is 1.7 compared to an average fertility rate of 1.48 in the EU 25 (Eurostat, 2008). Life expectancy at birth averages 80.1 years overall, 76.6 years for males, and 82.2 years for females (Eurostat, 2008).

The relatively small Luxembourg population is distributed in rural and urban areas; the industrialized south of Luxembourg represents the most populated part of the country. A further distinctive feature of the

Table 29.1

Age Groups and Sex Ratios of the Luxembourg Population in 2008
(Proportions of the Total Population)

Age groups	2008	M	F
Active age (15–64 years)	67.9%	9.3%	8.8%
Children (0–14 years)	18.2%	34.3%	33.5%
Third age (65 years and older)	14%	5.8%	8.2%
	100%	49.4%	50.5%

Source: STATEC. (2008). *Population et emploi* [Population and labor]. Retrieved July 21, 2008, from the National Statistical Bureau of Luxembourg Web site: http://www.statis tiques.public.lu/fr/population/index.html

Luxembourg population is its relatively high amount of foreign persons, which has progressively grown since the 1960s. The current ratio of native Luxembourgish to foreign persons amounts to 1.35; native Luxembourgish represent 57.4% and foreign persons 42.6% of the total population. Luxembourg is by far the richest country in the European Union, with Ireland second at almost half its gross domestic product (GDP) per capita. In terms of purchasing power parity, GDP per inhabitant in Luxembourg in 2006 was almost three times the EU average at 276 units (GDP €71,600; EU-27: €26,600; USA: €35,000; see Eurostat, 2008). This is in part artificially boosted, given the large number of cross-border workers who work in Luxembourg but do not live there. In March 2006, a total of 318,600 persons were employed in Luxembourg, and 43% of these were foreigners, the so-called frontaliers who enter the country daily for their work (STATEC, 2007). The high economic standard in Luxembourg is due to a stable, high-income economy, characterized by solid growth, low inflation, and comparatively low unemployment. Comparing Luxembourg to the other members of the European Union, senior citizens are retiring rather early from professional activities, with a relatively high income. Even at the age of 80, four out of five persons show a solid functional status, allowing them to live in an autonomous manner (Ferring & Weber, 2005).

   Luxembourg thus represents a wealthy country where life expectancy will heighten for men and be even more pronounced for women in the years to come. Policy-makers have reacted to this with a legal act in 1998, when dependency insurance was established. Parallel to this, health and care services for the elderly—like nursing homes and especially home-care facilities—have been developed during the last two decades (see below).

This positive outline certainly has to be relativized, given that the social security and pension system rely heavily on the steady migration of cross-border workers, and on stable economic growth. With respect to these developments, Luxembourg, as well as its European neighbors, will have to reflect upon changes in its welfare and social security system (Ferring, Thill, & Leners, 2007; Schroeder, 2007).

RESEARCH ON AGING IN THE GRAND-DUCHY

Given the demographic development in Europe (Communication from the Commission [COM], 2006), the need for research in the various domains of aging has increasingly gained attention from funding agencies in Luxembourg during the last five years. In 2005, the First National Forum on Aging Research was held, bringing together researchers from several fields of aging research for exchange and better coordination of existing research facilities. The meeting covered five research domains: (1) health and active aging; (2) autonomy and dependency in old age; (3) diagnosis and treatment of age-associated disorders; (4) intergenerational relations; and (5) social security and employment models in age and old age. These topics give a first overview of aging research in Luxembourg, which covers both basic fundamental research as well as applied research within life sciences and social sciences.

Public research funding involves several ministries (Ministry of Culture, Higher Education and Research; Ministry of Social Security, Ministry of National Health, Ministry of Family and Solidarity), the National Research Fund (NRF), and the University of Luxembourg, founded in 2003. Furthermore, funding from the European Union is available for various programs, such as Ambient Assistant Living, described below. Three programs have been launched by the NRF, covering more or less explicitly different aspects of population aging: biological and medical aspects of aging; sociodemographic and socioeconomic development of Luxembourg, as well as population aging and its various consequences; and a third program, which covers several issues of crucial importance for the development of the Luxembourg population, and among these, aging represents one area under consideration.

Projects in the biological and medical aspects of aging utilize different methodological approaches, including experimental animal models, as well as clinical field research and epidemiological studies. An example of the latter is the prospective evaluation of neuropsychological and biological characteristics of mild cognitive impairment (MCI) and of associated subclinical health problems for Alzheimer's disease-type dementia

(ADTD; Perquin, 2007). A second prospective longitudinal study focuses on patients with recent onset of Parkinson's Disease (PD) and compares them to age-matched control subjects in order to find out if subclinical non-motor signs can be early disease markers (Diederich, Vaillant, Rufra, Blyth & Pieri, 2007; Hipp, Vaillant, Blyth, Pieri, & Diederich, 2007; Pieri, Vaillant, Blyth, Hipp & Diederich, 2007). In a further model, new therapeutic strategies to prevent neurodegeneration are investigated following an experimental design in animal models (Niclou, 2007).

The sociodemographic research initiative covers thematic priorities within the social sciences and humanities, in order to develop competences and steering knowledge with respect to ongoing demographic and social changes. The program includes (a) the evolution of the Luxembourg population, from a demographical, social, cultural, and historical point of view; (b) the development of human resources and the educational and training system; (c) the era of information and communication and its consequences for society; (d) the place of a small country like Luxembourg within the greater region, the European Union, and a global world, with a specific focus on the perspectives of the Luxembourg financial market; and (e) the organization of space, town, and country planning. Even though some of these priorities are not directly related to aging, the aging population has implications for each of them. The ongoing project on intergenerational relations in family and society directly explores essential aspects of an aging society (Ferring, Michels, Boll, & Filipp, 2008).

Besides these programs, the NRF has launched a new research program that covers 10 thematic priorities for the country. Among these, the domains of regenerative medicine in age-related diseases and translational bio-medical research especially will give further rise to biomedical research. The research priority characterized as "Identities, diversity and integration" covers aging from the perspective of social sciences and humanities; research questions to be analyzed here comprise social inclusion and exclusion processes with respect to the elderly, or the situation of elderly migrants, to give just two examples.

Importantly, the NRF is a member of the European Research Area in Aging (ERA-AGE) coordinated by the University of Sheffield (University of Sheffield, 2008). This four-year project, funded by the European Commission, is aimed at promoting the development of a European strategy for research on aging, comprising 12 European public authorities (including Israel) responsible for the funding and coordination of national research programs. Several activities link Luxembourg to its European partners, including the program on Future Leaders of Aging Research, which will be continued in the coming years. With respect to various EU-financed programs, Ambient Assisted Living especially should be highlighted. Specific goals of the program comprise (1) encouraging the development of technology for ameliorating the quality of life of the elderly, of family members, and of informal and formal caregivers; and (2) promoting the collaboration between the public and private sector (especially small-medium enterprises).

The main *research institutes* in Luxembourg include the University of Luxembourg, several specialized Public Research Centers (Centres de Recherche Publics; CRP) as well as the socioeconomic research center CEPS/INSTEAD (Centre d'Etudes de Populations, de Pauvreté et de Politiques Socio-Economiques/International Network for Studies in Technology, Environment, Alternatives, Development). The University of Luxembourg (UL) comprises three faculties, and research on aging is primarily located within the Faculty of Language and Literature, Humanities, Arts and Education. Research at the university is organized in the form of multidisciplinary research units that combine scholars from differing disciplines. Aging and intergenerational relations represent an explicit research objective of the Integrative Research Unit on Social and Individual Development (INSIDE); this unit includes researchers from psychology, sociology, social work, and educational sciences who study social change phenomena from a life-span perspective. Aging research in the unit focuses on the social construction of aging (Ferring, Haller, Meyer-Wolters, & Michels, 2008) as well as on personal and contextual factors contributing to autonomous living in old age. In detail, current research projects deal with the quality of intergenerational relations (Ferring, Michels, et al., 2008), the psychosocial situation of family carers in Luxembourg and Europe (e.g., Albert, Michels & Ferring, 2008), as well as the use of technology and its usability in old age, including research on user empowerment (Otjacques, 2007). All projects are designed as multidisciplinary endeavors and involve cooperation with European and/or other international partners. Projects already conducted include the European Study on Adult Well-being (Burholt et al., 2007; Drooglever-Fortuijn et al., 2006; Ferring & Hoffmann, 2007; Ferring et al., 2004) and the study of Services for Supporting Family Carers in Luxembourg (Ferring & Weber, 2005). Further research on biological aspects of aging is realized within the biological science unit at the UL (Grandbarbe et al., 2007).

Luxembourg also has several public research institutes that are not directly dedicated to aging research but that investigate research questions clearly associated with aging. The public research center on health (CRP Santé) does fundamental, clinical, and applied health research covering the domains of health care, public health, and biotechnology. Research at this multidisciplinary center is conducted in close cooperation with partners in the medical and care sector as well as industry. The CRP Santé is also interested in the planning of Health Policy and the monitoring of health in society, including epidemiological studies. The CRP Henri Tudor—a second public research center that is not only dedicated to aging research—has specialized in technology support to health and health services (e.g., hospital and medical information systems, telemedicine, home care and monitoring, and clinical engineering). It goes without saying that research questions related to care and health provision of the elderly are involved in all of these topics. The CRP-Gabriel Lippmann, another public research center, is dedicated to technological development, technology transfer, and high-level training. Its emphases lie on material research, management of natural resources, equipment for the automobile industry, and technologies of the information society. Especially within the latter domain, research is realized with respect to the application of IT solutions for the elderly, and a joint project is currently conducted here with the INSIDE research group at the UL.

Finally, the CEPS/INSTEAD is a research institute dedicated to demographics, socioeconomic, and social policy issues. The center is a member of the Consortium of Household Panels for European Socio-economic Research (CHER), and has conducted a socioeconomic panel study on income dynamics in Luxembourg since 1985 (Panel Socioéconomique Liewen zu Letzebuerg; PSELL I since 1985; PSELL II since 1994). The institute thus undertakes a rich data collection that allows for the comparison of Luxembourg with its European neighbors. The panel covers the domains of demography, household and family, living conditions, labor market, education, income, health, and housing, and renders longitudinal data sets on all of these issues. Here lies a big potential for secondary and follow-back analyses concerning socioeconomic aspects of aging.

In closing, it is clear that research on individual and social aspects of aging is well underway in Luxembourg. This corresponds with activities in the educational sector dealing with the challenges of population aging in Luxembourg, which will be presented below.

EDUCATION IN GERONTOLOGY

Basic training, as well as continuous training in gerontology and geriatrics, takes a central position in Luxembourg, since a shortage of competent and motivated care staff is predicted, a trend that is already appearing in our neighboring countries (e.g., Bundesministerium für Familie, Senioren,

Frauen und Jugend [BMFSFJ], 2003). Luxembourg's Ministry of Family and Solidarity has responded to this challenge with a set of initiatives: training for specific functions in socio-family support; implementation of a master's program in gerontology at the University of Luxembourg; and continuous training programs organized by various services or associations, such as socio-family service organizations, the Luxembourgish Alzheimer Association, and the Association for Training in Palliative Care. Moreover, two help networks, Hellef doheem (Help at Home) and Help, have been established since the installation of dependency insurance in 1998; these programs support primary caregiving tasks and also offer professional training for formal as well as informal carers.

The master's program in gerontology at the University of Luxembourg addresses practitioners in the field of gerontology and geriatrics (i.e., medical doctors, nurses, psychologists, social workers, and care assistants); the credential can be accomplished as in-job or further training (Ferring, 2008). The teaching comprises two units, both validated by 60 European credit points involving scholars from different disciplines. The first unit comprises the following modules: (1) introduction to geriatrics and psychogeriatrics; (2) geriatric intervention; (3) psychogerontology and social gerontology; (4) psychological and psychosocial interventions in old age; (5) historical and philosophical issues; (6) legal and socioeconomic aspects of aging; and (7) research methodology and statistics. While this first unit gives an overview and an insight into the various perspectives, domains, and dimensions associated with human aging, the second unit allows for further specialization in the domains of geriatrics and psychogerontology. Courses offered here deal with the diagnosis, treatment, and rehabilitation of various forms of age-associated diseases, especially neurodegenerative diseases; further topics include violence in care situations, sexuality in old age, drug dependency in old age, psychological problems of the elderly, palliative care, and euthanasia. Students obtain training in quantitative and qualitative research methods, and they have to develop their own research project and complete a master's thesis.

Training in gerontology is an interdisciplinary program that clearly benefits from the different but complementary inputs coming from the various disciplines involved: medicine, psychology, sociology, economics, and humanities. Specific to the Luxembourg situation, the program is bilingual; courses are held in French and German. Furthermore, the master's degree is realized in close cooperation with colleagues from neighboring European countries, including Belgium, France, Germany, and Switzerland. The initial master's program started in 2002 and was elaborated in close cooperation with the Ministry of Family and Solidarity and the Belgian

University Centre Benelux. Given the development in the health provision and care sector, as will be described in the following section, the master's program meets a crucial need for qualified personnel in this area who will also be capable of doing research in their specific work areas.

PUBLIC POLICY ISSUES IN AGING

The Ministry of Family and Integration, as well as the Ministry of Social Security, have leading roles in social policies concerning the elderly population (Ferring & Weber, 2005; Majerus, 2008). The national policy framework for older people, as published in the activity report of the Ministry of Family and Integration (2003) lists several general considerations. First, it is stated that older people *do not represent a homogeneous group*, and that policy actions are focused with high priority to people who are in a dependent situation, as well as to the members of their socio-familial environment. Older people are defined here as those with an age range of 55–60 to over 100 years. Second, the Ministry holds that policies should not only be planned *for* older people, but should also be planned together *with* older people. This objective is achieved through a close cooperation between the Ministries and the Higher Council for Older People.

Care policy has been formally implemented by the 1998 Dependency Insurance Act. Under this framework, the financial provision for professional care is secured and, for the first time, care services delivered at home by a family member or other informal carer can be financially compensated. Thus, the dependency insurance covers the costs of care for a dependent person; these services are independent of the place where the older dependent person is living. Payment for care services delivered by family members promotes the "aging at home approach" for dependent people, a policy adopted by the government in recent years within the general policy for older people. This is further facilitated by the above-mentioned help networks Hëllef Dohéem (Help at Home) and Help, which were created in the wake of the dependency insurance; both have the legal status of foundations and directly cooperate with the Union des Caisses de Maladies (Union of Sickness Funds). The model underlying dependency insurance relies on close cooperation between the national government and these two service systems. This formal cooperation allows for a clear-cut definition of services and assistance, as well as an establishment of quality criteria to be realized by the providers of services. Moreover, this direct link inhibits the development of a private, profit-oriented *care market*, since the Union of Sickness Funds discounts services only with the help networks. The service networks do cooperate and try to complement their services.

Considerable supports for care at home are provided by the help networks: technical adaptations, home-delivered meals, assistance on call, specialized day centers, holiday placement, geriatric rehabilitation and gerontological revalidation, advice and training for informal caregivers, a non-paid leave for care assistance for employed family members, and benefits for informal caregivers (family care) on the basis of the dependency insurance. In the home-care system, institutional placement is seen as the last alternative, since the majority of affected persons prefer to stay in their own homes as long as possible.

Existing service structures for the elderly in Luxembourg are summarized in Table 29.2. A guiding principle behind policies and programs is the notion of social inclusion, which aims at a decentralization of service provisions through the development of regional service networks. Furthermore, efforts are made toward revaluing older people by training frontline staff in person-centered assistance concepts, as well as strategies for preventing dependency. Finally, in order to promote the opportunity to live at home as long as possible, an extensive respite care system supports families in their caregiving efforts by offering incentives for caring family members, reinforcing the sense of family responsibility, and strengthening family values (Ferring & Weber, 2005).

In addition to the services systems designed to meet the functional and physical needs of older people, a complementary structure has been elaborated during the last 10 years—the so-called Clubs Senior or Regional Centres Offering Animation and Guidance for Older Citizens. The Clubs Senior are dedicated to primary prevention; they offer social, leisure, and cultural activities, as well as meals, and counseling services on various issues, such as retirement preparation and physical and mental health.

Finally, the country of Luxembourg offers assistance to terminally ill patients, many of whom are older people. The assistance of terminally ill persons is acknowledged to be a major social challenge. The Luxembourg government, in February 2006, elaborated a legal proposition introducing the right of each citizen to receive palliative care. Within this proposition, emphasis is put on high-quality provision of services to persons in need, be it in the hospital, in the nursing home context, or at home. The initiative called for a highly diversified mixture of out-of-hospital measures that have been implemented, comprising support and palliative care at home, hospices, and vacation for employed family caregivers without salary; furthermore, training in palliative care for various caregivers—professionals, informal, as well as family carers and volunteers—is promoted.

Summing up, one may conclude that Luxembourg has achieved a high standard in the provision of services to the elderly, be it the availability

Table 29.2
Overview of Existing Service Structures in Luxembourg

Type of Structure	Number
Integrated centers for older people	33
Nursing facilities	16
Assisted accommodation settings for older people	10
Psychogeriatric centers	28
Regional centers for activities and guidance of older people (Club Senior)	17
Support at home	8
Care at home	8
Food delivery at home ("repas sur roues" [Meals on Wheels])	67
External assistance hotline	9
Senior activity program	8

Source: Ministry of Family and Solidarity. (2007). *Rapport d'activité 2007* [Activity report 2007]. Retrieved July 21, 2008, from http://www.gouvernement.lu/publications/rapportsactivite

of hospital beds, places in nursing homes, and the availability of at-home care. Additional programs offer services promoting the prevention of functional and physical impairments and offering leisure-time activities. With respect to its European neighbors, Luxembourg offers a premium range of services beyond the average European standards (Mestheneos & Triantafillou, 2005), and it will be a challenge for all actors in the field to uphold these standards.

CONCLUSION AND OUTLOOK

Research and education with respect to population aging has increasingly gained prominence in Luxembourg in recent years. Social policy in Luxembourg has sought to guarantee the provision of health-care services for the elderly, as well as primary prevention services. It is, however, an open question as to whether Luxembourg will be able to keep these high standards of a social welfare state for an aging population.

Economic globalization will have a major influence on the Luxembourg situation. Aging society is highly challenged by ongoing global economic developments, which are sometimes not even foreseeable by political and economic institutes (e.g., the subprime mortgage crisis). Economies depend more and more on the demands of the global market, thus challenging long-existing national industries and the economic basis of many European states. The distribution of resources with respect to education, health, and the labor market—to name three central domains—will be linked to the question of resource fairness and the investment of society in these domains. Also in line with this broader speculation, one may ask whether the social welfare state can be preserved or if it will become obsolete as other models take shape (Giddens, 1998). Given the high financial resources of the Grand-duchy (Schroeder, 2007), these projections do not represent models that will become a reality in the near future of Luxembourg.

Nevertheless, national resources will be challenged within the next 20 years, given that cross-border workers will strain the Luxembourg pension system more and more. Luxembourg's economic development will continue to depend on a steady migration as well as a growing flow of cross-border workers to keep the GDP high. According to recent projections, the Luxembourg population will have to grow within the next 40 years by up to 30% of its current size (Langers, 2007). The size of the labor force as well as labor productivity (especially with respect to the senior labor work force) will thus pose central challenges when it comes to the quality of aging in Luxembourg, as well as in Europe.

REFERENCES

Albert, I., Michels, T., & Ferring, D. (2008). *Assessing responsibilities for elder care within families.* Paper presented at the 20th Biennial ISSBD Meeting, Würzburg, Germany.

Bundesministerium für Familie, Senioren, Frauen und Jugend (BMFSFJ) (Ed.). (2003). *Qualitätsmängel und Regelungsdefizite der Qualitätssicherung in der ambulanten Pflege—Nationale und internationale Befunde* [Quality and regulation deficits in in-house care—National and international findings]. Retrieved July 21, 2008, from http://www.familien-wegweiser.de/bmfsfj/generator/Kat egorien/Forschungsnetz/forschungsberichte,did=13762.html

Burholt, V., Windle, G., Ferring, D., Balducci, C., Fagerström, C., Thissen, F., et al. (2007). Reliability and validity of the Older Americans Resources and Services (OARS) social resources scale in six European countries. *Journals of Gerontology: Social Sciences, 62B*(6), S371–S379.

Communication from the Commission (COM). (2006). *The demographic future of Europe—From challenge to opportunity.* Retrieved July 21, 2008, from the European Commission Web site: http://ec.europa.eu/employment_social/ news/2006/oct/demography_en.pdf

Diederich, N. J., Vaillant, M., Rufra, O., Blyth, S., & Pieri, V. (2007). Searching for subtle sleep abnormalities by polysomnography in early Parkinson's disease. A prospective case-control study. *Movement Disorders, 22,* 166.

Drooglever-Fortuijn, J., van der Meer, M., Burholt, V., Ferring, D., Quattrini, S., Rahm.-Hallberg, I., et al. (2006). The activity patterns of older adults: A cross-sectional study in six European countries. *Population, Space and Place*, 353–369.

Eurostat. (2008). *Europe in figures. Eurostat yearbook 2008.* Luxembourg: Office for the Official Publications of the European Communities.

Ferring, D. (2008). *Master en gerontologie* [Master's in gerontology]. *Program description.* Retrieved July 21, 2008, from the University of Luxembourg Web site: http://wwwen.uni.lu/formations/flshase/master_en_gerontologie_master_professionnel

Ferring, D., Balducci, C., Burholt, V., Thissen, F., Weber. G., & Hallberg-Rahm., I. (2004). Life satisfaction in older people in six European countries: Findings from the European Study on Adult Well-being. *European Journal of Ageing, 1*, 15–25.

Ferring, D., Haller, M., Meyer-Wolters, H., & Michels, T. (Eds.). (2008). *Soziokulturelle Konstruktion des Alters: Interdisziplinäre Perspektiven* [Sociocultural construction of age: Transdisciplinary perspectives] (pp. 63–72). Würzburg: Könighausen & Neumann.

Ferring, D., & Hoffmann, M. (2007). Still the same and better off than others? Social and temporal comparisons in old age. *European Journal of Ageing, 4*, 23–34.

Ferring, D., Michels, T., Boll, T., & Filipp, S. H. (2008). *Emotional relationship quality of adult children with ageing parents: Solidarity, conflict, and ambivalence.* (Manuscript submitted for publication.)

Ferring, D., Thill, J., & Leners, J.-P. (2007). *Ist Altern noch bezahlbar? Perspektiven für Luxemburg* [Can we afford aging? Perspectives for Luxembourg]. *Reports from the Research Unit INSIDE, No. 1.* Luxembourg: University of Luxembourg.

Ferring, D., & Weber, G. (2005). *Services for supporting family carers of elderly people in Europe: Characteristics, coverage and usage (EUROFAMCARE). National background report on Luxembourg.* Retrieved July 21, 2008, from the University of Hamburg Web site: http://www.uke.uni-hamburg.de/extern/eurofamcare-de/publikationen.php?abs=2

Giddens, A. (1998). *The third way: The renewal of social democracy.* Cambridge, UK: Polity Press.

Grandbarbe, L., Michelucci, A., Heurtaux, T., Hemmer, K., Morga, E., & Heuschling, P. (2007). Notch signaling modulates the activation of microglial cells. *Glia, 55*, 1519–1530.

Hipp, G., Vaillant, M., Blyth, S., Pieri, V., & Diederich, N. J. (2007). Subtle executive dysfunction in early Parkinson's disease: A case-control study. *Parkinsonism and Related Disorders, 13*, 57.

Langers, J. (2007). Le vieillissement au Grand-Duché de Luxembourg : Quelques considérations démo-économiques [Aging in the Grand-duchy of Luxembourg: Some demo-economic considerations]. In D. Ferring, J. Thill & J.-P. Leners (Eds.), *Ist Altern noch bezahlbar? Perspektiven für Luxemburg* [Can we afford aging? Perspectives for Luxembourg] (p. 12–22). *Reports from the Research Unit INSIDE, No. 1.* Luxembourg: University of Luxembourg.

Majerus, M. (2008). Politik der Lebensalter. In D. Ferring, M. Haller., H. Meyer.-Wolters & T. Michels (Eds.), *Sozio-kulturelle Konstruktion des Alters: Interdisziplinäre Perspektiven* [Sociocultural construction of age: Transdisciplinary perspectives] (p. 63–72). Würzburg, Germany: Könighausen & Neumann.

Mestheneos, E., & Triantafillou, J. (2005). *Supporting family carers of older people in Europe—The Pan-European background.* Retrieved July 21, 2008, from the University of Hamburg Web site: http://www.uke.uni-hamburg.de/extern/eurofamcare-de/publikationen.php?abs=1

Ministry of Family and Integration (2003). *Rapport d'activité 2003* [Activity report 2003]. Retrieved July 21, 2008, from http://www.gouvernement.lu/publications/rapportsactivite

Ministry of Family and Solidarity (2007). *Rapport d'activité 2007* [Activity report 2007]. Retrieved July 21, 2008, from http://www.gouvernement.lu/publications/rapportsactivite

Niclou, S. P. (2007). *Functional validation of a new therapeutic strategy to prevent neurodegeneration and subsequent cognitive impairment in mouse models of Alzheimer's disease.* Retrieved July 21, 2008, from the National Research Fund of Luxembourg Web site: http://www.fnr.lu/SIML_FNR/Channel/FNR.nsf/fs_Root?OpenFrameset

Otjacques, B. (2007). *TIVIPOL—Information technologies to support ageing of the Luxembourg population.* Retrieved July 21, 2008, from the National Research Fund of Luxembourg Web site: http://www.fnr.lu/SIML_FNR/Channel/FNR.nsf/fs_Root?OpenFrameset

Perquin, M. (2007). *Neuropsychological and biological characteristics of mild cognitive and impairment (MCI) and of associated subclinical health problems for Alzheimer's disease-type dementia.* Retrieved July 21, 2008, from the National Research Fund of Luxembourg Web site: http://www.fnr.lu/SIML_FNR/Channel/ FNR.nsf/fs_Root?OpenFrameset

Pieri, V., Vaillant, M., Blyth, S., Hipp, G., & Diederich, N. J. (2007). Are there multisensory deficits in early Parkinson's disease? A case-control study. *Parkinsonism and Related Disorders, 13,* 40–41.

Schroeder, G. (2007). La pension de vieillesse à Luxembourg, une garantie ou un souci ? [The pension system in Luxembourg: A guarantee or a worry?]. In D. Ferring, J. Thill & J.-P. Leners (Eds.), *Ist Altern noch bezahlbar? Perspektiven für Luxemburg* [Can we afford aging? Perspectives for Luxembourg] (p. 5–11). *Reports from the Research Unit INSIDE, No. 1.* Luxembourg: University of Luxembourg.

STATEC. (2007). *Luxembourg in figures.* Luxembourg: Statistical Office of Luxembourg.

STATEC. (2008). *Population et emploi* [Population and labor]. Retrieved July 21, 2008, from the National Statistical Bureau of Luxembourg Web site: http://www.statistiques.public.lu/fr/population/index.html

University of Sheffield. (2008). *European Research Area in Ageing (ERA-AGE).* Retrieved July 21, 2008, from http://era-age.group.shef.ac.uk/flare_results.php

30

·▪·

Malaysia

Tey Nai Peng and Ng Sor Tho

POPULATION AGING

The population of Malaysia is still relatively youthful. However, declining fertility and increasing life expectancy have brought about a rapid increase in the number and proportion of older persons in the country. In 1970, out of a total population of 10.4 million, only 546,000 or 5.2% were aged 60 and above, but this had increased to 1.45 million, or 6.2%, by 2000 (Department of Statistics, 1983, 2001). The number of older persons aged 60 and above is projected to increase to 5.2 million or 14.1% by 2030. The shape of the population pyramid up to 2000 still reflects a young population with a broad base. However, in 2030, the population pyramid takes on the shape of a rectangle, which is typical of a population that has completed the demographic transition.

Table 30.1 presents the indicators of population aging in Malaysia. The median age increased from 21.9 years in 1991 to 23.6 years in 2000 and is projected to increase to 32 years by 2030. The aging index increased from 15.9% in 1991 to 18.7% in 2000. With fertility decline, the younger population is projected to increase at a much slower pace compared to the older population, resulting in a sharp rise of the aging index to 60.2% by 2030. The declining fertility has resulted in a rather sharp reduction in youth dependency while the old-age dependency burden remained flat between 1991 and 2000, such that the overall dependency has declined considerably. Looking into the future, Malaysia will continue to reap the demographic dividend as the youth dependency continues to decline from 53% in 2000 to 35% in 2030, more than offsetting the increase in old-age dependency from 6.2% to 14.4%. However, the potential support ratio is projected to decline to 6.9 after holding constant at about 6.2 between 1991 and 2000, indicating the dwindling family support for the older persons. The proportion of the old–old to the population aged 60 and over is not expected to change significantly, at about 21 to 22% between 1991 and 2030.

Declining fertility and increasing life expectancy have resulted in a shifting age structure and population aging in Malaysia. Between 1970 and 2005, the total fertility rate had declined from 5.0 to 2.5 children per woman. During the same period, life expectancy for males and females increased from 61.6 and 65.6 years to 71.5 and 76.2 years, respectively. At age 60, male life expectancy is about 17.4 and female life expectancy about 19.7 years (Department of Statistics, 2006).

The older population grew at an average rate of about 3.3% per annum between 1970 and 2000 as compared to 2.7% for the total population. The rate of growth of the total population is projected to decelerate to 1.5% per annum between 2000 and 2030, but that of the older population will be increasing at about 4.3% per annum during the same period.

The longer life expectancy among women compared to men has resulted in an unbalanced sex ratio among the older population. The sex ratio of older persons aged 60 and over is about 91 males per 100 females. At ages 75 and over, the sex ratio decreased further, to 79 males per 100 females (Table 30.1).

Besides having a longer life expectancy, women typically marry men 4–6 years older. Hence, older women are much more likely than older men to be widowed. In 2000, there were 333,582 widows aged 60 and above, but only 75,926 widowers in the same age range. Among older persons, the number of divorced women also outnumbered divorced men (15,298 versus 5,752). On the other hand, there were more currently married older men as compared to currently married older women (573,034 as compared to 366,322 in 2000). Interestingly, there was an almost equal number of never-married older men and women (14,534 and 14,010).

Owing to the differentials in fertility and mortality, the different ethnic groups in Malaysia have rather different age structures. The Chinese and Indians are much more advanced in the demographic transition compared to the Malays. While the former had attained replacement fertility by the turn of the new millennium, the fertility level of the latter remains relatively high at about 2.8 children per woman. The Chinese have the oldest age structure, with a median age of 28.9 years in 2000, followed by the Indians (25.1 years) and the Malays (21.0 years). The median age of these three

Table 30.1
Actual and Projected Aging Indices, Malaysia

	1991	2000	2030
Total population	18,379,655	23,274,690	36,950,000
Median age	21.9	23.6	32.0
Number age 60 and over	1,068,531	1,451,665	5,210,000
% aged 60 and over	5.8	6.2	14.1
Aging index (60+)/(0–14)*100	15.9	18.7	60.2
Youth dependency ratio (0–14)/ (15–64)*100	61.0	53.0	35.0
Old age dependency ratio (65+)/ (15–64)*100	6.2	6.2	14.4
Potential support ratio (15–64)/(65+)	16.1	16.2	6.9
Population (75+)/(60+)*100	20.9	20.0	22.0
Sex ratio of population aged 60+	89.7	90.9	91.5

Sources: Department of Statistics. (1995). *General report of the 1991 population census* (Vol. 2). Kuala Lumpur, Malaysia.
Department of Statistics. (2001). *Population distribution and basic demographic characteristics, 2000. Population Census.* Putrajaya, Malaysia.

ethnic groups is projected to increase to 41, 37, and 30 years respectively by 2030. Between 2000 and 2030, the proportion of population aged 60 and over is projected to increase from 5.7% to 12.2% for the Malays, 8.8% to 23.1% for the Chinese, and 5.6% to 17.6% for the Indians.

RECENT RESEARCH ON AGING

Population aging has gained increasing attention from the government and researchers. In 2002, the Institute of Gerontology (IG) was established at University Putra Malaysia (UPM) to spearhead research and education in gerontology. The Institute, is at the forefront of research and education on gerontology in Malaysia. Since its inception, it has undertaken and coordinated most research on aging in this country.

The government, through the Ministry of Science, Technology and Innovation (MOSTI) has funded a good number of large-scale research projects on the health and socioeconomic aspects of aging, under the Intensification of Research in Priority Areas (IRPA) program. Some of these research projects are multidisciplinary, involving researchers from different universities and disciplines. The Ninth Malaysia Plan stated that more research on the needs of older adults will be undertaken and that the findings will be used for the formulation of relevant policies and programs (Government of Malaysia, 2006, p. 315).

During the Eighth Malaysia Plan period (2001–2005), a total of 17 research projects were carried out by researchers from the University Putra Malaysia, the National University Malaysia, and the University of Malaya, under the IRPA program. These research projects concentrated mainly on the health and socioeconomic aspects of aging. The titles of these research projects are listed in Appendix 1.

Under the Ninth Malaysia Plan (2006–2010), the Institute of Gerontology is currently undertaking research on the following aging issues with funding from MOSTI:

1. Access and Utilization of Computers and the Internet among Older Malaysians
2. Perception, Awareness, and Risk Factors of Elder Abuse
3. Patterns of Social Relationships and Psychological Well-being among Older Persons in Peninsular Malaysia
4. Perception of Needs and Barriers of Older Road Drivers in Malaysia: Investigating and Assessing the Risk Factors, Mobility, and Behavioral Patterns
5. Diabetes Mellitus Type 2, Impaired Glucose Tolerance, Cognitive Decline, and Aging
6. Falls and Risk Factors among Older Malaysians at Home and in Institutional Settings

Case studies on Intergenerational Living Arrangements and Intergenerational Transfer and Relation were carried out by researchers from the University of Malaya in 2004 and 2006, with funding from the Japan Society for the Promotion of Science, Grant-in-Aid for Scientific Research. A study on Injuries among the Elderly in Alor Gajah District and a survey on Traffic and Aging were carried out in 2006. Research projects that are currently being carried out by researchers from the National University of Malaysia are Lifestyle of the Elderly in Rural and Urban Malaysia and Study of Religious Participation, Self-Concept and the Need of Counseling amongst the Elderly at Rumah Sri Kenangan (eldercare facilities) in Malaysia.

International agencies also play a role in gerontology research in Malaysia. As a follow-up to the project on Evaluating Program Needs of Older Persons in Malaysia, which was completed in 1998 under the IRPA program, the United Nations Population Fund provided funding to researchers of the University of Malaya for a project on Strengthening Community Participation for Reproductive Health Service (1998–2003). The implementation of this project led to the establishment of the Petaling Jaya Community Centre (PJCC). The PJCC has since become a model community center for intergenerational community work and activities. In 2003, researchers from the University of Malaya participated in a WHO-sponsored project titled Towards Age-friendly Primary Health Care, and the findings were incorporated into the intercountry report (WHO, 2004). The Institute of Gerontology completed a research project on Promoting Active and Productive Aging in Malaysia in 2007, with funding from the United Nations Population Fund, and a project on Integrated Response of Health Care Systems to Rapid Population Aging in 2006 with funding from the WHO. The Institute has secured additional funding from UNFPA to conduct an action-oriented research project on lifelong learning for older Malaysians during 2008–2012.

EDUCATION IN GERONTOLOGY

Courses on gerontology have been offered in many public and private institutions of higher learning in Malaysia. Social gerontology has been taught as an elective course in the Faculties of Arts and Social Sciences at the University Science of Malaysia, University of Malaya, and International Islamic University. The Tun Abdul Razak University incorporated gerontology into the course called Cognitive Science, Psychology, and Other Related Sciences in Education.

Gerontology and geriatric nursing constitute part of the Bachelor of Nursing or Diploma in Nursing at University of Malaya, National University of Malaysia, University Putra Malaysia, University Malaysia Sarawak, International Medical University, University College Sedaya International, and SEGI College.

Geriatric pharmacy and geriatric dentistry are offered at the University Science of Malaysia at the postgraduate level. Courses on geriatric health, geriatric nutrition, and geriatric orthopedics are offered as part of the degree program. The National University of Malaysia offers geriatric dentistry and gerontology and geriatric care at the undergraduate level. Geriatric optometry, geriatric psychiatry, geriatric nutrition, psychology of adults and older adults, life-span cognitive processes, growth and aging, and nutrition and aging are offered in the postgraduate program.

The Faculty of Medicine of the University of Malaya has a psychogeriatric unit that provides training in old-age psychiatry in medical and allied health disciplines at the postgraduate level, as well as in a professional development program. Various faculties at University Putra Malaysia (UPM) offer education in gerontology. The Faculty of Educational Studies offers a course on gerontology and counseling as part of the Master of Education (with specialization in Mental Health and Community Counseling); the Faculty of Human Ecology offers courses at the master's level, such as Family Gerontology, Economics of Aging, and Sociology of Aging; and the Faculty of Medicine and Health Sciences offers courses on geriatric health and nutrition at the undergraduate level. Theories on gerontology are offered in the doctoral program of the Institute of Gerontology in the fields of geriatric community, gerontechnology, gerontology, and social gerontology. Courses such as Consumer Behavior of Older Adults and Creative Music Experience with Older Adults are offered at the postgraduate level at UPM.

Besides the degree/diploma program or postgraduate program, the Institute of Gerontology, in collaboration with the International Institute on Aging, United Nations, organized the first *in situ* satellite training program—Demographic, Social, and Economic Issues of Aging—on August 19–26, 2007, and the second *in situ* satellite training program was conducted in August 2008.

In addition to the formal courses on gerontology and geriatric care, seminars, symposia and workshops on issues of population aging have also been conducted by the universities, government departments, the Employee Provident Fund, and nongovernmental organizations (NGOs) such as the Gerontology Association of Malaysia, National Council for Senior Citizens Organizations Malaysia, Petaling Jaya Community Centre, and Community Support Networks. Various talks have been conducted at governmental and community levels to promote awareness of elderly psychiatric illnesses like depression, neglect and abuse of elderly patients, and Alzheimer's disease.

The University of Malaya, in collaboration with the Ministry of Health, the Social Welfare Department, and the Social Welfare Council, and with the support of Tsao Foundation, Singapore, has conducted a series of caregiver training workshops. However, these workshops were discontinued in 2004.

CURRENT POLICY ISSUES IN AGING

The General Policy Framework

Although population aging is a rather recent phenomenon in Malaysia, aging issues have gained increasing attention in recent years. In the past, the needs of older people were incorporated into the National Welfare Policy. Older adults, especially the poor, have all along been identified as a target group for assistance. Various amenities and privileges have been made available to them. These include the provision of special counters and seating areas in public spaces and a 50% rebate on fares for domestic air and rail travel.

In 1995, the government adopted a developmental approach in dealing with issues pertaining to population aging by formulating the National Policy for the Elderly to "improve the potential of older persons so that they can continue to be productive in national development, while encouraging the provision of facilities for older persons so as to ensure care and protection for them" (Government of Malaysia, 1996, p. 571). A National Senior Citizens Policy Technical Committee was set up by the Social Welfare Department in July 1996, with six subcommittees, for social and recreational issues; health; education, religion and training; housing; research; and publicity. Various ministries and departments are involved in the action plans and activities for older persons, and these are coordinated by the Ministry of Women, Family and Social Development. The 1999 Malaysian Plan of Action does not adequately cover employment and income security, but the emphasis appears to be on social aspects that contribute to the overall well-being of older persons (Ong, 2002).

The National Policy for the Elderly was aimed at encouraging the continued participation of older people in national development. The Ninth Malaysia Plan (2006–2010) stated:

> Programmes introduced emphasized on community participation that included promotion of healthy lifestyles, social and recreational activities. These programmes also encouraged volunteerism among older persons as well as intergenerational activities, lifelong learning programmes and learning skills such as ICT [Information and Communication Technology] to enable their continued contribution to family, society and country. (Government of Malaysia, 2006, p. 311)

In the Ninth Malaysia Plan (2006–2010), the emphasis is on increasing employment opportunities for older persons. Under the Plan, employers are allowed to claim a 100% tax rebate on retraining costs for older persons taken in as employees. Despite the stated intention of the Ninth Malaysia Plan to involve older people in the mainstream of the economy, employees in the formal sector are forced to stop working upon reaching the mandatory retirement age of 55 in the private sector and 56 in the public sector (the latter has been revised to 58, effective July 2008). Most of the retirees are still healthy and able to continue working to support themselves and their families. Nevertheless, only a small number of retirees continue to work as contract workers, engage themselves in NGOs/community activities, or venture into their own businesses.

There is no official policy on long-term care for older adults. However, the Care Centre Act 1993, Care Centre Regulations 1994, and the Private Healthcare Facilities and Services Act 1998 were enacted to ensure the minimum standards that protect the interests of older persons.

It has always been the government's policy to encourage the family to take care of their aging relatives. Children are entitled to a tax rebate of RM5,000 for their parents' medical expenses. With the gradual erosion of family support for the older people, efforts are being taken to strengthen community participation and to facilitate the integration of older people into society.

Social Security Schemes

The two main social security schemes that cater to the financial needs of older persons are the Employment Provident Fund (EPF) and the Government Pension Scheme for Civil Servants. These two schemes cover about half the labor force. The EPF is a defined-contribution plan based on a prescribed rate of contributions by employers and employees, accumulated as savings in a personal account with full withdrawal capacity upon retirement. The scheme is mandatory for those in the formal sector, but it also allows those who are self-employed to contribute toward the fund. The rate of contributions is 12% and 9% for employers and employees, respectively, regardless of the age of the employee. The pension scheme is only for government employees. The benefits are extended to the widows/widowers of the pensioners.

Questions arise as to whether these two social security schemes are adequate to provide for the financial needs of Malaysians in their old age, especially with the longer life span and the rising cost of living. Most retirees tend to have only a rather small amount of savings in their EPF, and in many instances, the fund is used up within three to five years of their retirement to pay for their living expenses, medical bills, and their children's higher education. Moreover, the value of the money continues to depreciate. For those under the pension scheme, the payout is only half of their last-drawn basic salary. Hence, those depending on these two schemes will not be able to sustain the standard of living they were accustomed to during their employed life (Ariffin & Tey, 2008).

The majority of those in the informal sector, including the self-employed, do not contribute to the EPF and will have to rely on savings and financial support from their children to cover their living expenses in their old age. With the escalating cost of living following hikes in the price of food, petrol, and other essential goods, the propensity to save is diminishing. Working children are struggling to cope with their own expenses, let alone providing financial support to their parents. More often than not, the financial support from children is insufficient to cover emergencies like medical care bills due to long illnesses.

CONCLUSION

While the population of Malaysia is relatively young, issues of population aging have caught the attention of the government and researchers, as the number and proportion of older persons has increased. Most gerontology research is funded by the government and undertaken by researchers from the universities. Some of the research has been accompanied by action-oriented programs such as the Petaling Jaya Community Centre and life-long training to facilitate the continued participation of older persons in social and economic activities. In terms of research design, most research on aging issues is cross-sectional and quantitative in nature, but there is a need for more longitudinal studies and qualitative research.

Formal training on aging issues has been incorporated into quite a number of courses in the various institutions of higher learning. The Institute of Gerontology at University Putra Malaysia is the only specialized institution that conducts regular research and offers a postgraduate degree in gerontology. Aging issues are rather widely discussed in the media, conferences, seminars, and workshops.

Although various programs have been drawn up under the National Policy for the Elderly, the effectiveness of these programs has yet to be systematically evaluated. There is also a need for effective utilization of research for formulating, implementing, and evaluating the programs for older people.

REFERENCES

Ariffin, J., & Tey, N. P. (2008). Social services and protection for Malaysian families in the context of socio-demographic change. Paper presented at the United Nations ESCAP Regional Seminar on Enhancing Social Services Policies to Strengthen Family Well-being in Asia and the Pacific, May 13–15, 2008. Macao, China.

Department of Statistics. (1983). *General report of the 1980 population census* (Vol. 1). Kuala Lumpur, Malaysia.

Department of Statistics. (1995). *General report of the 1991 population census* (Vol. 2). Kuala Lumpur, Malaysia.

Department of Statistics. (2001). *Population distribution and basic demographic characteristics, 2000. Population Census.* Putrajaya, Malaysia.

Department of Statistics. (2006). *Abridged life tables, Malaysia, 2002–2005.* Putrajaya, Malaysia.

Government of Malaysia. (1996). *Seventh Malaysia Plan (1996–2000).* Kuala Lumpur, Malaysia.

Government of Malaysia. (2006) *Ninth Malaysia Plan (2006–2010).* Putrajaya, Malaysia.

Ong, F. S. (2002). Ageing in Malaysia: A review of national policies and programmes. In D. R. Phillips & A. C. M. Chan (Eds.), *Ageing and long-term care: National policies in the Asia Pacific.* Singapore: Institute of Southeast Asian Studies and Ottawa, Canada: International Development Research Center (ISEAS/IDRC).

World Health Organization (WHO). (2004). *Active aging: Towards age-friendly primary health care.* Retrieved July 16, 2008, from http://whqlibdoc.who.int/publications/2004/9241592184.pdf

APPENDIX 1: RESEARCH ON AGING CONDUCTED DURING THE EIGHTH MALAYSIA PLAN (2001–2005) UNDER THE IRPA PROGRAM

Title of Research	Name of Institution
A Community-Based Intervention Study of Promotion of Healthy Aging and Identification, Prevention and Management of Malnutrition among Rural Elderly Malays	National University of Malaysia (NUM)
A Study of Oxidative Damage in Down Syndrome and Aging	NUM
A Study on the Mechanism of Down Syndrome and Aging Using an Animal Model	NUM
An Elderly-Friendly Housing Environment for Older Malaysians	Gerontology Institute, University Putra Malaysia (IG, UPM)
Antioxidants in Preventing Degenerative Damage in Down Syndrome and Aging	NUM
Consumption Behaviors of Older Persons in Malaysia	University of Malaya (UM)
Chemo-intervention Studies Using Antioxidant VIT C & E in Reducing Oxidative Stress in the Aging Process	NUM
Economic and Financial Aspects of Aging	IG, UPM
Influence of Lifestyle (Exercise) on Oxidative and Immune Status in Aging	NUM
Mental Health and Quality of Life of Older Persons	IG, UPM
Molecular Mechanisms of Antioxidants in the Prevention of Degenerative Damage in Aging	NUM
Optimizing the Potential of Older Persons as Critical Resources for Development	UM
Poverty among Elderly Malaysians: Towards Productive Aging	IG, UPM
Psychosocial and Intergenerational Relationships of Older Persons	NUM
Quality of Life of Older Malaysians	IG, UPM
Social Support Towards Older Persons: A Study on the Role of Family	IG, UPM
Volunteerism among Retirees: A Potential Resource for Community Development	IG, UPM

31

..■..

Malta

Joseph Troisi

RECENT HISTORY OF AGING IN MALTA

The Maltese population of the Maltese Islands, as of the end of December 2006, was estimated at 393,933 persons, consisting of 195,466 males and 198,467 females. This does not include work- and resident permit-holders and foreigners residing in Malta, who, for the same period, amounted to 13,877 persons, bringing the total population to 407,810 (National Statistics Office [NSO], 2007). In Malta, the old segment of the population, namely those aged 60 years and over, has been steadily increasing during the past 50 years and now represents 19.7% of the Maltese population (NSO, 2007).

According to the 2005 national census, the mean age of the Maltese population was 49.43 years, while for the 1995 census, it was 35.73 (Central Office of Statistics [COS], 1997; NSO, 2007). This clearly shows the aging of the population. In the period between the two censuses, the 0–14 age group registered a decline of 11.1% (from 74,900 to 66,600), while the 15–59 and the 60+ age group recorded an increase of 2% and 20%, respectively. When one takes into account the fact that the Maltese population increased only by 1.8% during 1995–2005, the increase in the 60+ population clearly shows that the Maltese population is aging fast, with the older population growing at a faster rate than the rest of the population. Population projections show that this trend of population aging will not only continue but will accelerate. In fact, it is projected that by 2025, 27% of Malta's population will be above the age of 60, a projected increase of 31.3% (Camilleri, 2000; NSO, 2003; Troisi, Formosa, & Navarro, 2004).

The gender distribution remained almost constant throughout 1995–2006, with 98.4 males per 100 females. However, as in most other countries, the preponderance of women over men becomes more pronounced with advancing age, reaching its highest among the old–old. Thus, in 2006, males accounted for only 46.5% in the 60–74 age group, yielding a sex ratio of 86.9. In comparison, the sex ratio for those aged 75+ stood at 61.7, with about 38% males and 62% females (NSO, 2007).

A striking feature of the Maltese population is the constant decrease in the crude birthrate. By the end of 2006, the crude birthrate stood at 9.56, compared to 12.44 in 1995. The number of deaths registered during 2006 was 3,216, with a crude death rate of 7.9. During this year, the number of deaths increased by 2.7% when compared to 2005. As a result, during 2006, the number of older persons exceeded that of children. In fact, there were 66,517 Maltese below the age of 15 as compared to 77,799 aged 60 and above. Thus, the ratio of older persons (60+) to that of children (0–14) for the Maltese population in 2006 was 117 older persons per 100 children. The Total Dependency Ratio for the same year stood at 24.6.

Advances in public health and medicine, improvements in child care, nutrition, and standards of living, have resulted in a gradual increase in life expectancy. Between 1995 and 2005, the male life expectancy at birth increased by 2.5 years compared to 0.9 years for females. The expectation of life at birth for 2006 was 76.8 for males and 81.2 for females. At the age of 65, males are expected to live a further 15.7 years, while females are projected to live a further 18.7 years (NSO, 2007).

Older persons in Malta are, in general, well supported; social security and welfare services are highly developed and progressive. The majority of Maltese older persons own their place of residence. Non-owners live in property with controlled rents. By and large, housing is of good standard, and almost all houses have adequate space and sanitation. One does not find evidence in Malta of older persons living in conditions of poverty. Health services are highly developed, with free hospitalization and environmental services. All residents have access to preventive, investigative, curative, and rehabilitative services in government health centers and hospitals (Xerri, 1998). Personal health services are widely available and free for all who need them. There is also a free drugs-distribution service for low-income persons, as determined by a means test, and for those suffering from multiple chronic diseases.

Over the past decades, the government of Malta and voluntary organizations, foremost among them the Catholic Church, have, through various policies, programs, and schemes, contributed to the care and well-being of the elderly population. Moreover, Malta also prides itself with a number of self-help groups that help older persons form new identities and remain active in their old age.

RECENT RESEARCH ON AGING

Studies have been carried out on various issues in the field of aging and also on the characteristics of older persons in the Maltese Islands, as well as on the wide range of services to improve the quality of life of older persons. The University of Malta aims to maintain and confirm its place as a research-intensive institution. Research activity is at the very heart of the University's vision. The majority of postgraduate programs from master's to doctoral levels offered by the various faculties, institutes, and centers of the University are based on original research. During the past 10 years, a number of postgraduates have carried out research in the field of aging, mostly in the Faculties of Arts, Economics, Medicine, and Theology, and in the Institute of Health Care.

It is the policy of the European Centre for Gerontology and Geriatrics to establish a close link between its academic courses and research. In 1992, the Centre started a research-based program leading to a Master's degree. The original research is carried out in the candidate's own country. Candidates reading for the Postgraduate Diploma in Gerontology and Geriatrics are also required to write a dissertation based on secondary sources in the field of aging. Under the auspices of the Centre, the University also offers the degree of Master of Philosophy.

Although candidates reading for a postgraduate diploma/degree are free to choose a topic for their research, the main areas of research are class analysis; education for older persons; gender differences; social policy issues; retirement; social change and social networks; and medical and social security issues. The Centre organizes annual symposia for the general public, during which results of the research done by the Centre are shared and discussed with those, young and old, who are interested in the specialized topics.

The staff of the Centre are also engaged in various research projects, including, among others, the situation of the Maltese family carers and elderly members; elder abuse; the image of older persons in Malta; the welfare state ideology and older persons; the effect of social change on older persons; the role of the private sector and voluntary associations in the field of aging; and government policies and aging. They also participate, with other universities and research institutes, in EU research projects funded by the European Commission.

Between 1994 and 1996, in collaboration with the Centre for Education and Development at the University of Reading, United Kingdom, the members of the University of the Third Age (U3A) carried out a research project on the Images of Older Persons in Malta. The aim of this research project, designed and carried out by older persons themselves, was to discover how older persons look at themselves and how other persons look at them. Around 1,000 persons were interviewed. The analyzed data and findings were then presented and discussed in a workshop organized specifically for all the members and the general public.

The Maltese government and its various ministries are fully aware of the fact that research activities are instrumental in formulating, implementing, and evaluating policies and programs aimed at ensuring the quality of life of older persons. It encourages and sponsors research on the social, economic, and health aspects of aging, aimed at achieving better and more efficient uses of resources; improvement in social, economic, and health measures; and coordination of the services involved in the care of older persons. Rich information on aging is collected through the national censuses, which are carried out every 10 years, especially during the past three censuses. In addition, very rich and up-to-date information on older persons in Malta is found in publications produced regularly by the National Statistics Office. Building on such sources, one can construct a representative profile of the Maltese older persons on health, education, housing conditions, participation in the labor force, and income and expenditure.

THE CURRENT STATE OF EDUCATION IN GERONTOLOGY

Following the First World Assembly on Aging in 1982, and the ensuing Vienna International Plan of Action on Aging, the United Nations General Assembly, in its Resolution 37/51, recommended *inter alia* the promotion of training and research, as well as the exchange of information and knowledge in order to provide an international basis for social policies and action. As a result of its Resolution 1987/51, the UN Economic and Social Council recommended to the Secretary-General the establishment of the International Institute on Aging (INIA) in Malta. In 1987, the United Nations signed an agreement with the Government of Malta to establish the Institute as an autonomous body under the auspices of the United Nations.

Its UN mandate is tripartite in nature, namely: (1) to train personnel from developing countries who are working or who intend to work in the field of aging or with older persons; (2) to provide advocacy to developing countries in matters concerning capacity building in the areas of aging and older persons; and (3) to act as a practical bridge between developed and developing countries in information exchange in the field of aging. INIA organizes in Malta four core international short training programs of two weeks' duration in (a) social gerontology; (b) economic and financial aspects of aging; (c) medical geriatrics; and (d) demographic aspects and implications of population aging. Over 1,700 persons from 137 countries have participated in the 93 international training programs carried out in Malta since 1990. To meet the growing demands from various countries, in 1995 INIA started organizing *in situ* training programs in various countries. During the past 13 years, 53 such training programs have been carried out in 23 countries, benefiting 1,680 participants.

Following the change of government in 1987, the University of Malta, taking into account the small size and limited resources of the country, began identifying a few main areas of knowledge in which the country had some comparative advantage and concentrating the available resources on making them areas of excellence. It was likely that such areas would be mostly interdisciplinary ones. Their choice was to be highlighted by setting up institutes to provide an organizational framework for research and other related initiatives in the chosen areas. One of the areas so chosen was gerontology, an area of great interest across the University.

Within the Faculty of Medicine and Surgery, gerontology and geriatrics form part of the courses offered in the departments of family medicine, pharmacy, psychiatry, clinical pharmacology, and public health. A degree program in nursing studies within the Institute of Health Care was set up in collaboration with the University of Liverpool. Within this program, attention to geriatric nursing is included. Persons applying for a caring role in any government residential home for older persons are required to obtain a certification in nursing from this Institute.

Notable attention is given to the moral and religious aspects of aging by the Faculty of Theology, particularly in relation to terminal situations, dying and bereavement. The same can be said of the Department of Psychology, within the Faculty of Education, and the Departments of Economics, Social Policy, and Social Work, within the Faculty of Economics, Management and Accountancy. In 1987, following the establishment of a Parliamentary Secretary for the Care of the Elderly, work started on the conversion of a former private hospital into a specialized geriatric hospital. Its aim is to concentrate on those frail older patients requiring assessment, management, and rehabilitation by an interdisciplinary team to enable them to return to live in their own homes. It provides teaching services in the field of geriatrics, consisting of clinical placements, tutorials, and site visits. Students from all health disciplines, both Maltese and foreign, attend regularly for tutorials and clinical placements. Staff professional development is considered essential in ensuring a high standard of care.

The Institute of Gerontology, which later came to be known as the European Centre for Gerontology and Geriatrics, was set up in 1989 within the University of Malta to develop interdisciplinary education and research in a wide range of areas in the field of aging. The postgraduate courses offered leading to the M.Phil. and Ph.D. present a unique opportunity for systematic multidisciplinary training in the areas of gerontology and geriatrics. Through a variety of courses, the Centre provides high academic opportunities to link theory and practice and to experience innovative practices, service planning, and service delivery.

The postgraduate program was designed by an international group of experts during an Expert Meeting on Long-Term Training in Gerontology and Geriatrics, convened in 1989 by the International Institute on Aging, United Nations-Malta, with the participation of representatives from a number of UN experts.

The Centre enjoys a good international reputation and collaborates very closely with a number of university institutes and centers in the field of aging, throughout the world. It cooperates very closely with the International Institute on Aging (INIA), which the United Nations established in Malta in 1989. In 1995, the World Health Organization designated the Centre as a WHO Collaborating Center for Healthy Aging. In 1997, the Centre became the home of the Mediterranean and Middle East Gerontological and Geriatric Association. In 2001, the Centre started forming part of a European consortium aimed at running the European Master's in Gerontology (EuMaG) program. Its international reputation can be witnessed by the high number of applications from foreign students received annually. During the years 1990–2008, the Centre attracted no less than 254 candidates from 49 countries throughout the world; they have successfully completed their postgraduate studies.

The government of Malta also firmly believes that education and training should be made available at all levels and for different functions. This includes all those who work with older persons at home, in the community or in institutions, be they volunteers, family members, or older persons themselves. To meet this need, in 1993, in collaboration with the Parliamentary Secretary for the Care of the Elderly, the Institute at the University initiated a series of in-service training programs for paraprofessionals and primary care workers working in the care of older persons in the statutory sector, aimed at ensuring that they would have the necessary knowledge, skills, and attitudes to facilitate good care. Aware of the growing number of retirees in Malta and of the longer life expectancy, the Institute in 1987 set up pre-retirement programs aimed at enabling older workers in the public and private sectors, who will be retiring from active employment, to prepare themselves for a new lifestyle. Every program consists of 14–16 sessions, each of two hours' duration. Although the topics deal with retirement from a multidisciplinary perspective, the main focus is on how to remain active after retirement.

One of the very effective ways of encouraging older persons to participate in the process of personal development is the establishment of Universities of the Third Age, or U3A (Troisi, 2003a). The objectives are different from those of other teaching institutions intended to prepare young persons for life and work, or for retraining a middle-aged person in mid-career. A U3A offers education for leisure. Its aim is knowledge for its own sake. It was precisely in this light that in January 1993, the Institute of Gerontology set up the University of the Third Age. The public response was very encouraging.

In January 1993, the Institute of Gerontology started producing and presenting a weekly one-hour educational radio program on one of the national radio channels, aimed at disseminating information on aging to the general public and particularly to older persons themselves. In its own way, this program is bringing about a change in perspective. It is helping older persons improve their quality of life. It is also promoting a positive image of older persons, eradicating the negative stereotypes and attitudes that often led to their segregation.

Malta has a wide variety of programs and services for older persons. This has, in turn, increased the variety of skills needed and, consequently, the level of training. A lot is being done in capacity building in the field of aging. The government of Malta firmly believes that paraprofessionals and primary care workers should have the necessary knowledge, skills, and attitudes to ensure the quality of life of older persons and to facilitate good care in their localities. In fact, training is compulsory for both part-time social assistants and carers in public residential homes. Before being hired, all part-time social assistants working in the field of aging are required to follow 15 days of training, aimed at giving caring personnel a better insight into the needs of older persons.

A number of residential homes send their staff for in-service training programs organized periodically by the European Centre of Gerontology at the University of Malta. Various short training programs also are conducted by the Malta Memorial District Nursing Association and by a number of voluntary organizations working in the field of aging. The Centre provides consultancy, advisory work, and is also responsible for running national and international seminars.

HISTORY AND STATUS OF POLICY ISSUES ON AGING

The attainment of self-government by the Maltese in 1921 was accompanied by the introduction of a number of social security measures. Following the end of the Second World War, three laws were introduced that improved and enlarged the coverage of the social security measures. In 1948, the Old Age Pensions Act was introduced, providing for a noncontributory and means-tested payment of pensions to all those aged 60 and above. Eight years later, in 1956, two new Acts were promulgated. The National Assistance Act provided for a noncontributory social and medical assistance, on a means-test basis, to those heads of households who, for some reason or other, were either unemployed or seeking employment, and whose relative financial means fell below the Social Security Act. The National Insurance Act introduced a scheme of social insurance covering sickness, occupational injuries and diseases, unemployment, widowhood, orphanhood, and old age. In 1965, the Act was extended to the self-employed. Fourteen years later, in 1979, as a result of amendments to the Act, a Two-Thirds Pension system was introduced. In the case of an employee, the pensionable income was calculated by taking the average yearly salary on which the relevant contribution had been paid, of the best three consecutive calendar years during the last 10 years prior to retirement.

In 1987, all social security measures and legislations were consolidated in the Social Security Act, which also introduced and incorporated a number of further benefits, including disability pension and gratuity, marriage grants, maternity benefits, family allowance, and so forth. In addition, nonmaterial needs are met by a multiplicity of social services provided by governmental and nongovernmental organizations. In May 1988, Malta signed the European Social Charter. Malta's accession to the European Union in May 2004 was without a doubt a challenging and important development in all the spheres of the country's progress, and also in the field of social protection.

The family in Malta also benefits from a number of social security measures, including children's allowance, family allowance, maternity and paternity leave, cost-of-living allowance, and so forth. As a result of these measures, the Maltese government, following the welfare state ideology, is expected to guarantee an acceptable standard of living and provide the basic needs for all Maltese citizens from the cradle to the grave, by providing a comprehensive system of basic security and income-related benefits.

The Maltese social protection system is based on two pillars, namely: (1) social insurance, which is aimed at safeguarding citizens' income by providing a comprehensive system of basic security and income benefits that guarantee an acceptable standard of living; and (2) social and health-care services. Both these pillars have, over the years, guaranteed social cohesion, fairness and equality, with specific emphasis on the most vulnerable members of society. Almost all households in Malta receive, from time to time, some kind of income transfer or use social and health services.

In Malta, the central role played by the family as the principal provider of care is still maintained, and the exchange of obligations is still the basis of family relations. The family plays an important role in providing financial, practical, emotional, and social support. Older persons value contacts with their families and need to feel security, recognition, respect, and love (Micallef, 2000, 1994; Troisi, 1984, 1991, 1995). Although many Maltese older persons live alone, they are deeply embedded in family support networks of interdependence, of giving and receiving.

Recognizing both the value of the family environment for older persons, as well as the various economic, social, and psychology strains that can accompany a family's traditional caring role, the Maltese government has developed various policies and programs to supplement family support to enable older persons to remain within their family environment as long as possible (Vella, 1990). In May 1987, the Maltese government appointed a Parliamentary Secretary within the Ministry of Social Policy, who is directly responsible for the country's older persons. The fact that it was placed under the Ministry of Social Policy was a clear manifestation that the government was fully aware that aging is not a sickness, that older persons are primarily not to be seen as a health issue, and that older people must be dealt with holistically.

Other recent policy initiatives have sought to replace the practice of segregating and marginalizing older persons with a strategy that enables them to participate in society to the greatest extent possible. To this effect, the Maltese government started planning a wide range of policies and programs to respond to the unique needs and requirements of older persons and aimed at socially integrating them within their society. These national policies on aging were formulated within the wider national, economic, and social development. Maintaining older persons in their communities is now the accepted perspective of social policy. A range of more than 30 services are available for the elderly population and their carers, aimed at improving the quality of life of the older persons while maintaining them in their own homes and communities. These include, among others, day centers, domiciliary nursing, home- and community-based services, and Telecare (Abela, 1988; Cachia, 1985; Troisi, 1994b, 1990, 1989).

The various efforts of the government to improve the care services being given to the ever-growing number of Maltese older persons and, at the same time, to help them remain in the community for as long as possible, are being significantly complemented by the sterling services provided by a number of voluntary organizations, foremost among which is the Catholic Church, which was the pioneer in Malta in providing most of the care and assistance to the needy, including older persons (Abela, 1988; Bonello, 1995; Troisi, 1994b).

The main source of voluntary action for the benefit of older persons is through Caritas Malta, which provides a powerful force of volunteers. The following schemes are among the most important services offered by Caritas, aimed at helping older persons continue living in their own homes: Good Neighbour Scheme; Social Clubs; Self-Health Care; and Awareness Programs in Schools (Troisi, 1989, 1990). Besides Caritas, there are various voluntary organizations, including the Catholic Action Movement, Legion of Mary, Social Action Movement, and the St. Vincent de Paul Society, which help older persons in a number of ways and settings. The Malta Memorial District Association and the Malta Hospice Movement are two other voluntary nonprofit organizations that are providing valuable work, though not exclusively to Malta's elderly population (Malta Memorial District Nursing Association, 2004, 2003; Malta Hospice Movement, 2004). Malta also prides itself on a number of self-help groups that assist the older persons to form new identities in their old age. Through the programs and services offered to their members, these groups help give a new meaning of life to older persons and ensure they remain an integral part of Malta's mainstream society (Troisi, 2003b).

For older people who need residential care in Malta, there are three types of residential homes, namely facilities run by the government, facilities run by the Catholic Church, and facilities run by private for-profit organizations. Aware of the growing demands of older persons living in the community, the government's policy is to build homes for older persons in each locality so that those who cannot live in their own homes will not have to live far away from where they used to live (Nationalist Party, 1986). All the homes have single and double rooms, each with its own bathroom, a small kitchenette and ample living space. There are also communal facilities, including dining rooms, recreation rooms, and prayer rooms. In addition to accommodation, residents are provided with all meals, laundry, and social and recreational activities. A medical practitioner visits the residents regularly. The residents can also benefit from the community nursing care offered. The Catholic Church provides most of the residential homes for older persons in the Maltese Islands. Since 1993, various private organizations have opened a number of residential homes for older persons, which also offer respite care (Vassallo, 1998). Frequent checks are made to ensure that these homes maintain a high standard of care.

In 1996, the government embarked on a partnership scheme with some private organizations to offer residential care services for older persons. The Department for the Elderly and Community Services has subcontracted the administration of a number of recently built, government-owned homes to CareMalta, Ltd., a private organization. Care Malta is a joint venture between a Maltese Construction Company and Care UK Plc, a highly successful U.K. public company operating over 40 nursing and residential homes for older persons and the mentally ill in the United Kingdom (CareMalta, 2004; Tranter, 2000). During recent years, a small number of private agencies started providing home and nursing care for older persons.

Care of older persons in the community has, especially during the past two decades, become a focus in the policy of the Maltese government (Mifsud, 1999; Troisi, 1994b). Community-based services help older persons stay in the community longer and, at the same time, enable families to cope. It is important to note that the wide range of services in the field of aging in Malta complement rather than substitute or replace care from family, friends, or neighbors. However important the supporting role of the State, it is equally important to recognize the fact that family members, especially women, are the main players in caring for their elderly family members. In times of need, older persons turn first to their own families for help, then to friends and neighbors, and finally to the bureaucratic agencies. This is the reason why the majority of policies in the field of aging in Malta are family focused (Cutajar, 1997; Miceli, 1994; Troisi & Formosa, 2002).

REFERENCES

Abela, N. (1988). *Enabling the needs of the elderly to be met in the community: The required roles of government and voluntary agencies*. Dissertation, Faculty of Arts, University of Malta.

Bonello, R. (1995). *The role of social clubs in the provision of community care*. Dissertation, Institute of Gerontology, University of Malta.

Cachia, J. M. (1985). Care of the elderly in Malta. Research conducted for the M.Sc. in Community Medicine, University of London.

Camilleri, R. (2000). *Maltese demography within a European perspective*. Malta: Central Office of Statistics.

CareMalta, Ltd. (2004). *Homes we operate*. Retrieved from http://www.care malta.com

Central Office of Statistics (COS). (1997). *A demographic view of the Maltese islands: 1996*. Malta: Central Office of Statistics.

Cutajar, M. (1997). *Negative images of elderly women in Malta*. Dissertation, Faculty of Arts, University of Malta.

Delia, E. P. (1982). *The classification and lifestyle of the aged in the Maltese islands*. Malta: Moviment Azzjoni Socjali.

Malta Hospice Movement. (2004). *Report for 2003*. Malta: Malta Hospice Movement.

Malta Memorial District Nursing Association. (2003). *Annual general meeting March 26, 2003*. Malta: Author.

Malta Memorial District Nursing Association. (2004). Retrieved from http://www.mmdna.com

Micallef, T. (1994). *The family as the caregiver for the Maltese elderly in their home*. Dissertation, Institute of Gerontology, University of Malta.

Micallef, T. (2000). *Stress experienced by the informal caregivers of older relatives within their homes*. Dissertation, Institute of Gerontology, University of Malta.

Miceli, P. (1994). The visibility and invisibility of women. In R. Sultana & G. Baldacchino (Eds.), *Maltese society: A sociological inquiry* (pp. 79–94). Malta: Mireva Publications.

Mifsud, J. (1999). *The role of the social worker in supporting informal carers of elder people living in their own home*. Dissertation, Faculty of Arts, University of Malta.

National Statistics Office (NSO). (2003). *Demographic review 2002*. Malta: National Statistics Office.

National Statistics Office (NSO). (2007). *Demographic review 2006*. Malta: National Statistics Office.

Nationalist Party. (1986). *Electoral manifesto 1987*. Pieta, Malta: Author.

Tonna, V. (1992). *The institutional element in residential care at St. Vincent de Paul*. Dissertation, Institute of Gerontology, University of Malta.

Tranter, A. (2000, August 28). Caring for the elderly in comfort. *The Malta Independent*.

Troisi, J. (1984). The Maltese family in a flux. In Social Action Movement (Eds.), *Malta: Center of peace* (pp. 33–40). Malta: MAS.

Troisi, J. (1989). *The organization of comprehensive services for the elderly in the community in Malta*. Copenhagen: World Health Organization Regional Office, IRP /HEE 115.2.3.

Troisi, J. (1990). Varieties of welfare provision for the frail elderly people in Malta. In *Council of Europe Steering Committee on Social Policy Committee of Experts on Varieties of Welfare Provision and Dependent Old People*. Strasbourg: Council of Europe.

Troisi, J. (1991). The role of the family in supporting the dependent elderly. In *Council of Europe Steering Committee on Social Policy Committee of Experts on Varieties of Welfare Provision and Dependent Old People*. Strasbourg: Council of Europe.

Troisi, J. (1994a). The Maltese elderly: From institutionalisation to active participation in the community. In R. G. Sultana, & G. Baldacchino (Eds.), *Maltese society: A sociological inquiry* (pp. 655–668). Malta: Mireva Publications.

Troisi, J. (1994b). Continuity of care of the elderly in Malta. In WHO (Ed.), *Proceedings of Consultative Meeting on Continuity of Care of the Elderly*. Copenhagen: WHO Euro.

Troisi, J. (1995). The elderly and changing family roles: The Maltese and European experience. In S. Formosa (Ed.), *Age vault* (pp. 55–66). Malta: International Institute on Aging.

Troisi, J. (2003a, February 16). The University of the Third Age comes of age. *The Sunday Times*.

Troisi, J. (2003b, September 4). Active aging. *The Sunday Times*, p. 11.

Troisi, J., & Formosa, M. (2002). Older women in Gozo. Research carried out in collaboration with the Ministry for Gozo. Government of Malta.

Troisi, J., Formosa, M., & Navarro, M. (2004). The role of the family in caring for Maltese elderly relatives. Research for EUROFAMCARE project. Malta: European Centre of Gerontology.

United Nations. (1983). *Vienna international plan of action on aging*. New York: United Nations.

Vassallo, N. (1998). *Providing residential care for older persons in Malta: The role of the private sector*. Dissertation, Institute of Gerontology, University of Malta.

Vella, C. G. (1990). *Integrating social and family policy for the 90s*. Malta: Ministry for Social Policy.

Xerri, R. G. (1998). *The vision behind the health sector reform*. Malta: Department of Health Policy and Planning, Health Division, Ministry of Health.

32

Mexico

Armando F. Pichardo

RECENT DEVELOPMENTS

The development of gerontology in Mexico over the last decade is very interesting because the population of old persons increased quickly and the country faced a great challenge because of this change. This situation was caused jointly by the significant decrease in the birthrate, which is approximately 2.1 per woman, and the diminution of the mortality rate. At present, the population of Mexico is more than 103 million people, and those 60 years or older represent 8% of the population (Consejo Nacional de Poblacion [CONAPO], 2005).

This situation has generated significant challenges in all aspects of society. A larger infrastructure is required for the proper health care of the population. One of the factors that presently contributes to the deterioration of adult health is the lack of appropriate programs for health care (Secretaria de Salud, 2005).

Another problem is caused by migration from rural areas to the megalopolis of Mexico City, as well as migration to the United States of America. This migration tends to leave older parents, women, and children behind in rural areas, resulting in populations where there are mostly old women, such as in the states of Michoacan, Oaxaca, and Chiapas. This urban outmigration of younger people has reinforced the need to pay more attention to health services in rural areas. Mexico is currently investigating ways to reduce the rate of such migration.

Also because of the growth in the number of older adults, coordinated institutions have been created to carry out the needed actions at the national level, but with adaptations that each state or county requires.

In the last 20 years, the different aspects of the problems of aging have resulted in different action plans. Among those that stand out is the creation of the Law of the Human Rights of Older Adults, promulgated in 2002, as well as the creation of Seniors' Centers in different places in the country, such as in Mexico City, Guadalajara, Monterrey, Puebla, and Veracruz. Centers have recently been extended to other cities, with the goal that within six years, these centers can serve the entire older population in Mexico.

As a result of the demographic growth of the older population, the Clerk of the Ministry of Health is working on creating a National Institute of Geriatrics, proposed to be in operation in 2009. Its fundamental functions will be investigation, teaching, and establishing the necessary conditions so that soon Mexicans can have an active, functional, and healthy later life.

RECENT RESEARCH

Gerontological research has been carried out informally in recent years, and in the last decade, it has been extensive and focused, in most cases, on the social problems of the aging population. This research has dealt with diverse aspects of aging; for example, the studies carried out by Dr. Roberto Ham-Chande (2003), of the School of the North Frontier of Mexico, on demography.

At the Medical School of the Autonomous National University of Mexico, researchers have investigated ways in which elders relate to their relatives and their illness. Dr. Dolores Ortiz de la Huerta and Dr. Juan Jose Garcia, as well as a group of professors teaching Health among Old People, publish an annual anthology that serves as a guide to medical students. At the National Institute of Nutrition, Dr. Savior Zubiran has carried out research related to geriatric medicine.

Through these investigations, we have been able to influence politicians in addressing problems faced by older Mexicans. Clinical geriatrics research has been carried out in diverse centers, such as in the Geriatrics Services of the General Hospital of Mexico, where this research has been done for more than 20 years.

In addition, the National Commission of Attention to the Aging (CONAEN) has carried out research in very diverse areas, some of which is conducted in collaboration with the Pan American Health Organization

(PAHO), and with the Pan American Health and Education Foundation (PAHEF). This research has been used to develop the National System for the Integral Development of the Family (DIF), which has resulted in agreed-upon action plans for each town across the country; these plans pay specific attention to at-risk groups in small communities. The results of these actions are evaluated nationally in an annual meeting in which psychologists, social workers, nutritionist, and geriatricians participate. The reports of many of these investigations have been published in *ARCHIVE GERIATRIC*, the publication of the Mexican Association of Gerontology and Geriatrics, as well as in the monthly discussion forums and the annual meetings of this organization. In addition, Mexico has had a center of advanced investigation into Alzheimer's disease since the 1990s, located in the National Polytechnic Institute, with Dr. Raul Mena as the head of the team.

EDUCATION IN GERONTOLOGY

In the 1980s, the Ministry of Health began attending to the problems of aging in Mexico with the goal of being able to establish educational policies in gerontology. However, the earthquake of 1985 in Mexico City caused the destruction of many files that would have helped with the formulation of the formal education in gerontology and geriatrics. Informally, courses had begun in gerontology and geriatrics in Mexico City at the General Hospital of Mexico, as well as at other sites since the 1970s. There are informal courses lasting 6 to 12 months at the General Hospital of Mexico, the National Institute of the Senile (INSEN), and the National Institute of the Older Adults (INAPAM).

Since 1984, geriatrics and gerontology classes have been included in the curricula for medical surgeons at UNAM's medical school. Originally this course was taught in the last year of medical school and focused fundamentally on medical topics, leaving little space to gerontology as a whole. In 1994, there was a radical change in the plan of studies, which relegated 40 theoretical hours in public health to health issues of older persons. This change allowed for modifications in the content of the course so that it focused more on gerontology and the prevention of illness. Starting in 2006, the goal has been that when students finish this training, they can give proper attention to helping older people achieve an active, functional, and healthy aging process.

However, although there are nearly 78 medical schools in Mexico, only about 28 schools and universities teach gerontology and geriatrics, and there is a range of approaches to these subjects. The Mexican Association of Faculties and Schools of Medicine (AMFEM) has tried to standardize these approaches. This has been only partially achieved in Mexico City, Guadalajara, Monterrey, and San Luis Potosi, which leaves a tremendous gap in the geriatric education of medical students.

There are some classes in gerontology and geriatrics taught in other schools, such as those of engineering, architecture, social work, psychology, economics, and law, but only at a few universities.

In the 1980s, technical courses in gerontology began to be offered at high-school level. Initially, only two schools offered such courses, one of them in Mexico City. Now the Graduate School of Medicine at the National Polytechnic Institute (IPN), in collaboration with the Graduate School of Nursing, offers a graduate program in gerontology. This program is for nurses who want to complete a postgraduate course in geriatrics.

The National School of Nursing of the Universidad Nacional Autonoma De Mexico (UNAM) offers a postgraduate degree in geriatric nursing. In addition, UNAM's Faculty of Graduate Studies Zaragoza has taught a specialized course in geriatric nursing for nursing assistants, but the number of students in this program is not sufficient to cover the needs of the country. Zaragoza also offers a master's degree in gerontology, but very few students are enrolled in the program.

A license program in gerontology exists in public universities, but it does not have the necessary focus to produce gerontologists able to meet societal demand. Most of the gerontology faculty in the country has been trained in Barcelona or in Israel.

Since 1986, courses in human resources and geriatrics have been taught, initially at the Hospital Regional Lic. Adolfo Lopez Mateos of the Institute of Security and Social Services of the Workers of the State (ISSSTE), and two years later, at the General Hospital of Mexico. The entrance requirement was to have finished the internal medicine specialization. But it was eight years later that UNAM's Graduate Faculty of Medicine approved a specialization course in geriatrics that requires two years to complete. Combined with the requirement of having finished a specialization in internal medicine, this education process requires a total of six years. There are now nearly 300 doctors specialized in geriatrics, which means that there is only one geriatrician for each 50,000 older people, and most of the geriatricians are concentrated in the big cities.

The Coordination of National Institutes of Health at the Ministry of Health is collaborating with universities where specialization courses in geriatrics are taught (UNAM, Guadalajara, Monterrey, and San Luis

Potosi) to find solutions for the shortage of geriatricians. A similar short-age of geriatricians is found throughout Latin America and the United States.

PUBLIC POLICY ISSUES

In the past, the problems related to aging in the country have been neglected because the population of Mexico was fairly young. High priority was given to problems of the young, such as vaccination of infants, and infant and maternal health. But now that these services are working appropriately, the search for solutions to the problems of aging has begun to intensify.

These solutions are being sought in such institutions as the National Commission of Attention to the Aging (CONAEN), the Ministry of Health, the renovation of the National Institute of Senility (INSEN) at the National Institute of Older Adults (INAPM), the Ministry of Social Development, and the System for the Integral Development of the Family (DIF), as well as the creation of the National Institute of the Aging within the Ministry of Health in 2008.

Through public programs, economic help is beginning to become available for older men, especially those over 75 years without a pension. This help includes basic groceries, contributions of milk from the National Commission Anonymous Society of Industrial Milk (LICONSA), and government industry, which covers the entire nation. In addition, social centers have been created. The Mexican Institute of Public Health (IMSS) of the Institute of Security and Social Services of the Workers of the State (ISSSTE), the Institute of Health of the Army (SEDENA), and the Mexican Petroleum workers (PEMEX) pay special attention to older persons. Also in 2004, Popular Insurance was established to assist with minimum payments to those who do not have benefits from the organizations listed above.

Day centers for seniors have been created by the Ministry of Health and nongovernmental organizations have been established to support older persons, such as the National Program of the Third Age (PRONATE). PRONATE provides social support without charge for older people who are retired and require partial or total help. Other significant public efforts include a program that sensitizes youth about older persons, and a proposal to create special institutions in which aging criminals complete their sentences.

In the National Plan of Development 2007–2012 (PND), the government states that it is necessary to act today, if we want to have a better quality of life in the future. The plan includes projected activities and programs until the year 2030. This proposal is a first step to putting Mexico on the path to sustainable development, which would benefit older adults, their families, and the communities. With regard to health, the PND intends to advance toward universal access to quality health care, through a functional and programmatic integration of public institutions under the administration of the Ministry of Health. The program also cooperates in strategic alliances between private initiatives and the civil society, public health campaigns to communicate risks, and educational actions aimed at preventing smoking, as well as other determinants of active and healthy aging.

REFERENCES

Consejo Nacional de Poblacion (CONAPO). (2005, May). *Envejecimiento de la poblacion de Mexico. Reto del siglo XXI [The aging populations in Mexico. The challenge of the XXI century.]* (1a Reimpresión, pp. 48–92). Mexico: Author.

Consejo Nacional de Poblacion (CONAPO). (2007, October). *Situación demográfica de Mexico serio on line [Demographic situation of Mexico is serious].* Mexico: Author.

Ham-Chande, R. (2003). El envejecimiento en Mexico. El Colegio de las Frontera Norte [Aging in Mexico. The School of the North Frontier]. A. C. *Primera edicion.* Mexico: D.F.

Secretaria de Salud. (2005). Estadísticas de Mortalidad en Mexico, muertes registradas en el ano 2003 [Mortality statistics of Mexico, registered deaths in the year 2003]. *Salud Publica de Mexico, 47,* 171–180.

Secretaria de Salud. (2007a). Estrategia Nacional de Promoción y Prevención para una Mejor Salud. Dirección General de Promoción de la Salud. Subsecretaria de Prevención y Promoción de la Salud [National Strategy of Promotion and Prevention for a better Health. General address of Promotion of Health. Undersecretary of Prevention and Promotion of the Health]. *Secretaria de Salud,* 1–10.

Secretaria de Salud. (2007b, October). Programa Nacional de Salud 2007–2012. Por un Mexico Sano: Construyendo Alianzas para una Mejor Salud [National of Health Programs 2007–2012. For a healthy Mexico: Building alliances for better health]. *Secretaria de Salud,* 81–120.

33

·■·

The Netherlands

Marja Aartsen

RECENT HISTORY OF AGING

The Netherlands—claimed to be the lowest point in Western Europe—is a densely populated country with currently 16.4 million inhabitants. The Netherlands is traditionally associated with windmills, clogs, and tulips, but the Dutch themselves are more proud of their dikes, living below sea level, and liberal policies toward drugs, prostitution, and homosexuality. As in many other countries, the population is graying. Nevertheless, the Netherlands is still one of the youngest countries in Europe, together with Ireland and Luxembourg. In January 2008, 14.7% of the total Dutch population was 65 or over, and this percentage is expected to increase sharply to 25% in 2040 (Statistics Netherlands, 2008). The most important reason for the delayed graying of the population in the Netherlands is the large and lengthy baby boom that started shortly after World War II (De Jong Gierveld, 2001). The oldest people of this generation reach the age of 65 in 2011. In addition, the number of oldest old is expected to increase significantly. Projections for 2050 indicate that 38% of the 65+ population will be 80 years or older, compared to 25% in 2007. This so-called double graying of society stimulates governments and scientists to gain a deeper knowledge of the aging process and its economical and societal implications for community.

In discussions about the impact of population graying on society, two positions emerge. On the one hand, concerns are expressed about the imbalance in the age dependency ratio and the deficit in informal care with consequences for affordability of state pensions and health care (Struijs, 2006; Van den Berg Jeths, Timmermans, Hoeymans, & Woittiez, 2004). On the other hand, there is increased recognition of the value of older people, judging by the labeling of older people as "social capital" and a "new bubble in our economy" (Van Campen, 2008), and the noticeable change in the awareness of "the richness and challenges of an ageing society" (Ministry for Health Welfare and Sports, 2005).

RESEARCH ON AGING

In the Netherlands, research in gerontology and geriatrics is a lively enterprise, concentrated on several interdisciplinary academic research groups with foci on epidemiology of aging, nursing home medicine, mental health care, or biology of aging. In addition, many smaller research projects (e.g., individual dissertations) are conducted at (mental) health-care institutes in collaboration with academic centers. In this section, only the larger projects are described. For a more complete overview of all research projects on aging currently conducted in the Netherlands, see www.narcis.info.

Studies

The Longitudinal Aging Study Amsterdam (LASA; www.lasa-vu.nl) is the first ongoing longitudinal study in the Netherlands. It was specifically designed to study determinants of the autonomy and well-being of older (55+) persons. Although basically scientific in nature, the study aims to provide a basis for developing and evaluating central and local government policy in the field of aging. It is expected that by using longitudinal data, policy-relevant aspects of aging can be identified, and new policy aims can be developed. Moreover, assumptions from which policy measures are developed can be tested, and effects of policy changes can be assessed. The first round of data collection took place in 1992 (N = 3,107, ages ranged between 55 and 85) and subsequent data collection has been done every three years. In 2007/2008, the fifth follow-up was done. In 2002, a new cohort (N = 1,002) of older people aged 55–65 was included and will be re-interviewed every three years, allowing for cohort comparisons. LASA is carried out primarily at the Department of Psychiatry (Faculty of Medicine; Institute for Research in Extramural Medicine), and at the Department of Sociology (Faculty of Social Sciences) of the VU-University Amsterdam. Since 1995, the Department of Endocrinology (VU Medical Center), has also been part of the LASA study. Furthermore, collaboration has been established with the Departments of General Practice, Nursing Home and Social Medicine (VU Medical Center), the Department of Education Sciences (Faculty of Human Movement Sciences), the Department of Social Psychiatry (Faculty of Psychology and Education), and the Department of Econometrics (Faculty of Economics).

The Maastricht Ageing Study (MAAS; www.np.unimaas.nl/maas) is a large-scale cross-sectional, 12-year, longitudinal study of almost 1,900 participants aged 25–82 years. The study is devoted to the age-related decline of memory and other cognitive functions in healthy adults and factors that may be involved in this process. Data in MAAS are collected by means of postal surveys, questionnaires, and laboratory testing. Four consecutive panel studies have been carried out, each involving 440 to 480 individuals, stratified for age in 12 discrete age groups. MAAS is carried out at Maastricht University and is based at the Maastricht Brain and Behavior Institute, in association with the ExTra institute for extramural research and the Registration Network of Family Practices (RNH).

The Rotterdam Study (www.epib.nl/ergo.htm) is a prospective cohort study that started in 1990 in Ommoord, a suburb of Rotterdam, among 10,994 men and women aged 55 and over. The main objective of the Rotterdam Study is to investigate the prevalence and incidence of risk factors for chronic diseases in the elderly. All inhabitants aged 55 years or over were invited to participate. In total 7,983 subjects (4,878 women and 3,105 men) (78%) agreed and were interviewed, including 897 subjects living in one of the six homes for the elderly. The baseline study comprised a home interview, followed by two visits at the research center for clinical examinations. In 2002, another 3,011 participants (55 years of age since 1990) were added to the cohort. The Rotterdam Study is one of the research programs of the University Medical Center Rotterdam, in the Department of Epidemiology and Biostatistics.

Elderly in Institutes (http://www.scp.nl/miss/OII.shtml) is a repetitive cross-sectional study of the living situation, social networks, health, and financial situation of the residents (65+) of nursing homes, residential homes, or mental health care institutes. The first study was conducted in 1996 among 1,108 residents derived from 221 institutes in the Netherlands. The study was repeated in 2000, 2004, and 2008. The study is conducted by the Netherlands Institute for Social Research (in Dutch SCP).

Research Centers

Research on the biology of aging has been conducted at Leiden University Medical Center (LUMC, www.lumc.nl). Research started with the Leiden 85-plus Study, a prospective population-based survey among the very old (85 years and over) citizens of Leiden. The first data collection took place in 1987. Data on survival were added to this originally cross-sectional survey after the inclusion of a second cohort in 1997. The Leiden Longevity Study is another study at LUMC and is rooted in the Leiden 85+ study. The sample consists of 500 very old sib-pairs together with 1,500 family members and 1,000 spouse-controls. This sample, for which the researchers have sophisticated phenotypes and biomaterials, provides unique instruments for applying genomic-, proteomic-, and metabolomic-platforms to further unravel the biomolecular pathways of the aging process.

The National Institute for Neurosciences (NIN; www.nin.knaw.nl) carries out fundamental neuroscience research with special emphasis on the brain and the visual system. The research focuses on development, plasticity, and aging, and is often linked to clinical research questions. In addition, the NIN includes the Netherlands Brain Bank, where tissue from donors with a large variety of diseases is stored and made available to researchers all over the world.

At the Department of Nursing Home Medicine of the VU Medical Center Amsterdam (www.vumc.nl), several research projects on nursing care are conducted. Recent projects have concentrated on good care for people with dementia, infrastructure for patient care, measuring the quality of dying and palliative care, and the support of nursing home residents with dementia and depression.

The Trimbos Institute (www.trimbos.nl), or the Netherlands Institute of Mental Health and Addiction, conducts several studies varying from short-term to long-term implementation programs. One recently started study is called Monitor Mental Health Care of the Elderly (MEMO). In this study, monitor data are collected in institutes for mental health (GGZ in Dutch) on the quality and effectiveness of mental health care. Trimbos's activities are intended to contribute to improvements in mental health and addiction care in order to elicit individual health gains within the Dutch population, promote more effective treatment methods, and provide models for more efficient care.

The Center for Research on Aging (www.cvo.vu.nl) is a working group on research and education in gerontology and geriatrics at the Vrije Universiteit and VU University Medical Center. The Center aims for more cooperation between researchers of medical, sociological, and psychological disciplines in order to increase the quality of research and education in gerontology and geriatrics.

Distinct medical research in older adults (i.e., focused on Alzheimer or other neurodegenerative diseases) is also underway in the Netherlands but is beyond the scope of this handbook and will not be further discussed here.

CURRENT STATE OF EDUCATION IN GERONTOLOGY

Every year, more than 30 dissertations in the field of gerontology, geriatrics, gerodontology, nursing home medicine, and epidemiology are published (www.narcis.info), and a wide variety of conferences on aging are organized. Recurring conferences, for example, include the biennial NVG-conference organized by the Dutch Society for Gerontology (www.nvgerontologie.nl), the yearly conference on elderly psychiatry organized by the Dutch Knowledge Centre of Elderly Psychiatry (www.elderlypsy chiatry.com), the yearly two-day conference on geriatrics (www.congress care.com), and the yearly conference for geriatricians, geropsychiatrists, and nursing psychologists (nvva. artsennet.nl).

Higher education in gerontology, especially the bachelor's and master's programs at the universities, is organized by the VU-University in Amsterdam (European Master's program in Gerontology [EuMaG]), and the Radboud University in Nijmegen (Psychogerontology). The University for Humanistics in Utrecht offer modules with a focus on interpretive gerontology within the program on human development. EuMaG (www.eumag.org) is a modular, two-year, part-time international training program with core modules on biogerontology, social gerontology, psychogerontology, and public health. The administrative center is at the VU-University Amsterdam, and four universities in Europe deliver the core program: the VU-University Amsterdam, the Institute of Gerontology of the University of Heidelberg (Germany), Keele University (United Kingdom), and the Université du Versailles Saint-Quentin-en-Yvelines (France). Many other European universities (and also four universities in the United States—Miami University in Ohio, Oregon State University, San Francisco State University, and the Appalachian State University) contribute to the educational program of the EuMaG network. The Radboud University in Nijmegen offers both bachelor and master's courses in psychogerontology. The curriculum focuses on life-span development of people in the second half of life.

The Avans University in the south of the Netherlands (Breda, 's-Hertogenbosch, and Tilburg) delivers courses in gerontology and geriatric physical therapy (www.avansplus.nl/geriatrie). The Windesheim University of Applied Sciences in Zwolle recently started a lectureship on innovation in elderly care (www.windesheim.nl).

CURRENT PUBLIC POLICY ISSUES

Labor Market Participation

To cope with the consequences of the aging population, governmental policies were developed along two main lines: reduction of government debt, and promoting labor force participation, especially by older workers. However, labor force participation is relatively low among people aged 55–65. Ekamper (2006) derived from Eurostat data that there is a tendency toward early retirement, which reached its low point in 1995 when merely 20% of men 60–65 years old and 8% of women of the same age participated in the labor force. Therefore, the government aims to raise the labor participation of 55–65-year-old workers to 40% in 2010 and to 50% in 2020 (Ministry of Social Affairs and Employment, 2005). Meanwhile, there is a reassuring percentage of men and women aged 65–69 who are still active in the labor market, which rose, respectively, from 4% and 0.8% in 1981 to 14% and 7.4% in 2005 (Ekamper, 2006).

Pensions

The Dutch pension system is built on three pillars. The first is the basic state pension (AOW; National Old Age Pension Act) and consists of a fixed amount paid to those residents aged 65 and over who have lived in the Netherlands for at least 50 years. For every year they have not lived in the Netherlands after the age of 15, the AOW is reduced by 2%. In 2009, the gross AOW amount is €1,038 (US$1,306) per month for single persons and €723 (US$900) for people living together (Social Security Bank of the Netherlands, n.d.). The second pillar consists of occupational pensions accrued as fringe benefits of employment. These supplementary pension arrangements are made for nearly all employees. The third pillar consists of individual retirement provisions, which anyone can buy on the insurance market (Ministry of Social Affairs and Employment, 2005).

Poverty

In 2006, 11.2% of single older adults (aged 65 and over) and 2.2% of married older adults lived below the poverty line, which is defined as less than €880 (US$1,136) per month for single persons and €1,200 (US$1,549) per month for couples (Otten, Bos, Vrooman, & Hoff, 2008). Mainly due to adaptations in the basic state pension (AOW), the percentage living below the poverty line decreased in 2008 to 6.8% of single older adults and 1.6% of married older adults.

Living Arrangements

The 2004 Study of Institutionalized Older Adults, by the Netherlands Institute of Social Research, investigated the living situation of older adults who live in nursing or residential homes (De Klerk, 2005). According to that study, 5% of all persons aged 65 or over lived in residential homes and 2% in nursing homes, which totals approximately 150,000 people. There are, in total, approximately 700 nursing and residential homes in the Netherlands. There are two main differences between nursing homes and residential homes: the level of care (with people who require more intense care living in nursing homes) and the available living area. In residential homes, people often have their own apartments, and in nursing homes, the bedroom is very often shared with one or more other residents.

In contrast to what is often intuitively believed, the study shows that the vast majority of older people live independently until a very advanced age. Only after the age of 95 do more than 50% have to give up their independent living and move to a nursing or residential home. The average age of the nursing or residential home resident is 84, and approximately three-quarters of all older residents are female (De Klerk, 2005).

Residents in nursing and residential homes are very often affected with one of more chronic diseases. Every 7 out of 10 residents have two or more chronic diseases, of which arthritis is the most common (50%). Thirty percent of the residents have anxious feelings, and 28% suffer from depression. Twenty-three percent of all residents have serious cognitive problems, and 16% have mild cognitive problems (De Klerk, 2005).

In the last five years, there has been a growing interest in small-scale living arrangements for older people with dementia. A small-scale living arrangement is a care facility for a small group of people in need of intensive care and assistance. People live together in a home and live as normal a life as possible. In 2005, there were 349 locations offering small-scale living arrangements for 4,442 demented elderly people. In 2010, the capacity of small group homes for dementia patients will increase to 10,834 (Aedes-Actiz Kenniscentrum Wonen-Zorg, 2008).

Community Services

There is a wide range of professional services available to help people live independently as long as possible. These services include, domestic help, nursing, mental health, social work, telecommunication services, transportation services and meal distributions. The new Social Support Act (Wet maatschappelijke ondersteuning, Wmo) established in 2007 in all municipalities in the Netherlands regulates the provision of domestic help. The aim of the Wmo is to involve all citizens in all facets of the society, whether or not they receive help from friends, family, or acquaintances (Ministry of Health Welfare and Sports, 2006). The Wmo puts an end to various rules and regulations for handicapped people and the older population. It encompasses the Services for the Disabled Act (WVG), the Social Welfare Act, and parts of the Exceptional Medical Expenses Act (AWBZ) (Ministry of Health Welfare and Sports, 2006). The first evaluation of the Wmo is to be expected in 2009 (Timmermans, De Klerk, & Gilsing, 2007).

The New Health-Care System

As of January 2006, a new insurance system for curative health care came into force in the Netherlands. Under the new Health Insurance Act (Zorgverzekeringswet), all residents are obliged to take out a health insurance policy; the insurers are obliged to accept every resident in their area of activity. Next to this private insurance scheme, there is a national insurance scheme for long-term care, and the Exceptional Medical Expenses Act (AWBZ). This scheme is intended to provide the insured with chronic and continuous care that involves considerable financial consequences, such as care for disabled people with congenital physical or mental disorders. Everyone who is legally residing in the Netherlands and nonresidents who are employed and therefore liable for payroll tax in the Netherlands, are insured with the AWBZ. As costs claimed via the AWBZ have increased dramatically since 2003, the cabinet is making plans to ensure that the AWBZ remains viable for the most vulnerable members of society in the future (Bussemaker, 2008).

Loneliness

Loneliness can be defined as "a situation experienced by the participant as one where there is an unpleasant or unacceptable lack of (quality of) certain social relationships. The extent to which the situation is experienced as serious depends upon the participant's perception of his or her ability to realize new relationships or to improve existing ones" (De Jong Gierveld, 1989, p. 205). A widely used instrument to assess the level of loneliness is the De Jong Gierveld Loneliness Scale (De Jong Gierveld & Kamphuis, 1985). Based on that measurement scale, approximately 30% of Dutch people feel lonely. Some are seriously lonely (10% of the population), and some feel lonely now and then (20%) (Van Tilburg & de Jong Gierveld, 2007). Many initiatives are aimed at reducing loneliness among older adults, ranging from meeting centers, house visits and personal activation, to information and training programs for older people and professionals (e.g., Linnemann, van Linschoten, Royers, Nelissen, & Nitsche, 2001).

Alcohol Abuse

Alcohol consumption among older adults in the Netherlands has seen a steep rise over the last 10 years. One in every five older persons aged between 55 and 65 drinks in excess of the limits recommended by the National Institute on Alcohol Abuse and Alcohol Disorder (Visser, Pluijm, van der Horst, Poppelaars, & Deeg, 2005). The number of older adults (55+) who seek treatment for their alcohol problems has more than doubled since 1996, up to an absolute number of 6,300 in 2005 (IVZ Stichting Informatie Voorziening Zorg [IVZ], 2006). Taking into account that alcohol problems among older adults are often underdiagnosed (O'Connell, Chin, Cunningham, & Lawlor, 2003), and given the fact that only a small fraction of those with an alcohol use disorder seek treatment, the actual number of older people with an alcohol use disorder in the general population is likely to be much higher.

Euthanasia

Euthanasia is a sensitive issue (see, for example, the Ministry of Health, Welfare and Sports and Ministry of Justice brochure on Euthanasia), and there has been a broad political and public debate over the past 30 years about the question of whether and how criminal liability for euthanasia should be restricted (Ministry of Foreign Affairs, 2008). In April 2002, the Termination of Life on Request and Assisted Suicide Act came into effect. Euthanasia is understood to mean termination of life by a doctor at the patient's request, with the aim of putting an end to unbearable suffering with no prospect of improvement. The voluntary nature of the patient's request is crucial: euthanasia may only take place at the explicit request of the patient.

The debate about the justice of euthanasia has by no means been resolved (for an intriguing discussion, see Hope, 2004). Some argue that the Dutch act for Euthanasia is a "license to kill" (Cloud & Daruvalla, 2001), leading to an increase in the intentional ending of people's lives. However, in a recent evaluation of the Termination of Life on Request and Assisted Suicide Act (Onwuteaka-Philipsen et al. 2007), one of the most remarkable findings was the decrease in euthanasia and assistance in suicide after the Act went into effect.

CONCLUSION

As with many other societies, Dutch society is aging. From 2011, the first people of the large and lengthy baby-boom generation will reach the age of 65, which further accelerates the graying of the population. Research on aging is lively and productive with foci varying from quantitative to interpretive, from housing characteristics to predictors of well-being, and from risk factors of chronic diseases to research of brain tissues. Research results have provided input for new political strategies. Recently developed study programs seem to reflect a growing interest in applied gerontology, such as care management or innovations of care programs for older people. However, judging by the unpopularity of master's programs in gerontology, we are less successful in attracting new generations of scientifically oriented gerontologists. Whether these developments threaten a successful adaptation to the graying of society can only be judged afterwards.

REFERENCES

Aedes-Actiz Kenniscentrum Wonen-Zorg. (2008). Retrieved December 30, 2008, from http://www.kenniscentrumwonenzorg.nl

Akerlind, I., & Hornquist, J. O. (1992). Loneliness and alcohol abuse: A review of evidences of interplay. *Social Science and Medicine, 34,* 405–414.

Begemann C., van Lieshout, H., & Scholten, C. (2005). *Vrijwilligers en beroepskrachten in samenwerking, een handreiking tot samenwerking* [Volunteers and professionals in cooperation, a hand of cooperation]. Utrecht, The Netherlands: Lemma en NIZW Zorg.

Bruinsma, M., Dirksen, I., Scholten, C., & Keesom, J. (2001). *Focus op de vrijwilliger. Nieuwe impulsen voor werving, bemiddeling en begeleiding.* Utrecht, The Netherlands: NIZW.

Bussemaker, J. (2008). *Security of care, today and tomorrow.* The Hague, The Netherlands: Ministry of Health Welfare and Sports.

Cloud, J., & Daruvalla, A. (2001). A licence to kill? Critics say a Dutch euthanasia law goes too far. *Time, 157*(16), 66.

De Jong Gierveld, J. (1989). Personal relationships, social support, and loneliness. *Journal of Social and Personal Relationships, 6,* 197–221.

De Jong Gierveld, J. (2001). Ouderen in Europa. *Index, 8,* 20–21.

De Jong Gierveld, J., & Kamphuis, F. (1985). The development of a Rasch-type loneliness scale. *Applied Psychological Measurement, 9,* 289–299.

De Jong Gierveld, J., & Van Tilburg, T. G. (1999). *Manual of the loneliness scale.* Amsterdam: Dept. of Social Research Methodology, VU-University.

De Klerk, M. (2005). *Ouderen in Instellingen: Landelijk overzicht van de leefsituatie van oudere tehuisbewoners.* The Hague, The Netherlands: SCP.

Ekamper, P. (2006). Werkende ouderen in Belgie en Nederland—de cijfers. *Tijdschrift voor Human Research Management, 9,* 6–20.

Fokkema, T., & van Tilburg, T. G. (2006). *Aanpak van eenzaamheid: Helpt het? Een vergelijkend effect- en procesevaluatieonderzoek naar interventies ter voorkoming en vermindering van eenzaamheid onder ouderen* [Tackling loneliness: Does it really help? A comparative impact and process evaluation to interventions to prevent and reduce loneliness among the elderly]. The Hague, The Netherlands: Interdisciplinair Demografisch Instituut.

Hope, R. A. (2004). *Medical ethics: A very short introduction.* Oxford: Oxford University Press.

Hortulanus, R., Machielse, A., & Meeuwesen, L. (2003). *Sociaal isolement, een studie over sociale contacten en sociaal isolement in Nederland* [Social isolation, a study on social contacts and social isolation in the Netherlands]. The Hague, The Netherlands: Elsevier Overheid.

IVZ Stichting Informatie Voorziening Zorg. (2006). *Alcohol and older adults in outpatient addiction care in the Netherlands (1996–2005).* Retrieved October 28, 2008, from http://www.sivz.nl

Linnemann, M., van Linschoten, P., Royers, T., Nelissen, H., & Nitsche, B. (2001). *Eenzaam op leeftijd. Interventies bij eenzame ouderen.* Utrecht, The Netherlands: NIZW.

Ministry of Foreign Affairs. (2008). *FAQ Euthanasia 2008: Official publication.* The Hague, The Netherlands: Author.

Ministry of Health Welfare and Sports. (2005). *Ouderenbeleid in het perspectief van de vergrijzing.* The Hague, The Netherlands: Author.

Ministry of Health Welfare and Sports. (2006). *Social Support Act: Act of 29 juni 2006, containing new rules for social support.* The Hague, The Netherlands: Author.

Ministry of Social Affairs and Employment. (2005). *National strategy report on adequate and sustainable pensions*. The Hague, The Netherlands: Author.

O'Connell, H., Chin, A. V., Cunningham, C., & Lawlor, B. (2003). Alcohol use disorders in elderly people—Redefining an age-old problem in old age. *British Medical Journal, 327,* 664–667.

Onwuteaka-Philipsen, B. D., Gevers, J.K.M., van der Heide, A., van Delden, J.J.M., Pasman, H.R.W., Rietjens, J.A.C., et al. (2007). *Evaluatie Wet Toetsing levensbeëindiging op verzoek en hulp bij zelfdoding* [Evaluation of the Termination of Life on Request and Assisted Suicide Act]. The Hague: ZonMw.

Otten, F., Bos, W., Vrooman, C., & Hoff, S. (2008). *Armoedebericht 2008*. The Hague/Heerlen, The Netherlands: Statistics Netherlands.

Social Security Bank of the Netherlands. (n.d.). Retrieved June 19, 2009, from http://www.svb.nl

Statistics Netherlands. (2008). *Statistics Netherlands Voorburg/Heerlen*. Retrieved December 29, 2008, from http://www.cbs.nl

Struijs, J. (2006). *Informal care*. Zoetermeer, The Netherlands: The Council for Public Health and Health Care.

Timmermans, J., De Klerk, M., & Gilsing, R. (2007). *Onderzoeksopzet. Evaluatie van de Wet maatschappelijke ondersteuning* [Research design. Evaluation of the Social Support Act]. The Hague: The Netherlands Institute for Social Research, SCP.

Van Campen, C. (Ed.) (2008). *Values on a grey scale: Elderly policy monitor 2008*. The Hague, The Netherlands: The Netherlands Institute for Social Research, SCP.

van den Berg Jeths, A., Timmermans, J., Hoeymans, N., & Woittiez, I. (2004). *Ouderen nu en in de toekomst: Gezondheid, verpleging en verzorging 2000–2020* [Older now and in the future: Health, nursing and care 2000–2020]. *RIVM-rapport nr. 270502001*. Bilthoven/The Hague, The Netherlands: RIVM/SCP.

van Tilburg, T. G., & de Jong Gierveld, J. (Eds.). (2007). *Zicht op eenzaamheid: Achtergronden, oorzaken en aanpak* [Loneliness: Backgrounds, causes and prevention]. Assen, The Netherlands: Van Gorcum.

Visser, M., Pluijm, S.M.F., Van der Horst, M.H.L., Poppelaars, J. L., & Deeg, D.J.H. (2005). Leefstijl van 55–64 jarige Nederlanders in 2002/03 minder gezond dan in 1992/93. Nederlands Tijdschrift Geneeskunde [Lifestyle of 55–64-year-old Dutch in 2002/03 less healthy than in 1992/93]. *Nederlands Tijdschrift Geneeskunde, 149,* 2973–2978.

34

▪ ▪ ■ ▪ ▪

New Zealand

Judith A. Davey

AGING OF THE POPULATION

Population aging—commonly measured as growth in the percentage of the population above a certain age, or by upward movement in the median age—began in New Zealand over a century ago, with the transition from high to low fertility and falling death rates (Khawaja, 2000). In 1900, the median age was 23 (half of the population was aged under 23). Children outnumbered people aged 65 and over by 8 to 1. Average life expectancy at birth for men was about 57 years and for women, 60 years. Low fertility during the Depression years of the 1930s and the ongoing improvement in life expectancy meant that by the 1946 Census, the median age had risen to 30. The post-World War II baby boom reversed the aging trend, but only temporarily. The subsequent drop in fertility below replacement level (generally taken as 2.1 births per woman) lifted the median age to a new high of 34 in 1999, an overall increase of 11 years since 1900.

The 1901 Census recorded 31,000 persons aged 65 or older and they made up 4% of the population of 816,000. Between 1901 and 1951, the number of New Zealanders aged 65 and over increased almost sixfold, to 177,000. By 1999, this had grown by another 151% to reach 446,000, rising much faster than the rest of the population. People aged 65+ now account for 12% of the population, and numbered nearly half a million in 2006, when the total New Zealand population was 4.027 million.

Life expectancy continues to grow. A newborn male can expect to live on average 74 years and a female about 80. At age 65, life expectancy for males is 16.7 years (average age at death 81.7) and for females, 20 years (average age at death 85) (Statistics New Zealand, 2004).

The latest projections suggest that the population aged 65 and over will grow by about 100,000 during the current decade, to reach 552,000 by 2011 (Dunstan & Thomson, 2006). The pace of increase will pick up after 2011, when the baby-boom generation begins to enter this age group. Between 2011 and 2021, the 65+ population is projected to grow by about 200,000, and in the following 10 years, by 230,000. From the late 2030s, this age group will make up over one-quarter of the population. By 2051, there is expected to be 1.33 million New Zealanders aged 65 and older out of a total population of 5.5 million. The median age was 35.9 in 2006 and is expected to be 40.3 in 2021 and 45.9 in 2051. Within the 65+ age group, the number of people aged 85 and over is growing rapidly, and tripled from 1970 to roughly 55,000 in 2005. Population projections suggest that there will be 320,000 people aged 85+ in 2051—an increase of 500% from the year 2000.

RESEARCH ON AGING IN NEW ZEALAND

Significant research in geriatric medicine is being carried out through the Otago and Auckland Medical Schools. Both have extensive research programs on health and related services for older people, as well as preventive interventions, such as falls research. Some of the research involves residential care, but also community-based service provision. One large-scale program is ASPIRE (Assessment of Services Promoting Independence and Recovery in Elders), which is a randomized controlled trial to evaluate services aimed at assisting older people to live at home (Ministry of Health, 2006).

The Population Studies Centre at Waikato University with the Family Centre Social Policy Research Unit has a program of research titled Enhancing Wellbeing in an Aging Society (EWAS), funded by the Foundation for Research, Science and Technology (FRST) (EWAS, 2007). The Health Research Council has funded a longitudinal program— Health, Work and Retirement (HWR)—in the School of Psychology at Massey University, Palmerston North. Two rounds of data have been collected with a qualitative dimension being carried out in association with the New Zealand Institute for Research on Aging (NZiRA) (Stephens & Noone, 2007). The Massey University group with the Family Centre Social Policy Research Unit is beginning work on a longitudinal study of aging in New Zealand that will extend the EWAS and HWR programs.

NZiRA was established at Victoria University of Wellington in 2000, dedicated to research on the social and economic implications of population aging. NZiRA has carried out research contracts for a range of clients, mainly public sector agencies, including the Ministries of Health, Transport, Social Development (and Office for Senior Citizens), the Retirement Commission, the Department of Labor, and the Centre for Housing Research (CHRANZ). Other individuals and small groups of researchers have interests in aging-related issues, for example in Sport and Leisure Studies, University of Waikato, and there is a Retirement Policy and Research Centre in the Auckland University Business School. But overall, the academic capacity for research on aging in New Zealand is small in relation to the importance of the topic. NZiRA has run three biennial symposia for postgraduate students carrying out research on aging in New Zealand. The response shows that such students are spread through a variety of institutions, schools, and disciplinary bases, including psychology, sociology, anthropology, economics, public policy, management studies, nursing, health science, education, social work, and Maori and Pacific studies. As a support to research initiatives, NZiRA has produced two bibliographies of New Zealand research on aging (Davey & Gee, 2002; Davey & Wilton, 2005).

The largest program of government research on aging is being conducted in the Ministry of Social Development. This has included work on the living standards of older New Zealanders, especially those living in material hardship; aging in place; benefits and retirement income; and the development of indicators of Positive Aging (linked to the government's Positive Aging Strategy) (Ministry of Social Development, 2007). In 2007–2008, a study was undertaken of the intentions and aspirations of people turning age 65.

The Ministry of Health is concerned about the impact of aging on health and disability services and the implementation of the Health of Older People Strategy. The Department of Labor has recently published several reports on older workers (Department of Labor, 2007). Data from the Population Census and other collections are made available by Statistics New Zealand, through its Web site and publications (Statistics New Zealand, 2007). The New Zealand Treasury and the Retirement Commission publish papers related to the economic impacts of aging and retirement income. Many government agencies contract out research to universities and research companies, and the resulting reports can be found on their Web sites.

Concern with increasing the capacity for research on aging in New Zealand has been expressed by NZiRA and by the New Zealand Association of Gerontology (NZAG). Both organizations emphasize the complexity of aging and the need for multidisciplinary approaches to research and policy-making, linking biomedical research to social research in order to fully appreciate the social and economic implications.

EDUCATION IN GERONTOLOGY

Most of the formal courses in gerontology in New Zealand are aimed at health professionals, with aspects of the health care of older people embedded in the undergraduate and postgraduate curricula of the medical schools, and in nursing training. The Australian and New Zealand Society for Geriatric Medicine aims to promote the training of medical practitioners (including continuing education for qualified geriatricians) and allied disciplines on the medical and related problems of older people. The study of gerontology and later life is rarely available in social science curricula at New Zealand universities, although such papers are offered in postgraduate social work training.

Training for workers in aged care, apart from nursing training, has developed only recently. A National Certificate in Support of the Older Person is currently under review (New Zealand Qualifications Authority [NZQA], 2008). This certificate has levels corresponding to basic and advanced trades training, with strands in community and residential care.

In terms of general community education on aging, Age Concern New Zealand's Information Centre has a wealth of resources, including fact sheets, videos, pamphlets, and posters (Age Concern, 2008). The booklets *Aging is Living: A Guide to Positive Aging* and *Aging Well* give advice on planning and living a positive older age, and on health and well-being, including topics as varied as mobility, skin care, sexual relations, and safety. Age Concern fact sheets cover a wide range of topics including legal, financial, and housing issues. The New Zealand Association of Gerontology has a role in education through conferences and branch meetings, discussing cross-sectoral topics.

PUBLIC POLICY ISSUES

An aging population will have major impacts on government services and expenditure. A quarter of government expenditure accrues to people aged 65+. As the numbers in this age group grow, the fiscal costs will increase. One of the key drivers is New Zealand Superannuation (NZS). The net cost of NZS is projected to increase from 4.9% of GDP currently to 6.5% by mid-century. Health costs are predicted to increase from 6.3% of GDP to 11.1% by 2050, with over 60% generated by people aged 65 or older (Bryant, Teasdale, Tobias, Cheung, & McHugh, 2004). The policy implications of population aging are explored in Boston and Davey (2006), with chapters relating to retirement income, labor market, health services, and housing distribution, among others.

Retirement Income

On reaching age 65, all New Zealanders who fulfill the residence qualifications become eligible for NZS, a flat-rate universal payment funded from taxation and payable whether or not the recipient is in paid work. NZS can be supplemented by means-tested benefits to cover housing, disability, and other costs. Before the introduction of Kiwi Saver in April 2007, the coverage of employment-related pension plans was not widespread. Kiwi Saver is a voluntary contributory retirement income scheme administered through employers, attracting government incentives and provided by private sector agencies. Benefits are locked in until age 65, but there is provision to withdraw contributions to assist first home purchase.

The long-term sustainability of NZS is supported by the New Zealand Superannuation Fund, into which the government contributes to smooth the ongoing cost as the population ages. Evidence suggests that NZS is a good basis for retirement income support, providing an adequate, if basic, level of income, as illustrated in the Living Standards Study (Fergusson, Hong, Horwood, Jensen, & Travers, 2001). At present, all political parties support the retention of NZS and Kiwi Saver. However, the programs' sustainability depends very much on the future of the New Zealand economy.

Health and Community Services

People aged 65 and over are high users of primary health and hospital services. This age group receives subsidies for general practitioner consultations and prescriptions. Treatment in public hospitals is free for all New Zealanders. Average costs for government-funded health and disability services rise steadily from the age of 50, with a strong acceleration from age 80 onwards, mainly from the cost of residential care (Bryant et al., 2004).

Looking to the future, an aging population will bring increases in incidence rates and health expenditure on cardiovascular diseases, cancers, strokes, diabetes, COPD, osteoporotic fractures and musculoskeletal diseases, visual and auditory deficiencies, and dementia. On the other hand, improvements in the general health of the baby-boom generation may moderate the need for health services as this cohort ages. Growth in numbers of people 85+ suggests a higher demand for long-term care, depending on disability rates and the incidence of dementia. Recent changes to the income and asset test for the Residential Care Subsidy (raising the level of assets that are protected) will increase fiscal costs for this service. A significant expansion of home and community care options could reduce pressure on residential care and allow greater numbers of older people to age in place. Investment in care coordination and case management, respite care, and other support for carers are all likely to be cost effective.

Other factors will influence the demand for health services as the population ages. Breakthroughs in medical technology could reduce the demand for health services and lower costs, or generate increased demand and raise costs. The attitudes of oncoming cohorts of older people may result in higher expectations about health-care services, fuelled by a wider variety of information about treatments. But labor supply may be the greatest challenge facing health systems as the population ages. The health work force itself is aging; New Zealand is experiencing difficulties in recruiting specialists in geriatric care; and there are challenges in retaining health professionals and care workers in the face of active international recruitment.

Issues for health services in an aging population link with challenges in other policy areas, such as housing, transportation, and service delivery. Policy objectives in the Health of Older People's Strategy seek to strengthen primary care services and emphasize a more preventative approach (Ministry of Health, 2002). These are consistent with aging in place and a reduction in the use of residential care. At the same time, a coordinated and comprehensive approach to health-care delivery is required, incorporating the integrated continuum of care concept.

Housing

Three-quarters of older New Zealander own their homes, the majority mortgage free. Most wish to live in their homes for as long as possible and do so until the end of their lives. However, homeowners still face issues of maintenance, adaptation and renovation. Current assistance in these areas is limited, even though the quality of housing is crucial to successful aging in place. There is a very limited supply of supported or intermediate housing available in New Zealand.

Care of Older People

The vast majority of older people in New Zealand live in private dwellings. The proportion in institutional care does not exceed 5% until past the age of 80. In the age group 85+, 19% of men and 31% of women are in residential care. The residential care population is aging and people are at higher levels of disability when they enter. This means that many very old people, even with significant disabilities, remain living in the community. The provision of informal care for dependent older people, by family members, neighbors, and friends, is likely to remain the most important form of support (OECD, 2005). This poses questions for policy that have yet to be tackled. Who should be expected to provide such care in the future, and how should responsibility for care be shared between families, government agencies, the community, and voluntary sectors? The provision of informal care still tends to be an expectation of female family members. However, oncoming cohorts of women have higher levels of paid work-force participation and financial independence and this will affect their attitudes toward family caring. Combining paid work with eldercare is likely to become a more salient feature in workplaces, with implications for human resource management, labor supply, and productivity (Keeling & Davey, 2008).

A high proportion of care for dependent people in families and communities is provided by older people themselves, for spouses, relatives with physical and mental disabilities, and for grandchildren, ranging from casual babysitting to full custodial care. Child care provided by older people often facilitates labor force participation by parents, especially mothers, which has economic consequences for families and also in terms of labor supply. Full-time custodial care by grandparents is an emerging issue in New Zealand. In many cases, this is the result of situations that have detrimentally affected the children's emotional or physical well-being (Worrall, 2005). As a result of caring for grandchildren, many older people suffer financial hardship, legal problems, and stress. Assistance from formal services and recognition of their quasi-parental status has only recently been promised through the welfare benefit system.

Employment

Population aging is expected to lead to serious labor and skills shortages, affecting economic prospects (Stephenson & Scobie, 2002). Almost 40% of the New Zealand labor force is already aged 45 or older. However, there has recently been an upturn in labor force participation rates for people 65+, rising from 14% in 1981 to 23% in 2006 for men, and from 3% to 11% for women. This reflects policy adjustments—increasing the age of eligibility for NZS and removing compulsory retirement (under the Human Rights Act, 1993). Given strong labor demand over the medium term, improving health, and the desire to supplement income, labor force participation rates for older people are likely to grow still further. Moves to enhance labor force participation by older people have potential advantages for the workers themselves, for their employers and for society as a whole, provided that such measures are matched by adjustments in working conditions to meet the needs of older workers (Davey, 2007).

CONCLUSION

New Zealand has many advantages in facing the challenges of population aging. It is still a relatively young country demographically, with a comparatively small population. The government, through its Positive Aging Strategy, is emphasizing policy settings that support older people to remain active and independent and to maintain their participation in communities and wider society (Office for Senior Citizens, 2008). Policies that promote increased employment of older workers will help fund the fiscal costs of an aging population. Support for older people as carers will improve labor force participation by younger workers and reduce health costs. Such initiatives will become increasingly important as the population ages.

REFERENCES

Age Concern New Zealand. (2008). Retrieved from http://www.ageconcern.org.nz/?/infocentre/resources

Boston, J., & Davey, J. (Eds.). (2006). *Implications of population aging: Opportunities and risks*. Wellington: Institute of Policy Studies.

Bryant, J., Teasdale, A., Tobias, M., Cheung, J., & McHugh, M. (2004). *Population aging and government health expenditures in New Zealand, 1951–2051*. New Zealand Treasury Working Paper 04/14. Wellington: The Treasury. Retrieved from http://www.treasury.govt.nz/publications/research-policy/wp/2004/04-14/twp04-14.pdf

Davey, J. (2007). *Maximising the potential of older workers—2007 update*. Wellington: New Zealand Institute for Research on Aging. Retrieved from http://www.victoria.ac.nz/nzira/publications/recent_publications.aspx

Davey, J., & Gee, S. (2002). *Aotearoa aging: An annotated bibliography of New Zealand research on aging 1997–2001*. Wellington: New Zealand Institute for Research on Aging.

Davey, J., & Wilton, V. (2005). *Aotearoa aging 2005: A bibliography of New Zealand research on aging 2001–2005*. Wellington: New Zealand Institute for Research on Aging. Retrieved from http://www.victoria.ac.nz/nzira/downloads/AotearoaAging2005.pdf

Department of Labor. (2007). *Older people in work: Key trends and patterns 1991–2005*. Wellington: Department of Labor. Retrieved from http://www.dol.qovt.nz/PDFs/olderpeople.pdf

Dunstan, K., & Thomson, N. (2006). Demographic trends. In J. Boston & J. Davey (Eds.), *Implications of population aging: Opportunities and risks*. Wellington: Institute of Policy Studies.

Enhancing Wellbeing in an Aging Society (EWAS). (2007). Retrieved from http://www.ewas.net.nz/Publications/index.html

Fergusson, D., Hong, B., Horwood, J., Jensen, J., & Travers, P. (2001). *Living standards of older New Zealanders*. Wellington: Ministry of Social Policy. Retrieved from http://www.msd.govt.nz/documents/publications/csre/liv ingintro.pdf

Keeling, S., & Davey, J. (2008). Working carers in New Zealand: Zones of care and contested boundaries. In A. Martin-Matthews & J. Phillips (Eds.), *Blurring the boundaries: Aging at the intersection of work and home life*. London: Psychology Press.

Khawaja, M. (2000). *Population aging in New Zealand. Key statistics Jan/Feb 2000*. Retrieved from http://www.stats.govt.nz/NR/rdonlyres/02677883-A742–4000-AA80–59D264E774F6/0/PopAgeNZ.pdf

Ministry of Health. (2002). *Health of older people strategy*. Wellington: Ministry of Health. Retrieved from http://www.moh.govt.nz/publications/hops

Ministry of Health. (2006). *Assessment of Services Promoting Independence and Recovery in Elders (ASPIRE)*. Retrieved from http://www.moh.govt.nz/moh.nsf/indexmh/aspire-factsheet

Ministry of Social Development. (2007). *Positive aging indicators*. Wellington. Retrieved from http://www.msd.govt.nz/documents/work-areas/social-research/positive-agingindicators-2007.pdf

New Zealand Qualifications Authority (NZQA). (2008). Retrieved from http://www.nzqa.govt.nz/framework/explore/domain.do?frameworkId=76296

Office for Senior Citizens. (2008). *New Zealand positive aging strategy*. Retrieved from http://www.osc.govt.nz/positive-aging-strategy/publication/index.html

Organisation for Economic Co-operation and Development (OECD). (2005). *Long-term care for older people*. Paris: OECD.

Statistics New Zealand. (2004). *Demographic trends 2004. Table 4.11*. Retrieved from http://www.stats.govt.nz/analytical-reports/dem-trends-04/exceltables.htm

Statistics New Zealand. (2007). *New Zealand's 65+ population: A statistical volume*. Retrieved from http://www.stats.govt.nz/NR/rdonlyres/2618D769-A4DF-403D-99BF-5FDE42C68EE3/0/nzs65pluspopulationreport1.pdf

Stephens, C., & Noone, J. (2007). *Health, work and retirement survey. Summary report for the 2006 data wave—Health*. Retrieved from http://hwr.massey.ac.nz/resources/health stephens-noone.pdf

Stephenson, J., & Scobie, G. (2002). *The economics of population aging. Treasury Working Paper, 02/05.* Retrieved from http://www.treasury.govt.nz/workingpapers/2002/twp02–05.pdf

Worrall, J. (2005). *Grandparents and other relatives raising kin children in Aotearoa/New Zealand.* Auckland: Grandparents Raising Grandchildren Charitable Trust. Retrieved from http://www.raisinggrandchildren.org.nz/supporting/Research%20Report%20final.pdf

35

Norway

Kirsten Thorsen

Like many other countries, Norway has a graying population. Services for elderly people are based on a Nordic welfare system, with mostly public and tax-based services and little involvement of private firms or voluntary nongovernmental organizations (NGOs). Adult children have no legal obligation to support and take care of elderly parents, even if moral norms and obligations are still strong foundations in family relations. Elderly people prefer and expect public services over help from the family except for minor practical assistance and social support (Daatland & Herlofson, 2004). Most health and social services for elderly people in Norway—except specialized health services—are administered and organized by the municipalities. The principle of local democracy is politically important in Norway and has been given priority over national standardization and equality of level of services. The argument is that people locally know best what services are needed.

An affluent oil-supported economy and immigration have spared Norway from setbacks and drastic cuts in services for older adults, even with a sharp increase in the eldest population during the last years. The Norwegian care system depends on local economy and working markets and political priorities. There are large local variations in the services for older people, and the pictures in the media are dominated by individual stories of neglect of elderly persons and lack of adequate services. What services are provided and what changes are taking place?

Research in gerontology in Norway is set within this context, welfare system, cultural tradition, and legal framework, and this position gives perspectives and reflections for international comparisons.

ELDERLY PEOPLE IN NORWAY AND
THE AGING OF THE POPULATION

Norway has 4.6 million people. In 2005, life expectancy at birth was 82.5 years for women and 77.7 for men (Brunborg, 2006; United Nations, 2005), placing Norway eighth in the countries with highest life expectancy at birth. In the last 30 years, the number of persons 67 years and older has increased to 122,300, with most of the increase occurring among people 80 years and older. The number of people in this age group has increased more than 100% in the last 30 years, from 2.6% of the population to 4.7% in 2006—or from 105,000 in 1976 to 215,000 people in 2006 (Amlo, 2006). Two-thirds of the number of people 80 years and older are women. The youngest portion of the population, 20 years and younger, decreased from 31% to 26% in the same period.

The number of people 80 years and older will be relatively stable until 2020, but afterwards a sharp increase is expected. There are expected to be twice as many people 80 years and older in 2040 as in 2005, an increase from about 213,000 to about 407,000 in 2040.

More than 10,000 full-time workers have been added to the health-care work force in the last four years, but many municipalities are experiencing difficulties in recruiting qualified workers. The relatively stable demographic period until 2020 will give the government and local administrations some time to prepare for the increased need in services (Ministry of Health and Social Care Services, 2006).

In 2005, there were about 66,000 people with dementia in Norway (Eek, 2007; Engedal & Haugen, 2005). This number is expected to increase to 130,000 in 2040, and to 180,000 in 2060—an increase of about 170% from 2005. The increase will represent a great challenge for the Norwegian welfare and care system in terms of financing and staff education.

RESEARCH AND RESEARCH
INSTITUTIONS IN GERONTOLOGY

Gerontological research and education (including both gerontology and geriatrics) in Norway will be presented within an institutional context, since organizational and institutional frames direct and give priorities to research themes, educational obligations, and developments. There are no master's degrees in gerontology at any of the six universities and colleges in Norway. Researchers in social gerontology are still mostly working outside the universities, at research institutes, while geriatrics and health-related research mostly happens at hospitals and medical schools.

Gerontological research in Norway is mostly funded publicly, channeled through Norges forskningsråd (Norwegian Research Council, NFR) and the Ministries. Some health-related projects are funded by the Rehabilitation and Health Fund (Rehabilitering og helse). Private funding is nearly nonexistent. Much social gerontological research has been funded by NFR through its welfare program. Typical research areas in gerontology are family relations, elder services personnel, aging organizations, and how these organizations meet the needs of elderly Norwegians. At the latest Nordic Congress in Gerontology, May 25–28, 2008, in Oslo, 286 papers and posters were presented. Ninety-five of these were research projects done by Norwegian researchers affiliated with Norwegian institutions, and some had national or international collaborators. Most of the medical studies presented at the Congress were based on patient populations, characterizing patients, evaluating diagnostic instruments, describing risk factors, and evaluating treatments. Dementia, stroke, and falls were the dominant themes. There were also many pedagogic, social gerontological, sociological, and psychological studies focusing, among others, on coping, generational relations, social inequality, migration, elderly workers, geographical mobility, and spiritual and existential needs. The topics of gerontology research in Norway are quite varied, but most of them focus on elderly people with health problems—patients and service receivers. Many researchers are newcomers to the field.

Studies of healthy older adults deserve more research attention. The papers presented at the Congress also showed a lack of Nordic comparative research of care systems and services. The greatest gap is in studies that evaluate changes in models, systems, and services for older adults, which in some cases retract the Nordic welfare model (Esping-Andersen, 1990; Szebehely, 2005). Below are selected Norwegian research institutes. This is not a complete list.

NORWEGIAN GERONTOLOGICAL INSTITUTE (NGI) AND NORWEGIAN SOCIAL RESEARCH (NOVA)

The Norwegian Gerontological Institute (NGI) was established in 1957 and was for many years the dominating and expanding center of social gerontological research in Norway. It was both a research center and a coordinating link between gerontological research, care, and services for older adults and the local authorities and the central government. NGI gives advice to organizations and municipalities and educates students and personnel. Eva Beverfelt was the dynamic director until 1994, and she was involved in a wide range of international networks. In 1996, the institute fused with three other institutes or research programs to become a larger social research institute, Norwegian Social Research (NOVA). The Norwegian name for the institute translates as the Norwegian Institute for Research on Youth, Welfare and Aging, with the purpose of carrying out research from birth to old age. It was expected that creating a larger institute would have synergistic effects. NOVA is now established as the central and vital institute for social and welfare research, with a broad and interdisciplinary outlook. Most NOVA researchers are psychologists and sociologists.

Their primary source of data is from the NorLAG study (Life Course, Aging, and Generation). Taking the life-course perspective, it is a large longitudinal study that interviews people every five years. The first wave of the study was done in 2002–2003 with adults aged 55–79 from 30 municipalities in Norway, representing different geographic regions and contexts. The NorLag1 sample contains 3,036 respondents. This is the largest social gerontological study of aging in Norway, covering four main themes: work and retirement, family and generational relations, health and care, and coping and quality of life. The second wave of interviewing is now completed. The NorLAG2 study was coordinated with the large international Gender and Generation study (GGS) and is now called the Life Course, Gender, and Generation study (NorLAG2/LOGG). Altogether 15 countries are cooperating in this international project. The Norwegian study includes people 18–84 years old and is based on a representative sample of about 16,000 people interviewed. Other research themes at NOVA in the last few years have been working life and retirement, migration, informal and formal care, family and generational relations, social contact and loneliness, quality of life, coping, life course and life histories, disability and aging, and social and psychological aging.

CENTER FOR RESEARCH IN THE ELDERLY IN TROMSØ (SAT)

In 1994, Professor Peter F. Hjort, in collaboration with colleagues, formulated a research program in geriatrics and social gerontology for the University of Tromsø—in the northern part of Norway—called Being Old in the Society of the Future. In 1996, the Program for Research on the

Elderly was established in Tromsø. The idea was to establish an interdisciplinary research program and recruit new scientists for gerontological research. The first yearly national conference on older adults took place in 1998. In 1999, Kirsten Thorsen joined the research program as Professor II.

In 2000, the research program was turned into a center called the Center for Research on the Elderly in Tromsø (SAT). The center is now one of Helse Nord's research programs. SAT provides grants for research projects on rehabilitation coordination of services across sectors. While the intention initially was to include both geriatrics and social gerontology and build an interdisciplinary research program that includes medicine, health sciences, and social sciences, Helse Nord has turned the focus onto clinical health research. The projects now receiving grants are mainly in the field of geriatrics.

SAT has supported a number of projects in medicine, biology, psychology, health science, and social science. The research themes have spanned a broad range such as stroke, osteoporosis, dementia, calcium deficiency, and cardiovascular diseases among older adults. Some sociological themes that have been explored include experiences of old age, changing life courses in late modernity, losing one's spouse in old age, and experiences of becoming a retiree.

AGING AND HEALTH: THE NORWEGIAN CENTER FOR RESEARCH, EDUCATION AND SERVICE DEVELOPMENT

The forerunners of the Center were two developmental programs supported by the Ministry of Health, one focusing on dementia (1990–1996) and one focusing on geropsychiatry (1992–1995). The Norwegian Center for Dementia Research was established in 1997, and reorganized in 2007 into the Aging and Health Center, a national center. The main focus areas of the Center's activities are health and dementia, disability and aging—including intellectual disabilities—and geropsychiatry. About 50 researchers and support staff are part of this center.

Disability and Aging (FoA) was established as a program in 1999 to generate more knowledge, disseminate information, and improve services for disabled people who are aging. The focus is on people who became disabled early in life. Aging in People with Intellectual Disabilities (UAU) is a three-year development program that started in 2004 to improve the quality of the services offered to elderly people with intellectual disabilities. Both FoA and UA are now established permanently as units within the Aging and Health Center, along with geropsychiatry. UAU and FoA are the only organized units in Norway that concentrate on aging among people with early disabilities.

Examples of research projects include studies and development of institutions, ways to improve services, social and physical environments for older adults, better diagnosis and technology for people with dementia, and monitoring of the services for this group in the municipalities. Some projects study the use of coercion and restraints, and the legal protection of people with dementia. Studies of disability and aging have, among others, focused on aging among people with physical disabilities such as polio and multiple sclerosis. A project of aging among people with rare diagnoses is just starting up. Several projects have studied aging of people with intellectual disabilities and have also focused on their family relations as they themselves and their parents are reporting it. Many projects are studying how disabled people experience their aging and life situations, the stigma and barriers they encounter in daily life, and their perceived needs for services. Some projects have a life-course perspective and are based on life histories.

HIGHER EDUCATION ON AGING IN NORWAY

Universities and colleges in Norway have special programs in aging at the master's level in several health-related areas. There is an effort now to establish a master's degree in gerontology. Postgraduate education in aging and care for the elderly is offered at several universities. The Norwegian Psychological Association offers specialist programs after graduation (e.g., geropsychology).

The research at universities is dominated by a clinical perspective, with nurses as the main professional group targeted, but other groups are forthcoming, like occupational therapists, physical therapists, and people with education in sports and physical training. The University of Buskerud, in Drammen, has established a master's degree in clinical health with three basic themes: aging and care for the elderly, palliative care, and mental health care, with three professors connected to the gerontological courses, education, and research.

The University of Bergen (UOB) has established a postgraduate program in clinical and developmental psychology. Recruiting and training students and junior faculty members, with a special focus on aging, has been an important task of the Faculty of Psychology for many years. Professor Inger Hilde Nordhus is responsible for the research activities and educational program in gerontology. Geropsychology is an integrated part of the scientific as well as clinical program in the study of psychology. Emphasis is placed on both normal and abnormal processes in aging. In the master's degree program, gerontology may be included in the students' optional courses (e.g., as a thesis project). The Ph.D. program includes an increasing number of students with aging issues as a subject area. The integrated developmental model of the study may have the potential of attracting gerontology students who otherwise would not have considered this area. Psychologists (mental health professionals) should, as at UOB, have aging as an integrated part of their educational program.

Many studies with geriatric themes originated at the geriatric wards at university hospitals, with professors in geriatrics at three universities—the University of Oslo, University of Bergen, and the Norwegian University of Science and Technology in Trondheim. At these universities, researchers are studying many topics, including dementia, stroke, geropsychiatry, medication, and outpatient treatment.

The specialized health services in Norway—hospitals and other health institutions, ambulance services, and rehabilitation centers—are organized into four health regions. They are owned by the State. The government decided in 2008 to establish a new local center for care research in each of the four health regions. One center for care research has already been set up in Gjøvik. The centers are to be related to the local care and health services, especially the nursing homes and home services, and they will study the coordination between services at different organizational levels.

Geriatrics is included in courses for medical students, and gerontology is included in courses for many professional groups, especially in further training of health personnel after their basic education. But research and education in gerontology in Norway is hampered by the lack of gerontological master's degree programs. The most relevant master's degrees at the moment are in health sciences, rehabilitation, and disability. These research milieus will be important centers for further expansion of gerontological education and research in Norway.

SERVICES AND PUBLIC POLICY

Trends and Changes

Norwegian care for the elderly is based on what is called the Nordic welfare model (Esping-Andersen, 1990), characterized by public responsibility and funding and mostly public production of services. In the last few years, there has been a transition of legal and economic responsibility for elderly services (Ministry of Health and Social Care Services, 2006).

- From the state and the counties (19) to the municipalities (431);
- From special services for different groups (e.g., for people with intellectual disabilities) to integrated and general services and legal principles;
- From institutional care to home-based services; and
- From public services to more services provided by private firms.

In the municipalities today, 200,000 people are given social services, 40,000 people live in nursing homes, and more than 160,000 receive services in their private homes. In Norway, the number of places in nursing homes increased between 1994 and 2003. Since then, the number of places in old-age homes has been dramatically reduced, while the number of adapted flats has markedly increased (Szebehely, 2005). An important trend is that the number of younger people receiving social services is increasing rapidly; the number of service users younger than 67 years of age has doubled in the last 10 years. Younger service users are people with intellectual disabilities, mental illness, and illnesses associated with the use of drugs and alcohol. In 2005, about 110,000 full-time workers were working in the care sector, about half of them in nursing homes and the other half providing services in private homes.

Daatland (2006) has characterized the different periods of old-age care in Norway as the *Introduction* (1950–1965), *Expansion* (1965–1980), *Leveling and revision* (1980–1990), and *New design* (1990–) periods. The recent Norwegian strategies in service development to meet the needs of the elderly population employ the concepts of *tailoring*—fitting the services to needs; *targeting*—fitting needs to services; and *tuning*—redesigning responsibilities. Tailoring includes the development of a continuum of care and de-institutionalization of housing; targeting implies lower access to services—services are restricted to people with more disabilities than a few years ago—but higher standards of services are then given; and tuning means decentralization, more market-based services and narrowing down some services (Daatland, 2006).

The Legal Framework

The general Norwegian legal framework relevant to people with disabilities and to older people includes (1) The Act Relating to Social Services (called the Social Services Act); and (2) The Municipal Health Services Act (called the Health Services Act). The purposes of the Social Services Act are to promote financial and social security, to improve the living conditions of disadvantaged persons, to contribute to greater equality of human worth and social status, and to prevent social problems.

In addition, it is supposed to contribute to giving individuals opportunities to live and reside independently and to achieve an active and meaningful existence in community with others. All services included under this law are intended to promote autonomy and independent life for all people, including elders, those with disabilities, and others.

The Health Services Act is designed to provide necessary health services to everyone living permanently or temporarily in the municipality. The services promote health and prevent illnesses and disabilities. The purpose of the Health Services Act is to give services to those who are not able to do necessary self-care, or have to depend on personal assistance to manage the tasks of daily life. All municipalities are obliged to have these specified services:

- Practical assistance to and training of people in need of help because of illness, disability, age, and other reasons;
- Relief care for those with heavy care work. Support contact for people needing it because of disabilities, age or social problems; and
- Institutional care or care in specially built apartments with 24-hour service.

These are general laws, and have no special regulations for elderly people or people with disabilities. These two Acts regulate services to be given *according to needs*, not to special categories of the population. They are regulating the services in the municipalities, where most of the services outside hospitals are given as primary health care and social services.

Specialist health-care services include hospital services such as outpatient clinics, medical specialists, and ambulance services. The four regional health authorities (Helseforetak) governed by the Norwegian State through the Ministry of Health and Social Care Services are, as mentioned, responsible for the specialist health-care services. In January 2001, four new laws regulating psychiatric services, specialist health care, patients' rights, and health professionals' duties were implemented. The state is funding specialist health services at the state level, through the four Health Regions. At the municipal level, health and social services are funded by budgets based on political priorities in the municipalities, resulting in great variations between the municipalities. The municipalities finance most of the services for elderly people and people with disabilities, principally given according to their needs, but also regulated according to the economy of the municipality. For some services, the users must pay user fees. The services given at the municipal level may have different levels of user fees, while user fees in nursing homes are regulated nationally. Nursing services at home are free of charge all over the country, but the user fees for services like home help vary.

Informal caregivers are entitled to apply for caregiver wages, but the municipalities make the decision as to whether their application is approved, and the wages are modest. In 2002, altogether 4,126 people received wages for their care work for adult persons.

It is a challenge that the laws regulating the services for people with disabilities and elderly people in need of help are divided between several laws, with a corresponding split in the organizational system. Another limitation in Norwegian law is that people do not have a legal right to special services; they only have rights to a minimum level of necessary services.

Services

Institutions: The main services for elderly people in need of much assistance are nursing homes and specially built apartments with services. The trend in the last few years has been to deinstitutionalize housing for elders and to build these special apartments. A total of 5–6% of people 65 years and older, and 16–17% of people 80 years and older, are living in nursing homes. The staff-patient ratio is 1.1, and about 95% have single rooms (Daatland, 2006). About 5–6% of elderly people 65 years and older are living in (assisted) sheltered housing, and 5–10% of people aged 80+ live in these settings. Increasingly, nursing homes are reserved for old people with more serious disabilities. About 75–80% of the inhabitants of nursing homes have dementia (Engedal & Haugen, 2005; Selbæk, 2008).

Home-based care: In recent years, services in the municipalities have multiplied and become more varied. These services include home help, home nursing, senior centers, Meals on Wheels, day centers, respite care, short-term care, rehabilitation, personal assistance, and more specialized services like centers for technical equipment. About 15–20% of people 65 years and older, and 30–35% of people aged 80+, have home help and/or home nursing (Daatland, 2006).

User-directed personal assistance (BPA) is a service regulated by law since 2000. It lets the service user hire and direct a personal assistant. All municipalities must provide this service according to the Social Services Act. The service is financed by the municipalities. Only 1,833 people in Norway had personal assistants in 2006. The age of the users is changing over time; more middle-aged and elderly people are now receiving this service (32% of the users are 50–66 years old; 5.9% are 67–79 years; and 1% 80 years and older). BPA is a success, giving people with disabilities more autonomy and independence. Studies of user satisfaction show that people find it to be a very good service.

The municipalities have special *economic support for transportation* for people with disabilities of all ages. But the level of support, the number of trips a person can take by taxi at a low rate, varies greatly. The cost of a taxi trip the person is paying is the same as a ticket for public transportation. The economic support for transportation is given according to needs, to all age groups, but most of the users are elderly people.

Most of the municipalities have voluntarily introduced a *companion certificate* that allows a person accompanying an individual with disabilities free access to arrangements and transportation. Unfortunately, many arrangements do not accept such a certificate.

Individuals can specify his or her service needs, and services are allocated according to a legal process (enkeltvedtak). Decisions are then made to specify the services granted. Individuals have the right to appeal the decisions through an administrative appeal system.

Quality of Services

No minimum standards exist for services in the municipalities, which are given great freedom to set the standards themselves according to political choices and the local economy. Consequently, the standards and quality of the services vary greatly.

As mentioned earlier, the trend in the last few years has been the introduction of private firms in the delivery of services, both in the nursing homes and home-based services. This is only starting and it is happening mostly in the larger cities. The argument has been that elderly people should be allowed to choose between service deliverers. Private firms are allowed to compete for contracts with the municipalities, which specify the quality of the services to be fulfilled. Municipalities and special services regularly carry out surveys of user satisfaction of different services.

The quality of the services is in general regulated by decrees (special regulations) and by circulars. First and foremost, qualities of social services are regulated by the Quality Regulation, which specifies that people receiving care will be given services that respect the individual's way of life. It also specifies several basic human needs the services must fulfill, ranging from basic physiological needs to privacy, autonomy, independence, self-control, social contact, activity, social inclusion, and participation. To retain quality, people have rights to an individualized service plan. One person will be responsible for coordinating the services. In reality, many people still do not have an individualized plan.

Notification from the Parliament: Stortingsmelding 25, 2005–2006, states that the quality of services will be increased through more research, better foundational knowledge, increased status for those working in the health-service sectors, efforts to promote interest in these services among professionals, and supporting better knowledge-based practices.

Advocacy and Participation by the Elderly

Important councils that serve the needs of older Norwegians are the National Council for Senior Citizens and councils at county and municipal levels. The National Council for Senior Citizens is an advisory body for public authorities and national institutions. There are also Councils for Senior Citizens in all counties and municipalities. These councils and other organizations give advice and express opinions and may be consulted in preparing laws, making plans, and implementation. There are also several interest organizations for people with special disabilities/illnesses, and some comprehensive organizations at the municipal, county, and national levels. Norway has a national ombudsman for patients, and some municipalities also have an ombudsman for elderly persons.

Plans

As a result of pressure from different organizations and councils, new action plans and reports to the Parliament have been created, such as: (1) the Action Plan for the Care for the Elderly (1998–2001); (2) the Action Plan for Increased Accessibility for Persons with Disabilities (2004), which is a plan for universal design in key areas of society; (3) the National Health Plan (2007–2010); and (4) the Comprehensive Plan for People with Dementia (2007), which includes models for day care; cooperation between specialist services and services at the level of municipalities regarding diagnostic work; courses and groups for relatives of demented persons; information campaigns about dementia; education programs for personnel without formal education; and the establishment of an interactive databank of experiences in the field. Altogether, the intentions of all these plans are more and better services, accessibility and participation of the elderly population in Norway.

Challenges

Services for elders are often not up to the needed and expected standards. Norway experiences difficulties in recruitment of staff and in maintaining competence and stability of staff in many sectors of services. These problems will become even more acute in the future.

Trends from a Nordic Perspective

In comparison with other Nordic nations, Norway and Denmark have not reduced in-home services as much as Sweden and Finland. In the latter two countries, the number of elderly people with in-home services has been reduced by 50%. New Public Management (NPM) organizational solutions have been introduced in nearly all Swedish, but few Norwegian, municipalities. NPM is gradually transforming the Scandinavian welfare system; this organizational system opens up the market for more private for-profit service providers, with competition between private firms and public services on prices and quality of services. An important difference in Norway when compared to these other Nordic countries is the many small municipalities in Norway, usually too small for profitable market solutions. Informal help seems to replace public help in Sweden, while in Norway they serve as a supplement, not a substitute (Szebehely, 2005).

CONCLUSIONS AND VISIONS

In the near future, until 2020, Norway will probably be able to expand and develop services and care for the elderly, with a working force supplied primarily by immigrant workers. An unexpectedly large number of immigrants in the last few years implies great uncertainty about Norway's demographics in the future. The immigrants are welcomed also as potential workers and carers for the elderly, and they will need special and adapted services when they themselves become old. Research on the needs for services in ethnic minorities is a new field in Norway. Longer lives also imply more people with Alzheimer's and multi-morbidity, and all frail elderly will need individually tailored services and help.

One possible, and probable, scenario will be more market solutions in the sector. The Conservative and Social Democratic parties have different viewpoints and strategies regarding the introduction of market solutions, with the former principally in favor of more competition and more market-driven initiatives. Maybe in the years ahead, Norway will have a larger market for health and social services in which, especially, more affluent people can buy services outside the public system. Norway is a high spender on health and social services, with about 2–3% of GDP spent on aging services in the Nordic countries, compared to medium (1–1.5%; as in UK, Germany, and Brazil) and low spenders (less than 1%, as in Spain and Japan) (Daatland, 2006). Welfare expectations among the population in Norway are quite high. Criticisms and disappointments are flourishing in the media and among the public, in a country that is ranked among the most affluent countries, with the highest quality of life and the lowest unemployment in the world. The gap between expectations and services may widen in the future as the welfare society is pressed to care for its growing elderly population.

This scenario may imply more market-based solutions and more varied services and a welfare society where the traditional Norwegian welfare model may be retracting in content, form and obligations. Families—especially women—may take on more care obligations; technical solutions and IKT e-equipment (information and communication technology; data technology) will make practical tasks easier; and smart houses may make it possible to stay at home longer. Researchers will prepare for better solutions and give suggestions and develop treatments for healthier lives. And luckily, in Norway there are still more than 10 years to prepare, expand, experiment, transform, profit, and reflect on the implications of the very good news: that more people are living much longer than before.

REFERENCES

Amlo, U. K. (2006). Becoming ever more Norwegians. *Samfunnsspeilet*. Retrieved from http://www.ssb.no/samfunnsspeilet/utg/200605/02/index.html

Brunborg, H. (2006). What are the demographic trends in Norway? *Samfunnsspeilet*, *3*, 20–27.

Daatland, S. O. (2006). Long-term care for older people in Norway. Presentation for a delegation from the Chinese Academy of Social Sciences, at NOVA, October 12, Oslo, Norway.

Daatland, S. O., & Herlofson, K. (2004). *Family, welfare state and changes: Family solidarity in a European perspective. NOVA Report 7, 2004.* Oslo: Norsk institutt for forskning om oppvekst, velferd og aldring.

Eek, A. (2007). How to meet the challenges of an increasing number of elderly people? Paper at Conference: Disability and old age, October 2. Arr: Nordiska samarbetsorganet för handicappfrågor, Helsinki.

Engedal, K., & Haugen, P. K. (2005). *Dementia. Facts and challenges*. Oslo: Nasjonalt kompetansesenter for aldersdemens [Aging and health: The Norwegian Centre for Research, Education and Service Development].

Esping-Andersen, G. (1990). *The three worlds of welfare capitalism*. Cambridge: Polity Press.

Ministry of Health and Social Care Services (2006). Notification from the Parliament: St.meld. nr. 25. (2005–2006). *Mastering, possibilities and meaning: Challenges for care in the future*.

Selbæk, G. (2008). *Behavioural and psychological symptoms of dementia in Norwegian nursing homes—Prevalence, course and association with psychotropic drug use.* Doctoral dissertation, Faculty of Medicine, University of Oslo, Oslo.

Szebehely, M. (2005). Care for the elderly in the Nordic countries; services, research and statistics. In M. Szebehely, *Research in the Nordic countries on care for the elderly: A review* (pp. 21–51). TemaNord: 508. København: Nordiska minsterrådet.

Thorsen, K. (2007). Norway: Ageing of people with disabilities and older people with disabilities. In *Report from European Council. Committee of Experts on ageing of people with disabilities and older people with disabilities (P-RR-VPH).* Strasbourg.

United Nations. (2005). *World population prospects.* Retrieved June 16, 2009, from http://esa.un.org/unpp/

36

Pakistan

Ra'ana Mahmood

In the course of its history, Pakistan traditionally enjoyed a joint family system, particularly in its rural areas, which house more than 70% of its population. Parents and grandparents were regarded as the heads of the family, which would accommodate six or seven brothers and their interwoven families, who unhesitatingly obeyed the commands of the head. Those were the sunshine days of the elders who not only exercised their authority, but also commanded respect. Their wisdom was considered an asset for the entire family. Their decision-making went beyond financial authority.

Life expectancy during the last 50–60 years ranged from 32 to 35 years and an average family consisted of 6–8 children. The elders distributed the family resources evenly and ensured simple living within their means. Life was also simple in most parts of Pakistan, as people preferred to walk or cycle to work. In that traditional society, people practiced religion, lived a simple life—which was basically confined to the essentials—and did not make special efforts to educate their children. As heads of the family, parents or grandparents stressed moral education and had a lot of time to share their love with their children and grandchildren. Society had a high degree of congeniality and harmony.

However, it was evident that lack of education and proper health care was affecting the society, which had a modest human development index and low level of life expectancy. Economic incentives and greater regard for modern health-care facilities as well as standard of living brought about a paradigm shift in attitudes. Due to globalization and access to media, people, especially younger people, started following new trends set by developed countries solely to pursue economic prosperity at the expense of the traditional strengths of their society in the domains of social, cultural, and Islamic values, as well as their traditions. This sudden and chaotic shift has affected society in a variety of ways, and most critically in the domain of our values and family structure.

This transition toward economic and social independence created a trend in which nuclear families and the joint family system suffered disintegration. The benefits of the nuclear family notwithstanding, the transition from the traditional style has affected the older generations badly. They are finding themselves lost in an ocean of confusion in a rudderless ship in which they have been left to fend for themselves, while previously they were the ones who would make all vital decisions for the family. This situation has brought about phenomenal problems for them, ranging from loneliness to depression resulting from their state of mind: they lost an empire in which they were the ones on the throne. Now they are suddenly fishing for support and financial means. Being a developing country, Pakistan does not cater to the requirements of its elders and, thus, their problems have been confounded. Women are the worst sufferers in this situation. They find themselves shelterless and incapable of taking care of themselves, particularly if their spouses die before them. They face both physical and mental abuse. Most of them experience emotional and psychological humiliation. This may be the result of poverty, but the most obvious reason is illiteracy and ignorance in a society that was not ready for this transition. Lack of education deprives societies of the real values and importance of the elderly. Older women are more likely to be poorer than older men, because they are already financially weak and dependent, in most cases.

Since marriage of the children and providing education are accepted as the major responsibilities of parents, they are left with hardly anything, after having fulfilled these obligations. Subsequently, they find themselves in greater misery. Once the children become preoccupied with their practical lives, they become less conscious of their obligations toward their parents and elders. Consequently, the elderly feel left out. They are deprived of the basic amenities in life. From the exalted status of decision-makers of the family, they are left to struggle for their survival. At this stage, they feel the deprivations brought about by old age.

As the concept of nuclear family gains currency, the miseries of the older population grow. Now they are becoming excessively lonely and depressed. The values of respect for the elderly population are fast diminishing. In many cases, if the son favors the joint family system, the daughter-in-law speaks out against it.

Elderly people are finding it difficult to be a part of the nuclear family system, in which they can exercise authority and enjoy respect. Even when neither husband nor wife has time for their children, they tend not to want to utilize the help of their elders in taking care of their children. Because they grow up away from their elders, the children do not develop that much love for their elders.

Several other factors contribute to the growing isolation of elderly people. These include the following:

- Migration of young persons to countries abroad for higher education and jobs;
- The increasing trend of urbanization; and
- Poverty and joblessness drives people to seek jobs in far off places, leaving their ancestral homes and their elders.

It is a misconception that elders in Pakistan enjoy a lot of respect in society. In actuality, they get only lip service, because they usually live a miserable life without financial and emotional support. Even the traditional concept of reverence for them is undergoing change.

In urban areas, the elderly have adjusted to the changing social values and are making an extra effort to pay attention to their health and livelihood. Elderly people in rural areas face a more difficult and painful situation. Because of illiteracy, they can't take care of their health, and due to poverty, they can't afford health care. As a result of urbanization, they are also left alone without any formal support system.

RESEARCH ON AGING

Lack of research on this subject is essentially due to two main reasons: there is little research in any field, and Pakistan is far behind in research compared to the developed countries, and unfortunately, nobody is interested in the issues of aging. There is little effort to provide desired facilities for the older population. Although general research has been gaining currency recently, there is still not much progress in gerontology. No major initiatives have been undertaken by the government, although awareness is increasing. The estimated population of Pakistan today is around 165 million, and those over the age of 60 number about 15 million (about 9%).

About 60% of elderly males in urban and rural areas are in the labor force, and most continue to work till their death because of poverty. The theoretical retirement age is 60, but most do not want to retire because of their economic situation. However, many are forced to retire.

According to United Nations estimates, in 2002, the percentage of people aged 60 and over was 5.8%; this will rise to 7.3% by 2025 and 12.4% in 2050. The recommendations of the Vienna and Madrid International Conferences on aging are not reflected in the provision of facilities for elders by the Pakistani Government. Based on a research and survey conducted by the Geriatric Care Foundation in Pakistan, 4.5% of male elders are never married, 78% are married, 17% are widowed, and 0.3% are divorced. The survey also found that 5.4% of female elders are never married and only 48.8% are married. The ratio of widowed female elders is very high compared to male elders: 45.2% of female elders are widowed. Less than 1% of female elders are divorced. This survey shows that many older females are living alone and most likely in impoverished conditions. Women are the physically weaker sex, and thus become vulnerable as targets of violence. The threat of physical torture and violence keeps them under tremendous pressure and serves to make them humble and subservient.

Depression, loneliness, and financial dependency, coupled with harassment of different sorts, become factors that accompany them into old age. With these general factors encompassing the lives of women in Pakistan, we might now look at the specific aspects of their lives in rural and urban settings. Some women face sexual harassment at work at some stage. These women, and other victims of rape and gang rape, develop depression and other physical and psychological problems. Sisters-in-law consider them a burden, and after the death of their parents, they live in absolute poverty in old age.

The surveys show that the proportion of lonely women is increasing day by day. There are many reasons for this; for example, because of the demand of an expensive dowry by the bridegroom, girls who belong to poor families are unable to get married. Similarly, those who are not so pretty cannot get married. In some cases, girls make a sacrifice to look after their sick parents or the younger siblings. With the passage of time, when they become old, nobody looks after them.

Social ills have many other dimensions in Pakistani society; some rural areas with little education do apply pressure on women, forcing young girls to marry older men. Sometimes girls as young as eight or nine years of age are forced to marry men several times their age (80 or 90 years old). Most of the time, the men are wealthy and influential, and have other wives and several children. After the death of the old husband, the previous wives and their grown-up male children throw the young stepmother out, and she enters old age in poverty.

Our survey shows that the life expectancy of females is higher than that of males, so women are often left alone in their old age. The reasons for loneliness among females are many because they are expected to stay confined to their homes and are not supposed to remarry, even if they are in good health. Even affluent people live lonely lives in big houses, if their children live separately in the same city or live abroad.

EDUCATION IN GERONTOLOGY

There is little awareness at the government level, or even at the academic level, of the need for education in gerontology. There is little awareness of how important such education is, and how helpful it is in properly diagnosing the health and other issues facing the older persons. There is not a single medical college in which geriatrics or gerontology is included in the syllabus and curriculum.

The Geriatric Care Foundation approached representatives of the government in various ministries to try to convince them of the desirability of making geriatrics and gerontology a part of the curriculum. But that has not produced results, although those representatives had agreed to do so. They affirmed the need for specific attention to social and health issues of the older population, but have failed to take practical steps.

Some diseases afflict older adults due to only minor lapses in hygiene. This could be avoided through better understanding of hygiene related to health. There are others in the field, including some in government positions, who stubbornly refuse to accept the importance of gerontology. They insist that in a developing country like Pakistan, which has limited financial resources, one cannot afford to go into "hyper-technical details about diseases." This is absurd because such a shift in focus on diseases does not require huge expenditures. They need to focus on the specific needs and specific medical care requirements concerning older adults, because specific diseases and issues, as well as signs and symptoms, change with age. If doctors don't understand the importance of including gerontology in the syllabus of medical colleges, how could others understand the importance of such an education?

Paramedical staff are also not trained in taking care of elders, and most elderly patients die because of misdiagnoses by doctors and mishandling by paramedical staff. There is neither geriatric ward nor nursing home for elders in any government hospital, but currently some private hospitals are planning to establish geriatric wards in their hospitals.

A National Expert Committee for Aging was established by the Ministry of Social Welfare and Special Education in 2002, and several experts, including the President of the Geriatric Foundation of Pakistan, were appointed as members to deliberate on the current status and suggest ways and means to bring about a paradigm shift in working for the well-being and welfare of the elderly population. However, it appears that the government wanted to pay only lip service to the matter, because only one meeting was convened and the recommendations made in that meeting were disregarded. All members had recommended that geriatrics should be included in the medical curriculum, and geriatric wards should be established in government hospitals, but six years have passed and nothing has been done so far. Even the host ministry does not know about the fate of the committee or of its recommendations.

In Pakistan, arthritis, hypertension, diabetes and its complications, heart diseases, stroke, depression, insomnia, and gastric ulcers are the most common diseases among elderly people. People are not used to consulting a doctor to get advice. Only a small percentage of people are aware of this need. There are very few people who are health conscious and have adopted healthy habits.

In old age, parents consider themselves a burden on their children and become reluctant to demand that they need medical attention and should be taken to a doctor or have medicine prescribed for them. They continue to function under a dilemma as to how dependent they might be on their children or whether they should preserve a façade of independence and not demand any favor involving financial spending. There have also been instances in which children abandoned their parents when they needed care and financial support due to a serious illness. Edhi Homes for the Homeless have confirmed that many children leave their parents at the homes because they cannot take care of their parents. It is a fact that there are serious breaches in the traditional family structure and society has undergone a radical shift from the essentials of the joint family system. Now individuals are more concerned about their personal welfare and self-fulfillment. Even young people who study gerontology abroad refuse to come back to their native land to take care of their ailing and elderly parents. If they come back to their native land to elderly patients, they soon realize that there is no role for geriatricians.

Even the pharmaceutical companies do not find it cost effective to produce medicines for geriatric care on a large scale, because they are not often purchased by the children, for financial reasons.

The government also has not been playing its role and functions well. It has not introduced any scheme or plan, such as Medicare or Medicaid, like those in developed countries. Only a small number of people who retire from a government or semi-government job receive medical treatment along with their pension. The rest of the persons retired from private jobs do not receive any kind of medical support and pension. Consequently, their medical, social, and economic problems increase after retirement. The majority of people in Pakistan are small businessmen, farmers, or laborers who continue to work with no retirement age. They face difficulties financially and with medical treatment in their old age. Elderly people feel left out of family matters and feel dependent, which causes depression. In Pakistani research and surveys, psychological problems and tendency to commit suicide are increasing among lonely older adults. Hospitals cannot cater to the large number of elderly patients who queue up for treatment. Most of them require hospitalization, which is not possible due to the scarcity of resources and facilities. Therefore they die in despair. Those who can afford the expensive medical attention are the few lucky ones.

In rural areas, the situation is worse than in urban areas. Access to a physician is impossible; there is no concept of hospitals. There are small government dispensaries, where most of the time a doctor is not available. Paramedical staff, who are not competent to treat them, often make things worse for them. Medical equipment, oxygen cylinders, and life-saving medicines are missing, because the staff embezzles them. Quacks usually misguide the patients. The most common example of such misguidance is a quack insisting that diabetic patients can eat plenty of sugar, with their fake medicine. Patients develop complications and eventually die, but relatives consider it "the will of God."

Due to illiteracy and lack of awareness, most elderly people become handicapped due to diseases that are easily curable; for example, cataracts in their eyes. They spend their life in blindness, rather than getting cured through easy surgery.

POLICY ISSUES

The issues facing the elderly are not a priority of the government, which does not pay serious attention to the need to frame policies for the welfare and benefit of elders. Nothing has been done so far to implement the United Nations Millennium Development Goals, which are supposed to be binding on all governments, as spelled out in resolutions of the UN General Assembly regarding the well-being of elderly citizens. Similarly, the recommendations of the Vienna and Madrid International Conferences on Aging are not reflected in the policy documents. In 1972, there was a Bill passed for the welfare of senior citizens, but it has still not been implemented. In 2002, the National Expert Committee for Aging was established and the Geriatric Care Foundation, as a pioneer in the field, was also requested to associate with it for the benefit of the elderly population, but nothing has been done so far.

In response to an initiative by NGOs in 2006, the government deliberated the matter and finally conveyed a bill titled Senior Citizens' Welfare Bill to the National Assembly for Legislation. After three years, the bill is still being vetted by the National Assembly's standing committee.

In 1998, the ex-Prime Minister, Mr. Mohammad Nawaz Sharif, took an initiative and called eminent senior citizens in Islamabad and announced some benefits for them; for example, some token pension after retirement, concession in airfare and railways, concession in utility bills, provision of shelters in old-age homes and free medical facilities. However, that was a dream too good to be true, because the government of Nawaz Sharif was toppled by Pervez Musharraf and the groundwork simply evaporated.

On 6 February 2008, a National Conference on Aging was held in Islamabad with the collaboration of the Ministry of Social Welfare, United Nations, and the University of Gujrat. The Vice-Chancellor of Gujrat University, Dr. Nizamudin, was able to organize a successful event and ensured the participation of many experts and concerned people. It made very far-reaching recommendations. However, those are still to materialize, because the resource constraints do not allow even step one to take place.

SUPPORTIVE SCHEMES FOR THE ELDERLY

Following are some of the most important schemes launched by the government to benefit the elderly population: the Employees' Old Age Benefit Scheme, Pakistan Baitul Maal, the Zakat System, the National Saving Scheme, and so on. However, there are major problems with implementing these schemes, and public awareness, along with special measures by the government, may help to make them succeed.

In conclusion, it can be safely said that the situation of elders in Pakistan is becoming worse because the social practices that favored them are being replaced by those that do not safeguard their interests, and no system is ready to provide a cushion to allow them to live their lives with at least a bare minimum of resources. Our society, unfortunately, is not ready or willing to do something about their plight. As a result, a sizeable segment of Pakistan's population is deprived of its basic human rights.

REFERENCES

Geriatric Care Foundation. (2005). *Geriatric survey*. Karachi, Pakistan: Author.

UN Population Division. (2007). *World population prospects: The 2006 Revision Population Database*. New York: United Nations.

37

·· ■ ··

The Philippines

Grace Trinidad-Cruz and Anna Melissa C. Lavares

AGING IN THE PHILIPPINES

The Philippines, like many countries in Asia, has yet to experience significant aging. The 2000 census counted a total of 4.6 million older Filipinos (defined as those aged 60 years and over), comprising 6% of the country's population. The slow tempo of aging in the country can be attributed largely to its young population structure. But while the number of aged population may be relatively low, the aging of the population is expected to assume prominence in the future, to reach over 10 million in 2020 under a moderate fertility and mortality decline assumption (National Statistics Office, 1997). This future scenario is likewise suggested by the fast rate of growth of the older population sector, which is the fastest-growing population sector in the country today. The older population growth rate from 1995 to 2000 is 4.6% and is projected to maintain its high growth momentum, even with the deceleration in the overall population growth rate.

The increasing longevity has contributed in part to the aging of the country's population. Large strides have been achieved in extending life expectancy, with females expecting to live 72.7 years at birth and males, 66.9 years. This represents about 10 years' gain from their counterparts in the 1970s. As the probability of reaching old age has increased, so has the chance of survival among those who reached old age. Gender differentials also show that older females have a greater chance of growing much older than males. In 1995, a woman who survived to age 60 could expect to live 19.3 more years on the average, and the average male, 16.8 years. Older females also gained years more rapidly than males between 1970 and 1995 (2.2 and 0.5 years, respectively).

While Filipino women outlive males, females can expect to live a greater part of their remaining life in a state of functional impairment (Cruz, 2005; Cruz, Saito & Natividad, 2007; Ofstedal, Zimmer, Cruz, Chan, & Chuang, 2004). Because males experience higher mortality rates in almost all age groups, they can anticipate a truncated life expectancy, although the period lived in impairment is relatively compressed compared to the females. Such gender differentials imply that while Filipina elders have experienced greater longevity gains, longer life does not necessarily mean better health for them.

PHILIPPINE AGING STUDIES

Reflective of its demographic stage of development, aging research in the country is still at its infancy stage. Up to about the early 1980s, data on older people were taken mostly from the census and, to a certain extent, from government agencies that serve older people (Domingo & Feranil, 1990). The scarcity of data was slowly addressed with the conduct of studies and surveys such as the pioneering Socioeconomic Consequences of the Aging of the Population (SECAP) project implemented by the Demographic Research and Development Foundation (DRDF) in 1984. The project, jointly funded by the Australian Government and the Commission on Population, was an exploratory study of 1,321 persons aged 60 and above in six survey sites in the country.

It was not until 1996 that the first nationally representative sample survey of older people, the 1996 Philippine Elderly Survey (PES), was conducted. The study was part of the Comparative Study of Elderly in Four Asian Countries, which included the Philippines, Singapore, Taiwan, and Thailand, and was coordinated by the University of Michigan. The study of 2,285 respondents aged 50 years and over was designed to investigate how rapid demographic change in these societies has affected the elderly. Population Research areas explored covered a wide range of social and health issues, including health and health-seeking behavior of older people, exchanges of support, living arrangements, and work and economic status of older people, among others.

A subsample of the 1996 PES was followed up in 2000, which was the first attempt to gather panel data on older people in the country. This study was a trailblazing methodological attempt in aging research in the Philippines and was conducted primarily to explore the feasibility of employing a panel study design in understanding the conditions of older people (Natividad & Cruz, 2002). The availability of panel data, albeit at a subnational level, pushed the aging research frontiers to emerging methodologies and concepts, including active life expectancy (ALE) and life transition patterns of older people (Cruz et al., 2007).

The research momentum on ALE is expected to continue with the recent collection of data for the first nationally representative panel study on aging in 2007. The Philippine Longitudinal Study of Aging (PLSOA), covering a sample of 3,105 respondents aged 60 and over, is a collaborative effort between the University of the Philippines Population Institute (UPPI) and the Nihon University Population Research Institute (NUPRI). The study covers a broader health framework that includes areas that have not been explored by previous studies, such as oral health, anthropometric measures, and vignettes, among others.

Research projects have also been conducted by the National Institutes of Health (NIH) of the University of the Philippines. In 2000, NIH Clinical Institute of Epidemiology and the Department of Health (DOH) conducted the Baseline Surveys for the National Objectives on Health (BSNOH), covering over 2,400 older persons nationwide. Besides examining sociodemographic, environmental, and living arrangements, the study also examined common morbidities, nutrition, and health services for older people. The study surveyed hospitals, primarily government hospitals, to assess their readiness to address the health needs of older persons.

More recent research conducted by the NIH and the Philippine Society of Geriatric Medicine has focused on improving elders' quality of life, emphasizing disease prevention, total well-being, community-based care, and geriatric education (dela Vega, 2006). In particular, studies have focused on physical health of older people, including heart diseases, diabetes, osteoporosis, pain and cancer, among others.

There are other aging studies at the subnational or local levels, among which is the Cebu Longitudinal Health and Nutrition Study (CLHNS), conducted by the University of San Carlos Office of Population Studies in collaboration with Duke University in the United States. Current research based on CLNHS data includes studies examining the effect of chronic diet patterns on cognitive, physical, and functional limitation associated with aging (Borja & Adair, forthcoming). Indeed, while aging research is a relatively new area of study in the country, there has been a significant amount of interest and collaboration in the field in recent years.

CURRENT STATE OF EDUCATION
IN GERONTOLOGY AND GERIATRICS

Despite the existence of several mandates for geriatric education and training, there is still a lack of trained geriatric health professionals in the Philippines (dela Vega, 2007). Only four medical schools offer geriatric content in their curriculum. These are the University of the Philippines Manila, St. Luke's College of Medicine, University of Santo Tomas, and Cebu Doctors' University College of Medicine (dela Vega, 2007). In these medical schools, geriatrics is seldom offered as a separate course, although it is integrated into various courses, usually under the Department of Internal Medicine or Department of Family Medicine.

The University of the Philippines Manila (UPM), the lead agency in the institutionalization of geriatric training, offers lectures on geriatrics in the departments of Internal Medicine, Family and Community Medicine, Adult Medicine, and Pharmacology, to name a few. Lectures cover topics such as physical and psychosocial development during aging, care of aging patients, and geriatric pharmacology, among others. Students undergoing clerkship may be assigned to the University of the Philippines-Philippine General Hospital (UP-PGH) Geriatric Clinic.

St. Luke's Medical Center offers the only geriatric fellowship program in the country. The program is a two-year hospital training program for internists and family medicine practitioners. A specialty board was created to certify graduates of the program as geriatric specialists. To date, about 30 fellows have graduated from the program, and most have been certified as geriatricians.

The Cebu Doctor's University College of Medicine (CDU-CM) in the Visayas region offers modules on physiology of aging, elderly maltreatment and geriatric syndromes, with special topics focusing on geriatrics, hospice care, counseling, and death and dying. Three geriatricians work as faculty members in CDU-CM. Other universities in the Visayas region, namely Southwestern University and University of the Visayas, have also been incorporating instruction into geriatric medicine since 2004. The inclusion of a Care for the Elderly module in caregivers' schools in Visayas has improved clinical skills among health workers (Ponce, 2006).

In the University of Santo Tomas (UST) College of Medicine, lectures on physiology of aging and geriatric pharmacology are integrated into the first- and second-year curriculum. Sessions on preventive geriatrics and comprehensive geriatric assessment are included in the Department of Preventive Family and Community Medicine curriculum. Geriatrics is also incorporated as a topic in the clerkship elective.

The Bachelor of Science in Nursing curriculum in the country also shows limitations in the training of nurses on the care of older persons (Balabagno & Manahan, 2006). Only the UP Manila College of Nursing offers a three-unit course on the care of older persons at the pre-service level. While non-formal, short-term courses on the care of older persons have been increasing, a more structured and organized program for nurses is still needed.

Other organizations and committees in the country offer courses on geriatrics to promote a better understanding of the conditions of older Filipinos. The Philippine Society of Geriatric Medicine (PSGM), composed of internists, family medicine practitioners, and other physicians and allied health professionals, organizes annual conventions and educational lay forums for those who want to gain knowledge and skills in the care of older patients. They also conduct outreach programs for physicians in the provinces, which update health workers in the field of geriatric medicine.

The Committee on Aging and Degenerative Diseases (COMADD) of the NIH conducts research and continuing education of medical students, allied medical professionals, family members, and physicians specifically involved in the care of older persons. COMADD has undertaken nine successful postgraduate courses in geriatric medicine for physicians, nurses, and allied medical professionals since 1997.

COMADD and PSGM conducted policy-making and geriatric evidence-based medicine workshops, which resulted in policy statements for geriatric education, long-term care and PhilHealth (the national health insurance plan) reimbursement. A direct result of the policy statement on education was the release by President Gloria Macapagal-Arroyo of 1 million pesos to the University of the Philippines Manila-SHS Palo Leyte for the incorporation of geriatrics into its ladderized curriculum (Committee on Aging and Degenerative Diseases Study Group, 2007).

The Philippine College of Gerontology and Geriatrics (PCGG) has 142 active members who are diplomates and fellows of the organization. PCGG offers modules on basic geriatrics, clinical geriatrics, and applied geriatrics. Two hundred individuals have finished the program and those who passed the specialty board examination earned the title of diplomate. There is also a two-year fellowship program in a hospital accredited by the PCGG, after which the trainee is eligible to take the specialty board exam in geriatrics.

While only a few tertiary hospitals have geriatric services, these geriatric clinics or centers also contribute to educating and training health professionals and lay people on issues in geriatric medicine. These include the Philippine General Hospital Geriatric Outpatient Clinic, the first and only government-run geriatric clinic, and other private geriatric centers such as St. Luke's Geriatric Center, the Medical City Center for Healthy Aging, and the Manila Doctors' Hospital geriatric multidisciplinary clinic.

Evidently, the Philippines has a long way to go in the institutionalization of geriatric medicine in formal medical education. This is largely due to three factors: (1) the persistent misconception of geriatric medicine as merely an extension of internal medicine or family medicine; (2) the lack of trained faculty in geriatrics; and (3) the fact that geriatrics is not yet a widely recognized subspecialty and is not as "glamorous" as other fields (Gatchalian & Ramos, 1993; Ramos, 2001). Perhaps it may also be due to the young population structure of the Philippines, which tends to draw attention away from the elderly population.

Gerontology education in the country is even more limited than geriatric education. Some universities offer courses and electives on gerontology, mostly at the graduate level, within their psychology or sociology departments. The Sociology Department at the University of the Philippines Diliman, for example, occasionally offers an elective on Sociology of Aging, while the graduate students of the Psychology Department are required to take a course that deals with issues of mid-life and later life. UPPI also includes aging as a topic in its Emerging Issues in Population and Theory and Methods of Demography courses. In 2008, the Miriam College Department of Psychology launched a 10-day certificate program on the fundamentals of gerontology. Topics include economics for older Filipinos, social-interpersonal issues of the elderly population, geriatrics, caring for the older adults, and retirement issues, among others.

PUBLIC POLICY ISSUES IN AGING

A legal framework ensures that older Filipinos receive due care from the family and the state. The Philippine Constitution mandates the state to adopt a comprehensive approach to health development that gives priority to the needs of the elderly population (Article XIII, Section 2 on Health/Social Services). It likewise stipulates that the Filipino family has a duty to take care of its older members, while the State may design a program of social security for them (Article XV, Section 4 on the Filipino Family).

Accordingly, significant state efforts have been exerted to advance the welfare of the elderly in the country, most of which have centered on the need to provide health care in the form of curative services. Worth mentioning are two major legislative milestones: Republic Act (RA) 7432 and Republic Act (RA) 7876. RA 7432 (the Senior Citizens' Act) is "An Act to Maximize the Contribution of Senior Citizens to Nation Building, Grant Benefits and Special Privileges and for Other Purposes." The most significant provision in this Act has been the grant of a 20% discount on medicines for older people, age 60 and over—regardless of socioeconomic status. A supplementary law to the Senior Citizens' Act, RA 9257 (the Expanded Senior Citizens' Act of 2003), expands the coverage of the benefits and privileges for senior citizens.

By virtue of RA 9257, an Inter-Agency Committee was formed to develop the Philippine Plan of Action for Senior Citizens for 2006–2010. This Plan includes strategies, programs, projects, and activities that will contribute to the attainment of the action plans for older persons outlined in the Medium-Term Philippine Development Plan, 2004–2010 (Taradji, 2007).

Republic Act 7876, entitled "An Act Establishing a Senior Citizens' Center in all the Cities and Municipalities of the Philippines, and Appropriating Funds Therefore," provides for the establishment of senior citizens' centers to cater to older persons' socialization and interaction needs, as well as to serve as the venue for conducting other meaningful activities.

Other statutes and legislation in support of older people's welfare include Republic Act 344, or the Accessibility Law of 1982, which provides for the minimum requirements and standards to make buildings, facilities, and utilities for public use accessible to persons with disability, including older persons who are confined to wheelchairs and those who have difficulty in walking or climbing stairs, among others (Taradji, 2007). The General Appropriations Act of 2006 under Section 32 also mandates that all government agencies and instrumentalities should allocate 1% of their total agency budget to programs and projects for older persons and persons with disability (Taradji, 2007).

Also worth noting is PhilHealth's effort to provide for social health insurance that endeavors to deliver accessible quality health care to all Filipinos. All these speak well of the continuing effort of the government to integrate the welfare of older persons into the development agenda.

Promulgation of laws and action plans do not necessarily guarantee a perceptible alleviation of the older person's welfare. The low government priority given to the older sector of the population has resulted in inadequacies in the implementation of laws, which has affected the medical and dental service access for older people. The very young population structure of the country has also affected the distribution of resources, as indicated by the health infrastructure, which is generally oriented toward infectious diseases and maternal and child health, making it less equipped to handle the health requirements of older people (Hermalin, 2002).

Deficiencies in government support for the older sector have passed the burden of care for elders mainly on to the Filipino family. While Filipinos generally are known for their strong filial obligation, their efforts to assume caregiving roles are far from sufficient and may be further undermined by changing family structure brought about by migration, including rural-urban and overseas labor migration. It is a common fact that a number of older people have been abandoned and/or left to the care of institutions. The growing number of aging homes/hospices managed by government, NGOs, religious groups, and even the private sector attests to some gaps in the safety net of old-age support that has traditionally been assumed as the exclusive domain of the family. Poverty is another factor that may get in the way of the family's ability to care for the elderly. This is particularly salient in the context of a high-poverty situation, with estimates showing 26.9% of Filipino families living in poverty (National Statistical Coordination Board, 2006). Poverty can erode the middle generation's capacity to provide economic assistance for the older generation. Furthermore, this economic situation and the need to provide for the basic needs of the family force older members to continue working despite their age and health status.

Although the family continues to assume a predominant caregiving role for their elderly members, as mandated by the Constitution, signs of family stress call attention to the need for greater government support and intervention to respond to the complex needs of the older population.

REFERENCES

Balabagno, A., & Manahan, L. (2006). Care of the older person: Implication to nursing education and practice. In dela Vega, S. (Ed.), *Maximizing the quality of life of the elderly through better health* (pp. 31–36). Manila: National Academy of Science and Technology.

Borja, J., & Adair, L. (Forthcoming). *Chronic diet patterns that influence cognitive, physical and functional limitation associated with aging: Results from the Cebu Longitudinal Health and Nutrition Study.* Paper presented at the 20th REVES Conference, Pasig City, Philippines.

Committee on Aging and Degenerative Diseases Study Group. (2007). Unpublished report.

Cruz, G. (2005). Health transitions among Filipino older people. Unpublished doctoral dissertation, University of the Philippines.

Cruz, G., Saito, Y., & Natividad, J. (2007). Active life expectancy and functional health transition among Filipino older people. *Canadian Studies in Population, 34,* 29–47.

dela Vega, S. (Ed.). (2006). *Maximizing the quality of life of the elderly through better health.* Manila: National Academy of Science and Technology.

dela Vega, S. (2007). President's report. *Philippine Society of Geriatric Medicine Newsletter,* p. 1.

Domingo, L., & Feranil, I. (1990). *Socio-economic consequences of the aging population: Insights from the Philippine experience.* Quezon City, Philippines: Demographic Research and Development Foundation.

Gatchalian, E., & Ramos, M. (1993). Geriatric medicine in the Philippines: Its problems, challenges and future directions. *Philippine Journal of Internal Medicine, 31,* 223–231.

Hermalin, A. I. (2002). *The well-being of the elderly in Asia: A four-country comparative study.* Ann Arbor, Michigan: University of Michigan Press.

National Statistical Coordination Board. (2006). *2006 official poverty statistics.* Retrieved April 28, 2008, from http://www.nscb.gov.ph/poverty/2006_05mar08/tables.asp

National Statistics Office. (1997). *1995 census-based national and regional population projections* (Vol. 1). Manila: Author.

Natividad, J., & Cruz, G. (2002). *A feasibility study on the use of the panel design for the study of the elderly and the course of aging in the Philippines: The Visayan sample.* Report submitted to the Center for Integrated Development Studies, University of the Philippines, Diliman.

Ofstedal, M. B., Zimmer, Z., Cruz, G., Chan, A., & Chuang, Y. L. (2004). Self-assessed health expectancy among older adults: A comparison of six Asian settings. *Hallym International Journal of Aging, 6*(2), 95–117

Ponce, N. (2006). Geriatric medicine in Cebu. *Philippine Society of Geriatric Medicine Newsletter* (August–October), p. 2.

Ramos, M. (2001). Geriatrics in medical education in the Philippines: A necessity or nice idea. *Philippine Journal of Internal Medicine, 39.*

Taradji, P. (2007). *Philippine country report.* Paper presented at the High-Level Meeting on the Regional Review of the Madrid International Plan of Action on Ageing, October 9–11. Macao, China.

38

▪

Romania

Luiza Spiru and Ileana Turcu

RECENT HISTORY

Scientific concerns about aging are long-standing in Romania (Representative Figures of Romanian Science and Technology, 2004). An intense polemic regarding aging mechanisms and the anti-aging fight, with the neurologist Gheorghe Marinescu and the biologist and immunologist Ilia Metchnikov as protagonists, evolved in the early 1900s. Later, the remarkable endocrinologist, neurologist, and psychiatrist C. I. Parhon pointed out in his book, *Aging and its Treatment*, published in 1948, that aging is a pathological state, meaning that far from being a fatalistic degradation of body and mind during late life, aging could be delayed and even counteracted. Parhon used his scientific and political prestige to support Ana Aslan's creation of the first worldwide Institute of Geriatrics in 1952, which was recommended as a model in 1964 by WHO (Poli, 1997). The main contributions of Ana Aslan's life work, and of the school she created, are the holistic attempt at aging research (from basic, clinical, and social perspectives); the creation of the first, original drug to delay aging processes and to exert geriatric actions—Gerovital H3 (and, in 1970, Aslavital); and the Aslan Method—a set of rules for their administration, but always adapted to the patient's biomedical particularities (in modern terms, a personalized therapeutic attempt). In 1958, the new concept of social gerontology was advanced by the creation of the Social Gerontology department within the Institute of Geriatrics at Bucharest, in order to investigate the impact of social factors on aging, and to evaluate the adaptive capacities of the aging body facing ever-changing social demands. This new department was also entrusted with the gathering of medico-social, economic, psychological, demographic, and cultural data to develop suitable social politics for the third-age population. The actual notions of aging delay and aging-related pathology prevention were also attempted by Ana Aslan and her school. Her aging prophylaxis concept was put into practice within a national network comprising 144 centers for monitoring people, beginning at 40–45 years of age, distributed in urban and rural areas, and 76 centers designed for geriatric and social assistance. The outcomes of this multidisciplinary endeavor—including a study on longevity, an intergenerational study regarding the social image of the elderly population, and a study on the demographics of aging—were background for the National Program for Medico-Social Assistance of Elderly People in Romania, developed in 1997. Ana Aslan is one of the first scientists worldwide who seized upon the population aging phenomenon. In 1974, she began advocating for the organization of an extraordinary session dedicated to the third age. In November 1981, the UNO's General Assembly decided that the World Assembly on Aging would be held in Vienna from July 26 to August 6, 1982 (UNO, 1981).

Between the 1950s and 1970s, Aslan's school of gerontology and geriatrics formed part of a golden period of the Romanian school of medicine and of the universal thinking about aging, but the progressive worsening of the economical and political situation in the late communist period and the tribulations of the prolonged post-communist transition pushed its bastion, the Ana Aslan Institute, into the shadows. Even so, the Romanian school of gerontology and geriatrics found inner resources to recover its avant-garde thinking, to reduce the research and clinical technology gap and pursue constant development. The development of private actors in aging research and medical and social assistance, the development of organizations of civil society, the access to the European Community and private funding resources, as well as the opening up of cooperation with top international organizations and specialists substantially contributed to this recovery and progress.

RECENT RESEARCH

The main research directions in aging established by Ana Aslan, the biomedical, clinical, and social studies aimed at deciphering the complexity of the aging process and transferring the acquired knowledge into practice, are still pursued in Romania and abroad. In Romania, research on aging is formally organized and developed within two dedicated institutions—Ana Aslan National Institute of Gerontology and Geriatrics as a public actor (http://www.ana-aslan.ro/cercetare.htm), and the new Ana Aslan International Academy of Aging (www.brainaging.ro), created in 2000 by a private organization, the Ana Aslan International Foundation. Additionally, research on the aging process in its basic, clinical, and social aspects is performed here and there, especially in universities. The Ana Aslan Institute develops studies/research projects related to biological age evaluation criteria/biomarkers, the biochemistry of oxidative stress in aging and related pathology, investigation of lipid and lipoprotein metabolism, the cellular and molecular mechanisms in aging muscle, the mechanisms of normal and pathological immunosenescence, and in vitro studies regarding cellular senescence. Studies regarding the clinical particularities at the third age, the therapeutic aspects of age-specific pathology, as well as the psychosocial aspects of aging, the aging demographic and its challenges, and the psychosocial adaptation of the elderly are also carried out. Access to national and international grants and cooperation allowed the development of research related to biomarkers of human aging, the relationship between oxidative stress and cellular immune response, apoptosis in cardiovascular diseases, plasmatic level of TNF-alpha and Fas soluble receptors in systemic atherosclerosis, methyl-metabolism and genomics and epigenetic aspects in neuroendocrine, cardiovascular and cognitive pathology, genomic and nutrigenomic aspects of normal aging and pathology, pathology of blood cells in cardiovascular diseases, photo-physical methods in post-traumatic therapy, comparative study of DHEA seric level and estrogenic hormones during menopause and in atherosclerosis and cognitive dysfunctions, gender aspects of the clinic-biological and psychosocial factors involved in aging, the value of osteoporosis screening in the global evaluation of Parkinsonian older adults and the initiation of a registry book comprising the reference values for blood immunological and genotoxical determinations.

The main private organization in the field of research and development in aging, the Ana Aslan International Academy of Aging, rebranded the Ana Aslan geriatric concept, taking into consideration the large dynamic of knowledge acquisition in the field of longevity medicine. The Ana Aslan Academy of Aging is the new Ana Aslan brand for medical services, in brain aging prevention and longevity medicine. It has oriented its research activities toward the assimilation and development of the most practical tendencies and themes in biomedical, clinical, and social gerontology research through a sustained cooperation and partnership with top national and international organizations, consortia, and universities, gaining in a short time an important international recognition, and a sustained access to national and international funding opportunities (Spiru, 2007, 2008a, 2008b, 2008c). In the field of basic research, Ana Aslan Academy elaborated two new research concepts, just promoted into practice under international cooperation. The first, related to the attempt of the critical "omes" in aging and neurodegenerative pathology, gravitates around the synergy between hypothesis-based research and the "omic" bioinformatic attempt (Weinstein et al., 1992), and promises a highly integrative approach, able to extract the most meaningful and intimate core of the field and drive it to practice improvement. In this conceptual framework, the NERO-MIND and DIONA projects/research paradigms aim to provide significant outcomes related to the integrative pursuit of different neuromes and of their interplay with certain environmental (ecomes, nutriomes, chronomes) and inner organism omes, such as metabolome, genome/epigenome, transcriptomes, proteomes, initially addressed to the progress of pre-dementia states toward dementia stages (Spiru, Cucu, Radu, & Turcu, 2008, 2009). Secondly, the same omic integrative attempt is pursued for the reconsideration of old and newly issued international research outcomes regarding the behavior of procaine as a longevity and geriatric drug, together with a recently opened, sustained, and strongly documented campaign for the inclusion of this molecule in the actual worldwide trend of discovering new pharmacodynamic properties of old drugs. A third research concept envisages the comparative metabolomic and genomic/epigenetic attempt of aging and cancer as the two extremes of a fundamental molecular intimacy. Other important research attempts comprise the partnership to the EADC's DESCRIPA project for the development of screening guidelines and diagnostic criteria for pre-dementia Alzheimer's disease with a recently completed study on the impact of comorbidities, their gender aspects and risk factors for the progress of pre-dementia states toward dementia stages (Turcu, Visser, & Spiru, 2008), a study on the impact of cholinergic treatment use (Impact of Cholinergic Treatment Use—ICTUS Project, QLK 6 CT 2002, 02455, http://eadc.alzheimer-europe.org/ictus.html) and a clinical trial on memantine. The research direction of e-Health and AmI Assisted Living was first introduced in Romania by the Ana Aslan Academy, whose expertise underlay the European model of Ambient Assisted Living developed in the Share-it and K4Care European Community's FP6-funded projects and the other two FP7 applications still under evaluation. The implementation of the intelligent assistive platforms in Romania will be facilitated by and within the new Otopeni Clinic of Ana Aslan Academy, performing tasks related to medical assistance, healthy-living and long-living medical services, physical and psychic rehabilitation for inpatients and outpatients, as well as peer-counseling of patients' families and other people involved in the health-care process (K4CARE, 2006; SHARE-it, 2005; Spiru, 2008a, 2008b, 2008c; Spiru, Annicchiarico, & Cortes, 2009a, 2009b).

There is a principle of the pioneers of Romanian gerontology and geriatrics that penetrated and impressed the mentality of Romanians: geriatric prevention must start at the age of 40–45, but geriatric education should begin in infancy. This was difficult to do during the communist regime, but it is now facilitated by the slow but constant amendments to the Romanian health system. The Ana Aslan International Academy of Aging has been developing, since 2003, its Excellence Memory Clinic, a member of the European Alzheimer's Disease Consortium, and its Center for Age-Related Diseases, Psychogeriatrics, Neurodegenerative Diseases and Brain Aging, where clinical studies are also performed. In 2008, the Ana Aslan International Foundation opened its new Geriatrics, Gerontology for Longevity, Healthy Aging and Brain Aging Prevention Clinic in Otopeni, as a result of a fruitful collaboration with the Romanian Academy of Sciences. Other research and development activities are oriented toward the assessment of home, day, and social assistance for the elderly population in Romania and the implementation of the most fruitful foreign strategies by sustained international cooperation.

The above two main organizations in aging research in Romania perform sustained activity regarding the development of the specific work force dealing with formal academic training and informal assistance. In this respect, two projects dedicated to the training of managers and medical staff from two underdeveloped Romanian counties, Valcea and Teleorman, are now beginning and aim to include the very difficult field of assistance to cognitively disabled elderly. The research outcomes of these two institutions are disseminated firstly by means of their own publications, the *Romanian Journal of Gerontology and Geriatrics* (Romanian and English editions) and the *Brain Aging International Journal*, and sustained efforts are made to promote this on the ISI publications list. They also actively participate in top international scientific events. Besides the Ana Aslan Academy, other private Romanian organizations are directly involved in research, education, and international partnership activities in the field of aging, such as the Geron Foundation, the Anti-Aging Medicine Association, the Romanian Society of Gerontology and Geriatrics, the University Society of Internal Medicine, Geriatrics and Gerontology (Iasi), among other tangent activities developed by a growing range of

NGOs, private labs and imagistic units, retirement and medical homes for the elderly population, and so on. The alternative medicine principles and means are carefully evaluated and gain their deserved involvement.

EDUCATION

The most important education feature in gerontology and geriatrics was the optimistic shift in the perception on aging initiated by G. Marinescu, C. I. Parhon, and mainly by Ana Aslan. In 1988, Prof. Aslan passed away. However, Ana Aslan's greatest dream was fulfilled after 11 years, when the first Academic Geriatric Department was created in the Carol Davila University of Medicine and Pharmacy in Bucharest. Since 2003, the Ana Aslan International Foundation, through its academic body, has developed international training in the field of geriatrics and psychogeriatrics, Every year the Ana Aslan International Foundation trains over 400 specialists in the field of geriatrics, psychiatry, neurology, and psychogeriatrics.

There are several publications issued by Romanian gerontologists and geriatricians, sharing their knowledge and experience that contribute to the development of gerontology and geriatrics (Balaceanu-Stolnici, 1998; Bogdan, 1997; Romosan & Szucsic, 1996; Spiru & Romosan 2002, 2004; Spiru, Vellas & Ousset, 2000, 2001; Susan, 2003).

Special attention is given to the training and upgrade of geriatric nurses and social workers, depending on the institutional framework of their activity: at home, ambulatory, hospital, temporary or long-term care in residential or medical homes. In 2000, the III.A.II Section of the National Program 2.12, For Geriatric Prevention and Protection, raised the problem of the organization of long-term care for the elderly. The Ana Aslan Academy recently produced a draft of a project addressing the organization of long-term care for the elderly with cognitive disabilities, in which their assistance at home as long as possible is carefully thought out and promoted. Even if still scarce, the organization and geriatric education of voluntary and informal forces dedicated to the assistance of the elderly is underway and the adaptation of European and international successful models, rules, and standards is assiduously envisaged.

PUBLIC POLICY ISSUES IN AGING

Due to the imbalance between working and retired groups, population aging overlaps a problem already felt in Romania: elderly people request more medical and personal care than is possible with the resources available to both themselves, and the insurance and social assistance. The European Social Charter adopted by the European Commission in May 1996 was signed by Romania in May 1997 and ratified through Law 74/1999. The National Development Plan comprises measures taken in the field of national health to continue the heath system reform from 2007 to 2013. The priorities of the strategic national plan have as final outcome the increase of the active life span.

The medical, sociomedical and psychological needs of older patients and their dependency needs are assessed based on the National Elderly Needs Evaluation Grille, approved by Governmental Decision (GD) no. 886/2000. In accordance with GD 886/2000, art. 1, degree of dependency is defined as the state of a person that needs significant assistance and medical care, due to physical or mental causes. An assessment of the functional, sensorial, and psychological status of an older person is necessary in order to evaluate the degree of dependency. The social assistance strategy is based on a social, economic, and medical analysis of the particular situation. Law no. 17/2000 stipulates that the community services include temporary or permanent home care; temporary or permanent care in an elderly home; and medical care in day centers. Community assistance includes social order services (avoidance of elderly social isolation and support for social integration), sociomedical services (personal hygiene, adapting the home environment to the patient's needs), and medical services (evaluation and care at home, dental care, medication, provision of sanitary and medical devices). The district councils are responsible for providing these services for free to elderly people with no income or insufficient incomes. Law no. 95/2006, referring to health system reform in Romania, and GD no. 1842/2006 regulate the provision of these services. The accreditation of the staff involved in home-care services provision is regulated by the set of norms regarding the organization and functioning of home care, approved by Government Order no. 318/2003. The access of an old person to a home for elders is based on certain priority criteria: the person needs permanent assistance that cannot be secured at home; is unable to accomplish basic activities of daily living; has no support; or has no home and insufficient income to get one. The medical services provided in a home for elders include evaluation and therapy, care services, medication, provision of needed medical devices, and dental care. Elderly people who have sufficient income on their own or from their supporting persons must pay a monthly fee, based on the mean monthly fee. For those who have no or insufficient income, the fee is covered by the local government budget.

Homes for the older adults are included in the category of units of medical and social assistance whose organization, functioning and financing is regulated by rule of April 2, 2003, approved by GD no. 412/2003. An important provision of law no. 17/2000 (art. 30), concerning the protection of the elderly population, stipules that older adults will be assisted by a representative of the local council in whose territorial area that person lives, on request or ex officio. Law no. 16/2000 created the National Council of the Elderly, in order to support state institutions in the accomplishment of the recommendations of the International Plan on Actions on Aging.

One of the most important legal regulations is Law no. 47/2006, on the national system of social assistance, and Law 705/2001, on the national social assistance. According to the above-mentioned laws, the principles underlying the functioning of social assistance are universality (each person is entitled to assistance under the law); respect for human dignity (each person has the guarantee of the free and full development of personality); social solidarity (i.e., community participates in supporting people with social needs); and subsidization (if the person or family cannot provide the social needs, then the task is assumed by local organizations and associations). In order to ensure the proper application of social policies for older adults, local and district councils are entrusted to set up and organize the specific social assistance.

In terms of legislation related to the social protection of the elderly population, there has been considerable progress by the development of an appropriate legislative framework related to the social protection of the elderly. The most important problem that remains to be put into practice is the establishment of the instruments of social protection.

The main aim of Romanian gerontology and geriatrics remains the fight against the dark vision of aging, and delaying or preventing specific pathology, with special commitment to the cognitive aspect, in the case of the Ana Aslan Academy. As everywhere in the world, healthy, active aging, the preservation of dignity and maintaining a place in society, and the reorientation and use of the elder person's remaining work capacity, are understood in Romania as successful answers to the challenges of demographic aging, and are imperatives to which the transfer of scientific and technological achievements must be oriented.

REFERENCES

Balaceanu-Stolnici, C. (1998). *Practical geriatrics.* Bucharest: Ed. Medicala Amalteea.
Bogdan, C. (1997). *Basics of practical geriatrics.* Bucharest: Ed. Medicala.

Brătescu, G. (2008). *I. I. Mecinikov, descendant of Nicolae Milescu. Repere iatro-istorice* [Iatro-historical marks]. Retrieved from http://www.unitbv.ro/facul ties/medicina/JMB/JMB%202008%20nr.2%20supliment%20ist%20med/ CD/articole%20extenso/ist%20med%20pdf/04%20Bratescu%20-%20 I.I.Mecinikov.pdf

K4CARE. (2004). *Knowledge-based homecare eservices for an aging Europe—IST—2004—026968, 2006.* Retrieved from http://www.k4care.net

Landmarks. (2008). JMB, no. 2, Hist. Supplement. Med.

Poli, T. (Ed.). (1997). *Ana Aslan—In memoriam* (pp. 22–28). Braila, Romania: ISTROS Publishing House.

Representative Figures of Romanian Science and Technology—Gheorghe Marinescu. (2004). Retrieved from http://www.ici.ro/romania/en/stiinta/ marinescu.html

Romosan, I., & Szucsic, I. A. (1996). *Gerontology.* Timisoara, Romania: Ed. Dinamis Print.

SHARE it (Supported Human Autonomy for Recovery and Enhancement of cognitive and motor abilities using information technologies). (2005). IST—2005—2.6.2, 2006. Retrieved from http://www.ist-shareit.eu/shareit

Spiru, L. (2007). Mild cognitive impairment. Is there available treatment? Should it be given? First World Congress on Controversies in Neurology, Berlin, Germany.

Spiru, L. (2008a). Brain aging—A holistic approach of preventive and treatment strategies, millennia 2015, "Women as actors of development for the global challenges." Liège (Wallonia).

Spiru, L. (2008b). Cutting-edge diagnosis in brain aging prevention. AMWC Anti-Aging World Congress, Paris, France.

Spiru, L. (2008c). Knowledge-based homecare e-services for an ageing Europe. Ana Aslan Academy's International Training workshop on Brain Aging Prevention. Bucharest, Romania.

Spiru, L., Annicchiarico, R., & Cortes, U. (2009a). Legal concerns regarding AmI Assisted Living in the elderly, worldwide and in Romania. *Proceedings of the International Work Conference on Artificial Neural Networks, June 10–12, Salamanca.* (In print.)

Spiru, L., Annicchiarico, R., & Cortes, U. (2009b), Normal versus pathological cognitive aging. Variability as a constraint of patients profiling for AmI design. *Proceedings of the International Work Conference on Artificial Neural Networks, June 10–12, Salamanca.* (In print.)

Spiru, L., Cucu, N., Radu, L., & Turcu, I. (2008). Critical "omes" in aging and neurodegenerative pathology. From Theory to Practice: International Conference on Association of Alzheimer's Disease—ICAD July 2008, Chicago, United States. *Alzheimer's & Dementia,* 4(4) (Suppl 2), Abstracts.

Spiru, L., Cucu, N., Radu, L., & Turcu, I. (2009). A pilot, comparative epigenomic and metabolomic study in healthy elderly, adult and young people.

Proceedings of the 9th International Conference on Alzheimer's & Parkinson's Diseases: Advances, concepts & new challenges. Prague, Czech Republic.

Spiru, L., & Romosan, I. (2002). *Geriatrics treatise* (Vol. I/Vol. II). Solness Publishing House.

Spiru, L., & Romosan, I. (2004). *Geriatrics treatise, actualized.* Bucharest: Ana Aslan International Academy of Aging Publishing House.

Spiru, L., Turcu, I., & Cortes, U. (2008, July). Intelligent ambiance for the cognitively and physically impaired elderly. The European model. *Alzheimer's & Dementia, 4*(4) (Suppl. 2), Abstracts, T650.

Spiru, L., Vellas, B., & Ousset, P. J., (2000). *Observation book for patients with Alzheimer's disease* (1st ed.). Bucharest: Carol Davila University of Medicine and Pharmacy Publishing House.

Spiru, L., Vellas, B., & Ousset, P. J. (2001). *Clinical tests in Alzheimer's disease* (1st ed.). Bucharest: Carol Davila University of Medicine and Pharmacy Publishing House.

Susan, L. M. (2003). *Geriatric semiology.* Timisoara, Romania: Ed. Orizonturi Universitare.

Turcu, I., Visser, P. J., & Spiru, L. (2008). Comorbidities as a hot topic in predementia conditions. A Romanian neuroepidemiological study. International Conference on Association of Alzheimer's Disease—ICAD 2008, Chicago, United States.

UNO 57th plenary meeting. (1981, November 13). A/RES/36/30. Retrieved from http://www.un.org/documents/ga/res/36/a36r030.htm

Weinstein, J., Kohn, K. W., Grever, M. R. et al. (1992). *Neural computing and cancer drug development: Prediction mechanism of action. Science, 258*(5081), 447–451.

39

▪ ■ ▪ ▪

Singapore

Kalyani K. Mehta

The turning point in Singapore's demographic history took place in the early 1980s, when the awareness of increasing numbers of older persons above 60 years in the population was noted in a governmental report (Ministry of Health, 1984). The implications of an aging population across the economic, health, social (i.e., family and community), infrastructure, and legal sectors are interrelated and tend to be long term. In the last decade, the proportion of older persons above 65 years increased from 7 to 8%, but is projected to rise to 19% by 2030. "At a rate of 3.1% per annum, Singapore's growth rate for those aged 65 and above surpasses even the developed countries for the same period. . . . In absolute numbers, the number of older persons in Singapore is expected to increase from 238,000 in 2000 to 796,000 in 2030" (Teo, Mehta, Thang, & Chan, 2006, p. 16). The rapid aging of this island state's population is attributed to the increased life expectancy and a dramatic fall in the birthrate, which is currently below replacement level. Of great concern for health and social services is the average annual growth rate of those aged 85 years and over; their growth rate is twice the annual growth rate for those aged 65 years and over. The challenge facing the state is not only to respond to an aging population within a short span of about 25 years, but also the prospect of catering to the needs of a large segment of the older population.

As compared to the profile of an aged population in a more developed country, Singapore's older people who are currently 65 years and above have relatively lower levels of education (Ministry of Community Development,

1999), and more than 80% co-reside with family members. "In 2005, 73.7% of senior citizens aged 55 years and above were owners or co-owners of the homes they lived in. Home ownership decreased with age" (Ministry of Community Development, Youth and Sports, 2007, p. 22). Singapore, being primarily an Asian country, endorses the principle of filial piety in its population. This is reflected in the finding that for the age groups 65–74 years and 75 years and above, the reliance on children as the main source of income was 55.8% and 63.7% (Ministry of Community Development, Youth and Sports, 2007).

Two major Eldercare Masterplans were formulated for the periods 2001–2005 and 2006–2010. The focus of the first was on funding policy for eldercare services, setting the key directions for such services and program, including support for caregivers and public education efforts (Ministry of Community Development, Youth and Sports, 2001). The second Masterplan had the following thrusts: (a) housing options for seniors; (b) accessibility for seniors; (c) health-care and eldercare services; and (d) promotion of active aging and positive attitudes toward older people (Ministry of Community Development, Youth and Sports, 2006). The government has prioritized aging issues and challenges in its national agenda.

RECENT RESEARCH

Since the mid-1990s, research on aging-related topics in the Singapore context has been increasing. However, most of it has utilized methods such as cross-sectional surveys, in-depth interviews/case studies, focus group discussions, cross-cultural comparisons, and analysis of census and other secondary data. There is a lack of multidisciplinary and multidimensional longitudinal studies. To date, two longitudinal datasets have been collected by a collaboration between the Singapore Action Group of Elders (SAGE) and Centre for the Study of Ageing (CENSA) (for more details, see Kua, Ng, & Goh, 2004) and the Gerontology Research Programme, housed at the Faculty of Medicine, National University of Singapore. The latter study is called the Singapore Longitudinal Ageing Study and includes focus on older adults' health and functional status, medical care needs and utilization, cognitive impairment, sociodemographic characteristics, and nutrition.

Gerontological research conducted in Singapore can be grouped under three main categories: (1) financial security and social security schemes; (2) health and disability among the older population; and (3) life transitions and family caregiving. As there is currently no national institute or centralized database for aging-related research in Singapore, reporting on all the research done in Singapore may not be comprehensive. Hence, the author will touch on the major and recent research only (i.e., in the last 12 years).

In the first category, much research has examined the adequacy and equity perspective of the current financial protection for Singaporean elders, with much focus on the government-established mechanism called the Central Provident Fund (CPF) (Asher, 1998, 2002; Chia, 2008; Choon, 1996). In relation to financial protection and older women, the studies have highlighted the high levels of dependency on family members due to their financial inadequacy (Lee, 1999; Mehta, 2002, 2005).

The studies on health status and health-care arrangements have captured the need for customizing the services and affordability issues (Jatrana & Chan, 2007; Lee & Tan, 1997; The Tsao Foundation, 2007). Disability among the older populations has gendered dimensions and is relatively less studied (Verbrugge, Mehta, & Wagenfeld-Heintz, 2006; Yadav, 2001). A study carried out in five Asian countries on functional limitations and disabilities found that contrary to the U.S. trend of decreasing levels of disability, there was an increasing trend in four of the five countries (Ofstedal et al., 2007).

The third category of research, focusing on life transitions such as widowhood, grandparenting, and retirement, portray how Singaporeans cope with these life changes, using their cultural, social, and financial resources. Teo and Mehta (2001) illustrate that widows have their own agency and try to carve a role for themselves within their families. Grandparenting in Singapore is experienced as a natural life journey; however, the older generations (70 years and above) are more willing to perform grandchild minding as compared to the young-old cohorts (55–70 years). Relationships between grandparents and grandchildren were examined in 15 three-generational families drawn from three major ethnic groups—the Chinese, Malays, and Indians. Three generations were interviewed from the same family to understand their perceptions of the grandparent-grandchild relationship, as well as the role played by the link parent toward this relationship. Interestingly, a majority of the grandchildren felt that their relationship with their grandparents was not influenced by the "link" (middle generation) parent (Mehta, 2007). In the same study, it was found that grandparents played a supportive role rather than a custodial role in most Singaporean families. It was common for Singaporean grandparents to become involved in caring for the grandchild so their adult children and children-in-law could be gainfully employed. In Singapore, which has high levels of inflation and standard of living, dual-income families are the norm. Grandparents give support to the working adult children by directly or indirectly supervising the children during the day when the middle generation is away from home. On retirement, it has been found that a large proportion of Singaporeans do not plan for their retirement, hence the need for more financial planning courses and safety nets for the poor elders (Mehta, 1999).

Research on family caregivers has been carried out in hospitals and social service agencies, as well as universities. Overall, findings show that they are a stressed and largely unappreciated group. One study indicated that there was an inverse relationship between the level of stress of family caregivers and the activities of daily living (ADL) of the care recipient (Mehta, 2006). Another study suggested that spousal family carers exercise their agency in their caregiving role and are not mere passive actors in the caregiving roles (Ng, 2008).

Very little research has been done in Singapore on professional caregivers, but an outstanding exception is the cross-national research spearheaded by Professor Albert Hermalin from the University of Michigan, Ann Arbor. Over a period of 10 years, he was principal investigator of a study that culminated in the book, *The Well-being of the Elderly in Asia: A Four-Country Comparative Analysis*, in which Singapore was represented. The research had a highly rigorous methodological and analytical approach. One of the important findings was that living alone and being single are key predictive factors of the vulnerable older person in Singapore (Hermalin, 2002).

GERONTOLOGICAL EDUCATION

Currently, very few courses are offered at the postgraduate level in gerontological education. A master's in gerontology (Health Science) is offered jointly by the Singapore Institute of Management and the University of Sydney, and a similar course is run by Parkway Healthcare Foundation, Singapore, and La Trobe University in Australia. The Faculty of Medicine, National University of Singapore, conducts a graduate diploma course in geriatric medicine for family physicians who wish to specialize in geriatrics (Koh, 2007). Several certificate courses in gerontology are offered by Nanyang Polytechnic, Lee Community College, and the Social Service Training Institute of the National Council of Social Service. These courses range from 1 to 10 days. Nurses who are interested in working with elders may choose to take advanced diploma courses in gerontological nursing, integrated eldercare, or gerontological counseling—all these courses are either part-time (may last two years) or full-time (one year). Finally, a certificate course that has been offered annually since 2000 is the ASEAN Social Gerontology Course, a 10-day intensive training organized by the International Institute on Aging (INIA) at Malta and the Singapore Action Group of Elders.

A study conducted a few years ago indicated that many Singaporean professionals are keen to sign up for gerontology-based courses, but factors such as cost, lack of time, and lack of appropriate courses are some of the hurdles.

At the undergraduate level, students at the National University of Singapore can choose modules in social gerontology (which is offered by the Department of Social Work) or sociology of the life course and aging (offered by the Department of Sociology). Undergraduate medical students are also required to do a module on geriatrics before they graduate.

In sum, although the need is great for more tertiary-level master's and Ph.D. courses in gerontology, these programs are currently not available at these levels. Those with postgraduate education in gerontology at present have obtained their degrees from countries like the United States, United Kingdom, or Australia.

PUBLIC POLICY ISSUES

The consequences of a rapidly aging population for a small nation that has no natural resources are manifold and pervasive. Despite the efforts of the government, as well as nongovernmental organizations such as the Tsao Foundation, Singapore Action Group of Elders, the Singapore Gerontological Society, Alzheimer's Disease Association, and Society for Geriatric Medicine, many important policy issues are yet to be addressed. Some of these public policy issues require the cooperation of different governmental ministries, such as the Ministry of Community Development, Youth and Sports, and the Ministry of Health. Hence, the concept of InterMinisterial Committees (IMC) aims to bring the various ministry representatives to the same table to orchestrate a holistic approach in the nation's preparation for an aging population. This is a cost-effective strategy, but it cannot be as effective as a centralized coordinating council to plug the gaps in research and policy evaluation.

In terms of social security arrangements, the Central Provident Fund (CPF) is a national mechanism for retirement savings for the working population. It was established in 1955 as a pay-as-you-earn provident fund, and now it has evolved into "the world's most extensive social policy on assets" (Sherraden, Nair, Vasoo, & Ngiam, 1995, p. 112). The safety net for those who have inadequate amount of savings in their CPF account, or none at all if they have never worked, needs strengthening. The two other schemes that such persons could apply for are the Public Assistance Scheme and the Medifund Scheme. The first is primarily for those who have no family and lack the ability to work due to health or disability; the second is for those who have been hospitalized but are unable to meet their medical expenses. Singapore does not have a universal pension scheme, and government policies advocate the family to be the first line of defense for someone who is in a crisis. Community support by voluntary welfare associations is active, and there are many social activity centers, day-care centers and rehabilitation centers for the families to turn to if they need these services. The issue sometimes is affordability and incongruity in matching the needs with the resources available. Cultural differences—language, diet preferences, lack of proximity, and timing of the services and programs—often deter utilization of the services.

Health-care costs are spiraling, and cost of medication is often a source of deterrence for older persons and their families in seeking medical help. While the government policies have facilitated the use of the CPF funds such as Medisave, for medication of chronic illnesses under the Chronic Disease Management scheme, some funding conditions and limits inconvenience service users. When stress levels of family caregivers are high, helping professionals are concerned about the possibility of elder abuse and neglect. Currently, the numbers are relatively small (i.e., between 100 and 150 known cases per year), but this could be the tip of the iceberg.

The government has rolled out its National Policy of Successful Ageing by advocating active aging among seniors. However, for this to be realized, transport infrastructure has to accommodate the mobility needs of all types of seniors: the healthy, the frail, and the wheelchair-bound. This is not yet a reality, although the issue of accessibility was a focus of the second Masterplan drawn by the Committee on Ageing Issues (Ministry of Community Development, Youth and Sports, 2006). Buses with low steps and elevators have been installed in all Mass Rapid Transit (MRT) stations as of 2006, for starters.

To enable older workers to be employed, there is a strong need to change employers' mindsets. The Tripartite Committee on Employability of Older Workers has recommended that the government introduce legislation by 2012 for continuation of employment beyond the retirement age of 62. The Ministry of Manpower was urged to target groups such as low-income workers and female workers, so older persons who wish to work beyond age 62 may find the job opportunities to do so (Ministry of Manpower, 2007). Ageist stereotypes of older workers continue to prevail among employers, so the challenge is to influence them to accept the reality of a mature work force. The government works closely with the National Trades Union Congress and the Singapore National Employers Federation to calibrate the policies in tune with the changing social landscape of Singapore.

The last policy issue to be discussed is the adequacy, funding, and quality of long-term care (LTC), both institutional and community-based. The model of LTC in Singapore weighs more heavily on community-based care as opposed to residential care. Only about 2–3% of the older population lives in residential institutions. The recent General Household Survey (Ministry of Trade and Industry, 2005) showed that 21,858 elders live alone and 41,490 lived with their aged spouses only. Eldercare services, both social and health, have to reach out to these seniors who may be isolated and/or frail and depressed. While it is also true that not all elders who live alone or as an independent couple are cut off from their offspring (if any), it is equally true that fulfilling daily social needs requires neighbors and friends. The policy issue is to determine how much public monies should be spent on these community-based services and how much manpower has to be projected for running these services. It is a known fact that trained professionals would deliver better quality services, but can enough of the "right" people be attracted to work in the eldercare sector?

Singapore is the fastest-aging country in Southeast Asia, but in terms of numbers, it has an advantage over countries like Indonesia or China. Singapore's total population is only 4.5 million (including citizens and permanent residents) in a land size of 697km^2 (Ministry for Information, Communications and the Arts, 2007). The family safety net complements the state's safety net for older people. However, shifts in values and priorities of both young and old indicate that future cohorts of older persons will have different characteristics from the current cohorts. Higher educational levels, stronger financial security and health status are some of these improvements to be expected. However, the reality of higher life expectancies compel the nation to be better prepared in terms of policies, services, legal measures and programs for the year 2030, when one in five of Singapore's population will be over 65 years.

REFERENCES

Asher, M. (1998). The future of retirement protection in Southeast Asia. *International Social Security Review, 51*, 3–30.

Asher, M. (2002). *Social adequacy and equity of the social security arrangements in Singapore*. Centre for Advanced Studies Occasional Paper, National University of Singapore, Singapore: Times Academic Press.

Chia, N. P. (2008). The Central Provident Fund and financing retirement needs of elderly Singaporeans. In H. G. Lee (Ed.), *Ageing in Southeast and East Asia: Family, social protection and policy challenges* (pp. 22–39). Singapore: Institute of Southeast Asian Studies.

Children visit more if they live near parents. (2007, February 24). *The Straits Times*, p. 24.

Choon, A. T., & Low, L. (1996). Social security: How Singapore does it. *Asia Pacific Journal of Social Work, 6,* 97–119.

Hermalin, A. (Ed.). (2002). *The well-being of the elderly in Asia: A four-country comparative study.* Ann Arbor, MI: University of Michigan Press.

Jatrana, S., & Chan, A. (2007). Do socioeconomic effects on health diminish with age? A Singapore case study. *Journal of Cross-Cultural Gerontology, 22,* 287–301.

Koh, G.C.H. (2007). A review of geriatric education in Singapore. *Annals of the Academy of Medicine in Singapore, 36,* 687–690.

Kua, E. H., Ng, T. P., & Goh, L. G. (2004) *Long lives.* Singapore: Armour Pub.

Lee, K., & Tan, T. (1997). Functional status of the elderly in Singapore—The trend over a decade. *Annals of the Academy of Medicine in Singapore, 26,* 727–730.

Lee, W.K.M. (1999). Economic and social implications of aging in Singapore. *Journal of Aging and Social Policy, 10,* 73–92.

Mehta, K. (1999). Singaporeans' perceptions and preparations for retirement: A cross-cultural enquiry. *Ageing International: The Journal of the International Federation on Ageing, 25,* 31–46.

Mehta, K. (2002). National policies for ageing and long-term care in Singapore: A case of cautious wisdom? In D. R. Phillips & A.C.M. Chan (Eds.), *Ageing and long-term care: National policies in the Asia Pacific* (pp. 150–180). Singapore: IDRC and Institute of Southeast Asian Studies.

Mehta, K. (2005). The ageing experience of Singaporean women. In K. Mehta (Ed.), *Untapped Resources: Women in ageing societies across Asia* (2nd ed., pp. 47–69). Singapore: Marshall Cavendish Academic.

Mehta, K. (2006). Stress among family caregivers of older persons in Singapore. *Journal of Cross-Cultural Gerontology, 3,* 319–334.

Mehta, K. (2007). Multigenerational relationships within the Asian family: Qualitative evidence from Singapore. *International Journal of the Sociology of the Family, 33,* 63–78.

Ministry of Community Development. (1999). *Report of the Interministerial Committee on the Ageing Population.* Singapore.

Ministry of Community Development, Youth and Sports. (2001). *Eldercare Masterplan (FY 2001 to FY 2005).* Singapore: Author.

Ministry of Community Development, Youth and Sports. (2006). *Committee on Ageing Issues: Report on the ageing population.* Singapore: Author.

Ministry of Community Development, Youth and Sports. (2007). *National survey of senior citizens 2005.* Singapore: Author.

Ministry of Health. (1984). *Report of the Committee on the Problems of the Aged.* Singapore: Author.

Ministry for Information, Communications and the Arts. (2007). *Singapore yearbook 2007.* Singapore: Author.

Ministry of Manpower. (2007). *Tripartite Committee on Employability of Older Workers: Final report.* Singapore: Author.

Ministry of Trade and Industry. (2005). *General household survey 2005.* Singapore: Author.

Ng, G. (2008). Singapore: Characteristics of family caregivers and care recipients and their caregiving experiences. *Hallym International Journal of aging, 10*(1), 41–62.

Ofstedal, M. B., Zimmer, Z., Hermalin, A., Chan, A., Chuang, Y.-L., Natividad, J., et al. (2007). Short-term trends in functional limitation and disability among older Asians: A comparison of five settings. *Journal of Cross-Cultural Gerontology, 22,* 243–261.

Sherraden, M., Nair, S., Vasoo, S., & Ngiam, T. L. (1995). Social policy based on assets: The impact of Singapore's Central Provident Fund. *Asian Journal of Political Science, 3,* 112–133.

Teo, P., & Mehta, K. (2001). Participating in the home: Widows cope in Singapore. *Journal of Aging Studies, 15,* 127–144.

Teo, P., Mehta, K., Thang, L. L., & Chan, A. (2006). *Ageing in Singapore: Service needs and the state.* London: Routledge.

The Tsao Foundation. (2007). *Report on the perceptions of primary health care for older persons in Singapore.* Singapore: Author.

Verbrugge, L., Mehta, K., & Wagenfeld-Heintz, E. (2006). Views of disability in U.S. and Singapore. *Research on Aging, 28,* 216–239.

Yadav, S. S. (2001). Disability and handicap among elderly Singaporeans. *Singapore Medical Journal, 42,* 360–367.

40

···■··

Slovakia

Ladislav Hegyi and Štefan Krajčík

RECENT HISTORY

The history of Slovak geriatrics can be characterized by four developmental phases. The study of geriatrics was initiated by members of the Slovak Internist Society. This first stage of Slovak gerontology history can be called the Topoľčany stage, after the town where the founder of Slovak Geriatrics, Dr. Eugene Gressner, worked as the head of internal medicine. Dr Gressner became the first president of the Slovak Gerontological Society, which was established in 1975.

Dr. Gressner's contribution to the development of Slovak health-care provision was remarkable. Many of his disciples became heads of departments, professors, and eminent researchers. He taught internal medicine and geriatrics at Slovak Medical University for many years and published over 40 papers. Dr Gressner reached the age of 90 in good mental and physical health.

Another significant event during the Topoľčany stage was the creation of the Subdepartment of Geriatrics, headed by Associate Professor Štefan Litomerický at Slovak Medical University in 1972.

The second developmental stage of Slovak gerontology lasted from 1975 until 1980. The Subdepartment of Geriatrics in Bratislava expanded its activities, geriatric departments in the medical schools in Bratislava and Košice were founded, and the Research Institute of Gerontology in Malacky was established in 1977. The first significant meeting on prevention in geriatrics was held in Bratislava in 1975. This congress initiated the tradition of organizing international conferences on prevention in geriatrics and markedly influenced Slovak gerontology in its orientation toward preventive aspects of aging in both health and disease. The book of abstracts from this congress, edited by Professor Štefan Litomerický, CSc., became the first significant publication on geriatrics in Slovakia. The development of Slovak geriatrics at this stage was significantly influenced by the appointment of Prof. Karol Virsík, MD, Ph.D., DSc., to the post of geriatric consultant to the Slovak Ministry of Health in 1976. Prof. Virsik replaced Dr. Gressner, gaining the presidency of the Slovak Gerontologic Society in 1977. Shortly thereafter, in 1979, the Ministry of Health issued the Concept of Geriatrics document, encouraging and enabling the development of geriatric care, both curative and preventive. The Slovak Government adopted the Gerontology Program in 1981, which emphasized the necessity of countrywide efforts to improve living conditions and also the health of older persons.

The third developmental stage of Slovak gerontology, which was the most fertile period for the development of geriatrics, lasted from 1980 until 1989. This progress was influenced by the nomination of regional consultants in geriatrics, and, therefore, the developments and achievements in gerontology were different in various parts of the country. A network of facilities, both inpatient and outpatient, was also created, and geriatrics as an independent specialty was introduced. Undergraduate education of geriatrics was started at the Medical Faculty of Comenius University and at Palacky University in the 1980s. The first qualification exams for geriatrics in Czechoslovakia were held in Bratislava in 1983. The activities of the Research Institute expanded during this period as well.

The Slovak Gerontological Society also became very active in the 1980s. The International Conferences on Preventive Gerontology in 1981 and 1986 and the National Geriatric Days, organized annually in various towns in Slovakia, did much to promote geriatrics in public medicine. The fourth and current stage of development in geriatrics and gerontology began in 1990, and is characterized by the transformation of Slovak society and health care. This transformation contributed to a more up-to-date view of geriatrics, which in turn manifested itself in the adoption of the new Concept of Geriatrics in 1993.

There were negative aspects in this period, however. Some administrators considered geriatrics to be a heritage of the old regime, and the Geriatric Department of the Medical Faculty in Košice was disbanded in 1991. Further, the Research Institute of Gerontology in Malacky was closed in 1994, and its successor, the Geriatric Centre in Malacky, was shut down in 1996. The program in which geriatric nurses provided community care was canceled, too.

But there were also many positives. The Geriatric Centre of St. Lucas was founded and later became the Geriatric Department of Safarik University in Kosice. The journal *Geriatria* was initiated in 1995, and the second Geriatric Department at the Medical Faculty of Comenius University in Bratislava was founded in 2004. In the same era, the Faculty of Public Health at Slovak Medical University in Bratislava incorporated social gerontology into its curriculum.

This period also witnessed the development of universities of the third age in Slovakia, as well as the reinforcement of the international standing of Slovak gerontology and geriatrics.

Another success during this stage is the renewed cooperation with the Czech Geriatric and Gerontology Society. The Slovak Gerontology Society had been a part of the Czechoslovak Gerontology Society, which vanished in December 1992 as result of the partition of Czechoslovakia. The Czechoslovak Gerontology Society was replaced by the Slovak Gerontology Society and the Czech Gerontology Society, which were admitted to IAG and EURAG in 1993. An important step in the development of Slovak gerontology was the adoption of the National Program for the Protection of Older Persons by the Government of the Slovak Republic in 1999.

The Slovak Gerontology Society was renamed the Slovak Gerontology and Geriatrics Society (SGGS) in the 1990s. The new president of SGGS was Professor Ladislav Hegyi, who was in charge from 1994 to 2002. The current president is Professor Zoltan Mikes.

Slovak gerontology and geriatrics has made considerable progress during the last 30 years. This process started by establishing geriatrics as a medical branch, and main achievements include the development of the geriatric health care provision network; a system of postgraduate education; the establishment and development of social gerontology; and the founding of a journal establishing active international collaboration.

RECENT RESEARCH ON AGING

The effort to build a base for gerontology research resulted in the founding of the Research Institute of Gerontology in Malacky (October, 1977) by Dr. Viliam Balaz, CSc., who became the institute's first director (1977–1989). The research there focused mainly on metabolic disorders and the institute was a coordinator of gerontology research in Czechoslovakia for about a decade. Dr. Zoltan Kallay, CSc., succeeded Dr. Balaz as the institute's director, and resigned in January 1991.

The Ministry of Health transformed the institute in 1991, and its new priority became clinical research. This research was carried out in close cooperation with the Malacky Hospital. The Department of Social Gerontology was created within the institute in 1992. The founding of this department was subsequent to social changes accompanying the transition of society after the 1989 revolution. The department's research focused on maladaptation syndrome and hyperlipidemias (mainly in their relation to ischemic heart diseases and diabetic retinopathy). The most prominent achievements of this period involved the determination of normal values of cholesterol, triglycerides, fatty acids, and selene in the elderly population of Zahorie (west Slovakian region). However, financial constraints caused the institute to close at the end of 1994. Its successor was the Geriatric Centre, directed by Dr. Ladislav Hegyi, DrSc., who was also the last director of the Institute.

The principal activity of the center was health-care provision, and research activity was very restricted. Despite a very good reputation in Slovakia as well as abroad, the center was closed for no apparent reason on March 31, 1996.

The closing of the Gerontology Research Institute and its successor, the Geriatric Centre, had a very negative impact on Slovak gerontology and caused the end of institutional research in gerontology in Slovakia. Current research in gerontology is restricted by a lack of grants and human and financial resources.

Research activity in Slovakia's last period, stage four, was aimed at mapping the functional status of elderly people living in the community in residential homes, and was also targeted toward patients of geriatric departments and long-term care facilities. Researchers also studied pharmacotherapy. This research focused on polypharmacy and the use of potentially inappropriate drugs, yet another area of research attempted to identify the prevalence of malnutrition in residential homes.

The Geriatric Department of Slovak Medical University (chair, Prof. Štefan Krajčík, M.D., Ph.D.) was involved in the European Commission Project Dignity of Older Europeans in 2000–2005. The project was coordinated by the University of Cardiff, and other participating centers included France, Ireland, Spain, and Sweden. The project's goal was to explore the attitudes of people regarding older persons' dignity, and the factors affecting this matter. The results of the project were:

1. Poster: Dignity Balance
2. Policy recommendations
3. "Educating for Dignity"—A Multidisciplinary Workbook

The department was also involved in research aimed at pharmocotherapy and the functional status of older people.

The Geriatric Department of Comenius University, headed by Prof. Zoltan Mikes, DrSC, was involved in the following research projects:

1. Longitudinal follow-up of physical fitness and activity and the risk factors of stroke and ischemic heart disease.
2. Effect of Enterococcus faecium M-74–I administration on dyslipidemias, colon cancer, and immunodeficiency in old age.
3. National program of health promotion: Effect of Enterococcus faecium M-74–II administration on dyslipidemias, colon cancer, and immunodeficiency in old age.
4. RAMES (Riziko Aterosklerózy Mestských Seniorov [Risk of Atherosclerosis in Urban Seniors]) (sponsored by a Pfizer grant).
5. Risk factors of atherosclerosis and some effects of probiotic microflora.

THE CURRENT STATE OF EDUCATION IN GERONTOLOGY

Geriatrics has been an optional part of the curriculum at the medical faculties in Bratislava and in Kosice since the mid-1990s, but interest from medical students is generally low.

The former Czechoslovakia was a pioneer in geriatrics postgraduate education in Central Europe. The first four geriatricians qualified in 1983, and more than 150 geriatricians have qualified since that time. The Geriatric Department for Slovak Medical University has coordinated postgraduate training since 1983. Its first chair was Dr. Štefan Litomericky, CSc. (1983–1993), and its current head is Prof. Štefan Krajčík, CSc.

Qualification in geriatrics is, as one would assume, a prerequisite for a leading post in a geriatric department, a long-term care department, and/or an after-treatment department.

Postgraduate education in geriatrics was transformed after Slovakia joined the European Union in 2006, to comply with the requirements of the European Union of Medical Specialists. The training starts after a two-year internist stint, which ends with an examination. The training lasts for 36 months, of which 26 months are spent in a geriatric department, a long-term care department, or an after-treatment department. The trainee must document at least 200 discharged patients.

The curriculum includes a two-month stay in a psychiatric department, a two-month stay in a department of neurology, a month's work in a geriatric outpatients department, a month's stay in an RHB department, and a two-week stay in a department of neurology. The rest of the training is optional, but trainees must document 200 performed assessment tests (e.g., ADL, IADL, MMSE, and other).

The training program entails 400 hours of theory, including 180 hours in courses organized by the institution responsible for postgraduate education. The rest of the schooling takes place at congresses, conferences, and seminars organized by the Slovak Gerontology and Geriatric Society and others. The training concludes with a month's stay in the geriatric department of Slovak Medical University and a final examination, which includes a test, a practical examination, an oral examination, and a written thesis.

Most of the medical care for elderly people is provided by general practitioners. Two editions of the book *Geriatrics for General Practitioners* have been published and should be of help to them, as should a special program, Geriatrics for General Practitioners, which was sponsored by the Merck Institute of Aging and Health in 2005 and 2006.

Social gerontology is part of the Master of Public Health curriculum at the Faculty of Public Health, which has been part of Slovak Medical University since 1996. Geriatrics is also included in the curriculum of Nursing and Rehabilitation at the Faculty of Nursing, which has also been part of Slovak Medical University since 2002. Additionally, gerontology and geriatrics are part of the curriculum of nurses, rehabilitation workers, and social workers at Trnava University.

CURRENT PUBLIC POLICY ISSUES

Health-care and social-care provisions are regulated by laws, and patients' rights are guaranteed by legislation. Basic preventive medicine (free medical checkups) is granted by law.

The provision of specialized geriatric care is based on the *Concept of Geriatrics*, the document adopted by the Ministry of Health. The first Concept was adopted in 1979, and the current document was adopted in 2006. Geriatrics is defined as a specialty providing care to persons aged 65 or over. Geriatric care involves changes in the body related to aging and multimorbidity, with ensuing frailty and decreased adaptability. Care is aimed at assessment of the functional state and capacity and respects the impact of social factors on health, as well as the social aftermaths of diseases.

The typical problem of geriatric patients is frailty, which impairs adaptation and causes complications. Geriatric health care includes prevention, diagnosis, treatment, and rehabilitation.

The priorities of geriatric care are life prolongation and the achievement of the best possible quality of life. Another goal is the achievement of the highest possible level of performance in activities of daily living. Geriatrics emphasizes assessment in order to achieve these goals. Preventive medicine includes the prevention or decrease of cardiovascular diseases, malignancies, infections, falls, malnutrition, and adverse effects of drugs.

The Slovak Government adopted the National Program for the Support of Elderly People in 1999. The program, funded by Ministry of Labor, Social Welfare and Family, is evaluated and improved regularly. A major improvement to the Program is currently underway.

The most important government document regulating health-care provision is the State Policy of Health, enacted by the Ministry of Health in 2000, which had healthy aging as one of its priorities; however, the current document, adopted in 2008, does not contain any mention of health issues related directly to seniors. This change, which started in 2002, is not favorable to older people and geriatrics in Slovakia. The support of local activities from government is insufficient. The fact that care for elderly people is not a priority retards its development. Also, there are not many preventive health programs for seniors. Still, some positive developments can be observed in social care.

REFERENCES

Hegyi, L. (1997). Z dejín gerontológie na Slovensku (1) [History of gerontology in Slovakia (1)]. *Geriatria, 3*(3/4), 25–28.

Hegyi, L. (1998). Z dejín gerontológie na Slovensku (2) [History of gerontology in Slovakia (2)]. *Geriatria, 4*(1/2), 52–56.

Hegyi, L. (1999a). Z dejín gerontológie na Slovensku (3) [History of gerontology in Slovakia (3)]. *Geriatria, 5*(1–2), 34–37.

Hegyi, L. (1999b). Z dejín gerontológie na Slovensku (4) [History of gerontology in Slovakia (4)]. *Geriatria, 5*(3–4), 65–71.

Hegyi, L. (2001). The position of social gerontology in public health. *EURO-REHAB, 11*(2), 78–80.

Hegyi, L., & Krajčík, Š. (2004). *Geriatria pre praktického lekára* [Geriatrics for general practitioners] (1st ed.). Bratislava: HERBA.

Hegyi, L., & Krajčík, Š. (2006). *Geriatria pre praktického lekára* [Geriatrics for general practitioners] (2nd ed.). Bratislava: HERBA.

41

·· ■ ··

Slovenia

Valentina Hlebec and Masa Filipovic Hrast

Slovenia, like many other countries, has faced extensive demographic changes in recent years. The notable changes are low fertility rates and rapid aging of the population. In this chapter, we will present the recent history of aging in Slovenia and describe how political and scientific communities have been reacting to these changes; we will describe changes, research initiatives, and education in gerontology.

RECENT HISTORY

There are three main demographic changes in European Union that are also visible in Slovenia: aging of the population, with increased life expectancy and low fertility rates. In Slovenia, as in some other countries, immigration has somewhat mitigated the impact of falling birthrates.

Life expectancy increased from 65.6 (men) and 72.4 (women) in 1968 to 74.1 years (men) and 81.3 years (women) in 2005 (Statistical Office of the Republic of Slovenia [SORS], 2007a). This will increase further to 79.8 (men) and 85.1 years (women) in 2050 (European Commission, 2006). The net reproduction rate in Slovenia has decreased from above 1.0 before the 1980s to 0.60 in 2005. The total fertility rate was 1.26 in 2005. This net reproduction rate has been constantly decreasing since 1997, and was -0.3 in 2005. The net migration from abroad is positive, and was 3.2 in 2005, which made for a positive total net increase of 2.9 (all numbers are per 1,000 population) (SORS, 2007a).

These trends indicate that Slovenia is one of the countries with a rapidly changing population. According to the Statistical Office of the Republic of Slovenia (SORS, 2007a), the population of Slovenia grew in the last 30 years (from 1975 to 2005) in all age groups aged above 24 years. In the age group 55–59, the population increased by 115.1%, while in the age group 80 or more, it increased the most; that is, 181.7%. The aging index (the ratio between the population aged 65 or more and the population aged under 15) also shows a rapid aging of the population in the last few years. It grew by 2.4 times in the last 30 years. Since 1985, the index has been constantly rising, but until 1991, its annual growth never exceeded 2 index points. However, after 1995 it never rose by less than 3.8 index points. Therefore, in the past 30 years, the aging index has increased by 63.5 index points and in mid-2005 came to 108.7 (SORS, 2007a, p. 67).

The ratio between the people who do not participate in the labor force (the sum of people younger than 15 years and people aged 65 or more) and those who do (people aged 15–64 years) is measured by the population dependency ratio. In the past three decades, its value rose by 10.2, meaning that in mid-2005, there were 42.3 dependent people per 100 working-age population living in Slovenia, compared to 32.1 three decades earlier. Since 1987, the population dependency ratio of elderly people has been rising. Since 2003, the population aged 65 or more has contributed the most to the rise in the age dependency ratio (SORS, 2007a, p. 69). It is projected that these trends will continue in the future. According to the scenario that takes into account changes in fertility, mortality, and migration rates, the population of Slovenia will increase until 2019, but after that year, it will start to decline. Such a development will be the result of constant increase in life expectancy at birth, modest increase in fertility, and a relatively modest net migration (SORS, 2008). Consequently, the future age structure of the population in Slovenia will become top heavy as the number of older people increases and the number of younger people decreases (SORS, 2008, First Release).

Research on Aging in Slovenia

Aging is still under-researched in many fields. An illustrative example is the absence of this topic in family research. Research including older people represents only 2.9% of the research carried out in the area of sociology of family (Rener, Sedmak, Švab, & Urek, 2006). However, aging research does exist in many fields; for example:

- *Sociology*. At the Faculty of Social Sciences, University of Ljubljana, a research project on social integration of the elderly has been carried out; social networks research has looked specifically at social support networks of older people (see, e.g., Filipovič, Kogovšek, & Hlebec, 2005; Hlebec & Mandič, 2005; Pahor, Domanjko, & Hlebec, 2006), and also research on poverty among the elderly population. In collaboration with EU partners, the SOPRANO project—Service-Oriented Programmable Smart Environments for Older Europeans—is currently underway. Also, regular public opinion polls carried out by the Faculty of Social Sciences include topics related to aging, such as value orientations toward older people.

- *Medicine and health studies*. The Faculty of Health Sciences at the University of Maribor is involved in numerous research projects (national as well as international), covering a range of topics including evidence-based health promotion, the provision of health care in a variety of settings, and education about and for an aging population. Other health- and nursing-related faculties—at University of Primorska and University of Ljubljana—have done research on other topics, including the role of health care in quality of life, holistic treatment for older adults, telemedicine, fall prevention, technology and quality of life, and healthy active old age.

- *Social work*. At the Faculty of Social Work, University of Ljubljana, there have been research projects on working with people with dementia and on supported housing for vulnerable groups, which includes people with dementia. The Anton Trstenjak Institute, a research institute on gerontology and intergenerational relations, has done research projects on loneliness of older people and its consequences, and the social networks of older people that are formed to meet their nonmaterial needs.

- *Urban and housing studies*. Housing conditions of older adults in Slovenia have also been studied (Housing Survey, 2005, Faculty of Social Sciences, University of Ljubljana). The research project titled Housing Needs of Retired and Other Older People (2002) was done by the Urban Institute in cooperation with Faculty of Social Sciences, University of Ljubljana. The Urban Institute has also completed other research projects on housing and urban planning to meet the needs of older people.

Research on aging has been increasing in the last decade, reflecting the growing importance of the theme. The majority has been done in connection to health issues, but also some in connection to social issues and new information technology issues. There are also several interdisciplinary research projects among those listed above.

Current State of Education in Gerontology

Formal education in gerontology is conducted in various fields and is quite unsystematic. It is mostly present in the field of health care, and partly also in other fields, like sociology and social work. In the College for Health Studies at the University of Ljubljana, a course called Nursing Care of Older Adults and Gerontology is included in the curriculum. Similarly, this subject is part of the curriculum in the Faculty of Health Sciences at the University of Maribor. The Faculty of Health Sciences at the University of Maribor is also developing a master's degree program in gerontology in collaboration with international partners. Also, the Faculty of Social Work and the Faculty of Social Sciences at the University of Ljubljana have included gerontological content in their curricula (e.g., social work with older adults and social gerontology).

On the other hand, in the medical field, there is a significant lack of education in aging-related issues, as there is no official specialization in geriatrics. At the undergraduate level of medical studies, there is a special course in geriatrics at the new Medical Faculty of the University in Maribor, which is just about to start, but no such course is available at the more established Medical Faculty of the University in Ljubljana, where gerontological issues are included in other themes and courses (Mencej, 2008).

Informal gerontology education compensates for the rare formal education in gerontology. The so-called third voluntary sector performs important educational tasks. For example, the Gerontological Association of Slovenia, a voluntary general humanitarian organization, provides educational activities for older people as well as for professionals dealing with older people. The Gerontological Association of Slovenia has been an important agent in informal education processes—publishing books and organizing seminars and public debates. Also important are local and national pensioners' organizations that train volunteers and publish bulletins and leaflets, and organize seminars and round tables.

In addition, volunteers working in various nongovernmental organizations (NGOs) receive specific education and training relevant to their activities. In 1997, the Anton Trstenjak Institute started the development of a network of volunteers to help older people support themselves. Since the beginning of the 1990s, the Institute has trained about 500 volunteers who are now facilitators of more than 500 self-supporting groups for older people. These groups include about 5,000 older people all over Slovenia.

The association of long-term care facilities and private educational organizations has also developed programs, courses, and lectures on institutionalized care since the mid-1990s (Mencej, 2008).

PUBLIC POLICY ISSUES

The social welfare system in Slovenia today is based on the state-socialist welfare system developed in Yugoslavia, and is described by several authors (see Kolarič, 1993; Kolarič, Črnak Meglič, & Vojnovič, 2002; Kolarič, Kopač, & Rakar, 2008). The main characteristic of this system was the dominant role of the state, which was primarily oriented toward developing public institutions to care for the aging population. The informal sector (close family members—women in particular—other relatives, and neighbors) was heavily burdened with the care of the older adults. Women were especially burdened because of the very high employment rate of women. Services for older adults in Yugoslavia were partly formalized, partly informal, partly professionalized, partly unpaid, and partly illegal. Production of services by voluntary organizations and associations was not developed.

The new welfare system can be described as a "welfare mix" and more closely resembles the Western European welfare systems. The state still has the dominant position as a financial force, whereas the production of social services has been redistributed to the private sector. This structure was established in the 1990s. It is a tripartite system of a well-developed and regionally dispersed network of public/state organizations and institutions (production and distribution of services and financial compensations by the state and by corporations for employed people), and voluntary and unpaid services within the informal sector (family, relatives, neighbors, friends). This is an area to which the state did not pay attention for a long time. There has been a gradual introduction of reforms in social policies for individuals after the transformation of the political and economic system. For example, pension and health system, care for older adults (as described below).

The structure of financing social welfare has been quite stable over the last few years. In 2005, 23.6% of the GDP was used mainly for the following social welfare programs: (a) old age (42.5%): old-age pensions, disability, and survivors' pensions; (b) health care (32.3%): physical or mental health benefits; (c) family and children (8.6%): pregnancy-related costs, childbirth, child-rearing benefits, and caring for other family members; and (d) disability (8.5%): disability pensions and provisions of goods and services (SORS, 2007b).

In response to the demographic and economic trends, reforms of the pension systems were introduced, the most significant is the Pension and Disability Insurance Act (PDIA) in 1999. Reforms are good examples of the gradual approach toward the reform of the social welfare system. The reforms introduced a three-pillar pension system, where the dominant role is still played by the first, public pillar. Changes in the first pillar (e.g., the introduction of the retirement age of 63 for men and 61 for women and related "penalties" and "bonuses," abolishment of early retirement, new state pension, etc.), although substantial, were introduced gradually, with numerous exceptions. The first pillar is (still) mandatory and covers the risk of old age, disability, and survivorship. The second pillar is voluntary and covers only the risk of old age. It is managed by pension funds. In 2004, about 46.36% of all insured persons within the first (public) pillar were included in this pillar. The third pension pillar consists of voluntary individual savings for old age, mostly in the form of life insurance, administered by insurance companies. Most of the rights (especially rights to pensions) are earning related. Some supplementary benefits are means tested and targeted at low-income pensioners, with one universal benefit—recreation grant. The pension reform in the 1990s stabilized public pension expenditures as a percentage of GDP. After the introduction of the 1999 PDIA, the actual retirement age started to increase. Further reforms are discussed to encourage people to work longer.

Stropnik, Stanovnik, Rebolj, and Prevolnik Rupel (2003) claim that the Slovenian health-care system is in general quite transparent, well structured and financially stable. The legal basis for health-care reform is the Health Care and Health Insurance Act (Ministry of Health, 1992a), Health Care Services Act (Ministry of Health, 1992b), and rules of Health Insurance Institute of Slovenia (HIIS) on compulsory health insurance. All of these acts have been amended several times. The coverage is almost 100%. The entry into the health-care system is insurance based, while rights are based on the principle of equity. The system is based on the principle of solidarity as funds are redistributed from rich to poor, from young to old, and from healthy to ill. Voluntary Health Insurance (VHI) covers payments for health services that are not covered by CHI (Compulsory Health Insurance). VHI could be regarded as compulsory, as the majority of the population cannot afford not to be insured. However, it has been criticized for enlarging social inequality in Slovenia (Stropnik et al., 2003). Supplementary insurance for services of a higher standard is available but not very common. Most of the health-care providers (hospitals and clinics) are state owned. So far, a relatively stable and balanced funding has been ensured for the health-care system (about 7% GDP).

However, in the future, the current system will not be financially sustainable. This will be a major issue. The estimated expenditure on long-term care for 2004 was 0.9% of GDP, which was the same as the European Union 25 average. However, the projections for 2050 show an increase to 2.1%, which is above the 1.6 average in EU 25. This increase is among the steepest in EU 25, only superseded by Finland and Sweden (European Commission, 2008).

There have been many changes in the welfare system in the last 17 years with regard to the care for older adults. The welfare system before the transition comprised a well-developed and regionally dispersed network of public/state organizations and institutions. The number of long-term care facilities has grown slightly in the last 10 years, with 69 facilities existing in 2006. These 69 facilities provided care for just 3.8% of the aging population in Slovenia (65 years and above). However, the number of applicants is rising and the waiting periods for acceptance into these facilities are becoming longer (Vertot, 2007). Along with long-term care facilities, other services are provided by the State for older adults, such as adult centers and centers to help elders who are living at home. Starting in the mid-1990s, the latter have developed very quickly and have been well received by users. Unfortunately, the supply is still not meeting the demand and such assistance is not available in some communities. The scope is also limited, as these centers do not offer assistance with health care (Hvalič Touzery, 2007, pp. 151–154). Support in the home by medical nurses has been diminishing due to changes in the health-care system (Ramovš, 2003, in Hvalič Touzery, 2007, p. 139). Palliative care is another important service that still has not been developed, even though it is envisaged in the Strategy for Care for the Elderly. Here the third sector plays an important role, along with the hospice organization.

The third sector (the nonprofit and voluntary sector) is becoming more and more important in supporting older adults and their caregivers. However, the role of voluntary organizations, though increasingly important, has been limited by the small growth of the third sector. Organizations working in the social or health sector represent only a small part of the third-sector organizations.

Aging is addressed in the policies of social security and social welfare. For example, the Social Security adopted in 2000 emphasized care for older people, mainly by ensuring that they can live in their community as long as possible. Also, in the *Resolution on the National Social Assistance Program 2006–2010*, special care for older adults who need help is listed as one of the national priorities. It states that family and social networks that care for older adults should be provided and new models of community-based care should be developed. Furthermore, an Act on long-term care insurance is currently being processed in Parliament.

In 1997, the first document specifically targeting older people was adopted, *The Development of Care for Older Adults in the Field of Social Security in Slovenia until 2005*. Its main goals were developing more complementary and balanced services for older people, mainly by further developing institutional care (with the goal of developing long-term care facilities that can accommodate 4.5% of the older adult population) and developing community-based services (ensuring coverage of 15% of the aging population). Among community-based services, the following were mentioned: adult day centers, subsidized housing, and help at home (personal, household help, health care, etc.). This program was further developed in the *Care Strategy for Older Adults 2006–2010*. Its goal is to keep solidarity among all generations and ensure quality of aging and care for the aging population. It wants to ensure optimum conditions are in place for older adults to participate in society, to be included socially, and to have high-quality health and social services. It also aims to educate people in intergenerational solidarity, and reduces prejudices about aging and older people that exist in society. More specifically, goals are set to increase participation of older people in the labor market; to ensure a financially sustainable health care and pension systems; to promote preventive health-care practices; to support research on aging; and to develop communication services and traffic arrangements that meet the needs of older persons.

REFERENCES

European Commission. (2006). *The demographic future of Europe—From challenge to opportunity (COM 571 final)*. Brussels: European Commission.

European Commission. (2008). Long-term care in the European Union. Employment, social affairs and equal opportunities. *Proceedings from Intergenerational Solidarity for Cohesive and Sustainable Societies Conference, 2008*. Brdo, Slovenia: European Commission.

Filipovič, M., Kogovšek, T., & Hlebec, V. (2005). Starostniki in njihova vpetost v sosedska omrežja [The elderly and their integration in neighbouring networks]. *Družboslovne razprave, 21*(49/50), 205–221.

Health Insurance Institute of Slovenia. (2007). *Compulsory health insurance in Slovenia: Today for tomorrow*. Retrieved July 20, 2008, from http://www.zzzs.si/zzzs/internet/zzzseng.nsf

Hlebec, V., & Mandič, S. (2005). Socialna omrežja starejših v obdobju tranzicije v Sloveniji [Social networks of the elderly population for the transitional period in Slovenia]. *Kakovostna starost, 8*(4), 2–16.

Hvalič Touzery, S. (2007). *Družinska oskrba starih družinskih članov* [Family provision for older family members]. Doctoral dissertation, Faculty of Social Work, University of Ljubljana.

Kolarič, Z. (1993). Privatizacija na področju socialnega varstva v slovenski, postsocialistični družbi [Privatization in the sphere of social security in the Slovene, post socialist society]. In M. Kovač (Ed.), *Privatizacija na področju družbenih dejavnosti* [Privatization in the sphere of social activities] (pp. 267–306). Ljubljana, Slovenia: Državna založba Slovenije.

Kolarič, Z., Črnak Meglič, A., & Vojnovič, M. (2002). *Zasebne neprofitno-volonterske organizacije v mednarodni perspektivi* [Private non-profit volunteer organizations in international perspective]. Ljubljana, Slovenia: Založba Fdv.

Kolarič, Z., Kopač, A., & Rakar, T. (2008). Schrittweise Reformierung statt "Schochtherapie": das slowenische Wohlfahrtssystem [Gradual reformation instead of "shock therapy": The Slovene social welfare system]. In K. Schubert, S. Hegelich & U. Bazant (Eds.), *Europäische Wohlfartssysteme* [The European social welfare system] (pp. 569–593). Wiesbaden: VS Verlag für Sozialwissenschaften.

Mandič, S., & Hlebec, V. (2006). *Razvojno raziskovalni projekt Stanovanjska anketa 2005* [Housing survey 2005, report]. Retrieved October 19, 2008, from http://www.stanovanjskisklad-rs.si/upload/mo_files/lang_slo/Stanovan jsko%20porocilo%20koncno.pdf

Mencej, M. (2008). White paper 2008 on European geriatric medicine. Unpublished report. Slovenia: Gerontological Association of Slovenia.

Ministry of Health. (1992a). *Zakon o zdravstvenem varstvu in zdravstvenem zavarovanju* [Health Care and Health Insurance Act]. (*Uradni list Republike Slovenije*, št. 9/1992: ZZVZZ). Ljubljana: Ministry of Health.

Ministry of Health. (1992b). *Zakon o zdravstveni dejavnosti* [Health Care Services Act]. (*Uradni list Republike Slovenije*, št. 26/1992: ZZDej.) Ljubljana, Slovenia: Ministry of Health.

Ministry of Labour, Family and Social Affairs. (1997). *Program razvoja varstva starejših oseb na področju socialnega varstva v Sloveniji do leta 2005* [The development of care for older adults in the field of social security in Slovenia until 2005]. Ljubljana, Slovenia: Ministry of Labour, Family and Social Affairs.

Ministry of Labour, Family and Social Affairs. (1999). *Zakon o pokojninskem in invalidskem zavarovanju* [The Pension and Disability Insurance Act (PDIA)]. (*Uradni list Republike Slovenije*, št. 106/1999: ZPIZ-1.) Ljubljana, Slovenia: Ministry of Labour, Family and Social Affairs.

Ministry of Labour, Family and Social Affairs. (2000). *Nacionalni program socialnega varstva do leta 2005* [Social security programme until 2005]. Ljubljana, Slovenia: Ministry of Labour, Family and Social Affairs.

Ministry of Labour, Family and Social Affairs. (2006). *Resolucija o nacionalnem programu socialnega varstva za obdobje 2006–2010* [Resolution on the national

484 The International Handbook on Aging

social assistance programme 2006–2010]. (Uradni list Republike Slovenije, št. 39/2006: ReNPSV06–10.) Ljubljana, Slovenia: National Assembly of the Republic of Slovenia.

Ministry of Labour, Family and Social Affairs. (2007). *Strategija varstva starejših do leta 2010—Solidarnost, sožitje in kakovostno staranje prebivalstva* [Care strategy for older adults 2006–2010—Solidarity, coexistence and quality ageing of population]. Ljubljana, Slovenia: Ministry of Labour, Family and Social Affairs.

Pahor, M., Domajnko, B., & Hlebec, V. (2006). Double vulnerability: Older women and health in Slovenia. In G. Backes, V. Lasch, & K. Reimann (Eds.), *Gender, health and ageing: European perspectives on life course, health issues and social challenges* (pp. 157–174). Wiesbaden: VS Verlag für Sozialwissenschaften.

Rener, T., Sedmak, M., Švab, A., & Urek, M. (2006). *Družine in družinsko življenje v Sloveniji* [Families and family life in Slovenia]. Koper, Slovenia: ZaložbAnnales.

Statistical Office of the Republic of Slovenia (SORS). (2007a). *Population of Slovenia 2004 and 2005*. Retrieved June 24, 2008, from http://www.stat.si/doc/pub/rr-828-07.pdf

Statistical Office of the Republic of Slovenia (SORS). (2007b). *Expenditure and receipts of social protection schemes, Slovenia, 2005—Provisional data*. Retrieved July 3, 2008, from http://www.stat.si/eng/novica_prikazi.aspx?id=1215

Statistical Office of the Republic of Slovenia (SORS). (2008). *Eurostat's population projections for Slovenia, 2008–2060, EUROPOP 2008, convergence scenario*. Retrieved June 24, 2008, from http://www.stat.si/eng/novica_prikazi.aspx?id=1683

Stropnik, N., Stanovnik, T., Rebolj, M., & Prevolnik Rupel, V. (2003). Country study Slovenia—Länderstudie Slowenien. In *Social protection in the candidate countries—Gesellschaft für Versicherungswissenschaft unf-gestaltung E. V.* (pp. 1–156). Berlin, Germany: AKA.

Vertot, P. (Ed.). (2007). *Invalidi, starejši in druge osebe s posebnimi potrebami v Sloveniji* [Invalids, the elderly population and the other persons with special needs in Slovenia]. Ljubljana, Slovenia: Statistical Office of the Republic of Slovenia (SORS).

42

··■··

South Africa

Jaco Hoffman

South Africa, as the country with the highest proportion of older people on mainland sub-Saharan Africa (SSA), may be described as in the intermediate stage of population aging (Kinsella & Phillips, 2005). This general description, however, masks the heterogeneity of aging patterns in this multiethnic society with its diversity of social contexts.

BACKGROUND

Life for most people in South Africa is currently being determined by the following major interrelated trends—cross-cut by changing family/household structures—namely, poverty, migration, HIV/AIDS, and government policies toward the extension of social assistance.

South Africa—considering life expectancy, adult literacy, school enrolment rates, and income—ranks 125th out of 179 countries in the updated 2007–8 *Human Development Report* of the United Nations Human Development Index (United Nations Development Programme [UNDP], 2008). Numbering 48.7 million people, South Africa is a middle-income country with one of the highest levels of economic inequality in the world. Although South Africa contributes one-third of the gross domestic product (GDP) of SSA, unemployment is still widespread, around 36% if the expanded definition of unemployment is used, which takes discouraged work-seekers into account. Such entrenched inequality—both racial and gender—and poverty, with Blacks falling into the lowest income brackets, are legacies of previous policies related to colonialism and apartheid (Bhorat, Leibbrandt, Maziya, Van der Berg, & Woolard, 2001, Statistics South Africa, 2008). Under apartheid, the population was classified into four racial categories, namely Blacks, Whites, Coloureds, and Asian/Indians, with Whites specifically advantaged. This legacy, since dismantled with the 1994 democratic elections, still shapes any understanding and analysis of the South African population - currently constituting around 79% Blacks, 9% Whites, 9% Coloureds and 3% Indians/Asians (Statistics South Africa, 2008).

With half of the total population surviving on R20 (less than US$3) a day, millions of South Africans remain trapped in poverty, resulting, among other effects, in massive rural-urban migration (Statistics South Africa, 2008). Despite efforts by the first democratically elected government to support vulnerable groups through a social protection network, chronic poverty is still an all-encompassing reality, even more so given the AIDS pandemic (Lund, 2008).

South Africa is one of the hardest-hit countries, with around 6 million persons living with HIV/AIDS (Joint United Nations Programme on HIV/AIDS and World Health Organization [UNAIDS/WHO], 2007). This high prevalence contributes to such demographic changes as lower life expectancy and might have a temporary accelerative effect on population aging (Actuarial Society of South Africa [ASSA], 2004; Kinsella & Phillips, 2005). The focus on HIV/AIDS, however, masks several other health realities such as a health-care system challenged by conditions related to poverty (e.g., malnutrition and tuberculosis); an increase in noncommunicable diseases; and a high rate of injuries and other infectious diseases (Joubert & Bradshaw, 2006).

Poverty, exacerbated by HIV/AIDS, and constitutionally guaranteed access to social security set the scene for the South African government to oversee what is currently one of the fastest-growing social welfare systems in the developing world. Approximately 12 million people—considerably expanded in the context of HIV/AIDS—now receive social grants. Research shows that this range of grants—the most important being Old Age Pension, Foster Care Grant, Care Dependency Grant, and Child Support Grant—indeed protects the most vulnerable individuals (especially children, women, and older persons) and helps the poorest households get access to at least basic services (Barrientos et al., 2003; Lund, 2008, Møller & Ferreira, 2003).

AGING IN SOUTH AFRICA

Although on the whole, South Africa is currently one of the oldest populations in SSA, different geographical areas and different race groups follow diverse and unique aging patterns: South Africa's total population numbers 48.7 million people, 3.5 million (7.2%) of whom are aged 60 and over (Statistics South Africa, 2008). This older population is projected to almost double by 2050 to 6.4 million, representing 13%. Among SSA countries, population aging in South Africa is thus comparatively advanced, trailing only the island states of Réunion (9.9%) and Mauritius (9%) (United Nations Population Division [UNPD], 2006).

Despite the fact that persons aged 60 and over constitute only 7.2% of the country's population, they represent 19.6% of the provincial population in KwaZulu-Natal and 18% in the Eastern Cape. This is a direct result of out-migration of young adults for work and study purposes, as well as the impact of HIV/AIDS (Statistics South Africa, 2005). These "left-behind" older generations, as well as those who resettled in urban areas, experience heightened vulnerability in, respectively, depopulated and overpopulated contexts.

It is furthermore important to note that rates of population aging vary across the respective racial groups of South Africa. Although Black older persons constitute only 4.7% of the total population, they represent 64% of the older cohorts. Of the 60 and over population, Coloureds constitute 5%, Indians/Asians 3.6% and Whites 24.2%. The absolute number of Black older persons is expected to increase dramatically in coming decades, which will, because of their historical socioeconomic disadvantage, have significant implications for future public sector care and service provision (Statistics South Africa, 2008; UNDP, 2006).

The majority of older South Africans live in multi-generational households, but living arrangements are largely determined by sociocultural preferences and socioeconomic factors, varying across the different racial groups: While White older women are more likely to live independently, Black, Coloured, and Indian/Asian older women prefer to co-reside with the family in multi-generational households. Overall, 72% of the non-institutionalized older population, across racial groups, co-resides with children and/or grandchildren, and almost all Black older persons who co-reside head these multi-generational households (United Nations Department of Economic and Social Affairs, 2005).

Important to note is that these households—due to unemployment, out-migration, HIV/AIDS, and personal dynamics—have much fluidity in form, and their boundaries are porous (Ziehl, 2002). For example, several authors indicate that the so-called skip-generational configurations, assumed to characterize AIDS-stricken Africa where younger children are left without parents in the care of grandmothers, actually are embedded in broader grandmother-headed multigenerational and multilocational support networks (Chazan, 2008; Madhavan, 2004). Neither growing old nor being a child is entirely shaped by the world of the family and kinship. We need a deeper understanding of the processes associated with being "generationed" together.

Older persons are increasingly affected—and infected—by HIV/AIDS. In South Africa in 2005, the number of so-called AIDS orphans was estimated to be between 830,000 and 1.2 million, and that number is predicted to rise to 2.3 million by 2020 (UNAIDS, 2006; UNAIDS, UNICEF & USAID, 2004). Around 60% of these orphans are estimated to live in grandparent-headed households (Makiwane, Schneider, & Gopane, 2004; Monasch & Boerma, 2004), and older women, in particular, often must assume care responsibilities for infected and/or affected younger adults and/or orphaned and vulnerable children. It is in this context that Wilson and Adamchack (2001) refer to HIV/AIDS as the "grandmothers' disease."

The effects of HIV/AIDS on older persons in South Africa are extensively described in the literature, which also highlights a dichotomy between their burden of care and the contributions they make (Ferreira, Keikelame, & Mosaval, 2001; Hosegood & Timaeus, 2006; Schatz & Ogunmefun, 2005). As there are virtually no institutional care options for either AIDS patients or orphans, poor households ultimately provide the necessary shelter and care. Nuxani (2004) furthermore notes a trend where HIV/AIDS-infected younger generations return to their rural homes to be cared for by older generations.

Although under-researched in South Africa, an increasing number of older persons is found to be infected with HIV, and two trends are observed: (1) HIV-infected age cohorts are surviving to enter the older age groups as a result of effective treatments, and (2) new HIV/AIDS cases are occurring in persons aged 60 and older (Ferreira, 2006b). The heightened prevalence of HIV/AIDS among women in Africa can be traced to a patriarchal ideology, among other causes; that is, increased vulnerability to HIV/AIDS is intricately linked to factors related to gender inequity (Maitse & Majake, 2005). In addition to having been disadvantaged by gender inequalities in many spheres over the life course, Black older women in South Africa are especially vulnerable to the effects of the HIV/AIDS epidemic—especially concerning care management.

Older women in particular use their income to support the multigenerational household: South Africa is one of only five countries in SSA (the others are Botswana, Lesotho, Mauritius, and Namibia) that provide a noncontributory, means-tested social pension to the majority of its older population (2.2 million women and men from the age of 60). Although grants averaging R940 (about US$100) a month are paid to individuals, benefits are pooled and redistributed—especially by Black females—at household and community levels (Barrientos et al., 2003; Ferreira, 2006c; Møller & Ferreira, 2003; Sagner & Mtati, 1999).

This support affects their own well-being: As clearly indicated in various studies, the social pension empowers beneficiaries by offering them pensioner status and identity (Ferreira, 2004; Ferreira & Van Dongen, 2004). However, a general clustering of different generations for different reasons around these pensioners and the subsequent multiple responsibilities faced by them are increasingly perceived as a burden and a violation of their human rights (Ministerial Committee on Abuse, Neglect and Ill-treatment of Older Persons, 2001; Møller & Sotshongaye, 2002). Important issues regarding current existing patterns of intergenerational support from old to young relate to the asymmetrical need and dependency of younger generations on older generations and the older generations' entrapped sense of responsibility (Aboderin & Ferreira, 2007).

Apart from the physical, health, and emotional effects of the burden of caregiving and the loss of kin, older persons may also neglect their own health because of caregiving challenges. By far, the majority of older persons depend on the public sector for health care, and although provided to pensioners for free, the accessibility and quality of appropriate care are still major challenges. Although years of colonial and apartheid policies compromised older South Africans' health across the life course, life expectancy at age 60 is 14 and 18 years for males and females, respectively. Life expectancy at birth has dropped, however, from 61.8 years in 1990–1995 to an estimated 50.3 years for males and 53.9 years for females due to AIDS-associated mortality (Statistics South Africa, 2008).

EDUCATION ON AGING IN SOUTH AFRICA

As far back as 1955, the National Council for the Aged and the Cape Peninsula Welfare Organisation for the Aged advocated for the need to establish gerontology and geriatric medicine at South African universities. Only in 1977 was a Chair of Geriatric Medicine negotiated at the University of Cape Town, and the William Slater Chair of Geriatric Medicine was established in 1981, but it currently is frozen. Presently, only the University of KwaZulu-Natal in Durban has a chair of geriatrics (Kalula, 2008).

The emphasis on primary care led to the de-prioritization of education and training in gerontology and geriatric medicine—both at systemic and institutional levels (Ferreira, 2006a). In a population of more than

48 million, there are fewer than 10 registered geriatricians, about 6 psychogeriatricians, and fewer than 30 registered nurses with specific training in geriatric medicine and gerontology (Ferreira, 2007; Kalula, 2008). In undergraduate nursing education, there is currently no module specific to geriatrics/gerontology. The only postgraduate diploma in geriatric nursing, offered by the University of South Africa (UNISA), terminated at the end of 2008 since it has not been able to attract more than 10 students per year. Physiotherapy has a special module in geriatrics in six of the eight training institutions; occupational therapy, speech therapy, and social work cover pathologies that affect older persons, but lack a formal module on geriatrics in their core curricula.

As part of only a few social work, practical theology, and psychology courses, several modules on the psychosocial aspects of aging are run by universities throughout South Africa. Facilitated by the African Research on Ageing Network (AFRAN), based at the University of Oxford, the United Nations International Institute of Ageing (INIA) and North-West University in South Africa, together with a consortium of universities and the National Departments of Social Development and Health presented a short course on Social Gerontology in South Africa during 2008. There is, however, still no dedicated, well-coordinated, multidisciplinary focus addressing the broad social aspects of gerontology.

RESEARCH ON AGING IN SOUTH AFRICA

In addition to the research already referred to, it is to be noted that earlier work on older persons in South Africa was based mainly on anthropological studies as well as *ad hoc*, one-off research projects. Research on aging in South Africa as a coordinated effort was greatly stimulated by the establishment of the National Research Programme on Ageing of the Human Sciences Research Council (HSRC) in 1987 (Human Sciences Research Council, n.d.). This interdisciplinary program aimed to promote research on aging in the human sciences and to expand its volume and improve its quality. It was transformed in 1991 into the HSRC/UCT Centre for Gerontology at the University of Cape Town. This center stimulated and coordinated high-quality research in South Africa and acted as a pivotal point for research in the broader southern African context. Linked to the center was also the highly regarded first and only African journal on aging, the *Southern African Journal of Gerontology* (since discontinued due to lack of funding) as well as the authoritative *National Multi-dimensional Survey of Older Persons* in 1992 (Ferreira, Møller, Prinsloo, & Gillis, 1992). Following the HSRC's withdrawal of support for the center, the interdisciplinary Albertina and Walter Sisulu Institute of Ageing in Africa was established in 2001.

The multiplicity of the aging experience is, however, often still lost through the ongoing homogeneity in the discourse on aging in (South) Africa. This can be partly ascribed to the tendency over the past decades to explain aging and old age mainly in terms of orthodox modernization theory (Ferreira, 1999; Sagner, 1999). Only since the later 1990s has there been a move away from structural functionalist approaches toward an understanding of the contexts, experiences, and contributions of older persons as dynamic human agents (Makoni & Stroeken, 2002).

Although relatively advanced compared with the rest of SSA, South African research on health and health care in relation to aging remains underdeveloped and poorly translated into practice. Often focused on defined communities and not representative of a multiethnic society, research on the health aspects of older persons and age-related noncommunicable disease in South Africa ranges from the burden of disease attributable to chronic diseases of lifestyle (Schnitzler, Schnaid, MacPhail, Mesquita, & Robson, 2005; Steyn, Fourie, & Temple, 2006) to the clinical aspects of illness and health care, including stroke (SASPI Project Team, 2004); musculoskeletal disease (Kalula, de Villiers, Ross, & Ferreira, 2006; Schnitzler, et al., 2005); neoplastic disease (Vorobiof, Sitas, & Vorobiof, 2001); pharmacology (Tipping, Kalula, & Badri, 2006); institutional care management (Perold & Muller, 2000; Van Staden & Weich, 2007); and attitudes of health-care professionals toward older patients (Ntusi & Ferreira, 2004).

The effective translation of relevant research information into policy and practice will remain a challenge. Policy needs to be informed by research, and several pan-African research initiatives, like the African Research on Ageing Network and the United Nations Programme on Ageing/International Association of Gerontology and Geriatrics, have potential to focus and enhance research endeavors on aging in South Africa (AFRAN, 2005; United Nations Programme on Ageing/International Association of Gerontology and Geriatrics, 2006).

CURRENT PUBLIC POLICY ISSUES IN AGING

The National Department of Social Development assumes primary responsibility for, and aims to facilitate, accessible, equitable, and affordable services to older persons. Broadly speaking, since 1994, policies have shifted from institutional to community-based care. To this extent, the *Older Persons Act* No. 13 of 2006 was enacted to maintain and promote their status, well-being, safety, and security; recognize skills and wisdom; and promote participation in the community and activities pertaining to their interests and needs. It specifically aims to protect older persons from abuse and exploitation (Ferreira, 2007).

Although South Africa has a progressive constitution and has signed several recent global policy instruments—the UN Madrid International Plan of Action on Ageing 2002 (UN, 2002) and the African Union's Policy Framework and Plan of Action on Ageing (African Union/HelpAge International, 2003)—and enacted legislation to protect older persons, it still lacks a comprehensive and integrated policy on aging and older persons. Also lacking is an effective institutionalized voice for older persons. The establishment in 2005 of the South African Older Persons' Forum with the aim to monitor and evaluate the implementation of the Act was a positive development toward the interpretation and translation of these policies and rights into practice. These include policies challenging age discrimination and abuse; ensuring that older persons have access to education and training; enabling participation in policy formulation and implementation; empowering them to access services, and offering protection and care when needed (Ferreira, 2007).

An all-encompassing policy issue is HIV/AIDS and how it affects older persons in relation to younger generations—information and awereness programs, the impact of grants, intergenerational relations, care management, and contributions by older generations. A challenge will be to ensure that the emphasis on addressing HIV/AIDS in younger generations does not mask the needs of older, vulnerable South Africans. Generally, any policies and programs that enhance age-segregation and the fragmentation of generations and households should be opposed.

TOWARD A (SOUTH) AFRICAN-APPROPRIATE GERONTOLOGY. . .

The ongoing challenge for gerontology in South Africa is the development of a (South) African-appropriate gerontology: although appropriate attention should be given to the processes associated with modernization, the complex realities and multiplicity of human patterns of social organization must be recognized. Researchers and educators should move toward a critical gerontology; mindful, on the one hand, of the danger and irrelevance of imposed outside models and, on the other hand, careful of a reductionist African approach to explain elderliness. This probably will be developed at the research and policy interface, at the explicit or subtle interconnections of older persons with their environment, community members and kin across the generations as well as the ancestral past and present (Hoffman, 2006).

REFERENCES

Aboderin, I., & Ferreira, M. (2007). *Linking Ageing to Development Agendas in sub-Saharan Africa: Challenges and Approaches*. The WDA—HSG Discussion Paper Series on Demographic Issues, No. 2008/1. University of St. Gallen: World Demographic Association. Retrieved from http://www.wdassocia tion.org/_project/uploads/1/1_Isabella_Aboderin.pdf

Actuarial Society of South Africa (ASSA). (2004). *ASSA AIDS and demographic models: ASSA 2002*. Retrieved from http://www.assa.org.za.

African Research on Ageing Network (AFRAN). (2005). *Understanding and addressing ageing, health, poverty and social development in sub-Saharan Africa: A research framework and strategy plan*. Oxford, UK: Oxford Institute of Ageing.

African Union/HelpAge International (HAI). (2003). *AU Policy Framework and Plan of Action on Ageing*. Nairobi, Kenya: HAI.

Barrientos, A., Ferreira, M., Gorman, M., Heslop, A., Legido-Quigley, H., Lloyd-Sherlock, P., et al. (2003). *Non-contributory pensions and poverty prevention: A comparative study of Brazil and South Africa*. London: Institute of Development Policy and Management (Manchester) and HelpAge International.

Bhorat, H., Leibbrandt, M., Maziya, M., Van der Berg, S., & Woolard, I. (2001). *Fighting poverty: Labour markets and inequality in South Africa*. Landsdowne, South Africa: UCT Press.

Chazan, M. (2008). Seven "deadly" assumptions: Unraveling the implications of HIV/AIDS among grandmothers in South Africa and beyond. *Ageing & Society, 28*, 935–958.

Ferreira, M. (1999). Editorial: Building and advancing African gerontology. *Southern African Journal of Gerontology, 8*, 1–3.

Ferreira, M. (2004). Advancing income security in old age in developing countries: Focus on Africa. *Global Ageing: Issues and Action, 2*, 24–39.

Ferreira, M. (2006a). Geriatric medicine in South Africa—A Cinderella subspecialty? Editorial. *South African Family Practice, 48*, 18.

Ferreira, M. (2006b). HIV/AIDS and older people in sub-Saharan Africa: Towards a policy framework. *Global Ageing: Issues and Action, 4*, 56–71.

Ferreira, M. (2006c). The differential impact of social-pension income on household poverty alleviation in three South African ethnic groups. *Ageing and Society, 26*, 337–354.

Ferreira, M. (2007). *Growing old in South Africa: Between AIDS, baobabs and longevity. The Harold Hatch Lecture in Geriatrics and Gerontology*. University of Cape Town: International Longevity Centre—South Africa. Retrieved from http://www.ilcsa.uct.ac.za/Growing%20old%20in%20South%20 Africa.doc

Ferreira, M., Keikelame, J., & Mosaval, Y. (2001). *Older women as carers to children and grandchildren affected by AIDS: Towards supporting the carers.* Cape Town, South Africa: University of Cape Town, Institute of Ageing in Africa.

Ferreira, M., Møller, V., Prinsloo, F. R., & Gillis, L. S. (1992). *Multidimensional survey of elderly South Africans, 1990–91: Key findings.* Cape Town, South Africa: University of Cape Town, HSRC/UCT Centre for Gerontology.

Ferreira, M., & Van Dongen, E. (Eds.) (2004). *Untold stories. Giving voice to the lives of older persons in new South African society: An anthology.* Cape Town, South Africa: University of Cape Town, Institute of Ageing in Africa.

Hoffman, J. R. (2006). Re-conceptualising elderliness in South Africa—A theoretical and methodological exploration. *Generations Review, 16,* 16–19.

Hosegood, V., & Timaeus, I. M. (2006). HIV/AIDS and older people in South Africa. In National Research Council, *Aging in sub-Saharan Africa: Recommendations for furthering research* (pp. 250–275). Washington, DC: The National Academies Press.

Human Sciences Research Council. (n.d.). *National Research Programme on Ageing.* Pretoria: HSRC.

Joint United Nations Programme on HIV/AIDS and World Health Organization (UNAIDS/WHO). (2007). *AIDS epidemic update.* New York.

Joubert, J., & Bradshaw, D. (2006). Population ageing and its health challenges in South Africa. In K. Steyn, J. Fourie, & N. Temple (Eds.), *Non-communicable disease in South Africa: 2005* (pp. 204–219). Cape Town, South Africa: South African Medical Research Council.

Kalula, S. Z. (2008). *Professional training in geriatric medicine and gerontology in South Africa.* Presentation at the Second AFRAN Research-Policy Dialogue on Ageing: Advancing Health Service Provision for Age-related Non-Communicable Disease and Older Persons in sub-Saharan Africa: Identifying Key Information and Training Needs. 8–10 July. Abuja, Nigeria.

Kalula, S., de Villiers, L., Ross, K., & Ferreira, M. (2006). Management of older patients presenting after a fall—An accident and emergency department audit. *South African Medical Journal, 96,* 718–721.

Kinsella, K., & Phillips, D. (2005). Global aging: The challenge of success. *Population Bulletin, 60,* 1–40.

Lund, F. (2008). *Changing social policy: The child support grant in South Africa.* Cape Town, South Africa: HSRC Press.

Madhavan, S. (2004). Fosterage patterns in the age of AIDS: Continuity and change. *Social Science and Medicine, 58,* 1443–1454.

Maitse, T., & Majake, C. (Eds.) (2005). *Enquiry into the gendered lived experience of older persons living in conditions of poverty.* Johannesburg: Commission on Gender Equality.

Makiwane, M., Schneider, M., & Gopane, M. (2004). *Experiences and needs of older persons in Mpumalanga: Research report for the Mpumalanga Department of Health and Social Services.* Pretoria, South Africa: HSRC.

Makoni, S., & Stroeken, K. (Eds.) (2002). *Ageing in Africa: Sociolinguistic and anthropological approaches.* Aldershot, UK: Ashgate.

Ministerial Committee on Abuse, Neglect and Ill-treatment of Older Persons, Department of Social Development, Republic of South Africa. (2001). *Mothers and fathers of the nation: The forgotten people?* (Vol. 1). Pretoria, South Africa: Government Printer.

Møller, V., & Ferreira, M. (2003). *Getting by . . . Impact of old-age pension income on poorer South African households.* Cape Town, South Africa: University of Cape Town, Institute of Ageing in Africa.

Møller, V., & Sotshongaye, A. (2002). "They don't listen": Contemporary respect relations between Zulu grandmothers and grandchildren. In S. Makoni & K. Stroeken (Eds.), *Ageing in Africa: Sociolinguistic and anthropological approaches* (pp. 203–225). Aldershot, Englund: Ashgate.

Monasch, R., & Boerma, J. (2004). Orphanhood and childcare patterns in sub-Saharan Africa: An analysis of national surveys from 40 countries. *AIDS 2004, 18* (Suppl. 2), 555–565.

Ntusi, N., & Ferreira, M. (2004). Medical practitioners' attitudes towards older patients. *South African Medical Journal, 94,* 600–601.

Nxusani, N. C. (2004). Late-life migration and adjustment of older persons: Between the Eastern Cape and the Western Cape. In M. Ferreira & E. Van Dongen (Eds.), *Untold stories: Giving voice to the lives of older persons in new South African society: An anthology* (pp. 13–24). Cape Town, South Africa: University of Cape Town, Institute of Ageing in Africa.

Perold, A., & Muller, M. (2000). The composition of old age homes in South Africa in relation to the residents and nursing personnel. *Curationis, 23,* 87–94.

Sagner, A. (1999). Guest editorial: Reflections on the construction and study of elderliness. *Southern African Journal of Gerontology, 8,* 1–6.

Sagner, A., & Mtati, R. Z. (1999). Politics of pension sharing in urban South Africa. *Ageing and Society, 19,* 393–416.

SASPI Project Team. (2004). Prevalence of stroke survivors in rural South Africa: Results from the Southern Africa Stroke Prevention Initiative (SASPI). Agincourt field site. *Stroke, 35,* 627–632.

Schatz, E., & Ogunmefun, C. (2005). *Caring and contributing: The role of older women in multigenerational households in the HIV/AIDS era. IBS Working Paper.* University of Colorado at Boulder, Research Program on Population Processes. Retrieved from http://www.colorado.edu/ibs/pubs/pop/pop2005-0004.pdf

Schnitzler, C., Schnaid, E., MacPhail, A., Mesquita, J., & Robson, H. (2005). Ascorbic acid deficiency, iron overload and alcohol abuse underlie the severe osteoporosis in black African patients with hip fractures—A bone histomorphometric study. *Calcified Tissue International, 76,* 79–89.

Statistics South Africa. (2005). *Stats in brief: 2005.* Pretoria, South Africa.

Statistics South Africa. (2008). *Mid-year population estimates: South Africa.* Pretoria, South Africa.

Steyn, K., Fourie, J., & Temple, N. (Eds.). (2006). *Chronic diseases of lifestyle in South Africa: 1995–2005. Technical report.* Cape Town, South Africa: South African Medical Research Council.

Tipping, B., Kalula, S., & Badri, M. (2006). The burden and risk factors for adverse drug events in older patients: A prospective cross-sectional study. *South African Medical Journal, 96,* 1255–1259.

UNAIDS. (2006). *Report on the global AIDS epidemic: A UNAIDS 10th anniversary edition.* New York: Author.

UNAIDS, UNICEF, & USAID. (2004). *Children on the brink 2004: A joint report of new orphan estimates and a framework for action.* New York: USAID.

United Nations. (2002). *Madrid International Plan of Action on Ageing 2002.* New York: Author.

United Nations, Department of Economic and Social Affairs. (2005). *Living arrangements of older persons around the world.* New York: United Nations.

United Nations Development Programme (UNDP). (2008). *Human development report 2008.* New York: Author.

United Nations Population Division (UNPD). (2006). *Population ageing 2006. Wallchart.* New York: Author.

United Nations Programme on Ageing/International Association of Gerontology and Geriatrics. (2006). *Report of an expert workshop to review the Research Agenda on Ageing for the 21st Century, June 23–26, 2005, Rio de Janeiro, Brazil.* New York: Author.

Van Staden, A. M., & Weich, D.J.V. (2007). Profile of the geriatric patients hospitalised at Universitas Hospital, South Africa. *South African Family Practice, 49,* 14.

Vorobiof, D. A., Sitas, F., & Vorobiof, G. (2001). Breast cancer incidence in South Africa. *Journal of Clinical Oncology, 19,* 125–127.

Wilson, A. O., & Adamchak, D. J. (2001). The grandmothers' disease: The impact of AIDS on Africa's older women. *Age and Ageing, 30,* 8–10.

Ziehl, S. (2002). Black South Africans *do* live in nuclear family households: A response to Russell. *Society in Transition, 33,* 26–49.

43

· ■ ■ ■ ·

South Korea

Sung-Jae Choi

POPULATION AGING

Fertility and mortality in South Korea have been in continual decline for the last four decades, while life expectancy has increased substantially; as a consequence, during that time the absolute number and proportion of the elderly population have increased, and they are projected to continue to grow at a significant rate during the first half of the current century.

As of 2000, the proportion of the South Korean population that was elderly was 7.2%, and it had already reached 10% in 2008. It is projected to be 24.3% in 2030, 32.5% in 2040, and 38.2% in 2050 (National Statistical Office, 2007). These estimates regarding elderly Koreans exceed the estimated average elderly population of Organization for Economic Cooperation and Development (OECD) countries from 2030 on, and Korea may become one of the countries whose elderly population is the largest proportion if its current fertility rate is not raised substantially.

The rapid growth of South Korea's elderly population is mainly a result of the rapid lengthening of life span and an ever-dropping fertility rate. The extension of life span has been conspicuous over the past 40 years, with life expectancy at birth for men increasing from 51.1 years in 1960 to 75.1 years in 2005, while the expectancy for women increased from 53.7 to 81.9 years. It is projected to reach 82.9 years for men and 88.9 years for women by 2050. During the first half of the 21st century, the proportion of the oldest-old South Koreans (85 and over) is projected to increase by approximately 20 times its current percentage (from 0.4% to 8.0%), whereas the proportion of those aged 65 and over will likely show a five-fold increase (from 7.2% to 38.2%).

Reducing the nation's fertility rate (the average number of children born to a woman of childbearing age) was one of government's main initiatives to facilitate economic development from the 1960s to the 1980s. As a result, the total fertility rate dropped drastically, to the level of 1.6 children per woman of childbearing age. The rate continued to drop throughout the 1990s, and this trend has persisted well into the 21st century, reaching 1.08 in 2005, which may be considered one of the world's lowest fertility rates. While the South Korean government has initiated a significant policy effort to reverse this fertility trend, it has not yet been successful, and it will not be an easy task to reverse such a declining trend. Therefore, the declining fertility rate can be understood as one of the major factors accelerating South Korea's rapid population aging in the first half of this century (Choi & Bae, 2005).

For the past 40 years, urbanization in South Korea has greatly advanced, with 81.5% of the total population residing in urban areas. The urbanization process, in particular, has expedited the migration of young populations from their rural hometowns into urban areas in search of opportunities for better education and jobs. This migration phenomenon has broadened the gap of median age between the urban and rural populations: 34.0 years in urban areas vs 46.5 years in rural areas. Urbanization also has resulted in a great difference between urban and rural areas in their population proportion aged 65 and over: 7.2% in urban areas vs 18.6% in rural areas as of 2005.

The structure of the elderly population has experienced several changes in the past few decades. While the proportion of married elderly couples has been increasing, the number of widowed elderly people has decreased, mostly due to the extended life span. As of 2005, 55.4% of the elderly population was married, while the rest reported being widowed. The living arrangement of elderly people in Korea has also undergone great changes. While the proportion of elderly South Koreans living with their spouses or alone made up only 19.7% of the entire elderly population in 1981, that proportion has since increased dramatically, reaching 61.8% in 2007 (National Statistical Office, 2007). Although the proportion of the elderly population in institutions is still very small compared to that in Western countries, the rate of increase in institutionalized elders has been somewhat conspicuous. Their proportion increased from 0.87% in 1981 to 1.24% in 2007, and it is expected to increase greatly in the near future because of the inception in July 2008 of the Elderly Long-Term Care Insurance System.

RESEARCH ON AGING

Gerontology research in South Korea is closely related to academic associations of gerontological disciplines. The first such academic association was the Korean Geriatrics Society, founded in 1968, which signaled the start of the disciplinary study of gerontology in the country. Despite its notable beginning, gerontological researchers were few in number until the 1970s. In 1978, the Korean Gerontological Society was created, mainly composed of researchers in the fields of social and behavioral sciences, social policy, and health sciences. The Korean Society for Gerontology was formed in 1989, mainly composed of researchers from the biomedical sciences, nursing, nutritional sciences, and food engineering. The Korean Association for Geriatric Psychiatry was founded in 1994. Until the middle of the 1990s, a relatively small number of research projects were conducted, and, as a consequence, only several hundred research papers, theses, and dissertations were published in the academic journals of these gerontological associations. A major step in the development of gerontological research in South Korea took place in 1993 when the three gerontological associations joined together to form the Federation of Korean Gerontological Societies (FKGS). The FKGS was incorporated in 1997 and accepted the Korean Association for Geriatric Psychiatry as a member association in 2003. The FKGS has played important roles in expanding multi- or interdisciplinary studies in gerontology by holding a variety of academic meetings and inviting prominent scholars from overseas.

A major impetus to the growth of South Korean gerontological research was the hosting of Asia/Oceana Regional Congress of Gerontology, International Association of Gerontology and Geriatrics (IAGG) in Korea in 1999 (Choi, 1998). Another impetus to further advancement of Korean gerontological research was the increased social awareness of the significance of population aging issues in the 2000s. The possible negative effects of an aging society were emphasized, along with the problems of Korea's falling fertility rate and rapidly increasing life expectancy.

As of 2008, eight gerontological research centers have been established under the auspices of universities. All these research centers were founded in the 2000s. It is estimated that the number of academic papers, theses, dissertations, and books on gerontological research published since the 1990s is well over 4,000. These research works range across a wide variety of disciplines: social and behavioral sciences, social policy and services, family relations, nutrition, health sciences, nursing, geriatrics, geriatric psychiatry, housing, education and others (Federation of Korean Gerontological Societies, 2005).

Additional research institutes are planned in the near future. The National Institute for Longevity is under construction and will open in 2010. The South Korean government currently holds a concrete plan to establish the National Institute on Aging, a multidisciplinary research institute modeled after the NIA in the United States and the National Institute for Longevity Sciences in Japan. These two new South Korean institutes are expected to contribute to the growth and expansion of gerontological studies and interdisciplinary and international collaboration in the near future. Similar to the effects of hosting the regional congress of IAGG in 1999, hosting the World Congress of IAGG in 2013 will further contribute to the expansion of gerontological studies in Korea. Korean gerontologists will be engaged in various research projects, using both single and multidisciplinary methods, as well as domestic and cross-cultural methods.

EDUCATION IN GERONTOLOGY

Gerontological education in South Korea began with concern for the welfare of the elderly population when aging began to be recognized as a social problem in the early 1970s (Hyun, 1983). However, no systematic content existed for courses such as Elderly Welfare until several textbooks on this topic were published in the late 1970s. Because gerontological education was founded upon the welfare perspective, most of the gerontological education to date has been provided in the social work/welfare departments of universities and colleges.

From the 1980s, the content of gerontological education became more comprehensive, and yet the focus was still limited to social gerontology. From the 1990s, educational units offering gerontological education were expanded to medical schools, nursing schools, departments of psychology, gerontological social welfare, home management, and many others. These schools and departments began to offer courses on psychological gerontology, biological/physiological gerontology, and gerontological nursing as electives. However, gerontological education in South Korea still mainly consists of single undergraduate courses offered in social work/welfare departments under the title of Elderly Welfare or Introduction to Gerontology.

As of today, South Korea has 201 four-year universities, 147 two-year colleges, and 21 distance learning universities. One hundred and twenty four of the 201 four-year universities have social welfare departments, from which approximately 5,000 students graduate every year. Twenty-four of these universities have separate departments for gerontological social welfare or gerontology, from which 100 students reportedly graduate each year. In addition to the social welfare departments at four-year universities, 104 schools with two-year programs also have social welfare departments offering gerontology courses (Korean Council for College Education, 2008; Korean Council for University Education, 2008). South Korea also has 118 graduate schools, of which social work/welfare schools make up the largest proportion. These offer courses on gerontological social welfare as electives. It is also noteworthy that an increasing number of public administration schools in Korea tend to have social welfare departments within them, offering courses on gerontological social welfare.

In addition to regular education in gerontology offered at universities and colleges, a gerontological educational program for medical doctors and those in health-care professions was created under the auspices of the Asia/Oceania Regional Council, IAGG in South Korea in 2007 with instructors from South Korea and other countries in Asia/Oceania region. This educational program was developed by the regional council of IAGG to equip doctors and professional workers in health care in the Asia/Oceania Region with gerontological knowledge, anticipating the increasing number of elderly patients. Given the success of this educational program, leading to other education programs for those engaged in other health and social care professions for the elderly population, it is recommended that such programs be replicated in other countries.

As mentioned above, gerontological education at universities and colleges in South Korea is, in most cases, limited to one course, though such a brief overview of biological, psychological, sociological, economic, and social welfare aspects of aging may not be adequate to elicit further interest by students in gerontological study. This single-course approach to gerontological education is also inadequate in direct application in the planning and delivery of human services. It would be desirable to offer several courses on biological, psychological, and social aspects and outcomes of aging, as well as gerontological social welfare (or gerontological social work) as electives in undergraduate programs. At a minimum, an introductory course on gerontology should be offered as a foundational course for undergraduate students. It also would be ideal to develop gerontological education programs for those who are engaged in human services for older adults or to offer more detailed gerontological courses as part of their continuing education programs.

PUBLIC POLICY ISSUES IN AGING

South Korean society entered an era of "aging society" in the year 2000. In South Korea and Japan, it is generally recognized that societies with an elderly population of 7% or more could be classified into three categories: societies with 7–14% of elderly population are called aging societies, those with 14–21% are called aged societies, and those with 21% and more are called super-aged societies (Cabinet Office, Government of Japan, 2005; Yoichi, 1992). The symbolic meaning of entering into an aging society has triggered many important policy discussions related to population aging across Korean society. The significance of moving into an aging society has contributed to the construction of a societal understanding for broad and long-term implications of population aging, beyond the range of welfare policies for the elderly population. Since 2000, several critical policies associated with population aging have been developed and initiated.

The National Pension (NP) system was originally designed for an income replacement rate (IRR) of 70% of the average standard monthly income, based on a maximum contribution rate of 9% over a 40-year insured period. However, such IRR proved to be too high in relation to the NP contribution rate, and the NP was destined to be insolvent by the mid 2030s. Given the trend of rapid population aging predicted early in the 21st century, adjustment of the IRR was inevitable. Accordingly, the IRR was revised to 60% in 1988, but the effect was to delay insolvency of the system only to 2047. So, in 2007, the system was once again revised to lower IRR to 40%. To supplement the lowered IRR of the NP, a new program called Basic Old Age Pension (BOAP) was created in 2007, which was designed as a noncontributory pension to be given to retirees in the lower 60% of income and assets. In response to the need for long-term care (LTC) services, widely recognized since the latter part of the 1990s under the Elderly Long-Term Care Insurance Law, a social insurance scheme was legislated in 2007 and implemented in July 2008.

In response to the need for a very comprehensive long-term policy plan to prevent and solve problems and issues associated with our rapidly advancing aging society, the Basic Law for Low Fertility and Aging Society (BLLFAS) was enacted in 2005. This law requires the establishment of the Presidential Committee for Population Policy and Aging Society (PCPPAS) as a statutory committee, with the President sitting as the chair of the committee. The committee is to propose a five-year plan for an aging society every five years. However, unfortunately the amendment of the law (BLLFAS) in 2008 downgraded the presidential committee to a ministerial committee under the Ministry of Health, Welfare and Family. The first five-year plan (2006–2010) for an aging society was initiated in 2006 and has been implemented since. Though most critical measures for an aging society are reflected in the first five-year plan, some other issues may arise during the implementation of the policy. Hence, expected issues are examined according to the four parts of the plan: (1) policy-making and implementation in general, (2) creation of an environment conducive to childbirth and child-rearing, (3) building foundations for quality of life in an aging society, and (4) securing the power of economic growth in an aging society.

Policy-making and Implementation in General

The amendment of the law (BLLFAS) to downgrade the presidential committee to a ministerial committee in 2008 may reflect a change in the government's perspective on our aging society from a wide to a narrow one, limiting its concern mainly to the welfare of the aging population; consequently, the effectiveness of the five-year plans for an aging society may be weakened.

Building Foundations for Quality of Life in an Aging Society

Two difficulties are paramount here. First, we cannot expect notable increases in the fertility rate without alleviating the burden of childcare and education. Second, attitudes toward gender equality at home are likely to lag far behind such changes in employment and education sectors.

Seven major issues can be identified as barriers to quality of life in an aging society.

1. Sustainability of the public pension system at the expense of retirees' shrunken pension. Lowering IRR to 50% to keep the public pension system financially solvent may not guarantee a national minimum level of living for a substantial portion of retirees.
2. Dubious Basic Old Age Pension (BOAP). How to finance the BOAP and how to integrate it into the NP system may evoke discontent within the current elderly generation regarding their economic security.
3. Barriers in building a three-tier income security system for old age. Within the three-tier system, the first tier would be the public pension. The second tier is the retirement pension, a new mandatory occupational pension for employees that was converted from the existing

retirement benefit system. The third tier is optional individual pensions, offered by the private financial market. Since the rate of workers converting retirement benefits to retirement pensions is not high, and there are no particular incentives for workers to do so, individual pensions have not been attractive to those insured under the NP. Since the tax exemption amount on monthly premiums and pensions is also limited, it is questionable how much the retirement pension and individual pension will contribute to the construction of a three-tier income security system.

4. Lower coverage for public long-term care insurance. Since the long-term care insurance system covers only 3.4% of the elderly population, and only 23% of all the frail elderly in need of LTC, such limited coverage has provoked dissatisfaction with the LTC system. Furthermore, the system may operate against its original intent and principles of prioritizing community care.

5. Social negligence of supplying elderly housing. The demand for elderly housing with convenient design for daily life will also increase. However, although the government has plans to remedy this situation, elderly housing is currently in short supply in South Korea with the exception of a very few retirement communities (called "silver towns"). It is expected that without an adequate supply of elderly housing, which may help older adults lead more independent lives, their long-term care needs may increase. In this sense, it is evident that the government's plan of supplying elderly housing is attentive to such possible outcomes.

6. Creation of jobs for the elderly population with a short-term (or near-sighted) perspective. Providing older adults with opportunities to work is one of the most effective measures for population aging. The government's plan to create jobs has mainly focused on socially created jobs, which are government funded, low-wage jobs offered only for a period of seven months. However, jobs for older adults need to be just as competitive as in the regular job market. Without any job creation through systematic training, the provision of jobs by the government would not produce its intended effects.

7. Lack of effective measures for population aging in rural areas. Most of the local government regions with large elderly populations depend on the national government's budget. The central concern of these aged regions is how to develop their regions economically and with what industries. In this sense, the task of how to develop rural areas with a large elderly population should be the challenge of both the local and national governments. The issue of how much financial support should be allocated to these regions is an important decision for the national government.

Securing Economic Growth in an Aging Society

Economic growth in the midst of an aging society presents several difficult challenges.

1. Readjustment of mandatory retirement age and the anti-age discrimination law. It has been proposed that the mandatory retirement age should be adjusted from age 55 to 60, with 55 currently being the most prevalent. It will take a long time to adjust the mandatory retirement age to 60, as most private corporations are reluctant to engage in upward adjustment, and their strong opposition to passage of this law is expected. Therefore, readjustment of the mandatory retirement age and legislation of laws prohibiting age discrimination will be a challenging issue, evoking controversies in society.

2. Issues in developing economic markets for the elderly population (senior market). All the services necessary to respond to the various needs of the elderly population, including quality services demanded by the well-to-do population, cannot usually be provided in the social market. Development of an economic market that may be referred to as the senior market is imperative in order to respond properly to these needs, to provide more efficient and effective services for elders, and to develop more services and manufacturing industries in South Korean society. However, many controversial issues exist regarding the senior market. These issues may range from whether the market is within the scope of social welfare; whether welfare services provided in the market on a for-profit basis are justifiable; whether welfare services provided by for-profit organizations can reasonably respond to the needs of citizens and promote equality; and how to control the senior market in order to secure the rights and safety of the elderly population.

REFERENCES

Cabinet Office, Government of Japan. (2005). *Annual report on the aging society.* Tokyo: Cabinet Office, Government of Japan.

Choi, S.-J. (1998). The role of gerontological associations in Korea. *Australasian Journal on Ageing, 17,* 128–131.

Choi, S.-J., & Bae, S-H. (2005). National policies in South Korea. In J. Doling, C. J. Finer, & T. Maltby (Eds.), *Ageing matters: European policy lessons from the East.* Burlington, VT: Ashgate Publishing Company.

Federation of Korean Gerontological Societies. (2005). A proposal to host the 20th World Congress of Gerontology. Unpublished proposal.

Hyun, O.-S. (1983). *A study on policy-making process for the elderly Koreans and its characteristics.* Master's thesis, Seoul National University.

Korean Council for College Education. (2008). *State of member colleges*. Retrieved from http://www.kcce.or.kr

Korean Council for University Education. (2008). *State of member universities*. Retrieved from http://www.kcue.or.kr

National Statistical Office. (2006). *Statistics on elderly population*. Daejeon: National Statistical Office.

National Statistical Office. (2007). *Population projection for 2005–2050*. Daejeon: National Statistical Office.

Yoichi, U. (1992). *Social policy for the aged*. Tokyo: Minerva Publishing Company.

44

··■··

Spain

Belén Bueno and M. Teresa Sancho

RECENT HISTORY AND OVERVIEW

Longevity recorded a spectacular increase in Spain over the course of the 20th century. Life expectancy in 1900 was 34.8 years; today it is 2.3 times higher: the average number of years a person lives in Spain stands at around 80.2 years—77.0 in the case of men and 83.5 for women. This means that the life expectancy of the Spanish population is among the highest in the European Union and anywhere in the world.

As a result of this greater longevity, the number of elderly people has soared since the beginning of the last century. This segment of the population has increased eightfold since 1900, when it numbered fewer than a million people. Furthermore, it is quite striking how important people in their 80s are becoming in our society; the 10 years that elapsed between 1991 and 2001 sufficed to increase the numbers of those 80+ by 42%. The arrival of the baby-boomer generations at retirement age, a situation that will come about in Spain around the third decade of this century (2020), heralds a further boost in this population group, which will lead to sea changes in our social structure.

The latest population data available (Spain's National Statistics Institute—INE, 2007) record 7,531,826 people aged 65 and over in Spain (16.7% of the overall population), of whom 3,189,968 are males and 4,341,858 females. Women are, therefore, the dominant sex in old age, and this is despite the fact that more males are born; a higher mortality rate among men means that this advantage is reversed at around the age of 50 and reaches its peak difference among the very old (with over two women for every man in the 85+ age group).

Greater female survival is in contrast to the data regarding the perception that elderly people have of their own health, as women claim to be in a poorer state of health than men. Nevertheless, generally speaking, it can be affirmed that the majority of Spain's elderly population make a positive assessment of their health; moreover, this has improved significantly over the past 10 years.

A recent survey found that about one-quarter of older Spaniards "have problems and require assistance in their everyday activities," with over three-quarters being independent (Abellán et al., 2007). Of the dependent group, only 3.3% are seriously or fully dependent, with 5.2% requiring moderate help, and 16.5% slight or light assistance.

Regarding models of cohabitation, and contrary to certain notions that are widespread throughout our country, the most common types of living arrangements among elders are with their families and in the very homes they made for themselves. The drop in the number of elderly people who move in with one of their children, together with a sharp increase in the number of single-person households (14.2% in 1998 vs 25.5% in 2006) are the trends that are gradually bringing us closer to other European living arrangements.

Spain's elderly population continues to report low levels of formal schooling. The Active Population Survey (INE, 2006) shows that 7.6% of Spanish people aged 65 or over are illiterate; moreover, 32.4% did not complete their primary school education, while only 11.4% have a secondary education, and 6.6% attended college. Furthermore, there are significant differences between men and women: female illiteracy (9.8%) is twice that of men (4.7%), and only 4.5% of women have a higher education, as opposed to 7% among men (Sancho, 2007).

Insofar as the economic position of the older population is concerned, in January 2008, the average state pension amounted to about €806 (US$1,011) and a widow's pension to €526 (US$660). The differences between men and women correspond largely to the different kinds of protection that each one enjoys, constituting one of the more outstanding aspects of our pension system. Out of the nearly 3.5 million pensions paid to women aged 65 or over in the state Social Security system, half are widows' pensions and the other half are retirement and sundry pensions. On average, the pensions paid to women are below the system's average pension, regardless of the age of the woman receiving it. The average pension falls with age and at its minimum expression, among women aged 85 over, the average pension is practically tantamount to two-thirds of the average for the system as a whole.

The Survey on Living Conditions conducted by the National Statistics Institute confirms the importance of ownership in the system of household occupation among Spanish people in general, and specifically among elderly people. Home ownership increases with age, whereby among the 45–64 age group, almost 9 out of 10 people live in a dwelling that belongs to them (Abellán et al., 2007). A comparison with neighboring countries testifies to the importance home ownership has in our country as the way of occupying dwellings.

ORGANIZATION AND STATE OF AGING RESEARCH

Over the past 25 years in Spain, research on aging has been conducted within the biohealth sector, linked mainly to hospitals, geriatric units, and primary care services, while in the psychosocial sector, it has been driven by those groups working in universities. Research calls made by the Ministry of Science and Education, the Health Research Fund (FIS), and the Institute for Elderly People and Social Services (IMSERSO; formerly, the National Institute for Social Services [INSERSO]) have helped to financially support a significant number of projects. Likewise, foundations, private organizations, and pharmaceutical laboratories have also helped to fund research work in this field. Since its creation in 1966, the *Revista Española de Geriatría y Gerontología (Spanish Journal of Geriatrics and Gerontology)*—which was called *Revista Española de Gerontología (Spanish Journal of Gerontology)* up to 1977 and *Revista Española de Gerontología y Geriatría (Spanish Journal of Gerontology and Geriatrics)* between 1977 and 1980—the official journal of the professional society of the same name, has been a platform for the dissemination, both at home and abroad, of the results reported by these projects.

Special mention should be made of research in aging and its consequences fostered by the IMSERSO within its two major programs. The Programa Nacional de Tecnologías para la Salud y el Bienestar (National Program of Technologies for Health and Well-being) subsidizes research related to new technologies and technical aids designed to help the elderly and/or disabled, as well as accessibility to the physical medium, to information and communications, and promoting universal design. In 2005, 32 research schemes were subsidized within this program, with a further 37 in 2006. The Programa Nacional de Ciencias Sociales, Económicas y Jurídicas (National Program on Social, Economic, and Legal Sciences) includes four lines of research, with the line related to active and healthy aging being one of the most popular, especially in research projects dealing with profiles and lifestyles that favor active aging and those that analyze intergenerational programs being pursued in Spain. The second line of research focuses on the needs of those people at risk or in a situation of dependency. A highlight within this line of research is the subline Prevention and Non-pharmaceutical Treatment of Alzheimer's Disease, which is consistent with studies on psychosocial care programs in Alzheimer's and other dementias being undertaken at universities and research centers outside the country. The third line of research, On the Influence of Aging on Sociodemographic Matters, addresses the economic consequences of having an older population, as well as the influence of this sociodemographic phenomenon on architecture. The Programa Nacional de Ciencias Sociales, Económicas y Jurídicas subsidized 29 research projects in 2005, 34 in 2006, and 37 in 2007.

As postulated by Salvá (2005), the development of biohealth research on aging in Spain has allowed for defining and verifying the state of health of elderly people, their prevailing illnesses, and their foremost health problems, paying special attention to those that lead to disability and dependence. Chronic illness is central to the health of elderly people and, to a large extent, determines their demand for health resources. Nearly all (94%) of elderly Spanish people have some kind of chronic illness, among which some of the more common, affecting more than 20% of the population, are the following: high blood pressure, high cholesterol, chronic obstructive pulmonary disease, degenerative osteoarthritis, back pain, cataracts, depression or anxiety, circulatory complaints, and varicose veins. There are other illnesses, which, despite being less prevalent, have a major individual and social impact, such as Alzheimer's disease, diabetes, cancer, and osteoporosis. The study of these and the so-called major geriatric syndromes (e.g., falls, urinary incontinence, malnutrition, and acute confusional state), as well as the fragility syndrome, together with their accompanying psychological and social consequences, have taken up a large part of the scientific publications related to geriatrics. In each one of them, progress has been made in their epidemiological description, and some of these clinical states now have recommendations and practical clinical guides that focus and systemize actions in everyday practice.

In addition to the study of illnesses and their evolution, in some cases over many years, attention has been paid to the preclinical or latent stage as the basis for designing preventive strategies that allow for understanding morbidity and disability toward the end of life. Studies have been performed that underpin the importance of acting upon health habits, especially avoiding smoking, keeping reasonably fit, eating a balanced diet, and pursuing an active intellectual and social life.

An analysis has also been made of the ways of providing the necessary social and health-care services for properly addressing the different situations in which old people may find themselves. A great deal of evidence has been gathered on different models and levels of health care. Today, new contributions are required for the development of specialist outpatient services, care at home and in hospitals for the acutely ill, or in rehabilitation and long-stay units.

Another major group of publications are those grounded in basic sciences that deal with genetic models, the theory of free radicals, the role of hormones and immunosenescence, seeking to explain the biological bases of aging.

Within the psychosocial sphere, and especially over the past 10 years, several lines of research have been conducted by experts in the social and behavioral sciences linked to higher education and research institutes. Some of these involve the identification of psychosocial characteristics and needs, not only of older people but also of the very old (85+), placing special emphasis on exploring personality traits, the expression of positive and negative emotions, the perspective of time, the use of common strategies and approaches for coping with the most frequent and serious problems at advanced ages and the sense of personal self-efficacy, the social network and support, and analyzing the impact of these factors on subjective and objective well-being and satisfaction (e.g., Navarro & Bueno, in press; Vega, Mayoral, Buz, & Bueno, 2004).

The analysis of intergenerational relationships is another relevant line of research, with valuable information forthcoming on the ties between dyads of grandparents and grandchildren in normative and non-normative situations (e.g., Triadó, Villar, Solé, Osuna, & Pinazo, 2005). Likewise, successful attempts have been made to systemize aging by analyzing the everyday activities of elderly people in rural environments (Villar, Triadó, Solé, & Osuna, 2006).

Elsewhere, the early detection, assessment and treatment of cognitive and language problems in the normal aging process have focused the work of a large number of researchers (e.g., Juncos-Rabadán, Pereiro, & Rodríguez, 2005), as has the study of the cognitive reserve in different pathologies affecting the central nervous system (e.g., Corral, Rodríguez, Amenedo, Sánchez, & Díaz, 2006). The prevalence of Alzheimer's-type dementia, its influence on the family unit, and the identification of developmental care strategies are also being investigated by a substantial number of researchers. At the Matia Foundation, the Estudio Longitudinal

Donostia is assessing the efficacy of nonpharmacological therapies for treating Alzheimer's-type dementia (Yanguas, 2007).

In addition to specific actions on the different aspects involved in dementia, the development and assessment of gerontological care programs is of significance in such varying fields as education in connection with university programs for elderly people, in the promotion of personal autonomy with old people who are both healthy and ill (e.g., Rueda, Bueno, & Buz, 2001), and in the support for the caregivers of dependent old people (Montorio, Pérez, Losada, Izal, & Márquez, 2004). There is no doubt that research into dementias in Spain is set to receive a major boost over the coming years through a specific line of research promoted by IMSERSO and linked to the Reference Centre for Alzheimer's and Other Dementias, located in the city of Salamanca.

ORGANIZATION AND STATUS OF GERONTOLOGICAL EDUCATION

Since the 1990s, several Spanish universities have offered degrees in the Psychology of Aging in the Faculties of Psychology, Education, Social Sciences, and Occupational Therapy, in subjects that cover—albeit labeled differently from one university to another—content in adult development and aging, assessment and care in old age, and gerontological education. There are also subjects on geriatrics in the study plans for medicine and occupational therapy. There is a high demand for instruction in these fields.

Furthermore, since the end of the 1980s, several Spanish universities began to organize and offer master's degrees in gerontology. Spain's postgraduate training in gerontology began in 1989 with the Máster Universitario en Gerontología de la Universidad de Salamanca (master's degree in gerontology at the University of Salamanca), promoted and directed, until his passing in 2004, by Dr. José Luis Vega, one of the foremost champions of gerontology in Spain.

José Luis Vega propounded an innovative approach among Spanish academia in the last third of the 20th century; namely, the psychological perspective of the life cycle for describing, explaining, and dealing with human development. He fostered multidisciplinarity and interdisciplinarity as the cornerstones upon which to base work on gerontology. He was a pioneer in gerontology in Spain, dedicating the greater part of his teaching and research career to it. He founded the first doctorate in adult development and aging in 1987 and the first master's degree in gerontology. Through both of these efforts, he pursued a path of excellence, directing a myriad of research projects and writing several university handbooks, chapters for books, and scientific articles in the field of aging, which have served to instruct numerous Spanish, European, and Latin American gerontologists.

The knowledge, skills, and competencies taught in the master's degree program at the University of Salamanca are interdisciplinary, striking a balance between social and behavioral sciences and health sciences. This degree has catered to students with 30 different degrees and from 16 different countries, having now trained almost a thousand gerontologists. In addition, since 2004 it has been part of the INTERGERO international project with another two European and three North American universities, which promotes the sharing of best practices for advanced training in gerontology and the exchange of students and teaching staff between Spain, Germany, and the Netherlands on the European side, and the United States in North America.

Other Spanish autonomous communities outside Castilla y León also organize their own master's degrees in gerontology. For example, in 1990, the Autónoma University of Madrid, with the support of what was then the National Institute of Social Services (INSERSO), introduced the Master's in Social Gerontology, directed by Dr. Rocío Fernández Ballesteros, providing training for a good number of professionals working with the elderly in the Community of Madrid, although many of the students attending have hailed from other autonomous communities. The program initially instructed professionals in all areas of gerontology, although over the course of time, different curricula were established: a Diploma in Social Gerontology, Diploma of Quality in Gerontological Services, and Master's Degree in Social Gerontology.

The Universidad of Granada also has a protracted record in gerontological instruction in higher education. The University of Valencia has had its own postgraduate course in social gerontology since 1994. In the case of the University of Barcelona, since 2000 it has organized a master's degree in psychogerontology and neurosciences, conducted largely by psychologists.

Since their implementation in Spain, master's degrees in gerontology have helped to significantly advance specialist knowledge in this field, furnishing professionals with the competencies and skills required to achieve the ultimate goals of improving the quality of life of old people and their families.

Insofar as Ph.D. studies are concerned, the University of Salamanca has also been a pioneer, offering since 1987 a doctoral program in adult development and aging. Since 2000, this program has evolved toward a

Ph.D. in the psychology of aging, responding to the need for greater specialization in this field. The University of Barcelona had specific programs between 1994 and 2002 (Psycho-gerontology: Change and Optimisation and Development, and Diversity: Research into Disability and Aging) and continues with related modules in its current programs. Likewise, other Spanish universities offer doctoral programs with modules or seminars specializing in psychogerontology in the fields of developmental and health psychology (e.g., University of Santiago de Compostela, University of Valencia) and also of psychobiology (Autónoma University of Madrid, University of Almeria).

At present, Spanish universities are fully immersed in the process of adapting to the requirements made by European convergence in higher education, converting some of the unofficial qualifications that existed beforehand into official ones (e.g., Universities of A Coruña and Zaragoza) or creating other new ones with a specific professional and research focus (such as the case of the interuniversity postgraduate course in psychogerontology, organized jointly by the Universities of Barcelona, Salamanca, Santiago de Compostela, Valencia, and Almeria).

On another level, and as part of lifelong training, local and/or regional authorities allocate funds for training and refreshing their professionals in the area of social services with a view to improving specific aspects of the design and assessment of care programs for the elderly, intergenerational programming, and other direct services. Moreover, numerous companies throughout Spain, responding to calls made by the authorities and/or sundry associations, are dedicated to providing instruction for elderly people in order to foster a healthy aging process by promoting personal autonomy and helping to prevent dependence. The Sistema de Autonomía y Atención a la Dependencia (SAAD; System for Autonomy and Care for Dependence), recently created in Spain and described in the next section, will undoubtedly help to increase the possibilities and specific training offered within the field of gerontology at different levels.

CURRENT ISSUES IN PUBLIC POLICY

The history of the implementation of a public system for caring for the needs of the elderly is a relatively brief one, coinciding with the end of Franco's dictatorship and the establishment of a democratic political system 30 years ago. This brought the curtain down on a long period in which care for the elderly was associated with charity and care institutions.

The 1980s ushered in major changes for this segment of the population: pensions systems became universal, as did access to health care, with a relatively speedy development of traditional resources; home care and residential services were introduced with scant planning criteria. The realization that a more accurate diagnosis needed to be made of requirements in this sector with planning of care policies for an extended time scale would arise over the ensuing years, leading to the Gerontology Plan (INSERSO, 1993), which immediately became a reference and framework for action in the 1990s. Its design, its approaches regarding the integral nature of care, and its orchestration into five action areas (pensions, health and health care, social services, culture and leisure, and participation) laid the foundations for subsequent programs.

Our present administrative-territorial arrangement, which divides Spain into 17 Autonomous Communities with very similar powers to those of a federal state, has meant that each of these territories now rolls out its own gerontology planning, with significant differences between them in the development of their care models.

The far-reaching changes that elderly people have experienced in recent years have led to the introduction of an extensive array of programs that seek to respond to their needs, currently characterized by intragenerational diversity and the continuity of adult lifestyles. There are two main blocks of action described below.

Programs Designed to Promote Active and Healthy Aging

Public authorities promote a myriad of schemes on leisure, educational and cultural activities, the prevention of dependency, the promotion of health, and the use of time for supportive purposes. This involves a wide-ranging series of educational activities that further the learning of a variety of skills. Almost all Spanish universities provide specific programs designed for elders. Furthermore, the so-called popular universities offer classes for older people and other similar projects that provide more elementary learning schemes, as well as other activities of a cultural and occupational nature, for personal development.

Moreover, 3.5 million people are currently enrolled as members of social centers designed for elderly people, in which all kinds of activities are organized: cultural, sports, recreational, voluntary work, courses, and workshops. A large part of the 4,500 existing centers also provide care services: meals, chiropodist services, physiotherapy, social and health advice, and coaching. Indeed, many of these centers are becoming the mainstay of a versatile set of programs and services provided within the immediate community environment.

Likewise, since the mid-1980s the public sector has been organizing subsidized holiday programs that are currently enjoyed by around a million people. They fulfill two basic aims: improving the well-being of elderly people, who can enjoy tourist activities at affordable prices; and creating and securing employment in the hotel and catering sector along Spain's coastlines, thereby counteracting its seasonal nature.

Something similar occurs with the two-week stays in thermal establishments (spas) that are arranged by different public institutions at very affordable prices and always with prior medical recommendation. These schemes have helped to re-launch this sector, whereby our country now has an extensive network of top quality spas, used by the rest of the population at market prices.

To conclude this section, we believe there is an urgent need to reconsider the boundaries of what is strictly gerontological in an aging society. There is a need to reformulate public policies segmented by age groups to explore other options that break down the rigid compartments of age groups and draw closer to people's interests and needs at any stage of their lives.

Social and Health Services for Dependent Elders

In Spain, a million people are suffering from circumstances of dependency, of whom 500,000 are classified as serious or very serious. The past few years have seen a major development in the resources allocated to caring for people in situations of dependency.

The generalization of basic home-care services, day centers, and homes is now a reality, and access is virtually guaranteed for those people with few socioeconomic resources and very serious circumstances of dependency. Nonetheless, our social services system continues to fall short.

For the first time ever, our care system has managed to exceed the demand for home-care services with regard to residential places. However, major shortcomings continue to be detected in home care, despite being in greatest demand. The scant provision is coupled with the unsuitability of the tasks performed, largely of a household nature, the few hours these are provided, and the scarce coordination with health home-care services. In short, it is a service that requires a thorough reorganization in order to respond to the needs arising from situations of dependency.

Institutional services have undergone spectacular development in recent years, marshaled by private initiative, which subsequently reaches an agreement with the public sector on a large number of its places. There has been a significant improvement in the quality of institutions, although there continue to be shortfalls of all kinds, especially in the organization of everyday life, care programs, and the training of staff, who are poorly paid and experience a high turnover. In short, we need to continue researching and piloting residential experiences that are closer to people's "normal" lifestyles and provide a more acceptable quality of life than at present.

In 2007, a law was enacted to promote personal autonomy and care for people in a situation of dependency (Act 39/2006 of 14 December) that will undoubtedly constitute a historical milestone for Spain's model of social protection (Ministry of Labour and Social Affairs, 2007). It acknowledges the universal right to benefits and equal opportunities for accessing them. The recognition of these rights is a decisive step forward in the public system for caring for dependent persons, regardless of their age. Nonetheless, as opposed to other public services, this law is to be partly paid for by users according to their financial status. It seeks to establish a care model based on the provision of resources and, in the second instance, on cash benefits. It will be implemented gradually through 2015. By means of a single assessment tool used for the country as a whole, people are classified into three levels of dependence. People assigned to one of these levels are entitled to receive care and attention through services (home care, day and night, or institutional centers) consistent with the seriousness of their situation. There are also different kinds of cash benefits.

To conclude, Spain is undergoing significant development in its system of social protection for people in need of help. It is a project with consequences in different spheres of action: economy, health care, employment market, training, and social services. Yet, above all, there is a clear expectation of improvement in the living conditions of people who need help and their families, mostly women, who currently have to forego their personal and professional lives to devote themselves wholly to the care of their parents or husbands.

ACKNOWLEDGMENT

The authors would like to express their gratitude to Penélope Castejón, a researcher at CSIC (Higher Council for Scientific Research), for her help in drafting the first part of this chapter.

REFERENCES

Abellán, A., Barrio Truchado, E. del, Castejón Villarejo, P., Esparza Catalán, C., Fernández-Mayoralas Fernández, G., Pérez Ortiz, L., et al. (2007). A propósito de las condiciones de vida de las personas mayors [Concerning the living conditions of older people]. Madrid: IMSERSO.

Corral, M., Rodríguez, M., Amenedo, E., Sánchez, J. L., & Díaz, F. (2006). Cognitive reserve, age and neuropsychological performance in healthy subjects. *Developmental Neuropsychology*, *29*, 479–491.

INE [National Statistics Institute]. (2007). *Encuesta de población activa* [Labor force survey]. Madrid: INE.

INSERSO [National Institute for Social Services]. (1993). *Plan gerontológico* [Gerontology plan]. Madrid: Ministry of Labour and Social Affairs. INSERSO.

Juncos-Rabadán, O., Pereiro, A. X., & Rodríguez, M. S. (2005). Narrative speech in aging: Quantity, information content and cohesion. *Brain and Language*, *95*, 423–434.

Ministry of Labour and Social Affairs. (2005). *White paper. Care for people in a situation of dependence in Spain*. Madrid: MTAS. Secretary of State for Social Services, Families and Disability. IMSERSO.

Ministry of Labour and Social Affairs. (2007). Act 39/2006 of 14 December on the Promotion of Personal Autonomy and Care for People in a Situation of Dependence.

Montorio, I., Pérez, G., Losada, A., Izal, M., & Márquez, M. (2004). Eficacia diferencial de dos intervenciones psicoeducativas para cuidadores de familiares con demencia [Differential efficacy of two psychoeducational interventions for the carers of family members suffering from dementia]. *Revista de Neurología*, *38*, 701–708.

Navarro, A. B. & Bueno, B. (In press). Coping with health problems in very old people. *International Journal of Clinical and Health Psychology*.

Observatory for the Elderly. (2007). Social services for elderly people in Spain. *Boletín Perfiles y Tendencias n° 32*. Madrid: IMSERSO.

Rueda, M. I., Bueno, B., & Buz, J. (Vega, J. L., Coord.). (2001). *Lecto: Iniciación a la lectura y estimulación cognitiva* [Lecture: Initiation into reading and cognitive stimulation]. Mérida: Asociación Síndrome de Down de Extremadura.

Salvá, A. (2005). Las publicaciones científicas, reflejo de la investigación en Geriatría y Gerontología [Scientific publications, a reflection of the research into geriatrics and gerontology]. *Revista Española de Geriatría y Gerontología*, *40*, 1–3.

Sancho, M. T. (Coord.) (2007). *Informe 2006: Las personas mayores en España* [2006 Report: Older people in Spain]. Madrid: Ministry of Labour and Social Affairs. Secretary of State for Social Services, Families and Disability. Institute for the Elderly and Social Services.

Triadó, C., Villar, F., Solé, C., Osuna, M. J., & Pinazo, S. (2005). The meaning of grandparenthood: Do adolescent grandchildren perceive the relationship and role in the same way as their grandparents do? *Journal of Intergenerational Relationships*, *3*, 101–120.

Vega, J. L., Mayoral, P., Buz, J., & Bueno, B. (2004). Dominios globales y específicos del bienestar de las personas muy mayores [Global and specific domains of the well-being of very old people]. *Revista Española de Geriatría y Gerontología, 39* (Suppl. 3), 23–30.

Villar, F., Triadó, C., Solé, C., & Osuna, M. J. (2006). Patrones de actividad cotidiana en personas mayores: ¿es lo que dicen hacer lo que desearían hacer? [Patterns of everyday activity of older people: Is what they say they do what they would really like to do?]. *Psicothema, 18,* 149–154.

Yanguas, J. J. (2007). *Modelo de atención a las personas con enfermedad de Alzheimer* [Care model for people with Alzheimer's disease]. Madrid: Ministry of Labour and Social Affairs.

45

Sweden

Torbjörn Svensson and Susanne Iwarsson

This chapter will include information on Sweden's demographics and their consequences for society, the organization of services to older people, and some examples of ongoing gerontological research.

Like other countries, Sweden has a steadily increasing elderly population. The Swedish population has already gone through a massive increase in the ratio of elderly people in society. What we see now and in the decades to come are more or less changes in the distribution within the population above the age of 65. The increasing number of the old-old group and, thereby, the more frail elderly people in the Sweden has changed the focus of public debate and priorities in gerontological research. Today there is a greater awareness of the differing needs of the young old and the old old. Greater efforts are made to understand these differences and to meet these differing needs.

Sweden ranks as number 8 among the 10 countries, having the highest median age of 40.2 years (United Nations, 2007). The median age is expected to rise to 43.3 years in the year 2050. Sweden has the 8th highest mean life expectancy in the world, with 80.9 years, which will increase to 85.2 in 2050, which will put Sweden 10th in the world. Sweden was the first country to have more than 5% of its population over 80 years of age. At the end of 2006, 5.4% of the Swedish population was over 80 (Statistics Sweden, 2008). So far, Italy is the only other country with over 5%. In 2050, at least 25 countries will have more than 10% of their population over the age of 80, but with 9.3%, Sweden will not be among these countries. Sweden has one of the lowest infant mortality rates, with 3.2 deaths per 100,000 born, which is expected to decline to 2.3. It is also one of the 10 countries with the least fertility changes over the last 50 years and is expected to stay that way up till 2050, with a rate of 1.89 today and 1.80 by then. The oldest old is the most rapidly growing segment of the population. In Sweden, as in most other European countries, it is noted that people in this age group are the ones who need care the most. In Sweden, this old-old population is mostly single or widowed women and they usually live in one-person households. Further details on these phenomena will be explored below.

DEMOGRAPHY

The Swedish population was 9.11 million in 2007, and is predicted to increase to approximately 9.7 million in 2020, and slightly over 10.5 million in 2050 (Statistics Sweden, 2008). The ratios of people above the age of 65 in these years are 17.4%, 22.2%, and 23.7%, respectively. If we look at the proportion of women aged 65+ in relation to the proportion of men aged 65+, we find that the difference in the three aforementioned years (2007, 2020, and 2050) declines from 4.2% more women to 3%, to 2.5%. This demonstrates the higher life expectancy for women, 82.7 years at birth in 2007, compared to men (78.22 years), but at the same time the diminishing gap in life expectancy between the sexes. In 2050, the difference in life expectancy will be only two years; that is, 86 years for women and 84 for men. While it is important to make a greater effort to better understand aging issues for women, it is also critical to explore aging issues for men.

The group aged 80 years and over is increasing at the fastest rate in Sweden. This has implications for the planning of services, as these elderly people are the highest consumers of domestic services and medical care, irrespective of whether they are living in their own home or a sheltered housing facility. It is important to stress here that the vast majority of older persons are healthy and live in their own homes. Only about 6% of persons 65 years and above live in sheltered housing.

The number of persons 65 years old and older doubled from 1950 to 1990, from 721,000 to 1,526,000 people. This number has been more or less unchanged since then. During the next decade, when the baby boomers will retire, there will be an increase of around 20%, to about 1.9 million older people in the year 2015. The increase will continue until 2040, but thereafter there will be a slight decline. As has been said, the dramatic increase will be seen in the old-old group; that is, people 80 years old and older. Noteworthy is the increase in the number of persons who reach at least 100 years of age. In 1919, there were 21 centenarians in Sweden; in 1970, there were 127 people; and in 2007, the number was 1,407. Thus, there has been a sixfold increase in centenarians in the first 50 years from 1919, and then an increase by more than 10 times during the latest 35 years.

Because of the increase of older people in Sweden, it has been extensively discussed whether the pension system and social services system will go bankrupt within the next 20 to 25 years. The proportion of persons in the work force, "the providers," will decrease over the coming 35 years and then rise slightly until 2050. This is based on calculations on the proportion of individuals aged 20–64 years in relation to those who are younger and older. In 2005, there were 0.7 persons outside the work force to every person in it. This will increase to 0.86 around 2040, and then slightly decrease again up to the year 2050. In the interval from today until 2050, the proportion of those below 20 years of age will decrease by 2%, while those over 65 will increase by 6%. That is, the relative "burden" of older persons will increase in relation to the youngest. At its worst, there is a drop of 4% in the "providers." So Sweden might have to reallocate public expenditures from nurseries, schools, and other services for the young to services for the old, such as adult day centers, sheltered housing, and pensions to alleviate the projected economic problem.

We will now move to some demographic aspects that point to differences between the young old—that is, those 65–79 years of age and the old old: those 80 years old and older. Since around 1960, the proportion of men and women among the young old has been relatively stable: 45% to 55% in the 1960s and 47% to 53% today. In the old old, the proportions were the same in 1960, but by 1980, it had changed to a situation where one-third were men and two-thirds were women. This proportion then stabilized from 1980 and is expected to remain the same until 2025. Today there are 36% men and 64% women in the old-old group. After 2025, it is expected that there will be a gradual change until the year 2050, when equal proportions of men and women in the young-old group are expected to occur for the first time: 49.4% men and 50.6% women. In the old-old group, there will be 44% men and 56% women; that is, the same proportions in this age category as in 1960. This means that we will have to shift from focusing only on issues relevant to aging women to focusing on aging issues of both sexes.

Another factor that has to be taken into consideration is the proportion of older adults who are married/cohabiting vs. those who are single. If we look at figures from 1960 up till 1990, we can see that the proportions of married/cohabiting vs. single have been stable for both the young old and the old old. However, we also have to recognize that there was a difference between the two age groups. While there were about equal proportions for single or married for those 65–79 years of age, for those 80 years old or older, one-fourth were still married, or lived under marital conditions, while three-quarters of them were single. Today, 59% of the young old and 33% of the old old are married. It is important to note here that these differences are cohort effects. It should also be noted that 31.6% of the men and 27.5% of the women in the younger age bracket, and 20.5% of the men and 12.5% of the women of the old old, were married; that is, it is much more likely for a man to be married than for a woman. This may also have implications for the differences between the sexes in the possibility of obtaining support and care and thereby avoid unwanted, and maybe sometimes unneeded, institutionalization.

This also presents us with problems that are to be considered in relation to the differences that exist between the younger and the older old. Those who are single have lost one important component in their social network and therefore have to rely more heavily on formal help and services. Several of these services are provided in the old person's home and only very few of even the oldest old live in some kind of sheltered housing.

POLICY

The Swedish parliament has decided upon the following objectives for the policy on aging and older persons: they will be able to lead an active life and have influence on both society and their own lives; be able to grow older in security and maintain their independence; be able to live in their own home for as long as possible; be treated with respect; and have access to good health care and social services. These goals force municipalities to invest more actively in different forms of activity programs for older persons. Swedish policy on retirement transition also stipulates that people going through this transition should be given information and support.

Although strong pressure exists to make it possible for elderly people to live in their own homes as long as possible, and to return to ordinary housing as soon as possible after admission to hospital, achieving this goal requires a greater investment in home care and services than is the case at present. As fewer opportunities to live in sheltered housing are available, investments in new forms of housing alternatives are required. Recently, such developments were suggested in an initiative for housing for older persons (Statens Offentliga Utredningar [SOU], 2007), asking for intermediate forms of housing facilities. Intermediate types of housing would be directed to older persons who feel too insecure to remain living in ordinary housing, and in need of home care. There is no good English translation for this new form of housing, but its main aim is to increase the feeling of security. In the current situation, it is not uncommon that elderly persons who themselves think they need to live in sheltered housing are refused because their functional capacity is judged sufficiently high for them to manage in ordinary housing with the support of home care. In many cases, these individuals are at an advanced age and feel that they need more security. This type of living circumstances was, in a way, covered by earlier forms of sheltered housing, just 15 to 20 years ago, while during later years, societal investments have been geared toward home care and sheltered housing.

HOUSING

In the past, institutional living was considered normal for most elderly people who needed long-term care. They were expected to give up their homes and live the rest of their lives in an institution with little outside contact. Today in Sweden, sheltered housing provides more normal living conditions. Current sheltered housing units are usually smaller and more homelike in structure, and people staying there have a lease on their room or apartment. Out of the 98,600 persons living in special housing in 2006, 56% had 1–1.5 rooms, cooking facilities, restroom, and a shower or bath. Fewer than 5,000 individuals had none of these facilities in their rooms, while the rest lived in housing facilities in between these two standards. Only around 2% have to share a room with a non-family member.

A more recent trend for providing housing and care options to frail elderly people, and especially persons with dementia, is group homes. These units are usually designed for six to eight persons to live together, where they have their own private rooms but share kitchen and living room areas. Quite often these units are remodeled flats and thereby naturally integrated into ordinary dwelling complexes.

In 2006, 239,000 individuals (15%) over the age of 65 were staying permanently in sheltered housing, of which about two-thirds provide 24-hour care (equal to nursing homes, although this term is no longer in official use in Sweden) (Socialstyrelsen 2001), or were receiving home care. Among those 80 years old or older, 37% used these services. Compared to the year 2000, there has been an increase of 19,500 persons receiving home care; this is an increase of 16%. During the same time interval, there has been a decrease in the number of persons staying in sheltered housing by 19,700; that is, a drop of 17%. Among those aged 80 and over, there has been a drop from 20% to 16% in the proportion of people who are able to receive permanent residence in sheltered housing (with/without 24-hour care). Among those aged 65+, of whom about two-thirds are women, the drop was from 8% to 6%. From 2006 to 2007, 3,400 sheltered housing beds were eliminated, reducing the total from 98,600 to 95,200 (National Board of Health and Welfare, 2008). That is, from the year 2000 up to 2007, there was a reduction of 23,100 beds in 24-hour care facilities. While the total number of individuals either receiving home care or living in sheltered housing increased from 239,000 in 2006 to 249,000 in 2007, there was a reduction in the number of beds in sheltered housing. It should be noted here that public statistics show that sheltered housing costs about twice as much as home care. For the geriatric rehabilitation units run by county councils, there has also been a reduction of beds, from 3,189 in 2000 to 2,292 in 2006.

SOCIAL AND MEDICAL SERVICES

In Sweden, the social and medical services rely upon three authorities (i.e., the social insurance office, the municipality, and the county council). For older people, the social insurance office (a governmental (state) office) is mainly responsible for pensions, housing supplement for pensioners, and housing allowance. Social insurances include means-tested, income-related, and universal benefits. The municipality (there are 290 of these local governmental units) is obliged to take care of social domestic assistance, special transportation services, assistive devices, and housing allowances. Lastly, the county council (there are 21 of these regional government units) is responsible for medical and health care. As of January 1, 1992, this partly changed, as the provision of sheltered housing, including units with 24-hour care, home health care, and geriatric rehabilitation, was transferred to the municipalities. The municipalities must provide health care to elderly people and persons with disabilities, delivered mainly by nurses, occupational therapists and physiotherapists. The county councils are only responsible for geropsychiatric units and medical care provided by physicians.

There is also a private sector that provides care and housing to older persons, although the municipalities have the ultimate responsibility. In 2006, around 11% of the home-care services were delivered by the private sector, compared to 7% in the year 2000. In 2006, the private sector provided 14% of special housing in Sweden.

All care services provided by the municipality, the county council, and the private sector are supervised by the National Board of Health and Welfare. Most social services are income related; namely, payment is based on the individual's assets. One exception is housing adaptation grants; these are independent of income. Slightly over 80% of the municipal health care and social services are financed by taxes; some are financed through federal grants; and around 4% are charges to the user. A minimum amount of money that a person must retain for private consumption is guaranteed. Thus, around 20% of older adults receiving home care do not pay any fees due to low income. Their costs are covered by public expenditures. As a consequence, most people do not have to purchase insurance, even if private pension plans to support the regular pensions are common.

RESEARCH ON AGING

In this section, some studies in major areas of gerontological research in Sweden will be exemplified. This will not provide a complete picture, as much research in the geriatric and biological fields is not included, although medical aspects are included—for example, in some of the longitudinal research presented, and in studies regarding dementia. Thus, the research presented should be regarded as examples of recent and ongoing research by different research groups and centers across Sweden, with quite a few being contributions by recently established researchers after completing their Ph.D. education.

Theoretical Contributions

In the theoretical field, a major contribution has been made by Tornstam (2005). His theory of gerotranscendence describes developmental changes in the way people define their life and existence. This theory triggered the collaborator and widow to the late Erik H. Erikson to add a ninth step to their well-known developmental model (Erikson & Erikson, 1997). In nursing practice, the theory has been used as a guideline for running reminiscence groups with good results (Wadensten & Häglund, 2006).

Health and Disability

Several longitudinal studies produce findings on health and disability and their relation to survival. Bravell, Berg, and Malmberg (2008) investigated how health, activities of daily living (ADL), and use of care changed over time in individuals aged 86, 90, and 94 years, and how differences in health and ADL affected survival. Based on data from the longitudinal sequential study Lund 80+, various combinations of number of diseases and symptoms were used to explore implications for mortality in a sample of 80-year-olds followed up to 95 years of age (Steij Stålbrand et al., 2007). This study showed that the experience of subjective signs of illness carries the same mortality risks as diagnosed diseases over a 15-year period. Meinow, Parker, Kåreholt, and Thorslund (2006) conducted a similar study with people aged 77 and older. The results suggested a worsening of health over a 10-year period and an increase of complex problems. Jakobsson and Hallberg (2006) investigated mortality among elderly persons aged 65–98 who received public long-term care. They found that the determinants of death were male gender, severe cognitive impairment, comorbidity, and problems in ADL.

In a study by Braungart Fauth, Zarit, Malmberg, and Johansson (2007), the Disablement Process Model was used to predict whether a sample of very old people maintained their disability or disability-free status during a two- and four-year follow-up, or whether their status changed over the period. The results indicated that demographic factors, physical impairments, physical and cognitive limitations, and psychosocial variables at baseline predicted which persons stayed non-disabled after two years. Most factors continued to distinguish between the groups after four years.

Most surveys of the health of the older population show successive improvement over time, suggesting support for the compression of morbidity hypothesis. To study this, changes in the health of the Swedish population aged 77 years and older from 1992 to 2002 were studied (Parker, Ahacic, & Thorslund, 2005). The findings revealed that although disability measures often show improvement, there is a simultaneous increase in chronic disease and functional impairments. For this reason, Parker and Thorslund (2007) argue that a concept of general morbidity is not sufficient when discussing health trends and the need for care services.

The Swedish government launched a major longitudinal study, the Swedish National Study on Aging and Care (SNAC), in 2001 to explore older adults' future needs of care (Lagergren et al., 2004). Using data from this study, health-care consumption in men and women aged 65 and above was investigated in the two years prior to decision about permanent municipal care at home or in special accommodation (Kristensson, Hallberg, & Jakobsson, 2007). The findings indicated a breakpoint in terms of having hospital admissions about five months prior to municipal care and service. Early detection and preventive interventions for these people in a transitional stage of becoming increasingly dependent on continuous care and services seem urgent to prevent escalating acute health-care consumption.

Dementia

As in many other countries, dementia research is an area of priority in Sweden. The Study of Dementia in Swedish Twins (HARMONY) includes procedures for complete ascertainment of all cases of Alzheimer's disease (AD) and other dementias in 14,435 individuals aged 65 and older from the national Swedish twin registry (Gatz et al., 2005; Gatz et al., 2006). It could be confirmed that heritability for AD is high and that the same genetic factors are influential for both men and women. It should be noted that nongenetic risk factors also play an important role and might be the focus for interventions to reduce disease risk or delay disease onset.

Dahl and her colleagues (Dahl, Berg, & Nilsson, 2007) compared the identification of dementia from different data sources with that of consensus diagnosis based on a sample enrolled in the Swedish population-based longitudinal twin study. The precision of medical records increased when recordings of cognitive impairment were at hand. The discharge registry was shown to be an uncertain source and of low value for dementia identification.

Both AD and depression are prevalent disorders in old age and may co-occur in the same individual. Using population-based samples, Berger and colleagues (Berger, Fratiglioni, Winblad, & Bäckman, 2005) examined if a diagnosis of depression in persons with AD had negative effects on cognitive functioning in the preclinical stage of the disease, as well as at the time when the diagnoses were established. They found that depression was not associated with a greater decline in cognitive functioning over three years.

Data from the Kungsholmen project were used to determine the occurrence of neuropsychiatric symptomatology and the relation to future development of AD in persons with and without mild cognitive impairment (MCI) (Palmer et al., 2007). The predictive value of MCI for identifying future AD is improved if the presence of anxiety symptoms is assessed. Based on data from the same study, Monastero and colleagues (Monastero, Palmer, Qiu, Winblad, & Fratiglioni, 2007) studied the relation of vascular, neuropsychiatric, social, and frailty-related factors to cognitive impairment, no dementia (CIND), and tried to verify their effect independently on future progression to AD. The results pointed to the fact that not only the AD-type neurodegenerative process but also neuropsychiatric and frailty-related factors may induce cognitive impairment in non-demented elderly people.

The experiential aspects of dementia are also of great interest. An example of this type of research is a study using constructivist grounded theory regarding the impact of dementia on the everyday life and relationships of older spousal couples (Hellstrom, Nolan, & Lundh, 2005).

Care and Policy

Family caregivers of relatives with dementia often report higher levels of psychological distress than other caregivers. Andrén and Elmståhl (2007), after interviewing 50 caregivers, concluded that persons with a low health profile and a low income, especially adult children, are more prone to experiencing a higher burden of care. To investigate quality of life in relation to loneliness, caregiving, social network, sex, age, and economic status among caregiving men and women, a study was done on a population-based sample aged 75+ (Ekwall, Sivberg, & Rahm-Hallberg, 2005). Overall, the results showed significant association between loneliness, weak social network, and low mental quality of life.

A study to describe the amount of formal and informal care for non-demented and demented persons living at home in a population-based sample was done in a rural community (Nordberg, von Strauss, Kåreholt, Johansson, & Wimo, 2005). The amount of informal care was much higher than formal care and also higher among demented than non-demented individuals. The authors concluded that informal care seems to substitute rather than complement formal care. An overview of how the expression of filial obligations has shifted over time in Sweden has been presented (Johansson & Sundström, 2006). In line with what public records and statistics show, it was concluded that intergenerational solidarity has not disappeared in Sweden; just the manifestations have changed. Given its relative ethnic and socioeconomic homogeneity, Sweden is an ideal nation for the study of variations in formal and informal care as a function of sex, disability, and advanced age. An analysis of the relationships between these factors and the formal care in 1994 and 2000 has been presented (Davey, Savla, Sundström, Zarit, & Malmberg, 2007). The conclusion is that Sweden's system of old-age care appears in broader terms to be equitable, although the quality of care could not be fully assessed or evaluated. Although home and community-based service provision (HCBS) has recently decreased, variations in the volume and mix of delivered formal services do reflect the variety of needs of the older population.

There is an increasing demand for services, and with limited resources, it is important to find ways to optimize the use of these resources. Nordberg and colleagues (2007) analyzed time use and costs in institutional care in relation to different levels of cognitive and functional capacity. The main finding was that when analyzing total care time use, the presence of dementia added more than 9h, while each loss of one ADL function added 2.9h. The estimated cost for institutional care increased, with more than 85% for people being dependent in 5–6 ADL activities compared to persons with no functional dependency, and with 30% for persons with dementia.

As more immigrants reach advanced age in Sweden, more studies in the area emerge. Emami and Torres (2004) studied older immigrants' experiences of receiving public care and found that they experienced health problems, painful losses, feelings of exposure and desertion, but still wanting to manage on their own.

Psychology and Cognition

Research on aging and psychological factors as well as cognitive functioning is high on the research agenda in Sweden today. In a study on cognition and mortality, using longitudinal data, individual changes in perceptual speed were modeled as a conditional function of age and time-to-death (Thorvaldsson, Hofer, & Johansson, 2006). In both an age-based and a death-based time-structured model, accelerated changes prior to time of death were observed that support the terminal-decline hypothesis. Also, when studying cognitive decline effects in twins, there is support of the terminal-decline phenomenon (Johansson et al., 2004). Latent growth models (LGMs) showed that both chronological age and time to death are consistent predictors of decline in measures of memory, reasoning, speed, and verbal abilities.

In a community-based sample, the association between blood pressure and the risk of subsequent cognitive decline in the oldest old was examined (Nilsson et al., 2007). The authors concluded that lower systolic blood pressure in the oldest old is associated with an increased risk of cognitive impairment even after adjusting for compromised vitality.

Rönnlund and his colleagues (Rönnlund, Nyberg, Bäckman, & Nilsson, 2005) studied five-year changes in episodic and semantic memory. Among other things, they found that cohort differences in educational attainment accounted for the differences between cross-sectional and longitudinal findings. This stresses the need to control for cohort effects when comparing individuals over time and age. Sex differences in declarative memory and visuospatial ability have been shown to be robust in cross-sectional studies. This was confirmed in a longitudinal study over a 10-year period (de Frias, Nilsson, & Herlitz, 2006).

Berg and her colleagues (Berg, Hassing, McClearn, & Johansson, 2006) examined factors associated with life satisfaction in the oldest old. Social network quality, self-rated health, sense of being in control of one's life, and depressive symptoms were significantly associated with life satisfaction. However, there were different sets of variables associated with life satisfaction in men and women.

Feelings of loneliness and fear are fairly common among elderly people. They seem to be related to each other and are both found to be "threats" to leading a good life. A study on feelings of loneliness and fear was done based on cross-sectional data (Jakobsson & Hallberg, 2005). Loneliness was significantly associated with gender, marital status, living in facilities for the elderly, fear, and need for help with instrumental activities of daily living (IADL); while fear was significantly associated with gender, number of children, having someone to trust, loneliness, and being in need of help with IADL.

Environment

Environmental gerontology is a growing area of research. Ståhl and colleagues (Ståhl, Carlsson, Hovbrandt, & Iwarsson, 2008) initiated a project aiming to identify and implement measures for increased accessibility and safety in a residential area. This included separating pedestrians/cyclists, lower speed limits, better maintenance, and specific measures for pedestrian walkways, such as wider sidewalks, levels and shape of curbs, and even surfaces on pavements. Results after four years demonstrated no effects in terms of increased outdoor mobility, but more appreciation of the environment regarding accessibility and safety.

Well-being, ill-health, ADL dependence, and person-environment (P-E) fit, especially regarding housing accessibility problems during the aging process, have been studied longitudinally over a 10-year period (Werngren-Elgström, Carlsson, & Iwarsson, 2008a, 2008b). Overall, the participants rated their subjective well-being as high, and stable over time, as was the prevalence of symptoms, while P-E fit problems increased over time.

The ENABLE-AGE Project is a European multi-center study involving five countries with the aim to explore the home environment as a determinant for autonomy, participation, and well-being in very old age

(Iwarsson et al., 2007). Overall, besides a wide range of valuable methodological contributions to the field, results showed that P-E fit in terms of housing accessibility problems has an important influence on health, while environmental barriers *per se* do not have such an influence. One example of more detailed results (Oswald et al., 2007) is that participants living in more accessible homes, who perceive their homes as meaningful and useful, and who think that external influences are not responsible for their housing situation, are more independent in daily activities and have a better sense of well-being. Qualitative studies among the very old showed that home was experienced as the locus and origin for participation (Haak, Dahlin Ivanoff, Fänge, Sixsmith, & Iwarsson, 2007) and a signification of independence (Haak, Fänge, Iwarsson, & Dahlin Ivanoff, 2007).

The body of literature on use of assistive devices in old age is rapidly increasing. In Sweden, occupational therapy researchers have investigated different aspects of need, use, and satisfaction with mobility devices. One retrospective longitudinal study demonstrated that the use, and especially the permanent use, of several mobility devices increased between 85 and 90 years of age (Dahlin-Ivanoff & Sonn, 2005). Focusing on another type of assistive technology, Nygård and colleagues have published substantial research on technology use among persons with dementia (e.g. Margot-Cattin & Nygård, 2006).

THE FUTURE

Sweden has for some years been stressing the importance of having older people living in their own homes as long as possible. This has meant allocating more funding to home care and services at the expense of sheltered housing options. In the near future, building of housing alternatives for older people with a minimum of service but with an optimum of safety and security may be expected. Overall in Sweden, aging issues have high political priority, implying that at least today's level of funding will be maintained, in services to older people as well as in research on aging. Since it has been shown that the vast majority of older persons prefers and can live in their own homes with adequate support and services, it is probable that additional efforts will be made to develop and study these types of services. Since both access to an activity and getting to it are prerequisites for societal participation, demands will arise for better transportation for older people. That is, most likely the interest in studying environmental conditions and ecological factors will increase.

Intervention studies are scarce today and more research is needed to support the development of evidence-based initiatives in the care of older persons. It is of utmost importance that more resources are invested in research on care options for older persons, especially regarding health promotion. A recent bill on research funding identified caring research as a priority area for the years to come.

The continued growth in the number and ratio of the oldest old points to the need to further knowledge on the aging process after the age of 80, and the special needs and demands of this population, maybe with an emphasis on women. Another area that will be of great importance in the future is the prevention of infirmity and disability. This will encourage gerontological research of younger cohorts also, in order to better understand what governs the transition to disability and illness during aging. This trend should be welcomed as a means of broadening our knowledge about old age and the aging process.

REFERENCES

Andrén, S., & Elmståhl, S. (2007). Relationships between income, subjective health and caregiver burden in caregivers of people with dementia in group living care: A cross-sectional community-based study. *International Journal of Nursing Studies, 44*(3), 435–446.

Berg, A. I., Hassing, L. B., McClearn, G. E., & Johansson, B. (2006). What matters for life satisfaction in the oldest-old? *Aging & Mental Health, 10*(3), 257–264.

Berger, A. K., Fratiglioni, L., Winblad, B., & Bäckman, L. (2005). Alzheimer's disease and depression: Preclinical comorbidity effects on cognitive functioning. *Cortex, 41*(4), 603–612.

Braungart Fauth, E., Zarit, S. H., Malmberg, B., & Johansson, B. (2007). Physical, cognitive, and psychosocial variables from the disablement process model predict patterns of independence and the transition into disability for the oldest-old. *The Gerontologist, 47*(6), 13–624.

Bravell, M. E., Berg, S., & Malmberg, B. (2008). Health, functional capacity, formal care, and survival in the oldest old: A longitudinal study. *Archives of Gerontology and Geriatrics, 46* (1), 1–14.

Dahl, A., Berg, S., & Nilsson, S. E. (2007). Identification of dementia in epidemiological research: A study on the usefulness of various data sources. *Aging Clinical and Experimental Research, 19,* 381–389.

Dahlin-Ivanoff, S., & Sonn, U. (2005). Changes in the use of assistive devices among 90-year-old persons. *Aging Clinical and Experimental Research, 17*(3), 246–251.

Davey, A., Savla, J., Sundström, G., Zarit, S. H., & Malmberg, B. (2007). How equitable is Sweden's changing care-mix? Linking individual and regional characteristics over time. *Ageing and society, 27*(4), 511–532.

de Frias, C., Nilsson, L.-G., & Herlitz, A. (2006). Sex differences in cognition are stable over a 10-year period in adulthood and old age. *Aging, Neuropsychology and Cognition, 13*(3–4), 574–587.

Ekwall, A. K., Sivberg, B., & Rahm-Hallberg, I. (2005). Loneliness as a predictor of quality of life among older caregivers. *Journal of Advanced Nursing, 49*(1), 23–32.

Emami, S., & Torres, S. (2004). Making sense of illness: Late in life migration as point of departure for elderly Iranian immigrants' explanatory models of illness. *Journal of immigrant health, 7*(3), 153–164.

Erikson, E. H., & Erikson, J. M. (1997). *The life cycle completed. Extended version with new chapters on the ninth stage of development.* New York: Norton.

Gatz, M., Fratiglioni, L., Johansson, B., Berg, S., Mortimer, J. A., Reynolds, C. A., et al. (2005). Complete ascertainment of dementia in the Swedish Twin Registry: The HARMONY study. *Neurobiology of Aging, 26*(4), 439–447.

Gatz, M., Reynolds, C. A., Fratiglioni, L., Johansson, B., Mortimer, J. A., Berg, S., et al. (2006). Role of genes and environments for explaining Alzheimer disease. *Archives of General Psychiatry, 63*, 168–174.

Haak, M., Dahlin Ivanoff, S., Fänge, A., Sixsmith, J., & Iwarsson, S. (2007). Home as the locus and origin for participation—Experiences among very old Swedish people. *Occupational Therapy Journal of Research: Occupation, Participation & Health, 27*(3), 95–103.

Haak, M., Fänge, A., Iwarsson, S., & Dahlin Ivanoff, S. (2007). Home as a signification of independence and autonomy—Experiences among very old Swedish people. *Scandinavian Journal of Occupational Therapy, 14*, 16–24.

Hellstrom, I., Nolan, M., & Lundh, U. (2005). Awareness context theory and the dynamics of dementia: Improving understanding using emergent fit. *Dementia, 4*(2), 269–295.

Hovde, B., Hallberg, I. R., & Edberg, A.-K. (2008). Older immigrants' experiences of their life situation in the context of receiving public care in Sweden. *International Journal of Older People Nursing, 3*, 104–112.

Iwarsson, S., Wahl, H.-W., Nygren, C., Oswald, F., Sixsmith, A., Sixsmith, J., et al. (2007). Importance of the home environment for healthy aging: Conceptual and methodological background of the European ENABLE-AGE Project. *Gerontologist, 47*, 78–84.

Jakobsson, U., & Hallberg, I. R. (2005). Loneliness, fear, and quality of life among elderly in Sweden: A gender perspective. *Aging clinical and experimental research, 17*(6), 494–501.

Jakobsson, U., & Hallberg, I. R. (2006). Mortality among elderly receiving long-term care: A longitudinal cohort study. *Aging clinical and experimental research, 18*(6), 503–511.

Johansson, B., Hofer, S. M., Allaire, J. C., Maldonado-Molina, M. M., Piccinin, A. M., Berg, S., et al. (2004). Change in cognitive capabilities in the oldest old:

The effects of proximity to death in genetically related individuals over a 6-year period. *Psychology and Aging, 19*(1),145–56.

Johansson, L., & Sundström, G. (2006). Policies and practices in support of family caregivers—filial obligations redefined in Sweden. *Journal of Aging & Social Policy, 18*(3/4), 7–26.

Kristensson, J., Hallberg, I. R., & Jakobsson, U. (2007). Healthcare consumption in men and women aged 65 and above in the two years preceding decision about long-term municipal care. *Health & Social Care in the Community, 15*(5), 474–485.

Lagergren, M., Fratiglioni, L., Hallberg, I. R., Berglund, J., Elmståhl, S., Hagberg, B., et al. (2004). A longitudinal study integrating population, care and social services data. The Swedish National study on Aging and Care (SNAC). *Aging clinical and experimental research, 16*(2), 158–168.

Margot-Cattin, I., & Nygård, L. (2006). Access technology and dementia care: Influences on residents' everyday lives in a secure unit. *Scandinavian Journal of Occupational Therapy, 13*, 113–124.

Meinow, B., Parker, M. G., Kåreholt, I., & Thorslund, M. (2006). Complex health problems in the oldest old in Sweden 1992–2002. *European Journal of Ageing, 3*(2), 98–106.

Monastero, R., Palmer, K., Qiu, C., Winblad, B., & Fratiglioni, L. (2007). Heterogeneity in risk factors for cognitive impairment, no dementia: Population-based longitudinal study from the Kungsholmen Project. *American Journal of Geriatric Psychiatry, 15*(1), 60–9.

National Board of Health and Welfare. (2008). *Statistics social welfare. Care and services to elderly persons 2007.* Social Welfare 2008:7. Stockholm.

Nilsson, S. E., Read, S., Berg, S., Johansson, B., Melander, A., & Lindblad, U. (2007). Low systolic blood pressure is associated with impaired cognitive function in the oldest old: Longitudinal observations in a population-based sample 80 years and older. *Aging Clinical and Experimental Research, 19*(1), 41–47.

Nordberg, G., von Strauss, E., Kåreholt, I., Johansson, L., & Wimo, A. (2005). The amount of informal and formal care among non-demented and demented elderly persons-results from a Swedish population-based study. *International Journal of Geriatric Psychiatry, 20*(9), 862–871.

Nordberg, G., Wimo, A., Jonsson, L., Kåreholt, I., Sjolund, B.-M., Lagergren, M., et al. (2007). Time use and costs of institutionalised elderly persons with or without dementia: Results from the Nordanstig cohort in the Kungsholmen Project—A population-based study in Sweden. *International Journal of Geriatric Psychiatry, 22*(7), 639–648.

Oswald, F., Wahl, H.-W., Schilling, O., Nygren, C., Fänge, A., Sixsmith, A., et al. (2007). Relationships between housing and healthy ageing aspects in very old age: Results from the European ENABLE-AGE Project. *Gerontologist, 47*, 96–107.

Palmer, K., Berger, A. K., Monastero, R., Winblad, B., Bäckman, L., & Fratiglioni, L. (2007). Predictors of progression from mild cognitive impairment to Alzheimer disease. *Neurology, 68*, 1596–1602.

Parker, M. G., Ahacic, K., & Thorslund, M. (2005). Health changes among Swedish oldest old: Prevalence rates from 1992 and 2002 show increasing health problems. *The Journals of Gerontology Series A: Biological Sciences and Medical Sciences, 60,* 1351–1355.

Parker, M. G., & Thorslund, M. (2007). Health trends in the elderly population: Getting better and getting worse. *The Gerontologist, 47,* 150–158.

Rönnlund, M., Nyberg, L., Bäckman, L., & Nilsson, L.-G. (2005). Stability, growth, and decline in adult life span development of declarative memory: Cross-sectional and longitudinal data from a population-based study. *Psychology and Aging, 20*(1), 3–18.

Socialstyrelsen. (2001). *Vad är särskilt boende för alder? En kartläggning.* Stockholm: Kunskapsöversikt.

Ståhl, A., Carlsson, G., Hovbrandt, P., & Iwarsson, S. (2008). "Let's go for a walk!"—User involvement when prioritizing measures in a residential area to increase accessibility and safety for older people. *European Journal of Ageing.* (In press.)

Statens Offentliga Utredningar (SOU). (2007). *Bo för att leva—seniorbostäder och trygghetsbostäder.* SOU 2007:103.

Statistics Sweden. (2008). *Statistical yearbook of Sweden.*

Steij Stålbrand, I., Svensson, T., Elmståhl, S., Horstmann, V., Hagberg, B., Dehlin, O., et al. (2007). Subjective health and illness, coping and life satisfaction in an 80-year-old Swedish population—Implications for mortality. *International Journal of Behavioral Medicine, 14*(3), 173–180.

Thorvaldsson, V., Hofer, S. M., & Johansson, B. (2006). Aging and late-life terminal decline in perceptual speed: A comparison of alternative modeling approaches. *European psychologist, 11*(3), 196–203.

Tornstam, L. (2005). *Gerotranscendence. A developmental theory of positive aging.* New York: Springer Publishing Company.

United Nations, Department of Economic and Social Affairs, Population Division. (2007). *World population prospects: The 2006 revision, highlights.* Working Paper No. SA/P/WP.202. New York: United Nations.

Wadensten, B., & Häglund, D. (2006). Older people's experience of participating in a reminiscence group with a gerotranscendental perspective: reminiscence group with a gerotranscendental perspective in practice. *International Journal of Older People Nursing, 1,* 159–167.

Werngren-Elgström, M., Carlsson, G., & Iwarsson, S. (2008a). A 10-year follow-up study on subjective well-being and relationships to person-environment (P-E) fit and activity of daily living (ADL)-dependence of older Swedish adults. *Archives of Gerontology and Geriatrics.* (In press.)

Werngren-Elgström, M., Carlsson, G., & Iwarsson, S. (2008b). Changes in person-environment fit and ADL dependence among older Swedish adults—A 10-year follow-up. *Aging Clinical and Experimental Research.* (In press.)

46

Switzerland

Jean-Pierre Michel, Christophe J. Büla,
Daniel Grob, Reto Kressig,
and Thomas Münzer

(Special acknowledgment: Andreas Stuck)

Switzerland was created in 1291 by the representatives of three cantons who signed an alliance treaty that still presides over the federal cohesion of the country. Today, each of the 26 cantons constituting the Swiss confederation benefits from a legislative and executive autonomy, which means that each canton establishes its own health policies and budget. In fact, there is no health ministry at the country level, while the interior affairs ministry supervises and coordinates universities'/high schools' activities. The government of each canton has a health and an education department responsible for the implementation of programs elaborated by the cantonal authorities. The rarity of the national sources of data and the cantonal diversity do not facilitate the gathering of comparable data at the national level (Michel, Stuckelberger, & Grab, 1993).

In 2006, Switzerland had 7,509,000 inhabitants, of whom 16.6% were aged 65 years and older and 4.7% were aged over 80 years. The life expectancy at birth is 79.1 years for men and 84.0 years for women, and life expectancy at the age of 65 averages 18.7 years for men and 21.6 years for women (Swiss Federal Statistical Office, 2008). Demographic prospects foresee an alarming increase in the aged population while the total population will stay constant. In 2050, the proportion of adults aged over 65 and 85 years will reach 27.7% and 12.4%, respectively (Figures 46.1 and 46.2; United Nations, 2007).

Figure 46.1
Switzerland: Population structure by age, in thousands (1900 vs 2005)

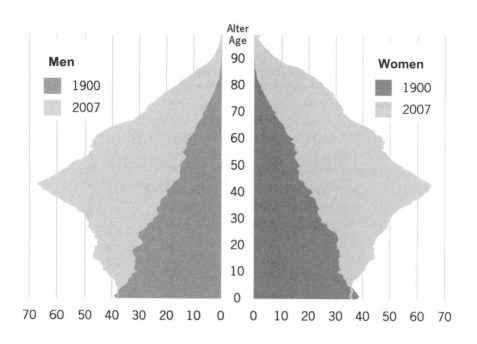

Source: Swiss Federal Statistical Office. (2008). *Statistical yearbook of Switzerland.*
Neue Zürcher Zeitung (NZZ).

RECENT HISTORY OF GERIATRICS

Created in 1992 under the leadership of the Swiss Gerontological Society (founded in 1953), the Swiss Professional Geriatric Society became
independent in 2003 after the recognition in 2000 of geriatrics as a board-
certified discipline (Foederatio Medicorum Helveticorum, 2000). The
process of specialization in geriatrics requires physicians to first obtain
board certification in internal or family medicine (five years), and then
complete an additional three-year training program specifically dedicated
to geriatrics (two years in a department of geriatrics, plus one year in a department of psychiatry—including at least six months of psychogeriatric
training) (Schoenenberger & Stuck, 2006). The geriatric board certificate is obtained after an overall training period of seven to eight years,
which corresponds more to a "supra-specialty" than a subspecialty of internal or family medicine. In 2008, 30 geriatric programs were accredited

Figure 46.2
Switzerland: Population age groups prospect from 1991 to 2050

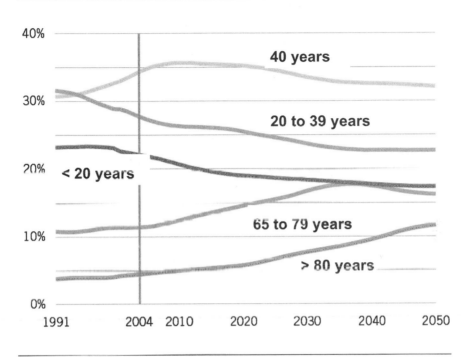

Source: Swiss Federal Statistical Office. (2008). *Statistical yearbook of Switzerland.*
Neue Zürcher Zeitung (NZZ).

in Switzerland, with only 8 recognized for a two-year fellowship program. Currently, there are 184 certified geriatricians in Switzerland, practicing mainly in urban areas.

The second recent and most significant progress in geriatric medicine in Switzerland was the creation of two new chairs of geriatrics in Bern (Prof. A. Stuck—2004) and Lausanne (Prof. Ch. Büla—2007), complementing the two existing chairs in Basle (Prof. R. Kressig, successor—2006) and Geneva (Prof. J.-P. Michel—1987). So among the five Swiss medical schools, only Zürich does not yet have a chair of geriatric medicine.

- In the Basle University hospitals, after the retirement of Prof. H. Staehelin, the geriatric ward was restructured. In 2008, under the leadership of Prof. R. Kressig, the geriatric activities were centralized within the university and cantonal hospital (in the medicine department) with a clinic of 28 acute-care beds, a memory outpatient clinic (for early dementia detection), and a mobility center (for assessment of older adults' function-ality, gait, balance, and falling risk). Geriatric medium- and long-term care wards are located in another hospital (Felix-Platter Hospital).

- In the Bern University hospitals, the geriatric department, chaired by Prof. A. Stuck, includes 70 acute-care beds, 48 rehabilitation beds, and 12 beds devoted to geriatric evaluation and management, as well as a day hospital and an outpatient assessment clinic that focuses on memory assessment and gait analysis.

- In the Geneva University hospitals, the geriatric and rehabilitation department is the largest academic medical department of the canton (of the 12 medical existing departments in Geneva). Since 2006, it has been chaired by Prof. R. Rizzoli, an internist specializing in bone metabo-lism. The department is composed of 700 beds divided into five clinical wards: 124 acute care beds of geriatric medicine (Prof. J.-P. Michel), 114 acute and post-acute care beds (providing care mostly for demented and depressed patients affected by somatic diseases—Prof. G. Gold), 104 acute care beds of internal medicine (including a special oncological supportive care program—Prof. A. F. Allaz), 56 beds specializing in gait disturbances analysis/fall prevention and early post-hip fracture rehabilitation (Prof. R. Rizzoli—head of the department), 30 beds for palliative care (with a specific liaison team for pain control within the other different wards of the department; Dr. G. Zulian), completed by medium- and long-stay care beds (260 beds—Dr H. Vuagnat). The geriatric and rehabilitation departments also have a specific geriatric team working in the emergency department (Dr. Th. Chevalley), an intensive care unit (Dr. J.-J. Per-renoud), and outpatient memory (Prof. G. Gold) and bone metabolism clinics (Dr. B. Uebelhart). This department works closely with a com-munity team of geriatricians belonging, for administrative reasons, to the Community health care department (Prof. C.H. Rapin).

- In the Lausanne University hospitals, the geriatric department is also considered a medical department on its own, under the leadership of Prof. C. Büla. The department includes acute, post-acute, and rehabilitation beds, as well as an ambulatory sector with a geriatrics consultation, an outpatient memory clinic, and a multidisciplinary team working in the community. Finally, the department also provides care to residents in hospital-affiliated long-term-care institutions.

- The Geriatric Hospital at St. Gallen is part of St. Gallen Excellence Cen-ter for Health and Aging. This center is unique in Switzerland, since it combines all aspects of aging under one organizational structure. The Center runs a senior citizen residency for persons living independently, providing individuals a choice of physicians within the region, a geri-atric hospital, and a nursing home. It delivers medical and nursing care to the geriatric hospital and the nursing home. The organization looks back to a history of more than 750 years. The "new" Geriatric Hospital (Prof. C. Hürny) was built in 1980 and has a capacity of 86 beds. It serves as a geriatric reference center for the eastern part of the country and is currently responsible for the establishment of new geriatric care units in other hospitals of the region as part of an official cantonal political mandate. Currently, the Geriatric Hospital covers the full range of geriatric medical care, such as acute geriatric treatment and assessment, geriatric rehabilitation, long-term care, and palliative care. In addition, the center offers ambulatory assessment of cognition in a memory clinic, as well as a day-care clinic for patients with advanced dementia or frailty, and psychological support for patients or family members.

• In the Zürich University hospital, a chair of geriatric medicine has not yet been established. Seventy-eight acute-care geriatric beds are located in Town-Hospital Waid, whose director (Dr. Daniel Grob) carries out some geriatric teaching tasks together with the chief-physician of Zürich (P.D. Dr. Albert Wettstein). In late summer 2008, the Center for Aging and Mobility was established through cooperation between the university and Town-Hospital Waid. This research center is located in both University Hospital and Town-Hospital Waid. The Director is Prof. Heike Bischoff-Ferrari and Dr. Daniel Grob represents clinical geriatrics.

RECENT RESEARCH

Research activities on aging have been essentially developed by, or with, the involvement of academic geriatricians. The most important development in gerontological research was in the Center of Interdisciplinary Gerontology at Geneva University. The main research activities were to constitute, follow up, and compare two cohorts of Swiss octogenarians living in urban and rural areas (Swiss Interdisciplinary Longitudinal Study on the Oldest Old), focusing on psychological changes with aging and the frailty process (Lalive d'Epinay, 2008; Armi, Guilley, & Lalive d'Epinay, 2008).

In Basel, three main research topics are in progress. Initiated with the well-known Basel Longitudinal Study, research on nutrition is now focusing more on micronutrient intake (Bisschoff, Staehelin, & Willett, 2006) and calcium metabolism (Bischoff-Ferrari et al., 2008). The second long-term research topic in Basel focuses on cognitive impairments: early detection of dementia (Steuerwald et al., 2007), conversion of MCI to dementia (Zehnder, Bläsi, Berres, Spiegel, & Monsch, 2007), clinical/functional course of the dementia progression (Taylor, Probst, Miserez, Monsch, & Tolnay, 2008), and new therapeutical approaches with disease-modifying drugs (in progress). The third and most recent research topic developed in Basel is related to gait analysis and fall prevention (Kressig, Herrmann, Grandjean, Michel, & Beauchet, 2008).

In Bern, A. Stuck's research focused first on home-care service organization and delivery, evaluating a large variety of outcomes (survival, hospital admissions, drugs use, daily functioning, quality of life, and cost effectiveness) (Stuck et al., 2005; Wagner et al., 2006). Next, he and his team focused their research activities on a related topic: individual risk appraisals. International comparisons were very useful for better understanding and then focusing geriatric priorities (Carmaciu et al., 2007; Stuck et al., 2005). Following these results, the Bern geriatric research team targeted main clinical problems of interest for increasing both quality of care and quality of life in community-dwelling adults, as well as organization and efficiency of hospital geriatric care: pain and cardiovascular diseases (Schoenenberger, Erne, Ammann, Gillmann, et al., 2008; Schoenenberger, Erne, Ammann, Perrig, et al., 2008).

In Geneva, the main research topic developed by R. Rizzoli and his team deals with bone metabolism. Lifelong longitudinal studies examine the two opposite extremes of life: (a) early life and the interrelation between genes and environment (Bonjour, Chevalley, Rizzoli, & Ferrari, 2007) to better date the peak bone mass and understand its constituting process (Bonjour, Chevalley, Ammann, Slosman, & Rizzoli, 2001); and (b) its decrease with aging, leading to the osteoporotic process and related complications. The relationship between protein nutrition and decrease of the bone density was deeply analyzed in animal models (Ammann et al., 2002), in normal aging individuals (Rizzoli & Bonjour, 2004), in post-hip-fracture patients, and the positive bone and muscle impacts of renutrition with amino acids and proteins were demonstrated in the same previously mentioned populations (Rizzoli, Ammann, Chevalley, & Bonjour, 2001). Indeed, many epidemiological studies have also focused on the possible prevention and treatment of osteoporosis, including traditional (Rizzoli et al., 2008) or more innovative therapeutic approaches (Reginster et al., 2008; Richert, Uebelhart, Engelhardt, Azria, & Rizzoli, 2008).

The second research interest of the Geneva geriatric and psychogeriatric academic teams is dementia. Many research areas have been covered, but vascular dementia was a specific area of interest, with a critical analysis of validated diagnostic scores using clinico-pathological confrontation (Gold, Giannakopoulos, Herrmann, Bouras, & Kövari, 2007; Kövari et al., 2007). But more and more collaborative research concerns the evaluation of the brain reserve using special EEG techniques to explore the working memory and determine the conversion from mild cognitive impairment to dementia (Missonnier et al., 2007). This question was studied by identifying risk factors of conversion to dementia in a longitudinal survey of community-dwelling patients (Zekry et al., 2008a).

The other Geneva geriatric activities can be divided into three main categories: (a) biology applied to clinically relevant geriatric problems (Vischer, 2006; Zekry et al., 2008b); (b) geronto-epidemiology and geriatric care prospects (Michel, Newton,& Kirkwood, 2008; Robine & Michel, 2004); and (c) clinical geriatric medicine focusing on metabolic disturbances and their age-related complications, cardiogeriatric, or palliative medicine (Weber, Merminod, Herrmann, & Zulian, 2008) and pain evaluation and control in demented patients (Pautex, Herrmann, Michon, Giannakopoulos, & Gold, 2007).

In Lausanne, research interests have focused on health-care delivery to older patients in the community, acute, rehabilitation, as well as long-term care settings (Bosshard, Dreher, Schnegg, & Büla, 2004; Büla, Ghilardi, Wietlisbach, Petignat, & Francioli, 2004). This includes issues related to the epidemiology, detection, and clinical management of geriatric syndromes such as depression, delirium, and dementia. A second area of research has been developed in falls, including gait and physical activity monitoring in older persons (Büla, Martin, Rochat, & Piot-Ziegler, 2008; Ganea et al., 2007). More recently, spirituality has become a focus of research interest in Lausanne (Monod, 2008). Finally, in 2004, a multidisciplinary collaboration started a cohort study of the determinants and outcome of frailty in community dwelling elderly persons (Santos-Eggimann et al., 2008).

In St Gallen, research interests focus primarily on endocrine changes and interventions in older patients. The first project was an observational study examining the question of whether the effects of nasal continuous airway pressure ventilation in patients with obstructive sleep apnea syndrome are influenced by the age of the patient. The study focuses on changes in the cardiovascular system, on body composition, hormones and quality of life. A new research initiative will examine the effects of different hormones on falls in pre-frail older individuals.

In Zürich, research activities in the new center for aging and mobility will focus on falls, fracture-rehab, and vitamin D metabolism. There is also research cooperation between Town-Hospital Waid and the federal technical university (ETH; Institute for movement sciences and sport).

EDUCATION IN GERIATRICS

As previously stated, the independence of each medical school makes it difficult to summarize the various teaching activities in geriatrics. At the graduate level, the number of hours varies from 40 to 120. However, it is important to say that in the four universities with a department of geriatric medicine, the medical students get instruction in the biology of aging and in geriatric and palliative care medicine throughout their medical curriculum, not only for a few designated hours a year. Various teaching activities are used in the different medical schools, such as problem-based learning, lectures, interactive workshops, clinical geriatric demonstrations to all the medical students (such as in the aging game), and bedside courses.

Another interesting point to mention is the involvement of geriatric teachers in the various schools of dentistry, dietetic, nursing, and other health-care professionals.

Postgraduate teaching in geriatric medicine is particularly well organized in the four above-mentioned universities, based on a consensual program established under the leadership of the Swiss professional society of geriatrics.

Continuing geriatric education is more problematic because all geriatricians working in private practice as well as in other care facilities (academic or not) have to participate in 40 hours per year of geriatric/psychogeriatric educational activities to maintain their specific competency in geriatric medicine. This mandatory educational participation has to be added to the 50 hours that they also have to report to keep their certification in internal or general medicine. So, the main obstacles are linked to the shortage of geriatricians working in private practice, and the difficulty of finding enough hours of geriatric educational activities, remembering that Switzerland is a country with four different official languages, some of which are not known by some geriatricians.

Two interesting initiatives are ongoing to promote geriatric education and research. First, in 1994, a small group of European professors of medical gerontology, including J.-P. Michel (Geneva) and H. Staehelin (Basle), founded an advanced postgraduate geriatric course for junior geriatricians, called the European Academy for Medicine of Aging (EAMA) to teach future teachers of geriatric medicine. It is a four-week residential course based on teachers' and students' lectures, group discussions, and intense tutorial activities that enhance scientific interactions and create an international geriatric network of competency in geriatric education and care (Bonin-Guillaume et al., 2005). From 1995 to 2006, 198 participants from 17 European countries and 13 other overseas countries obtained the EAMA diploma. Among these participants, 91% upgraded their professional position and of them, 30% got a geriatric professorship. Many of the 24 Swiss participants were already promoted and the others will constitute the future geriatric Swiss and/or international geriatric supply.

The second initiative is the creation of the Robert Bosch Foundation (Stuttgart, Germany) to support young German-speaking research investigators. This outstanding initiative will probably stimulate translational research in the wide field of aging (Robert Bosch Foundation, 2006).

PUBLIC POLICY ISSUES

Switzerland has the second most expensive health-care system worldwide, with 11.5% of the gross domestic product. Switzerland has a health-care system with universal insurance coverage and a social insurance system, ensuring an adequate financial situation for 96% of the oldest population (Schoenenberger & Stuck, 2006). Because a recent and very comprehensive paper from the Bern University geriatric department detailed all the challenges faced by Switzerland, this chapter will only point out the newest available data:

- Recent national votes concerning the financing of the insurance confirmed the current status.
- A recent calculation of the dependency ratio, defined as the number of people aged 0–19 + number of aged >65 divided by the number aged 20–64, and an oldest-old support ratio, defined as the number of people aged over 85 divided by the number aged 50–74, testifies to the drastic changes in the Swiss age structure. In 1890, for one old dependent adult, there were 139.7 young/middle-aged adults, while in 1990, there were only 16.2, and in 2050, there will be only 3.5 young/middle-life adults to care for each old dependent person.
- These figures shows the need for the different cantonal governments to promote community care networks. In Geneva, a cantonal vote allowed an increase in taxes of 2% to pay for the development of a professional public network of home care. Lausanne Canton is structuring a network to assure the best possible continuity of care from home to nursing home, integrating and favoring the role played by geriatricians.
- At the same time, the various Swiss cantons that are not yet involved (such as Basle and Geneva) in the diagnostically related groups (DRGs) payment of hospital stays are planning to introduce this payment method, which will change all of health care functioning.

CONCLUSION

Although not exhaustive, this review of Swiss research and development in geriatrics is very encouraging, with the recent creation of two new chairs of geriatric medicine (Bern and Lausanne) doubling the number of previously existing full professorship in geriatrics (Basle and Geneva), and the establishment of a research center for aging and mobility in Zürich. Finally, the role played by Switzerland in promoting high-level education programs for the next generations of geriatric teachers (EAMA) and researchers (Robert Bosch Foundation) is very promising.

REFERENCES

Ammann, P., Laib, A., Bonjour, J. P., Meyer, J. P., Rüegsegger, P., & Rizzoli, R. (2002). Dietary essential amino acid supplements increase bone strength by influencing bone mass and bone microarchitecture in ovariectomized adult rats fed an isocaloric low-protein diet. *The Journal of Bone and Mineral Research, 17,* 1264–1272.

Armi, F., Guilley, E., & Lalive d'Epinay, C. J. (2008) Health: Support provided and received in advanced old age: A five-year follow-up. *Z Gerontol Geriatr, 41,* 56–62.

Bischoff, H. A., Staehelin, H. B., & Willett, W. C. (2006). The effect of under nutrition in the development of frailty in older persons. *Journals of Gerontology Series A: Biological Science and Medical Science, 61,* 585–589.

Bischoff-Ferrari, H. A., Can, U., Staehelin, H. B., Platz, A., Henschkowski, J., Michel, B., et al. (2008). Severe vitamin D deficiency in Swiss hip fracture patients. *Bone, 42,* 597–602.

Bonin-Guillaume, S., Herrmann, F. R., Boillat, D., Szanto, I., Michel, J.-P., Rohner-Jeanrenaud, F., et al. (2006). Insulinemia and leptinemia in geriatric patients: Markers of the metabolic syndrome or of under nutrition? *Diabetes Metabolism Research & Review, 32,* 236–243.

Bonin-Guillaume, S., Kressig, R., Gavazzi, G., Jacques, M.-C., Chevalley, T., & Pautex, S., et al. (2005). Teaching the future teachers in geriatrics: The 10-year success of the European Academy for medicine of Ageing. *Geriatrics & Gerontology International, 5,* 82–85.

Bonjour, J. P., Chevalley, T., Ammann, P., Slosman, D., & Rizzoli, R. (2001). Gain in bone mineral mass in prepubertal girls 3.5 years after discontinuation of calcium supplementation: A follow-up study. *Lancet, 358,* 1208–1212.

Bonjour, J. P., Chevalley, T., Rizzoli, R., & Ferrari, S. (2007). Gene-environment interactions in the skeletal response to nutrition and exercise during growth. *Medical Sports Science, 51,* 64–80.

Bosshard, W., Dreher, R., Schnegg, J. F., & Büla, C. J. (2004). The treatment of chronic constipation in elderly people: An update. *Drugs Aging, 21,* 911–930.

Büla, C. J., Ghilardi, G., Wietlisbach, V., Petignat, C., & Francioli, P. (2004). Infections and functional impairment in nursing home residents: A reciprocal relationship. *Journal of the American Geriatrics Society, 52,* 700–706.

Büla, C. J., Martin, E., Rochat, S., & Piot-Ziegler, C. (2008). Validation of an adapted falls efficacy scale in older rehabilitation patients. *Archives of Physical Medicine & Rehabilitation, 89,* 291–296.

Carmaciu, C., Iliffe, S., Kharicha, K., Harari, D., Swift, C., Gillmann, G., et al. (2007). Health risk appraisal in older people 3: Prevalence, impact, and context of pain and their implications for GPs. *British Journal of General Practice, 57,* 630–635.

Carmona, G. A., Hoffmeyer, P., Herrmann, F. R., Vaucher, J., Tschopp, O., Lacraz, A., et al. (2005). Major lower limb amputations in the elderly observed over 10 years: The role of diabetes and peripheral arterial disease. *Diabetes Metabolism, 31,* 449–454.

Foederatio Medicorum Helveticorum. (2000). Formation approfondie en gériatrie. *Bulletin of Swiss Medicine, 81,* 82S-86S.

Ganea, R., Paraschiv-Ionescu, A., Salarian, A., Büla, C., Martin, E., Rochat, S., et al. (2007) Kinematics and dynamic complexity of postural transitions in frail elderly subjects. *Proceedings of the IEEE Engineering in Medicine & Biology Society, 2007,* 6118–6121.

Gold, G., Giannakopoulos, P., Herrmann, F. R., Bouras, C., & Kövari, C. (2007). Identification of Alzheimer and vascular lesion thresholds for mixed dementia. *Brain, 130,* 2830–2836.

Kövari, E., Gold, G., Herrmann, F. R., Canuto, A., Hof, P. R., Bouras, C., et al. (2007). Cortical microinfarcts and demyelination affect cognition in cases at high risk for dementia. *Neurology, 68,* 927–931.

Kressig, R. W., Herrmann, F. R., Grandjean, R., Michel, J.-P., & Beauchet, O. (2008). Gait variability while dual-tasking: Fall predictor in older inpatients? *Aging Clinical & Experimental Research, 20,* 123–130.

Lalive d'Epinay, C. S. D. (2008). *Les années fragiles: La vie au-delà de quatre-vingts ans.* Quebec: Presses de l'Université Laval.

Michel, J.-P., Newton, J. L., & Kirkwood, T. B. (2008). Medical challenges of improving the quality of a longer life. *Journal of the American Medical Association, 299*(6), 688–690.

Michel, J.-P, Stuckelberger, A., & Grab, B. (1993). Switzerland. In E. B. Palmore (Ed.), *Development and research on aging: An international handbook* (pp. 299–315). Westport, CT: Greenwood Press.

Missonnier, P., Deiber, M. P., Gold, G., Hermann, F. R., Millet, P., Michon, A., et al. (2007). Working memory load-related electroencephalographic parameters can differentiate progressive from stable mild cognitive impairment. *Neuroscience, 150,* 346–356.

Monod, S. R. E., Martin, E., et al. (2008). Spirituality in post-acute rehabilitation: Appraisal by interdisciplinary team members. *Journal of the American Geriatric Society, 56,* S110.

Pautex, S., Herrmann, F. R., Michon, A., Giannakopoulos, P., & Gold, G. (2007). Psychometric properties of the Doloplus-2 observational pain assessment scale and comparison to self-assessment in hospitalized elderly. *Clinical Journal of Pain, 23,* 774–779.

Perrenoud, J. J., & Büla, C. (2005). Is geriatric cardiology different? *Swiss Review of Medicine*, *1*, 2499–2500.

Reginster, J. Y., Felsenberg, D., Boonen, S., Diez-Perez, A., Rizzoli, R., Brandi, M. L., et al. (2008). Effects of long-term strontium ranelate treatment on the risk of nonvertebral and vertebral fractures in postmenopausal osteoporosis: Results of a five-year, randomized, placebo-controlled trial. *Arthritis and Rheumatism*, *58*, 1687–1695.

Richert, L., Uebelhart, B., Engelhardt, M., Azria, M., & Rizzoli, R. (2008). A randomized double-blind placebo-controlled trial to investigate the effects of nasal calcitonin on bone microarchitecture measured by high-resolution peripheral quantitative computerized tomography in postmenopausal women—Study protocol. *Trials*, *9*, 19.

Rizzoli, R., Ammann, P., Chevalley, T., & Bonjour, J. P. (2001). Protein intake and bone disorders in the elderly. *Joint Bone Spine*, *68*, 383–392.

Rizzoli, R., & Bonjour, J. P. (2004). Dietary protein and bone health. *Journal of Bone Mineral Research*, *19*, 527–531.

Rizzoli, R., Boonen, S., Brandi, M. L., Burlet, N., Delmas, P., & Reginster, J. Y. (2008). The role of calcium and vitamin D in the management of osteoporosis. *Bone*, *42*, 246–249.

Robert Bosch Foundation. (2006). Retrieved from http://www.forschungskolleg-geriatre.de

Robine, J. M., & Michel, J.-P. (2004). Looking forward to a general theory on population aging. *J Journal of Gerontology Series A: Biological & Medical Sciences*, *59*, M590–597.

Robine, J. M., Michel, J.-P., & Herrmann, F. R. (2007). Who will care for the oldest people in our ageing society? *British Medical Journal*, *334*, 570–571.

Santos-Eggimann, B., Karmaniola, A., Seematter-Bagnoud, L., Spagnoli, J., Büla, C., Cornuz, J., et al. (2008). The Lausanne cohort Lc65+: A population-based prospective study of the manifestations, determinants and outcomes of frailty. *BMC Geriatrics*, *8*, 20.

Schoenenberger, A. W., Erne, P., Ammann, S., Gillmann, G., Kobza, R., & Stuck, A. E. (2008). Prediction of arrhythmic events after myocardial infarction based on signal-averaged electrocardiogram and ejection fraction. *Pacing Clinical Electrophysiology*, *31*, 221–228.

Schoenenberger, A. W., Erne, P., Ammann, S., Perrig, M., Bürgi, U., & Stuck, A. E. (2008). Prediction of hypertensive crisis based on average, variability and approximate entropy of 24-h ambulatory blood pressure monitoring. *Journal of Human Hypertension*, *22*, 32–37.

Schoenenberger, A. W., & Stuck, A. E. (2006). Health care for older persons in Switzerland: A country profile. *Journal of the American Geriatric Society*, *54*, 986–990.

Steuerwald, G. M., Baumann, T. P., Taylor, K. I., Mittag, M., Adams, H., Tolnay, M., et al. (2007). Clinical characteristics of dementia associated with argyrophilic grain disease. *Dementia & Geriatric Cognitive Disorders*, *24*, 229–234.

Stuck, A., Amstad, H., Baumann-Hölzle, R., Fankhauser, A., Kesselring, A., Leuba, A., et al. (2005). Treatment and care of elderly persons who are in need of care: Medical-ethical guidelines and recommendations. *Journal of Nutrition and Health in Aging, 9*, 288–295.

Swiss Federal Statistical Office. (2008). *Statistical yearbook of Switzerland.* Neue Zürcher Zeitung (NZZ).

Taylor, K. I., Probst, A., Miserez, A. R., Monsch, A. U., & Tolnay, M. (2008). Clinical course of neuropathologically confirmed frontal-variant Alzheimer's disease. *National Clinical Practical Neurology, 4*, 226–232.

United Nations. (2007). *World population ageing.* New York.

Vischer, U. M. (2006). von Willebrand factor, endothelial dysfunction, and cardiovascular disease. *Journal of Thrombosis & Haemostasis, 4*, 1186–1193.

Wagner, J. T., Bachmann, L. M., Boult, C., Harari, D., von Renteln-Kruse, W., Egger, M., et al. (2006). Predicting the risk of hospital admission in older persons Validation of a brief self-administered questionnaire in three European countries. *Journal of the American Geriatric Society, 54*, 1271–1276.

Weber, C., Merminod, T., Herrmann, F. R., & Zulian, G. B. (2008). Prophylactic anti-coagulation in cancer palliative care: A prospective randomised study. *Support Care Cancer, 16*, 847–852.

Zehnder, A. E., Bläsi, S., Berres, M., Spiegel, R., & Monsch, A. U. (2007). Lack of practice effects on neuropsychological tests as early cognitive markers of Alzheimer disease? *American Journal of Alzheimer's Disease & Other Dementia, 22*, 416–426.

Zekry, D., Herrmann, F. R., Grandjean, R., Meynet, M.-P., Michel, J.-P., Gold, G., et al. (2008a). Demented versus non-demented very old inpatients: The same comorbidities but poorer functional and nutritional status. *Age Ageing, 37*, 83–89.

Zekry, D., Herrmann, F. R., Irminger-Finger, I., Ortolan, L., Genet, C., Vitale, A.-M., et al. (2008b). Telomere length is not predictive of dementia or MCI conversion in the oldest old. *Neurobiology of Aging.*

47

·· ■ ··

Taiwan

Ching-Yu Chen

TRENDS

The tempo of population aging in Taiwan is one of the world's fastest. With its residents aged 65 years and older accounting for 7% of the total population, Taiwan stepped into an aging society in 1993. The percentage of elderly population moved up to 9.9% in 2006 (one senior citizen in every 10 residents) and is predicted to escalate to 10.5% in 2010, 16.1% in 2020, and 24.5% in 2030, due to the entry of baby boomers into old age and the global trend of baby bust. The absolute number of older adults in Taiwan, according to a forecast by the Council of Economic Planning and Development (CEPD), will rocket to 3.02 million in 2016, 4.75 million in 2026, and 6.86 million in 2036. By 2050, the percentage of the population who are elderly may be as high as 35.5% (Department of Manpower Planning, Council for Economic Planning and Development, 2002).

According to statistics from the Department of Health, the total number of deaths among people aged 0–64 years old increased by 6% over the past two decades from 1985 to 2005 (44,216 in 1985; 46,701 in 1995; and 47,026 in 2005). However, the growth in the number of deaths among people aged 65–79 during the same period is over 50% (33,556 in 1985; 46,005 in 2005; and 50,430 in 2005). Even more alarming is the number of deaths among people over the age of 80, which escalated from 13,349 in 1985 to 25,248 in 1995 and to 41,401 in 2005, with a growth of 211%. Moreover, the percentage of deaths of older adults in Taiwan climbed from half of the total number of deaths in 1985 to nearly two-thirds in 2005. During those two decades, the percentage of older adults in Taiwan rose from 3.5% to 9.68%. To sum up, the older adults in Taiwan, while making up less than 10% of the country's total population, accounted for a third of the overall death toll in 2005. As Taiwan's population continues to age, its impact on health care and the entire society will become severe.

An aging population affects not only the number of deaths; growth in age also leads to an increased number of chronic diseases. More and more older people will find their quality of life seriously deteriorating as they suffer from chronic diseases and related complications. According to the CEPD study, the percentage of people aged over 75 is rising. They accounted for 40% of the total number of people aged 65 and over in 2004 and the figure is estimated at 54% in 2050. The growth in the number of older elders outpaces the increase in the number of younger elders. The continuous growth in elderly population is bound to trigger a corresponding rapid increase in the demand for long-term care. This demand is predicted to triple in the next 30 years (Wu, 2002).

Due to the trend toward rapid aging, the number of elderly patients is expected to sustain swift growth. Medical professionals will have to take care of elderly patients with multiple diseases who require greater attention and patience. As a result, gerontology and geriatrics have come to play an increasingly crucial role in Taiwan. In response to its rapidly aging population, Taiwan needs to build up an integrated, comprehensive eldercare system that relies to a great extent on the expertise and dedication of specialists and professionals in the geriatric interdisciplinary teams (Department of Health and National Health Research Institutes, 2008).

PROGRESS IN GERONTOLOGICAL AND GERIATRIC RESEARCH

A search using the key words "gerontology," "old age," and "Taiwan" led to 200–300 papers, most of which were related to long-term care and nursing. There were hardly any large-scale or full-fledged geriatric/ gerontological studies performed in or for Taiwan prior to the establishment of the Division of Gerontological Research at the National Health Research Institutes in 2003. Founded with the mission to promote successful aging for the elderly people in Taiwan, the National Health Research Institutes (NHRI) Division of Gerontological Research strives to initiate and supervise a wide spectrum of gerontological and geriatric research based on various scientific models. Three recent research activities are summarized as follows:

1. Clinical assessment and treatment of common geriatric syndromes and diseases. With the development of a geriatric specialty, geriatric syndrome assessment and intervention have been emphasized at newly established geriatric clinics and services. Frailty, as a core pathophysiologic phenomenon of declining functions during the aging process, has triggered increased discussions and research in recent years. Major concepts and definitions of frailty currently in use encompass a variety of domains, such as physical characteristics and function, cognitive function, other psychological characteristics, and psychosocial factors. A potential clinical implication of frailty is that this syndrome can be detected early and treated. The consequent disabilities, comorbidities, and death could be prevented. Hip fracture, another common disease in elderly people associated with postoperative quality of life, has been examined and public education on fall prevention is being addressed.

2. Community epidemiological study of aging. In Taiwan, population aging is increasing the prevalence of chronic diseases and geriatric problems, including disability. Population-based long-term observational aging and functioning studies based on self-report and physical and biological measures of health have been carried out since 1989, such as the Taiwan Longitudinal Study of Aging (TLSA), the Social Environment and Biomarkers of Aging Study (SEBAS), and the National Health Interview Study (NHIS). A NHRI pilot community intervention study of frail elders with or without osteoporosis and depression is ongoing in a local community. Another new project, called Health Aging Longitudinal Study in Taiwan (HALST), plans to conduct a baseline examination on a sample of about 5,000 men and women aged 50 years or older, with the majority of these examinees drawn from the participants of the 2007 health survey conducted by the Department of Health. The proposed study will provide a unique opportunity to enhance our understanding of cardiovascular disease risk factors, physical and mental performance and functioning, quality of life, and morbidity and mortality in a representative cohort in Taiwan.

3. Development of novel biomarkers of geriatric syndrome in aging. A few basic studies on aging have been reported. With the development of geriatric medicine in teaching hospitals, early diagnosis and intervention of geriatric syndrome were studied. Frailty is a major clinical manifestation in aging, and sarcopenia is a leading cause of frailty. The severity of muscle wasting not only exerts a great impact on the effect of treatment, prognosis, and survival of elderly patients, but is also closely related to the quality of their life. It is commonly believed that a variety of cytokines produced by inflammatory cells jointly cause metabolic disturbances in older adults. In recent years, the medical community has gained more understanding of the mechanism of energy homeostasis. In addition to macrophage, adipose tissue is also able to secrete a variety of

adipokines to affect energy metabolism in humans. The detailed mech-anisms for proinflammatory cytokines to disturb energy homeostasis are not known. Therefore, identifying biomarkers through understanding pathophysiology of sarcopenia is a very important issue. After prelimi-nary studies with some potential biomarkers, further endeavors will be undertaken to elucidate the relationships between these markers and sarcopenia in animals and *in vitro* studies.

GERONTOLOGY EDUCATION AND TRAINING OF GERIATRICIANS

With the advent of an aging society, institutes related to gerontology and geriatric medicine have been established to promote the develop-ment of aging studies and eldercare in Taiwan. However, the need for these institutes to recruit teaching faculties and research specialists ex-poses Taiwan's failure to train and supply sufficient professionals in the field of gerontology and geriatrics. Not until recent years have substantial efforts in gerontology education and geriatrician training been initiated by the NHRI Division of Gerontology Research and the Taiwan Associa-tion of Gerontology and Geriatrics.

Although founded in 1982, the Taiwan Association of Gerontology and Geriatrics (TAGG) was not authorized to administer geriatrics specialist certification examination until 2001 because geriatrics was not recognized as an independent specialty when the Department of Health implemented the certification system for medical specialists in 1987. The NHRI Divi-sion of Gerontology Research, on the other hand, launched Taiwan's first formal geriatric fellowship training program in 2003.

In this fellowship program (July 2004–June 2007), fellows were trained in the practice of comprehensive professional geriatric services, including placing elderly patients in proper settings (outpatient clinic, acute care, hospitalization, nursing home, home care, etc.) in accordance with their individual needs for integrated, long-term care; providing interdisciplin-ary geriatric care; facilitating early diagnosis and treatment of common health problems of elderly people (such as falls, incontinence, delirium, osteoporosis, and other geriatric syndromes); helping elderly people avoid disability and achieve successful aging; and contributing to develop-ment in related fields like aging-related medical ethics, palliative care, hospice, and treatment of chronic illnesses (NHRI Division of Geron-tology Research, 2007). Fifteen geriatric fellows have been successfully trained and serve as the pioneer physicians for promoting geriatric care at their hospitals. Ongoing efforts have led to the establishment of geriatrics departments in seven leading teaching hospitals in Taiwan (three in 2007 and four in 2008), all of which have passed the TAGG accreditation to host their own geriatric fellowship training programs.

Though the NHRI geriatric fellowship program took the first step to trigger recognition of the importance of cultivating specialists in clinical geriatrics, the geriatrician training system in Taiwan is still in its infancy, and the general shortage of geriatricians and eldercare-related medical professionals poses a bottleneck in the development of geriatric medicine and studies in Taiwan. DOH and related government agencies should work together to provide local medical centers with sufficient support and resources to expedite and expand geriatric medical education and training. There are around 35,000 certified physicians practicing in Taiwan, only 700 of whom have passed the geriatrics specialist certification examination. It is simply impossible to expect these certified geriatricians alone to shoulder the huge load of taking care of the elderly people who need geriatric care in Taiwan. The best way to solve the problem at its roots is to incorporate gerontology- and geriatrics-related courses into the core curriculum of Taiwan's basic medical education. Students majoring in medicine and geriatrics-related fields (such as nursing, rehabilitation, pharmacy, and social work) should be given the opportunities to learn basic gerontology and geriatric knowledge and skills relevant to their individual specialties, just as medical students are required to study both internal medicine and surgical science regardless of their chosen specialties. Moreover, medical students receiving training in an area of specialization that may involve treating elderly patients (notably internal medicine and family medicine) should be required to learn essential knowledge and skills from the geriatrics/gerontology department. The same requirement should also be applied to medical interns. Implementation of these measures can be expected to activate rapid growth in the number of medical professionals capable of meeting the diverse and complicated needs of elderly patients. There would be no need to stake the development of Taiwan's gerontology and eldercare solely on the TAGG-certified geriatricians and geriatric fellows trained by medical centers.

In addition to facilitating gerontology education and geriatric training for medical and nursing professionals, basic eldercare knowledge should be included as an essential part of the health education at elementary, junior high, and high schools, to familiarize students with gerontology at an early age. Both the central and local governments should initiate comprehensive, national assessments on eldercare manpower requirements and work with related medical institutes and academic associations to train the needed eldercare professionals, such as nursing specialists, physical and occupational therapists, pharmacists, dieticians, social workers and hospital volunteers.

CURRENT ISSUES IN SOCIAL POLICIES

Crucial issues and problems in the current status of geriatric care and long-term care in Taiwan are summarized as follows (Wang et al., 2005; Wu & Chou, 2006; Wu et al., 2003).

1. The two systems—social welfare and health administration—should be integrated. Health and social care of elderly people in Taiwan remains under the supervision of two separate administrative systems, and the failure of the two systems to agree in terms of missions, policies, and visions has resulted in the government's inability to allocate and optimize available resources and to deliver continuous and integrated eldercare services. Regulations concerning long-term care can be found scattered throughout the social administration system (Senior Citizens Welfare Act, Protection Act for Physically and Mentally Disabled Citizens, etc.), the health administration system (Medical Care Act, National Health Insurance Act, Nurse Act, Mental Health Act, etc.) and the veteran affairs administration system (Veterans' Assistance Act). Some of the administrative rules should be upgraded to regulations, and some are in need of official authorization by related laws. Moreover, regulations about the establishment of nursing homes and long-term care institutions are similarly in need of coordination and integration.

2. The capacity of home- and community-based care fails to reach one-third of the estimated demand. Day-care centers have been established as a model of providing local senior citizens with necessary nursing services. The current status of day-care centers, however, is marked by a serious imbalance between supply and demand for various factors. As for home-based care that serves mainly elderly people with lower income, major services remain focused on assistance in the so-called three-tube (Endo, Foley, and NG) procedures. The highly important home- and community-based rehabilitation and other health-care services are still at the trial stage. And respite care has not been able attract enough attention from its target users, in spite of active promotion by the central and local governments. Realization of aging in place, the ultimate goal of long-term care, thus still has a long way to go in Taiwan.

3. Potential impact of the new national health insurance payment system. With the case-based DRG (Diagnosis Related Group) payment system cited as one of the solutions to the serious financial problems facing the 12-year-old national health insurance system, the length of hospitalization is expected to be reduced. Comprehensive supporting

measures thus need to be provided to help patients receive the quality treatment and nursing services necessary for restoring functions and sustaining full recovery after they are discharged from hospital. However, there are not enough nursing centers with sufficient and proper facilities, and the expenses spent on nursing home and home-based care are not covered in the national health insurance program.

Moreover, there is no increase in the permitted amount of home-based care. Provision of different post-acute care models for different diseases remains an issue to be addressed; also to be designed is a prospective payment system for hospitals focusing on rehabilitation, chronic diseases, and other specialties. At present, most of the elderly patients in desperate need of post-acute care, notably those suffering from stroke or hip fracture, have to face the predicament of having nowhere to go. The Bureau of National Health Insurance therefore must design a set of comprehensive supporting measures about post-acute care before the case-based DRG payment system can be implemented.

4. Financial support needed for long-term care services. It is beyond the ability of an ordinary family to finance quality long-term care, no matter whether it is home care, community-based day care, or other forms of institutional health care. Providers in their turn entertain no interest in making investments to promote the quality of the cost-intensive and highly demanding eldercare services by hiring qualified professionals and introducing advanced equipment and facilities.

5. Professional geriatric interdisciplinary teams remain in short supply. An ideal geriatric interdisciplinary team, as previously stated, is composed of geriatricians, physicians in related medical specialties, geriatric nursing specialists, physical and rehabilitation specialists, respiratory specialists, psychiatrists, dieticians, social workers, and other supportive members so as to be able to perform comprehensive geriatric assessment, devise effective treatment plans, and conduct individual case management, follow-up, outreach, and other desirable services. However, as the government has yet to implement related incentives and supporting measures, geriatricians and the other members of the geriatric interdisciplinary team have not received proper attention from most local hospitals. The relatively poorer pay and greater responsibilities further aggravate the shortage of eldercare professionals in Taiwan. So far, hospitals with a geriatric interdisciplinary team remain a rare minority.

6. Service delivery and management systems have not yet been established. The "long-term care management centers" planned and established in local governments for nearly 10 years have not been able to fulfill their role as integrators and managers of local eldercare resources, due to discrepancies in the criteria of assessing eligibility, in the adopted assessment tools, in the standards for subsidy, in the degree of adherence to the assessment guidelines, and in the preparations for residents' discharge.

A set of standard assessment tools and uniform assessment criteria for evaluating applicants' eligibility for long-term care are needed, and the mechanism for preparing residents for discharge also needs to be standardized. The differences in the services provided between cities and counties should be eliminated; more education and training activities need to be provided; and a review and supervision system must be established to prompt local governments to improve their performance. The private sector should also be encouraged to help develop eldercare services in remote regions through strategic partnership or collaboration. Moreover, there is no mechanism for integrating medical and nursing resources. The city or county management center fails to integrate and optimize the resources available in the primary and community medical-care systems, and this failure in turn cripples the delivery of integrated and continuous medical treatment and nursing services.

7. Eldercare-related medical ethics are in need of further promotion. While it is important to provide the elderly with quality medical care, it is also imperative to respect elderly patients during the treatment. Any medical treatments or procedures that may compromise the quality of life and dignity of elderly patients, such as insertion of nasogastric tubes, tracheotomy, and subsequent use of ventilator, should be approved by either the patients themselves or their families. Related medical professionals should be thoroughly trained in the removal of unnecessary tubes or ventilators without considering factors other than the benefits to the patient. Both the number of applications and the amount of average expense for health insurance payment for tube insertion have increased with the growth in the number of respiratory wards. The idea of a peaceful death embraced by hospice/palliative care for terminally ill patients may merit active promulgation, especially to the medical professionals dedicated to eldercare.

REFERENCES

Department of Health and National Health Research Institutes. (2008). *Healthy people 2020* (pp. 214–219). Taipei City: Department of Health, Executive Yuan.

Department of Manpower Planning, Council for Economic Planning and Development. (2002). *Taiwan population projection: 2004–2051* (p. 15). Taipei City: Executive Yuan.

National Health Research Institutes (NHRI) Division of Gerontology Research. (2007). *Geriatric subspecialty training manual.* Taipei City: Author.

Wang, T. Y., Chou, U. M., Lin, L. Z., Chang, H. J., Gou, D. C., & Chen, W. C. (2005). *Planning and study for the delivery of long-term care services in Taiwan.* Taipei City: Ministry of the Interior.

Wu, H. C., & Chou, S. C. (2006). *Planning and study for Taiwan's long-term care system and related regulations.* Taipei City: Ministry of the Interior.

Wu, S. C. (2002). *Evaluation of national demand for long-term care: First-year result report.* Taipei City: Department of Health, Executive Yuan.

Wu, S. C., Wang, C., Liu, B. J., Chuan, K. Y., Chang, M., & Tai, Y. C. (2003). *The third-year plan for the pilot study to establish the national long-term care system.* Taipei City: Long-Term Care Special Taskforce of the Social Welfare Promotion Committee, Executive Yuan; Ministry of the Interior; and Department of Health, Executive Yuan.

48

.. ■ ..

Thailand

Rossarin Soottipong Gray
and Aphichat Chamratrithirong

Aging issues, as in many other countries in the world, are increasingly important for Thailand, since the number of older persons is growing rapidly. This phenomenon is due to a rapid decline in fertility and an increase in longevity. The total fertility rate declined from over 6 children per woman in the early 1960s (Knodel, Chamratrithirong & Debavalaya, 1987) to 1.5 children per woman in 2008 (Institute for Population and Social Research, 2008). Life expectancy at birth increased from 58.0 for males and 63.8 for females in 1975 (National Statistical Office, 1997) to 70.2 for males and 76.9 for females in 2008 (Institute for Population and Social Research, 2008). As a result of such changes, the proportion of older persons increased significantly, from 4.6% in 1960 to 9.5% in 2000. Based on the population projections carried out between 2005 and 2025, the percentage of older persons will increase, while that of children and the working-age population will gradually decline (Institute for Population and Social Research, 2006). In 2025, the percentage of older persons will exceed that of children (Table 48.1). It should be noted that the elderly in Thailand are defined by the 2003 Elderly Persons Act as those 60 years and older, which is different from the age used in most developed countries.

Table 48.2 compares selected Asian countries in terms of their 60-and-over populations and shows that between 2000 and 2050, the number of older persons in almost all countries listed was projected to increase about three times or slightly more. Japan has shown the highest proportion of older persons among selected countries since 1950, while

Table 48.1
Total population and age structure of the population of Thailand, 1960–2025

| Year | Total Population (In Thousands) | Age group (%) | | |
		0–14	15–59	60 and over
1960	26,257.9	43.2	52.2	4.6
1970	34,397.4	45.1	50.0	4.9
1980	44,824.5	38.3	56.2	5.5
1990	54,548.5	29.2	63.4	7.4
2000	60,916.4	24.4	66.1	9.5
2005	62,162.6	23.0	66.7	10.3
2010	63,652.3	20.7	67.4	11.8
2015	64,647.6	19.0	67.0	14.0
2020	65,138.3	17.2	66.0	16.8
2025	65,088.8	16.0	64.1	19.8

Source: Authors' calculation from 1960–2000 population censuses and Mahidol University population projections for Thailand, 2005–2025

the number of Thailand's older persons is projected to increase to 27.1% in 2050.

According to the population censuses, the proportions of Thai population living in rural areas have been declining, from 87.5% in 1960 to 68.3% in 2000. While the age structure is almost the same among both urban and rural populations, the proportion of older persons is slightly higher in rural areas, which is likely due to rural-urban migration among young adults. As in many other countries, elderly women outnumber elderly men, due to higher life expectancy among females, and older women are more likely to be widowed than are older men (Bryant & Gray, 2005; Soonthorndhada, Gray, Soonthorndhada, & Viswanatham, 2008). Educational attainment of Thai older persons is still low; in 2007, about 16.7% had no formal education at all, and about 74% had completed only elementary education or less. This is mainly because mass education in Thailand began only in the 1950s.

As in other Southeast Asian societies, the Thai family traditionally takes primary responsibility for older members, who usually live with at least one of their children. However, there has recently been some reduction in co-residence. The proportions of older persons living with at least one child declined from about 80% in 1986 to 74% in 1995 and

Table 48.2
Percentage of population aged 60 and over of selected Asian countries, 1950–2050

Year	China	Indo-nesia	Japan	Malaysia	Philip-pines	Republic of Korea	Singapore	Thailand	Vietnam
1950	7.5	6.2	7.7	7.3	5.5	5.4	3.7	5.0	7.0
1975	6.9	5.4	11.7	5.6	4.9	5.8	6.7	5.0	7.5
2000	10.1	7.6	23.2	6.6	5.5	11.0	10.6	9.5*	7.5
2025	19.5	12.8	35.1	13.4	10.4	24.1	30.0	19.8*	12.6
2050	29.9	22.3	42.3	20.8	19.5	33.2	35.0	27.1	23.5

Source: United Nations Department of Economic and Social Affairs, Population Division. (2002). *World population ageing 1950 2050.* New York: United Nations.
*From Table 1.

to 68% in 2002. According to a 2007 survey of the elderly by the National Statistical Office, the proportion of co-residence was 62.5% (original calculations). However, intergenerational exchanges of support and services remain pervasive (Knodel, Kespichayawattana, Wiwatwanich, & Saengtienchai, 2007). Co-residence can be expected to decline further due to the changes in socioeconomic conditions that lead young adults to migrate away from home for work. Additionally, the number of living children per old person is falling due to fertility decline over recent years. It is projected that the mean number of living children will decline from about 5 persons in 1994 to 2.4 persons in 2020 (Bryant & Gray, 2005).

Old age is a period of mental and physical changes that often result in health problems. It was found that in 2003–2004, for example, 4 in 5 Thai people aged 60–69 and 9 in 10 aged 80 and over had one or more chronic illnesses. Rates of disability increased from 5.8% in 2001 to 15.3% in 2007. Both illness and disability rates increase with age and are higher for women than men (Institute for Population and Social Research & the Health Promotion Foundation, 2007; National Statistical Office, 2008). It is projected that by 2015, about 18% of older persons will be disabled, and most will require assistance with everyday living. As they age further, many will be unable to leave the house unassisted, and some will become bedridden (Jittapunkul, Kunanusant, Phoolcharoen, & Suriyawongpaisal, 1999).

With lower physical capacities, people may be unable to continue working. In 2007, about 36.4% of older persons were working, but only 38.5% of this working group were engaged in paid employment. Thus, they are in need of financial support, and family remains the main source of support for older persons. Although the trend in employment in the agricultural sector has been declining due to the transformation from agriculture to industry in Thailand, over 60% of those over 60 who are employed are working in the agricultural sector. Among those who do have income, about 70% have an average annual income of less than 50,000 baht (about US$1,500), and about 23.1% of those who have income report that their income is not sufficient (National Statistical Office, 2008).

EDUCATION AND RECENT RESEARCH IN GERONTOLOGY

In Thailand, interest in aging issues began in the early 1960s. The first senior citizens' group was set up in 1962 by a group of medical doctors. In 1982, the government established the first National Commission on the Elderly. However, it was not until 1990 that the growth in gerontology and programs for older persons increased dramatically, due to the increase in the number of older persons. The Division of Geriatric Medicine within the Faculty of Medicine at Siriraj Hospital, Mahidol University, which is the oldest hospital school of medicine in Thailand, was established in 1990. Nowadays, studies in geriatric medicine are available in almost all medical schools in Thailand. Similarly, education in gerontological nursing has been included in all faculties of nursing. In 1992, several courses relating to social gerontology were offered in many universities, and the Institute of Geriatric Medicine was established under the Ministry of Public Health, primarily devoted to research, training, and development of caring models for the elderly using a multidisciplinary approach. The Thai Society of Gerontology and Geriatric Medicine (TGG) was established in 1997 and is now a member of the International Association of Gerontology and Geriatrics (IAGG).

With regard to recent research in gerontology, this article focuses on social gerontology research since 2000. The broad theme covers both the subjective and objective well-being of the elderly, described below.

Subjective Well-Being

Subjective well-being refers to an individual's perceptions of overall quality of life. Specific concepts that have been used to assess subjective well-being among the Thai elderly include psychological well-being (Ingersoll-Dayton, Saengtienchai, Kespichyawattana, & Aungsuroach, 2001, 2004), happiness (Gray, Rukumnuaykit, Kittisuksathit, & Thongthai,

2008), and self-esteem (Nanthamongkolchai, Makapat, Charupoonphol, & Munsawaengsub, 2007).

Using both qualitative and quantitative methods, Ingersoll-Dayton and her colleagues (2004) developed a measure of psychological well-being based on the indigenous expertise of older Thai persons. They found that the psychological well-being of elderly Thai is different from that of older people in the West. While psychological well-being in the West is predominantly intrapersonal and characterized by self-acceptance, autonomy, and personal growth, in Thailand it is found to be related to both intrapersonal and interpersonal factors (Ingersoll-Dayton et al., 2001, 2004). These consist of five components: (1) harmonious relationships within one's family and with neighbors; (2) reliability in the provision of assistance among themselves, children and relatives, neighbors, and communities; (3) having a peaceful mind (coaxing the mind to be happy) and being accepted by others; (4) being respected; and (5) having activities with friends and going to temples.

Gray et al. (2008) explore the determinants of happiness among Thai elderly in Chai Nat province. The determinants are divided into external and internal factors. The external factors—which include economic hardship, living arrangements, physical functional ability, perceived social environment, and consumerism—significantly influence the level of happiness. The strongest predictor of happiness is, however, the internal factor—that is, a feeling of relative poverty in relationship to their neighbors. The respondents who said they do not feel poor showed the highest level of happiness compared to those who said they feel as poor as or poorer than their neighbors. This is self-interpreted as a feeling of contentment with what one has, which has been influenced by Buddhism, the religion of most Thais.

Self-esteem is an important factor that maintains the subjective well-being of the elderly. It is also an important factor in individuals' ability to cope with problems in daily life and to behave in such a way as to be a reflection of their worthy intrapersonal and communal lives, all of which leads to a high level of subjective well-being. Nanthamongkolchai et al. (2007) identified factors affecting self-esteem of rural Thai elderly in Nakhon Sawan province; namely, monthly income, activities of daily living, personality, participation in family or social activities, and social support. Additionally, they found that social support was the most important predictor. This finding confirms the importance of interpersonal factors and external factors, as measured by perceived social environment, in predicting subjective well-being among Thai elderly (Gray et al., 2008; Ingersoll-Dayton et al., 2001, 2004).

Other research that may be related to subjective well-being was carried out by Yuji (2006) among Tai-Lue elders, an ethnic minority group in Nan province. This study deals with their adaptation in response to the national policies toward local cultures and the elderly, or to the stream of "welfarization."

Economic Security

Thanakwang and Soonthorndhada (2007), using a nationally representative survey, provided evidence that nearly one-third (32%) of the Thai population aged 60 and over had incomes below the poverty line. Economically vulnerable seniors were mainly found among the following groups: women, the very old, rural inhabitants, the disabled, those with low levels of education, those engaged in low-status occupations, and those unprepared financially for old age.

Another study, of the effect of population aging on agricultural production and rural poverty, was carried out by Bryant and Gray (2005). Using data from the 1985–2003 Labor Force Surveys and the 2003 Agricultural Census, the results show that agriculture has the oldest work force of any economic sector in Thailand.

Gender and Well-Being

Recent studies on gender among Thai older persons show a complex association between gender and various aspects of aging. Older Thai women do face certain disadvantages compared to their male counterparts, including lower education and literacy, far higher levels of widowhood and living alone, and a lower likelihood of receiving formal retirement benefits. Older Thai men, however, face other disadvantages, including worse survivorship, a lower likelihood of receiving money from adult children, and a greater probability of financial problems (Sobieszczyk, Knodel, & Chayovan, 2003). Additional research shows some other disadvantages of older females, including higher levels of functional disability and unemployment. Additionally, most of the caregivers for adult children with HIV/AIDS are mothers (Soonthorndhada et al., 2008).

Living Arrangements and Intergenerational Solidarity

In Thailand, as in many Asian countries, family has traditionally taken primary responsibility for older persons. Recent research shows that even though there has been a decline in co-residence, intergenerational exchanges of support and services remain pervasive (Knodel, Chayovan, Graiurapong, & Suraratdecha, 2000; Knodel, Chayovan, Mithranon, Amornsirisomboon, & Arunraksombat, 2005). Additionally, a study of the social and economic consequences of the migration of adult children to urban areas for rural parents shows that, despite concerns in the media about the erosion of traditional family values, children still maintain contact and visits through improvements in transportation and communication; namely, mobile phones (Knodel, Kespichayawattana, Wiwatwanich, & Saengtienchai, 2007; Knodel & Saengtienchai, 2007). The researchers also found that migration of children to urban areas contributes positively to the material well-being of the elderly.

Another research project concerning intergenerational relations between migrant children and parents was carried out in the agricultural setting of Nang Rong by Piorrowski (2008). His finding is consistent with an intergenerational bargaining perspective; that is, returning and visiting migrants are more likely to help with the rice harvest if the original household owns securely titled land, and if the migrant has lower human capital achievements. It is suggested that parents may use land as a strategic bequest to elicit support.

Health

Active aging is one of the important goals that the Thai government has set for older persons. Research by Thanakwang and Soonthorndhada (2006) assesses active aging among older Thai persons using the WHO framework, which consists of three components: health, community participation, and security. This research found that most active aging occurred among males, younger elderly, married elderly, those with rather high-prestige occupations, those with high levels of education, and those suffering from no chronic illness.

Concerning health-promoting behavior, Lortrakul, Chaiwan, and Lasuka (2001) and Thanakwang and Soonthorndhada (2008) found that family support had a prominent influence on elderly subjective well-being, which in turn facilitated health-promoting behavior. Additionally, research on a community-based health promotion program for older persons in Kanchanaburi was carried out (Boonchalaksi, Muensakda, Ek-Sarn, & Channotip, 2003; Boonchalaksi, Muensakda, Nguenbodhi-Klangdee, & Henprasert, 2008). The results showed that older persons who joined the program were healthier than those who did not, as measured by a lower proportion receiving hospital treatment.

Additionally, a community elderly club and group and a community elderly fund were set up.

HIV/AIDS

In Thailand, comprehensive empirical research on the impact of the AIDS epidemic on parents has been carried out. High priority has been given to this issue, since the adult prevalence of HIV/AIDS in Thailand, at 2%, although modest compared to the worst-hit African countries (UN-AIDS, 2000), is second only to Cambodia in Asia. Parents are the primary caregivers for their adult children with HIV/AIDS who return to their parental homes due to their illness and need for care near the end of their lives (Saengtienchai & Knodel, 2001). Most such adult children died within a few months of their return (Knodel & VanLandingham, 2003). Consequently, parents lost financial contributions from children before the children were ill, and orphaned grandchildren often ended up with grandparents (Knodel & Im-em, 2004; Saengtienchai & Knodel, 2001).

Research has also assessed the potential health impacts of caregiving on older parents who had a child die of AIDS (Kespichayawattana & VanLandingham, 2003). It was found that large proportions of older persons provided a variety of time-consuming and strenuous caregiving services to their children. However, mothers shouldered most of this burden. Such parents reported lower levels of overall happiness than those who did not have a child afflicted with AIDS, and many AIDS parents experienced health problems such as anxiety, insomnia, and head- and stomachaches during the time they cared for their ill children.

Using demographic analysis and computer microsimulation, Wachter, Knodel, and VanLandingham (2002, 2003) projected the number of older Thais who would lose children to AIDS during their own lifetimes. The lower projections of the HIV/AIDS epidemic still imply that 13% of Thais over the age of 50 in 1995 will lose at least one child to AIDS before their own deaths. About 12% of those over age 50 will lose more than one child. The chance of losing an adult child during one's lifetime was estimated to be 70% higher than if there were no AIDS epidemic.

There have also been a few studies on the sexuality of older persons and their own risk of AIDS (Knodel & Chayovan, 2001; VanLandingham & Knodel, 2007), revealing that substantial proportions of married and unmarried older Thais remain sexually active. The currently unmarried (including ever-married, ever-separated, ever-divorced, or ever-widowed) do not appear to be at great risk of acquiring HIV, since they engage primarily in noncommercial sexual relations with a cohort of women who are not for the most part at high risk of being infected with HIV. However, most worrisome is the prospect that some engage in unprotected intercourse with both sex workers and with women who are not sex workers (Chamratrithirong & Ford, 2008). Additionally, although older persons generally have good knowledge about AIDS, misperceptions are occasionally reported (Im-em, VanLandingham, Knodel, & Saengtienchai, 2002).

NATIONAL POLICY ON AGING

The purpose of this section is to provide an overview of public programs both currently in place and under development. Social security and health-care programs are emphasized. The Thai government established the first long-term National Plan for Older persons for the period 1982–2001. It was influenced by the first World Assembly on Aging in Vienna in 1982. The Plan aimed to serve as an instrument to promote, support, and develop guidelines on the implementation of support for the elderly in five areas: health, education, social and income stability, social and cultural integration, and social welfare. In 1999, the same year as the UN's International Year of Older Persons, the Thai government drafted its Declaration on Older Persons.

In 2002, the Madrid International Plan of Action on Aging was adopted following the second World Assembly on Aging in Madrid. Thailand also adopted its second National Plan for Older Persons (2002–2021). This plan has content and scope covering and in compliance with the contents of the Madrid International Plan of Action on Aging.

In 2003, the Act on Older Persons was enacted (Ministry of Social Development and Human Security, 2005). The National Commission on the Elderly was established to serve as the national mechanism working for the elderly according to the Act. Section 11 of the 2003 Act states that the elderly should be granted:

1. Immediate, rapid, and convenient medical and health services;
2. Education, news, and information that are helpful for their lives;
3. Access to appropriate occupations and suitable occupational training;
4. Opportunities for self-improvement, integration, and participation in social activities and assisting networks;
5. Safe access to facilities and buildings, places, vehicles, and other public services;
6. Support and assistance for fares and tickets in public transportation;
7. Exemption from fees to government-run facilities;
8. Emergency support in case of family abandonment;

9. Counseling services in legal proceedings on family problems;
10. Provision of housing, foods, and clothing according to their needs;
11. Provision of a monthly allowance when necessary;
12. Provision of funeral assistance; and
13. Other assistance as defined by the Commission.

Although the family remains the main source of support for older Thai persons, several government programs provide formal sources of assistance, particularly social security programs and health-care programs. Social security programs can be separated into two schemes: compulsory saving schemes and voluntary saving schemes.

Compulsory Saving Schemes

Thailand has been developing its social security programs for many years. Regarding pension provisions, there are two major programs: a social security system for private sector employees and a government pension fund. These programs are run by the government.

Social Security System (SSS)

Thailand's social security program was undertaken with the passage of the 1990 Social Security Act. However, it was not until 1999 that the program on old-age benefits was included in the social security system (SSS) under the Office of Social Security, Ministry of Labor. The aim is to provide benefits to all private sector workers in enterprises of one employee or more. Funding from the programs is provided by the contributions from three parties: employee, employer, and government. Two types of benefits are available from the SSS: old-age allowance and old-age pension. The old-age allowance is paid to workers who reach age 55, while the old-age pension will be paid monthly for life to those workers who are at least 55 years of age and have at least 15 years of covered service. Thus, the first pension will not be paid until 2014 (Ramesh & Asher, 2000). The Government Pension Fund was established in 1997. It is a contributory type and is paid to public servants from the civil service sector when they reach the retirement age of 60 years.

Voluntary Saving Schemes

These funds are managed by private organizations under the supervision of the government. There are two types of fund: the provident fund (PVD) and the retirement mutual funds (RMF). The PVD serves both workers in private and government sectors and state-owned enterprises. Workers need to pay into the fund at a rate of 2–15% of their monthly income. The RMF is for long-term savings. Anybody can buy into the fund with at least 5,000 baht (US$150) per unit each year for a minimum of five years before they can request their principal and interest. Payments made into the fund are tax-deductible.

But these funds cover only a small minority of older persons. There are also self-organized community savings plans based on self-reliant individual contributions, and the Thai government is preparing to establish an obligatory National Pension Fund. This project is under study (Ministry of Social Development and Human Security, 2007). The National Pension Fund will serve as a measure to strengthen income stability apart from the existing social security system. It is expected that the National Pension Fund will cover all workers in the formal sector. Moreover, there are several ongoing studies in preparation for setting up funds that would cover all Thai people.

The government has introduced various other programs for old-age security. They include tax incentives to encourage support from children toward their elderly parents; namely, tax deductions for children who earn income and take care of their own older parents and parents-in-law, and tax deductions for health insurance policies purchased by any children for their older parents or their parents-in-law (Ministry of Social Development and Human Security, 2007).

A government program to provide economic assistance (a monthly allowance) to indigent elders has been in effect since 1993. In 2007, the allowance was increased from 200 baht to 500 baht (from about US$6 to about US$15), and only 25% of the total eligible older persons are covered by this program (Ministry of Social Development and Human Security, 2007).

In 2009, the program was expanded to cover all senior citizens who are not eligible for any other welfare or privilege from government organizations, state enterprises or local administrative organizations, and who do not live in state-owned homes for the elderly.

Finally, the Elderly Fund was set up in 2004 under the prescription set forth in the 2003 Act on Older Persons. The Elderly Fund provides financial support and resources for activities arranged by elderly clubs, associations, or networks, and it promotes activities that will broaden job opportunities for the elderly.

Health-care Programs

Since 2001, all Thai people have been covered by one kind of health benefit scheme or another. They are the Universal Coverage Scheme

(UC) (covering low-cost health services for the general public), the Social Security Scheme (SSS), the Civil Servant Medical Benefit Scheme (CSMBS), and state enterprises benefit. In 2006, a universal free government health service was initiated for Thai people, regardless of age, who were not covered by any other plan. In fact, Thai people aged 60 and over have received free health services from government hospitals and health centers since 1989 (Ramesh & Asher, 2000).

There is still no long-term care for the elderly in public hospitals in Thailand. However, there is such care in some private hospitals in Bangkok (Ministry of Public Health & Ministry of Social Development and Human Security, 2007). Long-term care is an important challenge for Thailand, since the number of older persons with disabilities will increase. Thailand needs to produce enough trained caregivers and develop appropriate models for long-term care.

The Home Health Care Program of the Ministry of Public Health (HHC) was introduced as a health-care service for the elderly at the community level and aims to prevent disease and illness from high-risk factors and to promote healthy living, effective treatment, and rehabilitation. The HHC also covers older persons who are discharged from hospitals with chronic illnesses or with disabilities (Ministry of Social Development and Human Security, 2007).

In 2003, a program to provide community volunteer caregivers for the elderly was initiated by the Ministry of Social Development and Human Security. This project is targeted at older persons in communities who have no caregivers and who need assistance in daily living at home. It was approved by the Cabinet to be expanded to cover all of Thailand in 2007.

The Thai government has a strong policy that a nursing home for the elderly should be the last choice. However, 20 government homes for the elderly exist in Thailand for those who encounter social problems such as lack of relatives and caregivers.

There are other programs aimed at helping the elderly in Thailand, several that promote positive attitudes toward aging and older persons. The Older Person's Brain Bank was established in 2000 as a coordination and information center to make use of the knowledge and skills of retired older persons from the public sector, state enterprises, and private entities. The data have been collected and a database has been set up so that they may be contacted as resources or for counseling assistance. Similarly, a Brain Bank of older persons at the community level was set up in 2004 by the Thai Development Foundation to serve as a clearinghouse for tapping intellectual resources of elderly people in local communities (Ministry of Social Development and Human Security, 2007).

For the sake of employment of older persons, apart from the programs for job placement and occupational training for the elderly in the private sector, the retirement age for workers in the government sector has been extended from 60 years to 70 years for senior judges and senior public prosecutors, based on assessment processes, and from 60 years to 65 years for lecturers in universities on a voluntary basis, and based on university assessments.

CONCLUSION

This review demonstrates the growth of aging-related policies and programs, and the expansion of gerontology research and education in Thailand. Given the demographic and socioeconomic characteristics of older persons, cultural context, and rapid social and economic changes in Thai society, it should not come as a surprise that the topics of intergeneration relations, internal well-being, and economic well-being have been major research focuses since 2000.

REFERENCES

Boonchalaksi, W., Muensakda, P., Ek-Sarn, N., & Channotip, R. (2003). *Designing a health promotion program for the elderly through collaborative action research with health centers in Thongphaphum, Kanchanaburi*. Nakhon Pathom, Thailand: Institute for Population and Social Research, Mahidol University.

Boonchalaksi, W., Muensakda, P., Nguenbodhi-Klangdee, S., & Henprasert, J. (2008). *Research and development of a health promotion program for the elderly in Kanchanaburi*. Nakhon Pathom, Thailand: Institute for Population and Social Research, Mahidol University.

Bryant, J., & Gray, R. (2005). *Natural Resources Management and Environment Department, SD dimensions. Rural population ageing and farm structure in Thailand*. Retrieved September 8, 2008, from http://www.fao.org/sd/dim_pe3/pe3_051001_en.htm

Chamratrithirong, A., & Ford, K. (2008). Post reproductive sexual relation: Natural and social change. In A. Archavanitkul. & K. Tangcholatip (Eds.), *Gender dimension in population society* (pp. 66–77). Nakhon Pathom, Thailand: Institute for Population and Social Research, Mahidol University. (In Thai.)

Gray, R. S., Rukumnuaykit, P., Kittisuksathit, S., & Thongthai, V. (2008). Inner happiness among Thai elderly. *Journal of Cross-Cultural Gerontology, 23,* 211–224.

Im-em, W., VanLandingham, M., Knodel, J., & Saengtienchai, C. (2002). HIV/AIDS-related knowledge and attitudes: A comparison of older persons and young adults in Thailand. *AIDS Education and Prevention, 14,* 246–260.

Ingersoll-Dayton, B., Saengtienchai, C., Kespichyawattana, J., & Aungsuroach, Y. (2001). Psychological well-being Asian style. *Journal of Cross-Cultural Gerontology, 16,* 283–302.

Ingersoll-Dayton, B., Saengtienchai, C., Kespichyawattana, J., & Aungsuroach, Y. (2004). Measuring psychological well-being: Insights from Thai elders. *The Gerontologist, 44,* 596–604.

Institute for Population and Social Research. (2006). *Mahidol University population projections for Thailand, 2005–2025.* Nakhon Pathom, Thailand: Institute for Population and Social Research, Mahidol University.

Institute for Population and Social Research. (2008). *Population gazette 2008.* Nakhon Pathom, Thailand: Institute for Population and Social Research, Mahidol University.

Institute for Population and Social Research & the Health Promotion Foundation. (2007). *Thai health 2007: The scent of the Lamduan flower preparing for an ageing society.* Bangkok, Thailand: Amarin Printing and Publishing Ltd.; Institute for Population and Social Research, Mahidol University and the Health Promotion Foundation.

Jittapunkul, S., Kunanusant, C., Phoolcharoen, W., & Suriyawongpaisal, P. (1999). *Health problems of Thai elderly (a national survey).* Bangkok, Thailand: National Health Foundation.

Kespichayawattana, J., & VanLandingham, M. (2003). Health impacts of co-residence with and caregiving to persons with HIV/AIDS (PHAs) on older parents in Thailand. *Journal of Nursing Scholarship, 35,* 217–224.

Knodel, J., Chamratrithirong, A., & Debavalaya, N. (1987). *Thailand's reproductive revolution: Rapid fertility decline in a third-world setting.* Wisconsin: University of Wisconsin Press.

Knodel, J., & Chayovan, N. (2001). Sexual activity among older Thais: The influence of age, gender and health. *Journal of Cross-Cultural Gerontology, 16,* 173–200.

Knodel, J., Chayovan, N., Graiurapong, S., & Suraratdecha, C. (2000). Ageing in Thailand: An overview of formal and informal support. In D. Phillips (Ed.), *Ageing in the Asia-Pacific regions: Issues and policies* (pp. 243–266). London: Rutledge.

Knodel, J., Chayovan, N., Mithranon, P., Amornsirisomboon, P., & Arunraksombat, S. (2005). *Thailand's older population: Social and economic support as assessed in 2002.* Bangkok, Thailand: National Statistical Office.

Knodel, J., & Im-em, W. (2004). The economic consequences for parents of losing an adult child to AIDS: Evidence from Thailand. *Social Science and Medicine, 59,* 987–1001.

Knodel, J., Kespichayawattana, J., Wiwatwanich, S., & Saengtienchai, C. (2007). *Migration and intergeneration solidarity: Evidence from Thailand, papers in population ageing no. 2.* Bangkok, Thailand: UNFPA Thailand and Country Technical Services Team for East and Southeast Asia.

Knodel, J. E., & Saengtienchai, C. (2005). Older-aged parents—The final safety net for adult sons and daughters with AIDS in Thailand. *Journal of Family Issues, 26, 665–698*.

Knodel, J. E., & Saengtienchai, C. (2007). Rural parents with urban children: Social and economic implications of migration for the rural elderly in Thailand. *Population, Space and Place, 13, 193–210*.

Knodel, J., & VanLandingham, M. (2003). Return migration in the context of parental assistance in the AIDS epidemic: The Thai experience. *Social Science and Medicine, 57, 327–342*.

Lortrakul, N., Chaiwan, S., & Lasuka, D. (2001). Social support and health promoting behaviors among the elderly with coronary artery disease. *Nurse Journal, 28, 49–61*.

Ministry of Public Health & Ministry of Social Development and Human Resources. (2007). *Thailand: Country report on social welfare and health care services for the elderly*. The 3rd ASEAN & Japan High Level Officials Meeting on Caring Society: Collaboration of Social Welfare and Health Services and Development of Human Resources and Community—Community Services for the Elderly, 27–30 August 2007. Tokyo, Japan.

Ministry of Social Development and Human Security. (2005). *The Act on Older Persons B.E. 2546 (2003 A.D.)*. Bangkok, Thailand: The Agricultural Co-operate Federation of Thailand, Ltd.

Ministry of Social Development and Human Security. (2007). *Thailand's implementation of the Shanghai Implementation Strategy (SIS) and the Madrid International Plan of Action on Ageing (MIPAA) 2007*. The Bureau of Empowerment for Older Persons, the Office of Welfare Promotion, Protection and Empowerment of Vulnerable Groups, Ministry of Social Development and Human Security.

Nanthamongkolchai, S., Makapat, A., Charupoonphol, P., & Munsawaengsub, C. (2007). Self-esteem of the elderly in rural areas of Nakhon Sawan province. *J Med Assoc Thai, 90, 155–159*.

National Statistical Office. (1997). *Report on the 1995–1996 survey of population change*. Bangkok, Thailand: National Statistical Office.

National Statistical Office. (2008). *Thai older persons 2007: Reflections from statistics*. Bangkok, Thailand: National Statistical Office. (In Thai.)

Piotrowski, M. (2008). Intergenerational relations in a context of industrial transition: A study of agricultural labor from migrants in Nang Rong, Thailand. *Journal of Cross-Cultural Gerontology, 23, 17–38*.

Ramesh, M., & Asher, M. G. (2000). *Welfare capitalism in Southeast Asia social security, health and education policies*. New York: St. Martin's Press.

Saengtienchai, C., & Knodel, J. (2001). *Parents providing care to adult sons and daughters with HIV/AIDS in Thailand*. UNAIDS Best Practice Collection. November 2001. Geneva: UNAIDS.

Sobieszczyk, T., Knodel, J. E., & Chayovan, N. (2003). Gender and well-being among older people: Evidence from Thailand. *Ageing & Society, 23, 701–735*.

Soonthorndhada, A., Gray, R., Soonthorndhada, K., & Viswanatham, P. K. (2008). Elderly women in Thailand: Roles and position. In J. Troisi & A. L. Pawliczko (Eds.), *The elderly woman in Asia: Her roles and position* (pp. 285–310). Malta: The International Institute on Ageing, United Nations—Malta; Veritas Press.

Thanakwang, K., & Soonthorndhada, K. (2006). Attributes of active ageing among older persons in Thailand: Evidence from the 2002 Survey. *Asia-Pacific Population Journal, 21*, 113–135.

Thanakwang, K. & Soonthorndhada, K. (2007). Determinants of economic security among Thai elderly: Evidence from a cross-sectional national survey. *Asia Journal of Global Studies, 1/2*, 35–49.

Thanakwang, K., & Soonthorndhada, K. (2008). Family relations and health-promoting behavior among older people in Nan province. *Journal of the Medical Association of Thailand, 91*, 1102–8.

UNAIDS. (2000). *Report on the global HIV/AIDS epidemic, June 2000*. Geneva: UNAIDS.

United Nations Department of Economic and Social Affairs, Population Division. (2002). *World population ageing 1950–2050*. New York: United Nations.

VanLandingham, M., & Knodel, J. (2007). Sex and the single (older guy): Sexual lives of older unmarried Thai men during the AIDS era. *Journal of Cross-Cultural Gerontology, 22*, 375–388.

Wachter, K. W., Knodel, J. E., & VanLandingham, M. (2002). AIDS and the elderly of Thailand: Projection familial impacts. *Demography, 39*, 25–41.

Wachter, K. W., Knodel, J. E., & VanLandingham, M. (2003). Parental bereavement: Heterogeneous impacts of AIDS in Thailand. *Journal of Econometrics, 112*, 193–206.

Yuji, B. (2006). Changing meaning of the elderly in Nan Province, Northern Thailand: From "Khon Thao Khon Kae" to "Phu Sung Ayu". *Southeast Asian Studies, 44*, 321–338.

49

·∎·

Turkey

Yesim Gökçe-Kutsal

One of the most significant phenomena of the 20th century has been population aging; that is to say, the dramatic increase in the number and proportion of persons aged 60 and above. It has become a major concern facing the whole world. In fact, the first quarter of the 21st century has often been called the Age of Aging. The demographic transition that, until recently, was mostly viewed as a phenomenon of the more developed countries is becoming a feature of many developing countries as well (Troisi & Gökçe-Kutsal, 2006).

BASIC DEMOGRAPHIC INFORMATION

With a surface area of 774,815 square kilometers, 97% of Turkey's territory is located in Asia and the remaining 3% in Europe. Its population density as of the year 2000 was 88 persons per km². The share of the elderly population within the overall population remained under 5% until the end of the 20th century. According to the 2000 census results, the population aged 65 and over, which was 3,858,949, represented 5.7% of the overall population. Men represent 45.3% and women 54.7% of the elderly population (State Planning Organization Publications, 2007).

In 2006, 72.9 million people were living in Turkey. The population is aging in Turkey, like many other countries in the world. According to the data from the Turkish National Population and Health Survey, elderly people now comprise 6.9% of the total population. While the percentage of the elderly population is 6% in urban areas, it is 9% in rural areas.

The life expectancy at birth has reached 74.2 for females and 69.3 for males. The longer life expectancy for women in Turkey gives them about 1.5 extra years of healthy life. According to WHO estimates for 60-year-olds in Turkey, the Health-Adjusted Life Expectancy (HALE) for women (14.2 years) is more than three years longer than that for men (12.8 years). There are over 3.5 million older persons and it is estimated that this figure will increase twofold and reach 7–8 million in the next 20 years and 12 million by the year 2050 (Hacettepe University Institute of Population Studies, 2004; World Health Organization, 2006).

Calculations based on the assumption that current demographic trends will continue signify that the 21st century will be a century of the elderly in Turkey as well, in parallel to the expectation worldwide. It is expected that together with the changing age structure, the elderly population will also gain importance on social, demographic, and economic terms in Turkey, especially in the second half of the century (State Planning Organization Publications, 2007).

According to Turkish Statistical Institute projections, the elderly population is forecasted to represent 19% of the overall population by 2050. Looking at the demographic changes in Turkey, the increase in the elderly population is evident. A significant decrease has been observed in the fertility rates since the 1950s, as a result of abandoning the post-Republic policies encouraging fertility, taking into consideration the worldwide demographic changes and the requirements of the country in the middle of the century. The fertility rate was estimated to be over 6 in the 1950s, but declined to as low as 2.2 in the forecasts of the 2003 Turkish Population and Health Survey. This decline accelerated especially in the 1970s, and a reduction of 61% was observed over a 30-year period. Besides the decline in the fertility rate, infant and child death rates also decreased rapidly, as a result of the increase in the antenatal and post-natal care and vaccination rates. The infant death rate, which was fore-casted to be over 230 per thousand, declined to as low as 29 per thousand by the 2000s, as a result of advancements in maternity and child health. Conversely, life expectancy has recorded a significant increase in all age groups, again as a result of the advancements in field of health care. Life expectancy at birth has seen an increase of approximately 25 years since 1950 until the present. Life expectancy at birth was forecasted as 71.1 for 2004.

Aging is an issue that needs to be assessed in terms of developing countries, as well; not just developed countries. Survey results signify that our

country is making a transition to a new demographic structure. The decrease in the child and young population over time and the increase in the
share of the elderly population within the overall population are foreseen as
the reasons for the fertility rate to drop to renewal level. Being informed of
the socioeconomic and demographic characteristics of elderly people is significant as far as meeting this group's needs and expectations and planning
of the services offered to all age groups of the population are concerned.

Even though the proportion of the elderly is small, and other indicators
of aging show that the age structure of Turkey is still relatively young when
compared to the populations of developed countries, the increase in the elderly population in absolute numbers is significant, and the number of older
adults is equal to the total population of some small European countries.

Recently a study was carried out that attempted to describe social,
demographic, and economic characteristics of the elderly population in
Turkey, using data from the latest nationwide 2003 Demographic and
Health Survey and the last population projections. It also intended to
determine the co-residence pattern of the elderly data and to find out
what sort of family structure, in the future, the elderly population will
live in, by employing the household projection method. In addition, it
tried to explain the economic demand that will be created by the change
in co-residence. The analysis of elderly characteristics has shown that
the percentage of female population is more than that of males in the
distribution of the 65+ population. Over 56% of the elderly live in urban
localities, while 43.5% live in rural localities.

There is an improvement in literacy by cohorts. Younger elderly are
more educated than oldest olds. It is observed that 30.8% of the elderly
are living in simple conjugal household type. The nuclear family household type contains 15.1% (Canpolat, 2008). The issue of aging in Turkey
remains less pressing than that of industrialized Western societies. Nevertheless, there are still problems in this respect. As it is forecast that in
the 2000s, the elderly population of Turkey will increase faster than that
of developed countries, the required measures have to be taken before
aging becomes a major problem in society. The issue of aging is, first of all,
a medical and social issue. In order to overcome any current challenges
regarding aging, ample importance must be placed on the field of preventive medicine. One of the major problems of gerontology is how to make
a distinction between changes deriving from aging and changes deriving
from diseases. To meet the challenges in this area, preventive medicine
should be promoted further.

It is important to be aware of the persons responsible for meeting the
needs of the elderly population, as far as planning of services offered is

concerned. According to survey results, 43% of the elderly population stated that they themselves have the principal responsibility for meeting their needs (State Planning Organization Publications, 2007).

LEGAL STATUS

In accordance with the new Metropolitan Municipality Law No. 5216, adopted on July 10, 2004, the duties and responsibilities of metropolitan, county and first-degree municipalities were substantially defined, and a general provision was included concerning elderly people, stating that methods suiting the conditions of the disabled, elderly, dependent and needy persons in offering relevant services. Based on Article 17 of Ministry of Health and Welfare Organization Law No. 3017, the Directorate General of Social Services was established in 1963 according to Article 4 of Law No. 225, with the purpose of organizing all kinds of social assistance and security services, caring for, lodging and rehabilitating dependent elderly people, children and disabled persons, and providing social security for poor people who are unable to work.

With the principles foreseen by Law No. 2828, current services aimed at elderly people are offered within the framework of the provisions of three regulations, which are:

1. Social Services and Child Protection Agency Regulations for Rest Homes and Rest Homes and Care and Rehabilitation Centers for Elderly People;
2. Regulations for Private Rest Homes and Nursing Homes for Elderly People; and
3. Regulations on Establishment and Performance Principles of Rest Homes for Elderly People, to be established within Public Institutions and Organizations.

SERVICES OFFERED TO ELDERLY PEOPLE

The Social Services and Child Protection Agency's Division on Services for Elderly People, established in accordance with Paragraph (f) of Article 10 of the Law, is assigned the following duties and functions (State Planning Organization Publications, 2007):

- Arranging, monitoring, coordinating and inspecting the services pertaining to detection, caring for, and protection of the elderly people who suffer from social and economic deprivation;

- Planning, implementing, and monitoring and coordinating the performance of activities pertaining to establishing of rest homes for elderly people and other social service facilities with similar qualities in a balanced manner across the country and on the basis of requirements and their dissemination within the framework of a program, organizing and ensuring the performance of the activities pertaining to protection of elderly people in the society; and

- Setting the principles for, providing guidance for, monitoring the implementation of, coordinating and inspecting the opening of, performance, and inspection of organizations for elderly people to be established by public institutions, real persons and corporate bodies.

SERVICES OFFERED BY PUBLIC INSTITUTIONS AND ORGANIZATIONS

Social Security

In Turkey, the number of people benefiting from social security programs who are insured in the literal sense has not reached an adequate level, and a comprehensive social security network has not yet been built. Therefore, in order to ensure they are looked after in their elderly years, people who remain outside the scope of the system choose to be covered within the scope of private pension plans, which are complementary systems of social security. Social security services offered to elderly people are implemented through the Law on Pension Fund for Civil Servants (Laws No. 5434 and 2022), Law on Social Insurance Institution (Law No. 506, Article 20 of this Law, and Law No. 2925), Law on Tradesmen and Craftsmen and Other Freelance Workers (Laws No. 1479 and 2926). Other than these, assistance is provided to elderly people who are not included in the scope of any social security institution and who are in need in accordance with the Law No. 3294 on Encouraging Social Help and Solidarity.

SOCIAL ASSISTANCE

Within the scope of the Prime Ministry General Directorate of Social Assistance and Solidarity and Law No. 3294 on Encouraging Social Help and Solidarity, which came into force in 1986, elderly people who are in poverty and deprivation, who are not subject to social security institutions and are not entitled to pension or any income (including individuals who are entitled for pension in accordance with Law No. 2022) from such institutions benefit from the Social Solidarity Fund.

SOCIAL SERVICES

The Social Services and Child Protection Agency Law No. 2828 has been enacted with the purpose of gathering under one umbrella all services offered by various volunteer organizations and public institutions, which were in an unmanageable and disorganized condition. Various paragraphs of Articles 3, 4, 9, 10, 34 and 35 of this Law include provisions pertaining to social service practices for elderly people. The Regulations for Private Rest Homes and Nursing Homes for Elderly People Numbered 23099 dated September 3, 1997, drafted in accordance with Articles 34 and 35 of Law No. 2828, have come into effect.

The provisions of the Regulations for Private Rest Homes and Nursing Homes for Elderly People provide that elderly individuals who are 55 years old or older, who are in social and/or economic deprivation and require long-term care by institutions, are cared for and protected in private rest homes or in nursing homes if they require special care. Establishments offering the services of private rest homes for elderly people can be classified under three headings, which are:

- Establishments of associations or foundations;
- Establishments of minorities; and
- Establishments of real persons.

According to Law No. 5434, on the Republic of Turkey Pension Fund for Civil Servants, delivery of services for elderly people are conducted through rest homes and nursing homes. Individuals who receive pension from the fund with the statuses of retired, disabled, widower, orphan, or those in the scope of the Service to Country Arrangement, and who are 60 years old, are not alcohol or drug addicts, do not have any contagious diseases, are not convicted of infamous crimes, and are able to conduct their daily activities by themselves will benefit from these institutions.

RETIREMENT POLICY

The retirement age in Turkey is 65 years of age. However, there are different retirement policies for different occupational sectors. On one hand, the retirement age for a person working either in public or private sector is 65 years of age; on the other hand, it is 67 years of age for academics. It is recommended that our main purpose should be not to discriminate against elderly people in any field, including retirement age, and governmental bodies should take this very important issue into consideration.

HEALTH-CARE SERVICES

Efforts for Healthy Aging and Health of Elderly People were initiated within the scope of Goal 5 of the Health for All in the 21st Century policy. Within the framework of this initiative, the current situation and the current problems were determined, and aims, goals, and strategies were specified through the intrasegmental and intersegmental meetings held. The work in this scope is currently in progress (State Planning Organization Publications, 2007).

As the length of life increases, older people can respond with lifestyle changes that can increase healthy years of life. Correspondingly, health-care systems need to shift toward more geriatric care, the prevention and management of chronic diseases and more formal long-term care (Aslan, 2008). Since people are living longer, measures to improve health and prevent disease need to focus on people of working age (World Health Organization, 2006). The Ministry of Health is currently working on the health policy of the total population, known as Health Reform. However, the coverage of the health insurance system is lacking in some ways. Although the majority of the inhabitants' health needs are covered by a state-funded insurance system, there are still a significant number of uncovered people (9%) (Aslan, 2008). This contributes to the inequalities in the utilization of the health services. As elderly people are one of the main vulnerable groups in the society, they are experiencing problems in this regard.

Health services should be accessible for all, including older persons. Financial, physical, psychological, and legal difficulties hindering accessibility should be minimized. It is essential to deliver rehabilitation, care services, and assistant techniques for older persons so as to meet their needs, while ensuring their full integration within their society. Services should be accessible, and the technology used should be simple, acceptable, and independently applicable. Regular and sufficient level of physical activity, mental stimulus, involvement in social life and communication with the surrounding environment make it possible for older persons to lead more independent lives.

EDUCATION

As the population is aging in Turkey, the importance of education has gained momentum compared to the past few years. The basics of geriatrics and gerontology are taught in medical faculties and in the sociology schools of some universities. Not only the medical doctors, but nurses, dentists, pharmacists, psychologists, and specialists of nutrition deal with aging as well. However, there is still a problem with the institutionalization process.

Geriatrics medicine and gerontology are taught in university undergraduate courses. Medical and social sciences contribute the content of the programs (Aslan, 2008). The improvement of geriatric medicine will take time in Turkey. Geriatric medicine should be a specific medical discipline (like pediatrics) and it needs a multidisciplinary approach. However, in some of the medical faculties, geriatrics is established as a branch of internal medicine. This is a very important issue that blocks the institutionalization of geriatric medicine with a more holistic approach, which would be an improvement. Not only the effective treatment but also the prevention and early diagnosis of the diseases should be evaluated in a multidisciplinary manner. In addition, increasing the awareness of the public about healthy and successful aging is an interdisciplinary issue.

CENTERS FOR RESEARCH AND TEACHING

Geriatrics and gerontology science is improving in a number of branches in Turkey. As there are many, we can classify the institutions into six major branches and give some examples (Aslan, 2008):

a. *Governmental bodies:* Ministry of Health plays the major role regarding this type of institutionalization. There are a few geriatric hospitals; e.g., Ministry of Health Ankara PMR Research and Education Center (http://www.saglik.gov.tr).

b. *University research and application centers:* These centers prioritize multidisciplinary work on education and research. Hacettepe University Research and Application Center of Geriatrics Sciences—GEBAM (http://www.gebam.hacettepe.edu.tr) is a multidisciplinary academic organization dealing with geriatrics and gerontology.

c. *Military-based centers:* For example, Ankara TSK Rehabilitation and Care Center (http://www.rehab..gata.edu.tr).

d. *Geriatric medicine:* In Turkey, some institutions have formed as a branch of internal medicine, such as Istanbul University School of Medicine Department of Internal Medicine, Division of Geriatrics (http://www.istanbul.edu.tr). However, some institutions also take a multidisciplinary approach to elderly health. For example, Baskent University Ayas Geriatric Rehabilitation Center (http://www.baskent-ank.edu.tr) and Hacettepe University ORAN Geriatric Rehabilitation Center (http://www.hacettepe.com.tr).

e. *Gerontology science:* These are located under the faculty of social sciences at some universities. Akdeniz University School of Sociology is an example of a department that offers education in gerontology (http://www.geroder.org). Another example: Hacettepe University School of Literature Division of Sociology (http://www.sosyoloji.hac ettepe.edu.tr).

f. *Non-governmental organizations*: Societies, associations, and so on. For example, Geriatrics Society-Turkey (http://www.geriatri.org).

g. *Private sector*: Private nursing homes, geriatric care units or centers, and so on.

RECENT RESEARCH ON AGING

In one study, a number of characteristics and living conditions of 1,300 older persons aged 65 and above and living in Ankara were examined by Hacettepe University Research Center of Geriatric Sciences (2004). And in another study, the cardiopulmonary and metabolic responses to maximum exercise and aerobic capacity, and relationship between the resulting data and motor disability in hemiplegic patients, were evaluated (Sezer, Kutay Ordu, Sutbeyaz, & Koseoglu, 2004). Research was undertaken to evaluate the possible association between low levels of serum cholesterol and depression in the elderly. In this study, there was no association between depression and low serum cholesterol levels after adjustment for confounding factors (Ergun et al., 2004).

To determine gender discrimination and risk factors in the elderly population and to assess the impact of that discrimination on elderly health, 168 elderly individuals were selected from the records by simple randomized sampling, and enrolled in a study. Data were obtained through face-to-face interviews at the residence of the elderly individuals. It was determined that 51.7% of the females and 21.3% of the males were exposed to negative gender discrimination. This discrimination was higher among women in all subgroups. In fact, older women and elderly individuals with only primary school education or less were significantly more exposed to gender discrimination (p = 0.008 and p = 0.043, respectively). It was found that only economic variables were related to poor health status, without gender discrimination. Despite the fact that freedom has been obtained in some areas, such as participation in household decision-making and dressing, the patriarchal family structure and sexual inequality continue in older age (Keskinoglu, Ucuncu, et al., 2007).

To compare the prevalence and risk factors of elder abuse in the elderly population in two different districts in Izmir, Turkey, a cross-sectional study was performed. The prevalence of physical and financial abuse among the elderly in the district of low socioeconomic status was 1.5% and 2.5%, respectively, while among the elderly in a district of high socioeconomic status, it was 2% and 0.3%, respectively. However, the prevalence of elder neglect in the two districts was 27.4% and 11.2%, respectively. Prevalence of neglect was associated with infrequent contact with relatives, little or no income, and fewer years of education among the elderly in the low socioeconomic district. In the high socioeconomic district, neglect was associated with fewer years in education, poor health status and having chronic status. The prevalence of abuse among the elderly living in the two different districts was low. However, nearly one-fifth of elderly people were exposed to neglect (Keskinoglu, Pıcakcıefe, et al., 2007).

The geriatric population is growing continuously; therefore, more aged patients are being admitted to dermatology clinics. Successful management of these patients requires a thorough understanding of the features of geriatric patients and prevalence of skin diseases in this group. Patients aged 65 years and older admitted to the dermatology outpatient clinic over a three-month period included the most common complaints in the chronic eczema-dermatitis group. However, the most commonly detected disorders were in the chronic sun exposure group. Some severe cutaneous and noncutaneous diseases were detected incidentally at total dermatological examination. Treatment satisfaction scores of patients and improvement scores of the doctor had a significantly good correlation. The study results indicated that in the management of elderly patients, social and physical evaluation should be carried out and treatment must be recommended accordingly. In all elderly patients, total dermatological examination must be performed because it may reveal some severe cutaneous or underlying noncutaneous diseases (Polat, Yalçın, Calışkan, & Allı, 2008).

Osteoporosis has recently been recognized as a major public health problem by some governments and health-care providers. Despite significant progress in knowledge about osteoporosis, public awareness is required for effective management if precautions are to be taken. The aim of this study was to evaluate the educational status of osteoporotic individuals, and their awareness about the disease and sources of information (Kutsal et al., 2004).

Another study was designed to assess the quality of life of retired Turkish physicians. The focus was on their working conditions, their health status, and the impact of their disabilities on activities of daily life. It is believed that planning for retirement in all its aspects should be a legitimate concern of all physicians. Recommendations for future retirees or the construction of guidelines for making this time of life enriching and a period of intellectual growth are awaited (Gökçe-Kutsal, Ozçakar, Arslan, & Sayek, 2004).

GERIATRIC REHABILITATION

Living longer and sustaining one's quality of life can be considered both a success and a never-ending struggle. This struggle requires not only the capacity for staying healthy, enjoying independence, enjoying social relations, being sociable, and having access to affordable health care, but also having a positive approach toward older persons and old age (Troisi & Gökçe-Kutsal, 2006). The recommendations are organization of training programs on healthy aging in order to prepare individuals for old age; provision of service units for those older persons who have difficulties in carrying out the activities of daily living; provision of consultancy services with regard to the use of health and social service units for older persons who are not covered by any form of social security; and formation of models of domiciliary health care for older persons in order to provide them with needed service at their own homes.

Maintaining the health and quality of life in an aging population is often accompanied by significant social and economic difficulties, hence the growing need to create new policies and strategies aimed at increasing the level of welfare. Rehabilitation services are very important in preventing or delaying chronic disabilities accompanying the unavoidable and irreversible process of old age. They ensure the better use of the existing potential of older persons and reintegrating them into their society as healthier and more productive individuals. This matter should be prioritized.

A multidisciplinary approach should be taken as the basis for the rehabilitation of older persons, particularly in offering them a comprehensive and integrated health service. Medical approaches should be applied in parallel to preventive and rehabilitative measures, psychological, sociological, nutritional approaches, and various other disciplines should be involved in order to work as a team with the patient and his or her family. Protective approaches should be developed aimed at preventing and, if possible, eradicating primary and secondary disabilities among older persons.

Another issue that should be taken into consideration is education. Raising awareness in the family, amongst caregivers of older persons and in society in general, regarding the phenomenon and the process of aging, the needs of older persons, possible diseases, and disabilities would prevent new problems from arising. The essential purpose is to ensure independent living conditions at home. When this is not possible, it is important to educate and to communicate with the family and the caregivers by providing assistance or making observations in order to allow for self-efficacy in the future.

COMPREHENSIVE GERIATRIC ASSESSMENT

Comprehensive Geriatric Assessment should be multidimensional and interdisciplinary. The diagnostic process should determine a frail elderly person's medical, psychosocial, and functional capabilities and problems as well.

The purposes of Comprehensive Geriatric Assessment are:

- To achieve a multidimensional diagnostic evaluation,
- To develop an overall plan for primary care and case management,
- To determine long-term care needs and optimal placement, and
- To make the best use of health-care resources.

A comprehensive geriatric assessment differs from a standard medical evaluation as follows:

- It concentrates on frail elderly people with complex problems.
- It emphasizes functional status and quality of life.
- It frequently makes use of interdisciplinary teams.
- Professional services for elderly are provided in more settings than with any other population (because of the great variety of needs, functional deficits, and needs for social support).

In caring for older patients, a clinician will get assistance from local clinics, acute-care hospitals, rehabilitation hospitals, skilled nursing facilities, residential care facilities, geropsychiatric units, and home-care agencies. Hospital-based geriatric services improve diagnosis and management, increase patient's functional level, increase quality of care, achieve appropriate placement, and reduce use of chronic institutions. The key to diagnosis and treatment in a difficult situation is social history. Many elders come to need medical attention because of some combination of economic constraints and social isolation (Gökçe-Kutsal et al., 2004).

THE MAIN ACHIEVEMENTS IN THE FIELD OF GERONTOLOGY AND GERIATRICS

Considerable increases in a number of activities listed below can be an indicator for evaluating achievements in the field of gerontology and geriatrics in Turkey:

- National and international education programs and courses;

- National and international scientific meetings (congresses, symposiums, panels, etc.);

- A scientific (national and international indexed) journal (*Turkish Journal of Geriatrics*);

- Societies and associations dealing with the multiple problems of the elderly;

- Activities held to increase public awareness about healthy aging;

- Increase in the number of nursing homes and geriatric care centers; and

- Increase in media attention.

REFERENCES

Aslan, D. (2008). Geriatrics society—Turkey. *Journal of Nutrition Health and Aging, Special Issue.* (In press.)

Aslan, D., & Üner, S. (2001). *Health status of Turkey* (p. 27). Ankara, Turkey: Hacettepe University Public Health Foundation Publications.

Canpolat, S. (2008). *The economic consequences of population aging in Turkey: A country at the onset of population aging.* Ph.D. thesis, Ankara, Turkey.

Ergun, U.G.O., Uguz, S., Bozdemir, N., Guzel, R., Burgut, R., Saatci, E., et al. (2004). The relationship between cholesterol levels and depression in the elderly. *International Journal of Geriatric Psychiatry, 19,* 291–296.

Gökçe-Kutsal, Y. (2007). *Aging in Turkey.* 60th Annual Scientific Meeting of the Gerontological Society of America, State of the Art Presidential Symposium, November 17, 2007. San Francisco, USA.

Gökçe-Kutsal, Y., Ozçakar, L., Arslan, S., & Sayek, F. (2004). Retired physicians: A survey study by the Turkish Medical Association. *Postgraduate Medical Journal,* Feb, 80(940), 101–3.

Hacettepe University Institute of Population Studies. (2004). *Research on Turkey's population and health, 2003.* Ankara, Turkey: Ministry of Health General Directorate for Maternity and Child Health and Family Planning, State Planning Organization, and the European Union.

Keskinoglu, P., Pıcakcıefe, M., Bilgic, N., Giray, H., Karakus, N., & Ucku, R. (2007, August). Elder abuse and neglect in two different socioeconomic districts in Izmir, Turkey. *International Psychogeriatrics* 19(4), 719–31. Epub April 16, 2007.

Keskinoglu, P., Ucuncu, T., Yildirim, I., Gurbuz, T., Ur, I., & Ergor, G. (2007, Nov.–Dec.). Gender discrimination in the elderly and its impact on the elderly health. *Archives of Gerontology Geriatric, 45*(3), 295–306. Epub March 6, 2007.

Kutsal, Y. G., Atalay, A., Arslan, S., Basaran, A., Cantürk, F., Cindaş, A., et al. (2004). Awareness of osteoporotic patients. *Osteoporosis International, 16*(2), 128–33. Epub June 10, 2004.

Polat, M., Yalçın, B., Calışkan, D., & Allı, N. (2008, April 30). Complete dermatological examination in the elderly: An exploratory study from an outpatient clinic in Turkey. *Gerontology*.

Sezer, N., Kutay Ordu, N., Sutbeyaz, S. T., & Koseoglu, B. F. (2004). Cardiopulmonary and metabolic responses to maximum exercise and aerobic capacity in hemiplegic patients. *Functional Neurology, 19*(4), 233–238.

State Planning Organization Publications. (2007). *The situation of elderly people in Turkey and the national plan of action on aging* (issue 2741, pp. 17–33). Ankara, Turkey: Author.

Troisi, J., & Gökçe-Kutsal, Y. (Eds.). (2006). *Aging in Turkey* (pp. 23–105). Malta: Hacettepe University Research and Application Center of Geriatrics Sciences (GEBAM) and International Institute on Aging (INIA) publication, Veritas Press.

World Health Organization. (2006). *Highlights on health in Turkey, 2005*. Geneva: Author.

50

■ ■ **■** ■ ■

Uganda

James Kakooza

AGING IN UGANDA

In this chapter, older persons' demographics will be discussed in terms of size, growth, density, distribution, and statistics. In this chapter, the terms "older persons," "the elderly," and "60+" will be used interchangeably to refer to persons aged 60 years and above.

Population Trends in Uganda

Statistical surveys in Uganda indicate that the population of older persons has been increasing over time. In fact, the population of older Ugandans has doubled over the past two decades (1991–2009). The 1991 Population and Housing Survey revealed that out of a total population of over 16.7 million, slightly over 686,000 were aged 60+, representing 4.1% of the population (Uganda Bureau of Statistics [UBOS], 2002). Ten years later, the national population and housing census results put the total population at about 23.9 million, of which 1.1 million (4.6%) were persons aged 60 years and above. The population of older persons estimated during the Uganda National Housing Survey (NHS) of 2005/2006 put the figure of the 60+ population at approximately 1.2 million. Further, projections for 2007/2008 indicated an estimated figure of about 1.7 million of 60+ population, which puts the proportion of the elderly in Uganda at 6.1%. When the above figures are used to calculate the annual increase among the 60+ population, it is found to be approximately 7.1%. Therefore, Uganda's 60+ population is among the fastest growing in Africa (United Nations Department of Social and Economic Affairs [UNDESA], 2006). At this rate, the population of older persons in Uganda is projected to increase to about 6 million by the year 2050.

Life Expectancy

In Uganda, like many other African countries, a bigger proportion of persons aged 60+ live in rural areas, with limited and poor quality social support services. In addition, the 60+ age group comprises more female older persons than males. The male-to-female ratio of persons above the age of 60+, however, varies by age bands. In the 60+ band, the ratio is 85%, while for the age band 80+, it is 76% (HelpAge International, 2007). This trend, of course, is not surprising, since it relates directly to the general population life expectancy model for Uganda. In Uganda, women have a higher life expectancy than men. Specific life expectancy figures for the older population tend to differ with age seniority. For example, for the 60+ age band, life expectancy is estimated at 15.2 years, while for the 80+ age band it is 5.5 years. By the year 2050, however, these figures are expected to increase to 19 and 6.7 for the 60+ and 80+ age bands, respectively (UBOS, 2006). This means that in Uganda, while at present the average living ages for the older person who has passed 60 and 80 years are 75.5 and 85.5 years, in 2050, the figures will increase to 79 and 86.7 years, respectively.

Role of Older Population in the Development of Uganda

The 60+ population in Uganda is composed of active and resourceful community members. For example, in 2004, among the voting population of 18+, 10% were persons above the age of 60+ (UNDESA, 2005). This means that 10% of the leadership mandate in Uganda is contributed by the 60+ age group. Another interesting contribution of the older population in Uganda is in the work force. The aging wall chart of UNDESA for the period 1950–2050 indicates that in Uganda, 81% of the males and 57% of the females aged 60+ are active members of Uganda's work force (UNDESA, 2006).

The increasing number of orphans in Uganda, especially children orphaned by HIV/AIDS, gives a burdensome opportunity to the 60+ to champion the caregiving role to their grandchildren. For example, by the year 2002, 50% of the approximately 1.2 million single and double orphans in Uganda were being cared for by their grandparents of age of 60+ years (United Nations Development Program, 2002).

The above demographic picture of older persons is not independent of other issues. In Uganda, there is a growing body of knowledge regarding the 60+ population in terms of what influences this population growth. Some of these issues will be discussed in detail in the section on recent research on aging in Uganda, but is worth mentioning the critical ones here: poor to no economic empowerment programs for the elderly; weak community support programs; and lack of specific social services support programs for the elderly, such as health, water, sanitation, food, nutrition, shelter, recreation, leisure, sports, and education. Older persons in Uganda also suffer from a lack of psychosocial support services and lack of support and care of older people with disabilities.

The above well-known aging history in Uganda, combined with the problems highlighted above, raises a question as to whether aging issues in Uganda have been studied satisfactorily. The next section explores the extent of research done in Uganda on the issue of aging.

RESEARCH ON AGING IN UGANDA

In Uganda, research on aging has not been given priority by any standard: academic, policy, or practice. For example, while in the developed world and other countries in Africa, there are centers developed to specifically research aging, to date there is no such center in Uganda. However, despite the absence of such specialized research centers, individual researchers from different establishments have done some significant studies. Most of these few investigations on aging conducted in Uganda are through individual initiatives, mostly by social scientists and medical personnel.

Historical Profile of Research on Aging in Uganda

The history of aging research in Uganda can be traced back to the 1970s, when a nine- developing-country study on aging was sponsored by the United Nations Social Development Section. This study was the first ever study on aging in developing countries or in Uganda. Uganda and Ghana were the two countries selected to represent Africa in this study (Apt & Grieco, 1994). Unfortunately, since that time, very little research on aging in Uganda has been done.

Reasons given by development and academic researchers regarding this very low response to research in aging are centered on the skepticism about the importance of aging in Uganda. This is because for a long time, the aged were viewed as a minority, and their responsibility was a burden for their families and not for the community or government. In Uganda, like in many African countries, aging is viewed as an issue of Western world concern. This ideology is worsened by the attitude carried in Uganda—probably as in most other African countries—that research should be focused on the escalating numbers of youth and children (AU/HAI, 2003).

It was only after the 1982 first United Nations Assembly on Ageing (UNAA) in Vienna that this entrenched perception started changing. At this assembly, aging was raised as a global issue with a great effect on the developing world as well. However, while this pronouncement raised research momentum in many developing countries, it was not the case in Uganda (Gillis, 2002). Following the UNAA in 1982, the first ever African discussion on aging took place in Dakar, Senegal, later in 1982, sponsored by the Senegalese government, the United Nations Population Fund (UNFPA) (UNFPA, 2005), and the United Nations Educational, Scientific and Cultural Organization (UNESCO).

In 1986, the UN Assembly officially approved the formation of the African Gerontological Association (AGES). However, AGES did not begin operation till 1989. AGES was formally launched at the 14th Congress of the International Association of Gerontology in Acapulco, Mexico. Unfortunately, out of the 55 African countries, only 12 were members at the time of inauguration, and Uganda was not a member. AGES was mandated to promote awareness of aging issues through research, publication, and all avenues of dissemination, including conferences. This would have been a very good opportunity for Uganda to assume some research responsibility, but since Uganda was not a member, this opportunity for research was again lost.

The good news about aging issues and research came about in 2001, when HelpAge International lobbied and introduced aging into the agenda of the African Union, in which Uganda is a very active member. The African Union would then mandate consideration of aging issues, including research, among member countries, including Uganda. Unfortunately, this initiative has not produced much fruit in Uganda on the side of aging research.

Importance of Aging Research for Uganda

Having given the above historical background on the position of aging research in Uganda, one would be interested to know whether research on aging is important to Uganda or not. This question arises since the Government of Uganda and its people have been in existence for centuries without any significant research on aging! The answer to the above question can only be "yes," due to two main reasons: (1) the need for research to sufficiently sensitize and convince policy-makers in Uganda about the urgent need to respond to population aging by documenting the scale of aging in Uganda and its implication for social service provision in the country; and (2) to provide a sound basis for the government to identify policy options and devise effective strategies to ensure the welfare of the growing numbers of older persons. It should be recalled that in Uganda, the population of older persons is increasing at a record rate of tenfold within 60 years—from 0.6 million (1991) to 6.0 million (2050). In line with the above two research needs for Uganda, the available research contributions are discussed below.

Some Contribution to Aging Research in Uganda

Like all other research fields, most of the popular studies on aging in Uganda are initiated and conducted by individual researchers at public and private universities, and specialized research centers. The institutions at which most research is done are Makerere University's Faculties of Arts and Social Sciences and the Institute of Statistics and Applied Economics (ISAE). Research centers include Makerere Institute for Social Research (MISR), Centre for Basic Research (CBR), and the National Union of Researchers and Research Users (NURRU). Nongovernmental organizations (NGOs) have also contributed nonacademic research on aging. These NGOs include HelpAge International (Uganda), The Aged Family Uganda (TAFU), and the Uganda Reach the Aged Association (URAA).

Research conducted by the above-mentioned organizations cover issues like health and HIV/AIDS, care provision, poverty, food, water and sanitation, disability, family structures, conflict and emergencies, and policy issues.

General Health

Studies indicate that poor health ranks highest among problems faced by older persons (Aboderin, 2007; The Uganda Chronic Poverty Report of 2005). A study jointly conducted by Uganda's Chronic Poverty Study Centre and the World Health Organization (WHO), highlighted the following: in comparison to other developing countries, older persons in Uganda faced higher mobility rates. WHO estimated that 91% of older persons above the age of 60 years had experienced episodes of illness at least one week prior to their research survey. Painful legs and backache were identified as the most common ailments. The Chronic Poverty Research Centre CPRC/WHO (2005) study put the percentages of older persons with painful legs and backache at 23% and 20.4% respectively.

The Uganda Human Development Report (United Nations Development Program [UNDP], 2005), Bevan (2003), and the World Bank (2003) reveal similar figures: about 50% of the elderly have visual impairment and physical disability. The Uganda Human Development Report (UNDP, 2005) reveals that the number of health facilities is limited, and many Ugandans live far away from them. The report further reveals that where facilities are available in meaningful proximity, the facilities lacked skilled personnel and medicines for the diseases affecting the elderly. The U.S. Centers for Disease Control (CDC) and the Institute of Public Health (IPH) at Makerere University report that trauma due to wars and HIV/AIDS-related deaths are major mental health problems affecting the elderly.

HIV/AIDS

While HIV/AIDS is one of the most researched subjects in Uganda, little has been done regarding HIV/AIDS among older persons in Uganda. Nevertheless, there have been a few studies of international standards on HIV/AIDS among the elderly. The most notable of this research is described below.

An age-cutting study by Kakooza and Kimuna (2005) focused on HIV/AIDS orphans' education in Uganda and the changing role of older people in the Kayunga District of central Uganda. They revealed that in Uganda, many older people's roles have been reversed, going from being provided for to being providers of care. Older people, who are already poor, face the loss of economic support from their adult children and unexpected social, psychological, and economic burden due to the caregiving role they are assuming. Using cross-sectional data from Kayunga District in central Uganda to examine the impact of HIV/AIDS on the role of older persons, these authors found that there were HIV/AIDS-related deaths in 82.3% of the surveyed households. In almost 34% of the households, the caregivers of HIV/AIDS orphans were older people over 50 years old. Almost all households headed by older people (97.8%) had on average three school-going orphaned children living in the household (Kakooza & Kimuna, 2005).

Other scholars of how HIV/AIDS is affecting the elderly are Kamya and Poindexter (2005) and Nampanya-Serpell (2002). The global implications of older adults raising children in the wake of HIV/AIDS are discussed in

Daphne Joslin's book on the subject. In these studies, it was revealed that older persons are sexually active; for women in their 70s and men up to age 95, this sexual activity exposes Ugandan elders to HIV/AIDS. Like Kakooza and Kimuna (2005), most of these researchers identified caregiving as a role shifting rapidly to the elderly.

Physical Disability and Abuse

Uganda Reach the Aged Association (URAA), through its implementation research accompanying its three-year action plan (2003–2005), identifies physical, economic, and social abuse as major problems affecting the elderly. Their study reveals that such abuse leads to loneliness, loss of self-esteem, and economic deprivation. Older women are sexually and physically abused. URAA specifically identifies allegations of witchcraft toward elderly women, leading to physical assault. The study further reveals there is a lack of protection mechanisms for older people, making them extremely vulnerable to all forms of abuse.

Survival Strategies

Nyanzi (2008), in his *Case Study on the Older Persons of Uganda*, conducted through The Aged Family Uganda (TAFU), reveals that despite major constraints in Uganda regarding older persons, this group of citizens have developed the survival strategy of selling of assets, including their land, to pay for treatment, school fees for the grandchildren, food and other essential commodities. As a result, older persons are left with the only option of depending on community volunteers and church members for support. As each of us would agree with Nyanzi, this deprives the elderly of their right to independence and dignity. Another strategy is doing petty jobs despite their lack of energy. The study reveals that older persons do casual labor, including quarrying, herding animals for others, cleaning toilets, and practicing witchcraft. Nyanzi (2008) further reveals that older persons living in urban centers go to the extent of scavenging garbage for food. Due to poverty, older persons avoid health centers and resort to natural curative mechanisms, often leading to death.

Another practitioner action research by HelpAge International (2007), reveals that "bride price" is another survival strategy adopted by the older persons, leading to underage marriages. HelpAge and TAFU both reveal that especially in the northern and eastern parts of the country, girls can be married off at 14 or even 13 years of age, leading to loss of family value and violation of these young girls' right to choice.

Summary on Research on Aging in Uganda

While research on aging is very important, and although there have been some quality studies done, these are insufficient to drive development of support systems and policies in Uganda. It is therefore imperative that in both the near and far future, research addressing issues of older persons be developed. These studies should have a Ugandan or (at most) an African context. Models and frameworks from the West could, however, be used for grounding the research. The research should emphasize issues of how family, community, and government resources can be harnessed and used to solve the social needs of older persons. As stated earlier, there is a need to develop specialized research centers in Uganda (at least one research center before 2014). Such a center could be established at an existing institution of higher learning, or even as a stand-alone Aging Research Center. This center would address research in both gerontology and geriatrics. Again as stated earlier, the government of Uganda should have not only a deliberate interest in development of such research centers, but also funding activities of these centers, including associated research studies.

EDUCATION IN GERONTOLOGY IN UGANDA

In this section, we address the status of gerontology education in Uganda. As any academic will recognize, aging is a multidisciplinary field. Gerontology is the study of the aging processes and individuals as they grow from middle age through later life. This means that the study of aging integrates information from several separate areas of study. Biology, sociology, and psychology are the core or basic areas, along with content from many other areas of study, such as public policy, humanities, and economics.

Gerontology Education in Uganda

In Uganda, while the core disciplines of biology, sociology, and psychology are highly developed academic areas, no specific course in gerontology is registered in any of the universities in Uganda. This applies even to Makerere University, which has been in existence since 1922. An assessment of all public universities—Makerere, Kyambogo, Mbarara, Busitema, and Gulu Universities—finds no course in gerontology at any level (certificate, diploma, bachelor's, master's, or doctorate).

As a result of the lack of courses in gerontology, Uganda lacks professionals competent in gerontology. Therefore, Uganda is a country with no gerontologists, with the exception of a very few general sociologists and psychologists with interest in aging issues. This means that with this deficiency, the country remains lagging with regard to understanding gerontological issues among its people. After recognizing this deficiency, the Government of Uganda, through its Department of Elderly and Disabled, Ministry of Gender Labour and Social Development, made a provision for a certificate course in gerontology.

Certificate Course in Gerontology—The Only Gerontological Education Initiative in Uganda

The Ministry of Gender, Labour and Social Development (MoGLSD), in collaboration with HelpAge International and UNFPA, has supported training of staff from MoGLSD and the Nsamizi Institute of Social Development in gerontology at the University of Malta. The knowledge and skills attained were utilized to develop a six-week Certificate Course in Gerontology at Nsamizi Institute of Social Development. Participants are usually drawn from government institutions and NGOs involved in implementing programs for older persons in Uganda.

The six-week course covers studies in physical, mental, and social changes in older people as they age; investigation of the changes in society resulting from the aging population; application of this knowledge to policies and programs; study of health and disease in later life and comprehensive health care of older persons; and the well-being of their informal caregivers. The course is flavored by experiences from the United Nations International Institute on Aging (INIA) and the Institute of Gerontology and Geriatrics at the University of Malta. This institute at the University of Malta offers a unique opportunity for systematic multidisciplinary training in a wide range of areas in the fields of gerontology and geriatrics. It consists of 13 study units, 2 practice placements, and a long essay in an approved area of study. The program was designed by an international group of experts during a meeting convened in 1989 by the United Nations International Institute on Aging, in collaboration with the University of Malta, WHO, and UNESCO.

Summary of Gerontology Education in Uganda

Unfortunately, while the six-week certificate course helps practitioners in the area of aging, in no way does it offer academic analysis. Therefore, Uganda has a dire need to develop and implement specific courses in the area of gerontology. It is important that at least in the next five years (2009–2014), certificate, diploma, bachelor's and master's degrees be developed at both public and recognized private universities. These courses should deliberately be developed with a strong research component and should be funded by the Government of Uganda, at least initially. Otherwise research, development, and policy will continue to suffer because they are based on uninformed decisions.

PUBLIC POLICY ISSUES ON AGING IN UGANDA

There has been a lack of national policy on older persons (60+ years) to guide government and donor action. Issues affecting the 60+ age group have therefore not been given the attention they deserve, leaving them marginalized, with little or no access to services and opportunities that would improve their standard of living. Therefore, a lot of effort and political will are needed to ensure successful development and implementation of a national policy on older persons once it is in place.

Uganda in the Face of Madrid International Plan of Action of Ageing

Uganda is a signatory to the Madrid International Plan of Action of Ageing (MIPAA), which was adopted by the Second World Assembly on Ageing in Madrid, Spain, in April 2002. Therefore, policy issues on aging will be analyzed in light of issues raised in MIPAA plan. The MIPAA action plan focuses on poverty eradication, health promotion, access to food and adequate nutrition, income security, access to knowledge, education and training, HIV/AIDS, housing and general care and support to the elderly.

Recognizing that to date, at least till the end of 2008, Uganda had no approved policy on aging and that policy issues concerning older persons' plight are multidimensional, the Government of Uganda put in place a steering committee to develop such a policy. This committee comprises members from central ministries, local governments, faith-based organizations (FBOs), NGOs, and community-based organizations (CBOs), the private sector, older persons themselves, and the community. The Ministry of Gender, Labour and Social Development was mandated to lead the process. Participation of older persons in the process to enhance ownership and sustainability of programs was proposed as a strategy. Whether the older persons are participants or just involved in the process is a question yet to be answered.

Responsibilities of the policy formulation team comprise, among others, policy formulation; development of guidelines to implement policy; provision of support supervision to local governments; networking with line ministries, NGOs, and other stakeholders; initiation of laws and re-view of the existing laws to address concerns and needs of older persons; and design of programs and activities for older persons and monitoring and evaluation of this policy.

Legal and Policy Frameworks that Provide for Aging in Uganda

Some of the legal and policy frameworks proposed to promote and pro-tect the rights of older persons are drawn from the official Government of Uganda policy documents, some of which are listed below:

Constitution of the Republic of Uganda (1995): Recognizes the rights of older persons and provides the basis for the enactment of laws to ad-dress their rights and needs. Under the National Objectives and Directive Principles of State Policy of the Constitution, it is stated, "The state shall make reasonable provision for the welfare and maintenance of the aged." Article 32 of the Constitution stipulates that, "Notwithstanding anything in this Constitution the state shall take affirmative action in favour of groups marginalized on the basis of gender, *age*, disability or any other reason created by history, tradition or custom, for the purpose of redress-ing imbalances which exist against them" (Government of the Republic of Uganda, 1995).

Local Government Act (1997): For effective participation of older persons in decision-making processes on matters that affect their lives, older persons are represented at various levels of local government from village to district level. In line with this, Local Governments Act of 1997; CAP 243 Section 10 (1) and 23 (6) provide for representation of two older persons, male and female, elected by older persons at all recognized Local Government Councils (District and Sub-County levels).

The Equal Opportunities Commission Act (2007): provides for mon-itoring and evaluating policies, programs, plans, activities, practices, trad-itions, culture usages, and customs to ensure that they are compliant with equal opportunities and affirmative action in favor of groups marginalized on the basis of sex, age, ethnic origin, religion, social and economic standing, gender or any other reason created by history, tradition or custom.

Vision 2025 is a long-term National Development Framework. Its per-tinent aspirations are that older persons will have easy access to basic services, infrastructure, and other social amenities. In line with this, the vision for the policy for the 60+ population aims to have "A society where older persons age with security and dignity" (Uganda Ministry of Finance, Planning, and Economic Development, 2000).

Poverty Eradication Action Plan (PEAP): This act provides an over-reaching framework to guide public action on eradication of poverty. It spells out priority action areas to support, mobilize, and empower vulnerable groups to participate in the economic growth and social development process. In order to implement the PEAP, various sector strategic plans were developed. Key sector strategies, as far as issues of older persons is concerned, include the Social Development Sector Strategic Investment Plan (SDSSIP); Plan for the Modernisation of Agriculture (PMA); Water and Environmental Sanitation Investment Plan (WESP); Education Sector Investment Plan (ESIP); Health Sector Strategic Plan (HSSP); and the Justice, Law and Order Sector Plan (JLOSP). Concerns and needs of older persons are being integrated during review of these planning frameworks.

Right of Older Persons to Associate: These associations have been established from village level to district level. They were formed for the following reasons: to mobilize older persons to participate in development activities; promote interaction and intergenerational linkages; enable government to extend special services to the elderly among other vulnerable groups; use executive committees of the associations as electoral colleges for electing their representatives to local councils; facilitate older persons to form Savings and Credit Cooperative Organizations (SACCOS) to access government loans known as Bonna ba Gaggawale (Luganda phrase meaning "prosperity for all").

Priority Areas of Focus for the National Policy on Aging in Uganda

The proposed policy is expected to focus on priority areas that seek to improve quality of life of the 60+ population. This will be achieved through economic empowerment of older persons; strengthening the formal and informal community support institutions; enhancing access to social services such as health, water and sanitation, food and nutrition, shelter, recreation, leisure and sports, education and training; psychosocial support; care and support of older persons with disabilities; and research and information dissemination.

Summary of Policy and Public Issues Affecting Older Persons in Uganda

Unfortunately, until the above-stated strategies are put in place, there is no evidence that Ugandan elders will be taken seriously. Second, the above cannot bear fruit unless the following are put into consideration:

(1) strengthening of sensitization of local governments and stakeholders to integrate programs of older persons in sub-county and district plans; (2) building capacity of stakeholders at all levels to enhance delivery and utilization of services for older persons; (3) promotion of research and dissemination of best practices and experiences with older persons to support interventions; (4) strengthening of collaboration and networking for collective utilization of resources for provision of quality services for older persons; and (5) establishment of a coordination body between government departments, other service providers, and older persons. This would act as a body at national level through which concerns, problems, and needs of older persons will be communicated to its agencies for action. All in all, Uganda is still far from meeting the basic social and economic needs of elderly persons in the country. Of course, without specific and clear policy on the elderly, seniors will continue to be marginalized. If this marginalization continues in this direction, it will be interpreted as a clear and deliberate violation of the rights of these senior citizens to good quality of life, which is contrary to the MIPAA, of which the government of Uganda is a signatory.

REFERENCES

Aboderin, I. (2007). Development and ageing policy in sub-Saharan Africa: Approaches for research and advocacy. *International Federation on Ageing: Global Ageing Issues and Action*, 4(3), 11.

African Union/Help Age International (AU/HAI) (2003) The African policy framework and plan of action on ageing. Nairobi, Kenya: HelpAge International Africa Regional Development Centre.

Apt, N. A., & Grieco, M. (1994). Urbanisation, caring for the elderly and the changing African family: The challenge to social welfare and social policy. *International Social Security Review*, 48, 111–122.

Bevan, D. (2003). *Discussion paper on economic growth, investment and export promotion*. Kampala, Uganda: Ministry of Finance, Planning and Economic Development (MFPED).

Chronic Poverty Research Centre in Uganda and World Health Organization (2005). *Chronic poverty in Uganda—The policy challenges*. Kampala, Uganda: Author.

Gillis, L. (2002). In honour of Monica Ferreira. In S. Makoni and K. Stroeken (Eds.), *Ageing in Africa* (pp. 285–286). Aldershot: Ashgate Publishing.

Government of the Republic of Uganda (1995). *The 1995 Constitution of the Republic of Uganda*. Kampala, Uganda: Author.

HelpAge International. (2007). *Age demands action in Uganda: Progress on implementation of the Madrid International Plan of Action on Ageing (MIPAA)*.

Kakooza, J., & Kimuna, S. R. (2005). HIV/AIDS orphans' education in Uganda: The changing role of older people. *Journal of Intergenerational Relationships*, 3, 63–81

Kamya, H., & Poindexter, C. (2005). Mama Jaja: The stresses and strengths of HIV/AIDS-affected Grandmothers. *Social Work in Public Health*, 24(1 & 2), 4–21.

Nampanya-Serpell, N. (2002). Global implication. In D. Joslin (Ed.), *Invisible caregivers: Older adults raising children in the wake of HIV/AIDS* (pp. 278–296). New York: Columbia University Press.

Nyanzi, F. (2008). *A case study on the older persons of Uganda*. The Aged Family Uganda (TAFU).

Uganda Bureau of Statistics (UBOS). (2002). *Uganda population and housing CENSUS report*. Kampala, Uganda.

Uganda Bureau of Statistics (UBOS). (2006). *The 2000/2001 Uganda demographic health surveys (UDHS)*. Kampala, Uganda.

Uganda Ministry of Finance, Planning, and Development (2005). *Poverty reduction strategy paper: Uganda's poverty eradication action plan summary and main objectives*. Kampala, Uganda: Author.

United Nations Department of Social and Economic Affairs (UNDESA). (2005). *World population prospects, 2004. The 2004 Revised Database*. New York: United Nations.

United Nations Department of Social and Economic Affairs (UNDESA). (2006). *United Nations population ageing wall chart (1950–2050)*. New York: United Nations.

United Nations Development Program (2002). *Uganda human development report*. New York: Author.

United Nations Development Program (2005). *Uganda human development report*. New York: Author.

United Nations Population Fund (UNFPA). (2005). *State of Uganda's population 2005*. New York: UNFPA.

World Bank. (2003). *World development report*. New York: Oxford University Press.

51

United States

Erdman B. Palmore

When the United States is compared with other countries in regard to its resources, research, and programs for its elders, several anomalies appear. The United States undoubtedly is one of the richest countries in the world in terms of natural resources, technical and scientific resources, and per capita national product. With one of the largest proportions of elders in the world, the United States was one of the first countries to develop substantial gerontological research, and it probably has more professional gerontologists and produces more gerontological research than any other country. It also spends more per capita on health care for its elders—about US$12,000 in 2006—than perhaps any other country.

Yet despite all these laudable facts, it has not solved the problems of its elders' health, social integration, and economic status as well as many other countries have. Some of the most important problems are indicated by the following facts. Life expectancy, 16 years at age 65 (Butler, 2008, Table 1.1), is less than that of 11 other industrialized countries. About 10% of elders have incomes below the official poverty threshold (Butler, 2008, Table 4.1). Millions are willing and able to work but cannot find employment because of age discrimination (Palmore, Branch, & Harris, 2005). Few elders (about 5%) participate in senior centers, and many are isolated from the mainstream of family and community life.

Despite some new programs for elders (such as Part D of Medicare, the prescription drug benefit), the United States continues to lag behind many European countries in offering a full spectrum of social and medical services. Federal long-term care benefits are mainly limited to the medi-cally indigent. Other evidence of *ageism* (prejudice and discrimination against the aged) is widespread (Palmore et al., 2005).

Several circumstances help explain this discrepancy between resources and programs. The United States has one of the most heterogeneous aged populations in the world. This has hampered efforts to deliver adequate programs and services, because different types of elders need different types of services. Also, while the United States has one of the most democratic forms of governments, it has an unusually elaborate system of checks and balances, which often frustrates attempts to develop needed programs. Since the September 11, 2001, attack on the World Trade Center, Home-land Security programs and wars in Iraq and Afghanistan have squeezed the federal budget and prevented the development of more adequate social and health programs for elderly persons.

On the positive side, it does appear that recognition and concern for elders are growing at an unprecedented rate. Certainly the number of per-sons over 65 has continued to grow rapidly. In 1990, when the last edition of this *International Handbook on Aging* went to press, about 31 million Americans were 65 and over, and the Census Bureau projects that there will be over 40 million by 2010 (U.S. Census Bureau, 2004). On the other hand, the percentage of the U.S. population 65 and over (12.4%) has not increased at all. It is true that this percentage is expected to increase to about 20% in 2040, when the peak number of baby boomers move into the over-65 category, which will increase their number to about 80 million. There has been much concern and controversy over what will happen to our Social Security system, and especially the financing of Medicare and Medicaid. Even more problematic is the increase in the numbers of persons over age 85: this will have almost tripled from 1980 to 2010 (from 2.2 to 6.1 million). Persons over 85 tend to need more programs and ser-vices than those aged 65–84. These services include not only health care, but also senior centers and nutrition centers, including Meals on Wheels, housing, and transportation.

However, it appears that growth in academic gerontology has leveled off: currently there are somewhat over 6,000 members of the Geronto-logical Society of America—about the same as in 1990. The number of journals and newsletters on aging published in the United States also has leveled off at about 50 (http://www.crab.rutgers.edu/~deppen/journals.htm), although there are probably an equal number published elsewhere.

On the other hand, growth in the number of nonacademic professionals and paraprofessionals serving elders in various ways continues to increase in step with the increasing numbers of elders.

An important development in professional organizations since our last edition (Palmore, 1993) is the move of the Association for Gerontology in Higher Education (AGHE) from an independently incorporated organization to a unit within the Gerontological Society of America (GSA). Since 1972, GSA had focused primarily on research in gerontology, while the AGHE focused on education. But by 1998, leaders of both the AGHE and the GSA came to the conclusion that a stronger partnership between these organizations, promoting both research and education, would be beneficial to all.

RECENT RESEARCH

Due to space limitations, we cannot review in detail the recent developments in research. The following summary is based on reviews of the major recent encyclopedias and handbooks on aging (Binstock & George, 2006; Birren, 2006; Birren & Schaie, 2006; Maddox, 2001; Masuro & Austad, 2006; Palmore et al., 2005; Schultz, 2006; Whittington, 2006).

We believe the following are the major developments in U.S. recent research:

- Research on health continues to dominate gerontology, but it has tended to become more quantitative, with more use of scales, typologies, and protocols for assessment and evaluation.

- Sophisticated methods of statistical analysis for cohorts, longitudinal studies, imputation of values for missing data, cluster and factor analysis, latent structure analysis, path analysis, interaction detector analysis, and so on, have become more common.

- New research technologies include genetic analysis, computer assisted tomography (CAT scans), magnetic resonance imaging (MRI), positron emission tomography (PET scans), and twin studies.

- On the other hand, there has been growing acceptance of various kinds of qualitative analysis to generate hypotheses for quantitative testing (when possible). This trend is reflected in the new journals, *Journal of Aging Studies* and *Journal of Aging, Humanities and Arts*.

- There has been somewhat less development of gerontological theory and conceptualization. The criticism is often made that gerontology remains data rich and theory poor. However, there have been significant developments in social theories of gerontology, such as in ageism, social construction and social exchange theories, the life-course perspective, feminist theories, age stratification, political economy, and critical gerontology. As for nonsocial theories of aging, significant developments have occurred in disposable soma theory, evolutionary theory, genetic programming theories, neuroendocrine theories, and oxidative stress theory.

- Another criticism is that there is usually a disconnect between the worlds of theory, research, and practice. Both theory and research are often neglected in the development of programs, policies, and techniques for solving the many problems (and fulfilling the promises) of aging.

- However, gerontological theory, research, and practice techniques are rapidly becoming more and more accessible by computer searches through Google, Ageline, Medline, and Wikipedia, for example.

- Concepts in the areas of the social and behavioral sciences that have generated considerable research and writing since our last edition include active life expectation, ageism, aging in place, antiaging, assisted living, assisted suicide, disabling conditions, diversity, end-of life/human rights, ethics of care, family care, financial gerontology, generational equity, globalization, health care and long-term care, homosexuality and gender identity, increase of older populations in developing countries, life styles, new technologies, neuroscience, the oldest old, public policy, quality of life, rationing of health care, religion, and women.

- Concepts in the area of biology generating considerable attention include age-associated diseases, AIDS/HIV, Alzheimer's disease, body size and longevity, dietary restriction, gene expression, immune systems, racemization (inversion of amino acids), short-lived models of aging, stem cells, and telomeres.

Education

Most education in gerontology is carried out by colleges and universities that belong to the Association for Gerontology in Higher Education (AGHE). AGHE was established in 1974 to help develop education, training, and service programs in aging, as well as research dealing with these areas. The current membership of the AGHE is about 300 institutions in the United States, Canada, and an increasing number of institutions outside North America. Members range from small two-year colleges to large research universities, as well as aging organizations outside higher education. The programs these members offer range from just a few courses to major centers on aging that offer various credentials and degrees in gerontology and geriatrics. There are now about 100 M.A. programs and 9 Ph.D. programs in gerontology.

AGHE has annual meetings, with workshops and seminars that share information and ideas about curriculum and program development and evaluation. AHGE also provides a range of publications including *The*

Directory of Educational Programs in Gerontology and Geriatrics, Gerontology Program Development and Evaluation, Standards and Guidelines of Gerontology Programs, and the *Brief Bibliography Series.*

The Database on Gerontology in Higher Education is a computerized listing of over 1,000 gerontology and geriatrics programs in the United States. The Program of Merit evaluates and recognizes educational programs at all levels, following national standards.

AGHE also advocates for the development and recognition of gerontology and geriatrics education, and undertakes analyses of programs to provide assistance in improving education in gerontology.

The AGHE is now the educational unit of the Gerontological Society of America and is a nonprofit organization with its headquarters in Washington, DC. More information can be obtained at its Web site, http://www.aghe.org.

Much informal education about aging takes place at various conferences and in publications of such organizations as the National Conference on Aging, the American Society on Aging, and the Gerontological Society of America.

Public Policy Issues

Most of the major public policy issues relating to aging in recent years have been affected by the remarkable double turnaround of the federal budget balances. When the last edition of this *Handbook* went to press (1992), the budget deficit was about $290 billion. Largely because of this deficit, some economists and politicians called for cutting back expenditures for Social Security, Medicare, and Medicaid, including privatization of these programs (proposals to reduce federal financing in favor of private financing). However, in 1998, the federal budget showed a remarkable *surplus* of $69 billion. This surplus continued to increase for several years and effectively relieved pressures to privatize these programs and reduced fears of their bankruptcy.

But with the invasions of Afghanistan and Iraq, coupled with significant tax cuts and a large new prescription drug benefit under Medicare, the budgets again went into the red and suffered bigger and bigger deficits. As a result, renewed calls for privatization and reducing expenditures for these programs began to gain strength. These expenditures were challenged on equity grounds—is too much being spent on older people compared to children?—and on ideological grounds—should some responsibilities borne by the federal government be transferred to individuals and the private sector?

At present (2008), the proposals for privatization have receded and the issues of prescription drugs and long-term care appear to have become more prominent. Part D of Medicare, which established some federal aid to help persons on Medicare pay for their prescription drugs, has been highly controversial. Supporters hail the fact that the government now helps pay for some drugs, while critics maintain that funding the program through private insurance agencies makes it inefficient, complex, and inadequate.

On the long-term care front, federal aid continues to be limited to persons on Medicare who are recovering from hospital stays, or to persons on Medicare who are too poor to pay for such care. Calls for expanding federal support for long-term care appear to be muted currently by the mounting federal deficit. The main policy issues appear to be how much the government should support home health care, assisted living institutions, and hospice (end-of-life) care. The underlying debate is at the heart of many policy decisions in the United States: who should be responsible for health and long-term care—individuals, families, communities, or the government? A related issue is the legalization of physician aid-in-dying (formally called assisted suicide). Such aid-in-dying is now legal in Oregon, and several other states are considering various forms of legalization.

The basic issue of age-related entitlements has been attacked from two directions: political conservatives say the government cannot afford to continue to finance these huge entitlements with the coming of the "boomer generation," without significant changes in program rules; and some liberals concerned with generational equity maintain that age-related entitlements are a kind of ageism because they discriminate against younger people (Palmore et al., 2005). The latter group suggests that the ageism could be reduced if Social Security benefits were based solely on years of contribution, rather than on a combination of age and contribution. Alternately, the ageism of programs such as Medicare (which is limited to older people) could be eliminated if health care were extended to persons of all ages.

Information Sources

If you prefer to get information from printed sources, we refer you to the references listed below. If you prefer to use Internet sources, the following can give you good leads:

- http://www.ageline.org/research/ageline
- http://agingstats.gov

- http://www.nasua.org/informationandreferral
- http://www.nia.nih.gov

Or you can usually find what you need on Google.

REFERENCES

Binstock, R., & George, L. (Eds.). (2006). *Handbook of aging and the social sciences* (6th ed.). San Diego, CA: Academic Press.

Birren, J. (Ed.). (2006). *Encyclopedia of gerontology* (2nd ed.). San Diego, CA: Academic Press.

Birren, J., & Schaie, K. (Eds.). (2006). *Handbook of the psychology of aging* (6th ed.). San Diego, CA: Academic Press.

Butler, R. (2008). *The longevity revolution*. New York: Public Affairs.

Federal Interagency Forum on Aging Related Statistics. (2004). *Older Americans 2004*. Washington, DC: U.S. Government Printing Office

Maddox, G. (Ed.). (2001). *The encyclopedia of aging* (3rd ed.). New York: Springer Publishing Company.

Masoro, E., & Austad, S. (Eds.). (2006). *Handbook of the biology of aging* (6th ed.). San Diego, CA: Academic Press.

Palmore, E. (1993). *Developments and research on aging: An international handbook*. Westport, CT: Greenwood Press.

Palmore, E., Branch, L., & Harris, D. (2005). *The encyclopedia of ageism*. Binghamton, NY: Haworth Press.

Schultz, R. (Ed.). (2006). *Encyclopedia of aging* (4th ed.). New York: Springer Publishing Co.

U.S. Census Bureau. (2004). *International database*. Washington, DC: U.S. Government Printing Office.

Whittington, F. (2006). You might be a gerontologist . . . if you decide to buy this book. *The Gerontologist, 46*, 840–4.

52

.. ■ ..

Zimbabwe

Sitawa R. Kimuna

The world's age structure has been changing as people have fewer children and live longer. The number of people aged 60 and older is rising rapidly and is expected to exceed the number of those aged between 15 and 24 years old within two decades (Population Reference Bureau, 2007). Population aging is now not only a concern for developed countries, but the process is also gaining momentum in developing countries, with sub-Saharan Africa projected to have more than 155 million older people by the year 2050 (United Nations Department of Economic & Social Affairs, 2007). This rapid increase is happening among people over the age of 60 despite—or perhaps because of—the impact of HIV/AIDS. Since women live longer, they outnumber older men; in sub-Saharan Africa (SSA), they often live in extreme poverty and material deprivation. Further, 25% of all households in SSA are headed by older people, and 68% of those households headed by older people take care of one or more children under the age of 15 years (Kimuna & Makiwane, 2007).

The growing awareness of the importance of aging in Africa is corroborated by the African Union (AU) Policy Framework and Plan of Action on Aging that was adopted in 2001. The AU Policy Framework binds all AU member countries to develop policies on aging that would improve the lives of older people on the continent (HelpAge International, 2008). Although the development of an aging policy without implementation does not bring about change, the AU Plan of Action on Aging has been lauded as an important step in recognizing aging in Africa.

HISTORY OF AGING IN ZIMBABWE

Zimbabwe is a southern African country with a population of approximately 13 million (United Nations, 2006), and, of this figure, approximately 800,000 people are aged 60 years and above. By 2050, the population of older people will rise to approximately 1.5 million, nearly 9% of the population (United Nations, 2006). The increase in sheer numbers of the population of older people in Zimbabwe is largely due to a lower fertility rate that started in the 1980s (Kimuna, 2005b), and the increase will continue despite the AIDS pandemic that is wreaking havoc in Zimbabwe. Not only will the number of older people increase more rapidly, but the length of time an older person will remain older also will increase (Kimuna, 2005c). For example, the 2006 United Nations population estimates indicate that 5% of Zimbabwe's population is aged 80 years and over, and this population will increase to 11% by 2050 (United Nations, 2006).

Aging in Zimbabwe is happening without the safeguards of traditional support systems. Family and social support are eroding due to a variety of factors related to rapid social change, changing family patterns, shrinking family size, and higher levels of HIV/AIDS, which is mowing down the economically active family members (Kimuna, 2005b, 2005c) and putting stress on existing household systems (Schatz & Ogunmefun, 2007). In the absence of social security and other formal social support programs that exist in more developed countries, older people in Zimbabwe and other developing countries of Africa are at considerable risk.

In Zimbabwe, a large proportion of older people are illiterate, live in rural areas, lack employment, and are generally poor (Kimuna, 2005b; Nyanguru, 2007). Since women tend to live longer and marry older men, older females are more likely to be widowed, divorced, or separated and thus heading households. A study by the World Health Organization (WHO, 2002) on caregivers of orphans and other vulnerable children in Zimbabwe found that 71.8% of caregivers were over 60 years, 74.2% of them women, and over 60% of orphaned children live in grandparent-headed households.

The environment (poverty, hunger, poor sanitation, HIV/AIDS epidemic, and conflict) in which vulnerable populations (children and older people) live in Zimbabwe has been exacerbated by the election crisis of 2008. According to a HelpAge International news release (July 4, 2008), the severe food shortages and the continuing ban on nongovernmental organizations' (NGOs) activities placed vulnerable people at critical risk of starvation. For example, most residents at care homes for older people who relied on support from NGOs have no family and nowhere else to get help (HelpAge International, 2008).

Further, the instability and attacks created displacement of people and humanitarian needs. Together, detrimental Zimbabwe policies such as Operation Murambatsvina (Shona for "clean up trash campaign" or what Nyanguru (2007) called "Operation Restore Order") in 2005 and the land reform program resulted in the loss of housing, displaced many people in both rural and urban areas, and increased Zimbabweans' vulnerability and poverty, especially for elders. The insecurity within the country and the disadvantage of living in inaccessible remote areas that lack basic health services further marginalized older people. This movement not only affected people's proximity to clinics and other health-care facilities, but wiped out the informal sector, which was providing employment and income for at least 40% of the labor force.

For older-female–headed households, the prevailing difficult political and socioeconomic situation in the country has had a devastating impact. Almost a decade of conflict between government and civil societies has made it impossible for Zimbabwe's vulnerable to surmount poverty, hunger, poor sanitation, and the HIV/AIDS epidemic. The detrimental social policies have been further compounded by the combined effects of depleted human capital, decreased economic support for older people, high unemployment rates, increased caregiving responsibilities, and the astronomical inflation at 231 million%, as reported by the British Broadcasting Corporation (BBC; October 9, 2008). The most vulnerable households in Zimbabwe that are hit the hardest are those that not only provide health care and support for their sick children, but are also responsible for financial support, emotional support, and rearing of grandchildren, some of whom are HIV/AIDS orphans. Research in South Africa and Uganda on older people as resources and as providers of education for HIV/AIDS-orphaned grandchildren indicates that grandparent-headed households have taken on all forms of parental responsibilities of caregiving and providing other resources such as school fees for orphaned grandchildren (Kimuna & Makiwane, 2007; Kakooza & Kimuna, 2005).

RESEARCH ON AGING IN ZIMBABWE

Scholarly research on aging in sub-Saharan Africa (SSA) is gradually increasing. According to the Committee on Population (United Nations, 2006), researchers are now beginning to ask how factors such as trends in socioeconomic conditions, changing cultural norms and values, changing levels of formal and informal social support, ongoing poor health conditions, and the AIDS crisis are combining to affect the well-being of older people. However, the report also notes that much of what is known today comes either from censuses, which often are not particularly reliable or particularly detailed, or from small cross-sectional surveys, which often suffer from problems of nongeneralizability. In addition, gerontology research in SSA has tended to be country specific, which tends to overlook similarities between countries as well as the heterogeneity within each country (Apt, 2002). Moreover, the body of scholarly literature on aging in Africa is in reference to other social issues on the continent (Makoni, 2008).

For example, in examining changes in societal arrangements for the support of older people in other settings, demographers have often used trend measures of living arrangements. Such analyses can be particularly complex in SSA due to the variety of household structures, including resident and nonresident household members and multiple household memberships. Zimmer and Dayton (2005, p. 295) used data from Demographic and Health Surveys (DHS) conducted in 24 SSA countries to examine the composition of households containing older people. The authors found that 59% of older people in SSA live with a child and 46% with a grandchild. They also found that older adults are more likely to be living with orphans in countries with high AIDS-related mortality, reconfirming the notion that research on aging in SSA is indeed in reference to other social issues.

Generally, research on aging in Zimbabwe has taken the same pathway as elsewhere in SSA. Studies have included discussions on intergenerational transfers; marginalization of the elderly, which relegates them to the bottom of most development program agendas (Kimuna, 2005a); the weakening family support systems for the elderly; and aging in the context of physiological changes, psychological changes, and changes in social role and status. Other studies have examined topics ranging from lack of social security protection (Kaseke, 2005); health, gender, and livelihoods (Adamchak & Wilson, 1999; Adamchak, Wilson, Nyanguru, & Hampson, 1991; Allain et al., 1997; Kasere, 1995), rural/urban migration and older people in Zimbabwe (Nyanguru, 2007); and the impact of President Robert Mugabe's government land reform on older people (Kanyenze, 2004).

Kaseke's (2005) study examined the social security system in Zimbabwe, highlighting the social exclusion of people employed in the informal sector. It also describes and evaluates the various social security schemes available to vulnerable groups such as older people, persons with disabilities, the chronically ill, and dependents of indigent people. Mapati (1998) outlines labor laws governing staff in age-care institutions. The study highlights the legal provisions of age-care institutions and also explains the rights of older people in Zimbabwe. While the research of Adamchak et al. (1991) and Adamchak and Wilson (1999) focused on intergenerational transfers, observing that lack of old-age support is the most frequently mentioned grievance in interviews with the elderly, Allain et al. (1997) highlighted disease and disability in elderly Zimbabweans. In addition, Kasere (1995) assessed the needs of older refugees at the Mazowe River Bridge Refugee Camp in Zimbabwe and highlighted their needs regarding health care, nutrition, and literacy training.

A more recent study has examined the types of migrants over age 60 living in Harare, Mutare, and villages up to 50 kilometers from the two cities and their overall life satisfaction (Nyanguru, 2007, p. 57). Results from this study note rural/urban differences in life satisfaction. Whereas urban residents reported a somewhat general life satisfaction, life for rural residents was miserable. Linked to life satisfaction of older people in both rural and urban areas is Kanyenze's (2004) study on the Mugabe government's land reform program and its impact on older people.

Other studies have documented the loss of financial support for older people taking care of kin (Agyarko et al., 2002; Kimuna, 2005b, 2005c). These studies suggest that older people, due to the loss of adult children who are expected to care for them, have taken on the role of caregivers to dependent children and grandchildren. The change in older people's roles has adversely affected their living arrangements and also impacted their familial support systems (Kimuna, 2005b, 2005c).

A United Nations Population Fund (UNFPA, 1998) report documents the needs of poor older people in Zimbabwe and recommends the development of indigenous infrastructures, research planning, and programs that directly assist older people, as well as policy development. Data used in this study were from a small survey that had been conducted in rural and urban areas. A World Health Organization (WHO, 2000) report provides insights on the outcomes of a workshop hosted in Harare, Zimbabwe, on creating a Minimum Data Set (MDS) for research, policy, and action on aging and older persons in four sub-Saharan African countries—Ghana, South Africa, Tanzania, and Zimbabwe. In addition, the report contains a summary of information regarding the situation of older people and aging-related data for the continent.

Other noteworthy reports on aging research in Zimbabwe include documents published by HelpAge Zimbabwe. Jazdowska (1992) (for HelpAge Zimbabwe) used a community survey to examine health-care infrastructure and its lack of resources to adequately provide services to people with HIV/AIDS and their caregivers. The report highlights cultural hindrances that affect the support systems of older people, especially those that provide care for people suffering from HIV/AIDS. It notes that not only are HIV/AIDS sufferers stigmatized, but so are caregivers. Consequently, community attitudes and prejudice exacerbate the burden of caregiving. HelpAge International's (1995b) Supplementary Report on the Africa Regional Workshop on AIDS and the Elderly held in Harare, Zimbabwe, acknowledges the lack of recognition of older people in HIV/AIDS interventions, even as they continue to be affected by the pandemic. The report addresses problems faced by older people in relation to the HIV/AIDS pandemic and proposes intervention measures.

Finally, to better understand the situation of older people in Zimbabwe, research is needed in the following areas: family support and social networks; changing roles, status, and responsibilities of older people in the era of HIV/AIDS; formal and informal social protection schemes for older people; health and quality of life of older people; and housing, nutrition, and living arrangements. Just as studies cited above are neither complete nor intended to be an exhaustive literature review of aging research in Zimbabwe, the topics listed as those needing research are neither complete nor exhaustive. Rather, both the topics and literature are drawn from a subset of the literature known to the author.

ZIMBABWE'S CURRENT STATE OF EDUCATION IN GERONTOLOGY

After Zimbabwe's independence in 1980, the new government embarked on expanding the education and health systems and was successful in training and recruiting skilled personnel to provide services more widely than in the past. Nurses and doctors were trained locally and abroad. Improvements in health care touched the lives of most people; clinics helped to fulfill aspirations for a better quality and standard of life. The clinics run by local authorities, municipalities in urban areas, and district councils in rural areas were affordable to many older people in both rural and urban areas.

However, gains in Zimbabwe's education and health systems have been eroded by the substantial devaluation of Zimbabwe currency, current hyperinflation, and policies instituted by the government, such as the introduction of structural adjustment programs in the early 1990s; the introduction of land reform at the beginning of 2000; and Mugabe's Project Murambatsvina. The structural adjustment programs led to layoffs in the formal sector, especially in the civil service, as well as the imposition of fees for all services, including health and education, which had been free. This adversely affected the availability, affordability, and accessibility of services for people, especially older Zimbabweans. The land reform program displaced many people in both rural and urban areas (Nyanguru, 2007). This movement might have affected their proximity to health-care facilities and schools.

The combination of the above measures and the economic problems being experienced in Zimbabwe today has resulted in the collapse of the majority of government-run facilities, some of which are in dire need of resources, including personnel and equipment. To function effectively, hospitals and schools need certain pre-existing infrastructural supports, such as a transportation network to move patients, students, and supplies from one location to another, and reliable electricity to run equipment. Currently, Zimbabwe lacks the infrastructure to maintain the most basic needs for her citizens.

Similar to other institutions, Zimbabwe's public universities have limited budgets, which are spent on meager salaries, leaving few resources to initiate gerontology and geriatric programs. In these public universities, there are very few courses in gerontology and even fewer courses in geriatric medicine, which affects the number of gerontologists and geriatricians being trained in Zimbabwe. Moreover, the meager salaries for faculty and lack of resources within the education and health systems has resulted in the demise of these universities and the flight of faculty into the private sector and to industrialized countries, seeking better working conditions. This trend has been accelerated by the volatile political and economic climate that has been witnessed in Zimbabwe since the 1990s. Consequently, the migration of not only faculty but also skilled personnel from the medical profession has been attributed to worsening of Zimbabwe educational institutions and the current health crisis (Chikanda, 2005).

Because of the poor state of education in gerontology and geriatrics in Zimbabwe, older people are faced with two major problems: (1) lack of doctors and nurses specialized in geriatrics and of personnel trained in gerontology in both rural and urban areas; and (2) negative attitudes toward elders from the health-care staff attending to their needs.

AGING POLICY ISSUES IN ZIMBABWE

Although the World Bank (2007) considers Zimbabwe's legislative and social policy framework for social protection to be strong, high levels of inflation and weak public financial management have affected the level of contributions made to social protection programs. Further, government policies and programs in Zimbabwe give low priority to the concerns of the elderly. Authorities generally expect families to continue to provide for the welfare of their elderly members.

Traditionally in Zimbabwe and elsewhere in sub-Saharan Africa, social protection for older people is provided by both formal and informal programs and practices that have been developed to reduce poverty and vulnerability in old age (Kaseke, 2004). But with per-capita income depleted and inflation rapidly increasing, it is no surprise to find that formal social security systems in Zimbabwe cover only a small fraction of the population. The self-employed, workers in the informal sector, domestic workers, and the vast majority of the population living in rural areas and engaged in subsistence agriculture or other forms of subsistence living are excluded from formal social security schemes and must rely on their families for support and protection when they can no longer work. Consequently, the extended family unit remains the main source of support for the vast majority of older people in Zimbabwe.

Formal Forms of Social Security

Prior to Zimbabwe's independence in 1980, all non-Africans of retirement age were eligible for means-tested pensions (Gist, 1994; Kaseke, 1995, 2004). Post-1980, the scheme has largely been dismantled, but pensions in existence in 1980 continue to be paid. This race-based scheme assists only a tiny fraction of elders. Since the mid-1980s, government coverage for the elderly has consisted solely of assistance from the Ministry of Social Welfare within a public assistance scheme for the destitute, which is means tested (Hampson, 1985; Kaseke, 2004). This noncontributory social security scheme is administered by the Department of Social Welfare after the Welfare Assistance Act enacted in Zimbabwe in 1988 (Kaseke, 1995).

However, there is an urban bias to this welfare assistance. The great majority of the populations in the rural areas have no access to welfare assistance. The situation is also exacerbated by the fact that many of those living in rural areas are not aware of the existence of the welfare assistance program and thus are automatically excluded on account of their ignorance. Moreover, most welfare offices in the rural areas are not within easy reach. Thus, those in need of assistance have to travel long distances to get to their nearest office, and many withdraw prematurely on account of the travel costs involved (Kaseke, 1995).

In October 1994, the government of Zimbabwe introduced a national social security pension scheme funded by a 3% contribution of monthly insurable earnings from both the employer and the employee. All people in formal employment, except domestic workers, are required by law to make monthly contributions to the scheme. The scheme is designed to provide retirement, survivors' and disability pensions and grants, and funeral grants to vested contributors, particularly for formal sector workers (Kaseke, 1995; Kimuna, 2005c). Again, this scheme provides limited coverage for only a small minority of older people, mostly professional and urban based. The scheme is administered by the National Social Security Authority (NSSA), formed in 1993 (Government of Zimbabwe, 1993). Other social protection schemes available in Zimbabwe are listed here.

Workers' Compensation

This program is provided under the Workers' Compensation Act of 1976 and administered by the Department of Occupational Health, Safety and Workers' Compensation (Kaseke, 1995). The objective of the program is to provide financial relief for employees and their families when the employee is injured or killed in an accident that occurred in the course of, or arising from, the employee's duties. The scheme is extended only to workers earning up to Z$500 (approximately US$6.12) per month. Again, this excludes domestic and casual workers.

State Services Disability Benefit and War Victims' Compensation

The scheme provided under the State Services Disability Benefits Act of 1980 provides noncontributory benefits to civil servants in the event of work-related injuries or death (Kaseke, 1995). The War Victims' Compensation program is governed by the Act of 1980 and administered by the Department of Social Welfare. It is a noncontributory social security scheme funded from government revenue (Kaseke, 1995). The scheme provides for the payment of compensation in respect of injuries or death of persons caused by the liberation war. The state assumes responsibility for those whose earning capacity is impaired by war-related injuries or those whose breadwinners died as a result of war.

Informal Forms of Social Security

Research has shown that there exists a wide variety of informal, community-based arrangements that have been developed in rural areas, aimed at spreading risk among friends and extended family members, with neighbors, or with other participants (Dhemba, Gumba, & Nyamusara,

2002). These often involve self-help or community-based initiatives that draw on African traditions of shared support and kinship networks. In parts of Zimbabwe, for example, the government has successfully reintroduced the concept of the *Zunde raMambo* (literally "the Chief's Granary"), which refers to the harvest from a common field that is stored in a common granary and used at the discretion of the chief in order to ensure that the community has sufficient food in the event of a drought or a poor harvest (Dhemba et al., 2002). Although informal schemes exist to help the poor, these schemes also suffer from a number of chronic problems and, in their current form, fail to provide much in the way of long-term protection against various forms of risk (Kaseke, 2005).

The above discussion indicates that Zimbabwe lacks a comprehensive social security program. The few schemes in operation rarely complement each other, and coverage is extended to a very small percentage of the population. This clearly implies the significant role played by the family in the welfare of elders in Zimbabwe. Stronger social safety nets are urgently needed to protect the most vulnerable in Zimbabwe.

CONCLUSION

This chapter has assessed the current aging research, education in gerontology, and aging policies in Zimbabwe aimed at improving older people's quality of life. We found that aging research in Zimbabwe is examined in conjunction with other social issues; there is a lack of gerontology programs; and aging policies are largely ineffective. For example, due to lack of resources in health and educational institutions, gerontology and geriatric programs are also lacking. Further, the flight of professionals from Zimbabwe to seek greener pastures elsewhere has greatly affected service delivery within the health and educational institutions. Most medical professionals have emigrated to South Africa and Britain. The government should enact policies without delay to retain its professional medical personnel.

To be able to increase capacity in education and health institutions, the government should draw up policies that are effective in retaining faculty at educational institutions and re-attracting and retaining professionals in health. There is an urgent need also to train more village health workers who live with people in the villages. For the Government of Zimbabwe to be successful in building capacity in the areas of education and health at all levels, it must include the Zimbabwe National Traditional Healers Association (ZINATHA) in an effort to integrate the traditional healers with the modern Western health-care systems. Currently, traditional medicine is seen as inferior to Western medicine, and is associated with witchcraft. However, traditional health care has been found to play a positive role in primary health care, and since the majority of traditional healers are located in the rural areas, this pool of professionals could alleviate the shortage of health care delivery in rural locations. Further, research directed to how Western medicine and traditional medicine could collaborate successfully should be encouraged. Finally, while there is a consensus that Zimbabwe has a strong aging policy framework (World Bank, 2007), given the current political conflict and economic downturn in Zimbabwe, the policy framework is no longer useful in addressing issues that affect older people.

REFERENCES

Adamchak, D. J., & Wilson, A. O. (1999). The situation of older people in Zimbabwe. In HelpAge International (Ed.), *The ageing and development report: Poverty, independence and the world's older people*(pp. 143–146). London: Earthscan Publications Ltd.

Adamchak, D. J., Wilson, A. O., Nyanguru, A., & Hampson, J. (1991). Elderly support and intergenerational transfer in Zimbabwe: An analysis by gender, marital status, and place of residence. *The Gerontologist, 31*(4), 505–513.

Agyarko, R. D., Madzingira, N., Mupedziswa, R., Mujuru, N., Kanyowa, L., & Matorofa, J. (2002). *Impact of AIDS on older people in Africa: Zimbabwe case study.* Geneva: World Health Organization.

Allain, T. J., Wilson, A. O., Gomo, Z.A.R., Mushangi, E., Senzanje, B., Adamchak, D. J., et al. (1997). Morbidity and disability in elderly Zimbabweans. *Age and Ageing, 26,* 115–121.

Apt, N. (2002). Preface. In S. Makoni & K. Stroeken (Eds.), *Aging in Africa: Sociolinguistic and anthropological approaches* (pp. ix–xii). Hampshire, England: Ashgate.

BBC News. (2008, October 8). Zimbabwe inflation hits new high. Retrieved from: http://news.bbc.co.uk/2/hi/africa/7660569.stm

Chikanda, A. (2005). Nurse migration from Zimbabwe: Analysis of recent trends and impacts. *Nursing Inquiry, 12*(3), 162–174.

Central Statistical Office (2002). *Census 2002: Zimbabwe national report.* Harare, Zimbabwe: Author.

Dhemba, J., Gumba, P., & Nyamusara, J. (2002). Social security in Zimbabwe. *Journal of Social Development in Africa, 17*(2), 111–156

Gist, Y. (1994). Aging trends: Southern Africa. *Journal of Cross-Cultural Gerontology, 9,* 255–276.

Government of Zimbabwe. (1993). *National Pension and Other Benefits Scheme (Statutory Instrument No. 393).* Harare: Government Printer.

Hampson, J. (1985). Elderly people and social welfare in Zimbabwe. *Ageing and Society, 5*(1), 39–67.

HelpAge International. (1995a). *Older women in development.* HelpAge International, London.

HelpAge International. (1995b). *Supplementary report on the HelpAge International Africa Regional Workshop on AIDS and the Elderly.* Harare: HelpAge Zimbabwe.

HelpAge International. (2008). *AU Policy Framework and Plan of Action on Ageing. Co-operation between HelpAge International Africa Regional Development Centre and the African Union.* Nairobi, Kenya. Retrieved November 26, 2008, from http://www.helpage.org.

Jazdowska, N. (1992). *Elderly women caring for orphans and people with AIDS, Ward Six, Hurungwe District.* Harare: HelpAge Zimbabwe.

Kakooza, J., & Kimuna, S. R. (2005). HIV/AIDS orphans' education in Uganda: The changing role of older people. *Journal of Intergenerational Relationships,* 3(4), 63–81.

Kanyenze, G. (2004). African migrant labor situation in Southern Africa. Paper presented at the ICFTU-Afro Conference on Migration Labor, March 15–17. Nairobi, Kenya.

Kaseke, E. (1995). Social security and redistribution: The case of Zimbabwe. In J. Dixon & R. P. Scheurell (Eds.), *Social security programs: A cross-cultural comparative perspective.* Westport, CT: Greenwood Press.

Kaseke, E. (2004). An overview of formal and informal social security systems in Africa. Paper presented at the National Academy of Sciences and University of Witwatersrand Workshop on Aging in Africa, July 27–29. Johannesburg, South Africa.

Kaseke, E. (2005). Social exclusion and social security: The case of Zimbabwe. *Journal of Social Development in Africa,* 18(1), 33–48.

Kasere, C. J. (1995). *Needs assessment for the elderly disabled at Mazowe River Bridge Refugee Camp, Zimbabwe.* Harare: HelpAge Zimbabwe.

Keller, I., Makipaa, A., Kalenscher, T., & Kalache, A. (2002). *Global survey on geriatrics in the medical curriculum.* Geneva: World Health Organization.

Kimuna, S. R. (2005a). Elderly women, economic growth and development in sub-Saharan Africa: Zimbabwe case study. In S. Boko, M. Baliamoune-Lutz, & S. R. Kimuna (Eds.), *Women in African development: The challenge of globalization and liberalization in the 21st century* (pp. 159–187). Trenton, NJ: Africa World Press.

Kimuna, S. R. (2005b). Living arrangements and conditions of older people in Zimbabwe. *African Population Studies,* 20(1), 143–163.

Kimuna, S. R. (2005c). Socio-economic support of older people in Zimbabwe. *Quarterly Journal of the International Institute on Ageing* (United Nations—Malta), 15(4), 13–27.

Kimuna, S. R., & Makiwane, M. (2007). Older people as resources in South Africa: Mpumalanga households. *Journal of Aging and Social Policy,* 19(1), 97–114.

Madzingira, N. (1997). Poverty and aging in Zimbabwe. *Journal of Social Development in Africa,* 12(2), 5–19.

Makoni, S. (2008). Aging in Africa: A critical review. *Journal of Cross-Cultural Gerontology, 23*, 199–209.

Mapati, L. (1998). *The legal framework of age-care institutions in Zimbabwe.* Harare: HelpAge Zimbabwe.

Ministry of Health & Child Welfare. (2005). *Zimbabwe national HIV/AIDS estimates, 2005 preliminary report.* Harare, Zimbabwe: Author.

Nyanguru, A. C. (2007). Migration and aging: The case of Zimbabwe. *Journal of Aging and Social Policy, 19*(4), 57–85.

Population Reference Bureau. (2007). *Today's research on aging, No. 4.* Washington, DC: Author.

Schatz, E., & Ogunmefun, C. (2007). Caring and contributing: The role of older women in rural South African multi-generational households in the HIV/AIDS era. *World Development, 35*(8), 1390–1403.

United Nations. (2002). *Report of the Second World Assembly on Ageing.* United Nations Publication A/CONF.197/9, Sales No. E.02.IV.4.

United Nations. (2006). *Population ageing 2006.* New York: Department of Economic and Social Affairs. Population Division. Retrieved from http://www.unpopulation.org

United Nations Department of Economic & Social Affairs. (2007). *World population ageing 1950-2050.* New York: Author. Retrieved from http://www.un.org/esa/populations/worldageing19502050

United Nations Population Fund (UNFPA). (1998). *Population ageing: Improving the lives of older persons. Report of the ICPD+5 Technical Meeting on Population Ageing.* New York: Author.

World Bank. (2007). *Zimbabwe social sector delivery analysis: A social sector public expenditure review. Draft report.* Washington, DC: World Bank.

World Health Organization. (2000). *Information needs for research, policy and action on ageing and older adults: Report of a workshop on creating Minimum Data Sets (MDS) for research, policy and action on ageing and the aged in Africa.* Geneva: Author.

World Health Organization. (2002). *Health statistics and health information systems.* Retrieved from http://www.who.int/healthinfo/systems/sage/en/index3.html

Zimmer, Z., & Dayton, J. (2005). Older adults in sub-Saharan Africa living with children and grandchildren. *Population Studies: A Journal of Demography, 59*(3), 295–312.

Afterword: Aging in the Global Century

Jon Hendricks

What are the lessons to be learned from a thoughtful review of this compendium on international aspects of aging? Both the intellectual depth and the localized focus of the entries deserve a keen conceptual eye on the part of the reader in order to draw out the most meaningful lessons. There is a great deal of substance in the entries themselves, and there is an equal amount to be gained through a critical juxtaposing of one with another.

Having delved into any number of the foregoing chapters in this *vade mecum*, readers will undoubtedly be convinced that the world is a far smaller place than it was as recently as a generation ago. As we move into what is already being called the global century, there have been qualitative as well as quantitative changes, and there are most certainly more to come. For example, the speed of technology means the furthest reaches of the world can be linked 24 hours a day. That same technology and other analogous innovations allow a global flow of ideas that are increasingly accessible and potentially influential for decision-making on even the most local level. As the door to the world has opened, it has also opened on what will most likely be the world of tomorrow, a far more relational and intertwined world. That is not to say it is a cohesive or unified world, but it is one in which any one part can be touched by the other parts, and transnational contacts reach to the level of daily life. These same advances also have the potential to contribute to what Beck, Bonss, and Lau (2003, p. 6) refer to as "revolution through side effects": societal segmentation revolving around the digital world divides populations into those who have access and are facile with new technology, and those who are uncomfortable with or have less access to this aspect of change.

VARIATION AND THEMES IN THE FACE OF GLOBALIZATION

The warp and woof of the strands running through the expositions of this third edition of the *International Handbook of Aging* are sufficiently clear to suggest that policies for older populations are being profoundly influenced by and formulated with an eye to another aspect of the global marketplace: the economic arena. Modernity and globalization occur in part because economic ties and transitions bring widely diverse countries into common ground. Those interactions and collaborations are crucial components of local, national, and international decision-making, whether made by governmental bodies or intergovernmental organizations (IGOs) such as the World Bank, the International Monetary Fund (IMF), and so on. The World Bank and the IMF, to take two examples, have stipulated that developing countries seeking their assistance would be wise to implement what they term structural adjustment policies (SAPs). Intended to spur economic development, these SAPs have an unintended consequence of imposing significant hardships on selected segments of the populations of those countries, including the elderly (Olson, 2006). The interconnectedness that accompanies globalization means that social and political processes are also interrelated with what is going on elsewhere in the world: as (Phillipson, 2009)avers, the construction of old age, not to mention deliberation of old-age policy and service, are now part of a global discourse and cannot help but influence norms of reciprocity in the most local of situations.

Globalization is not merely a macro-level phenomenon from which everyday life is somehow insulated. As a number of discussions in this *Handbook* make clear, immediate relationships, the shape of well-being, life expectancy, and health status all reflect the impact of cultural context and intercultural ties. Inequality, lifestyle diseases, and poverty do as well; social advantage or social risks also accrue to individuals based on their connection to the flow of international currents. This is as true of nation-states as it is for individuals; in fact, the two are closely linked, and country after country must weigh its priorities and its options in light of global participation.

In terms of nation-states, some estimates have income differentials between the richest countries and poorest countries at more than 50 to 1 (Clark, 2007). In terms of personal and per capita income, the fact that over 2.5 billion people live on less than US$2 a day or that more than a billion do not even have a single $1 daily is ample evidence that global problems run rampant and are likely to portend an unpleasant specter in the coming decades, perhaps magnified for the older population. Income differentials are not merely economic indicators; they also signal powerful indices of quality of life, education, structured dependencies, and exclusions resulting from policy decisions. The United Nations, the World Bank and other IGOs and NGOs, national governments, and policy-makers are all well aware of the impending issues facing our planet and the re-examination of priorities that will be necessitated. As historical conditions change, values are redefined and the social contract is revised and revised again; new relationships and priorities emerge and countries respond to the presence of transnational and non-sovereign powers that have become an ever-present part of the negotiation process. As has been noted in this essay and in this book, a new politics of aging has emerged, one that affects older people in all countries regardless of the contours of their lives. Unfortunately, the new politics of aging does not ensure substantial sanctuary based on past contributions (Townsend, 2007; Walker, 2006).

The prospects of lifelong employment, economic security, and wage and benefit packages, as well as the spread of technological innovation, are sure to manifest significant if uneven alterations as we move into the global century. Townsend (1981) was the first to refer to the structured dependency of the elderly as a consequence of societal-level redefinitions. Workers closing in on what is locally considered to be old age may find their earned credits and entitlements redefined as other priorities rise to the top of the agenda. As has been noted by a number of concerned commentators, the risks and the benefits do not accrue equally to men and women, nor on the economic ladder, at any age and especially in old age. As Lash and Urry (1987) noted several years back, the disorganization and precariousness that sometimes accompanies the shift to post-industrialism are not distributed equally between different status groups or across the life course. In the face of rapid social change, one generation is likely to have a different set of expectations from that of subsequent generations about what is considered fair and just. Chen and Turner (2006) characterize the emoluments on which the elderly commonly depend as reflecting the invisible hand of market forces, the invisible handshake of tradition, as well as the invisible foot of political decisions. Many of the chapters in this book reflect the powerful intersecting impacts of those invisible forces.

The design of policies for old age rest on three dominant pillars that have differing degrees of prominence depending on local circumstances (World Bank, 1994). Discussion of those pillars is evident in many of the foregoing entries. The three pillars revolve around publicly managed and tax-financed mandatory safety nets; mandatory but privately managed individual savings systems; and voluntary occupational or private savings plans. Together and individually, these pillars represent options for protecting elders against the risks of old age, yet ensure that a government has the latitude to participate in global market-oriented opportunities and to foster growth of GDP. Not too surprisingly, what has emerged to varying degrees in different nations, however, is an emphasis on market-led welfare policies for all segments of the population and a de-emphasis of public welfare provisions. In the interval since that original publication, the World Bank has underscored the importance of neoliberal and privatized public welfare provisions as part of its criteria for screening loan and economic support proposals made by developing nations.

Another theme emerging from the many empathetic entries in this volume is that none of us grows old in isolation from what is going on around us. Whether an individual is aging in one of the relatively isolated social systems, or in the heart of one moving at breakneck speed, that person is involved in numerous relational networks defined by custom, position, and public policy. These networks are the source of social capital available as one negotiates the life course; these networks are also the foundation for the social norms by which one marks progress, decline, and expectations. In short, life's scripts are grounded in life circumstances, and as the latter change, so too will the former. These scripts embody cues relevant for self-appraisals and self-assessments drawn from those "webs of significance"—that relational life space in which individuals find themselves (George, 2003). It does not take much reflection to appreciate how as the one changes, so does the status and standing of those individuals who are part of that world. As opportunity structures open or close, long-standing identities are unsettled and many aspects of one's being, including sense of mastery and even cognitive functioning, come into alignment. The interconnectedness between physical and social *milieus* on the one hand and individual characteristics are well represented in the notion of the "ecology of human development" and by the phrase "environmental press" (Bronfenbrenner, 1979; Hess, 2006; Lawton & Nahemow, 1973).

Transformations in the global century will, as all historic changes always have, touch all aspects of our lives; these changes will encompass economic rationalities, commodification, standardization, secularization, and shifting rationalities, but also shifts in broader cultural patterns. Virtually every entry in this *Handbook* has alluded to some aspect of these changes, and virtually every one provides a basis for assessing whether what is regarded as fair and just is altering the experience of growing old. In the face of rapid social change, the solidarity sustaining the continuities between generations becomes a casualty of age segmentation where one generation may not seek and has a hard time obtaining consensual validation from other generations. As utile symbols lose their relevance to others, interpersonal bonds of solidarity are lessened, and the status of those not versed in the most current ways moves from venerable to vulnerable (Cole & Durham, 2007).

THE IMPACT OF AREA STUDIES

The organization of the foregoing materials may be described in terms of archetypical area studies. Area studies, typically referring to in-depth perspectives on particular countries or regions of the world, have a long history. Gerontologists may be most acquainted with the Human Relations Area Files (HRAF), brought together at the end of the 1940s from five pre-existing databases scattered around the United States, later augmented several times and now housed at more than 20 institutional affiliates. Intended as a ready resource for comparative analyses, the precursor to the HRAF served as a crucial component of Leo W. Simmons's (1945)classic *The Role of the Aged in Primitive Society*—one of the benchmarks of early comparative analysis of aging. The entries above parcel out in-depth analyses of the nature of aging in one country after another without particular attention to cross-border interaction or the effects of globalization, *per se*.

Yet, tightly focused and coherent summaries of aging processes in distinct regions and nation-states exceed the value of their insights about a given region. They have the potential to permit the reader of a compendium such as this to look cross-culturally, at least from an armchair vantage point, and begin to draw out patterns of their own, depending on their personal agenda. Of course, each country is unique and has a style that is uniquely its own. But that is not to say that properties do not recur in one country after another. The same is true of relational space wherein the circumstances of older persons are contingent on the ebb and flow of local as well as more broadly based interactions. There are lessons to be learned from juxtaposing, but the lessons necessarily involve the active and critical attention of the readers, in this case, and observers.

As an illustration: If one were to look at India, the intricacies of caste, class, language groupings, religion, and other facets of life on the subcontinent, along with the burgeoning of the population over the past few decades, would quickly become overwhelming. The same could be said of many developing countries and throughout the Third World. Sticking with India as a case in point, there has also been an exponential increase in the older population, up more than sixfold in the 20th century, even as the average age of the population has hovered in the early 20s (Liebig & Ramamurti, 2006). With more than one in seven of the world's elders living in India at the moment (and more than half living across Asia), the potential for generational segmentation is nowhere any greater, unless one wants to make a case for China, despite strong cultural traditions to the contrary.

Paradoxically, in the past decade or two India, a country of more than one billion people, has taken off in terms of technology, entrepreneurship—what other country has a National Knowledge Commission?—and productivity; India has built a skilled labor pool that ranks near the top, perhaps second, in the world with a sustained growth in GDP in the neighborhood of 6%. In addition to the infusion of foreign capital, the population boom has provided the human capital that has been at the forefront of the dramatic economic expansion of knowledge industries. However, these same boons are implicated at least in part for the increasing difficulties of its elderly population; the government is caught on the horns of the dilemma of whether to support economic growth or care for its aged members. Of course, one obvious question is what should the government do? How does a country decide on a course of action amidst so many priorities? The same is true for all developing countries, as for India: the government must be mindful of both priorities and create a dynamic balance between caring for its own and playing a role on the world's economic stage.

BRINGING THE GLOBAL DOWN TO EARTH

One aspect of the globalization of aging not yet touched upon revolves around questions of personal agency. What happens to old people when the system they grew to know, to cognitively and emotionally depend upon, and to fold into their anticipated life scripts, falls by the way as they reach their later years? As O'Rand (2006) and others have pointed out, long-term structural shifts in the economy and social safety nets are not due to fate or random occurrences, but rather can be traced to moral economies and value frameworks grounded in market conditions. It is not too much of an exaggeration to say that tradition and custom become scripts to live by, until those traditions and customs themselves begin to erode in the face of global contacts.

Getting to the doorstep of old age with assumptions about who will help in the face of declines that are sure to come in the latter years does not provide much solace if urbanization and industrialization mean support networks are attenuated and governmental provisions lag behind. Institutions and types of social insurance thought to be the bedrock of palliative provisions in old age are being challenged; risks are being shifted onto the backs of individuals. Issues of personal agency matter not only in terms of relational life space but in terms of an older person's perceived worth in the context of modernity and rapidly changing social circumstances. Among the possible casualties is the status accorded older people and their own perceptions of their personal worth when the context no longer has much use for what they know or the wisdom they embody.

With a comparative analytic mindset firmly in place, the reader can approach these questions and myriad others raised in the foregoing articles. The editors are to be congratulated for bringing together materials and the authors capable of pointing to answers to the quandary of old age in the global century.

REFERENCES

Beck, U., Bonss, W., & Lau, C. (2003). The theory of reflexive modernization: Problematic, hypotheses and research programme. *Theory, Culture & Society, 20,* 1–33.

Bronfenbrenner, U. (1979). *The ecology of human development: Experiments by nature and design.* Cambridge, MA: Harvard University Press.

Chen, Y.-P., & Turner, J. (2006). Economic resources: Implications for aging policy in Asia. In H. Yoon & J. Hendricks (Eds.), *Handbook of Asian aging* (pp. 67–90). Amityville, NY: Baywood.

Clark, G. (2007). *A farewell to alms: A brief economic history of the world.* Princeton, NJ: Princeton University Press.

Cole, J., & Durham, D. (2007). Introduction: Age, regeneration, and the intimate politics of globalization. In J. Cole & D. Durham (Eds.), *Generations and globalization: Youth, age, and family life in the new world economy* (pp. 1–28). Bloomington, IN: Indiana University Press.

George, L. K. (2003). Well-being and sense of self: What we know and what we need to know. In K. W. Schaie & J. Hendricks (Eds.). *The evolution of the aging self: The societal impact on the aging process* (pp. 1–35). New York: Springer.

Hendricks, J., & Leedham, C. (1991). Dependency or empowerment? Toward a moral and political economy of aging. In M. Minkler & C. L. Estes (Eds.), *Critical perspectives on aging: The political and moral economy of growing old* (pp. 55–74). Amityville, NY: Baywood.

Hess, T. L. (2006). Attitudes toward aging and their effects on behavior. In J. E. Birren & K. W. Schaie (Eds.), *Handbook of the psychology of aging* (pp. 379–406). San Diego, CA: Academic Press.

Lash, S., & Urry, J. (1987). *The end of organized capitalism*. Cambridge, UK: Polity Press.

Lawton, M. P., & Nahemow, L. (1973). Ecology and the aging process. In C. Eisdorfer & M. P. Lawton (Eds.), *The psychology of adult development and aging* (pp. 619–674). Washington, DC: American Psychological Association.

Liebig, P., & Ramamurti, P. V. (2006). Living arrangements and social support for older adults in India. In H. Yoon & J. Hendricks (Eds.), *Handbook of Asian aging* (pp. 237–260). Amityville, NY: Baywood.

Olson, L. K. (2006). The politics and policies of aging, Asian style. In H. Yoon & J. Hendricks (Eds.), *Handbook of Asian aging* (pp. 91–115). Amityville, NY: Baywood.

O'Rand, A. M. (2006). Stratification and the life course: Life course capital, life course risks, and social inequality. In R. H. Binstock & L. K. George (Eds.), *Handbook of aging and the social sciences* (6th ed., pp. 145–162). San Diego, CA: Academic Press.

Phillipson, C. (2009). Social welfare, aging and globalization in post-industrial society. In J. L. Powell & J. Hendricks (Eds.), *The welfare state in post-industrial society* (pp. 57–70). New York: Springer.

Simmons, L. (1945). *The role of the aged in primitive society*. New Haven, CT: Yale University Press.

Townsend, P. (1981). The structured dependency of the elderly: A creation of social policy in the twentieth century. *Aging and Society, 10*, 5–28.

Townsend, P. (2007). Using human rights to defeat ageism: Dealing with policy-induced "structured dependency." In M. Bernard & T. Scharf (Eds.), *Critical perspectives on ageing societies* (pp. 27–44). Bristol, UK: Polity Press.

Walker, A. (2006). Aging and politics: An international perspective. In R. H. Binstock & L. K. George (Eds.), *Handbook of aging and the social sciences* (6th ed., pp. 339–359). San Diego, CA: Academic Press.

World Bank. (1994). *Averting the old age crisis: Policies to protect the old and promote growth*. New York: Oxford University Press.

International Directory of Gerontological and Geriatric Associations

This list of the names and addresses of the major international, regional, and national gerontological and geriatric associations was derived from various sources, including the United Nation's *Department of Public Information Online Directory for Organizations Active in the Field of Aging*, the International Association of Gerontology and Geriatrics's *Online Directory for Member Societies*, American Society of Aging's *Online Listing of National Organizations Focusing on Aging and Aging Issues*, Gerontological Society of America's *Online Directory for Foreign and Regional Societies*, Norway Department of Public Health and Primary Health Care's *Primary Care Internet Guide*, and some of the individual organizations' Web sites. Only organizations whose primary activity is in gerontology and/or geriatrics are included. After the international organizations, the others are listed in alphabetical order by continent, and then by region/country.

INTERNATIONAL

AARP International
601 East Street NW
Washington, DC 20049, USA
http://www.aarpinternational.com/

American Association for International Aging
1133 20th Street, NW Suite 330

Washington, DC 20036, USA
http://www.unm.wdu/~aging/AAIAwelc.html/

European Federation of Older Persons
Stubenring 2/4A
1010, Vienna, AUSTRIA
http://www.eurag-europe.org/

European Research Area in Ageing
Department of Sociological Studies
University of Sheffield
Elmfield Building
Sheffield S10 2TU, UNITED KINGDOM
http://era-age.group.shef.ac.uk/

International Association of Gerontology and Geriatrics
Rua Hilário de Gouveia 66
1102 Copacabana, Rio de Janeiro
RJ 22040–020, BRAZIL
http://www.iagg.com.br/

International Federation on Ageing
Castleview Wichwood Towers (CWT)
351 Christie Street
Toronto, Ontario, M6G 3C3, CANADA
http://www.ifa-fiv.org/

Information Gérontologique Internationale
Route Aloys-Fauquez 84
1018 Lausanne, SWITZERLAND

International Institute on Ageing
United Nations, Malta
117, St. Paul Street
Valletta, VLT1216, MALTA
http://www.inia.org.mt/

International Network for the Prevention of Elder Abuse
Arenales 1391 8* "B" (1061)
Buenos Aires, ARGENTINA
http://www.inpea.net/

International Psychogeriatric Association
550 Frontage Road, Suite 3759
Northfield, Illinois 60093, USA
http://www.ipa-online.org/

International Society for Gerontechnology
Matrix 1.06 P.O. Box 513
5600 MB Eindhoven,
THE NETHERLANDS
http://www.gerontechnology.info/

Nordic Gerontological Federation (Nordisk Gerontologisk Förening)
c/o NISAL, ISV
Linköpings Universitet
SE-601 79 Norrköping, SWEDEN
http://www.ngf-geronord.se/

United Nations Programme on Ageing
Division for Social Policy and Development
Department of Economic and Social Affairs
United Nations, DC2—1320
New York, NY 10017, USA
http://www.un.org/ageing/

World Health Organization: Health and Aging
FCH/ALC
Main Building, World Health Organization
Avenue Appia 20
1211 Geneva 27,
SWITZERLAND
http://www.who.int/ageing/en/

AFRICA

African Research on Ageing Network
c/o Oxford Institute on Ageing
University of Oxford
3rd Floor Manor Road Building, Manor Road
Oxford OX1 3UQ,
UNITED KINGDOM
http://www.ageing.ox.ac.uk/afran/index.html/

Asociación guineo ecuatoriana para cuidado y defensa a la edad avanzada
P.O. Box 612
Malabo, EQUATORIAL GUINEA

African Gerontological Society
P.O. Box 01803
Osu-Accra, GHANA

International Network for the Prevention of Elder Abuse—Africa
Focus on Elder Abuse
P.O. Box 92 Plumstead
7801 Cape Town, SOUTH AFRICA

Age-in-Action (formerly South African Council for the Aged)
P.O. Box 2335
8000 Cape Town, SOUTH AFRICA

South African Gerontological Association
P.O. Box 23845
7700 Claremont, SOUTH AFRICA

South African Geriatrics Society
P.O. Box 19168
7505 Tygerberg, SOUTH AFRICA

Tunisian Association of Gerontology—ATUGER
Policlinique CNSS—Boite Postale 560—3018 SFAX
TUNISIA

ASIA AND THE OCEANIA REGION

Australian Association of Gerontology
Suite 154, 236 Hyperdome
Loganholme QLD 4129,
AUSTRALIA
http://www.aag.asn.au/

Australian Council on the Ageing
GPO Box 1583
Adelaide, SA 5001, AUSTRALIA
http://www.cota.org.au/

Australian and New Zealand Society for Geriatric Medicine
ANZSGM Secretariat
145 Macquarie Street
Sidney, NSW 2000, AUSTRALIA
http://www.anzsgm.org/

National Ageing Research Institute
35–54 Poplar Road (via Gate 4)
Parkville, Victoria 3052, AUSTRALIA
http://www.mednwh.unimelb.edu.au/

Bangladesh Association for the Aged and Institute of Geriatric Medicine
Agargaon, Sher-e-Bangla Nagar
Dhaka -1207, BANGLADESH
http://www.baaigm.org/

Chinese Taipei Association of Gerontology and Geriatrics
17F-18, No. 50, Sec. 1 Chung Shiao W. Road
100 Taipei, TAIWAN
http://www.tagg.org.tw/

Gerontological Society of China
Jia 57 Anwaidajie, Dongcheng District,
Beijing, Post code 10001, PEOPLE'S REPUBLIC OF CHINA
http://www.chinagsc.org.cn/

Hong Kong Association of Gerontology
GPO Box 10020, HONG KONG
http://www.hkag.org /

Hong Kong Geriatrics Society
Department of Medicine & Geriatrics,
TWGHs Fung Yiu King Hospital,
9 Sandy Bay Road, Pokfulam, HONG KONG
http://www.fmshk.com.hk/hkgs/home.htm/

Hong Kong Psychogeriatric Association
c/o Psychogeriatric Team, Castle Peak Hospital
Tuen Mun, N.T., HONG KONG
http://www.hkpga.org/

Association of Gerontology (India)
Department of Zoology
Banaras Hindu University
Varanasi 221005, INDIA
http://www.agindia.org/

Geriatric Society of India
K-49, Green Park Main
New Delhi—110 016, INDIA
http://www.geriatricindia.com/

Indonesian Society of Gerontology
Jalan Iskandarsyah Raya 7
Jakarta 12160, INDONESIA

Japan Association of Gerontology
Maniwa Hospital
2204 Maniwa Yoshimachi
Tanogun Gunma, 370–12, JAPAN

Japan Geriatrics Society
Kyourin 702,
4-2-1 Yushima, Bunkyou-ku,
Tokyo, 113–0034, JAPAN
http://www.jpn-geriat-soc.or.jp

Japan Gerontological Society
Kyorin Building, 702
4-2-1 Yushima, Bonkyo-ku
Tokyo, JAPAN

Japan Society for Biomedical Gerontology
c/o Sociology Department
Tokyo Metropolitan Institute of Gerontology
35–2 Sakae-cho, Itabashi-ku
Tokyo 173–0015, JAPAN

Japan Society for Social-Gerontology
c/o Sociology Department
Tokyo Metropolitan Institute of Gerontology
35–2 Sakae-cho, Itabashi-ku
Tokyo 173, JAPAN

Federation of Korean Gerontological Societies
Suite 714, Shinhan Nextel Bldg., #14
Dosun-dong, Sungdong-ku
Seoul, 133–040,
SOUTH KOREA
http://www.fkgs.org/

Korea Gerontological Society
Seoul National Univ., Public Health
#28 Yonkeun-Dong
Seoul, 110–499, SOUTH KOREA

Korean DRP Society of Gerontology and Geriatrics
c/o WHO Collaborating Centre in Gerontology & Geriatrics
P.O. Box 109
Pyongyang, NORTH KOREA

Gerontological Association of Malaysia
507C 4th Floor Diamond Complex
Jalan Medan Bangi, OFF Persiaran Bangi Business Park
43650 Bandar Baru Bangi, Selangor Darul Ehsan, MALAYSIA

Age Concern New Zealand
P.O. Box 10–688, Wellington 6143
4th Floor, Education House,
178 Willis Street, Wellington,
NEW ZEALAND
http://www.ageconcern.org.nz/

New Zealand Association of Gerontology
P.O. Box 22–126
Wellington 6030,
NEW ZEALAND
http://www.gerontology.org.nz/

New Zealand Institute for Research on Ageing
Victoria University of Wellington
P.O. Box 600
Wellington,
NEW ZEALAND
http://www.victoria.ac.nz/nzira/

Geriatric Care Foundation Karachi
58, National Chambers Arambagh Road
Karachi, PAKISTAN
http://www.iaed.org/gcfk/index.html/

Philippine Association of Gerontology
4th Street BBB Marulas
Valenzuela Metro Manila, PHILIPPINES

Gerontological Society of Singapore
80 Marine Parade Road, #07–0708 Parkway
Parade, Singapore 449269,
SINGAPORE
http://www.gs.org.sg/

Gerontological Society of Taiwan
National Taiwan University Hospital
No. 7, Zongshan South Road
Taipei 100, TAIWAN

Thai Society of Gerontology and Geriatric Medicine
Ayurasat Building, Chulalongkorn Hospital
Rama 4 Road Prathumwan
Bangkok 10330, THAILAND

EUROPE

Albanian Association of Gerontology and Geriatrics
Rr. E Dibres, Pallati 312/1, Shkalla 3,
Apt 24 Univ. Hospital Centre Mother Theresa
Tirana, ALBANIA

Austrian Society of Geriatrics and Gerontology
Sophienspital, Apollogasse 19
A-1070 Wien,
AUSTRIA
http://www.geriatrie-online.at/

Belgian Society of Gerontology and Geriatrics
Gen.Jungbluthlaan, 11
B-8400 Oostende,
BELGIUM
http://www.geriatrie.be/

Bulgarian Association on Ageing
Boulevard Vitosha 36
1000 Sofia,
BULGARIA

Czech Society of Gerontology and Geriatrics
Gerontocentrum
Simunkova, 1600
CZ-182 00 Praha 8, CZECH REPUBLIC

Danish Gerontological Society
Aurehojvej, 24
DK-2900 Hellerup, DENMARK
http://www.gerodan.dk/

Danish Institute of Gerontology
Aurehøjvej 24
DK—2900 Hellerup,
DENMARK
http://www.geroinst.dk/

Danish Society for Geriatrics
http://www.danskselskabforgeriatri.dk/

Estonian Association of Geriatrics and Gerontology
Lembitu 8
Tartu 50406,
ESTONIA
http://www.egga.ee/

Finnish Gerontological Society
Haartmannink, 4
FIN-00290 Helsinki,
FINLAND
http://www.gernet.sci.fi/

Société Française de Gériatrie er Gérontologie
(French Society of Gerontology and Geriatrics)
CO Fondation Nationale de Gérontologie
49 Rue Mirabeau
75016 Paris, FRANCE

National Foundation of Gerontology
Hopital Broca, Center of Gerontology,
54–56, rue Pascal
75013 Paris, FRANCE

Georgian Gerontology and Geriatrics Society
4, Chachava Street
380059 Tbilisi, GEORGIA

German Centre of Gerontology
Deutsches Zentrum für Altersfragen, DZA
Manfred-von-Richthofen-Strasse 2
12101 Berlin-Tempelhof, GERMANY
http://www.dza.de/nn_13036/EN/Home/homepage__node.
html?__nnn = true/

German Society of Gerontology and Geriatrics
Universitaetsklinikum Eppendorf
Intitut fuer Medizin-Soziologie
Martinist. 40
D-20246 Hamburg,
GERMANY
http://www.dggg-online.de/

Institute for Gerontology
Institut für Gerontologie
Bergheimer Str. 20
69115 Heidelberg, GERMANY
http://www.gero.uni-heidelberg.de/

Hellenic Association of Gerontology and Geriatrics
23 Kaningos Street
10677 Athens, GREECE
http://www.gerontology.gr/

Hungarian Association of Gerontology
Semmelweis University
Faculty of Health Sciences 1st
Department of Medicine & Geriatrics
Budapest 1135 Szabolcs utca 35, HUNGARY
http://www.geronto.hu/

Irish Gerontological Society
Dr. Denis O'Mahony
Department of Geriatric Medicine
University Hospital, Wilton,
Cork, IRELAND
http://www.gerontology.ie/

National Council on Ageing and Older People
11th Floor Hawkins House
Hawkins Street
Dublin 2, IRELAND
http://www.ncaop.ie/

Israeli Gerontological Society
Habonim 8
Ramat-Gan 52462, ISRAEL

Societa Italiana Di Gerontologia E Geriatria
Via Giulio Cesare Vanini,
5 to 50129 Florence, ITALY
http://www.sigg.it/

Association Luxembourgeoise de Gérontologie et Gériatrie
13, Rue Prince Jean—Grand Duchy of Luxembourg
L-9052 Ettelbruck, LUXEMBOURG

Maltese Association of Gerontology and Geriatrics
European Centre of Gerontology, University of Malta
Msida, MSD 06, MALTA
http://soc.um.edu.mt/magg/

Netherlands Society of Gerontology
P. O. Box 222
3500 AE Utrecht, THE NETHERLANDS
http://www.nvgerontologie.nl/

Dutch Society for Clinical Geriatrics
P. O. Box 2704
3500 GS Utrecht, THE NETHERLANDS
http://www.nvkg.nl/

Centre for Research on Aging
University of Tromsø,
Faculty of Medicine
9037 Tromsø, NORWAY
http://uit.no/medfak/

Nasjonalt kompetansesenter for Aldring og helse
(Norwegian Centre for Dementia Research)
Division of Internal Medicine
Ulleval University Hospital
N-0407 Oslo, NORWAY
http://www.nordemens.no/english.html/

Norwegian Geriatrics Society
Department of Internal Medicine
Aker University hospital
N-0514 Oslo, NORWAY
http://www.legeforeningen.no/index.gan?id = 17534&subid = 0/

Norwegian Gerontological Society
c/o National Centre for Aging and Health
Medical Division, Geriatrics Department,
Ulleval University Hospital
N-0407 Oslo, NORWAY

Polish Society of Gerontology
Medical Academy—Department of. Gerontology
Ul. Kilinskiego 1
15–230 Byalystok, POLAND

Sociedade Portuguesa De Geriatria E Gerontologia
(Portuguese Society for Gerontology and Geriatrics)
Av. Joao XXI 64–3 DT.
1000 Lisbon, PORTUGAL

Ana Aslan National Institute of Gerontology and Geriatrics,
9 Caldarusani St.
Bucharest 011241
P.O. Box 2-4,
ROMANIA
http://www.brainaging.ro/

Romanian Society of Gerontology and Geriatrics
9 Caldarusani St.
78178 Sector 1 Bucharest, ROMANIA

Gerontological Society of the Russian Academy of Sciences
68, Leningradskaya, Str., Pesocnhy-2
St. Petersburg 189646, RUSSIA

Society of Gerontology of the Republic of Serbia
Krfska St. 7
11000 Beograd, SERBIA

Slovak Society of Gerontology and Geriatrics
Department of Geriatrics, Faculty of Medicine
Comenius University, Dumbierska 3
831 01 Bratislava, SLOVAKIA

Gerontological Association of Slovenia
Teslova 17, SL-1000
Ljubljana, SLOVENIA

Spanish Society of Geriatrics and Gerontology
Principe de Vergara, 57–59—esc. B 1
28006 Madrid, SPAIN
http://www.segg.es/

Spanish Society of Geriatric Medicine
c/o Hospital Monte Naranco
Av. Dres. Fernandez Vega, 107
33012 Oviedo, SPAIN
http://www.semeg.es/

Swedish Gerontological Society
c/o Stockholm Gerontology Research Center
Box 6401 Stockholm, S-113 82 SWEDEN
http://www.dfr.se/sgs/

Swiss Society of Gerontology
Spital Bern-Ziegler, Postfach
CH-3001 Bern, SWITZERLAND
http://www.sgg-ssg.ch/

Geriatrics Society of Turkey
Billur Sokak 29/9
Kavaklidere—Ankara, TURKEY
http://www.geriatri.org/

National Association of Social and Applied Gerontology—Turkey
Liman Mahallesi 27.Sokak Tunalı Apt.No:26/C
Antalya, TURKEY
http://www.geroder.org/

Gerontology and Geriatrics Society of the Ukraine
67, Vyshgorodskaya Str.
254114 Kiev, UKRAINE

Institute of Gerontology
Ukrainian Academy Medical Sciences
Vyshgorodskaya, 67
252114 Kiev, UKRAINE

Age Concern England
Astral House
1268 London Road London SW16 4ER, UNITED KINGDOM
http://www.ageconcern.org.uk/

British Geriatrics Society
Marjory Warren House
31 St John's Square
London EC1M 4DN, UNITED KINGDOM
http://www.bgs.org.uk/

British Society of Gerontology
Department of Applied Social Science
University of Stirling
Stirling FK9 4LA, UNITED KINGDOM
http://www.britishgerontology.org/

British Society for Research on Ageing
c/o Dr Sian Henson
Dept Immunology and Molecular Pathology
University College London,
46 Cleveland Street
London W1T 4JF, UNITED KINGDOM
http://www.bsra.org.uk/

Centre of Policy on Ageing
25–31 Ironmonger Row
London EC1V 3QP, UNITED KINGDOM
http://www.cpa.org.uk/

Centre for Social Gerontology
Keele University
Keele, Staffordshire ST5 5BG, UNITED KINGDOM
http://www.keele.ac.uk/research/lcs/csg/index.htm/

The Institute of Human Ageing
University of Liverpool Muspratt Building
Quadrangle, Brownlow Hill
Liverpool L69 3GB, UNITED KINGDOM
http://www.liv.ac.uk/~cas/home.htm#About/

LATIN AMERICA AND THE CARIBBEAN

Gerontological Association of Argentina (AGA)
Paso de los Andes 1497/1505 (CP: 5500)
Mendoza, ARGENTINA
http://www.gerontogeriatria.org.ar/

Sociedad Argentina de Gerontología y Geriatría (SAGG)
San Luis 2538 C1056 AAD
Buenos Aires, ARGENTINA
http://www.sagg.org.ar/

Brazilian Geriatrics Society
Av Indianopolis 2343
Sao Paulo 04063–004, BRAZIL

Brazilian Society of Geriatrics and Gerontology
Av. Ipiranga 5311/405
Porto Alegre RS CEP 90610–001, BRAZIL
http://www.sbgg.org.com.br/

Chilean Geriatrics and Gerontology Society
Alameda 390
Piso 3, Santiago, CHILE
http://www.socgeriatria.cl/

Asociación Colombiana de Gerontología y Geriatría
(Colombian Gerontological and Geriatric Society)
Carrera 13 No. 38—65 oficina 203
Bogotá, COLOMBIA
http://www.acgg.org.co/

Costa Rican Association of Geriatrics and Gerontology
300 mts norte y 25 mts este de al Iglesia
Santa Teresita, Barrio Escalante,
Apartado 5956–100, COSTA RICA

Sociedad Cubana De Gerontologia Y Geriatria
Calle L # 406 / 23 y 25
27 and G Place
City of Havana, 10400, CUBA
http://www.sld.cu/sitios/gericuba/

Ecuadorian Society of Gerontology and Geriatric

Asociación Mexicana de Gerontología y Geriatría (AMGG)
Puebla No. 212, Despacho 205
C. P. 06700
Col. Roma, Deleg. Cuauhtémoc, MEXICO, D.F.
http://www.amgg.com.mx/

National Institute of Seniors (INSEN)
419 Petén Col. Narvarte , Del. Narvarte, Del. Benito Juárez
P.O. Box 03020,
Mexico City, MEXICO
http://www.inapam.gob.mx/

Sociedad de Geriatria y Gerontologia de Mexico (GEMAC)
Society of Geriatrics and Gerontology of Mexico A.C.
Prolongacion Division Del Norte 4271 C. P. 14350
Col Prado, Coapa Delg. Tlalpan, MEXICO

Asociación Panameña de Geriatría y Gerontología
P.O. Box 0823–04377,
Panama City, 7, REPUBLIC OF PANAMA

Panamanian Council of Geriatrics and Gerontology
Apartado 870 097
Panama City 7, REPUBLIC OF PANAMA

Gerontology and Geriatric Paraguayan Society
Gobernador Irala and Coronel Lòpez (Sajonia)
Asunciòn 543, PARAGUAY

Sociedad de Gerontología y Geriatría del Perú
(Peruvian Gerontology and Geriatric Society)
Av. Arequipa 2524—1407
Lima 14, PERU
http://www.sggperu.org/main/

Sociedad de Gerontologia de Puerto Rico
P.O. Box 363472
San Juan, 00936–3472,
PUERTO RICO
http://www.socgerontologiapr.org/

Sociedad Uruguaya de Gerontología y Geriatría
Lallemand 1666
CP: 11400
Montevideo, URUGUAY
http://www.sugg.com.uy/

Sociedad Venezolana De Geriatria Y Gerontologia
Caracas. Piso 5 Consultorio: 513 Apto
Postal: 1010, Caracas, VENEZUELA

NORTH AMERICA

Aging Research Network
10951 90 Ave
Edmonton, AB, T6G 1A4, CANADA
Canadian Association of Retired Persons
Suite 1304, 27 Queen St. E.
Toronto, ON M5C 2M6, CANADA
http://www.carp.ca/

Canadian Association on Gerontology
222 College St. Suite 106
Toronto, ON M5T 3J1, CANADA
http://www.cagacg.ca/

Canadian Geriatrics Society
162 Cumberland Street, Suite 300
Toronto, ON M5R 3N5, CANADA
http://www.canadiangeriatrics.com/

Institute of Aging
Canadian Institutes of Health Research
The University of British Columbia
2080 West Mall, Room 038
Vancouver, BC, V6T 1Z2, CANADA
http://www.cihr-irsc.gc.ca/e/193.html

National Advisory Council on Aging
200 Eglantine Driveway
Ottawa, ON K1A 0K9, CANADA

American Association for Geriatric Psychiatry
7910 Woodmont Avenue, Suite 1050
Bethesda, MD 20814–3004, USA
http://www.aagpgpa.org/

American Association for Retired Persons (AARP)
601 E Street NW
Washington, DC 20049, USA
http://www.aarp.org/

American Association of Homes and Services for the Aging (AAHSA)
2519 Connecticut Avenue, NW
Washington, DC 20008–1520, USA
http://www.aahsa.org/

American Federation for Aging Research (AFAR)
55 West 39th Street, 16th Floor
New York, New York 10018, USA
http://www.afar.org/

American Geriatrics Society
The Empire State Building
350 Fifth Avenue, Suite 801
New York, New York 10118, USA
http://www.americangeriatrics.org/

American Physical Therapy Association—Geriatrics Section
1111 North Fairfax Street
Alexandria, Virginia 22314, USA
http://geriatricspt.org/

America Society on Aging
833 Market Street, Suite 511
San Francisco, California 94103, USA
http://www.asaging.org/

Association for Anthropology & Gerontology
Bloomington Hospital
P.O. Box 1149
Bloomington, Indiana 47402, USA
http://www.slu.edu/organizations/aage/

Association for Gerontology Education in Social Work
1416 Fama Dr. NE
Atlanta, Georgia 30329–3308, USA
http://www.agesocialwork.org/

Association for Gerontology in Higher Education
1220 L Street, NW, Suite 901
Washington, DC 20005, USA
http://www.aghe.org/

Gerontological Society of America
1220 L Street, NW, Suite 901
Washington, DC 20005, USA
http://www.geron.org/

Hawaii-Pacific Gerontological Society
P.O. Box 3714
Honolulu, Hawaii 96812, USA
http://www.hpgs.org/

Midwest Council for Social Research on Aging
University of Minnesota,
Department of Sociology
Minneapolis, Minnesota 55455, USA

National Council on Aging
1901 L Street, NW, 4th Floor
Washington, DC 20036, USA
http://www.ncoa.org/

National Gerontological Nursing Association
NGNA National Office 7794 Grow Drive
Pensacola, Florida 32514, USA
https://www.ngna.org/

National Hispanic Council on Aging
2713 Ontario Road NW
Washington, DC 20009, USA
http://www.nhcoa.org/

National Indian Council on Aging
10501 Montgomery Boulevard NE, Suite 210
Albuquerque, New Mexico 87111, USA
http://www.nicoa.org/

National Institute on Aging
Building 31, Room 5C27
31 Center Drive, MSC 2292
Bethesda, Maryland 20892, USA
http://www.nia.nih.gov/

New England Gerontological Society
81 Cutts Road
Durham, New Hampshire 03824, USA

Northeastern Gerontological Society
4 Country Club Drive
West Simsbury, Connecticut 06092, USA

The Society of Geriatric Cardiology
7910 Woodmont Avenue, Suite 1050
Bethesda, Maryland 20814–3004, USA

Southern Gerontological Society
PMB Suite 144
1616—102 W. Cape Coral Pkwy.
Cape Coral, Florida 33914, USA
http://www.southerngerontologicalsociety.org/sgs/index.asp

Southwest Society on Aging
P.O. Box 13346, UNT
Denton, Texas 76203–6346, USA

United States Administration on Aging
One Massachusetts Avenue, Suites 4100 & 5100
Washington, DC 20201, USA
http://www.aoa.gov/

Index

About the Editors
and Contributors

EDITORS

SUZANNE KUNKEL is director of the Scripps Gerontology Center, and professor of sociology at Miami University, where she has been involved in several international initiatives, including a project funded by the U.S Department of Education to establish an international exchange program for the study of social and health policy in aging nations. She has served President of the Association for Gerontology in Higher Education, chaired the International Task Force for that organization, and served on editorial boards for the Journals of Gerontology: Social Sciences and the Journal of Applied Gerontology.

ELIZABETH LOKON combined her background in art, gerontology, and education to found Opening Minds through Art (OMA), an art program for people with dementia. She is a Research Associate at Scripps Gerontology Center at Miami University. She has presented her work in the United States, Europe, and Asia, and her publications include over 40 journal articles, chapters, instructional manuals, and books, mostly in the field of education.

SAMUEL M. MWANGI is a doctoral student in Social Gerontology at Miami University of Ohio. Prior to joining Miami, he obtained his Master of Arts (Gerontology) degree from Wichita State University in Kansas. Originally from Kenya, Mwangi developed his interest in aging when he was a school teacher in his home town of Thika. He identified the lack of restorative and social services for the elderly, as well as their lack of income and health security, as major problems in Kenya. Mwangi has made several presentations at conferences on aging issues in Kenya. He also contributed to this volume by writing two chapters, one on his native Kenya and the other on the international NGOs active in the field of aging.

ERDMAN B. PALMORE is Professor Emeritus of Medical Sociology at the Duke University Center for the Study of Aging and Human Development. He has written or edited 20 books, including the *Normal Aging* series, the *Handbook on the Aged in the U.S.*, *Facts on Aging Quiz*, *Ageism*, *Encyclopedia of Ageism*, and the first two editions of the *International Handbook on Aging*. He has also published 118 articles in professional journals. He is a past president of the Southern Gerontological Society and a Fellow of the Gerontological Society of America.

FRANK WHITTINGTON is Professor of Gerontology and Associate Dean for Academic Affairs in the College of Health and Human Services at George Mason University in Fairfax, Virginia. He previously was Director of the Gerontology Institute and Professor of Sociology at Georgia State University in Atlanta. Dr. Whittington received his Ph.D. from Duke University, and he is a Fellow of the Gerontological Society of America and Past-President of the Southern Gerontological Society. He currently serves as Book Review Editor of The Gerontologist. His publications include 9 books and over 50 articles and chapters on long-term care and health behavior of older people. Dr. Whittington's recent research, funded by the National Institute on Aging, sought to identify supports and barriers for independence, autonomy, and quality of life of residents of assisted living facilities. His most recent book, co-authored with Mary Ball and four other colleagues at the Georgia State Gerontology Institute and published by Johns Hopkins University Press, is entitled Communities of Care: Assisted Living for African American Elders.

CONTRIBUTORS

MARJA AARTSEN, Ph.D.
Programme Director, European Master's in Gerontology
(EuMaG), Vrije Universiteit—University Amsterdam
Postal address: Vrije Universiteit/FSW/SCW, De Boelelaan
1081, 1081 HV Amsterdam, THE NETHERLANDS
Email: MJ.Aartsen@fsw.vu.nl

ISABELLA ABODERIN, Ph.D.
Research Fellow
Oxford Institute of Ageing University of Oxford
Manor Road Building, Manor Road
Oxford, OX1 3UQ, UNITED KINGDOM
Email: isabella.aboderin@ageing.ox.ac.uk

ABDEL MONEIM ASHOUR, M.D.
Head Psychogeriatric Research
Ain-Shams University
Obour Building 3rd Fl. Apt. 33
Salah Salem Street N. 12, Cairo, EGYPT
Email: ashour200835@yahoo.com

MAURO DI BARI, M.D., Ph.D.
Department of Critical Care Medicine and Surgery
Unit of Gerontology and Geriatric Medicine, University
of Florence and AziendaOspedaliero-Universitaria Careggi
Florence, ITALY
Email: mauro.dibari@unifi.it

BÁLINT BOGA, M.D.
Hungarian Association of Gerontology
1035 Berend u.4, Budapest, HUNGARY
Email: bboga_md@freemail.hu

DON E. BRADLEY, Ph.D.
Assistant Professor, Department of Sociology
East Carolina University
442-A Brewster Building
Greenville, NC 27858 USA
Email: bradleyd@ecu.edu

JENNY BRODSKY
Director, Center for Research on Aging
Myers-JDC-Brookdale Institute
JDC Hill, POB 3886
Jerusalem 91037, ISRAEL
Email: jennyb@jdc.org.il

BELÉN BUENO
Programme Director, Master's in Gerontology and Ph.D. in
Psychogerontology Professor, Department of Developmental & Educational
Psychology University of Salamanca, Faculty of Psychology
Avda. La Merced, 109–131, Salamanca 37005, SPAIN
Email: bbueno@usal.es

CHRISTOPHE J. BÜLA, M.D.
Professor of Geriatric Medicine
University of Lausanne Medical School &
Chief, Service of Geriatric Medicine & Geriatric Rehabilitation
University of Lausanne Medical Center (CHUV)
Rue du Bugnon 21 CH—1011 Lausanne, SWITZERLAND
Email: christophe.bula@chuv.ch

LAURIE BUYS, Ph.D.
Professor, School of Design, Institute for Sustainable Resources
Queensland University of Technology
2 George Street, GPO Box 2434
Brisbane Old 4001 AUSTRALIA
Email: l.buys@qut.edu.au

APHICHAT CHAMRATRITHIRONG, Ph.D.
Emeritus Professor
Institute for Population and Social Research (IPSR)
Mahidol University, Salaya, Nakhon Pathom 73170
THAILAND
Email: pracr@mahidol.ac.th

ALFRED C. M. CHAN, Ph.D.
Chair Professor of Social Gerontology
Department of Sociology and Social Policy and
Asia-Pacific Institute of Ageing Studies (APIAS)
Lingnan University, HONG KONG
Email: sscmchan@ln.edu.hk

NEENA L. CHAPPELL, Ph.D., FRSC
Canada Research Chair in Social Gerontology
Professor, Centre on Aging and Dept. of Sociology
University of Victoria P.O. Box 1700 STN CSC
Victoria, British Columbia, V8W 2Y2, CANADA
Email: nlc@uvic.ca

CHING-YU CHEN, M.D.
Director of Geriatric Research, Population Health Science Institute
National Health Research Institutes
Professor of Family Medicine
National Taiwan University Medical College
Taipei, TAIWAN
Email: chency@nhri.org.tw

SHEUNG-TAK CHENG, Ph.D.
Professor, Department of Applied Social Studies
City University of Hong Kong
Email: tak.cheng@cityu.edu.hk

ANTONIO CHERUBINI, M.D., Ph.D.
Institute of Gerontology and Geriatrics
Department of Clinical and Experimental Medicine
University of Perugia Medical School
Policlinico Santa Maria della Misericordia
Piazzale Menghini 1, 06156 Perugia, ITALY
Email: acherub@unipg.it

SUNG-JAE CHOI, Ph.D.
Department of Social Welfare
Seoul National University
San #56–1 Shinrim dong Kwanak = ku
Seoul 151 742, KOREA
Email: sjchoi@snu.ac.kr

NIKI CHONDROGIANNI, Ph.D.
National Hellenic Research Foundation (NHRF)
Institute of Biological Research & Biotechnology (IBRB)
48 Vas Constantinou Ave., Athens 11635, GREECE
Email: nikichon@eie.gr

JUDITH A. DAVEY, Ph.D.
Associate Professor and Senior Research Associate
Institute of Policy Studies
Victoria University of Wellington
Box 600, Wellington, NEW ZEALAND
Email: Judith.Davey@vuw.ac.nz

KATE DAVIDSON, Ph.D.
Senior Lecturer
Department of Sociology, University of Surrey
Guildford, GU2 7XH, UNITED KINGDOM
Email: K.Davidson@surrey.ac.uk

ISIDORO FAINSTEIN, M.D.
President of the Argentina Gerontology & Geriatric Society
San Louis 2538 C1056 AAD
Buenos Aires, ARGENTINA
Email: presidencia@sagg.org.ar

MONICA FERREIRA, D.Phil.
President, International Longevity Center—South Africa
University of Cape Town
Faculty of Health Sciences
Observatory 7925, SOUTH AFRICA
Email: monica.ferreira@uct.ac.za

DIETER FERRING, Ph.D.
Professor of Psychology
Director, Integrative Research Unit on Social and
Individual Development
Université du Luxembourg
L-7220 Walferdange, LUXEMBOURG
Email: dieter.ferring@uni.lu

MASA FILIPOVIC HRAST, Ph.D.
Research Associate
Faculty of Social Sciences
University of Ljubljana
Kardeljeva ploscad 5, 1000 Ljubljana, SLOVENIA
Email: masa.filipovic@fdv.uni-lj.si

BEATRICE GASPERINI, M.D.
Institute of Gerontology and Geriatrics
Department of Clinical and Experimental Medicine
University of Perugia Medical School, Policlinico Santa Maria della
Misericordia, Piazzale Menghini 1, 06156 Perugia, ITALY
Email: beatricegasperini@hotmail.com

YESIM GÖKÇE-KUTSAL, M.D.
Director, Research Center of Geriatric Sciences—GEBAM
Hacettepe University Medical School
Billur Sokak 29/9, Kavaklidere—Ankara, TURKEY
Email: ykutsal@hacettepe.edu.tr

EFSTATHIOS S. GONOS, Ph.D.
Director, Institute of Biological Research and Biotechnology
National Hellenic Research Foundation
48 Vas Constantinou Avenue, Athens 11635, GREECE
Email: sgonos@eie.gr

ROSSARIN SOOTTIPONG GRAY, Ph.D.
Institute for Population and Social Research (IPSR)
Mahidol University, Salaya, Nakhon Pathom 73170, THAILAND
Email: prrgr@mahidol.ac.th

DANIEL GROB, DR.MED. MHA
Medical Director
Department for Acute Care Geriatrics
Town-Hospital Waid
CH—8037 Zürich, SWITZERLAND
Email: daniel.grob@waid.zuerich.ch

RENATO MAIA GUIMARÃES, M.D.
Director, Geriatric Medical Centre
Hospital Universitario de Brasilia
Avenida L2, Norte 604/605
Brasilia, Distrito Federal, BRAZIL 70840 050
Email: remaig@uol.com.br

ALEJANDRO GUTIERREZ DELGADO, M.D.
Geriatics and Gerontology Resident
Raúl Blanco Cervantes Nacional Hospital for the Elderly
Universidad de Costa Rica, San José, Costa Rica
Email: alegutidel@latinmail.com

LADISLAV HEGYI, M.D., Ph.D., Sc.D.
Slovak Medical University
Faculty of Public Health
Limbová 14, 833 03 Bratislava 37, SLOVAKIA
Email: ladislav.hegyi@szu.sk

JON HENDRICKS, Ph.D.
Associate Provost
International Programs
Oregon State University
444 Snell Hall, Corvallis, OR 97331, USA
Email: joe.hendricks@oregonstate.edu

VALENTINA HLEBEC, Ph.D.
Associate Professor of Sociology and Head of Sociology Department
Faculty of Social Sciences University of Ljubljana, SLOVENIA
Email: valentina.hlebec@fdv.uni-lj.si

JACO HOFFMAN, Ph.D.
James Martin Research Fellow
Oxford Institute of Ageing
University of Oxford Manor Road Building, Manor Road
Oxford, OX1 3UQ, UNITED KINGDOM
Email: jacobus.hoffman@ageing.ox.ac.uk

YANG HUI, Ph.D.
Institute of Gerontology
Renmin University of China, CHINA
Email: rucyanghui@163.com

SUSANNE IWARSSON, Ph.D.
Professor, Centre for Ageing
and Supportive Environments
Department of Health Sciences, Lund University
Health Science Centre, Baravägen 3
Box 157, SE-221 00 Lund, SWEDEN
Email: susanne.iwarsson@med.lu.se

D. JAMUNA, Ph.D.
Professor, Center for Research on Ageing
Department of Psychology
S.V. University Tirupati A.P. 517502, INDIA
Email: jamunad123@yahoo.co.in

JOSÉ R. JAUREGUI, M.D.
Sociedad Argentina de Gerontología y Geriatría
San Luis 2538 C1056AAD Ciudad Autónoma de Buenos Aires
República, ARGENTINA
Email: jose.jauregui@hospitalitaliano.org

JAMES KAKOOZA, Ph.D.
Senior Researcher, Makerere Institute for Social Research (MISR)
Lecturer, School of Education
Makerere University
P.O. Box 937, Kampala, UGANDA
Email: jakakooza@yahoo.com

SITAWA R. KIMUNA, Ph.D.
Associate Professor, Department of Sociology
East Carolina University
A-408 Brewster Building
Greenville, NC 27858, USA
Email: KIMUNAS@ecu.edu

KATHRIN KOMP, M.A.
Department of Sociology
VU University Amsterdam
De Boelelaan 1081 1081 HV Amsterdam
THE NETHERLANDS
Email: K.komp@fsw.vu.nl

ŠTEFAN KRAJČÍK, M.D., Ph.D.
Department of Gerontology
Slovak Medical University
Krajinská 101 Bratislava-Podunajské Biskupice SLOVAKIA
Email: stefan.krajcik@szu.sk

RETO KRESSIG, M.D.
Professor and Chief of Geriatrics
Basel University Medical Faculty and University Hospital
Medical Department
Petersgraben 4 CH-4031 Basel,
SWITZERLAND
E-mail: rkressig@uhbs.ch

ANDREAS KRUSE, Ph.D.
Professor and Director, Institute of Gerontology Dean
Faculty of Behavioral and Cultural Studies University of Heidelberg
Bergheimer Str. 20 69115 Heidelberg, GERMANY
Email: andreas.kruse@gero.uni-heidelberg.de

SUZANNE KUNKEL, Ph.D.
Director, Scripps Gerontology Center
Professor, Department of Sociology & GerontologyMiami University
Oxford, OH 45056, USA
Email: kunkels@muohio.edu

ANNA MELISSA C. LAVARES
Demographic Research and Development Foundation, Inc.
C/o UP Population Institute
Palma Hall, University of the Philippines
Diliman, QC, PHILIPPINES
Email: mlavares@yahoo.com

HOWARD LITWIN, D.S.W.
Professor, Paul Baerwald School of Social Work and Social Welfare
The Hebrew University of Jerusalem
Mount Scopus 91905-IL, Jerusalem, ISRAEL
Email: mshowie@huji.ac.il

ELIZABETH LOKON, Ph.D.
Graduate Student Scripps Gerontology Center
Miami University,
Oxford, OH 45056, USA
Email: lokon@yahoo.com

GEORGE L. MADDOX, Ph.D.
Director, Duke Long Term Care Resources Program
Duke University Medical Center
Box 2920, DUMC Durham, NC 27710, USA
Email: glm@geri.duke.edu

DAISAKU MAEDA, Ph.D.
Professor, Social Gerontology Statistical Analysis
Japan Lutheran College, Graduate Program
Department of Social Work
Ohsawa 3–10–20, Mitaka City, Tokyo, JAPAN
Email: dmaeda@luther.ac.jp

RA'ANA MAHMOOD, M.D.
President, Geriatrics Care Foundation of Pakistan
58 National Chambers, Arambagh Rd.
Karachi, PAKISTAN
Email: raanamahmood@yahoo.com

KALYANI K. MEHTA, Ph.D.
Department of Social Work, Blk AS3, #04–08, 3 Arts Link
National University of Singapore
Singapore 117570, SINGAPORE
Email: swkkkm@nus.edu.sg

JEAN-PIERRE MICHEL, M.D.
Professor of Medicine
Geneva Medical School and University Hospitals
Department of Rehabilitation and Geriatrics
Chemin Pont Bochet, 3
CH-1226 Thonex-Génève, SWITZERLAND
Email: Jean-pierre.michel@hcuge.ch

EVONNE MILLER, Ph.D.
Senior Lecturer, School of Design
Faculty of Built Environment and Engineering
Queensland University of Technology, AUSTRALIA
Email: e.miller@qut.edu.au

JIM MITCHELL, Ph.D.
Director, Center on Aging
Professor, Sociology and Family Medicine
East Carolina University
A-403 Brewster Building
Greenville, NC 27858 USA
Email: mitchellj@ecu.edu

KENEILWE MOLOSI
Department of Adult Education
University of Botswana
P/Bag 0022, Gaborone, BOTSWANA
Email : MOLOSIK@mopipi.ub.bw

KAREN MUNK, Ph.D.
Associate Professor
Centre for Humanistic Health Research
Department of Philosophy, University of Aarhus
Building 1465, Room 418 Jens Chr. Skous vej 7 Nobelparken
Denmark-8000 Aarhus C, DENMARK
Email: filkpm@hum.au.dk

THOMAS MÜNZER, M.D.
Geriatrische Klinik
Kompetenzzentrum Gesundheit und Alter
St. Gallen and Geriatric University Hospital, Bern
9000 St. Gallen
SWITZERLAND
Email: thomas.muenzer@geriatrie-sg.ch

SAMUEL M. MWANGI, M.A.
Graduate Student
Scripps Gerontology Center
Miami University
Oxford, OH 45056, USA
Email: munanus@yahoo.com

AKPOVIRE ODUARAN, Ph.D.
Professor of Lifelong Learning
Department of Adult Education
University of Botswana
P/Bag 0022, Gaborone, BOTSWANA
Email : ODUARANA@mopipi.ub.bw

DESMOND O'NEILL, M.D.
Director, Centre for Ageing
Neurosciences and the Humanities
Trinity College Dublin
Trinity Centre, Adelaide & Meath Hospital
Dublin 24, IRELAND
Email: doneill@tcd.ie

FRANCESCO ORSO, M.D.
Department of Critical Care Medicine and Surgery
Unit of Gerontology and Geriatric Medicine
University of Florence and Azienda
Ospedaliero-Universitaria Careggi, Florence, ITALY
Email: francesco.orso@anmco.it

EAMON O'SHEA, M.A., M.Sc., Ph.D.
Irish Centre for Social Gerontology
National University of Ireland, Galway
University Road, Galway, IRELAND
Email: eamon.oshea@nuigalway.ie

ERDMAN B. PALMORE, Ph.D.
Professor Emeritus
Duke University Medical Center (DUMC)
P.O. Box 3003, Durham, NC 27710, USA
Email: ebp@geri.duke.edu

DU PENG, Ph.D.
Professor & Director, Gerontology Institute
Renmin University of China
Beijing 100872, CHINA
Email: dupeng415@yahoo.com.cn

TEY NAI PENG, M.Sc.
Faculty of Economics and Administration
University of Malaya
50603, Kuala Lumpur,
MALAYSIA
Email: teynp@um.edu.my

DAVID R. PHILLIPS, Ph.D.
Chair Professor of Social Policy
Department of Sociology and Social Policy and
Asia-Pacific Institute of Ageing Studies (APIAS)
Lingnan University, HONG KONG
Email: phillips@ln.edu.hk

ARMANDO F. PICHARDO, M.D.
Association Mexicana de Gerontologia y
Geriatria, Uebla No. 212, Despacho 205 Co. Roma, Deleg
Cuauhtemoc C.P. 06700, MEXICO, D.F.
Email: pichardo2@prodigy.net.mx

P. V. RAMAMURTI, Ph.D.
Hon. Director (emeritus)
Center for Research on Ageing
Department of Psychology
Sri Venkateswara University
Tirupati.A.P.517502, INDIA
Email: ramu142004@yahoo.co.in

NELIDA REDONDO, Ph.D.
Researcher in Sociology of Ageing
Isalud University, ARGENTINA
Email: nredondo@fibertel.com.ar

KAREN ROBINSON
Executive Officer, Australian Association of Gerontology
Suite 154, 236 Hyperdome,
Loganholme QLD 4129, AUSTRALIA
Email: karen.robinson@qut.edu.au

KAI SAKS, Ph.D.
Associate Professor
Department of Medicine University of Tartu
Puusepa 6, Tartu 51014, ESTONIA
Email: Kai.Saks@kliinikum.ee

M. TERESA SANCHO
Technical and Institutional Adviser
Fundación Instituto Gerontológico Matia in Madrid, SPAIN
Email: msancho@fmatia.net

ERIC SCHMITT, Ph.D.
Vice-director, Institute for Gerontology,
University of Heidelberg
Bergheimer Str. 20, 69115 Heidelberg, GERMANY
Email: eric.schmitt@gero.uni-heidelberg.de

LUIZA SPIRU, M.D., Ph.D.
President, Ana Aslan International Foundation
Executive President, Ana Aslan International Academy of Aging
Head, Memory Clinic-Elias Univ. Hospital
Head of Ana Aslan International Clinic for Longevity
Healthy Aging and Brain Aging Prevention
Head, Department of Geriatrics-Gerontology-Gerontopsychiatry
Carol Davila University of Medicine and Pharmacy
Bucharest, ROMANIA
Email: lsaslan@brainaging.ro

TORBJÖRN SVENSSON, Ph.D.
Associate Professor
Centre for Ageing and Supportive Environments
Department of Health Sciences, Lund University
Health Science Centre, Baravägen 3
Box 157, SE-221 00 Lund, SWEDEN
Email: torbjorn.svensson@med.lu.se

JAMES T. SYKES, Ph.D.
Senior Advisor for Aging Policy
Population Health Sciences
University of Wisconsin
625 N. Segoe Rd. #908
Madison, WI 53705, USA
Email: jtsykes@wisc.edu

NG SOR THO, M.Econ.
Department of Applied Statistics
Faculty of Economics and Administration
University Malaya, 50603 Kuala Lumpur, MALAYSIA
Email: ngst@um.edu.my

KIRSTEN THORSEN, Ph.D.
Senior Researcher/Professor
Norwegian Social Research (NOVA)
P.O. Box 3223 Elisenberg
N-0208 Oslo, NORWAY
Email: kirsten.thorsen@nova.no

EVA TOPINKOVÁ, Ph.D.
Professor, Department of Gerontology & Geriatrics
First Faculty of Medicine, Charles University in Prague
Institute of Postgraduate Medical Education
Londýnská 15, Prague 2, 120 00, CZECH REPUBLIC
Email: topinkova.eva@vfn.cz

GRACE TRINIDAD-CRUZ, Ph.D.
Director, Population Institute
University of Philippines
3rd Floor, Palma Hall, UP Diliman, QC, PHILIPPINES
Email: gustcruz@yahoo.com

JOSEPH TROISI, Ph.D.
Director, European Centre for Gerontology
Professor, Department of Sociology, Faculty of Arts
University of Malta, MSD 2080, MALTA
Email: joseph.troisi@um.edu.mt

IOANNIS P. TROUGAKOS, Ph.D.
National Hellenic Research Foundation (N.H.R.F.)
Institute of Biological Research & Biotechnology (I.B.R.B.)
48 Vas. Constantinou Ave., Athens 11635, GREECE
Email: itrougakos@eie.gr

ILEANA TURCU, Ph.D.
Director of Scientific Research and Publishing
Ana Aslan International Academy of Anti-Aging
P-ta Mihail Kogalniceanu no 1, Sc. A, Ap. 17
050064 Bucharest, ROMANIA
Email: it@brainaging.ro

CILLIAN TWOMEY, M.B. FRCPI
Consultant Physician in Geriatric Medicine,
Cork University Hospital, Wilton, Cork, IRELAND
Email: Cillian.Twomey@hse.ie

ENRIQUE VEGA, M.D.
Regional Advisor on Aging and Health
Pan American Health Organization/World Health Organization
525 Twenty Third Street, NW
Washington, DC, 20037, USA
Email: vegaenri@paho.org

LUCIE VIDOVICOVÁ, Mgr., Ph.D.
Institute for Research on Social Reproduction and Integration
Faculty of Social Studies Masaryk University
Jostova 10, 602 00 Brno, CZECH REPUBLIC
Email: lucie.vidovic@seznam.cz

FRANK WHITTINGTON, Ph.D.
Associate Dean for Academic Affairs
George Mason University
Robinson B 413A
Fairfax, VA, 22030, USA
Email: fwhittin@gmu.edu